WITHDRAWN

2006 LECTURES

PROCEEDINGS OF THE BRITISH ACADEMY · 151

2006 LECTURES

Published for THE BRITISH ACADEMY
by OXFORD UNIVERSITY PRESS

Oxford University Press, Great Clarendon Street, Oxford OX2 6DP

Oxford New York
Auckland Cape Town Dar es Salaam Hong Kong Karachi
Kuala Lumpur Madrid Melbourne Mexico City Nairobi
New Delhi Shanghai Taipei Toronto

© The British Academy 2007
Database right The British Academy (maker)
First published 2007

All rights reserved. No part of this publication may be reproduced,
stored in a retrieval system, or transmitted, in any form or by any means,
without the prior permission in writing of the British Academy,
or as expressly permitted by law, or under terms agreed with the appropriate
reprographics rights organization. Enquiries concerning reproduction
outside the scope of the above should be sent to the Publications Department,
The British Academy, 10 Carlton House Terrace, London SW1Y 5AH

You must not circulate this book in any other binding or cover
and you must impose this same condition on any acquirer

British Library Cataloguing in Publication Data
Data available

ISBN 978–0–19–726424–9
ISSN 0068–1202

Typeset in Times
by J&L Composition, Filey, North Yorkshire
Printed in Great Britain
on acid-free-paper by
Antony Rowe Limited, Chippenham, Wiltshire

The Academy is grateful to Professor P. J. Marshall, CBE, FBA
for his editorial work on this volume

Contents

The Child in Poetry: Foundlings, Lostlings, Changelings MARGARET REYNOLDS (*2005 Warton Lecture on English Poetry*)	1
Coercion and Consent in Nazi Germany R. J. EVANS (*Raleigh Lecture on History*)	53
A. E. Housman's Rejected Addresses ROBERT DOUGLAS-FAIRHURST (*Chatterton Lecture on Poetry*)	83
Condorcet and the Meaning of Enlightenment LORRAINE DASTON (*Master-Mind Lecture*)	113
The Search for Perfection: Atlantic Dimensions BERNARD BAILYN (*Isaiah Berlin Lecture*)	135
The Origins of Fair Play KEN BINMORE (*Keynes Lecture in Economics, with discussion*)	159
Judicial Independence: Who Cares? NEIL MacCORMICK (*British Academy Law Lecture*)	195
Nation and Covenant: The Contribution of Ancient Israel to Modern Nationalism ANTHONY D. SMITH (*Elie Kedourie Memorial Lecture*)	213
Bonjour Paresse: Literary Waste and Recycling in Book 4 of Gower's *Confessio Amantis* JAMES SIMPSON (*Sir Israel Gollancz Memorial Lecture*)	257
Kinds of People: Moving Targets IAN HACKING (*British Academy Lecture*)	285
Shakespeare, Jonson, and the Invention of the Author IAN DONALDSON (*Shakespeare Lecture*)	319
'Now Shall I Make My Soul': Approaching Death in Yeats's Life and Work R. F. FOSTER (*Warton Lecture on English Poetry*)	339

Recovering Maya Civilisation NORMAN HAMMOND (*Albert Reckitt Archaeological Lecture*)	361
The Devil in the Holy Water: Political Libel in Eighteenth Century France ROBERT DARNTON (*2007 British Academy Lecture*)	388
Einstein JOHN STACHEL (*2005 Master-Mind Lecture*)	423
Abstracts and Notes on Lecturers	459
Lecture series published in the *Proceedings of the British Academy*	473

2005 WARTON LECTURE ON ENGLISH POETRY

The Child in Poetry: Foundlings, Lostlings, Changelings

MARGARET REYNOLDS
Queen Mary, University of London

Displacements, Diagonals

TO BEGIN WITH A POEM. This is from *The Usborne Book of Poems for Young Children*. It is by Anon, and it is called 'Strange Story'.

> I saw a pigeon making bread
> I saw a girl composed of thread
> I saw a towel one mile square
> I saw a meadow in the air
> I saw a rocket walk a mile
> I saw a pony make a file
> I saw a blacksmith in a box
> I saw an orange kill an ox
> I saw a butcher made of steel
> I saw a penknife dance a reel
> I saw a sailor twelve feet high
> I saw a ladder in a pie
> I saw an apple fly away
> I saw a sparrow making hay
> I saw a farmer like a dog
> I saw a puppy mixing grog
> I saw three men who saw these too
> And will confirm what I tell you.[1]

Read at the Academy 26 May 2005.
[1] *The Usborne Book of Poems for Young Children*, chosen by Philip Hawthorn, illustrated by Cathy Shimmen, edited by Sam Taplin (London, 2004), p. 61.

Depending on how familiar you are with poetry as bedtime reading, or how quickly your eye adjusts the space to make sense out of nonsense, then you will see how to read this poem of displacements. ('I saw a pigeon' is the odd phrase out: otherwise each first half line connects to the second half line above—'I saw a girl . . . | making bread' etc.)

To go with that poem that works on the idea of displacement and diversion, here is another digression, another 'strange story' about 'out of place'. In 2004 the popular radio journalist, Nicky Campbell, published a memoir. His title was *Blue Eyed Son* and the first line reads: 'I was committing adultery in Room 634 of the Holiday Inn in Birmingham when my wife rang to say they'd found my mother.'[2]

It is a deliberately flaunting first line. Everything is inappropriate: the wife (let alone the mother), suddenly intrudes into this scene of illicit sex. But a glance at the sub-title of Campbell's book makes clear why his tactic is legitimate. For this is *The Story of an Adoption*. The mother—whose own secret sexual life had led to his birth—had just been traced, found, named, for the first time, for the son who had never known her.

Of course, Campbell means to shock. He is a journalist. But it may be that his pressurised sense of contradiction—paradox, lack of propriety—is one that appeals to him because it connects to something in himself. As an adopted child, taken far from where he began, and placed in an elsewhere to which he does (and does not) belong, which he conceives (but which is not where he was conceived), his keynote is displacement.

Displacement explains how to read the anonymous riddle poem 'Strange Story'. It is a double text. The nonsense version set out on the page makes poetic sense because poetry deals in figurative substitutions and unlikely comparisons: 'I saw a pigeon making bread'. But the good sense version is still there—provided the reader chooses to see it: 'I saw a girl . . . | making bread'. One is Nonsense, and the other is Sense, but neither one quite obliterates the other, and readers—young and old—are entirely capable of keeping both patterns in focus at once.

---

[2] Nicky Campbell, *Blue-Eyed Son: The Story of an Adoption* (Basingstoke and Oxford, 2004), p. 1.

I. Foundlings

Displaced children

This lecture is about children out of place. It is about how children in general, from the eighteenth century onwards, came to be seen as always out of place, somewhere other. And it is about how poetry images and repeats that displacement. To begin with, I will talk about Foundlings. I will be going on to Lostlings, and to Changelings, but in each case I am dealing with the doubles and puns, with the strange presences and uncanny absences that mark physical, emotional and social displacements.

Since the 1960s and the publication of the pioneering work of Philippe Ariès, many scholars and cultural critics have accepted the notion of the 'invention' of childhood taking place at around the end of the seventeenth and beginning of the eighteenth century.[3] Before that— goes the argument—very small children were construed as null. They were devoid of value until they had survived infancy. Thereafter, they were regarded as small adults, subject to the same social expectations in relation to the exploitation of their labour, their commodification, and their imaginative world view. They wore smaller versions of the same adult clothes, and they functioned as adjuncts of their parents' lives.

But then, after that key historical moment, Ariès and his followers proposed that a special place was accorded to children which was supposed to set apart the world of the child, usually in a pastoral setting, and blank and untrammelled. However problematic this argument, it is certainly true that the 'simplicity school' of childhood and children was so effective in its propaganda from the eighteenth century onwards, and in the nineteenth and early twentieth centuries especially, that for many years scholars working on literature written on, for and by children, felt themselves constrained to argue against continuing notions of the 'easiness' of children's literature.[4] But no literary work exists entirely independent of its context; all writing is complicated by the particular historical and cultural frameworks that produced it. This is true for the

---

[3] Philippe Ariès, *L'Enfant et la vie familiale sous l'ancien régime* (Paris, 1960: English trans., New York, 1962). See also Lawrence Stone, *The Family, Sex and Marriage in England 1500–1800* (New York, 1977) and Randolph Trumbach, *The Rise of the Egalitarian Family: Aristocratic Kinship and Domestic Relations in Eighteenth-Century England* (New York, 1978).
[4] See Karin Lesnik-Oberstein, 'Introduction', in Karin Lesnik-Oberstein (ed.), *New Approaches to Children's Literature* (Basingstoke and Oxford, 2004), pp. 1–3.

> I have a home wherein to dwell,
> And rest upon my bed.
>
> While others early learn to swear,
> And curse, and lie, and steal;
> Lord, I am taught thy name to fear,
> And do thy holy will.
>
> Are these thy favours day by day
> To me above the rest?
> Then let me love thee more than they,
> And try to serve thee best.[6]

This poem, like others in the collection, is interesting not so much for its conventional pieties—the succinct introduction to the first, third, ninth and eighth Commandments is particularly impressive—but for the fact that it does introduce something new to poetry—the voice of a child, and a child who observes other children. What is also new here—though it is so familiar to us now as to make it virtually invisible—is the idea of the intense urbanisation, the web of narrow streets and close rooms. It is only because of the sudden springing up of ragged suburbs, with hundreds of people living in confined quarters, that the child can see so much in a 'walk abroad'; that beggars can go 'from door to door'; that children can be seen 'in the street'; and that 'poor wretches' can be forced into rapid change of lodging with no responsibility being taken for them either by the community or the state.[7]

Mother Goose

The other important children's book, also remaining long in print, was *Mother Goose's Melody or Sonnets for the Cradle,* printed from the papers of the well-known publisher John Newbery (with the selection and arrangement attributed to Oliver Goldsmith) and first appearing about the end of 1780. It was not the first book of nursery rhymes—that was *Tommy Thumb's Pretty Song Book* published in 1744—but *Mother Goose* was the most popular.[8]

---

[6] Isaac Watts, *Divine and Moral Songs for Children*, 13th edn. (1715: Richard Ford at the Angel in the Poultry, London, 1735), no. 4.

[7] The 1835 'New Edition' includes engraved illustrations of streets and close walls which are still more explicitly realised: see Isaac Watts, *Divine and Moral Songs for Children*, 13th edn. (1715: R. Miller, London, 1835), no. 4.

[8] *Songs for the Nursery, or Mother Goose's Melodies* was reportedly published in Boston in 1719 but, according to Marina Warner, this is a 'ghost' volume and no copy has ever been found. It

The order and selection of the rhymes varies in the many different versions of the volume, but generally in the late eighteenth century the order of the poems goes: 'A Love Song'—about a 'little man' who asks a 'little maid' to marry him, 'A Dirge', about Betty Winckle's pig who died—whereupon so did she, 'A Melancholy Song', a warning from a mother about the dangers risked by girls going abroad—'she bid me tread lightly, | And come again quickly, | For fear the young men should do me some harm', and 'Cross patch': 'Cross patch, draw the latch, | sit by the fire and spin; Take a cup and drink it up, | Then call the neighbours in.' Over and again the concerns of the rhymes are the same: sex, death, procreation, anxiety over food, clothing and housing, and, perhaps above all, a preoccupation with social exchange perhaps brought on by an awareness of the dangers of living in the urban environment.

Though both Isaac Watts's *Divine Songs* and *Mother Goose* were advertised and promoted as for the use of children, they are clearly also designed to appeal to the adults who were to buy them and use them. Grown ups as well as children appear in the woodcuts that head each poem or rhyme. In the images for editions of Watts's volume they are often portrayed supervising the child's education or catechism. In *Mother Goose* they alternate between comic figures with hooked noses and sprouting hairs, and comfortable-looking mothers or nurses. But the assumed presence of an adult reader and an adult sensibility is most clear in those editions of *Mother Goose* which include a satirical and usually wholly irrelevant 'moral' to conclude each rhyme. As with the Disney film *Shrek II*, there is a sophisticated double layering of relevance designed to keep the interest of both those doing the reading (the adults) and those to whom they are reading (the children).

One subject that haunted the eighteenth century was of interest to both adults and children alike and appears even in these pages. Watts's child-speaker in 'Praise for Mercies Spiritual & Temporal' does not specifically mention babies—abandoned babies, babies wrapped in paper or rags, left in doorways, on church steps, by bridges, or in market

---

was followed by another similar title published by John Newbery in London, *Mother Goose's Melody, or Sonnets for the Cradle* (London, 1765). Many later versions include *Mother Goose's Quarto, or Melodies Complete* (Boston, c.1825). See Marina Warner, *No Go the Bogeyman: Lulling, Scaring and Making Mock* (1998: London, 2000), p. 195. See also Nigel Tattersfield, introduction to the facsimile of a 1780 edition in the Bodleian Library, Douce Adds. 36 (3), *Mother Goose's Melody or, Sonnets for the Cradle,* with the original wood engravings by Thomas Bewick (Oxford, 2003), pp. 1–5.

thoroughfares—but Watts's readers knew that this was a common contemporary phenomenon lying behind his poem.

It was not so much that people were having more children for which they could or would not care. Nor was this excess of abandoned infants due to the failure of the Poor Law, the harsh conditions of the workhouse, or even the public opprobrium meted out to illegitimates and unchaste mothers—though of course all of these were factors. Rather, it was the fact of the rapid expansion of urban dwelling. Even today, this is still the case. In those countries where (whether for reasons political—as in China with its one-child policy combined with a preference for boys, or social—as in India with its anxiety about the need to provide dowries for daughters) children are relinquished in this extreme way (whether wanted or not by their parents). They are, typically, carried by country-dwelling parents away from their village and the small community where pregnancy makes a coming baby all too visible, to the nearest city, to be left in places of public resort (markets, bridges, big shops) in the hopes that in a populous area the babies will soon be seen and rescued.[9]

In 1720, five years after the first publication of Watts's *Divine Hymns*, Thomas Coram found himself semi-retired, without regular employment, living on the outskirts of London and making frequent trips to the City. He began to notice the children by the roadside 'exposed, sometimes alive, sometimes dead, and sometimes dying'—all of them displaced, separated from their biological, and often geographical, origin.

Born in Lyme in Dorset in 1668, Coram trained as a shipwright, worked with modest success in New England, and returned to Britain to attempt various philanthropic projects for the American colonies. When these failed, he looked nearer home and by 1722 had made up his mind to do something about the problem of exposed babies. Coram encountered many difficulties in gaining influential support for his project, even though there were a number of such establishments for abandoned infants abroad—in Florence, in Paris, and in Amsterdam. That in Rome had been going since 1185, while that in Dublin was just being set up and would finally be established under the auspices of the Workhouse in 1730.

---

[9] Many letters and personal testimonies attest to this in the pages of the newsletters published by such independent support organisations as OASIS (Overseas Adoption Support and Information Service), the Inter-Country Adoption Centre and CACH (Children Adopted from China). See also Emily Prager, *WuHu Diary: The Mystery of my Daughter Lulu* (London, 2001), Karin Evans, *The Lost Daughters of China: Abandoned Girls, Their Journey to America, and the Search for a Missing Past* (New York, 2000), and Emily Buchanan, *From China with Love: A Long Road to Motherhood* (Chichester, 2006).

But Coram persisted, and in 1739 the Governors of the 'Hospital for the Maintenance of Exposed and Deserted Young Children' held their first meeting. In 1741 the first children were received into what became popularly known as 'the Foundling Hospital'.[10]

In spite of this seventeen-year delay, the Foundling Hospital rapidly captured the imagination of the public. Fashionable ladies came to view it on the regularly appointed days when distressed mothers could present themselves to beg admission for their child. Whole families would attend at the Chapel to watch the orphans pray, and then go on to watch them consume their strictly frugal diet in the dining hall. As Isaac Watts's ever popular *Divine Songs* remained in print well into the nineteenth century there were doubtless not a few well-off children who had the lessons of their visit to the Hospital reiterated with a bracing Sunday reading of his 'Praise for Mercies Spiritual and Temporal'.

The publicity attending Coram's venture is usually attributed to the extraordinary success of the institution in attracting support from well-known artists and musicians. William Hogarth was a dedicated supporter: he designed the Hospital's seal, painted a major portrait of Coram, regularly included images of infants 'lost'—or should that be 'found'?—in his famous engravings, as well as fostering children both at his own expense and in his own home. Even more famously, Handel gave concerts, including parts of *Messiah*, at the Foundling Hospital which were attended by the whole fashionable world. The Hospital still owns a fair copy of the manuscript bequeathed by the composer.[11]

But more was at stake here. The rise of print culture—books and engravings—combined with the shock of urbanisation, its close ways of living and the resulting new visibility of children in the streets and byways of towns—destitute or otherwise—meant that the idea of the Foundling Hospital rapidly entered the popular imagination. By these

---

[10] For Thomas Coram see Gillian Wagner, *Thomas Coram: Gent: 1668–1751* (Woodbridge, 2004). For Italy see 'The Lives of Foundlings in Nineteenth-Century Italy' by David I. Kertzer and 'Five Centuries of Foundling History in Florence: Changing Patterns of Abandonment, Care and Mortality' by Pier Paolo Viazzo, Maria Bortolotto and Andrea Zanotto, both in Catherine Panter-Brick and Malcolm T. Smith (eds.), *Abandoned Children* (Cambridge, 2000), pp. 41–56 and pp. 70–91. For Ireland, see Joseph Robins, *The Lost Children: A Study of Charity Children in Ireland, 1700–1900* (Institute of Public Administration, Dublin, 1980). In the process of setting up his 'darling project' Thomas Coram requested and received information about similar projects in the cities of Amsterdam and Paris. These documents are still in the Foundling Hospital collection: see Wagner, *Thomas Coram*, p. 136.

[11] See Wagner, *Thomas Coram*, on Hogarth, pp. 135, 139–42, 184 and on Handel, pp. 130, 165, 182–3. See also *The Foundling Museum Guidebook* (London, 2004), pp. 22–6, 52, 60, 74, 78.

means, and because of these facts, children were seen anew as vulnerable, unformed (and yet about to be formed), and society as a whole might be held responsible for their welfare. The connections between the Hospital and literature are borne out by some cross-fertilising stories. The Hospital went into the imagination of the literary world, and the worlds of poetry and fiction came into the Hospital.

The Foundling Hospital for Wit

In 1743, just four years after the official establishment of the Foundling Hospital, a new popular magazine appeared allegedly edited by one Samuel Silence and called *The Foundling Hospital for Wit*. Its title page declared that this was

> The
> Foundling Hospital
> for
> WIT,
> INTENDED
> For the Reception and Preservation of
> such Brats of WIT and HUMOUR,
> whose Parents chuse to drop them.
> CONTAINING
> All the SATIRES, ODES, BALLADS, EPIGRAMS, &c.
> that have been wrote since the Change of the Ministry, many of which have never before been printed.[12]

An elaborate Preface set out the aims of this new publication in terms borrowed from the language of the Royal Charter that enacted the founding of the Hospital itself. That 'Samuel Silence' could so clearly expect his audience to recognise these terms is one thing. Even more important are the ironic ways in which he uses the well known facts of the plague of abandoned infants so common in London life at this period, and as reported day after day in the newspapers and the courts:[13]

> The Royal Charter of Apollo and the Muses, for Establishing an HOSPITAL for the Reception and Preservation of such Brats of WIT and HUMOUR, whose Parents chuse to drop them.
> Apollo, *God of Wit, Father of Light, King of* Parnassus, *and all the*

---

[12] *The Foundling Hospital for Wit,* Number 1. To be continued Occasionally (London: Printed 1743, Reprinted for W. WEBB, near St. Paul's, M DCC LXIII), title page.
[13] See Josephine McDonagh, *Child Murder and British Culture, 1720–1900* (Cambridge, 2003), pp. 1–5.

Territories thereunto belonging; to all to whom these Presents shall come, Greeting.

WHEREAS our Trusty and Well-beloved Subject Samuel Silence, Gentleman, in Behalf of great Numbers of *Mental Infants* daily exposed to Destruction, has, by his Petition, humbly represented unto us, that many Persons of WIT and HUMOUR of both Sexes, being sensible of the frequent Murders committed on these beautiful Infants by the inhuman Custom of exposing them to perish and starve in the common News Papers, or to be bury'd and suffocated in Dunghils of Trash in the Monthly Magazines, have, by the Instruments of Writing, declared their Intentions to contribute liberally towards the erecting and supporting an Hospital for the Reception and Preservation of such exposed and deserted Productions, as soon as We should be graciously pleased to grant our Letters Patent for the good Purpose . . .

The editor was surnamed 'Silence' because—like the Foundling Hospital itself—he undertook absolute discretion in relation to the provenance and heritage of such literary progeny as came under his hand, advising 'such modest Parents as would dispose of their Issue privately, that Letters directed for *Samuel Silence*, Esq; [were] to be left at *Brown's Coffee House* in *Spring Gardens*'. Also, in the manner of the practice at the Hospital, he took to himself the 'full and sole Power to refuse whatever Brats he shall think proper, particularly such as shall be judged infected with any dangerous Distemper, as also all misshapen, weak, or sickly Productions, neither such as are untoward, wicked, and licentious: forasmuch as the Admission of such might tend to Disgrace of our *Hospital*, and change what was intended as a Nursery for spritely and beautiful Infants, into an Infirmary for Invalids'.[14]

The verses collected in *The Foundling Hospital for Wit* were, for the most part, political and social satire directed against eminent men and women. One copy in the Bodleian Library has names filled into the blanks, among them Pitt, Walpole and the Duchess of Marlborough. The publication continued for six issues to 1764, then ceased until a new edition began to be published, *The New Foundling Hospital for Wit*, running

---

[14] *The Foundling Hospital for Wit* (London, 1743), pp. i-iv. The Preface goes on: 'And finally we will, for the universal Encouragement of all our loving Subjects, in the delightful Occupation of begetting Children, that whether their Offspring shall speak in the musical and sublime Language of Rhime, or in the plain and natural Cadence of Prose; whether they shall appear in the finer Dress of Epistles, Satires, Odes, Songs, and Epigrams; or in the plain and modest Garb of Letters and Essays, they shall be equally fitted an Apartment in this our *Hospital*, and as carefully attended and provided for, as if they were under the Eye of their own dear Parents.'

from 1768 to 1773 and this time with contributions from Lord Chesterfield, Lord Lyttelton, Mr Garrick, Dr Akenside, Elizabeth Carter and Lady Mary Wortley Montagu.

Tokens and tags

At the Foundling Hospital itself, many parents left their infants with tokens and tags to assist in later recognition and acknowledgement (Fig. 1). Some would also leave poems as a way of expressing and dignifying their loss. Each of these was scrupulously preserved by the institution—though they were never restored to the child. One such, about a male child reckoned to be about fourteen days old, was discovered on 10 May 1759. A scrap of its clothing was pinned in the register along with this poem:

> Hard is my Lot in deep Distress
> To have no help where Most should find
> Sure Nature meant her several Laws
> Should men as strong as Women bind
>   Regardless he, Unable I
> To keep this Image of my Heart
>   'Tis Vile to Murder! Hard to Starve
> <u>And</u> Death almost to me to Part
> If Fortune should her Favours give
> That I in better Plight may Live
> I'd try to have my Boy again
> And Train him up the best of Men.
>
> Joseph—in London. Born Apr 28.1759
> *Va! Mon Enfant prend ta Fortune.*[15]

As the unfortunate parents of these children reached for literary means to describe and shape their suffering, so too did literature influence the concept of the foundling from within the institution. On admission—whether an infant was deposited at the door, or brought by some woman who petitioned for her child's admission—each child was given a new name, his or her previous existence wiped out.

To begin with the children were named after the illustrious living. Not surprisingly, this began to cause problems. So the process settled on names drawn from the illustrious dead—Julius Caesar, Edward

---

[15] From the Foundling Hospital collection in the London Metropolitan Archives, and quoted in *The Foundling Museum Guidebook* (2004), p. 46.

Figure 1. Tokens given by mothers to their children on leaving them at the Foundling Hospital (mixed media) by English School (18th century) (©The Foundling Museum, London, UK/The Bridgeman Art Library).

Plantagenet, Philip Sidney, Oliver Cromwell, Perkin Warbeck. Or they reflected aspirational or moral qualities—Diana Thrifty, Judith Bright, Alice Hope, Eliza Meek, Michael Angel. Otherwise the children were given geographical names, presumably alluding to their beginnings in life—Mary Islington, Thomas Africa, Frances Ladbrooke. Finally the children were given appropriate names drawn from legend and literature. Of these Moses was immensely popular, but so was Aaron, and there was even an Ishmael and an Epaminondas. There was also a Clarissa Harlowe, a Sophia Western, a John Blifil, a George Allworthy, and—perhaps unsurprisingly—there were several named Tom Jones.

Songs of Innocence (and Experience)

By the latter part of the eighteenth century the idea of the lost and found, the abandoned child and the many charitable institutions that took them in, had become a familiar topic in literature. William Blake wrote several poems of Innocence and Experience about lost children, city children, and charity children. His first 'Holy Thursday' poem published in *Songs of Innocence* (1789) is about the special service held in St Paul's on the first Thursday in May for the children of London's charity schools:

> 'Twas on a Holy Thursday, their innocent faces clean,
> The children walking two and two in red and blue and green,
> Grey-headed beadles walked before with wands as white as snow;
> Till into the high dome of Paul's they like Thames waters flow.

Blake's *Innocence* 'Holy Thursday' poem was illustrated with an image of the procession, but his other 'Holy Thursday' poem in *Songs of Experience* (1793) was altogether different. The text of the poem may not be explicit, but it hardly needs the very striking illustration of the stylised woman standing looking down on the body of the naked babe on the ground, to convey its own strange logic. It is not clear whether this woman in the illustration is the surprised finder or the stricken abandoner, and the poem itself allows for both:

> Is this a holy thing to see,
> In a rich and fruitful land;
> Babes reduced to misery,
> Fed with cold and usurous hand?
>
> Is that trembling cry a song?
> Can it be a song of joy?
> And so many children poor?
> It is a land of poverty!
>
> And their sun does never shine,
> And their fields are bleak and bare,
> And their ways are filled with thorns;
> It is eternal winter there.
>
> For where'er the sun does shine,
> And where'er the rain does fall—

Babe can never hunger there,
Nor poverty the mind appal.[16]

Half sheltered by a naked wall I

Many other poets wrote about children, or to and for children, in the late eighteenth century, but it was the abandoned baby, the orphaned child, the foundling, that came to put all the concepts of 'child' and 'childhood' most powerfully under pressure.

A small and naked child bears no marks of origin, and no identity. Displace that child from its points of origin and there is nothing to show the way back to those beginnings. The child has no language, no memory and no consciousness which will allow him to explain who he is. His body will bear no marks that link him to any other person or place. It is only that other person or place that can identify him, the 'naming' and recognition can only go in one direction. Only the developed consciousness—whether that of an adult or another child—can say 'he looks like his father', or recognise the baby's moles or birthmarks, or claim external markers like the child's clothing, or the kinds of tokens left with the babies of the Foundling Hospital. Recognition and identity is here an entirely one-way process. [17]

But at the same time that child must have a past beyond his beginning, on the other side of birth and the scene of relinquishment. The facts of biology mean that he must have had a father (however briefly) and a mother, a mother whose voice will be familiar to him and whose face he is quite likely to have seen, if only once. But the key idea is that the child is alone. Unaided, without support and without name or place in an alien world, the abandoned child must construe his own identity and shape his own landmarks.

---

[16] William Blake, *Songs of Innocence and Experience*, (1789 and 1793), ed. Richard Willmot (Oxford, 1990), pp. 18 and 29–30. Josephine McDonagh notes that Blake's poem, combined with its engraving, 'encourages us to see the child's death as the responsibility of the "cold and usurous hand" of society more generally': *Child Murder and British Culture*, pp. 69–70.

[17] Nonetheless, the adults whose lives are marked by the experience of abandoned children (perhaps as parents driven to this extreme, or perhaps as adoptive parents pondering the 'mystery' of their child's origins) often seem driven to create, or to believe in, the possibility of the mark that will always distinguish their child. Internet websites for self-help support groups for adoptive parents often cite stories about abandoned babies bearing distinctive scars or marks on their bodies. It may only be an urban myth, but it still indicates the power of the drive for claiming an identity and knowledge of origin.

William Wordsworth wrote a poem about an abandoned baby in the story of Martha Ray in 'The Thorn', published in *Lyrical Ballads* in 1798. But in a well-known passage from *The Prelude* he writes one of his best accounts of the abandoned child; yet it is, in fact, about himself. It is a passage that appears (only minimally revised) in all the versions of the poem from the two-part *Prelude* of 1805 to the last version of 1850. It also bears some relation to other sections on his early life in *The Prelude* and to many of the major poems such as 'Tintern Abbey' and 'Intimations of Immortality based on Recollections of Early Childhood'.

This is from Book One of the two-part *Prelude*, lines 330–53:

> One Christmas time,
> The day before the holidays began,
> Feverish, and tired, and restless, I went forth
> Into the fields, impatient for the sight
> Of those three horses which should bear us home,
> My brothers and myself. There was a crag,
> An eminence, which from the meeting point
> Of two highways ascending overlooked
> At least a long half-mile of those two roads,
> By each of which the expected steeds might come—
> The choice uncertain. Thither I repaired
> Up to the highest summit. 'Twas a day
> Stormy, and rough, and on the grass
> I sate half sheltered by a naked wall.
> Upon my right hand was a single sheep,
> A whistling hawthorn on my left, and there
> Those two companions at my side, I watched
> With eyes intensely straining, as the mist
> Gave intermitting prospects of the wood
> And plain beneath. Ere I to school returned
> That dreary time, ere I had been ten days
> A dweller in my father's house, he died,
> And I and my two brothers, orphans then,
> Followed his body to the grave.

This passage includes both the site and the sight of orphaning—of the certainty of knowing himself to be alone in the world, even though the orphaning has actually not yet happened, and he is, strictly speaking, not alone. Thus it is the feelings, the apprehension of isolation *in itself* that makes the significance of the moment, not the facts.

The poet-speaker is supposed to be going 'home' but—as far as poetic logic is concerned—he never makes it, for we never see the anticipated horsemen arrive. The poet looks out from a 'summit', a high point of vision then, and sees two roads which represent 'the choice uncertain'. In the poetic landscape of the mind these might be roads leading both to the past and to the future. This is a day 'stormy' and 'rough' wherein he is exposed. At the centre are three apparently uncomplicated constituents of the scene which displace and 'carry across', which become metaphors representing the vulnerable self. Like many (literally) exposed babies he is 'half-sheltered' by a 'wall', while the close juxtaposition of the adjective 'naked' creates a slippage, so that the child is more easily visualised as 'naked' than the wall can ever be. The 'sheep' on his right hand is 'single', like the lost sheep sought by the good shepherd in Christ's parable. The 'whistling hawthorn' on his left is bare, and makes a sound without language, as the cry of the infant child. His eyes 'strain' to see the 'intermitting prospects' but far from being 'plain' he sees a dark wood only through a mist. From having been a 'dweller in my father's house'—with all the New Testament implications that go with the phrase—he finds himself an 'orphan' in the world.

The episode, he tells us immediately, stays in his mind, its elements slightly displaced again, reordered and 'translated', made into a nexus of metaphors once again as he repeats the scene which, he says, he will go on repeating compulsively:

> And afterwards the wind and sleety rain,
> And all the business of the elements,
> The single sheep, and the one blasted tree,
> And the bleak music of that old stone wall,
> The noise of wood and water, and the mist
> Which on the line of each of those two roads
> Advanced in such indisputable shapes—
> All these were spectacles and sounds to which
> I often would repair, and thence would drink
> As at a fountain. And I do not doubt
> That in this later time, when storm and rain
> Beat on my roof at midnight, or by day
> When I am in the woods, unknown to me
> The workings of my spirit thence are brought.[18]

But in this second refrain there is one fundamental change. The 'old stone wall' and the 'wood and water' make a 'noise', specifically a 'bleak music' and it is to these 'spectacles and sounds' to which he 'repairs'—with all the puns of restitution—and drinks 'As at a fountain'. Paradoxically, the moment of loss is the moment of most gain. The poet

---

[18] William Wordsworth, from the two-part *Prelude* of 1799, in Jonathan Wordsworth, M. H. Abrams and Stephen Gill (eds.), *The Prelude: 1799, 1895, 1850* (New York, 1979), pp. 9–11.

is lost in the world, he is orphaned. But in recognising, naming and recording in the displacing poetic language of metaphor and music, he finds himself.

Wordsworth's scene of self-discovery is one that was to go on to be highly influential in the vocabulary and images of his Victorian successors writing in both poetry and prose. Tennyson established himself as a major poet with the publication of *In Memoriam* (1850) where he re-visited the child's lonely moment of loss. Elizabeth Barrett Browning's poet-heroine in *Aurora Leigh* (1857) discovers a sense of the conscious self at the moment when she loses her father. And the opening chapter of Dickens's *Great Expectations* (1861–2) puts the scene of Pip's recognition of 'the identity of things' beside the grave of his father and mother.[19]

Of course the nineteenth century is full of orphan heroes and heroines and this is usually seen as a trope for the young person—or any person—negotiating an entry into society. But to know that you are alone, to understand the concept, let alone to 'name' yourself and go on to create an identity, requires language, and this is where poetry—and particularly the poetry of the nursery—comes into play.

Half sheltered by a naked wall II

The earliest children's books recognised the importance of poetry. In his Preface to the *Divine Songs* addressed 'to all that are concerned in the Education of Children', Isaac Watts gave four reasons for instruction through poetry: because there is 'great delight in the easy learning of Truths and Duties this way' due to Rhyme and Metre being 'so amusing and entertaining'; because 'What is learned in Verse is longer retained in Memory and soon recollected'; because children will thus 'have something to think upon when alone, and sing over to themselves'; and

---

[19] 'So runs my dream: but what am I? | An infant crying in the night: an infant crying for the light: And with no language but a cry.', Alfred Tennyson, *In Memoriam* (1850), canto LIV, in Christopher Ricks (ed.), *The Poems of Tennyson* (London and Harlow, 1969), p. 909. 'I was just thirteen, | Still growing like the plants from unseen roots | In tongue-tied Springs,—and suddenly awoke | To full life and life's needs and agonies | With an intense, strong, struggling heart beside | A stone-dead father . . .', Elizabeth Barrett Browning, *Aurora Leigh* (1857), ed. Margaret Reynolds (New York, 1996), p. 11. 'My first most vivid and broad impression of the identity of things, seems to me to have been gained on a raw afternoon towards evening. At such a time I found out for certain, that this bleak place overgrown with nettles was the churchyard; and that Philip Pirrip, late of this parish, and also Georgiana wife of the above, were dead and buried', Charles Dickens, *Great Expectations,* with an introduction by David Trotter and edited with notes by Charlotte Mitchell (1860–1: London, 2003), p. 3.

because such songs provide 'pleasant and proper Matter for their daily or weekly Worship, to sing over in the Family, or at such times as the Parents or Governors shall appoint'.[20]

Over a hundred years later Lucy Aikin made much the same point in her 1825 *Poetry for Children, Consisting of Short Pieces to be Committed to Memory*:

> The magic of rhyme is felt in the very cradle—the mother and the nurse employ it as a spell of soothing power. The taste for harmony, the poetical ear, if ever acquired, is so almost during infancy. The flow of numbers easily impresses itself on the memory and is with difficulty erased. By the aid of verse a store of beautiful imagery and glowing sentiment may be gathered up as the amusement of childhood, which, in ripe years may sooth the weary hours of languor, solitude and sorrow; may strengthen feelings of piety, humanity and tenderness; may sooth the soul to calmness, rouse it to honourable exertion, or fire it with virtuous indignation.[21]

In each case, while the fact of poetry's being easy to recall is emphasised, it is interesting that both these writers see poetry as contributing to the formation of the child's identity and character. It is also interesting to note that they both construe poetry as a private resource, something they may 'sing over to themselves' or turn to in 'solitude', much as Wordsworth turns his 'inward eye' in 'the bliss of solitude' to the scenes—above Tintern Abbey, along the daffodil-strewn shores of Lake Esthwaite, or on that hill overlooking the two roads—that made him as a poet and that he made into poetry.

Lucy Aikin's remark about mothers and nurses, and 'the magic of rhyme' being felt 'in the very cradle' raises another issue. As parents will know, rhythm, rhyme, assonance, alliteration, repetition, metaphor, and poetic shape are very often the first kinds of speech directly offered to the new-born baby; except that it comes out as 'And who's my darlingist most delishingest itty bitty honey bunny baby then?' Rocking your baby according to the poetry of your own intimate body rhythms—and almost everybody's is slightly different—poetry is what you offer to the child; except that this comes out as

> Eleanor, Eleanor,
> Dropped the baby on the floor

---

[20] Isaac Watts, *Divine and Moral Songs for Children* (London, 1835), pp. i-iv.
[21] Lucy Aikin, *Poetry for Children: Consisting of Short Pieces to be Committed to Memory* (London, 1825), p. iv.

> Knocked her brains out with a smack,
> Mopped them up and put them back.

Or else,

> Whose Daddy put her in the microwave
> In the microwave
> In the microwave?
> Whose Daddy . . .[22]

and so on for several verses.

While vocabulary and cognitive activities and knowledge, such as numerical calculations, belong to the left, or dominant, cerebral hemisphere, poetry—distinguished by its free associating displacements and illogical connections—is an activity belonging to the right, or non-dominant, cerebral hemisphere. Of course it also needs the attributes of the dominant hemisphere to bring it into being, but its musical and emotional qualities are similarly associated with the non-dominant right hemisphere. In new-borns, the right hemisphere is larger than the left and this remains the case until the third or fourth year.

In a fascinating account of lullabies, and their functions in relation to what psychologists call 'Motherese', or 'BT' (Baby Talk), Marina Warner explains why mothers hold and cradle babies on their left side. It used be thought that it was to do with the mother's heartbeat, but new work suggests that it is to do with the child's accessing and learning language—and the world through the associative processes of the right brain, which are of course connected to the left side of the body. So the child cradled with its right side against the mother's left breast has his left ear and eye free to experience vocal and visual stimulus, all the web of associations, emotions and reactions that make up the infant's learning of the world which is 'independent of verbal meaning'.[23]

The Australian psychologist and poet Craig Powell takes this further. In an article entitled 'On Poetry and Weeping' he suggests that the very moment of the acquisition of language is a moment of loss. As the developing child begins to understand that he and his mother are not one, but different—a process learned through the sound of the mother's voice, as he begins to distinguish the specificity of the noises which he makes from the sounds made by her, so he experiences loss,

---

[22] I am indebted to Paul and Vicky, Eleanor Shearer's father and mother, for their inventions.
[23] Warner, *No Go the Bogeyman*, pp. 232–3.

and mourns the separation where the security of one becomes two.[24] The realisation that comes to the child as he recognises that the mother is no longer a 'self-object' but distinctively other, is one that comes with language and with naming. The child names his mother. And at that very point he loses her. He is orphaned. Now this does work very neatly where children do indeed utter 'Mama' as their first word. Even 'Dada' fits the theory. But I am left wondering what to do with the children whose first words are 'cat', or 'ball' or 'book', which was the case with my nephew and nieces, let alone the child whose first word was 'hoover'.

Still the point remains. Entry into language is always a site of mourning, and specifically mourning for the imaginary mother (whether that child has an actual mother present at the time or not). So poetry—the most associative, displacing, transmuting language form—will always recall that essential moment of childish loss. A loss which in fact, biologically speaking, begins even further back with parturition when the child is no longer part of two, self and other, surrounded by and part of the mother's body, blood, heartbeat. In poetry then, we are all foundlings—separate, displaced and alone. But what we might find there is everything—and ourselves.

Different and yet the same

I keep saying 'the child', as if there were only one. Or as if children were all the same. In fact, of course, the only thing that all children share is what we all share by virtue of being alive, and which, in turn makes us all feel that we are qualified to know what 'children' are—the fact that we have all been one.

This conviction of certainty took the nineteenth-century idea of the child on to some peculiar consequences. 'The child' was supposed to be living in a land of 'childhood' which was different, special, pure maybe, certainly a blank page. It might be tinged with sadness at both ends—because of the first loss which comes with birth and separation, and the second loss which comes at the entry into grown-up life, but it is definitely alienated from the adult world, strange and separate, not at home in

---

[24] Craig Powell, 'On Poetry and Weeping' in *Free Associations*, 3, part 2, no. 26 (1992), 185–8. See also Craig Powell, 'Poetry on the Brain' in *Meanjin: New Writing in Australia on Psychology*, 63, no. 4 (2004), 116–21.

the world of commerce, politics, work, social engagement and sexual relations.

But think back to the tokens left with the babies of the Foundling Hospital. The parents of those children tried desperately to give them an individual identity and to leave some trace of their child in the world. Or, to put it the other way round, to leave a trace of their world with the child. But the Foundling Hospital locked away those tokens. They dressed the children alike in a uniform. They trained them for the same jobs—girls for service, boys for the military—and they gave the children new names, which was often the same name, because it was just a different way of saying the same thing—'this is an orphan': Moses Thames, Philip Sidney, Hope Thrifty, Mercy Angel, Tom Jones.

Because the Foundling Hospital was dealing with children *en masse* they could turn them all into identikits of 'the child'. But funnily enough, that is exactly what was going on out in the world too, most especially in middle-class homes. Here too, children were dressed alike in a special 'uniform' that was ungendered and said 'this is a child'. They were relegated to their own special world, the nursery and the schoolroom, to be dealt with by specialist nurses and tutors, they were given the same specially produced books and poems to read. And writers began to write for that special, but generalised, audience. Everyone knows the story of how Lewis Carroll began to tell stories for one little girl called Alice, or how Edward Lear entertained his employer's children, or how Robert Browning composed 'The Pied Piper of Hamelin' for Macready's little boy when he was ill. But so orthodox by now was the idea of the universality of 'the child' that publishers knew that there was profit to be made when you have two audiences—children themselves, and more importantly still, the masses of adults with ready money and a vested interest in preserving their idea of 'childhood' in 'the child'.

II. Lostlings

Exiled from childhood

But what then of the Lostlings? The children who are displaced from where they belong, but who are never found, and who yet remain as a memory, a shadow, an empty place, or a ghost. What then of the children who never did live in 'childhood'? After all, in the nineteenth century the idealised sexless, ageless, fairy world of 'the child' was not where most children lived.

In 1842 the Children's Employment Commission investigating the working conditions for mines delivered its report. Illustrated with engravings, one of the pictures that caused most reaction showed two children—a boy and a girl, but on the verge of puberty—being drawn up out of a mine on a rope together, their legs wrapped around each other. The children are clearly naked from the waist up, and modern commentators say that even the breeches worn by the children in this picture were drawn in at a late stage before publication.[25] The report caused a lot of comment. Elizabeth Barrett Browning wrote a poem about it. It caused a lot more comment than had been occasioned three years earlier when a 9-year-old boy was hanged at Chelmsford for arson. To my knowledge, no one wrote a poem about that.

By the 1850s sensationalist reports on prostitution calculated the numbers of children sold or selling themselves on the street in thousands. Child beggars, some deliberately mutilated, were often to be seen by tourists in Italy but they were common in England too. In 1856 there were 1,990 children under the age of 12 in prison. Burial societies paid out on insurance, no questions asked, for dead children. Baby farms grew up that would take unwanted children off your hands and, it has to be said, pretty shortly off their own. The press was full of stories of mysterious houses in the suburbs where heavily pregnant women went in, stayed for a while, only to come out slim and with no baby. In the late 1850s and into the 1860s there was another epidemic of abandoned babies both dead and alive, in ponds, in privies, but also this time, typically, in railway carriages, in canals and by roadsides.[26]

Adult literature dealt with all of this, but books for children—by definition a middle-class production designed for a middle-class audience—

---

[25] *Children's Employment Commission (Trades and Manufactures)*, Parliamentary Papers, 1843, Volume XIV, Appendix to 2nd report, pt. I, Appendix. III, Cols. 6–7. See Peter Kirby, *Child Labour in Britain, 1750–1870*, (Basingstoke, 2003), pp. 99–101.

[26] See George Behlmer, *Child Abuse and Moral Reform in England 1870–1908* (Stanford, 1982), pp. 17, 20–1, 27–8 and McDonagh, *Child Murder and British Culture* pp. 101–14, 123–7. McDonagh quotes Henry Humble's 'Infanticide, Its Cause and Cure' from Revd Orby Shipley (ed.), *The Church and the World: Essays on Questions of the Day* (1866), p. 57: '. . . bundles are left lying about the streets, which people will not touch, lest the too familiar object—a dead body—should be revealed, perchance with a pitch plaster over its mouth, or a woman's garter around its throat. Thus, too, the metropolitan canal boats are impeded, as they are tracked along by the number of drowned infants with which they come into contact, and the land is becoming defiled by the blood of her innocents.'

became very schizophrenic. Even an apparently innocuous book of poems by 'safe' women writers like Jean Ingelow, Dora Greenwell and Dinah Mulock, published in 1865 and guaranteed by its title of *Home Thoughts and Home Scenes*, carried illustrations by Arthur Boyd Houghton that displaced and unsettled, that even contradicted the poems.[27] The children are shown 'in nature'—much as Wordsworth depicted himself in nature, with that 'single sheep' and the 'blasted tree' in *The Prelude*—because of the prevailing idea of the childlike as 'natural' and 'innocent'. But the children look lost, alienated, and afraid and the adults are shown turning away, taking no notice, or asleep.

The Infant Life Protection Act

At the end of December 1872 Christina Rossetti published *Sing-Song*, subtitled *A Nursery Rhyme Book* and with a hundred-and-twenty illustrations by Arthur Hughes.[28]

Ten years earlier in 1862 Rossetti had had no intention of writing for children. In a letter dated 7 March [1862] to a correspondent not identified in Anthony H. Harrison's scholarly edition of her letters, she wrote:

> My dear Sir,
> I should be very happy for something of mine to come out in a volume so ably illustrated and containing contributions by Miss Greenwell and Miss Ingelow; but it so happens that children are not amongst my suggestive subjects and I could not venture to promise you anything at all worthy of such plates.[29]

Rossetti's correspondent was clearly George Routledge, the publisher of *Home Thoughts and Home Scenes*, and it would also seem from this letter that some—if not all—of the poems were written to the engravings and

---

[27] *Home Thoughts and Home Scenes* : Original poems by Jean Ingelow, Dora Greenwell, Mrs Tom Taylor, the Hon. Mrs Norton, Amelia B. Edwards, Jennett Humphreys, and the author of 'John Halifax, Gentleman' [Dinah Mulock Craik], illustrated by Arthur Boyd Houghton (London, 1865). See also Christine Sutphin, 'Victorian Childhood. Reading Beyond the 'Innocent Title': *Home Thoughts and Home Scenes* in Karin Lesnik-Oberstein (ed.), *New Approaches to Children's Literature*, pp. 51–77.
[28] Christina Rossetti, *Sing-Song. A Nursery Rhyme Book* with 120 illustrations by Arthur Hughes (London, 1872).
[29] *The Letters of Christina Rossetti*, ed. Antony H. Harrison (Charlottesville and London), I (1997), pp. 158–9.

not the other way around.[30] But that leaves one important question. What happened to make Rossetti change her mind about writing for children?

In 1872, the same year as the publication of *Sing-Song*, the Infant Life Protection Act was passed. It set up the first legal requirement for the registration of the births—and the deaths—of infants; it provided for the regulation of houses used for lying-in; and it required the registration and regulation of nurses caring for two or more children under the age of one year. Among the groups which had pressed for this legislation was the Association for the Preservation of Infant Life established in 1862, the very year in which Rossetti refused to contribute to *Home Thoughts*. To begin with, the Association's campaigning in Parliament and in the press was directed at reform of the 1844 Poor Law Amendment, arguing that if the stigma of illegitimate birth fell equally upon father as upon mother, it might help to prevent the high incidence of infanticide. In 1863 the Association had gone on to establish the National Society and Asylum for the Prevention of Infanticide with a view to offering practical help to mothers. But by the time Parliament actually took up the cause, it had become clear that it was not just mothers (or fathers) but complete strangers, that were also disposing of infants—for a fee: hence the terms eventually enshrined in the 1872 Infant Life Protection Act.

In his book on *Child Abuse and Moral Reform* George Behlmer says that the Act was not very successful in implementation.[31] But the publicity devoted to the problem of unnatural infant death—and the problem of mistreated children generally—had been so much canvassed in public that it did have results. Political and reforming results, as I will explain, but also literary results. Arthur Hughes's Frontispiece illustration to Rossetti's *Sing-Song* repairs Wordsworth's site of orphaning (Fig. 2). Here there are lots of sheep and a burgeoning tree sheltering guardian angels. Above all, the image supplies the lost mother, who is here (literally) knitting all the displacements back together (though she is also holding the baby on her right, rather than her left side). Rossetti's text, on the other hand, is not as innocent as it looks. Her work never is.

---

[30] Christine Sutphin comments on a certain 'disjunction' between the sinister character of the engravings in *Home Thoughts and Home Scenes* and the relatively more sentimental tone of the poems, but this may be explained by the fact that the engravings seem to have come first: see Christine Sutphin, 'Victorian Childhood. Reading Beyond the "Innocent Title": *Home Thoughts and Home Scenes*' in Lesnik-Oberstein (ed.), *New Approaches to Children's Literature*, pp. 51–77.
[31] See Behlmer, *Child Abuse and Moral Reform in England*, p. 38.

Figure 2. Arthur Hughes's frontispiece illustration to Christina Rossetti's *Sing-Song*.

Sing-Song

While Rossetti was working on her collection of 'nursery rhymes' she was very particular about the ordering of the poems, and about the illustrations which she envisaged as essential to the whole. In the manuscript, now in the British Library, she included little instructive sketches in pencil and red crayon for each of the poems, even while claiming that 'I cannot draw'.[32] As the manuscript did the rounds of publishers, she made it clear that her own sketches were not to be included, but were designed to 'explain my meaning' to whichever artist would eventually undertake the commission.

The settling on a choice of artist proved to be a problem. At one stage the work was offered to Rossetti's friend Alice Boyd, but then Rossetti did not like the sketches Boyd submitted. Eventually, William Michael Rossetti suggested Arthur Hughes. The key point of all this is that the illustrations—as eventually produced by Hughes—are very much an integral part of the book.[33] The title of the collection itself, while it looks simple enough, sets up some of the key concepts and patterns in the book: it is paradoxical, oppositional, punning, riddling and tautological. If there is singing, then there is a song. If there is a song, then there is singing. If there is an up—as in a 'sing-song' voice—then there is a down. The whole collection is arranged around this set of oppositions, or displacements. This is the first poem in the collection and Hughes's accompanying illustration shows a baby in a cradle watched over by one adult angel and two winged cherubs (Fig. 3).

> Angels at the foot,
>   And Angels at the head,
>   And like a curly little lamb
>   My pretty babe in bed.

If one reads the whole collection as a self-contained narrative poem, then it completes a circle or a round. The volume begins and ends with a

---

[32] The autograph manuscript is in the British Library, Ashley. 1371.
[33] *The Letters of Christina Rossetti*: Christina Rossetti to Frederick Startridge Ellis, 23 Feb. 1870 (I, 341); Christina Rossetti to Ellis, 25 Feb. 1870 (I, 342); Christina Rossetti to the Dalziel Brothers, 26 April 1871 (I, 369–71); Christina Rossetti to the Dalziel Brothers, 3 Aug. 1871 (I, 375); Christina Rossetti to William Michael Rossetti, 1 Sept. 1871 (I, 379–80); the Dalziel Brothers to Christina Rossetti, 1 Sept. 1871 (I, 381); Christina Rossetti to the Dalziel Brothers, [21 Sept. 1871] (I, 382); Christina Rossetti to Dante Gabriel Rossetti, 20 [Nov. 1871], and Christina Rossetti to the Dalziel Brothers, [25 Nov. 1871], (I, 385–6); Christina Rossetti to Dante Gabriel Rossetti, [1 Dec. 1871], (I, 387).

Figure 3.

cradle—actually the same illustrated cradle that reappears several times in the volume, as does its little carved heart design, which figures at one point hung over mother's bed, and, in another illustration, carved on a baby's grave. The illustrations to the first and last poems in the collection make a kind of mirror image. The adult angel in the illustration to the opening poem kneels on the right-hand side of the cradle. The adult woman in the illustration to the final poem in the volume is positioned on the left-hand side of the cradle. The angel and the mother here make a pair of 'book ends' to the whole collection, and this visual image reflects a similar 'mirroring' in the text: in the first poem baby is 'like a curly little lamb'; in the last poem baby is 'bo-peep'.

The second poem emphasises the mother/child dyad by setting up mirrors that guarantee reciprocity. Love goes back and forth, the song is both high and low, mother's arms are under and her eyes are above.

> Love me,—I love you,
>   Love me, my baby:
> Sing it high, sing it low,
>   Sing it as may be.
>
> Mother's arms under you,
>   Her eyes above you
> Sing it high, sing it low,
>   Love me,—I love you.

Then the tone changes; the third poem in the collection presents at one and the same time, the certainty of security on the inside, and the place outside or beyond, where there is the risk of the motherless, the fatherless, the forlorn and the poor. Arthur Hughes's image is similarly ambiguous and double (Fig. 4). Is this simply a mother lying asleep as her baby tugs at her dress? Or does her couch resemble a marble slab, making this a monument to the dead? Whichever way you look at it—and both possibilities are there—the adult turns her head away, as the adults so often do in Arthur Boyd Houghton's illustrations to *Home Thoughts*.

> My baby has a father and a mother,
>   Rich little baby!
> Fatherless, motherless, I know another
>   Forlorn as may be:
>   Poor little baby!

By poem 4—which offers the other side of Poem 3—the link is explicit.

> Our little baby fell asleep.
>   And may not wake again,
> For days and days, and weeks and weeks;
>   But then he'll wake again,
> And come with his own pretty look
>   And kiss Mamma again.

Now the baby is the one lost, and in Hughes's illustration (Fig. 5) the child is carried away by the adult angel we have already seen illustrating the first poem. The angel is represented horizontally (like the mother in the illustration to Poem 3) but, conversely and importantly, she is looking directly at the child in her arms.

After the four prefatory poems the 'story' of the collection marks out its true beginning at Poem 5 with daybreak 'springing':

Figure 4.

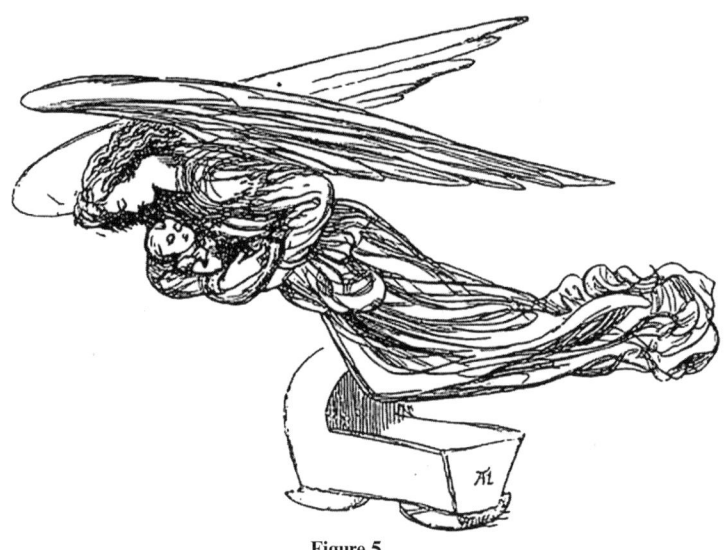

Figure 5.

'Kookoorookoo! kookoorookoo!'
   Crows the cock before the morn;
'Kikirikee! kikirikee!'
   Roses in the east are born.

'Kookoorookoo! kookoorookoo!'
   Early birds begin their singing;
'Kikirikee! kikirikee!'
   The day, the day, the day is springing.

Essentially the whole of *Sing-Song* contains only three kinds of poems. Firstly, there are broadly defined 'nature' poems, like this one, that emphasise the positioning of the 'innocent' child in the natural world and that follow on from Rousseau and Wordsworth.

Secondly, there are the liminal 'inside/outside' poems, like 'Bread and milk for breakfast', which is helpfully illustrated with an actual window out of which the child leans:

      Bread and milk for breakfast,
         And woollen frocks to wear,
      And a crumb for robin redbreast
         On the cold days of the year.

Similarly, in 'There's snow on the fields', Rossetti repeatedly sets the warmth, consistency and security of home against the cold, the contingency and the risk of 'beyond home';

> There's snow on the fields,
>   And cold in the cottage,
> While I sit in the chimney nook
>   Supping hot pottage.
>
> My clothes are soft and warm,
>   Fold upon fold,
> But I'm so sorry for the poor
>   Out in the cold.

Then, thirdly, there are the utterly typical Rossetti poems that riddle.

> A city plum is not a plum;
> A dumb-bell is no bell, though dumb;
> A statesman's rat is not a rat;
> A sailor's cat is not a cat;
> A soldier's frog is not a frog;
> A captain's log is not a log.

These 'riddling' kinds of poems represent, repeat and reinforce—at a very sophisticated level—the key moment when the child enters into language. As the child says 'Mama' and identifies 'Mama' as 'other' and not part of himself—realises that they are two and not one—so here the poem is structured around the dualistic character of language, of the word or sign as separated from the thing, idea or object that that word or sign represents.

These riddle poems are also, of course, about poetic language and the duality of metaphor and poetic method. But I wonder too whether Rossetti's riddle poems also have a more practical and worldly side. 'A city plum is not a plum' may be a whimsical tease, but it is also about finance, sport, politics, the military and commerce. It may be that within the sequence of poems in *Sing-Song* there is not just a simple 'inside/outside' concerned with houses, and with worldly power and possessions (and the lack thereof), but also a complicated 'inside/outside' concerned with the meta-text of the 'masculine' worlds of social engagement, as opposed to the 'feminine' world of family and home. It may be too that the lesson of ambivalence and doubleness that underlies so many of Rossetti's poems in this collection is all the more necessary in learning how to negotiate that grown-up 'masculine' world where things are quite likely *not* to be what they seem.

As the collection goes on, Rossetti's poems insist on mourning, risk and loss. 'A baby's cradle with no baby in it' is illustrated with the empty cradle and the mourning mother:

> A baby's cradle with no baby in it,
>   A baby's grave where autumn leaves drop sere;
> The sweet soul gathered home to Paradise,
>   The body waiting here.

'Crying, my little one' is illustrated with the mother cradling the child on her shoulder and trudging through the snow:

> Crying, my little one, footsore and weary?
>   Fall asleep, pretty one, warm on my shoulder:
> I must tramp on through the winter night dreary,
>   While the snow falls on me colder and colder.
>
> You are my one, and I have not another;
>   Sleep soft, my darling, my trouble and treasure;
> Sleep warm and soft in the arms of your mother,
>   Dreaming of pretty things, dreaming of pleasure.

The poems insist too on inside and outside, security and danger, and they play with the failures of language and explanation. In 'Why did baby die', the same sound rhyme is repeated throughout, linking all the words to do with the voice—'sigh', 'cry' and 'no reply'—with the definitive 'die' and the eternally repeated question 'why?' It looks astonishingly simple. It is remarkably complex.

> Why did baby die,
> Making Father sigh,
> Mother cry?
>
> Flowers, that bloom to die,
> Make no reply
> Of 'why?'
> But bow and die.

Finally, the collection reiterates the necessities of contrast and measurement, and the contradictions and oppositions that make the only kind of sense:

> If all were rain and never sun,
>   No bow could span the hill;
> If all were sun and never rain,
>   There'd be no rainbow still.

And yet Rossetti takes that sensible key fact of life—that there can be no joy without sorrow, no life without death, no positive without a negative, and takes it to its necessary conclusion in depicting the everyday nonsense of language and the social contract:

> If a pig wore a wig,
>> What could we say?
>> Treat him as a gentleman,
>> And say, 'Good day.'
>
> If his tail chanced to fail,
>> What could we do? –
>> Send him to the tailoress
>> To get a new one.

Through the whole collection Rossetti emphasises the riddling language that exists in poetry, in the nursery and in the 'real' world:

> A pin has a head, but no hair;
> A clock has a face, but no mouth there;
> Needles have eyes, but they cannot see;
> A fly has a trunk without lock or key;
> A timepiece may lose, but cannot win;
> A corn-field dimples without a chin;
> A hill has no leg, but has a foot;
> A wine-glass a stem, but not a root;
> A watch has hands, but no thumb or finger;
> A boot has a tongue, but is no singer;
> Rivers run, though they have no feet;
> A saw has teeth, but it does not eat;
> Ash-trees have keys, yet never a lock;
> And baby crows, without being a cock.

The message in *Sing-Song* for children—or perhaps for adults *about* children—is that this is a world which cannot be trusted, where children are always vulnerable and at risk. At first sight Hughes's illustration to 'A pin has a head' seems peculiarly irrelevant—or else deceptively simple. It shows a mother chatting to the toddler she holds to her shoulder. But the two look down on a homemade broody box where a cat seems to be safely shut up away from the little chicks that peck around at mother's feet (Fig. 6).

And yet even in Rossetti's elaborate contradictions of risk and loss, inside and outside, there is the possibility of a poetic resolution.

> Motherless baby and babyless mother,
> Bring them together to love one another.

This poem is the shortest in the volume—perhaps the shortest in Rossetti's whole *oeuvre*—and yet it clearly demonstrates Rossetti's method and effect (Fig. 7). Like the collection as a whole, it is a kind of palindrome, because it reads the same backwards and forwards. Like the

Figure 6.

Figure 7.

title of the collection, it is also tautological, for everything is repeated and mirrored. Even the vocabulary itself is repeated—two 'baby's in the first line, two 'mother's and two 'less's. In the second line 'them together' and 'one another' are repetitions, just as the two verbs 'bring' and 'love' are similar, both being about doubleness; you can only 'bring' something from one place to another, and can only 'love' something when there is a consciousness to do the loving and an object to be loved. The only slightly varied words in the whole poem are the conjunction 'and' in the first line, and the preposition 'to' in the second. But in terms of the poetic function of *Sing-Song* as a whole, even those two tiny words are relevant, for every poem—whether a safety and loss poem, or an inside and outside poem, or a riddling poem—is about 'and', about additions and connections; there is one thing and there is another. Every poem in the collection has a 'to' in the sense of 'in order to achieve', in order to bring about some purpose or meaning.

> Crimson curtains round my mother's bed,
>   Silken soft as may be;
> Cool white curtains round about my bed,
>   For I am but a baby.

The collection concludes with a series of poems that head us off to bed and back towards the baby in the cradle. Superficially they look like soothing evening poems closing the 'day' or the seasons of childhood. But look more closely, and they are about transition and change, about the difference between 'baby' and 'mother'—about growing up then.

Rossetti thumbs back through poems about the lost child:

> Baby lies so fast asleep
>   That we cannot wake her:
> Will the Angels clad in white
>   Fly from heaven to take her?

> Baby lies so fast asleep
>   That no pain can grieve her;
> Put a snowdrop in her hand,
>   Kiss her once and leave her.

She intersperses them with cheerful poems about the 'found' child:

> I know a baby, such a baby,—
>   Round blue eyes and cheeks of pink,
> Such an elbow furrowed with dimples,
>   Such a wrist where creases sink.

> 'Cuddle and love me, cuddle and love me'
>   Crows the mouth of coral pink:
> Oh, the bald head, and, oh, the sweet lips,
>   And, oh, the sleepy eyes that wink!

She runs again through the nursery songs, the comfort of mother's voice, through the processes of learning the world through the associative right brain, and the dichotomies of inside and outside. Here, in the illustration to 'Lullaby, oh, lullaby!' baby is being held the right way round:

> Lullaby, oh, lullaby!
> Flowers are closed and lambs are sleeping;
> Lullaby, oh, lullaby!
> Stars are up, the moon is peeping;
> Lullaby, oh, lullaby!
> While the birds are silence keeping,
> Lullaby, oh, lullaby!
> Sleep, my baby, fall a-sleeping,
> Lullaby, oh, lullaby!

And so to the final poem in the collection which is clearly about the sanctity of the cradle in the nursery, and the safety of home and mother's love:

> Lie a-bed,
> Sleepy head,
> Shut up eyes, bo-peep;
> Till daybreak
> Never wake:—
> Baby, sleep.

Or not.

For this mother—in Hughes's illustration (Fig. 8) to 'Lie a-bed'—kneels over her baby from the left, thus mirroring the angel who knelt over the baby from the right in the first poem in the collection 'Angels at the foot | And angels at the head'. More than that, only three poems back we read 'Baby lies so fast asleep | That we cannot wake her; | Will the Angels clad in white | Fly from heaven to take her?' As so often with Rossetti, words, once said, cannot be unsaid. The *sense* of this poem's ending—and so the ending to the whole collection—is indeed that baby should sleep only 'till daybreak'. But the *feeling* remains—once 'Never wake:—' has been uttered, that is all too probably what will happen.

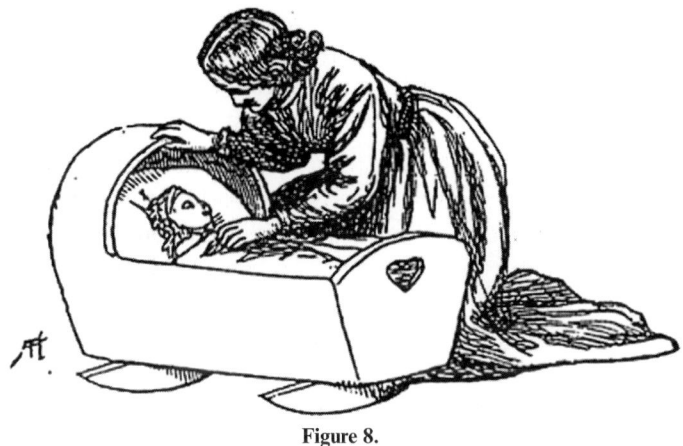

Figure 8.

Nursery Rhymes? Home and the '*unheimlich*'

In 1865 John Ruskin in 'Of Queen's Gardens' had published one of his best-known pieces of propaganda about home and the family, and particularly about women's role. 'This', he wrote,

> is the true nature of home—it is the place of Peace; the shelter, not only from all injury, but from all terror, doubt, and division. In so far as it is not this, it is not home; so far as the anxieties of the outer life penetrate into it, and the inconsistently-minded, unknown, unloved, or hostile society of the outer world is allowed by either husband or wife to cross the threshold, it ceases to be home; it is then only a part of the outer world which you have roofed over, and lighted fire in.[34]

However innocuous *Sing-Song* may appear to us now, the truth is that Rossetti does let in 'terror, doubt and division'. Over and again critics have described her most famous poems as 'uncanny', 'wayward', 'haunting', 'unsettling' and 'ambiguous', and the poems in *Sing-Song* are that, just as much as any of the others.[35] Like *Goblin Market*, 'Winter, My

---

[34] John Ruskin, 'Of Queen's Gardens', *Sesame and Lilies,* in *The Works of John Ruskin* (London, 1903–12), 18, 122.

[35] See, for instance, Angela Leighton in Angela Leighton and Margaret Reynolds (eds.), *Victorian Women Poets* (Oxford, 1995), pp. 353–7 and Angela Leighton, *Victorian Women Poets: Writing Against the Heart* (Hemel Hempstead, 1992), pp. 118–63. See also Isobel Armstrong, 'Christina Rossetti: Diary of a Feminist Reading', in Sue Roe (ed.), *Women Reading Women's Writing* (Brighton, 1987), pp. 117–37 and Isobel Armstrong, *Victorian Poetry: Poetry, Poetics and Politics* (London and New York, 1993), pp. 344–54.

Secret' or 'Remember', *Sing-Song* is a sequence that is haunted by repetitions, by silences, by mirrors and doubles, by animals that are human, and inanimate objects that live, by *déjà vu,* premature burial, by danger and risk, and by death. Above all, when read against the backdrop of contemporary events and reforms with respect to children, Rossetti does indeed let 'the anxieties of the outer life' and 'the hostile society of the outer world' enter into the sanctity of the home—and into the nursery.

But of course that is what poetry—including poetry for, to and about children—often does do. The texts of lullabies and nursery rhymes court and negotiate the threats that encompass the child, even while the mother's voice magically chants 'home', sings evil away out into the other side of this safe space with the reassurance of her presence.[36] Marina Warner quotes a piece of 'etymological guesswork' on the part of an eighteenth-century lexicographer who proposed that the very word 'lullaby' means 'to sleep (lull) at home' on the grounds that 'by' is derived from the old word for 'home' (as in 'Selby' or 'Grimsby').[37] But, as we have seen, even in the 'nursery' poems under discussion here, 'home' is a place always threatened by the hostile outside, as in the anxious poems about children in the city by Isaac Watts or William Blake. Or else 'home' is a place one never reaches, just as we never get to see the anticipated horsemen in *The Prelude* who were to come to take the young William Wordsworth back 'home' to be 'a dweller in my father's house'.

Home and its discontents

Christina Rossetti carried on with her new interest in children's literature—and in children. She went on to publish a collection of stories in *Speaking Likenesses* and she corresponded with other writers for children, like Lewis Carroll and Caroline Gemmer, who had once written under the name of 'Gerda Fay' and who published *Babyland, or, Pretty Rhymes for the Little Ones* in 1877. With Gemmer, Rossetti also shared a common interest in the welfare of animals and the efforts of the anti-

---

[36] Gilles Deleuze and Felix Guattari in '1837: Of the Refrain' in *A Thousand Plateaus: Capitalism & Schizophrenia*, trans. Brian Massumi (1988: London and New York, 2004), p. 343.

[37] Warner *No Go the Bogeyman*, p. 204. The whole of Marina Warner's section on lullabies is important and instructive; as she says, 'Odd as it may seem, lullabies obsessively spell out such dangers, attempting to encompass every possibility', op. cit., p. 201. It should also be noted here that when Rossetti translated her *Sing-Song* into Italian she called it *Ninna-Nanna* which has the same alliteration and onomatopoeia as the English, but which also means 'lullaby' in Italian—the connection being to the mother, nurse or grandmother '*nan*' doing the singing.

vivisection campaigners. It is one of the ironies of the nineteenth century that even while the idealised image of 'the child' was at its most prevalent, actual children in the real world were the last vulnerable group to benefit from reform and legislation. They came after factory workers, after women, after animals.

Rossetti herself worked on behalf of all of these vulnerable groups. Though she declined, when asked in 1888, to become Patron of the Society for the Protection of Women and Children, earlier in the decade she had assiduously collected signatures for a petition in support of the Criminal Law Amendment Bill. One of the many important reforms supported by Josephine Butler, this Bill was introduced into Parliament in May 1883 and proposed the introduction of significant prison sentences for the seduction of girls under sixteen. It was eventually passed in 1885, but it attracted a lot of public comment in the process, and it was not the only reforming project concerned with the welfare of children in the 1880s.

In 1873, the year after the publication of *Sing-Song*, Benjamin Waugh published a controversial book entitled *The Gaol Cradle: Who Rocks it?*[38] Here he argued that sending juveniles to prison only turned them into hardened criminals and fostered the generations of adults filling up Britain's prisons. Waugh was later to become a leading figure in the London Society for the Prevention of Cruelty to Children which was established in 1884 on the model of a similar society set up in Liverpool in the previous year. Something happened to the ways in which society thought about children in the two decades from 1870. In France, substantial changes were made to the Napoleonic code which reduced the significance of the *puissance paternelle*, and this innovation seems to have filtered across the Channel. On the one hand, the idealisation of 'the child' in middle-class homes had turned children into a generic entity without individuality. At the same time that very difference had deprived poorer class children of their very humanity; they were construed as animals, chattels, objects.

Christina Rossetti, along with other important writers for children, blurred the boundaries and challenged the false categories. She did not

---

[38] For Benjamin Waugh see ch. 2, 'Benjamin Waugh and the Founding of the Society' in Anne Allen and Arthur Morton, *This is Your Child: The Story of the National Society for the Prevention of Cruelty to Children* (London, 1961), pp. 15–33. Hesba Stretton was another writer who was interested in the work of the Society: op. cit., pp. 18–19. The first line of Allen and Morton's book is 'This book deals with terrible things'.

subscribe to the idealisation of 'the child', or see a separation between the adult world and the world of the child. She let the 'hostile society of the outer world' into her poetry for children, and wrote poetry for adults which was apparently about children, but which really dealt with the grown up subjects of sexual violence and sexual commerce. (Her best known work in this area is the poem *Goblin Market*, where even Dante Gabriel's opening illustration, showing a fully grown up Lizzie and Laura asleep in each others' arms, suggests the ambivalences of Christina Rossetti's poem.)

In the second half of the nineteenth century reformers, and then legislators, began to realise just how besieged real children were, how many lostlings had been cast aside, neglected, abused, murdered. An early history of the National Society for the Prevention of Cruelty for Children is illustrated with harrowing photographs from the late nineteenth and early twentieth centuries that testify to this new concern. The captions alone make the point: 'Starvation was common in the early days', 'Victims of brutality', 'Children lived in these places', 'Four neglected babies'. One picture of four terrified and haunted-looking children was labelled: 'Their home had *One* chair, *One* cup; They took turns to drink from a jam jar. Their Kitchen floor was slippery with dirt; Their parents were gaoled for six months for *Neglect.*'[39]

Between 1870 and 1908 no less than sixty-nine Acts of Parliament were passed concerning child-welfare. They dealt with everything ranging from elementary education to chimney sweepers, from the sale of drink and gunpowder to minors, to the punishment of incest and indecent assault, from consent to sex and the prevention of cruelty, to legislating on pawning and betting by infants.[40] If the 'hostile society of the outer world' had just begun to recognise the dangers that surrounded children, the literature of the nursery—in the very inner sanctum of home—had always known it.

---

[39] Allen and Morton, *This is Your Child*, pp. 6, 38, 39, 55, and 57.
[40] See Behlmer, *Child Abuse and Moral Reform in England*, Appendix A, 'Child Welfare Legislation 1870–1908', pp. 229–30.

III. Changelings

Displacements and Daddies

Toward the end of the nineteenth century, and partly because of the efforts of reformers and legislators, children once again became more visible in the imagination of society. But shortly thereafter—just as had been the case in the mid-eighteenth century—the results of particular social and political events meant that more children were actually on the streets, and not in the nursery. So in order to get on to Changelings and my last kind of displaced child, here is an entirely unscientific sample of music hall songs dating from 1883 through to 1916, selected solely on the grounds that they each have the word 'Daddy' in the title.

The first is 'Daddy Long Legs', dating from 1883, where the singer explains how he was brought up as the 'school goody goody' until the 'fates made a slight alteration' when he met a girl in the street:

> Her eyes and her—well, altogether,
> I felt as I'd not felt before . . .
> . . . After tea I said 'I'll see you home'. She said 'Halfway'. I said 'All the way,
> I'm jiggered if I don't'. When to my surprise she said,
> [—and chorus –]
> 'Old Daddy Long Legs wouldn't say his prayers . . .'

As the verses go on, we meet the girl's brother and then another child, and eventually it becomes clear that these are the lostlings, and that 'Daddy Long Legs' is the spider who is all too willing to pay for their services.

'Goodbye Daddy' and 'The Boers have got my Daddy', both published in 1900, are self evidently sentimental songs designed to shore up public morale. But 'Don't be Angry Daddy' from 1901 offers a slightly different moral perspective, for this tells the story of a man who has deserted his family and who is subsequently haunted by the pleas of his child. 'Daddy, don't leave us dear' from 1902 tells a similar tale.

On the other hand, in 'Where Does Daddy Go, When He Goes Out' from 1913 we gradually realise all that is really going on, as the child tries to comfort his mother by explaining that he knows the answer to this question because he had heard father say 'I'll meet my fairy fine or wet'. The comic song 'When Daddy Comes Home Tonight' might be the sequel to the above, as the child begs mother not to 'black his eye tonight . . . as you did the other day'. 'Put Me Through To Daddy Christmas', from 1917, tells of a little girl making a phone call:

> Put me through to Father Christmas
> Hello Santy is that you?
> I don't want my dolls and toys
> Take my share to other girls and boys
> All I want is just my Daddy
> Who is fighting o'er the sea
> Won't you drive, right away, in your sleigh, to the fray
> And bring him back to me.

Finally, from 1916, 'The Empire Now Will Be Your Daddy'—which does not need any explanation.[41]

It may be unscientific, but it is revealing. From the recognition in popular culture of the moral threat that exercised so many of the reformers of the late nineteenth century, through a sentimental valuing of the family—even while it reflects the facts of fathers' desertions—to a kind of anti-Suffragette joke about strong-minded women, and the recognition that war means many fatherless children, this is a social history in little.

I set myself this exercise in the first place because I was posing a question about fathers at the turn of the century. As mentioned earlier, legislation in France had reduced the *puissance paternelle*, and in Britain too, legislation meant that actual fathers of real children no longer owned them as chattels as had once been the case. Instead, in very many ways the state had taken over that individual role, had systematised responsibility, so that patriarchy—instead of being made up of individual acts and general social expectations—was encoded in the law and the apparatus of the state; 'The Empire Now Will Be Your Daddy'.

At the turn of the nineteenth century Freud had also vested the idea of 'the father' with a key importance—as indeed he had the idea of 'the child'. In some ways Freud's recognition of the incidence and importance

---

[41] 'Daddy Long Legs', written by A. Maynard and composed by W. G. Eaton (Howard and Co., London, 1883); 'Goodbye Daddy', written by Laura Barclay, composed by Lucy Everard and sung by Miss Vesta Victoria (Francis, Day and Hunter, London, 1900); 'The Boers Have Got My Daddy', by Mills and Castling, and sung by Tom Costello (Francis, Day and Hunter, London, 1900); 'Don't Be Angry Daddy' written by Carl Howard and composed by E. Joughmans and sung by Tom Costello (Francis, Day and Hunter, London, 1901); 'Daddy, Don't Leave Us Dear', written by Frederick Buxton, composed by Arthur Jules and sung by Mrs Frederick Buxton (1902); 'Where Does Daddy Go When He Goes Out?', written and composed by Frederick Gardner and Billy Williams, and sung by Billy Williams (Francis, Day and Hunter, London, 1913); 'When Daddy Comes Home Tonight', written, composed and sung by Robert Henry (Keith Prowse, London, n.d.); 'Put Me Through To Daddy Christmas', words by James Wilson, composed by Sidney Lennox (E. Osbourne and Co., London, 1917); 'The Empire Now Will Be Your Daddy', written by R. P. Weston, composed by Herman Darewski (Francis, Day and Hunter, London, 1916). All of these items are in the Sheet Music collection in the Bodleian Library.

of childhood trauma, no matter how flawed it may have been, grew directly out of the nineteenth-century idea of 'the child'. It was a kind of skewed version of the argument that made childhood separate, special, different and alien, even while it would go on to recognise how that experience bled into the life of the adult. That this took Freud on to think first about *fathers*—not mothers, not nurses, not siblings—is what marks him as a man of his time. In psychoanalytic theory the importance of mothers and mothering begins to come into view essentially with the work of later analysts, like Anna Freud, Melanie Klein, and D. J. Winnicott. It is only with John Bowlby's theory of attachment developed—significantly—after the Second World War, in the light of his study of the mass evacuation of children from London that it showed its results. It is at that stage that bonding and attachment, based on the model and the role of the mother, comes into clinical discourse.[42] But again, in literature, and even in legislation, the importance of the idea of the mother, or the mother substitute, had been there all along.

Adoption law and the welfare of the child

By the end of the nineteenth and the beginning of the twentieth century there were a lot of displaced children in Britain. There were several reasons for this. One—bizarrely, but obviously—was the result of the Factory Acts which regulated the child labour market. In 1851 children under 15 had made up 6.9 per cent of the total workforce, but by 1881 they represented only 4.5 per cent.[43] No longer useful to parents as producers of labour, many children were left to their own devices. John Barnardo had set up his first institution for homeless children in the East End of London in 1866. By 1885 he had nine such establishments, but there were still reckoned to be some 20,000 homeless children living in London.[44] The Boer War, the First World War and the post-war influenza epidemic exacerbated the situation.

Officially, institutional care was the only option, partly because the old nineteenth-century practice of 'baby farming' had given private

---

[42] John Bowlby, *Maternal Care and Mental Health* (World Health Organisation, Monograph Series No. 2. 1951), and John Bowlby, *Attachment and Loss*, vol. I, *Attachment* (London, 1969), 2nd edn. (1982); vol. II, *Separation: Anger and Anxiety* (London, 1973); vol. III, *Loss: Sadness and Depression* (London, 1980). See also Jeremy Holmes, *John Bowlby and Attachment Theory* (London, 1993), *passim*.
[43] Behlmer, *Child Abuse and Moral Reform in England 1870–1908*, p. 46.
[44] Ibid., p. 58.

adoption a bad name. This is one advertisement that had appeared over many weeks during 1870 in *Lloyd's Weekly Newspaper*:

> Adoption—a good home with a mother's love and care is offered to any respectable person wishing her child to be entirely adopted. Premium £5 which sum includes everything. Apply by letter only to Mrs Oliver, Post Office, Grove-Place, Brixton.

On 12 June 1870 two dead babies were found in Brixton, one by a railway line, another in a pile of rubbish. In the previous weeks there had been sixteen other such finds in and around Brixton. The police investigation uncovered a scrap of paper with one of the dead babies that led to a particular house run by a Margaret Waters, who also went under the name of 'Oliver'. Waters was hanged for child murder on 11 October 1870.[45]

Nevertheless—given pressing contingent circumstances—in the early twentieth century private adoption was increasingly common, and promoted by several agencies such as the National Child Adoption Association. In 1920 Edward Shortt, the then Home Secretary, appointed a committee presided over by Sir Alfred Hopkinson to look into the desirability of making legal provision for the adoption of infants—that is, anyone under 21 years old. They decided that the need was urgent, but over and again, across the debates that took place on some six private Members' bills in the following years to 1926 (when the Adoption of Children Act was passed), Members of Parliament worried about the 'very serious effect of severing the tie between mother and child'.[46] The provisions of the Act itself allowed married couples to adopt jointly, and single persons to adopt. There were restrictions on a single man adopting an infant female—which some members of the House of Lords felt cast 'an unnecessary slur on the morals of the male sex'—while other Lords regretted that there was no provision for 'two maiden ladies' to adopt.[47] The evidence of these debates is interesting because it suggests how, even in the 1920s, the concept of the 'family' and of what that might consist, was far from the supposed ideal of father, mother and two children.[48]

---

[45] Behlmer, *Child Abuse and Moral Reform in England 1870–1908*, p.29.
[46] 'The Adoption of Children Bill', 26 Feb. 1926: *Parliamentary Debates, Commons* (1926), vol. 192, Feb. 22–March 12, column 919.
[47] *Parliamentary Debates, Lords* (1926), vol. 65, 28 July 1926, column 325.
[48] Human geographers generally recognise that the imagined 'universal' unit of father, mother and two children is one which only came anywhere near to actually existing (and even then, mostly in the popular imagination and in the hopes of the legislators) during the twenty years following the 1939–45 war.

But the overriding focus of the 1926 Adoption of Children Act, as is clear from the debates as well as the legislation itself, was that any adoption order 'will be for the welfare of the infant, due consideration being for this purpose given to the wishes of the infant, having regard to the age and understanding of the infant'.[49] That principle remains the same in adoption practice in Britain today and it has had widespread influence on adoption legislation throughout the world.

When We Were Very Young

A. A. Milne's collection *When We Were Very Young* was published in 1924. His second volume of poems for children, *Now We Are Six*, appeared in 1927, so the two dates span the period of the passing of the 1926 Adoption Act.[50] *When We Were Very Young* is, like the other poems and collections discussed in this essay, of its time. It is about a family order where the child is at the centre and yet, at the same time, this is a collection which composes and wards off the dangerous 'corner of the street | Where the three roads meet'. 'Corner-of-the-Street' is the first poem in the collection:

> Down by the corner of the street,
>   Where the three roads meet,
>   And the feet
> Of the people as they pass go 'Tweet-tweet-tweet',
> Who comes tripping round the corner of the street?
>   One pair of shoes which are Nurse's;
>   One pair of slippers which are Percy's . . .
>   Tweet! Tweet! Tweet!

As with Christina Rossetti, Milne's poems look simple enough. They probably seem all the simpler to readers reading now in middle age because they are familiar from their own childhood and from their parents' childhood. But, as with Christina Rossetti, these poems have their antecedents in other poems about and for children. In his Preface to *When We Were Very Young*, A. A. Milne wrote:

> At one time (but I have changed my mind now) I thought I was going to write a little note at the top of each of these poems, in the manner of Mr William

---

[49] 16 & 17 Geo. V (1926), c. 29, 3 (b).
[50] A. A. Milne, *When We Were Very Young* (1924), and *Now We Are Six* (1927), in *Winnie-The-Pooh: The Complete Collection of Stories and Poems*, with illustrations by E. H. Shephard (London, 2001), pp. 250–335 and 336–432.

Wordsworth who liked to tell his readers where he was staying, and which of his friends he was walking with, and what he was thinking about, when the idea of writing his poem came to him.

In fact, Milne's annotations were not necessary because the secure world Christopher Robin inhabits is so sure. Or rather, because the *fantasy* of the secure world that Christopher Robin inhabits is so sure *in the wishful imagination of his readers* (old and young) that it needs no explanation. In 'Buckingham Palace' it is easy to construct the image of Christopher Robin's world: he lives in a patriarchal order where Daddy hardly ever appears but where his controlling presence is over all, where Alice—Mummy's substitute and second—is marrying one of the guards, and where the larger life of the Empire is certain, like the little life of the cared-for child, because the King 'knows all about me' and it is always 'time for tea':

> They're changing guard at Buckingham Palace—
> Christopher Robin went down with Alice.
> Alice is marrying one of the guard.
> 'A soldier's life is terrible hard,'
> > Says Alice.

But the real reason why it is so very easy to conjure up Christopher Robin's world is because it is not a real world, but an imagined world that we can all share. At the same time this is also a book about the child alone, secure in his own identity (in poems like 'Happiness'), and capable of shaping and naming his own world in poems like 'The Christening':

> What shall I call
> > My dear little dormouse?
> His eyes are small,
> > But his tail is e-nor-mouse.
>
> I sometimes call him Terrible John,
> 'Cos his tail goes on—
> And on—
> And on.
> And I sometimes call him Terrible Jack,
> 'Cos his tail goes on to the end of his back.
> And I sometimes call him Terrible James,
> 'Cos he says he likes me calling him names. . . .
>
> > But I think I shall call him Jim,
> > 'Cos I *am* fond of him.

If Christopher Robin's happy family and national life is a phantasm, the promotion of his secure sense of identity and purpose is propaganda designed both to inculcate those virtues in the child and to reassure adults of the child's independence and resilience in the face of the horrors of the world. Almost all of the poems in *When We Were Very Young* repeat these patterns and concerns to do with identity and naming and self assurance. They go on right up to the concluding pages which, like Rossetti's *Sing-Song*, end with a poem that is a lullaby, and a prayer, and where Christopher Robin is, crucially, on his own:

> Oh! *Thank you, God, for a lovely day*
> And what was the other I had to say?
> I said 'Bless Daddy', so what can it be?
> Oh! Now I remember it. *God bless me.*[51]

Now We Are Six

Now We Are Six begins and carries on in the same way; the opening poem in the volume is 'Solitude':

> I have a house where I go
>   When there's too many people,
> I have a house where I go
>   Where no one can be;
> I have a house where I go,
> Where nobody ever says 'No'
> Where no one says anything—so
>   There is no one but me.

There are very few adults here either in the pictures or the poems, and if that means that the child in this poetry flirts with the risk of being displaced, of being lost and forgotten and alone in the world, his independence, and individuality of will is still guaranteed as in the opening and ending to 'Forgotten':

> Lords of the Nursery
>   Wait in a row,
> Five on the high wall,
>   And four on the low;
> Big Kings and Little Kings,
>   Brown Bears and Black,
> All of them waiting
>   Till John comes back . . .

---

[51] It is indicative of the national and social psychological investment in ideas to do with childhood at this time that this particular poem was written for, and still belongs to, the library of Queen Mary's dolls house.

> *What's become of John boy?*
>   *Nothing at all,*
> *He played with his skipping rope,*
>   *He played with his ball.*
> *He ran after butterflies,*
>   *Blue ones and red;*
> *He did a hundred happy things—*
>   *And then went to bed.*

With 'In The Dark' the collection again ends with the child alone though safe and secure because 'they've all of them been | And kissed me lots | They've all of them said "Good-night"'. Once this background is filled in, the child can turn inward untrammelled and self-directed, and imagine himself into a new existence, into a future of self-construction and self-definition as he falls asleep. In all these seemingly innocent poems the new contemporary attitudes to children, as enshrined in the Adoption Act, allowed for some autonomy, for the 'wishes' of the child to be taken into account.

> So—here I am in the dark alone,
>   There's nobody here to see;
>   I think to myself
>   I play to myself,
>   And nobody knows what I say to myself;
> Here I am in the dark alone,
>   What is it going to be?
> I can think whatever I like to think,
> I can play whatever I like to play,
> I can laugh whatever I like to laugh,
>   There's nobody here but me.
>
> I'm talking to a rabbit . . .
>   I'm talking to the sun . . .
> I think I am a hundred—
>   I'm one.
> I'm lying in a forest . . .
>   I'm lying in a cave . . .
> I'm talking to a Dragon . . .
>   I'm BRAVE.
> I'm lying on my left side . . .
>   I'm lying on my right . . .
> I'll play a lot tomorrow . . .
>   . . . .
> I'll think a lot tomorrow . . .
>   . . . .
> I'll laugh. . ..
>   a lot . . .

> tomorrow . . .
> (*Heigh-ho!*)
>
> Good-night.

'So I think I'll be six now for ever and ever'

Who speaks children's poetry?

It is a question that A. A. Milne himself addresses in his Preface to *When We Were Very Young,* but his very formulation allows for freedom of choice, according to the wishes of the child:

> You may wonder sometimes who is supposed to be saying the verses. Is it the Author, that strange but uninteresting person, or is it Christopher Robin, or some other boy or girl, or Nurse, or Hoo? If I had followed Mr Wordsworth's plan I could have explained this each time; as it is, you will have to decide for yourselves.

Far from having one voice, the child in poetry has many. And far from 'children's poetry' and 'children's literature' always being the same, an identifiable genre, it varies to reflect the concerns of its own time and the treatment of real children in its own time. If the ideal of childhood—innocent, unwritten on, removed and separate from contemporary social concerns—was always a phantom even at the times when it was supposed to be most real, that is from the late eighteenth to the early twentieth century, then the idea that the literature of childhood was similarly isolated—removed, special, involved in its own magic space and separate from contemporary social concerns—is equally phantasmagoric.[52]

In historical fact, real children lived lives in a world that was the same as the adult world—complicated, messy, difficult, painful. Far from being an oddity, it was the displaced child—translated from the supposed 'ideal' of the family unit—who was the normal child. It was those real displaced children who—at different times and in different ways—drove the imaginative energies that formed children's literature. It was the idea of the Foundling, alone and isolated in nature, by the roadside, or in the

---

[52] In her article on *Home Thoughts and Home Scenes* Christine Sutphin tells a very revealing story about a book by Fred Cody called *Make-Believe Summer: A Victorian Idyll* (New York, 1980). Cody was inspired by Arthur Boyd Houghton's illustrations to *Home Scenes* to write a story based on them. But the narrative which he composes is one that insists on 'a charming depiction of middle-class Victorian life . . . to tell the story of the children and their idyllic summer on an English farm'. See Christine Sutphin, 'Victorian Childhood. Reading Beyond the "Innocent Title": *Home Thoughts and Home Scenes*' in Lesnik-Oberstein (ed.), *New Approaches to Children's Literature*, pp. 68–71.

busy street, that lay in the margins of Isaac Watts's collections and in *Mother Goose,* and that reappeared in Blake's writings or Wordsworth's picture of himself on the hill overlooking the two roads. It was the idea of the Lostlings, the suffering children on the outside, attested to by the Factory Acts and the Infant Life Preservation Act and all the rest of the late nineteenth century's reforming legislation, who haunted the contradictory, ever shifting boundaries of Christina Rossetti's not-so-safe nursery in *Sing-Song*. It was the notion of the Changeling—removed from one place to another with its 'wishes' taken into account, because of an autonomy, apparently legally guaranteed by the Adoption Act, but, in reality, forced upon the many children who had to take care of their own lives because there was no one else to care for them—it was that Changeling child that informed the peculiarly solitary poems of A. A. Milne.

While the old, idealised, pretty image of the child and childhood never did exist either in the real world, nor in literature by, for and to children, it *did* exert a pull on the popular imagination and it did have an effect. To some extent, all the various charitable efforts and moral reforms directed at children's lives were driven by that ideal (however imaginary), and represented a striving towards it. But then, sometimes an absence can be more powerful than a presence. Think of the apocryphal story of the discarded scrap in Samuel Beckett's waste paper basket where he had written: 'Act I, scene 1 . . . Enter Godot'.

In the early twenty-first century we still hanker for the phantom ideal of 'childhood'. Our nostalgia for an innocence in children and childhood makes us anxious to protect something that never did exist and may not be possible. Worse still, on the Alice Miller model of 'the drama of being a child' we are nostalgic for our own lost childhoods of uncluttered happiness and security that—more than likely—we never did have and never could have had.[53] In spite of the facts and contrary to all the evidence—in the history of social ills and social reform, and in the literature that reflects that history—we still want to be six 'for ever and ever', just as Christopher Robin says in 'The End':

> When I was One,
> I had just begun.
>
> When I was Two,
> I was nearly new.

---

[53] Alice Miller, *The Drama of Being A Child and the Search for the True Self* (London, 1987).

> When I was Three,
> I was hardly Me.
>
> When I was Four,
> I was not much more.
>
> When I was Five,
> I was just alive.
>
> But now I am Six, I'm clever as clever.
> So I think I'll stay six now for ever and ever.

It may be, that the best kind of children's literature being produced now is that which recognises that children live in a real world that is puzzling and painful, but which is still sophisticated enough to know about the phantom of this lost ideal—in time, place, childhood and youth—and allows for its haunting, persistent resilence. One example might be in Nick Sharratt's strange and hallucinatory illustrations for Jacqueline Wilson's *Midnight*—a story for today about adoption and dispersed families and displaced children. But Sharratt's illustrations draw on and re-interpret the cradle from *Mother Goose* or from Arthur Hughes's pictures for *Sing-Song*. They remind us too of the haunting lostlings in Arthur Rackham's illustrations to *Peter Pan*—who is also part of the long history of the foundling.[54]

It may be that the best poetry about, for and to children is that which acknowledges 'the child' as multiple, various, difficult. 'The child' is not a blank page, but written over, many layered, a palimpsest of the displacements of imagery and metaphor, found, lost, changed—just like poetry itself.

Angela Leighton's 'Icarus on the Beach' was written for me, and I cannot now recall how much of our discussions about literature—and about life—might have gone into the poem. What I do recognise is the imagery of the geological stratifications that layer the facts of history with the ideas of literature. I recognise too the haphazardness of the encounter, and the slipperiness of the 'sandlings' that 'flicker' into being my foundlings, lostlings and changelings of the past and the present.

> They seem to shoulder air with ease, these bony children,
> buckling to, like sudden folding Z's,

---

[54] Jacqueline Wilson, *Midnight* (London, 2003), pp. 2 and 150. J. M. Barrie, *Peter Pan in Kensington Gardens* (London, 1906), and J. M. Barrie, *Peter Pan in Kensington Gardens,* ed. Peter Hollindale (Oxford, 1999).

on hassocked sand,
landing themselves on its slippery territory.

Tricked out of air, were they? Into shins and elbows and knees,
hitched into limbs, the thin rigging of bone
underpinning
self's strange sense, its reach and ending.

That paper-pattern fragility is ours, rearranged.
Consistencies survive and leave a print.
Shadowy,
as shale laminae layered in bedding-planes,

the understated, oscillating shoulder-blades—
gear-shifts behind the flickering adept hands
that build, in play,
landownerships: small castles against the waves.

Children come like homing creatures here, sandlings,
still summering for a season, feeling the sea
repeat, revise
its long, slow breathing exercise.

They seem like tidings left by the turned, returning tide,
a story's incomplete completion told
through each self's
visible risky precision, its lonely device.

Turning now, I see them only where, so far,
sea's fluent border shifts a weight.
Waves and dunes
absorb them. Matter haunts them like a ghost.

Out of our hands, they seem, so distantly composed,
cradled from air and water, quartz and schist,
children found
in the making of what goes, and has to live.[55]

Note. Text by A. A. Milne (c) The Trustees of the Pooh Properties reproduced with permission of Curtis Brown Group Ltd, London. The poem 'Icarus on the Beach' is reproduced by kind permission of the author.

---

[55] Angela Leighton, 'Icarus on the Beach' (2003).

RALEIGH LECTURE ON HISTORY

Coercion and Consent in Nazi Germany

RICHARD J. EVANS
Fellow of the Academy

IN THE DECADES THAT immediately followed the end of the Second World War, there was a general consensus that Nazi Germany was a police state. Its all-encompassing apparatus of surveillance and control allowed the individual citizen little freedom of thought or action. The view that what principally characterised the Third Reich was the total destruction of civil freedoms and the rule of law in what the German political scientist Karl Dietrich Bracher called 'the German dictatorship' in his classic book of that title, went together with an emphasis on the top-down nature of decision-making in the Nazi regime, putting Hitler at its centre in what came to be known as the 'intentionalist' approach to the study of Nazi policy, in which things were seen to have happened because the Nazi leader wanted them to.[1] From the late 1960s onwards, however, this interpretation began to be pushed aside, as a new generation of historians began to explore the inner contradictions and instabilities of the Third Reich's system of rule. Local and regional histories uncovered a wide and changing variety of popular attitudes towards the Third Reich and its policies. This research emphasised by implication ordinary Germans' relative freedom of choice to resist or not to resist, and thus restored an element of voluntarism to their relationship with the Nazi regime.[2]

Read at the Academy 24 May 2006.
[1] Karl Dietrich Bracher, *The German Dictatorship: The Origins, Structure and Consequences of National Socialism* (New York, 1970); Tim Mason, 'Intention and Explanation: A Current Controversy about the Interpretation of National Socialism', in Gerhard Hirschfeld and Lothar Kettenacker (eds.), *The 'Führer State': Myth and Reality* (Stuttgart, 1981), pp. 23–40.
[2] Useful historiographical surveys include Ian Kershaw, *The Nazi Dictatorship: Problems and Perspectives of Interpretation*, 4th edn. (London, 2000) and John Hiden and John Farquharson, *Explaining Hitler's Germany. Historians and the Third Reich*, 2nd edn. (London, 1989); classic

At the same time, the apparatus of the police state began to look a good deal less coercive than it had done in the 1950s. A variety of studies showed that the Gestapo, once portrayed as a universally intrusive institution of surveillance and control, was in fact a relatively small organisation, certainly when compared to the State Security Service of Communist East Germany, the Stasi.[3] And recently, a large-scale and methodologically sophisticated opinion survey of elderly Germans conducted in the 1990s by the American historian Eric Johnson and the German sociologist Karl-Heinz Reuband has claimed that a majority of those questioned admitted to being 'positive' or 'mainly positive' about Nazism at one time or another during the regime. Only a small minority ever feared being arrested by the Gestapo. 'Hitler and National Socialism', Johnson and Reuband have argued, 'were so immensely popular among most Germans that intimidation and terror were rarely needed to enforce loyalty.' The regime's popularity could also be clearly seen in the results of the elections and plebiscites it held at various intervals during the 1930s. The 99 per cent support the electorate gave to Hitler and his policies, according to the historian Robert Gellately, provided 'remarkable' evidence of 'popular backing' for the regime, a view endorsed by Hans-Ulrich Wehler, perhaps Germany's leading historian, who has claimed in his survey of the period that 'a systematic strategy of manipulation was not pursued' by the Nazis on these occasions.[4] The

---

studies include Franz Neumann, *Behemoth. The Structure and Practice of National Socialism 1933–1944*, 2nd edn. (New York, 1944); Martin Broszat, *Der Staat Hitlers: Grundlegung und Entwicklung seiner inneren Verfassung* (Munich, 1969); Martin Broszat, et al. (eds.), *Bayern in der NS-Zeit*, 6 vols. (Munich, 1977–83); Jeremy Noakes, 'The Oldenburg Crucifix Struggle of November 1936: A Case Study of Opposition in the Third Reich', in Peter D. Stachura (ed.), *The Shaping of the Nazi State* (London, 1983), pp. 210–33; Tim Mason, *Social Policy in the Third Reich: The Working Class and the 'National Community'* (Providence, RI, 1993, first published in German in 1977). For the *Sopade* reports, a major source for social historians, see Klaus Behnken (ed.), *Deutschland-Berichte der Sozialdemokratischen Partei Deutschlands (Sopade) 1934–1940*, 7 vols. (Frankfurt am Main, 1980).

[3] For a sample of this work, see Klaus-Michael Mallmann and Gerhard Paul, 'Omniscient, Omnipotent, Omnipresent? Gestapo, Society and Resistance', in David F. Crew (ed.), *Nazism and German Society 1933–1945* (London, 1994), pp. 166–96; Reinhard Mann, *Protest und Kontrolle im Dritten Reich: Nationalsozialistische Herrschaft im Alltag einer rheinischen Grossstadt* (Frankfurt am Main, 1987); more generally, Robert Gellately, 'Die Gestapo und die deutsche Gesellschaft: Zur Entstehung einer selbstüberwachenden Gesellschaft', in Detlef Schmiechen-Ackermann (ed.), *Anpassung, Verweigerung, Widerstand: Soziale Milieus, Politische Kultur und der Widerstand gegen den Nationalsozialismus in Deutschland im regionalen Vergleich* (Berlin, 1997), pp. 109–21.

[4] Eric A. Johnson and Karl-Heinz Reuband, *What We Knew: Terror, Mass Murder, and Everyday Life in Nazi Germany: An Oral History* (Cambridge, Mass., 2005), pp. 329–33 and jacket flap

most sweeping claims in this respect have been made by the left-wing German historian Götz Aly, who has recently argued that 'the Third Reich was not a dictatorship maintained by force'. Instead, it was a popular regime, sustained by the enthusiasm of the vast majority for its achievement, early on, of material prosperity and social equality. Its decision-making structures were not 'top-down' but 'flat', giving maximum opportunity to people for participation in the formulation and implementation of policy.[5]

These arguments have been driven not least by a strong moral imperative, fuelled by the re-emergence of war crimes cases since the fall of Communism, and the launching of compensation and restitution actions on a variety of fronts, from looted art to slave labour. Anything that implies constraints on the free will of historical actors puts a potentially serious obstacle in the way of establishing their culpability. The language of the courtroom has been imported into history, as everyone who lived in Germany or Europe between 1933 and 1945 is categorised as a 'perpetrator', a 'bystander' or, less often, a 'victim'. Hans-Ulrich Wehler has argued that it would be 'mistaken to characterize the *Führer* state primarily as a terror regime in which a band of deperadoes under the leadership of an Austrian social outcast exercized a kind of alien rule over Germany to which the decent but defenceless majority had to bow'. Such a view, commonly found in West Germany in the immediate post-war period, provided an alibi for the majority, he argues, while it conveniently ignores the fact that there was a 'broad consensus' in support of the regime from the outset. This consensus, he argues, was maintained above all by the charismatic appeal of Hitler and by a mixture of 'bread and circuses' for the masses. In consequence, there existed in Nazi Germany an 'unreserved agreement' between the rule of the *Führer* and the opinion of the people'.[6] For Wehler, admitting such a consensus underpins the postulate of collective guilt that provides the primary integrating factor in Germany's post-unification national identity. This identity has never been uncontested, and there have been repeated attempts to provide an alternative,

---

text; Robert Gellately, *Backing Hitler. Consent and Coercion in Nazi Germany* (Oxford, 2001), pp. 14–16; Hans-Ulrich Wehler, *Deutsche Gesellschaftsgeschichte*, IV: *Vom Beginn des ersten Weltkrieges bis zur Gründung der beiden deutschen Staaten 1914–1949* (Munich, 2003), pp. 614, 652. Here, as elsewhere, translations are mine unless otherwise noted.

[5] Götz Aly, *Hitler's Beneficiaries. Plunder, Racial War, and the Nazi Welfare State* (translated by Jefferson Chase, New York, 2007), p. 28.

[6] Wehler, *Gesellschaftsgeschichte*, IV, pp. 675–6 (the section is entitled 'Die Konsensbasis von Führerdiktatur und Bevölkerung').

or to undermine its premises by portraying the Germans as victims of war and conquest as much as anybody else was. But it has achieved hegemonic status none the less. It rests on a shared sense of responsibility for Nazism's crimes that can now be observed almost everywhere in Germany, but above all in Berlin, where a monument and museum to Nazism's principal victims have been placed at the very heart of the nation's new capital city.[7]

But the emphasis on a national consensus behind Nazism in the 1930s and early 1940s is not confined to those whose primary interest is in providing historical legitimation for a left-liberal concept of nationhood. It is now widespread amongst historians of Nazi Germany in whatever country they are based. 'In their successful cultivation of popular opinion', Robert Gellately has written, 'the Nazis did not need to use widespread terror against the population to establish the regime.' 'The Nazi revolution', he argues, 'did not begin with a sweeping onslaught on German society, but moved forward in tune with what the great majority of people wanted or would tolerate.' Terror, he says, was directed above all at small groups of social outcasts, and did not threaten the lives of the vast majority of ordinary Germans. Most Germans were indeed aware of the concentration camps and the terror apparatus, but their reaction was one not of fear but of approval. If terror did play a role in consolidating the regime, then it was the terror the Gestapo and the criminal police exercised against social outsiders, which helped convince the overwhelming majority of ordinary Germans that law and order were at last being restored after the chaos and disorder of the Weimar Republic. 'The silent and not-so-silent majority', says Gellately, 'backed the regime.' This is not an isolated view. Indeed, a new consensus seems to have emerged according to which the Third Reich was thus, to use a phrase used recently by a number of historians, both German and non-German, a 'dictatorship by consent', a *Zustimmungsdiktatur*, to quote the title of a chapter by Frank Bajohr in a recent collaborative scholarly history of Hamburg in the Nazi era.[8]

---

[7] Bill Niven, *Facing the Nazi Past: United Germany and the Legacy of the Third Reich* (London, 2002), provides a balanced assessment.
[8] Robert Gellately, 'Social Outsiders and the Consolidation of Hitler's Dictatorship, 1933–1939' in Neil Gregor (ed.), *Nazism, War and Genocide. Essays in Honour of Jeremy Noakes* (Exeter, 2005), pp. 56–74, at p. 58 (also quoting Wehler, *Gesellschaftsgeschichte*, IV, p. 676); and Gellately, *Backing Hitler*, p. 257; Frank Bajohr, 'Die Zustimmungsdiktatur: Grundzüge nationalsozialistischer Herrschaft in Hamburg', in *Hamburg im 'Dritten Reich'*. Herausgegeben von der Forschungsstelle für Zeitgeschichte in Hamburg (Göttingen, 2005), pp. 69–131.

In what follows, I will take a critical look at three central propositions, or groups of propositions, on which this new consensus rests. These are:

1 The Nazis did not seize power but won it legally and by consent. They only applied coercion to small minorities of social outsiders, and had the approval of the vast majority of the population in doing so.

2 Nazi repression, exercised through the Gestapo and the concentration camps, was on a small scale and did not affect the majority of the population.

3 The overwhelming popularity of the regime from the outset is demonstrated by the staggeringly successful results it achieved in national elections and plebiscites, by later opinion surveys of people's memories of the regime, by ordinary people's willingness to denounce to the authorities anybody who stepped out of line, and by the widespread publicity given to the concentration camps, which thus appeared to be generally accepted as useful institutions by the German public.

I will return at the end to draw some general conclusions in the light of the points I have raised in these introductory remarks.

I

The first, and in many ways the most obvious problem with the argument that Nazi Germany from the very outset was a 'dictatorship by consent' lies in the nature of the Nazi seizure of power. Of course, it has become conventional to criticise this concept, and to point out that Hitler did not seize power. Rather, he was allegedly handed it on a plate by representatives of the conservative elites and the military establishment, who secured his appointment as Reich Chancellor on 30 January 1933. Wehler, indeed, gives his description of Hitler's appointment the title 'The Handing-over of Power'.[9] What followed was, Robert Gellately maintains, a 'legal revolution', whose actions were legitimated by decrees and laws passed by elected legislative assemblies up to and including the Reichstag, thus reassuring the mass of the population that everything was in order.[10] But of course the Nazis were not handed power on 30 January 1933. There was instead, as Bracher pointed out long ago, a power vacuum in Germany, in which no government and no political force, not even the army, was able to assert itself or gain popular legitimacy for its

---

[9] Wehler, *Gesellschaftsgeschichte*, IV, p. 380.
[10] Gellately, 'Social Outsiders', p. 58.

actions. Moreover, although Hitler did become head of the Reich government on 30 January, there were only two other Nazis in the cabinet, which was dominated by conservatives, headed by the Vice-Chancellor Franz von Papen, whose aim it was to outmanoeuvre Hitler and use his mass support to legitimise their own policies of establishing a counter-revolutionary authoritarian regime of their own. The Nazi seizure of power did not end on 30 January; in fact it only began at that point.

Nor was it legal, as Bracher, who actually coined the phrase 'legal revolution', pointed out. Hermann Göring's crucial actions as Minister-President of Prussia, for instance, lacked legal foundation because the status of his appointment was invalidated by the lawsuit brought by the Social Democratic government of Prussia that had been illegally deposed by Papen the previous June. The Enabling Act that provided much of the foundation for Hitler's legislative powers was passed illegally because Göring, as President of the Reichstag, broke the law in refusing to count the absent but legally elected Communist deputies in the total from which he reckoned the two-thirds majority needed for the Law's passage. The fact that it would have passed even without this illegal action did nothing to make it legal. Göring's appointment of hundreds of thousands of Nazi stormtroopers as auxiliary Prussian police was of dubious legality given his own position's lack of legitimacy. And even if it had been legitimate, this would not in any way have legalised the numerous physical attacks, murders, lootings and other acts they went on to commit over the first half of 1933, as the many thousands of criminal prosecutions brought against them by state prosecutors' offices in the course of 1933—all of them subsequently quashed on Hitler's orders—eloquently testified.[11]

Against whom was Nazi violence directed? Gellately in particular claims it was from the outset only visited upon small minorities. Both during 1933 and afterwards, he argues, the concentration camps were overwhelmingly used as so-called re-education centres for social outsiders, including not only Communists but also habitual criminals, the work-shy, vagrants, homosexuals, alcoholics and the like. In fact, however, in 1933 the Communists were by some distance the largest category of people imprisoned in the camps. It was only later that social outsiders became a majority. And the Communists can only with difficulty be

---

[11] For these arguments, see Richard J. Evans, *The Coming of the Third Reich* (London, 2003), pp. 451–6, with further references; also Norbert Frei, '"Machtergreifung": Anmerkungen zu einem historischen Begriff', *Vierteljahrshefte für Zeitgeschichte*, 31 (1983), 136–45, and Bracher, *The German Dictatorship*, pp. 246–50.

described as social outsiders, since they were strongly integrated into working-class communities all across the industrial regions of Germany; they were only social outsiders from the perspective of the middle classes, a perspective which Gellately too often unconsciously adopts. Nor were the Communists a tiny or marginal minority: in the Reichstag elections of November 1932 they gained a hundred seats, more than half as many as the Nazis did.[12]

Much more important, however, is the fact that Nazi violence in 1933, and indeed well before that, was not directed exclusively against the Communists but also targeted the Social Democrats, whose representatives sat in councils and parliaments across the land and who had led not only the Prussian but also the Reich government at various times before the Nazi seizure of power. Gellately dismisses Nazi violence against the Social Democrats as insignificant,[13] but even a cursory glance at the evidence reveals its shocking intensity and extent in the first six months of 1933 as the Nazis moved to crush what they called 'Marxism', by which they meant not Communism (which they termed 'Bolshevism'), but Social Democracy. Three thousand leading members of the party were arrested immediately after it was banned on 21 June 1933, beaten up, tortured and in many cases killed. An attempt at armed resistance in the Berlin suburb of Köpenick prompted the immediate arrest of five hundred Social Democrats by Nazi stormtroopers, who in the course of the so-called 'Köpenick blood-week' tortured them so severely that ninety-one of them died. Senior political figures, far from being immune, were specifically targeted: the Social Democratic Minister-President of Mecklenburg, Johannes Stelling, was tortured to death and his body tied up in a sack and thrown into a river, from which it was fished out soon after along with the bodies of twelve other Social Democratic Party functionaries killed the same night. The Social Democratic mayor of Stassfurt was shot dead by Nazis as early as 5 February 1933. The ex-mayor of Breslau, the former editor of the town's daily paper, and the recently sacked chief administrator of the Breslau district, all of them Social Democrats, were arrested and imprisoned in a newly opened concentration camp by the

---

[12] Gellately, 'Social Outsiders', pp. 58–60; November 1932 election results summarised in Evans, *The Coming*, p. 299, and analysed authoritatively in Jürgen W. Falter, *Hitlers Wähler* (Munich, 1991), esp. pp. 34–8.
[13] Gellately, 'Social Outsiders', p. 58 ('far fewer members of the SPD were "persecuted" in any way', i.e., compared to the Communists); Gellately's use of the inverted commas to distance himself from the term 'persecuted' suggests in any case that the persecution was largely a figment of the victims' imagination.

stormtrooper leader Edmund Heines, who paraded one of them through the streets of the town dressed as a harlequin: Heines also kidnapped and arrested the former President of the Reichstag, Paul Löbe, another Social Democrat, and put him in the camp too.[14]

A characteristic incident occurred in Braunschweig on 13 March 1933 when stormtroopers burst into a session of the town council, hauled off the Social Democratic mayor, and forced him to resign; to underline the point, a gang of SS men then stripped him, beat him insensible, and threw a bucket of water over him, after which they dressed him again and paraded him through the streets to the town prison. Social Democratic councillors and officials in the town were threatened with similar violence should they fail to resign their posts; one of them was beaten to death when he refused. The leading Social Democrat in Cologne, Wilhelm Sollmann, was tortured at Nazi Party headquarters and made to drink a mixture of castor oil and urine, while the director of the Social Democratic newspaper in Chemnitz was shot dead when he refused to tell a gang of stormtroopers where the party funds were. Incidents of this kind were repeated in different forms all across Germany in the spring of 1933 as the Nazis moved to take over town councils and city administrations. Five hundred municipal administrators and seventy mayors had been forcibly removed from office by the end of May 1933; not all of them were Social Democrats of course, but many were.

These people were hardly members of a despised minority of social outcasts. Indeed, between them, the Social Democrats and the Communists had won 13.1 million votes in the Reichstag elections of November 1932, a good many more than the Nazis, who won only 11.7 million. In the Weimar Republic's system of proportional representation, these figures translated directly into parliamentary seats, which gave the combined working-class parties 221 to the Nazis' 196. The two working-class parties were, of course, bitterly divided against each other, and the many proposals for common action to stop the Nazis never stood a serious chance of success. These parties, particularly the Social Democrats, were closely affiliated to Germany's massive trade union movement, rendered largely ineffective by mass unemployment. Its premises were invaded across the land on 2 May 1933 by gangs of stormtroopers, their furniture and equipment looted, their assets seized, and their

---

[14] These and many other, similar incidents, are detailed in Evans, *The Coming*, pp. 320, 341, 347, 360–1; for a good regional study, see Richard Bessel, *Political Violence and the Rise of Nazism; The Storm Troopers in Eastern Germany 1933–1934* (London, 1984).

functionaries arrested and thrown into concentration camps, where they were brutally mishandled; in the industrial town of Duisburg, four union officials were beaten to death in the cellars of the trade union headquarters.[15]

Overt coercion was applied in 1933, then, not to despised minorities of social outcasts, but above all to the working class and its organisations. Many recent authors have failed to recognise this crucial fact, and have differentiated simply between 'social outcasts' and the rest, describing the latter as a more or less uniform majority of 'the people', 'the masses', or 'the Germans', as Wehler, for example, frequently does. Both Gellately and Johnson and Reuband also fail to differentiate between social classes. They fail to recognise the fact that the major obstacle to the regime in generating support for its policies and actions both in 1933 and subsequently was posed by the mass allegiance of millions of workers to the ideals and principles of Social Democracy and Communism, an allegiance whose formal expression could only be broken by terror. Not surprisingly, as soon as the regime collapsed, in 1945, trade unions, Social Democratic and Communist party organisations, strikes, and other expressions of this allegiance reappeared almost instantly, and on a remarkably widespread basis, testifying to the inability of the Nazis to win the positive support of the great majority of working-class Germans.[16]

The middle classes and the peasantry were more amenable to the Nazi message, given their fear of Communism and their support in varying degrees for an authoritarian solution to Germany's political, social and economic crisis. Thus they required a much less concentrated application of violence and intimidation to force them to capitulate to the new regime and agree to the dissolution of their parties. It was real enough all the same. The only other party with mass support besides the Nazis, the Social Democrats and the Communists was the Catholic Centre. Its Reichstag deputies were persuaded first to vote for the Enabling Law, then to wind the party up, with some prodding from the Papacy, when the

---

[15] Evans, *The Coming*, p. 341. Numerous documented examples of violence against Social Democrats and others (including, especially, Jews) were provided in the *Brown Book of the Hitler Terror and the Burning of the Reichstag*, ed. World Committee for the Victims of German Fascism, President [Albert] Einstein (London, 1933).

[16] Dick Geary, 'Working-class Identities in the Third Reich', in Gregor (ed.), *Nazism*, pp. 42–55; Rüdiger Hachtmann, 'Bürgertum, Revolution, Diktatur—zum vierten Band von Hans-Ulrich Wehlers "Gesellschaftsgeschichte"', *Sozial.Geschichte*, 19 (2004), 60–87, at 80; Geoff Eley, 'Hitler's Silent Majority? Conformity and Resistance under the Third Reich', *Michigan Quarterly Review*, 42 (2003), 389–425 and 555–9.

imminent prospect of a Concordat between the Vatican and the Third Reich was dangled before their eyes. Yet the party wanted a Concordat not least because of the massive intimidation to which it had been subjected since the end of February 1933. This included violent attacks on Centre Party meetings during campaigning for the elections of 5 March 1933, during one of which the Centre Party politician and former government Minister Adam Stegerwald was severely beaten by Nazi stormtroopers (on 22 February). One after another in the spring and early summer of 1933, Catholic lay organisations were being forcibly closed down or merged with their Nazi counterparts, Catholic journalists and newspaper editors were arrested, especially if they had attacked the Nazi-led coalition government in print, and leading Catholics were brutally mistreated by the SA. The Württemberg State President Eugen Bolz, a leading Centre Party politician, was arrested and severely beaten on 19 June 1933, only the most prominent of many. In Bavaria, the new chief of the political police, Heinrich Himmler, ordered on 26 June 1933 the placing in 'protective custody' of all the Reichstag and Landtag deputies of the Bavarian People's Party, the autonomous Bavarian equivalent of the Catholic Centre in the rest of Germany: indeed, he went even further and ordered the arrest of everyone who had been 'particularly active in party politics', no matter what party they belonged to. The Catholic Trade Unions suffered the same fate as their socialist equivalents, and, crucially, Catholic civil servants were openly threatened with dismissal unless they resigned from the Centre Party. Not surprisingly, it was fear of the complete destruction of its lay organisations and the reversal of all the progress that Catholic laymen had made towards gaining equality of status with Protestants in the civil service and the professions over the previous decades that provided the major impetus behind the agreement of the Centre to dissolve itself in return for a Concordat in which the new regime would commit itself—with how little sincerity would soon become apparent—to preserving the integrity of the Catholic community and its institutions.[17]

Between them, the working-class parties and the Catholic Centre represented a majority of the electorate. Together they had won 291 seats to the Nazis' 196 in the last free Reichstag elections of the Weimar Republic,

---

[17] Details in Evans, *The Coming*, pp. 322–3, 363–6; also Martin Broszat, 'The Concentration Camps 1933–1945', in Helmut Krausnick *et al.*, *Anatomy of the SS State* (London, 1968), pp. 397–496, 409–11; more generally Günther Lewy, *The Catholic Church and Nazi Germany* (New York, 1964), pp. 45–79.

in November 1932. The other parties had lost virtually all their electoral support since 1930 and were thus a less serious obstacle. Here too, however, violence and the threat of violence played a part. Like the Catholic Centre Party, the liberal State Party voted for the Enabling Law not least because of Hitler's bloodcurdling announcement in the debate that their decision whether to support or oppose the Law was a decision 'as to whether it is to be peace or war', or, in other words, if the Law was rejected, he would set two and a half million stormtroopers loose on everyone who had opposed it. All the same, many State Party politicians at every level from local councils upwards were subsequently arrested and the party forced to dissolve itself by the end of June 1933. The continuing dismissal of its members from the civil service seems to have been the main impulse behind the People's Party's decision to wind itself up, though its self-immolation did little to save their jobs in many cases. Hitler's Nationalist Party coalition partner, which like the People's Party and the Centre Party had no real commitment to the Weimar Republic or indeed to democracy by this time, was all in favour of the suppression of the labour movement and the parties of the left. What it did not expect, however, was that it would itself be suppressed. At the end of March 1933 the house of Ernst Oberfohren, the party's parliamentary floor leader in the Reichstag, was raided and his office searched, and a few weeks later he was found dead in suspicious circumstances. The warning was clear enough, and it was backed by explicit threats. Meeting with Hitler on 30 May 1933 to complain about the violence and intimidation to which their party representatives were being subjected, the Nationalist leaders were treated to what one of them called a 'hysterical outburst of rage' in which the Reich Chancellor announced that he would let the SA 'open fire' on the Nationalists and their paramilitary affiliates and 'arrange a bloodbath lasting three days long' if they refused to dissolve their party. To underline the point, he had one of their leading figures, Herbert von Bismarck, arrested. Within a few weeks, both the Nationalist Party and the paramilitary units associated with it were no longer in existence.[18]

These events did not entirely subdue Hitler's conservative coalition partners, who became increasingly concerned about the violence of the

---

[18] Evans, *The Coming*, pp. 367–74. The best account of the enforced dissolution of the non-Nazi political parties and the accompanying violence is still the heavily documented collection edited by Erich Matthias and Rudolf Morsey, *Das Ende der Parteien 1933: Darstellungen und Dokumente* (Düsseldorf, 1960), in which Friedrich Freiherr Hiller von Gaertingen's account of the Nationalists (the DNVP), on pages 541–642, is particularly valuable.

SA, four and a half million strong by 1934, by the increasingly openly declared ambition of its leader Ernst Röhm to replace the army, and by their own progressive political marginalisation. In the early summer of 1934, the imminent prospect of the death of Reich President Hindenburg prompted in the Vice-Chancellor, von Papen, the ambition of regaining power by replacing him, hinted at in speeches denouncing the revolutionary rhetoric of the SA. Hitler quelled the restlessness of the SA at the end of June, arresting a number of its leading figures and having them shot by the SS. But it is important to remember that in the so-called Röhm Purge, or 'Night of the Long Knives', Hitler also struck a blow against the conservative right. Those killed included not only Röhm and his associates but also Papen's secretary Herbert von Bose, his speechwriter Edgar Jung, the leader of the Catholic Action organisation, Erich Klausener, former Chancellor Kurt von Schleicher, and others who were on a list compiled by Jung as possible members of a post-Hitler government. Papen was placed under house arrest, and his predecessor as Chancellor, the Catholic politician Heinrich Brüning, escaped with his life only because he was outside Germany at the time. The warning to conservative and Catholic politicians to stay quiet was unmistakeable. Coercion across the board was seldom more openly in evidence than in the 'Night of the Long Knives'.[19]

II

Nazi violence, real and threatened, was unevenly applied in the months of the seizure of power from February to June 1933. Physical coercion was directed with massive ferocity against Communists, Social Democrats and Trade Unionists, and with discriminating and symbolic or exemplary force against those such as liberals, Catholics, Nationalists and conservatives who were less diametrically opposed to the politics of the emerging Third Reich. Nevertheless, it operated across the board. As Richard Bessel has remarked, 'violence . . . during the early months of 1933, was used deliberately and openly to intimidate opposition and potential opposition. It was used to create a public sphere permeated by violence and it provided a ready reminder of what might be in store for *anyone*

---

[19] Richard J. Evans, *The Third Reich in Power* (London, 2005), pp. 31–6, with further references. For a well-documented narrative, see Heinz Höhne, *Mordsache Röhm: Hitlers Durchbruch zur Alleinherrschaft 1933–1934* (Reinbek, 1984).

who stepped out of line, who failed to show loyalty to the new order.'[20] How, then, have some historians failed to recognise this fact and claimed instead that Nazi violence was directed only against small and socially marginal minorities? This brings me to the second proposition or group of propositions I want to discuss, namely that Nazi repression was exercised through the Gestapo and the concentration camps, it was on a small scale, and it did not affect the majority of the population.

Wehler barely mentions the repressive apparatus of the Nazi state, except in passing, and when he does, it is to allude to 'the instruments of terror: Gestapo, protective custody, revocation of citizenship, concentration camps'.[21] Gellately's most recent statement of his views does not mention other sanctions besides arrest by the Gestapo and imprisonment in a concentration camp.[22] Aly backs up his assertion that 'most Germans simply did not need to be subjected to surveillance or detention' by pointing out that 'the Gestapo in 1937 had just over 7,000 employees' who, 'with a far smaller force of security police ... sufficed to keep tabs on more than 60 million people'. By 1936, he adds, 'only 4,761 people—some of whom were chronic alcoholics and career criminals—were incarcerated in the country's concentration camps'.[23] Similar assumptions are evident in Johnson and Reuband's statement, taking up a wider historiography, that:

> In the light of the large number of individuals arrested by the Gestapo and temporarily detained in concentration camps and the cruelty of the Gestapo's conduct—especially where the extortion of confessions was concerned—many authors have assumed that fear of falling into the hands of the Gestapo constantly plagued everyone in the Third Reich and concluded that fear and terror were the decisive factors in shaping the German population's everyday behaviour. Our survey evidence, however, does not support this assumption and conclusion.[24]

There is a real circularity about these arguments, as the assumption that the Gestapo and the concentration camps were the only agents of control and repression in the Third Reich inevitably produces the answer, when this assumption is made the basis of interview questions, that they were not very significant, and so leads on to the sweeping conclusion that

---

[20] Richard Bessel, 'The Nazi Capture of Power', *Journal of Contemporary History*, 39 (2004), 169–88, at 182 (my italics).
[21] Wehler, *Gesellschaftsgeschichte* IV, p. 676; Hachtmann,'Bürgertum', 80.
[22] Gellately, 'Social Outsiders', pp. 63–4.
[23] Aly, *Hitler's Beneficiaries*, p. 29.
[24] Johnson and Reuband, *What We Knew*, p. 354.

control and repression did not feature at all in the lives of the great majority of Germans.

Two points need to be made here. The first is that the principal instrument of terror in Nazi Germany was not the concentration camp but the law—not, to use Ernst Fraenkel's terminology, the prerogative state but the normative state, not in other words the state apparatus created by Hitler, notably the SS, but the already existing state apparatus dating back decades or even centuries.[25] This is not to belittle the camps' role in 1933, of course. During 1933 perhaps 100,000 Germans were detained without trial in so-called 'protective custody' across Germany, most but by no means all of them members of the Communist and Social Democratic Parties. The number of deaths in custody during this period has been estimated at around six hundred and was almost certainly higher. By 1935, however, the vast majority of these prisoners had been released on good behaviour and there were fewer than 4,000 of them left. Almost all the early camps had already been shut down by the end of 1933.[26] A major reason for this decline lay in the fact that the leading role in political repression was now being carried out by the regular courts and the state prisons and penitentiaries. A whole new set of laws and decrees passed in 1933 vastly expanded the scope of the treason laws and the death penalty. A law of 24 April 1933, for example, laid down that anyone found guilty of planning to alter the constitution or to detach any territory from the German Reich by force, or engaging in a conspiracy with these aims, would be beheaded: the concept of 'planning' included writing, printing and distributing leaflets, altering the constitution included in due course advocating the return of democracy or the removal of Hitler as Leader, conspiring included anyone associated with the guilty parties. A law of 20 December 1934 went even further and applied the death penalty to aggravated cases of 'hateful' statements about leading figures in the Nazi Party or the state. Another law made 'malicious gossip' illegal, including spreading rumours about the regime or making derogatory remarks about its leaders. A whole system of regional Special Courts, crowned by the

---

[25] Ernst Fraenkel, *The Dual State: Law and Justice in National Socialism* (New York, 1941).
[26] Ulrich Herbert, Karin Orth and Christoph Dieckmann, 'Die nationalsozialistischen Konzantrationslager. Geschichte, Erinnerung, Forschung', in Herbert, Orth and Dieckmann (eds.), *Die nationalsozialistischen Konzentrationslager*, 2 vols. (Frankfurt am Main, 2002), I, 17–42, at 26.

national People's Court, the *Volksgerichtshof*, was created to implement these and other, similar laws.[27]

It is important to remember the extreme extent to which civil liberties were destroyed in the course of the Nazi seizure of power. In the Third Reich it was illegal to belong to any political grouping apart from the Nazi Party or indeed any non-Nazi organisation of any kind apart from the Churches (and their ancillary lay organisations) and the army; it was illegal to tell jokes about Hitler; it was illegal to spread rumours about the government; it was illegal to discuss alternatives to the political status quo. The Reichstag Fire Decree of 28 February 1933 made it legal for the police to open letters and tap telephones, and to detain people indefinitely and without a court order in so-called 'protective custody'. The same decree also abrogated the clauses in the Weimar Constitution that guaranteed freedom of the press, freedom of assembly, freedom of association and freedom of expression. The Enabling Law allowed the Reich Chancellor and his cabinet to promulgate laws that violated the Weimar Constitution, without needing the approval of the legislature or the elected President. The right of judicial appeal was effectively abolished for offences dealt with by the Special Courts and the People's Court. All this meant that large numbers of offenders were sent to prison for political as well as ordinary criminal offences. In 1937 the courts passed no fewer than 5,255 convictions for high treason. These people, if they escaped the death penalty, were put into a state prison, often for a lengthy period of time. From 1932 to 1937 the prison population increased from 69,000 to 122,000. In 1935, 23,000 inmates of state prisons and penitentiaries were classified as political offenders. The crushing of the Communist and Social Democratic resistance ensured that these numbers had fallen by more than 50 per cent by the beginning of 1939; nevertheless, they were still far more significant than the numbers of political offenders in the camps after 1937, when the camps expanded again; this time they really did function mainly as places of confinement for social rather than political deviants.[28]

---

[27] Evans, *The Third Reich in Power*, pp. 67–75; Richard J. Evans, *Rituals of Retribution. Capital Punishment in Germany 1600–1987* (Oxford, 1996), pp. 620–45; Nikolaus Wachsmann, *Hitler's Prisons. Legal Terror in Nazi Germany* (New Haven, 2004), esp. pp. 165–83; Gerhard Fieberg (ed.), *Im Namen des deutschen Volkes: Justiz und Nationalsozialismus* (Cologne, 1989), p. 68. For the early camps, see Jane Caplan, 'Political Detention and the Origin of the Concentration Camps in Nazi Germany, 1933–1935/6', in Gregor (ed.), *Nazism*, pp. 22–41.

[28] Evans, *The Third Reich in Power*, pp. 79, 85–7.

The second point to be made is that legal condemnation for treason, malicious gossip and similar offences, and quasi-legal 'preventive detention' in concentration camps, were only the most severe of a vast range of sanctions that reached deep into German society in pursuit of the regime's efforts to prevent opposition and dissent. Local studies give a good picture of the range of coercive measures open to the regime and its servants in these respects. In the small north German town of Northeim, for instance, the subject of William Sheridan Allen's classic study *The Nazi Seizure of Power*, first published in 1965, the Communists were arrested in the early months of 1933, along with some of the town's leading Social Democrats; the Social Democratic town councillors were forced to resign after attending a council meeting in which the walls were lined by brownshirts who spat on them as they walked past. Forty-five council employees were sacked, most of them Social Democrats working in institutions as varied as the town gas works, the local swimming pool, and the municipal brewery. At a time of continuing mass unemployment they were unlikely to find other jobs. The local Nazis put pressure on landlords to evict Social Democrats from their apartments, and made sure the police subjected their homes to frequent searches in the hunt for subversive literature.[29]

At every level, too, the regime used coercion of a kind that did not involve arrest or incarceration when it sought to implement particular policies and secure the appearance of public support for them. Members of the Catholic, liberal and conservative political parties were coerced into joining the Nazis in the spring of 1933, and above all after the civil service law of 7 April, by the direct threat of losing their jobs in state employ, which in Germany included not only civil servants and local officials but also schoolteachers, university staff, prosecutors, policemen, social administrators, post office and public transport officials, and many others. When, some years later, it moved to abolish denominational schools and force parents to enroll their children in state-run secular educational institutions, in order to subject them more completely to Nazi indoctrination, the regime ran local plebiscites on the policy, and threatened parents who refused to vote in favour with the withdrawal of welfare benefits, including child support. A massive propaganda campaign was unleashed against monks and priests who staffed private schools run by the Catholic Church, accusing them of pederasty and bringing a large

---

[29] William Sheridan Allen, *The Nazi Seizure of Power: The Experience of a Single German Town, 1922–1945*, 2nd edn. (New York, 1984), pp. 218–32.

number of them before the courts in widely publicised trials. Parents, even schoolchildren, were then pressured to petition against being taught by alleged deviants such as these. Here, then, was a major proportion of the population, the Catholics, getting on for 40 per cent of all Germans, consisting of far more than mere social deviants or outcasts, that was subjected to persistent coercion and harassment when it stood in the way of a key policy of the regime.[30]

There were thus many kinds of coercion in Nazi Germany. It was particularly evident in the area of charity and welfare, where stormtroopers knocked on people's doors or accosted them in the street demanding contributions to Winter Aid. In all schools, pupils who failed to join the Hitler Youth were liable to be refused their school-leaving certificate when they graduated, destroying their prospects of an apprenticeship or a job. Because the Nazi regime acquired powers to direct workers to where it felt they were needed, it was able to use the threat of reassignment to dirty and difficult jobs as a sanction against troublemakers. Over a million German workers had been compulsorily reassigned to work in munitions and war-related industries by 1939, often being forced to live a long distance from their families, and sometimes transported to their destinations escorted by prison warders. Increasingly, as the rearmament programme began to create labour shortages and bottlenecks, skilled workers in key industries were punished by lesser sanctions such as these, rather than by measures, such as imprisonment, that would deprive the state of their labour. Being sent to work on the defensive fortifications of the West Wall, with its twelve-hour shifts of backbreaking manual labour, became a favourite instrument of coercion on the part of employers under pressure from the government's Four-Year Plan Office to produce more and keep costs down, and faced with workers demanding more wages or shorter hours, or overheard making derogatory remarks about their bosses, or about the regime, on the shop-floor.[31]

The very wide range of coercive measures used by the regime at every level was enforced by an equally wide range of coercive agents. It is a mistake to focus exclusively on the Gestapo on the assumption that it was the sole, or even the principal instrument of control in Nazi Germany. Detlev Schmiechen-Ackermann, for instance, has recently drawn attention to the 'Block Warden' or *Blockwart*, a popular name given to low-level officials of the Nazi Party, each of whom was responsible for a block of apartments

---

[30] Evans, *The Third Reich in Power*, pp. 244–7.
[31] The classic study of coercion on the shop-floor is Mason, *Social Policy*, pp. 266–74.

or houses, where he had to ensure that people took proper air-raid precautions, hung out flags on Hitler's birthday and similar occasions, and refrained from engaging in illegal or subversive activities. The Block Wardens kept a close watch on former Communists and Social Democrats, listened out for expressions of dissatisfaction with the regime, and could punish political or social deviance by a variety of means ranging from stopping the offenders' welfare benefits to reporting their names to the district Party organisation for forwarding to the Gestapo.[32] In the workplace, Labour Front officials carried out a similar function, and were able to transfer recalcitrant workers to unpleasant jobs, increase their hours, or deny them promotion. Surveillance, control and political discipline were exercised by Hitler Youth leaders, who were normally a good deal older than their charges. By 1939 membership was compulsory, and some 8.7 million out of a total of 8.9 million Germans aged 10 to 18 belonged to this organisation, so its effects were not limited to the deviant or the marginal.

Taken together, all these agencies of coercion added up to what one historian has recently called a polymorphous, uncoordinated but pervasive system of control, of which the Gestapo formed only one small though important part. Here too, of course, their animus was directed most forcefully against former Communists and Social Democrats in working-class areas, but it was present as a looming threat in middle-class society as well.[33] It was not surprising, therefore, that most of Johnson and Reuband's respondents recalled that they had to be careful about what they said when speaking to strangers or to people they knew to be Nazis, 'such as the ubiquitous Nazi Party block leader'. One interviewee recalled: 'In the course of time, all people became cautious. They simply didn't speak with people anymore.' Ordinary Germans, as Johnson and Reuband rightly conclude, 'knew well that rash, politically unacceptable remarks and corresponding behavior could lead to serious punishment and possibly endanger their lives'.[34] In consequence, they withdrew more and more into the private sphere. Johnson and Reuband do not draw the obvious conclusion that people were living in a climate of fear, but even

---

[32] Detlef Schmiechen-Ackermann, 'Der "Blockwart". Die unteren Parteifunktionäre im nationalsozialistischen Terror- und Überwachungsapparat', *Vierteljahrshefte für Zeitgeschichte*, 48 (2000), 575–602.

[33] Dieter Nelles, 'Organisation des Terrors im Nationalsozialismus', *Sozialwissenschaftliche Literatur-Rundschau*, 25 (2002), 5–28; Evans, *The Third Reich in Power*, pp. 114–18, 272, 276, 485–6.

[34] Johnson and Reuband, *What We Knew*, pp. 359–60.

on the evidence they present, it seems justifiable to conclude that they were. Ultimately, too, as their respondents suggest, the fear that formed the permanent backdrop to their daily lives was not a fear of the Gestapo, still less of ordinary citizens, friends or relatives, but a fear of active Nazis, low-level Party officials, and committed supporters of the regime: if you fell into conversation with a stranger, you might be able to tell whether he belonged to one of these categories by small signs such as, for example, whether he used the Hitler greeting, but you could never be entirely certain, so it was best to be circumspect, and if you knew the person you were talking to was an active Nazi, then you certainly had to be cautious.

III

Why was such a vast apparatus of coercion and control necessary if, as historians like Wehler, Gellately, Johnson and Reuband and others claim, the Nazi regime was viewed in such a popular light by the mass of the German people? This brings me to the third proposition or bundle of propositions I want to examine: that the overwhelming popularity of the regime from the outset is demonstrated by the extraordinarily successful results it achieved in national elections, by later survey data on people's memories of the time, by ordinary Germans' willingness to denounce to the authorities anybody who stepped out of line, and by the public support given to the concentration camps as indicated by the prominence given to them in the Nazi press. Certainly, to begin with the plebiscites and elections that were held at intervals under the Third Reich, the regime regularly won over 90 per cent of the vote when it put its policies to the people for approval. But were these results really such striking indicators of the regime's popularity as some have claimed? A wide range of contemporary reports strongly suggests that they were not. In the plebiscite on Hitler's appointment as Head of State following the death of Hindenburg in 1934, for instance, and in the plebiscite of April 1938 on union with Austria, and on other occasions, gangs of stormtroopers rounded voters up from their homes and marched them to the polling stations. Here the electors were usually forced to vote in public, since in many places the polling booths had been removed, or were labelled 'only traitors enter here'; this was more than mere rhetoric, since in 1938, when the plebiscite was coupled with a vote of confidence in Hitler, anyone voting 'no' was voting against Hitler and would therefore—as Nazi officials and propaganda agents did not fail to point out—be committing an offence under the treason laws.[35]

At all these elections, polling stations were surrounded by stormtroopers whose minatory attitude made clear what would happen to anybody who failed to conform. Suspected opponents of the regime were given specially marked ballot papers, and in many places rumours were circulated beforehand that all the papers were secretly numbered, so that people who voted 'no' or spoiled their ballot papers could be identified and punished; and indeed people who took this course, or refused to vote, were beaten up by the brownshirts, or dragged through the streets with placards round their neck calling them traitors, or even committed to mental hospitals. Just to ensure an overwhelming 'yes' vote, many former Communists, Social Democrats and other critics of the regime were arrested before the vote and only released when it was safely over, and ballot papers in many areas were already marked with a cross in the 'yes' box before electors arrived at the polling station; in some areas it was reported that so many 'no' votes and spoiled papers were replaced with one or more forged 'yes' ballots that the number of 'yes' votes actually exceeded the number of electors. None of this meant, of course, that in a plebiscite on an issue like unification with Austria, the government would have failed to obtain a majority for its actions; but it is surely safe to say that in a free vote, it would not have obtained the 99 per cent 'yes' vote it got by the tactics of manipulation and intimidation I have just outlined; in the plebiscite of 1934 it might even have failed to win a majority.[36]

Let us turn to evidence for the Nazi regime's supposedly overwhelming popularity from 1933 onwards provided by later opinion survey data. Johnson and Reuband claim that their interviews of elderly Germans during the 1990s show that 'Hitler and National Socialism were [so] immensely popular among most Germans'.[37] Yet their sample consisted overwhelmingly of people born between 1910 and 1928, people who therefore would have been between the ages of 5 and 23 at the beginning of the Third Reich and 17 and 35 at the end. In the nature of things, more of them would have been born towards the end of the period chosen than

---

[35] Otmar Jung, *Plebiszit und Diktatur: Die Volksabstimmungen der Nationalsozialisten. Die Fälle 'Austritt aus dem Völkerbund' (1933), 'Staatsoberhaupt' (1934) und 'Anschluss Österreichs' (1938)* (Tübingen, 1995); Theodor Eschenburg, 'Streiflichter zur Geschichte der Wahlen im Dritten Reich', *Vierteljahrshefte für Zeitgeschichte*, 3 (1955), 311–18; Evans, *The Third Reich in Power*, pp. 109–13.

[36] For detailed evidence, see Evans, *The Third Reich in Power*, pp. 109–13.

[37] Johnson and Reuband, *What We Knew*, jacket flap text.

towards the beginning. All we know about Nazi Germany, from the *Sopade* reports to the diaries of people like the Jewish professor Victor Klemperer, underlines the fact that Nazi propaganda was most effective in the younger generations of Germans, who after all had had few chances to form their own firm values and beliefs before the regime began, and who were subjected to massively intense and unremitting indoctrination from their schools, from the Hitler Youth, and from the mass media orchestrated by Goebbels. It was overwhelmingly young people, for example, who joined in the antisemitic violence of the *Kristallnacht* and shouted insults at Victor Klemperer in the streets.[38] And Johnson and Reuband themselves note that 'younger people ... were disproportionately receptive to National Socialism'.[39] Their survey shows that 62 per cent those of their respondents born in Berlin between 1923 and 1928 admitted to having been 'positive or mainly positive' about National Socialism, compared to only 35 per cent of those born between 1911 and 1916; in Dresden the comparable figures were 65 per cent and 39 per cent, in Cologne 45 per cent and 21 per cent. It would not be unreasonable to suppose that the figures for people born, say, before 1890 or 1880 would have been lower still. Their *overall* results, therefore, are skewed by the fact that most of their respondents were born in the 1920s.[40]

Moreover, as the authors themselves point out, when faced with their three questions—whether they believed in National Socialism, whether they admired Hitler and whether they shared Nazi ideals—only a minority (18 per cent) answered in the affirmative to all three, while 31 per cent answered yes to two. Thus only 49 per cent of those who took part in the survey gave a clear yes to more than one of these three questions. Only when those whose answers appeared as ambivalent or neutral were added in did this become a majority. Johnson and Reuband's careful and exemplary detailed analysis of their survey data shows that the attitudes of most of the people they questioned were mixed: some viewed some aspects of Nazism positively but not others, while many people's attitudes changed quite markedly over time, a factor that emerges more clearly from some of the in-depth interviews than from the statistics provided by the opinion survey. All these variations and qualifications are spelled out in convincing detail in the text of Johnson and Reuband's book; it is

[38] Evans, *The Third Reich in Power*, pp. 585–7.
[39] Johnson and Reuband, *What We Knew*, pp. 332, 335.
[40] Ibid., p. 335.

a pity that they disappear entirely when it comes to summarising and presenting their conclusions.[41]

The third major strand of evidence presented by some historians in favour of the regime's popularity is the practice of denouncing law-breakers to the authorities. How much does the practice of denunciation actually reveal about people's attitudes to the regime? What it does not reveal, to begin with, is that Nazi Germany was a 'self-policing society', as Gellately has claimed, for people did not denounce offenders to each other, they denounced them to the authorities, including the Gestapo, and if the Gestapo and other agencies of state and party control had not been there to act, either legally or extra-legally, against the objects of denunciation, then denunciation would have been meaningless. In practice, of course, denunciation was extremely rare: there were only between three and fifty-one denunciations a year in Lippe, where the population was 176,000, during the Third Reich, for instance; and a relatively high proportion of denouncers were members of the Nazi Party—42 per cent in Augsburg, for example. In Düsseldorf, some 26 per cent of Gestapo investigations were triggered by denunciations from members of the general population; the other three-quarters were initiated by Gestapo officers or informers, Nazi Party organisations, the criminal police and the SS, and state authorities of one kind and another. In addition, a study of recently declassified Gestapo files for the Koblenz and Trier region has revealed that the Gestapo made extensive use of paid informers and also kept a register of unpaid informers, whom they did not scruple to use repeatedly; around a third of these people were members of the Nazi Party or its affiliated organisations.[42]

In the case of contraventions of the Nuremberg racial laws, the proportion of cases that arose from denunciations was a good deal higher, but this was not least because such offences were largely committed in private, and few were likely to know about them apart from neighbours, acquaintances and family. In any case, as I have already noted, people were generally very cautious about what they said to strangers, so the relative prominence of family members, relatives and neighbours in denouncing people to the Gestapo might reflect among other things the fact that people often lowered their guard when talking to them. 'Malicious gossip' cases were more often than not begun by denunciations, above all, at

---

[41] Johnson and Reuband, *What We Knew*, pp. 325–45.
[42] Claire Hall, 'The Gestapo Spy Network 1933–1945' (Ph.D. thesis, University of Hull, forthcoming).

least in the early years of the regime, from innkeepers and drinkers in bars, where alcohol loosened the tongue: significantly, however, as the consequences of loose talk gradually became clear, the proportion of malicious gossip cases in the Augsburg court, the focus of a particularly illuminating study, that derived from denunciations in pubs and bars fell from three-quarters in 1933 to one-tenth by the outbreak of the war. As Gellately has pointed out, moreover, many denunciations from ordinary citizens were made from personal motives, and say nothing about their overall attitude to the regime, its ideologies or its policies.[43]

In many cases, of course, denunciation would lead to prosecution, appearance before a Special Court, and imprisonment — not in a concentration camp but in a state-run jail. Nevertheless, above all in the first two years of their rule, the Nazis made a point of publicising the concentration camps and their function, at a time when the repressive efforts of state and Party were directed mainly against political opposition and dissent. To claim, as Gellately does, that camp prisoners in 1933–4 were 'social outsiders of one kind or another' is simply incorrect. Not only were Communists not social outsiders, unless one wants to stigmatise the entire German working class — by some estimates, fully half the entire population of Germany — as social outsiders; the camps, as anyone who has paid any attention to the events of 1933 will know, were intended for Social Democrats too; and the 'good citizens' of Germany in 1933, who Gellately portrays as rejoicing in the 'crackdown', included, as we have seen, large numbers of Social Democratic mayors, councillors, deputies, officials, civil servants and others. Far from rejoicing, they were themselves now liable to be thrown into the camps.[44]

Articles and even pictures were printed prominently in local newspapers when the Dachau camp was opened in 1933, as Gellately notes. They advertised the fact that not only Communists but also Social Democrats or 'Marxists' and political opponents of every hue were being 're-educated'. Once more, local evidence is telling on this point. In Northeim in 1933,

---

[43] Bernward Dörner, 'NS-Herrschaft und Denunziation. Anmerkungen zu Defiziten in der Denunziationsforschung', *Historical Social Research*, 26 (2001), 55–69; Werner Röhr, 'Über die Initiative zur terroristischen Gewalt der Gestapo — Fragen und Einwände zu Gerhard Paul', in Werner Röhr and Brigitte Beierkamp (eds.), *Terror, Herrschaft und Alltag im Nationalsozialismus: Probleme der Sozialgeschichte des deutschen Faschismus* (Münster, 1995), pp. 211–24; Gerhard Hetzer, 'Die Industriestadt Augsburg. Eine Sozialgeschichte der Arbeiteropposition', in Broszat *et al.*, (eds.), *Bayern*, IV, 1–234; Gisela Diewald-Kerkmann, *Politische Denunziation im NS-Regime oder die kleine Macht der 'Volksgenossen'* (Bonn, 1995); Evans, *The Third Reich in Power*, pp. 96–118.
[44] Gellately, 'Social Outsiders', p. 59.

for example, the local and regional papers ran stories on Dachau and the nearby camp at Moringen, and carried regular reports on the arrest of citizens for making derogatory remarks about the regime and its leaders. The guards at Moringen were drawn from the local population, and prisoners were released mostly after only a few weeks inside, so that knowledge of the camp must have been widespread in Northeim and the surrounding district.[45] Of course, here as elsewhere there were multifarious contacts of other kinds with the local population, who were involved in constructing and supplying the camp and carrying out maintenance and repairs; but these did not necessarily indicate only support for its objectives: a plumber could repair leaky water-pipes in the camp office building and still be afraid of what might happen if he stepped out of line or uttered an incautious remark. On occasion, the regime was explicit in its general use of the threat of the camps for people who made trouble: 'Concentration camp', declared the front page of Germany's newspapers in the immediate aftermath of the 'Night of the Long Knives', 'is threatened . . . for rumour-mongering and offering slanderous insults to the movement itself and its Leader.' Mostly the threat was implicit.[46] Nevertheless, it was directed potentially at anybody, not just at social outsiders. It was only after the initial wave of repression in 1933–4 that the camps, having ceded their function of political 're-education' to the Special Courts and the state prisons, became repositories for social outsiders.

IV

Recent historiography has been rightly critical of older studies that reduce popular opinion in the Third Reich to no more than the product of coercion and propaganda. But to belittle the former and ignore the latter in favour of a wholly voluntaristic approach is not very useful as a means of explaining how the Third Reich operated. Propaganda was important, but it did not operate of course on a blank slate as far as most people's views were concerned. Nazi propaganda was at its most effective where it tapped into already existing beliefs, as Ian Kershaw demonstrated in his classic study of popular opinion in Bavaria under the Third Reich some years ago.[47] Where people, notably Social Democrats,

---

[45] Allen, *The Nazi Seizure of Power*, pp. 218–32.
[46] Evans, *The Third Reich in Power*, pp. 37–8.
[47] Ian Kershaw, *Popular Opinion and Political Dissent in the Third Reich: Bavaria, 1933–1945* (Oxford, 1983).

Communists and Catholics, had formed their values and taken up their political stance well before the beginning of the Third Reich, it was less than wholly effective. Propaganda also had an effect where it bore at least some relationship to reality: the Nazis won widespread if sometimes grudging approval for instance by the reduction of unemployment, the restoration of order on the streets, and the successful re-establishment of Germany's international prestige and freedom of action. In the latter part of the war, by contrast, Goebbels's assurances of imminent victory were believed by few.

Yet the more people clung to alternative values to those of Nazism, the more important terror was as a means of coercing them into submission. The Nazis themselves were the first to admit this. On 15 March 1933, referring to the semi-free elections that had taken place ten days previously, giving the Nazi Party and its Nationalist coalition partners a bare absolute majority of the vote, Goebbels declared that the government would 'not be satisfied for long with the knowledge that it has 52 per cent behind it while terrorising the other 48 per cent but will, by contrast, see its next task as winning over that other 48 per cent for itself.' Goebbels's speech was as remarkable for its frank admission of the role of terror in the establishment of the Third Reich as it was for its bold declaration of the importance of obtaining the ideological support of the whole of the German people. The story of the following years is in part the story of how the Nazis succeeded in key respects in doing this. Yet Goebbels's aim of winning over the majority of the people to wholehearted enthusiasm for Nazism was only partially fulfilled. The Nazi leadership knew by 1939 that most Germans paid its most loudly and insistently proclaimed ideals little more than lip-service: they conformed outwardly while keeping their real beliefs for the most part to themselves. Nazism had succeeded in shifting the attitudes and beliefs of most Germans, particularly in the younger generation, some way in the direction it wanted, but it had not reached the ambitious goal it had set itself. This situation, attested above all in local studies such as Allen's *The Nazi Seizure of Power*, was in turn a reflection of the fact that, in the end, coercion was at least as important as propaganda in its impact on the behaviour of the vast majority of people who lived in Nazi Germany.[48]

---

[48] Goebbels's speech of 15 March 1933 in David Welch (ed.), *The Third Reich: Politics and Propaganda*, 2nd edn. (London, 2002), pp. 173–4; on the effects of propaganda more generally, see the judicious assessment by Ian Kershaw, 'How Effective was Nazi Propaganda?', in David Welch (ed.), *Nazi Propaganda: The Power and the Limitations* (London, 1983), pp. 180–203.

Who operated the system of coercion, therefore? How many people were involved in its implementation? The fact that a great many agencies were involved implies that it was put into effect by a far larger range of people than those who belonged to the relatively small organisation of the Gestapo. The SA was nearly three million strong by the beginning of 1934, four and a half million if incorporated paramilitary and veterans' associations like the *Stahlhelm* are included. There were around 200,000 'Block Wardens' by 1935, and no fewer than 2,000,000 of them, including their assistants and deputies, by the beginning of the war. Hundreds of thousands of Germans occupied official posts in Nazi Party organisations of one kind and another, such as the Hitler Youth, the Chambers of Culture, the Nazi Teachers' and university students' leagues, the Labour Front, and so on. Particularly important in this context were the legal and judicial professions, including the regular police force and the Gestapo, most of whose officers were already serving policemen under the Weimar Republic. In Prussia only three hundred out of around 45,000 judges, state prosecutors and officials were dismissed or transferred to other duties for political reasons by the Nazis in 1933; the rest stayed on and enforced the new laws enacted by the regime with only minimal and sporadic objections. If we count in all those many other Germans who held positions of responsibility in the state, the number of people who were willing to some degree or other to play a role in the coercive apparatus of the regime must have run into several millions. Even so, in a nation with a population of 80 million, they remained a minority. Just as important, too, they also knew, like everyone else, that they would fall foul of the regime if they stepped out of line: as many as 22 per cent of people tried for 'malicious gossip' in Augsburg in the mid-1930s were actually members of the Nazi Party. Nevertheless, exercising various kinds of coercion and violence, real or threatened, that would not be tolerated in a democratic society, had become a way of life for millions of Germans by the outbreak of the war.[49]

It is only by recognising that large numbers of Germans had become willing administrators of coercion and repression, and that millions of younger Germans had been heavily influenced by Nazi indoctrination, that we can explain the extraordinarily savage behaviour of the forces that invaded Poland in 1939. The invasion of Poland took place under

---

[49] Hetzer, 'Die Industriestadt Augsburg', pp. 146–50; Schmiechen-Ackermann, 'Der "Blockwart"'; Evans, *The Third Reich in Power*, p. 22; Evans, *The Coming of the Third Reich*, p. 383.

favourable conditions, in good weather, against an enemy that was swept aside with contemptuous ease. The invading troops did not need to be convinced by political indoctrination that the enemy posed a huge threat to Germany's future; clearly the Poles did not. Primary group loyalties in the lower ranks of the army remained intact; they did not have to be replaced by a harsh and perverted system of discipline that elbowed traditional military values aside in favour of an extremist racial ideology.[50] Almost everything that was to happen in the invasion of the Soviet Union from June 1941 onwards had already happened in the invasion of Poland almost two years before. From the very beginning, SS units entered the country, rounding up the politically undesirable, professionals and the intelligentsia and shooting them or putting them in concentration camps, massacring Jews, arresting local men and sending them off to Germany as slave labourers, and engaging in a systematic policy of ethnic cleansing and brutally executed population transfers. From the very beginning, too, Nazi Party officials, stormtroopers, civilian officials and especially junior army officers and ordinary soldiers joined in, to be followed in due course by German settlers moved into Poland from outside. Arrests, beatings and murders of Poles and especially Jews became commonplace. Just as striking was the assumption of all the invading and incoming Germans that the possessions of the Poles and Jews were freely available as booty. The theft and looting of Jewish property in particular by German troops was almost universal.[51]

Toughness, hardness, brutality, the use of force, the virtues of violence, had been inculcated into a whole generation of young Germans from 1933 onwards. Among older troops and officials, propaganda also built on a deeper-rooted feeling that Slavs and Eastern Jews were subhumans. The violence meted out to Poles and especially Jews from the beginning of September 1939 continued and intensified actions and policies already established by the Third Reich. So too did the looting and expropriation to which they were subjected, in the same way as Communist, Social Democratic and trade union assets had been looted and expropriated in Germany in 1933 and Jewish assets at the same time and continuously thereafter. It was in direct imitation of the November 1938 pogrom in Germany that SS units burned down synagogues in some

---

[50] Thus the arguments in Omer Bartov, *The Eastern Front 1941–1945: German Troops and the Barbarization of Warfare* (London, 1985); and Omer Bartov, *Hitler's Army* (Oxford, 1991), dating these processes from the invasion of the Soviet Union onwards.
[51] Richard J. Evans, *The Third Reich at War* (London, 2008), ch. 1, for details.

Polish towns in September and October 1939. And the regime's policy towards the Jews of Poland, which moved quickly towards ghettoisation, can only be understood in the light of its previous policy towards the Jews of Germany, who over the preceding six and a half years had been pushed out of their jobs, expropriated, deprived of their citizenship and their rights, and cut off by law from mixing in most ways with the rest of the population.

The substantial minority of Germans who implemented such policies of coercion, terror and mass murder had become accustomed to such things from the experience of the previous six years in Germany itself. Did the majority of the population give its consent to all this? Dick Geary has pointed out that to talk of 'consent' is meaningless unless it is freely given: 'consent', he writes, 'can only be measured in situations in which individuals can choose between real alternatives.'[52] It is worth calling to mind, too, the fact that the legal definition of 'consent' (for example, in rape cases) lays down the principle that a person consents if he or she agrees by choice and has the freedom and capacity to make that choice. A threat of violence is held in law to rule out consent. Categories such as 'tacit consent' or 'passive consent' are in this context little more than vehicles of negative moral judgement based on an extreme and unrealistic model of active citizenship that assumes that if you do not openly protest against a government policy then you are giving your consent to it.

A more sophisticated approach to the question of consent in Nazi Germany has recently been offered by Peter Longerich, using the example of the regime's policies towards the Jews, but in a way that has implications for other areas as well. The more radical the regime's antisemitic policies became, he argues, the less willing the mass of Germans became to go along with them. Before contacts between Jewish and non-Jewish Germans became in many respects illegal, with the Nuremberg Laws of 1935, it had proved extremely difficult to persuade the mass of Germans to ostracise the Jewish minority. Both in the pogrom of November 1938 and later on, during the war, the majority of people, rather than being indifferent, disapproved of violence and murder towards the Jews. But they felt unable to do anything concrete because of fear of this violence being turned against themselves by the regime and its agents, because of fear of arrest and prosecution, or sanctions of other kinds. This fear reached an extreme in the last eighteen months of the war, as the regime,

---

[52] Dick Geary, 'Working-Class Identities in the Third Reich', in Gregor (ed.), *Nazism*, pp. 42–55, at p. 52.

backed by the judicial and law enforcement system, ruthlessly suppressed so-called 'rumour-mongering' about its extermination of Europe's Jews. At the same time, the mass of the German population, who knew what had been happening in Auschwitz and Treblinka, began to repress their knowledge in the face of looming defeat, as the prospect of Allied revenge or retribution for the mass murder began to become more certain. What appeared as indifference was thus in fact something far more active, namely an increasingly desperate search for a way of denying responsibility for actions that almost everybody recognised as crimes. Here too, therefore, fear played a key role in shaping people's behaviour, as indeed it had done throughout the Third Reich in other areas too.[53]

What implications, finally, does this conclusion have for the task, if we wish to pursue it, of reaching a moral judgement on these people's behaviour between 1933 and 1945? As Neil Gregor has recently pointed out in a critique of what he calls 'the voluntarist turn' in historical studies of the Third Reich, reaching a moral judgement does not require that all those who lived under the Third Reich 'were faced with completely free choices, the outcomes of which were determined only by their own personal convictions, moral codes, or desire for blood'.[54] 'Human agency', as Tim Mason pointed out, 'is defined or located not abolished or absolved by the effort to identify the unchosen conditions' under which it is exercised.[55] What we have to recognise in this context, hard though it may be, is the absolute centrality of violence, coercion and terror to the theory and practice of German National Socialism from the very outset. As Richard Bessel has remarked, 'Nazi ideology was, at its core, about violence . . . The horrors unleashed by the Third Reich were a reflection of the fact that the Nazis made their ideology real.'[56] It is impossible to understand the terror vented by the Nazis upon people in the regions they conquered, especially in eastern and south-eastern Europe, and upon the Jews across the whole of the occupied areas of the Continent, unless we grasp the fact that they had already vented it upon large sectors of their own people before 1939: and not merely on despised and tiny minorities of social outcasts, but on millions of their fellow-citizens, indeed at one level or another, to one degree or another, on the great majority of them.

[53] Peter Longerich, *'Davon haben wir nichts gewusst!'. Die Deutschen und die Judenverfolgung 1933–1945* (Berlin, 2006), pp. 313–29.
[54] Gregor, 'Nazism', p. 20.
[55] Mason, 'Intention and Explanation', p. 229, quoted in ibid.
[56] Bessel, 'The Nazi Capture of Power', 183.

CHATTERTON LECTURE ON POETRY

A. E. Housman's Rejected Addresses

ROBERT DOUGLAS-FAIRHURST
Magdalen College, Oxford

I

THOMAS GRAY'S FRIEND AND COLLEAGUE JAMES BROWN recalled how quietly the poet approached his death: 'He never spoke out, but I believe from some little expressions I now remember to have dropped from him, that for some time past he thought himself nearer his end than those about him apprehended.'[1] Matthew Arnold was quick to pick up a hint so closely aligned with his own interest in the large implications of 'little expressions'. In their original context, he admits, these words 'fell naturally, and as if by chance, from their writer's pen', but 'let us dwell upon them, and press into their meaning, for in following it we shall come to understand Gray . . . *He never spoke out.* In these four words is contained the whole history of Gray, both as a man and as a poet.'[2] Crystallising a 'whole history' into just four words risks sounding ungenerous or strained, as Arnold recognises with his choice of 'contained', which balances a breezy confidence in his own powers of summary against the suspicion that writing contains the unruly contingencies of a life only in the way that one might try to contain a fire or a riot. But 'He never spoke out' is not the only phrase in Brown's letter which Arnold dwells on and presses into; 'nearer his end than those about him apprehended' is equally

---
Read at the Academy 19 September 2006.
[1] 'Thomas Gray' (1880), repr. in R. H. Super (ed.), *The Complete Prose Works of Matthew Arnold*, 11 vols. (Ann Arbor, 1960–77), 9. 189. Place of publication for all other works cited is London unless otherwise stated.
[2] Arnold, 'Thomas Gray', p. 189. The phrase '*He never spoke out*' is applied to Housman by Archie Burnett in 'Silence and Allusion in Housman', *Essays in Criticism*, 53: 2 (2003).

Proceedings of the British Academy **151**, 83–111. © The British Academy 2007.

charged with emblematic significance, because according to Arnold what primarily prevented Gray from speaking out was an unhappy misalignment of character and circumstance:

> If Gray, like Burns, had been just thirty years old when the French Revolution broke out, he would have shown, probably, productiveness and animation in plenty. Coming when he did, and endowed as he was, he was a man born out of date, a man whose full spiritual flowering was impossible.[3]

The idea that speaking out could be the historical equivalent of speaking out of turn is sympathetically echoed in Arnold's allusion to Gray's 'Elegy Written in a Country Churchyard' ('Full many a flower is born to blush unseen | And waste its sweetness on the desert air'),[4] which acknowledges that in some ways Gray was in an even worse position than the anonymous ranks of the churchyard dead described in his poem. Whereas they were denied the receptive ears of an audience, flinging out words like seeds into the desert, his voice was not even permitted a full flowering, repeatedly stinted and stunted in its passage through the world. Although the survival of his name prevents him from being a 'mute inglorious Milton', Arnold suggests, muteness is not a matter of all or nothing: like an allusion, what Gray could bring himself to say is only a fragment of what might have been; his poems offer themselves to the reader not as a set of fully realised intentions but as something more like an anthology of disappointment.

It is not only writers 'born out of date' whose work is likely to register the reciprocal pressures which speech and silence can exercise on each other. Any act of writing involves choice, and choice requires rejection: deciding what to shut out, when to shut up, how to approach that moment where a design is both achieved and abandoned. This process is likely to be etched in especially sharp relief when writing a poem, because although, as Adrienne Rich points out, 'every poem breaks a silence that had to be overcome',[5] in order to satisfy the requirements of its form a poem must also contain itself, emerging on the page as a shapely compromise of eloquence and muteness. However, few poets have set out to

---

[3] Arnold, 'Thomas Gray', p. 201. Arnold compares Gray to his contemporary Joseph Butler, a man 'impelled by the endowment of his nature to strive for a profound and adequate conception of religious things, which was not pursued by his contemporaries, and which at that time, and in that atmosphere of mind, was not fully attainable' (p. 201).
[4] Roger Lonsdale (ed.), *Gray, Collins and Goldsmith: The Complete Poems* (Harlow, 1969), p. 127.
[5] Adrienne Rich, *What Is Found There: Notebooks on Poetry and Politics*, rev. edn. (New York, 2003), p. 85.

occupy this creative no-man's land with Housman's particular blend of self-assertion and self-restraint. 'If I were obliged, not to define poetry, but to name the class of things to which it belongs,' he explained in 'The Name and Nature of Poetry', 'I should call it a secretion.'[6] It is a standard idea—poets from Pope to Eliot have referred to their poems as 'secretions'[7]—but Housman's use of the word has a particular edge, balancing as it does the twin loyalties of his verse to keeping secrets and confessing them, holding back and holding forth. Repeatedly, his writing invites interpretation and resists it, as if teasing his readers with the thought that a secret cannot be a secret unless someone else knows you have it.

There is a large gap between proximity and intimacy in Housman's verse, and it is seldom traversed by words:

> Lovers lying two and two
> Ask not whom they sleep beside . . .[8]

> But now you may stare as you like and there's nothing to scan;
> And brushing your elbow unguessed-at and not to be told . . .
> (*ASL* XXIII, p. 25)

> . . . before us
> Goes the delightful guide,
>
> With lips that brim with laughter
> But never once respond . . .
> (*ASL* XLII, p. 44)

> When I heard I did not answer, I stood mute and shook my head . . .
> (*MP* XLVI, p. 145)

---

[6] A. E. Housman, 'The Name and Nature of Poetry' (1933), repr. in Christopher Ricks (ed.), *A. E. Housman: Collected Poems and Selected Prose* (Harmondsworth, 1989), p. 370.

[7] *Of the Art of Sinking in Poetry*, ch. III, 'Poetry is a natural or morbid Secretion from the Brain' (Ricks's note in *Collected Poems and Selected Prose*, p. 515); *The Use of Poetry and the Use of Criticism* (1933, repr. 1964), p. 145 n. Given his discriminating interest in how easily some forms of self-expression can ossify into thoughtless prejudices (discussed below), Housman may also have had in mind Gide's warning in *L'immoraliste*: 'I depicted artistic culture as a welling up in a whole people, like a secretion, which is at first a sign of plethora, of a superabundance of health, but afterwards stiffens, hardens, forbids the perfect contact of the mind with nature, hides under the persistent appearance of life a diminution of life, turns into an outside sheath, in which the cramped mind languishes and pines, in which at last it dies'; Gide's comment is discussed in Jeffrey Meyers, *Homosexuality and Literature, 1890–1930* (1977), p. 35.

[8] *A Shropshire Lad*, XI (p. 15). All quotations from Housman's poems are taken from Archie Burnett (ed.), *The Poems of A. E. Housman* (Oxford, 1997). Futher references adopt the section headings of Burnett's edition, abbreviated as follows: *A Shropshire Lad* (*ASL*), *Last Poems* (*LP*), *More Poems* (*MP*), *Additional Poems* (*AP*), *Notebook Fragments* (*NF*), *Light Verse and Juvenilia* (*LVJ*), *Latin Verse* (*LV*), followed by page number.

Even when speech is possible in Housman's verse it is rarely easy, whether describing a 'blackbird's *s*train' ('Then my soul within me | Took up the blackbird's strain', *ASL* VII, p. 11), in which full-throated bursts of birdsong are made to sound like a reproach to the stresses and tensions of a human voice, or using the blankness of the page to draw attention to the silence against which speech is always pressing:

> In the land to which I travel,
>   The far dwelling, let me say—
>   (*ASL* XI, p. 15)

—where the dash both introduces utterance and threatens to cut it off. Some of these moments come close to being examples of paralipsis, a rhetorical sleight in which a speaker 'pretends to pass over a matter and so draws attention to it',[9] as Shakespeare's Mark Antony flourishes Caesar's will before the mob:

> Let but the commons hear this testament—
> Which, pardon me, I do not mean to read—
> And they would go and kiss dead Caesar's wounds . . .
> Have patience, gentle friends; I must not read it.
> It is not meet you know how Caesar loved you . . .[10]

So too, in Housman's poetry, withdrawals turn out to be confidences; circling a subject becomes a way of highlighting it rather than avoiding it. Even lines which drop away into the blank space of the margin can look as if they are pausing to gather their strength before picking up the thread of the poem again, so making his line-endings into both the breaking-points of his voice and the most concentrated hiding-places of his imagination. At their best, such moments transform his short poems into the literary equivalent of icebergs: small peaks of eloquence which rise above the indifferent surface of the page and are sustained by the hidden mass of the unsaid.

> Ask me no more, for fear I should reply;
>   Others have held their tongues, and so can I,
>   Hundreds have died, and told no tale before:
>   Ask me no more, for fear I should reply—
>   (*AP* VI, pp. 151–2)

---

[9] Brian Vickers, *In Defence of Rhetoric* (Oxford, 1998), p. 496.
[10] William Shakespeare, *Julius Caesar*, III. ii. 130.

The phrase 'no more' mattered to Housman, who could be reduced to tears by Milton's line 'Nymphs and shepherds, dance no more'.[11] This poem extends the logic of paralipsis into his syntax, which keeps appealing to the silent listener for a prompt before flinching back into a refusal to say any more, so dramatising the idea that loss is a process to be endured rather than a mere fact to be stated. But this double movement of approach and recoil is also carried in every other aspect of the poem: in the dash that follows 'reply', like an unanswered appeal for conversation, 'reply' in this stanza answering only to 'I' and itself; in the repetitions, which allow the speaker to carry on speaking without necessarily saying more; and especially in Housman's use of allusion. Even as Housman's speaker is reconciling himself to remaining alone, his lines reach out for company, like hands groping for each other in the dark. (The same is true of his use of rhyme: one of the most delicately insinuating patterns in *A Shropshire Lad* is that on each of the nine occasions 'alone' appears it is as a rhyme word.) The poem is generated and structured by the appeal 'Ask me no more', but this is itself an answer to Tennyson:

> Ask me no more: what answer should I give?
> I love not hollow cheek or faded eye:
> Yet, O my friend, I will not have thee die!
> Ask me no more, lest I should bid thee live;
> Ask me no more.[12]

—just as Tennyson's poem was an answer to Keats:

> Twice hast thou ask'd whither I went: henceforth
> Ask me no more! I may not utter it,
> Nor may I be thy love.[13]

Finally, hanging heavily over these lines as it does over so much of Housman's verse, there is the injunction he marked in his copy of the

---

[11] 'The Name and Nature of Poetry', *A. E. Housman: Collected Poems and Selected Prose*, p. 369; in the same lecture Housman also quotes Shakespeare ('Fear no more the heat o' the sun') and Blake ('Turn away no more').
[12] Alfred, Lord Tennyson, 'Ask me no more', in Christopher Ricks (ed.), *The Poems of Tennyson*, 3 vols. (Harlow, 1987), 2. 279.
[13] John Keats, *Endymion*, IV. 755–8, in Miriam Allott (ed.), *Keats: The Complete Poems* (Harlow, 1970), p. 275; the passage is marked in Housman's 1888 copy of Keats's poems. Archie Burnett notes the parallel (*The Poems of A. E. Housman*, p. 467) and compares Thomas Carew's 'A Song', each stanza of which begins 'Aske me no more'.

Apocrypha: 'Some man holdeth his tongue, because he hath not to answer: and some keepeth silence, knowing his time.'[14]

Housman had good private reasons for knowing why some silences might be both necessary and impossible to keep. 'Ask me no more' was almost certainly addressed to Moses Jackson, the Oxford contemporary to whom Housman devoted himself, but from whom, in the carefully chosen words of his brother Laurence, 'there was no response in kind'.[15] He was Housman's first and lasting love. Housman once explained that 'I did not begin to write poetry in earnest until the really emotional part of my life was over',[16] and given his double creative flowering in *A Shropshire Lad* (published soon after his break with Jackson) and *Last Poems* (published soon after he heard that Jackson was dying of cancer) a good case could be made for viewing all his poems as elegies, in which his rejection by one individual signalled a far greater loss that would continue to happen—the death of possibility. Housman's lop-sided loyalty has often been singled out by critics seeking a creation myth to explain his career. Historians of homosexuality have been especially quick with their pity, usually weighing him unfavourably against Wilde as two different models of response to a time that enjoined them to keep silent.[17] One is a prophet of gay pride, the other a relic of gay shame. Wilde put himself in the dock to make his notorious defence of 'the love that dare not speak its name'; Housman hid himself away in Trinity College Cambridge, his refusal to speak out being seen by later critics as broadly equivalent to a refusal to come out. Wilde claimed to have feasted with panthers; Housman was rumoured to have introduced crème brûlée to Trinity high table. Wilde died on the cusp of the twentieth century but transcended his time; Housman lived on to 1936 burdened by an imagination that never outgrew its Victorian roots. In this view, summarised in Stephen Spender's

---

[14] Eccles. 20: 6, Housman's marking is noted in Burnett (ed.), *The Poems of A. E. Housman*, p. 467.
[15] Laurence Housman, *Alfred Edward Housman's 'De Amicitia'* (1976), p. 23.
[16] Letter to Maurice Pollet (5 Feb. 1933), in Archie Burnett (ed.), *The Letters of A. E. Housman*, 2 vols. (Oxford, 2007), 2. 329.
[17] See, e.g., Keith Jebb, 'The Land of Lost Content', in Alan W. Holden and J. Roy Birch (eds.), *A. E. Housman: A Reassessment* (Basingstoke, 2000), p. 38: 'The possibility of a homosexual lifestyle, given a disguised but real treatment in Wilde's writings, appears to be a non-issue in A. E. H.'s poetry', and Ruth Robbins, '"A very curious construction": masculinity and the poetry of A. E. Housman and Oscar Wilde', in Sally Ledger and Scott McCracken (eds.), *Cultural Politics at the Fin de Siècle* (Cambridge, 1995), p. 146: 'It is difficult to think of a greater contrast than that of the poetry of Wilde and Housman. Where Wilde is verbose, pleasure-seeking, list-making and adventurous in form and substance, Housman is restrained, restricted . . .'.

part-admiring, part-admonishing characterisation of him as 'the lyricist of English repression',[18] Housman's poems are a series of self-exposures masquerading as self-concealments, each one a precise but unwitting calibration of 'the pressures which social *mores* impose upon the individual voice'.[19] The burden of these pressures in the late nineteenth and early twentieth centuries has often been vividly described, particularly where conditions of active opposition find themselves being answered by forms of passive obedience. For Edmund Gosse, writing in the 1890s, 'the position of a young person so tormented is really that of a man buried alive'[20]—a claim which reverberates in Freud's later comparison of repression to the choking deaths suffered in Pompeii,[21] and surfaces again in memoirs of Housman like *A Buried Life*, written by the aptly named Percy Withers.[22] But the tradition of depicting Housman as a victim of repression has been an unfortunate one, not least because often it has created the very problem it claims to describe.

'The most inveterate fault of critics', Hopkins observed, 'is the tendency to cramp and hedge in by rules the free movements of genius'.[23] Few have been able to resist the urge to create a version of Housman that is more narrowly predictable than his poems. This takes different forms according to each reader's priorities and blind-spots. Summary judgements are popular,[24] as are summaries of the poems which are themselves judgements on Housman's perceived limitations, such as the list of ingredients which Virginia Woolf thought made up the 'peculiar scent' of his poems ('May, death, lads, Shropshire'),[25] or Frank Harris's crushing review in *The Invention of Love*: 'No one gets off; if you're not shot, hanged or stabbed, you kill yourself. Life's a curse, love's a blight, God's

---

[18] Stephen Spender, *The Making of a Poem* (1955), p. 158.
[19] Geoffrey Hill, 'Tacit Pledges', in Holden and Birch (eds.), *A. E. Housman: A Reassessment*, p. 75 n.
[20] Cited in Colin Spencer, *Homosexuality: A History* (1995), p. 297.
[21] On 'the equation between repression and burial' see 'Delusions and Dreams in Jensen's *Gradiva*' (1907), trans. James Strachey, in *The Standard Edition of the Complete Psychological Works of Sigmund Freud*, 24 vols. (1953–74), 9. 40.
[22] Percy Withers, *A Buried Life: Personal Recollections of A. E. Housman* (1940).
[23] G. M. Hopkins, letter to A. W. M. Baillie (6 Sept. 1863), discussed in Robert Bernard Martin, *Gerard Manley Hopkins: A Very Private Life* (1991), p. 71.
[24] See, e.g., Stephen Spender's comment that 'what one might call the Essential Housman' might be reduced to 'perhaps less than fifty poems, in which Housman really says all he has to say', or E. M. Forster's even more reductive conclusion that 'about half-a-dozen' of *More Poems* 'are marvellous, and purists may wish that these alone had been printed'; both comments are repr. in Philip Gardner (ed.), *A. E. Housman: The Critical Heritage* (1992), pp. 377, 316.
[25] Virginia Woolf, letter to Julian Bell (2 May 1936) in Nigel Nicolson (ed.), *The Letters of Virginia Woolf*, 6 vols. (1975–80), 6. 33.

a blaggard, cherry blossom is quite nice.'²⁶ An alternative is to quote lines which are blinkered from the full imaginative range of their context, as when Mr Emerson in *A Room with a View* borrows four lines from *A Shropshire Lad* and then dismisses them as cripplingly one-sided:

> In his ordinary voice, so that she scarcely realized he was quoting poetry, he said:
>
> > 'From far, from eve and morning
> > And yon twelve-winded sky,
> > The stuff of life to knit me
> > Blew hither: here am I.
>
> George and I both know this, but why does it distress him? . . . Let us rather love one another, and work and rejoice. I don't believe in all this world-sorrow.'²⁷

'I don't believe in all this world-sorrow'—but Housman's speaker continues by making it clear that neither does he:

> Now—for a breath I tarry
> Nor yet disperse apart—
> Take my hand quick and tell me,
> What have you in your heart.
>
> Speak now, and I will answer;
> How shall I help you, say . . .
> (*ASL* XXXII, pp. 33–4)

Another critical gambit is to accuse Housman's verse of being 'adolescent'—a judgement which often says less about Housman than it does about the critic's desire to keep him in a state of arrested development.²⁸ Take Harold Bloom's regular returns to Housman's lines about 'The happy highways where I went | And cannot come again' (*ASL* XL, p. 40): 'Like many of Housman's poems it has been in my head for sixty years. As a boy of eight, I would walk about chanting Housman's . . . lyrics to myself, and I still do, less frequently yet with undiminished fervor.'²⁹ Such

---

²⁶ Tom Stoppard, *The Invention of Love* (1997), p. 86.
²⁷ E. M. Forster, *A Room With a View* (1908, repr. 1977), pp. 26–7.
²⁸ Christopher Ricks summarises the argument that Housman's poetry is 'adolescent' ('[a] word used with quite different valuations by critics as different as R. P. Blackmur, George Orwell, Conrad Aiken, W. H. Auden, and Hugh Kenner') in his introduction to *A. E. Housman: A Collection of Critical Essays* (Englewood Cliffs, NJ, 1968), pp. 4–5; the same volume reprints John Wain's comment that 'Housman's major faults as a poet—the things that keep him a *minor* poet—are (a) the immature and commonplace nature of his subject-matter, all self-pity and grumbling; (b) the lack of any development', p. 27.
²⁹ Harold Bloom, *How to Read and Why* (2000), p. 71.

incantations allow Bloom to conjure up his own past, as if to affirm that he has not changed his mind or his tunes in the intervening years, but they carefully ignore Housman's own refusal to settle into a single home-key, his skill at evading the patterns he has established for himself. At its best, this sort of cramping and hedging confuses the desire to pin Housman down with the desire to keep him in his place. At its worst, it resembles a set of variations on Housman's unhappy experience at school, where he was nicknamed Mouse and, according to his sister, 'boys would tread on him pretending they had not seen him'. Still, as she goes on to say, Housman was 'by no means the sort of boy to be downtrodden', and another story she tells about a tree planted to commemorate his birth might serve as an alternative emblem of his career: 'Alfred's tree was planted nearest to our family graves in the south-west corner of the churchyard. Some time ago it came to grief through age or storm and was cut down to a stump, which, however, sprouted instead of dying.'[30]

The conjunction of Housman and graves is a natural one. Indeed, given the 'corpse-strewn landscape' of Housman's Shropshire,[31] there is a special felicity in the stark title page of Richard Graves's biography *A. E. Housman: The Scholar-Poet*:

<blockquote>
Graves

A. E. Housman[32]
</blockquote>

Poem after poem shows Housman striking out in different directions before circling back to the gibbet or the churchyard, as death exerts its gravitational pull. Individual lines warp their syntax to make the grave the permanent axis around which they revolve: 'There in their graves my comrades are, | In my grave I am not' (*MP* XXXIX, p. 138). The relentless downward pressure can create what look like creative misprints, where a dream of liberty is twisted away from America to another united state, the 'free land of the grave' (*MP* XXIII, p. 129), or tangle together creation and destruction by using 'grave' to mean 'inscribe': 'Tell me of runes to grave' (*MP* XLV, p. 143). Indeed, so often do Housman's poems seek dead ends that there is a glumly self-conscious humour in the conclusion of both volumes he saw through the press.

---

[30] Katharine E. Symons, *Alfred Edward Housman: Recollections* (Bromsgrove, 1936), pp. 8, 12.
[31] Alan Hollinghurst, introduction to *A. E. Housman: Poems* (2001), p. x.
[32] Richard Perceval Graves, *A. E. Housman, The Scholar-Poet* (1979), p. i.

A Shropshire Lad:

> ... When I am dead and gone.
> THE END
> (p. 66)

Last Poems:

> ... To air the ditty,
> And to earth I.
> THE END
> (p. 109)

Set out like that, his poems can start to look like suicide notes, albeit of a peculiarly ineffective sort, given that, as Paul Valéry argued, unlike more pragmatic forms of speech a poem 'does not die for having lived', but instead is 'expressly designed to be born again from its ashes', forever renewing itself in the eyes and lungs of its readers.[33]

It is this resilience which distinguished Housman's voice during his life, and has helped to project it far beyond his death; his poetry makes the pressures of his time tell, in ways that are imaginatively enlivening rather than depressing or deadening, but he also outstrips this time through the very strength with which he observes it. In addressing the circumstances in which he wrote ('address' in the double sense of appealing to them and putting them to rights), his poems speak in a way that presses back against the cultural conditions which helped to shape them; to borrow Seamus Heaney's fine insight into the possible worlds that poetry creates, Housman's voice opens up 'a glimpsed alternative, a revelation of potential that is denied or constantly threatened by circumstances'.[34] And if we sometimes find it hard to hear this voice, that may be not because it has nothing to say to us but because it has so successfully become our own.

II

The idea that Housman could speak out at all would have come as a surprise to some of his contemporaries. 'Even in the most intellectual

---

[33] Paul Valéry, 'Poetry and Abstract Thought', repr. in *The Art of Poetry*, trans. Denise Folliot (1958), p. 72.
[34] Seamus Heaney, *The Redress of Poetry* (1995), p. 4.

company', Laurence Housman reported, 'he preferred to remain silent.' Wilfrid Blunt agreed: 'He would, I think, be quite silent if he were allowed to be.'[35] This could lead to problems; Percy Withers recalled how when they were out walking his chatter was often ignored by Housman, who preferred to express himself in other ways: 'Sometimes it would happen during the morning walk that he was morose and ill-tempered . . . and, one of the dogs crossing his path, he would lunge out with a foot, and appeared to derive satisfaction if the mean assault were effected. Those mornings were the most difficult.'[36] Himself a generous soul, Withers dismisses Housman's silence as no more than a personal quirk, like his preference for elastic-sided boots or sturdy underwear. But although Housman could certainly be 'difficult', many of his silences seem to have been a response to a more general difficulty: how to speak to someone in a way that discovers what you have in common without thereby exposing your differences. Far from revealing how unsociable he was, Housman's refusal to speak is just as likely to have been a sign of how far he idealised sociability, an ideal always likely to be disappointed by the risks and misunderstandings of ordinary conversation. He marked these lines in his copy of T. E. Lawrence's *Seven Pillars of Wisdom*:

> There was my craving to be liked—so strong and nervous that never could I open myself friendly to another. The terror of failure in an effort so important made me shrink from trying; besides, there was the standard; for intimacy seemed shameful unless the other could make the perfect reply, in the same language, after the same method, for the same reasons.[37]

Beside this passage, Housman wrote 'This is me.'[38] It may be that he saw this admission as a way of addressing his fears of being too unlike other people, too unlikeable, for his affections to be recognised and returned. On the page he could open himself to another, just as he did with his allusions, even if the act of reading also allowed him to keep intimacy literally at arm's length. But even here he worried that most replies were far from perfect, given the difficulty in knowing exactly how something on the page was being offered and so how it should be taken. Housman's unpublished poem about the need to separate from Moses Jackson ends

---

[35] Laurence Housman, *A. E. H.: Some Poems, Some Letters and a Personal Memoir by his Brother* (1937), p. 95; Blunt's comment is quoted in Archie Burnett, 'Silence and Allusion in Housman', p. 152.
[36] Percy Withers, *A Buried Life: Personal Recollections of A. E. Housman*, p. 55.
[37] T. E. Lawrence, *Seven Pillars of Wisdom*, 2 vols. (1935), 2. 580.
[38] Laurence Housman, *A. E. H.*, p. 99.

with the plea 'Be good to the lad that loves you true' (*MP* XXX, p. 132); Jackson's last letter to Housman was signed 'Yours very truly'.[39] But how could one express true feelings to someone with such a different understanding of what it meant to be true?

This can produce a certain stiffness in Housman's own letters, which even to his family are signed 'A. E. Housman', almost as if they could have been written by someone else. It also produces a degree of wary self-involvement in his poetry, which often extends itself and then recoils, as if asking a question, pausing for a response, and then carrying on where it left off:

> I met a statue standing still.
> Still in marble stone stood he . . .
> (*ASL* LI, p. 54)

> You smile upon your friend today,
> Today his ills are over . . .
> (*ASL* LVII, p. 60)

> Where you would not, lie you must,
> Lie you must, and not with me.
> (*LP* XXXIII, p. 102)

These syntactic stutters take a number of different forms. Lines curl back on themselves to reflect on the inconsequentiality of our hopes; or the gap between one line and the next is used to confirm that nothing has happened in this brief pause to change the direction of the speaker's thoughts:

> Now are he and I asunder
> And asunder to remain . . .
> (*AP* II, p. 150)

Other poems offer miniature dramas of abandonment, as the speaker returns to his words in ways that could suggest either the blank repetitions of shock or the keening of grief:

> He would not stay for me; and who can wonder?
> He would not stay for me to stand and gaze.
> (*AP* VII, p. 152)

Or, again self-consciously playing on the ambiguity of 'stay' (suggesting both pause and endurance), they respond to the speaker's loneliness by

---

[39] Laurence Housman, *Alfred Edward Housman's 'De Amicitia'*, p. 26.

asking for company and then rejecting it, narcissistically wrapping the lines up in themselves:

> Stay, if you list, O passer by the way;
>   Yet night approaches: better not to stay.
>   (*AP* XII, p. 154)

What these examples share is the recognition that a voice unwilling or unable to make contact with others could retreat into a form of private brooding; someone who 'repelled advance' might produce verse that ended up sticking in a rut of its own making.[40] Similar anxieties animate much nineteenth-century poetry, and Housman would have come across them in the work of Matthew Arnold, who often worries that a shared language cannot articulate our most intimate longings, and that failing to take preventative measures will leave us with nothing in common but our loneliness:

> And long we try in vain to speak and act
> Our hidden self, and what we say and do
> Is eloquent, is well—but 'tis not true![41]

Arnold's poems cautiously offer themselves as just such preventative measures. A sentence such as 'Ah, love, let us be true | To one another!' starts by trying to distinguish this love from all other loves,[42] and then breaks itself on 'true' to warn of the difficulty in being true to someone else. Rounding the corner of the line, though, it recognises the temptation to turn back on itself with the local chime 'true | To' before resisting it: 'true | To one another'. The appeal faces down its own fears and emerges braced by the ordeal, a lifeline thrown across a gulf of potential misunderstanding.

This need to find shadings of private significance within a public language might be true of any lover, whose protestations of single-heartedness always risk sounding shared or second-hand, just one more episode in the same old story. But the problem is likely to be especially acute for someone who finds his voice slipping into the grooves of commonplaces that can never speak for him. Consider the selective deafness in one of the *OED*'s definitions of 'reject': 'To repel or rebuff (one who makes advances); to refuse to accept, listen to, admit, etc. **b)** Of a woman: To

---

[40] G. U. Yule, cited in Graves, *A. E. Housman: The Scholar-Poet*, p. 168.
[41] 'The Buried Life', in Kenneth Allott (ed.), *The Poems of Matthew Arnold* (Harlow, 1965), p. 274.
[42] 'Dover Beach', in Allott (ed.), *The Poems of Matthew Arnold* (1965), p. 242.

refuse (a man) as lover or husband.'⁴³ Dictionaries offer definitions rather than justifications, but they also draw attention to the intimate relationship between linguistic norms and norms of behaviour: the pressures of expectation that gradually mould words like 'reject' to fit the contours of social life; the dangerous ease with which everyday speech can settle into comforting but thoughtless routines.

From the start of his career, Housman recognised this as both a threat and an opportunity.

> 'Hallelujah!' was the only observation
>   That escaped Lieutenant-Colonel Mary-Jane,
> When she tumbled off the platform in the station
>   And was cut in little pieces by the train;
>   Mary-Jane, the train is through ye,
>   Hallelujah! Hallejulah!
> We will gather up the fragments that remain.
>
> (*LVJ*, p. 256)

Housman might have been attracted to this parody by the thought that the Salvation Army was already a parody of a real army—a mixed-sex troop where death could come only by accident—although the hint of deliberate malice in the train which cuts her in pieces opens the disquieting possibility that we are always at war with a world in which, to borrow the Resistentialist slogan, 'things are against us'.⁴⁴ The joke of the poem is that Salvation Army hymns sometimes looked forward to taking a train to heaven, so there is a sly spoof of predestination in the way that 'Lieutenant-Colonel Mary-Jane' is drawn out until it is met with 'train', as if God had started using the railway tracks as a convenient way of organising his providential scheme. However, the sharpest bit of comic business is kept until last, because 'Gather up the fragments that remain' is itself a fragment of the Bible set to a new and sprightly tune: 'Gather up the fragments that remain, that nothing be lost.'⁴⁵

Such fragments often rise to the surface of Housman's verse, like the debris of a shipwreck, as the battered remains of old ways of thinking and speaking that no longer answer to present needs. Yet as Housman knew from his classical studies, what has happened to the Bible is what can happen to any speaker whose words are taken on by other voices. A

---

⁴³ *OED*, 'reject', 5.
⁴⁴ 'Les choses sont contre nous' is Paul Jennings's parody of Sartre in his 'Report on Resistentialism', first published in *The Spectator* (1948).
⁴⁵ John 6: 12.

sentence he cut from 'The Name and Nature of Poetry' describes how difficult it is 'to tell the truth when one knows it, to find words which will not obscure it or pervert it';[46] but even if a writer did manage to find the perfect match between word and idea, like fitting a key to a lock, it could still end up being warped or corroded by misinterpretation. Housman's entire career as a classical editor could be viewed as an attempt to clear away these confusions. Faced with an author like Manilius, whose intentions had been muffled by the buzz and static created by two thousand years of editorial interference, his version set out to see the object as in itself it really had been: restoring the author's words to him; redeeming error; journeying into the past in search of a land of lost *con*tent. It was a habit of thought he extended to his reading of English poetry: his copy of William Allingham's British ballads,[47] one of *A Shropshire Lad*'s key sources, is full of marginal jottings which suggest alternative readings for particular words and phrases, showing Housman's awareness that an oral tradition was especially vulnerable to producing lines that had taken a wrong turning over the years. The same habit of thought is also one he could turn to creative account, in lines that use sudden swerves of syntax to control the threat of error while simultaneously casting a wary ear on bits of second-hand speech:

> Bells at sunrise making babel:
> Christ is born, I hear men say.
> (*NF* XLV, p. 186)

The reader is alerted to how quickly a message can be corrupted in the stretching out of 'bells' into 'babel', and this gives 'I hear men say' a slightly sceptical curl of the lip, reminding us how much trust and doubt will be involved in any information that arrives as hearsay. The *OED* has a helpful definition of 'hearsay' ('Oral tidings; report; tradition; rumour; common talk; gossip'), which not only generously accommodates the different forms of speech it could encompass, but also does not discriminate between them, and so suggests how easily 'common talk' might become infected with the self-generating rhythms of 'gossip'. Several of Housman's notebook fragments show him exploring a similar set of ideas:

---

[46] Letter to Laurence Housman (24 May 1933), in Burnett (ed.), *The Letters of A. E. Housman*, 2. 349.
[47] William Allingham, *The Ballad Book* (1892 edn., first published 1864); the volume is now in the library of St John's College, Oxford.

> He called me all the names he knew,
> And that was more than he could spell;
> I gave him stuff to think of too,
> The tale about his sister Nell
> And Martin Hughes, and what folks thought
> And folks expected: then we fought.
> (*NF* XVIII, p. 176)

The dangerous effects of such tittle-tattle are suggested in that sudden collapse of 'folks thought' into 'fought', warning how divisive gossip could turn out to be once its illusion of solidarity is stripped away. This is a common worry during Housman's lifetime: both Kierkegaard and Hegel make some sharp observations on the damaging effects of 'idle words',[48] while religious tracts such as *Village Gossip Investigated* are equally suspicious of the false sense of community that gossip encourages:

> The instances which have been introduced are mainly such as have come before the notice of the writer, (many of a more dangerous character being purposely omitted), who has tried to weave then into a somewhat connected narrative, earnestly hoping that all who read it may find some benefit to themselves, and convey some benefit to others in the strength of the prayer
> 'Set a watch, O Lord, before my mouth: and keep the door of my lips.'[49]

One problem with this hope is that the narrator risks sounding complicit with the very problem he is describing: those brackets around 'many of a more dangerous character being purposely omitted', which aim at a soothing confidence, could easily be taken as a gossipy aside. Yet it is hard to see how any story could altogether avoid the accusation of peddling gossip, given that the gossip's key activities are also central to the workings of fiction: reporting, guessing, insinuating, surmising, telling tales. From *Cranford* and *The Tenant of Wildfell Hall* to one of Housman's favourite novels, Bennett's *The Old Wives' Tale*, this is something that Victorian novelists often play out and play on, as the relationship between narrator and reader—the intimacy that comes with shared knowledge—is used to reflect on the power of fiction to transform the world, while also questioning how far this differs from the tendency of gossip to twist the truth into the more compliant shape of a story. Poets are still more vulnerable to this charge, because their use of stanzas, rhythm and so on means that frameworks of 'common talk' are what they must write in, whatever they are writing about, and where the poet finds his voice set-

---

[48] See Patricia Meyer Spacks, *Gossip* (New York, 1985), pp. 16–18.
[49] 'A. Bird', *Village Gossip Investigated* (c.1895), Preface.

tling into the traditional measures of verse, it always risks weakening 'oral tidings', poetry's bardic origins, into little more than a form of refined cultural 'gossip'. 'The essential business of poetry, as it has been said, is to harmonise the sadness of the universe':[50] but how might the poet harmonise this sadness without it drowning out the melody of his own voice?

Housman's original title for *A Shropshire Lad* was 'Poems of Terence Hearsay': 'Terence' presumably because Housman's sense of exile chimed with the experience of an author originally brought to Rome as a slave, a stranger in a strange land; 'hearsay' because from the start of his volume he is concerned to show how the repetition of ideas can hollow them out into meaningless jingles.

> From Clee to heaven the beacon burns,
>   The shires have seen it plain,
> From north and south the sign returns
>   And beacons burn again.
>
> Look left, look right, the hills are bright,
>   The dales are light between,
> Because 'tis fifty years to-night
>   That God has saved the Queen.
>
> Now, when the flame they watch not towers
>   About the soil they trod,
> Lads, we'll remember friends of ours
>   Who shared the work with God.
>
> To skies that knit their heartstrings right,
>   To field that bred them brave,
> The saviours come not home to-night:
>   Themselves they could not save.
>   (*ASL* I, p. 3)

The first rhyme words of this lyric are 'returns' and 'again': appropriate for a poem about the Queen's birthday, perhaps, but the unpredictable reappearances of 'God save the Queen' in various mangled forms are not happy returns. 'The saviours come not home to-night: | Themselves they could not save': as so often in Housman, refrain is used to put the past in

---

[50] Letter to Katharine Symons (5 Oct. 1915), in Burnett (ed.), *The Letters of A. E. Housman*, 1. 346–7, referring to a passage in Leslie Stephen's *A History of English Thought in the Eighteenth Century* (1876): 'Nothing is less poetical than optimism; for the essence of a poet's function is to harmonise the sadness of the universe.' Burnett notes that the passage is copied out on p. 44 of Housman's Notebook X.

its place. It sets the tone for the rest of the volume, which repeatedly upends clichés—"Tis now the blood runs gold' (*ASL* V, p. 8), 'the morning clocks will ring | A neck God made for other use | Than strangling in a string' (*ASL* IX, p. 13), 'Let us endure an hour and see injustice done' (*ASL* XLVIII, p. 52)—while suspiciously invoking the anonymous power of the public voice: 'A Grecian lad, as I hear tell' (*ASL* XV, p. 18); 'miles around they'll say that I | Am quite myself again' (*ASL* XVIII, p. 20); 'On banks of Thames they must not say | Severn breeds worse men than they' (*ASL* XXXVII, p. 38).

As Housman grew older, retreating into the carefully chosen discomfort of his rooms in Trinity, he would have had good private reasons for distrusting the power of hearsay. The less he said, the more stories circulated about him. One concerned a dinner at which he and J. M. Barrie sat next to each other but did not exchange a word, after which Barrie wrote to apologise for being so shy, and Housman replied with exactly the same words, but with his own name correctly spelt.[51] Another concerned Wittgenstein, who had even more spartan rooms above him in Trinity, and was desperate to use his lavatory; Housman replied that as a philosophical hedonist he would not grant the request.[52] Colleges are both private and gossipy places, so it is not surprising that his silence resulted in other people eagerly swapping stories that seemed like spyholes onto his hidden life, a form of social revenge on the unsociable. But Housman was aware of how much conversation relies on borrowed words long before he went to Cambridge, and he could turn this in different directions, from gravely caricaturing snatches of received opinion in his letters ('Cancer is worse, they say'),[53] to adopting a voice which carefully settled itself in the gap between discriminating politeness and thoughtless *politesse* ('My heart always warms to people who do not come to see me, especially Americans, to whom it seems to be more of an effort'),[54] to the heartbreaking flatness of the note about Moses Jackson he wrote in his diary: 'I heard he was married.'[55] His poems, too, frequently approach conventions of address before neatly sidestepping them, in ways that range from reply to retort to reproof. Comic ideas are given slow and solemn atten-

---

[51] See Maas (ed.), *The Letters of A. E. Housman*, p. 262. Barrie's letter to 'Mr Houseman' (one 'so often misquoted', according to the sales catalogue in which it appeared in 1936) is accurately quoted in Burnett (ed.), *The Letters of A. E. Housman*, 1. 529 n.
[52] See Graves, *A. E. Housman: The Scholar-Poet*, p. 254.
[53] Letter to Percy Withers (4 May 1920), in Burnett (ed.), *The Letters of A. E. Housman*, 1. 439.
[54] Letter to Neilson Abeel (4 Oct. 1935), in Burnett (ed.), *The Letters of A. E. Housman*, 2. 496.
[55] Laurence Housman, *Alfred Edward Housman's 'De Amicitia'*, p. 34.

tion; serious ideas are set to jaunty tunes; sometimes his verse straddles both possibilities at once, as when he adopts a stanzaic form made popular by 'Drury's Dirge',[56] one of the parodies in Horace and James Smith's *Rejected Addresses* (1812), and uses it to carry a rhythm that could either be dragging its feet or kicking its heels.

> Up, lad, up, 'tis late for lying:
> Hear the drums of music play;
> Hark, the empty highways crying
> "Who'll beyond the hills away?"
> (*ASL* IV, p. 7)

'Hear the **drums** of **music play**', or '**Hear** the **drums** of **mus**ic **play**'? Light and cheery iambics play over a more cautious trochaic beat, and the result is disquieting, just as a military drummer's brisk tattoo can be slowed down to the muffled beat that accompanies death; the line both extends an invitation and reflects on where it could lead.

However, it is in the poems which address the unsettled, unsettling problem of homosexuality that Housman made his most far-reaching attempts to measure hearsay against a different voice, one which sounds both weary and urgent, despairing and demanding. Indeed, in its tonal flexibility and discriminating resistance to easy characterisation, it might be described as the voice of tolerance, especially if 'tolerance' is understood to mean not only the traditional virtues of generosity and patience, but also—a sense that was just starting to come into the language from mechanics—a legitimate variation from the norm.[57]

III

'Shot? So quick, so clean an ending?' was written shortly after Housman read about a young Woolwich cadet who had killed himself, partly because he worried that his love too was of a kind that could not be answered, and partly because he worried that it could:

> I wish it be clearly understood that I am not what it commonly called 'temporarily insane' . . . There is only one thing in this world that would make me thoroughly happy; that one thing I have no earthly hope of attaining . . . I have absolutely ruined my own life; but I thank God that, as yet, I have not morally injured—or 'offended', as it is called in the Bible—any one else. Now I am

---

[56] The same stanza is also used in *ASL* XXXV, *LP* VIII and *AP* I.
[57] OED, 'tolerance' 4b: 'the allowable amount of variation in any specified quantity' (from 1909).

quite certain that I could not live for another five years without doing so . . . Of the dreadful blow I am dealing to my mother and the few other people who care for me I am quite aware. . . . I hope that they will live to forgive and, perhaps, to forget me. May God, in His infinite mercy, forgive me for what I am doing.— HARRY C. MACLEAN.[58]

> Shot? so quick, so clean an ending?
>   Oh that was right, lad, that was brave:
> Yours was not an ill for mending,
>   'Twas best to take it to the grave.
>
> Oh you had forethought, you could reason,
>   And saw your road and where it led,
> And early wise and brave in season
>   Put the pistol to your head.
>   (*ASL* XLIV, p. 47)

There is much in the cadet's suicide note that would have chimed with Housman: the strained use of Biblical language, working alongside the ghostly rhymes and dactylic beat which play across the proverbial phrasing of 'they will live to forgive and, perhaps, to forget'; the unhappy felicity of the cadet's name, Harry Ma*clean*, grimly apt (on the page if not on the tongue) for one determined to have a *clean* ending; the way in which 'There is only one thing in this world that would make me thoroughly happy' strains between melodramatic posturing and modest self-restraint. Given his sceptical interest in the power of hearsay, Housman is especially likely to have sympathised with the scornful rejection of the officialese so often used to hush up such deaths, which holds 'temporarily insane' in quotation marks as one might pick up something unpleasant with a pair of tweezers. Housman takes the hint and stretches it further, by borrowing a word ('clean') regularly used by his contemporaries to fulminate against sexual transgression, but then opening it to ridicule by placing it in conjunction with the phrase 'in season'. This could refer to the warning in Ecclesiastes that to all things there is a season, 'A time to be born and a time to die . . . A time to embrace, and a time to refrain from embracing . . . A time to keep silence, and a time to speak',[59] but in this context it seems awkwardly bound up with the idea that the cadet may have been going through a phase of what was euphemistically described as 'beastliness', as animals find themselves wanting to be more

---

[58] Reprinted as part of the coroner's report in *The Standard* (10 Aug, 1895) and cited by Archie Burnett in *The Poems of A. E. Housman*, p. 353; Housman kept a cutting of the report in his copy of *ASL* at XLIV.
[59] Eccles. 3: 2–7.

than just good friends when they are 'in season', and perhaps muddles it up too with the thought that a homosexual in the 1890s deserves no more sympathy than any other creature shot when it is 'in season'. At the same time, the poem makes it clear that abstract theories of human conduct are not always reliable guides to the actualities of human behaviour, just as the speaker's voice refuses to be satisfied within the boundaries of a set form. 'Shot? So quick, so clean an ending?'—but the line itself does not have a clean ending, going beyond our metrical expectations in a small rebellion against necessity. As the poem develops, masculine endings continue to be played off against feminine endings, possibly with half an ear on the ancient and stubborn theory that homosexuality is actually a compromise of the sexes, but with the effect of making the speaker sound both certain and uncertain at once. Like the lines about Oscar Wilde's trial which Housman wrote but chose not to publish ('Oh a deal of pains he's taken and a pretty price he's paid | To hide his poll or dye it of a mentionable shade', *AP* XVIII, p. 157) the voice of this speaker sets public outrage against private indignation; it starts by agreeing with ordinary folk wisdom, but agrees so heartily it ends up sounding like a parody of compliance, as those repeated 'Oh's simultaneously hit a rhetorical peak of gloating and withdraw into private shock and regret. Like all of Housman's best poems, the tone settles into a polished double-act of knowing comedian and impassive stooge, straightforwardness and stealth. It is a tone which finely samples the unstable atmosphere in which these poems were written, and the unpredictable reaction which could be provoked by throwing a word like 'Invert' or 'Uranian' or, eventually, 'Homosexual' into conversation: sincerity and irony; praise and blame; acceptance and rejection. Like the reception that greeted Wilde's famous speech in the dock, it brings together 'loud applause mingled with some hisses'.[60]

There are occasions on which this sort of equivocation could be an essential strategy. Graham Robb describes the tactics that might be needed in the nineteenth century to sound out someone's sexual preferences without being either beaten up or locked up, producing a rhetorical equivalent of the dance of courtship which Charlus performs in the vicinity of Jupien in Proust's *A la recherche du temps perdu*, at once leading on and backing off. Characterised by 'labyrinthine syntax' and 'petticoat layers of allusion around the central silence',[61] such encounters encouraged

---

[60] Newspaper report, cited in Paul Hammond, *Love Between Men in English Literature* (1996), p. 2.
[61] Graham Robb, *Strangers: Homosexual Love in the Nineteenth Century* (2003), p. 149.

a form of speech which allowed admissions to be made and unmade in a breath.[62] This can produce its own form of literary game in Housman. According to William Empson, 'Obscurity in a writer may be due not to concentration, but to a refusal to speak out';[63] but many of Housman's poems are not even clear over how far they are being unclear; if they flirt with revelation, they also flirt with the prospect of not having anything to reveal, like the patter of a conjurer with nothing up his sleeves. A poem like this could mean everything or nothing:

> The street sounds to the soldiers' tread,
>   And out we troop to see:
> A single redcoat turns his head,
>   He turns and looks at me.
>   (*ASL* XXII, p. 24)

The pronouns here stage a teasing and elusive drama, as 'we', 'he' and 'me' revolve enquiringly around each other. The repetition of 'turns', carried over the line-break, dramatises the speaker's excited double-take, but the look itself is wholly blank: invitation? warning? indifference? Is this the syntax of cruising, or just a self-conscious literary joke, based on the Latin root of 'verse' in 'vertere' ('to turn')? Like a number of words in the poem, such as 'single' or 'My man', it invites us to construct loving narratives and then smiles at us for getting ahead of ourselves.

The double plot of such poems makes their natural home pastoral, in which two worlds, two stories, come into uneasy contact with each other. But Housman did not need to rely on plot to suggest the different narrative possibilities open to the same set of events. The single word 'lad' is equally caught between two worlds. *A Shropshire Lad* was published at the end of a period that had seen a number of other lads in print: *Lads' Love: An Idyll of the Lands of Heather*, *The Fighting Lads of Devon*, *War Times; or, The Lads of Craigross*, *Lads of Kingston: A Tale of a Seaport Town*, *A Lad from the Country*, *The Luckiest Lad in Libberton,* and several more.[64] Many of these are boys' adventure stories, but 'lad' can refer

---

[62] Colim Toíbín's fictional biography of Henry James, *The Master* (2004), finely investigates the ambiguous allure of same-sex friendships at a time when personal reserve could signal mutual recognition rather than (or as well as) antagonism or indifference: 'Everyone he knew carried within them the aura of another life which was half secret and half open, to be known about but not mentioned. In those years, you searched each face for what it might unwittingly disclose and you listened carefully for nuances and clues', p. 5.

[63] Cited in Adam Phillips, *Side Effects* (2006), p. xi.

[64] Respectively by S. R. Crockett (1897), William Murray Graydon (1900), 'Sarah Tytler' [Henrietta Keddie] (1893), James Capes Story (1888), John Maddison Morton (1879), Ruth Lamb (1885).

to a young man (often a soldier) as well as a boy: the 'lads of Lunda' are 'handsome, athletic boys, brimful of animal life and happiness';[65] the 'lad of Lovelyn' is 'big, bronzed and bearded'.[66] What they share is a sense of geographical and historical displacement from the cultural centre: almost all the stories are set in the provinces and in the past; many involve a 'lad' leaving home, not always to return—a detail which would gain a new pathos when the word was adopted by poets of the Great War.[67] Two other features of these stories are likely to have been of particular interest to Housman. The first is that in the border ballads that lie behind *A Shropshire Lad*, a 'lad' is always potentially a sweetheart, as in the stanza marked by Housman which ends 'I never lo'ed a lad but ane, | And he's drown'd in the sea.'[68] (The same is true of Uranian poems written in the 1880s and 1890s, in which references to 'lads' uneasily attempt to reconcile a spirit of classical pederasty with lingering descriptions of youthful bodies.) The second feature is a sense of community: the *OED* records that from the 1880s, 'lad' could refer to 'Men of any age belonging to a group sharing common working, recreational, or other interests, esp. with the implication of comradeship and equality.'[69] This too animates Housman's poems, as the repetitions of 'lad'—a word which in *A Shropshire Lad* 'occurs sixty-seven times in sixty-three poems', as Cyril Connolly tetchily pointed out—call out for companionship while remaining anxiously separated from each other,[70] just as the title itself remains stranded between referring to an individual and a type.

The link between homosexuality and comradeship was a popular one in the 1890s. Laurence Housman belonged to the Order of Chaeronea, a secret society named after the 300 pairs of Theban lovers who died together in battle, brothers in arms, and the phrase most often associated with their fate was the 'love of comrades'.[71] A delicately balanced phrase, pivoting around 'of' to suggest a form of perfectly reciprocated affection, it was echoed and re-echoed by so many different writers that it came

---

[65] Jessie Margaret E. Saxby, *The Lads of Lunda* (1887), p. 6.
[66] 'Old Cornish', *Ste, or the Lad of Lovelyn* (1898), p. 196.
[67] See Paul Fussell, *The Great War and Modern Memory*, rev. edn. (2000), and Martin Taylor, *Lads: Love Poetry of the Trenches*, rev. edn. (1998).
[68] Allingham, *The Ballad Book*, p. 132.
[69] *OED*, 'lad' 2d (from 1886).
[70] Cyril Connolly, 'A. E. Housman: A Controversy' (1936), repr. in Ricks (ed.), *A. E. Housman: A Collection of Critical Essays*, p. 36.
[71] See Matt Cook, *London and the Culture of Homosexuality, 1885–1914* (Cambridge, 2003), pp. 125–42; the link with Whitman was first noted by William Whallon, 'A. E. Housman and "The Love of Comrades"', *Housman Society Journal*, 14 (1988), 51–4.

close to doing what it described, creating a democratic community brought together by a set of common ideals.[72]

Walt Whitman:

> I will make inseparable cities with their arms about each
>   other's necks,
>   By the love of comrades,
>   By the manly love of comrades.[73]

Edward Carpenter:

> Though there is historic evidence of the prevalence of the passion we may say of this period that its ideal was undoubtedly rather the chivalric love than the love of comrades.[74]

John Addington Symonds:

> Homer himself raises no question in our minds about the relation of lover and beloved. Achilles and Petroclus are comrades. Their friendship is equal . . . Still, it may be worth while suggesting that Homer, perhaps, intended in Hector and Achilles to contrast domestic love with the love of comrades.[75]

Finally—more mournfully, more sceptically—Housman:

> And Theseus leaves Pirithoüs in the chain
> The love of comrades cannot take away.
>   (*MP* V, p. 119)

The love of comrades offered an alternative to the world of marriage, an elsewhere which had one foot in the present (the New World ruminations of Whitman) and one foot in the past (the Golden Age of Greece). Drawing out a Greek ideal like this could produce a sense of strain, cultural stretch-marks, as in the conversation about the Olympic Games between Wilde and some Cockney rent-boys which Frank Harris claimed to have overheard in the Café Royal: '"Did you sy they was niked?" "Of

---

[72] The phrase also migrated into a number of Whitmanesque poems on bonds of friendship in the American army: see, e.g., John Hay, 'Miles Keogh's Horse', on Custer's last stand as proof that 'the love of comrades, the honor of arms, | Have not yet perished from the earth', *The Complete Poetical Works* (1916), p. 77; Richard Hovey, 'Comrades', on an old soldier's nostalgia for Dartmouth College: 'for the love of comrades only, thou!', *Along the Trail* (1899), p. 45; Richard Watson Gilder, 'When With Their Country's Anger', on the 'noblest memory' of soldiers: 'the Love of Comrades,—| That flower forever blows', *Poems* (1908), p. 274.

[73] Walt Whitman, 'For You O Democracy', *Leaves of Grass* (1881, reprinted in its original form in 1902 as one of the 'Rejected Poems'), Michael Moon (ed.), *Leaves of Grass and Other Writings* (New York, 2002), p. 101.

[74] Edward Carpenter, *Homogenic Love, and its Place in a Free Society* (1894), p. 9.

[75] John Addington Symonds, *Studies of the Greek Poets*, 3rd edn. (1893), p. 103.

course," Oscar replied, "nude, clothed only in sunshine and beauty." '[76] In Housman's hands, similarly, references to 'a Grecian lad' or Shakespeare's 'golden lads' (*LP* II, p. 73) can sound as if they occupied several times and places at once. Yet in his case these lyrical strains are both more knowing and more ambitious, as they resolve themselves into lines which not only hark back to the past but also reach out enquiringly into the future.

The modern conservative textual critic, Housman once noted, was 'a creature moving about in worlds not realised'.[77] He was referring to the tendency of his rivals to blunder around inside a book like tourists who misunderstand or ignore local customs, but the same description might differently be applied to his own poems: what drives their sense of unappeased longing is his consciousness of moving about in a world not realised.

> I see the country far away
>   Where I shall never stand;
> The heart goes where no footstep may
>   Into the promised land.
>   (*MP* II, p. 115)

This could be the land of lost content: the famous poem about Shropshire's 'blue remembered hills' is on the opposite page in Housman's notebook, and the use of common metre then adds another layer of historical distance, making it sound like a muted chorus of 'There is a green hill far away'. However, 'the promised land' could equally refer to the undiscovered country of the future, as the sudden reversal of the rhythm on 'Into'— '**In**to the **pro**mised **land**'—shows present-tense speech urgently pressing up against a visionary ideal. Among Housman's contemporaries, such pastoral thinking increasingly offered itself as a more optimistic alternative to the usual fate of same-sex relationships in literature: madness, exile, death.[78] As Robb suggests, with a carefully judged passing allusion to Housman, such geographical and historical displacements were also a way

---

[76] Frank Harris, quoted in Linda Dowling, *Hellenism and Homosexuality in Victorian Oxford* (Ithaca, 1994), p. 145.
[77] One of Housman's editorial notes to *M. Manilii Astronomicon Liber Primus* (1903), repr. in Ricks (ed.), *Collected Poems and Selected Prose*, p. 384.
[78] Summaries of the popular literary association of homosexuality and tragedy are given in Gregory Woods, *A History of Gay Literature: The Male Tradition* (New Haven, 1998), ch. 18, Meyers, *Homosexuality and Literature*, p. 18, and Robb, *Strangers*, pp. 209–16; as Robb observes, even in the hands of its defenders during the late nineteenth century, 'Almost every scene of homosexual passion took place in or near the grave' (p. 210).

of modelling alternative futures that writers might help to bring into being: 'The land of lost content was also a dream of future bliss.'[79] It is a mode of thought that may have been especially attractive to Housman because of the name he associated with both regret and desire: Moses Jackson, another Moses who would never see the promised land, although in his case as much through choice as historical necessity. But it is not necessary to personalise this mode of thought to recognise how often Housman returned to it—an imaginative pattern that is sunk into his writing like a watermark. It can be heard in his addiction to words beginning with 'un-' —unbegot, unbeknown, undone, unheeded, unkind, and many more— which, as in Hardy's poems, cast a shadow plot of fulfilment across a seemingly fated world, it being impossible to think of what is undone or unheeded without also thinking about how it might be done and heeded. It works its way into his stanzas, which can sound uncomfortably restrained, like miniature cages, but also show his skill as an escape artist, creating hidden entrances into alternative worlds more suited to his imaginings. It even makes its presence felt in his strategic placing of 'if',[80] a word which always embodies a small refusal of inevitability, or what George Steiner has described as one of grammar's 'passwords to hope'.[81]

It is certainly true that Housman sometimes shied away from such openness, and not only by making this 'promised land' into a patch of earth just big enough for a coffin—an imaginative trajectory that is traced both in his narratives and in the internal stitching of individual poems, as with the small but relentless shifts of *ASL* LIV from 'laden' to 'lad' to 'laid'.[82] The lyric 'Oh were he and I together' was withdrawn from

---

[79] Robb, *Strangers*, p. 216; compare Mark Mitchell and David Leavitt (eds.), *Pages Passed From Hand to Hand: the Hidden Tradition of Homosexual Literature in English from 1748 to 1914* (1998), which cites Bayard Taylor's 1870 novel *Joseph and His Friend* as a plea for 'a valley of bliss . . . a new world where men might love each other without fear of conventional society' (p. 48), and Woods, *A History of Gay Literature: The Male Tradition*, ch. 9, 'Pastoral Elegists', on nineteenth-century uses of pastoral which inflect the traditional association of homosexuality and elegy with an alternative perspective that is 'forward-looking and capable of envisaging positive change' (p. 118).
[80] See, e.g., *ASL* IX ('A better lad, if things went right, | Than most that sleep outside', p. 13) and XXXIII ('If truth in hearts that perish | Could move the powers on high', p. 34).
[81] George Steiner, *Grammars of Creation* (2002), p. 5.
[82]   With rue my heart is laden
          For golden friends I had,
       For many a rose-lipt maiden
          And many a lightfoot lad.

       By brooks too broad for leaping
          The lightfoot boys are laid . . .   (p. 58)

Last Poems when it was in page proof, while the Latin verses he added to his translation of Manilius, dedicated to Moses Jackson, adopted the Roman formula used when one soldier chose another, 'uirque uirum legi', but was buried away in a subclause, a confession about loving his comrade that was made to sound both central and peripheral at once:

> *non ego mortalem uexantia sidera sortem*
> *aeternosue tuli sollicitare deos,*
> *sed cito casurae tactus uirtutis amore*
> *humana uolui quaerere nomen ope,*
> *uirque uirum legi fortemque breuemque sodalem*
> *qui titulus libro uellet inesse meo.*
> [*LV*, p. 290]

[I did not endure, not I, to importune the stars that blast our mortal lot, or the eternal gods, but smitten with love for valour that would swiftly fall I resolved to seek a name with human help, and man to man I chose a brave and brief companion who should be willing to stand at the head of my book.]

Such comradeship does not last for ever, the poem concludes, and that seems to be that—a suitably downbeat ending for a relationship that never happened. The original draft, though, continued more optimistically:

> maioraque somnia mundo
> attollens populis \gentibus attollens/ orientia signa futuris
> at nostrum neutri conspicienda polus
> (*LV*, p. 291)

[... and greater dreams for the world; the heaven that holds up the rising stars for the peoples to come; but for neither of us to see ...][83]

The lines were rejected, as if Housman wanted to protect Jackson from even a glimpse of what neither of them would see, but the same idea successfully made its way into another published poem, 'Hell Gate', where once again Housman imagines 'greater dreams for the world' than his own world seemed capable of satisfying.

The poem's speaker describes how he travels down to hell, thinking about what he lightly but equivocally refers to as 'the loves of men', until finally he recognises one of the sentries:

> Then the sentry turned his head,
> Looked, and knew me, and was Ned.
> (*LP* XXXI, p. 99)

---

[83] Leofranc Holford-Strevens's translation, in Burnett (ed.), *The Poems of A. E. Housman*, p. 566.

A look of mutual recognition this time, rather than the lonely standing and staring that preoccupies other poems, and one that is potentially comic, with a meeting that brings together the idealism of Plato[84] and the square-jawed action of a Rider Haggard adventure story in a rhyme that is made to sound both perfectly inevitable and joyously unexpected. 'The whole thing is on the edge of the absurd', Housman noted; 'if it does not topple over, that is well so far.'[85] But what ensures the poem's status as a comedy rather than a farce is the way it too generously topples over beyond its own ending, as the two men leave Hell and gradually make the ascent back to life:

> Silent, nothing found to say,
> We began the backward way;
> And the ebbing lustre died
> From the soldier at my side,
> As in all his spruce attire
> Failed the everlasting fire.
> Midmost of the homeward track
> Once we listened and looked back;
> But the city, dusk and mute,
> Slept, and there was no pursuit.
> (p. 100)

Depart from me ye cursed *out of* everlasting fire? On one level the narrative is a redemptive reworking of Horace's 'Diffugere Nives', in which the bonds of comradeship are tested against the chains of death, with the key difference that in this version of the story, as John Bayley points out, 'The love of comrades *can* take away the chain, at least in the world of poetry and the imagination.'[86] At the same time, looking back at a fiery city starts to blur hell with Sodom, although this time the two people escaping are not a man and his wife—not even a man and his almost-wife, like the lovers in *The Eve of St Agnes*, another poem which these lines seem to have in their sights—but two men, walking out of the grave together. They do not speak, perhaps because they have nothing to say, but also perhaps because they silently understand each other; like so many fantasies of perfect comradeship in the period, the love that dare not speak

---

[84] Compare Phaedrus's speech in the *Symposium*, quoted as evidence of the ennobling and enlivening character of same-sex love in Edward Carpenter's *Homogenic Love*: 'who would desert his beloved and fail him in the hour of danger? The veriest coward would become an inspired hero, equal to the bravest at such a time; love would inspire him' (p. 23).
[85] Letter to J. W. Mackail (25 July 1922), repr. in Burnett (ed.), *The Letters of A. E. Housman*, 1. 506.
[86] John Bayley, *Housman's Poems* (Oxford, 1992), p. 157.

its name is also the love that does not need to speak.[87] There is no pursuit, and like Forster's *Maurice*, another fictional space created to allow the imagination to press back against reality, the poem ends with the pair walking into the future, past the frontier separating the real world from the possible world which the last line represents. It is in every sense a moving poem. It is also Housman's most far-sighted and provocatively secular reworking of what he called 'the most important truth which has ever been uttered': 'Whosoever will save his life shall lose it, and whosoever will lose his life shall find it.'[88]

Note. I am grateful to Adrian Poole, Mac Castro, Eric Griffiths, Anne Henry, Robert Macfarlane and Daniel Neill, each of whom helped me with the writing of this piece.

---

[87] See, e.g., the anonymous pornographic fantasy *Teleny; or the Reverse of the Medal* (1893), on 'the soft, hushed, and pleading tones of the lover who would fain be understood without words', repr. in Mitchell and Leavitt (eds.), *Pages Passed From Hand to Hand*, p. 243.

[88] 'The Name and Nature of Poetry', in Ricks (ed.), *Collected Poems and Selected Prose*, p. 364, quoting Luke 17: 29–33: 'the same day that Lot went out of Sodom it rained fire and brimstone from heaven, and destroyed them all. Even thus shall it be in the day when the Son of man is revealed. . . . Remember Lot's wife. Whosoever shall seek to save his life shall lose it; and whosoever shall lose his life shall preserve it.'

MASTER-MIND LECTURE

Condorcet and the Meaning of Enlightenment

LORRAINE DASTON

Max Planck Institute for the History of Science, Berlin

I. Enlightenment at full strength

0.999993: THIS IS THE PROBABILITY calculated in 1785 by Marie-Jean-Antoine-Nicolas de Caritat, Marquis de Condorcet, to express the acceptable risk of a false conviction in a just society.[1] It is also perhaps the most concise expression of everything that is at once attractive and repellent, coldly calculating and warmly visionary about not just Condorcet but the Enlightenment credo he embodied, for friends and foes alike. His friend, the *salonnière* Julie de Lespinasse, who always apostrophised him as 'le bon Condorcet', cheered him on in his fight for 'the cause of reason and humanity';[2] his later foe, the conservative literary critic Charles-Augustin Sainte-Beuve, reviled him as the 'extreme product' of eighteenth-century rationalism, 'a monstrous brain' hell-bent on 'remaking the human heart'.[3]

Read at the Academy 10 May 2006.
[1] Condorcet expressed the probability as a fraction rather than as a decimal: 144,767/144,768: M. J. A. N. Condorcet, *Essai sur l'application de l'analyse à la pluralité des décisions rendues à la pluralité des voix* (Paris, Imprimerie Royale, 1785), pp. cxiii–cxiv.
[2] Letter from Julie de Lespinasse to Condorcet, May 1775, in Charles Henry (ed.), *Lettres inédites de Mademoiselle de Lespinasse à Condorcet, à d'Alembert, à Guibert, au Comte de Crillon* (Paris, 1887), p. 149. Unless otherwise specified, all translations are my own.
[3] Charles-Augustin Sainte-Beuve, 'Oeuvres de Condorcet', *Causeries du lundi*, 3 (1868), 260–77 at p. 268.

Both descriptions hit the mark, and what is more, they hit the mark in the same place. Condorcet was not a Janus-faced figure riven by contradictions and blurred by ambiguities, so that proponents and opponents can pick and choose among contrasting aspects of his thought, all equally his. Although his thinking on various scientific, philosophical, and above all political matters certainly traced a developmental curve over the course of his life, he was remarkably consistent on the main points. Indeed, his relentless consistency accounts for much of what is remarkable in his writing. A mathematician by training, he followed the implications of general propositions with bulldog tenacity, lead where they may. The endpoints he reached in his reasoning can seem, read over two centuries later with the benefit of twenty-twenty hindsight, either dazzlingly prescient — e.g. his defence of female suffrage or prediction of doubled human life expectancy — or weirdly wrongheaded — e.g. his attempts to quantify the reliability of witness testimony or the likelihood that a tribunal of a certain construction would arrive at a true verdict. Yet it is all of a piece, and it is, as Lespinasse and Sainte-Beuve both recognised, Enlightenment *pur*, love it or hate it.

This is my motive for returning to the Marquis de Condorcet (1743–94). As a mathematician, as a philosopher, as a political theorist (much less as a political strategist), he was not a Master Mind, even as measured against only his eighteenth-century competitors in these domains. But as an Enlightenment thinker, as a thinker about, for, and of Enlightenment, he remains without peer. Whatever Enlightenment means, Condorcet lived, breathed, and radiated it; he even died for it. Right now, when the meaning of Enlightenment is probably more ferociously debated than at any time since the period in which Enlightenment first became a fighting word, Condorcet is a guide to what is at stake.

In order to appreciate just how embedded Condorcet's life and works were in the project of Enlightenment, it will be helpful to recall at least the outline of his career as mathematician, *philosophe*, and politician. Marie-Jean-Antoine-Nicolas Caritat, Marquis de Condorcet, was born into a family of the military nobility stemming from the Midi in France. His father was killed in the siege of Neuf-Brisach a few days after he was born; he was raised by a pious mother, who came from a bourgeois family in Picardy, and schooled by Jesuits in Reims and the Collège de Navarre in Paris. There he took up the study of mathematics and became a protégé of the mathematician and *Encyclopédist* Jean d'Alembert, who introduced him to the salons of Mlle de Lespinasse and Mme Helvétius and paved his way to election to the Académie Royale des Sciences in

1769. Condorcet became Perpetual Secretary of this body in 1776 and a lifelong defender of scientific academies against revolutionary detractors like Marat. Starting in the 1770s, largely through his friendship with Anne-Robert-Jacques Turgot, the reforming minister to Louis XVI, he became increasingly interested in economic, social, and political reform. He sought to wed his mathematics to his liberal politics in numerous works that attempted to apply probability theory to insurance, the design of tribunals, and voting procedures. He held the office of inspector of the mint, was inducted into the Académie Française in 1782, and married Sophie de Grouchy, herself the translator of Adam Smith and Tom Paine into French.

From the outbreak of the French Revolution in 1789, he threw himself into liberal politics, first as a member of the Paris Municipal Council and, after 1791, as a delegate to the Legislative Assembly and, after 1792, the Convention. He was especially active in projects on the reform of weights and measures and public instruction. He fell foul of the Jacobin-dominated Convention by publishing a ferocious attack on its hurriedly drafted constitution; on 8 July 1793 a warrant was issued for his arrest. He was hidden by a Mme de Vernet for nine months in what is now the rue de Servandoni by the Jardin du Luxembourg; it was here that he wrote the first draft of the *Sketch of a Historical Picture for the Progress of the Human Mind*. On 24 October 1793 he was condemned to death *in absentia*; on 25 March 1794, convinced that he was a danger to Mme de Vernet, he fled his refuge. He was soon apprehended and found dead in his prison cell—some say of a stroke, others by poison administered by his own hand—on 27 March 1794, a martyr for—some say of—the Enlightenment.[4]

My aim in this lecture is to view the meaning of Enlightenment afresh through Condorcet's eyes. This is a peculiarly disorienting experience, a perspective that is at once familiar and surpassingly strange. I hope to be able to show that both familiarity and strangeness are obverse and reverse of the same coin, the Enlightenment currency of *lumières*.

I shall begin with the notion of *lumières* itself, a word best translated as 'enlightenment', but this time written minuscule, preserving the associations of wisdom and deeper insight that still cling to the word in English (as in the phrase 'spiritual enlightenment'). In Condorcet's usage, *lumières* is at once an inner and outer light, a quality that can be acquired through

---

[4] The story of Condorcet's final days is movingly told by Charles Coulston Gillispie, *Science and Polity in France: The Revolutionary and Napoleonic Years* (Princeton, 2004), pp. 326–38.

instruction, the mastery of a body of knowledge, but which also requires the internalisation of certain habits of thought and feeling. Although the content of *lumières* may be as straightforward as the principles of arithmetic and political economy, its inner workings involve a moral component, a sensibility and an attitude towards the world that more closely resembles the illumination of the sage than the expertise of the technocrat.

Yet for Condorcet, one of the principal—if not *the* principal— expression of *lumières* was calculation, understood not only as a technique, but also as a form of intelligence and a spiritual exercise. I shall explore these multiple senses of calculation in the second part of my paper. One might regard this fondness for calculation as simply the *déformation professionelle* of the mathematician. It is true that Condorcet's work, especially on the applications of probability theory to everything from legal contracts to the design of tribunals, does include some striking examples of quantiphrenia.[5] But Condorcet's concept of *calcul* extended far beyond mathematics, even if it began there. To calculate was for Condorcet an education in both epistemology and civics, a way of analysing ideas in order to fix the boundary between the known and the unknown as well as an exercise in poltical autonomy, an assertion of independence against priestcraft and tyranny.

In Condorcet's view, the most effective weapon of priests and despots was not violence but fear. Like many Enlightenment thinkers, he was steeped in the works of the Roman Epicureans and Stoics; Lucretius and Seneca were still commonplace points of reference for an educated elite schooled (as Condorcet was) by Jesuits.[6] Lucretius had prescribed a heavy dose of natural philosophy to dissolve religious terrors: 'This terror of mind, therefore, and this gloom must be dispelled, not by the sun's rays nor the bright shafts of day, but by the aspect and law of nature.'[7] In his final work, *Sketch of a Historical Picture of the Progress of the Human Mind* (post-1795), written while in hiding at the height of the revolutionary Terror in 1793, Condorcet characteristically went one better

---

[5] On this aspect of Condorcet's work, see Gilles-Gaston Granger, *La Mathématique sociale du marquis de Condorcet* (Paris, 1956); Keith Michael Baker, *Condorcet: From Natural Philosophy to Social Mathematics* (Chicago, 1975); and Lorraine Daston, *Classical Probability in the Enlightenment* (Princeton, 1988).

[6] On the *philosophes*' debt to Latin classical authors, see Peter Gay, *The Enlightenment: An Interpretation*, 2 vols., vol. 1: *The Rise of Modern Paganism* (New York, 1977).

[7] Lucretius, *On the Nature of Things*, trans. W. H. D. Rouse, rev. Martin Smith (Cambridge, MA, 1992), p. 99.

than Lucretius: 'There does not exist any religious system, any supernatural extravagance not founded on ignorance of the laws of nature.'[8] Hence to study the laws of nature was to combat the fear that kept humanity in chains. But Condorcet also identified fears among the philosophers who knew too much, as well as among the people who knew too little. Philosophers, including natural philosophers, who cultivated a praiseworthy scepticism concerning the dogmas of religions and discarded systems were prey to epistemological doubts, the fear of making a mistake. The fear of the ignorant led to slavery; that of the learned, to paralysis. How Condorcet sought to combat both variants, the one with *lumières* and the other with calculation, will be the topic of the third section of my paper. I shall conclude with some reflections on Enlightenment, enlightenment, and the probability 0.999993.

II. *Lumières*

Amongst the Condorcet manuscripts preserved at the Bibliothèque de l'Institut in Paris there is a draft of a letter from an imaginary Picard gentleman to the bishop of Amiens on the occasion of a condemnation of the Chevalier de la Barre read from the pulpit at Easter Sunday mass. François-Jean le Febvre de la Barre had been tortured and executed for blasphemy at the age of nineteen in the Picard city of Abbeville, a case that drew the crusading attention of Voltaire and various other *philosophes* (including Condorcet)[9] as a flagrant example of injustice and brutality fuelled by religious fanaticism. The letter defends the current century against the bishop's charges of decline:

> You say Monseigneur that our century is frivolous. Is it not true that mathematics, chemistry, natural history are cultivated in France as never before and that the study of the profane sciences has never been so widespread among fashionable folk? It is true that women who in other times read nothing but novels and their breviaries now read Montesquieu and Rousseau, that men who travelled in former times only on pilgrimages are now going to educate themselves throughout all of Europe. What frivolity. Our savants occupy themselves in learning about the number of kinds of earths, of which fluids the air we

---

[8] M. J. A. N. Condorcet, *Esquisse d'un tableau historique de progrès de l'esprit humain*, ed. O. H. Prior, édition présentée par Yvon Belaval (Paris, 1970), p. 192.

[9] As in, for example, an April 1775 letter from Condorcet to M. Target, 'avocat au Parlement', pleading for a retrial of La Barre in order to clear his name and the honour of France: F. Arago and A. Condorcet-O'Connor (eds.), *Oeuvres de Condorcet* (Paris, 1847–9), 1. 292.

breathe is composed. We are busy with canals, with machines that carry water to cities, agricultural experiments . . . poor century.[10]

The increase of knowledge and industry described here is the primary sense of *lumières*: more people know ever more about more things. This knowledge pertains not only to scientific and technical but also moral and political matters—everything that is necessary 'for the common use of life' for all men and women.[11] Convinced by the example of his own country and century that *lumières* 'constantly increased' from generation to generation,[12] Condorcet reversed not only the ancient trope of time as amnesia and decay, but also the fear of some *philosophes* that an outbreak of warfare or plague could once again engulf Europe in a new Dark Ages. For Condorcet, truth was indeed revealed by time.

For Condorcet and many of his fellow *philosophes*, the steady spread of *lumières* had a moral as well as an intellectual component. The truth will not only make us free, but virtuous as well—and by means of the same unmasking gesture. In contrast to seventeenth-century accounts of obstacles to the discovery of truth, which indicted human infirmity (dim senses, weak intellects, imperfect language, false theories), the eighteenth-century culprit is considerably more sinister: outright fraud, perpetrated by the powerful and cunning few upon the many in the form of prejudices instilled by upbringing. Condorcet's category of 'prejudice' is a capacious one, including religious bigotry, erroneous opinions in the moral and physical sciences, and various forms of injustice, such as the use of torture to extract confessions. But not every error qualifies as a prejudice in Condorcet's book. Prejudices are not just false beliefs; they are false beliefs instilled by authority and supinely, stubbornly, even slavishly held. Prejudices are *culpable* false beliefs, originating in deception and perpetuated by timidity and sloth, and hence a matter for moral reproach as well as intellectual regret.

Condorcet's psychology of belief was entirely passive, in stark contrast to active reason. The ghost of the scholastic opposition between (and asymmetric evaluation of) activity and passivity haunts Enlightenment

---

[10] 'Lettre d'un gentilhomme Picard à l'Evêque d'Amiens', Bibliothèque de l'Institut, Paris, Manuscrit Condorcet 857, ff. 1–13.
[11] M. J. A. N. Condorcet, *Vie de Turgot* [1786], in Arago and Condorcet-O'Connor (eds.), *Oeuvres de Condorcet*, 5. 204.
[12] M. J. A. N. Condorcet, 'Première mémoire: nature et objet de l'instruction publique', in Condorcet, *Cinq mémoires sur l'instruction publique*, ed. Charles Coutel and Catherine Kintzler (Paris, 1989), p. 61.

sensationalist psychology and Condorcet's morality of *lumières*. On this account, beliefs etch themselves into consciousness the way water wears down rock. Repetition of impressions at either first- or second-hand gradually cements belief; more vivid impressions, amplified by sensibility and passion, accelerate the process. In some cases, the tendency to believe on the basis of repetition is wholly reasonable, because the repetition depends on the uniformity of nature: we believe that the sun will rise tomorrow because it has repeatedly done so since time immemorial. But in other cases, it is textbooks and catechisms that drum in beliefs, often substituting intensity (the schoolmaster's rod or the church's ornament) for the frequency of impressions.[13] The imagination also conspires in this passivity, retreating to an inner world of pleasing fantasies and (in the case of savants) seductive systems. These mechanisms were so effective that prejudices imbibed in youth could rarely be rooted out in adulthood. Even in science, Condorcet claimed, geniuses who proclaim new ideas seldom win advocates except among 'their equals and some young people raised far from the prejudices of the public schools'.[14]

The only antidote to the automatism of belief was the exercise of active reason, which demanded both the courage to defy authority and the sagacity to sift, select, and above all analyse impressions. By practising a Lockean analysis upon our acquired ideas and beliefs, we will, so Condorcet hoped, be able to weed out those prejudices unsupported by evidence.[15] In contrast to later, nineteenth-century epistemological ideals that exhorted scientists to self-restraint, on the motto 'Let Nature speak for herself', eighteenth-century savants intervened resolutely to order and prune the data of experience. This was not so much a distinction between passive observation versus active experiment (which was of nineteenth-century coinage), as one between passive receptivity to and active organisation of experience. Condorcet admired the artificial classification system of Linnaeus, although he recognised that it deliberately excluded a great deal of observational detail about plants in order to focus on a few key characteristics that defined the species.[16] More generally, Condorcet was an enthusiast for tables that revealed the entire state of a science at a glance, the new analytical language of chemistry that decomposed

[13] Condorcet, *Essai*, pp. x–xiv, cxc–cxci.
[14] M. J. A. N. Condorcet, 'Eloge de Mariotte', in *Eloges des académiciens de l'Académie Royale des Sciences morts depuis 1666, jusqu'en 1699* (Paris, Hôtel de Thou, 1773), p. 52.
[15] Condorcet, *Esquisse*, p. 157.
[16] Keith Michael Baker, 'An Unpublished Essay by Condorcet on Technical Methods of Classification', *Annals of Science*, 18 (1962), 99–123, at p. 101.

compounds into elements on the page, and (as we will see in the next section) algebraic calculations that were the formal prototype for all analysis and combination of ideas.[17] These were the concrete practices of abstract reason in the Enlightenment.

Just as the passive harbouring of prejudices was at once a cognitive and moral failing, so the active flexing of reason to scrutinise belief and organise experience was praiseworthy on both counts. Condorcet's curious conviction that *lumières* entailed virtue as well as knowledge, that the Good followed in the wake of the True, requires some explanation for those persuaded by the history of science and technology in the intervening centuries between his day and ours that there is alas no necessary correlation between scientific and moral progress. What *lumières* made possible, according to Condorcet, was independence: the *homme éclairé* knew his rights before the law, enough mathematics and science not to be duped by charlatans or terrified by priests, and the difference between fact and opinion. The telos of human perfection envisioned in the Tenth Epoch of the *Sketch of a Historical Picture of the Human Mind* would be reached when 'all will have the *lumières* necessary to conduct themselves according to their own reason.'[18] This hope echoes Kant's definition of Enlightenment as emergence from 'self-imposed tutelage', although it is unlikely that Condorcet knew Kant's essay and still more unlikely that he would have approved of the restrictions Kant recommended to be imposed upon the public exercise of reason. Moreover, Condorcet did not consider reason alone sufficient for autonomy; reason must be supplemented by *lumières*.

The kind of life made possible by independence is a recurring theme in Condorcet's writings, which hint at an exemplary vita that is neither saintly nor Stoic, neither military nor political, but nonetheless virtuous and heroic.[19] That independence is desirable for the individual perhaps requires no further explanation, but it is noteworthy just *how* desirable it was felt to be by Enlightenment thinkers who otherwise diverged sharply in their political and social views. Condorcet would never have subscribed to the prayer Rousseau offers up in the *Discourse on the Sciences and Arts* (1750): 'Almighty God, thou who holds all spirits in thy hands, deliver us from the enlightenment and fatal arts of our forefathers, and give back to

---

[17] Condorcet, *Esquisse*, pp. 233, 180, 174.
[18] Ibid., pp. 204–5.
[19] See the excellent discussion of these themes in Emma Rothschild, *Economic Sentiments: Adam Smith, Condorcet, and the Enlightenment* (Cambridge, MA, 2001), especially pp. 201–2.

us ignorance, innocence, and poverty, the only goods that can give us happiness and are precious in thy sight.'[20] Yet he might well have assented to the passages in which Rousseau railed against the way in which civility and emulation in the arts and sciences placed people under the 'perpetual constraint' of cultivating the good opinion of others: 'Incessantly politeness requires, propriety demands; incessantly usage is followed, never one's own inclinations.'[21] Even the debauched title character of Diderot's dialogue *Rameau's Nephew* cannot bring himself to grovel in front of his wealthy, boorish patrons in order to be taken back as a pampered pet, although his own cynical principles would dictate a return to well-fed dependence on even the most humiliating terms: 'I feel something here [putting his right hand on his heart] which swells in pride and says to me, "Rameau, you'll do no such thing". A certain dignity attaches to the nature of man that nothing must destroy.'[22] Condorcet himself defended Voltaire's wealth, so unbefitting a philosopher according to the standards of the ancient sages, as a guarantee of independence: 'Let us then not blame a philosopher for having preferred, in order to assure his independence, the resources that the customs of our century presented him to those which suited other customs in other times.'[23]

But what made independence not just desirable, but virtuous? The answer must be framed largely in negative terms, as a reply to the converse question: what made dependence vicious? Condorcet assumed that dependence, whether financial or intellectual, inevitably corrupts both parties to the relationship. Slavery renders the slave devious and the master brutal; ignorance renders the peasant superstitious and the priest deceptive; tyranny renders the subject timorous and the despot cruel; patronage renders the client servile and the patron vain. Condorcet's opposition to dependence was principled as well as pragmatic: judged by the standards of natural rights, such relationships were profoundly unnatural, however entrenched in custom—as in the oppression of women by men, children by fathers, the poor by the rich.[24]

---

[20] Jean-Jacques Rousseau, *Discourse on the Sciences and Arts* [*The First Discourse*, 1750] in Jean-Jacques Rousseau, *The First and Second Discourses*, ed. Roger D. Masters, trans. Roger D. and Judith R. Masters (New York, 1964), p. 62.
[21] Rousseau, *Discourse on the Sciences and Arts*, p. 38.
[22] Denis Diderot, *Le Neveu de Rameau* [comp. c.1762], in Diderot, *Rameau's Nephew and Other Works*, trans. by Jacques Barzun and Ralph H. Bowen (New York, 1956), p. 21.
[23] M. J. A. N. Condorcet, *La Vie de Voltaire*, in *Oeuvres complètes de Voltaire* (Paris, 1831), 1. 30.
[24] Condorcet, *Vie de Turgot*, pp. 195–6.

The normative force of nature is mighty in Condorcet's thought, and it derives primarily from nature's uniformity and universality. He was scandalised by Montesquieu's defence of local custom over uniform criminal, civil, and commercial laws: 'Just as truth, reason, justice, the rights of man, the interests of property, of liberty, of security are the same everywhere ... A good law must be good for all people, as a proposition is true for all.'[25] In the same breath he defended a uniform system of weights and measures, preferably one based on a unit set by nature itself.[26] It would be easy, too easy, to dismiss Condorcet's appeals to the moral, legal, and political authority of nature as yet another commission of the naturalistic fallacy, a misguided attempt to derive 'ought' from 'is'. For Condorcet, uniform and universal nature underwrote all expressions of uniformity and universality—including not only the generalisations of mathematics but also the verdicts of justice. As such, nature served as a bulwark against all that was arbitrary, all that was blindly habitual in human affairs, against the caprices of the tyrant and the prejudices sanctioned by custom.

A law based upon natural rights was *ipso facto* one rooted in reason, and therefore transparent to all citizens, not just to the guild of lawyers who profited from complexity and obscurity. Moreover, the power of generalisations derived from uniform and universal natural rights could be breathtaking, because so contrary to accepted norms and venerable institutions. Relentless in his consistency, Condorcet turned uniformity and universality to utopian ends, using them to extrapolate to a future in which slavery would be abolished, public education would be available to all, life expectancy would double, and women would be the legal and political equals of men: 'But woman is also a sensitive being, capable of reasoning and of acquiring moral ideas: the natural rights of man therefore do not exist—there are none which woman should not share.'[27] Since the mid-nineteenth century, the authority of nature has usually been invoked by political conservatives, as the reason why reform is futile, because the current order is the necessary order: a position evoked by

---

[25] M. J. A. N. Condorcet, 'Observations de Condorcet sur le vingt-neuvième livre *De l'Esprit des lois*', in Antoine Louis Claude Destutt de Tracy, *Commentaire sur l'Esprit des lois de Montesquieu* (Paris, 1828), pp. 330–8. Book 29 of *De l'Esprit des lois* is entitled 'De la manière de composer les lois'.

[26] Condorcet, 'Observations', p. 380; cf. Condorcet, *Vie de Turgot*, p. 71, and [Borda, Lagrange, Laplace, Monge, and Condorcet], 'Rapport fait à l'Académie royale des sciences sur le choix d'une unité de mesures', *Histoire de l'Académie royale des sciences 1778* (Paris, Imprimerie Royale, 1781), pp. 7–16.

[27] M. J. A. N. Condorcet, 'De l'influence de la révolution en Amerique', Bibliothèque de l'Institut, Paris, Manuscrit Condorcet 857, f. 562v.

phrases such as 'anatomy is destiny', 'the struggle for existence', or, more recently, 'it's genetically hard-wired'. For Condorcet and his contemporaries, however, nature was on the side of the reformers and the radicals, a standing reproach to the social status quo. Nature had enlisted in the cause of *lumières*.

III. Calculation

For Condorcet, *lumières* as knowledge, as virtue, as world view stood four-square opposed to inert, submissive habit—with one notable exception, the habit of calculation. Perhaps no other word divides the friends and foes of the Enlightenment so sharply and so vehemently as 'calculation'. For those who reject the Enlightenment and all its works, 'calculation' conjures up the hypertrophy of head at the expense of heart, Sainte-Beuve's 'monstrous brain', an inexorable machine indifferent to human fate and foibles. In the course of the nineteenth century, calculation became further tarred with associations with the brutish as well as with the brutal. Massive calculations needed to compile logarithm tables or reduce astronomical data were performed first by low-paid workers (often women) and then by machines. Calculation came to be seen at best as soul-numbing, a kind of labour better delegated to machines, and at worst as soul-destroying, the mark of someone who knows all about the rationality of means and none about that of ends. Condorcet's enchantment with calculation can only strike these critics as confirmation of their worst fears about the icy inhumanity of the Enlightenment. Yet Condorcet's notion of calculation as both theory and practice was embedded in an entirely different field of associations, one that linked it to intelligence and *lumières* rather than to machines and heartlessness.

Calculation in the Enlightenment had not yet become mechanical, the paradigmatic example of processes that were mental but not intelligent. The 1778 edition of the *Dictionnaire de l'Académie Française* gave the following illustrative sentence for the word *calculateur*: 'This astronomer is a great and good calculator.'[28] Calculation was still the distinctive activity of the scientist or mathematician, not the anonymous drudge. Until the early nineteenth century, prodigious feats of mental reckoning were a topos in the eulogies for great mathematicians, Carl Friedrich Gauss's

---

[28] 'Calculateur, s. m.', *Dictionnaire de l'Académie Française*, 2 vols. (Nîmes, Pierre Beaume, 1778), 1. 162.

lightning arithmetic being perhaps the last of these stock legends. When the great French mathematician Pierre-Simon Laplace, Condorcet's colleague at the Académie Royale des Sciences and one-time protégé, described probability theory as 'good sense reduced to a calculus', he intended to disparage neither good sense nor probability by the comparison.[29] Indeed, intelligence itself was conceived as essentially a form of calculation.

Eighteenth-century usage of the term *intelligence* overlaps but does not coincide with its current meaning. Both denote mental agility, particularly in problem solving and learning. But the questions that now tax us about intelligence—inborn or acquired through education? the property of individuals or groups? unitary or multiple in its faculties?—could not have been easily accommodated within the Enlightenment framework for understanding the workings of the human mind. Rather, the sensationalist inquiries into the mind pursued by Locke and his successors posed questions about the origins and limits of human knowledge, straddling the boundary that now separates psychology from epistemology and which eighteenth-century philosophers (just to make the terminological confusion complete) often called 'metaphysics'. The sensationalist project, which Condorcet wholeheartedly endorsed as a cure for prejudice, was at once explanatory and therapeutic: to reveal how we came by our ideas was simultaneously to test their soundness. Etienne Bonnot de Condillac, whose version of Lockean sensationalism influenced many of the *philosophes*, described this investigation into the origins and validity of ideas as the method of 'analysis', which consisted 'only in composing and decomposing our ideas, in order to compare them differently, and to discover the relations they have among themselves, together with the new ideas they are capable of producing'.[30] Genius itself was nothing more than a mind more penetrating in analysis, more fertile in combinations.[31]

For Condorcet, analysis was simultaneously a method for investigating the mind's operations and a description of those operations. The healthy mind, unperturbed by passions or an unruly imagination, was endlessly taking apart its ideas and sensations into their minimal elements, then comparing and rearranging these elements into novel permu-

---

[29] Pierre-Simon Laplace, *Essai philosophique sur les probabilités*, 3rd edn. [1820], in Laplace, *Oeuvres complètes*, 14 vols. (Paris, 1886), 7. cliii.
[30] Etienne Bonnot de Condillac, *Essai sur l'origine des connoissances humaines*, 2 vols. in 1 (Amsterdam, 1746), 1. 101–2.
[31] Condillac, *Essai*, 1. 104.

tations and combinations. Condorcet could wax rhapsodic over this method of Lockean analysis, a 'universal instrument' as applicable to morals, politics, economics, and the rules of good taste as it was to the physical sciences. It discovered new truths, certified their degree of certainty, and erected 'an eternal barrier between the human species and the old errors of its childhood'.[32] His manuscripts contain many fragmentary plans for universal languages,[33] universal classification systems,[34] including even universal systems of legal contracts,[35] all based on the calculation of combinations and permutations.

This all sounds like the monomania of the mathematician. But Condorcet was quite capable of rejecting the results of calculation when they conflicted with 'common reason' or seemed insufficiently grounded in observation.[36] Clarity must not be sacrificed to rigour, as he reprimanded a political economist who had tried to quantify the desire to buy and sell.[37] More generally, he drew a distinction between mathematical calculation as a problem-solving tool and as a study 'suitable for forming reason, for strengthening it'.[38] Calculation was much more than a tool, much more even than a philosophical method for Condorcet; it might be described, borrowing a term from the historian of ancient philosophy Pierre Hadot, as a 'spiritual exercise',[39] repeated routines of the mind designed to strengthen and shape the soul as athletic exercises strengthened and shaped the body: 'Generally, they consist, above all, of self-control and meditation. Self-control is fundamentally being attentive to oneself: an unrelaxing vigilance for the Stoics; the renunciation of unnecessary desires for the Epicureans.'[40] The meditations of Marcus Aurelius

---

[32] Condorcet, *Esquisse*, pp. 156–7.

[33] Ibid., p. 174.

[34] Baker, 'An Unpublished Essay', p. 104.

[35] See the manuscript report, dated 30 April 1785, concerning a proposed prize to be offered by the Académie Royale des Sciences, Archives de l'Académie des Sciences, Paris, Dossier Condorcet.

[36] See for example M. J. A. N. Condorcet, 'Mémoire sur le calcul des probabilités: Quatrième partie. Réflexions sur la méthode de déterminer la probabilité des événemens futurs, d'après l'observation des événemens passés', *Mémoires de l'Académie royale des sciences 1783* (Paris, Imprimerie Royale, 1786), pp. 539–53, at p. 553; also Condorcet, *Essai*, p. lxxv.

[37] Condorcet to the Count Pierre Verri (7 Nov. 1771), in Arago and Condorcet-O'Connor (eds.), *Oeuvres de Condorcet*, 1. 283–7.

[38] Condorcet, *Vie de Turgot*, pp. 159–60.

[39] Pierre Hadot, *La Philosophie comme manière de vivre*. Entretiens avec Jeanne Carlier et Arnold I. Davidson (Paris, 2001), pp. 159–91.

[40] Pierre Hadot, 'Forms of Life and Forms of Discourse in Ancient Philosophy', in his *Philosophy as a Way of Life*, ed. Arnold I. Davidson, trans. Michael Chase (Oxford, 1995), pp. 49–70, on p. 59.

train the imagination to dwell upon scenes of human insignificance (the forgotten rulers of past epochs, the processes of decay already at work even among the living), much as Seneca took a cosmic perspective to shrink the entire planet earth to a pinpoint. What calculation taught its practitioners was, however, not the vanity of human ambitions, but what Condorcet called the 'exactitude of the mind [*justesse d'esprit*]'.

Like *lumières*, exactitude of mind was an attainment that combined intellectual, moral, and even aesthetic dimensions. In a textbook on arithmetic and geometry written for the public elementary schools he hoped that the revolutionary National Assembly would make universal, Condorcet used the simplest arithmetic identities—'three plus four equals seven'—to teach children the meaning of self-evidence and justified belief: 'From this, they will learn that the distinct memory of having had the perception of the identity of the two ideas that form a proposition, that is to say the self-evidence of this proposition, is the only motive they have to believe it . . . and that the memory of merely having always repeated or written this proposition, without having felt its self-evidence, is not a motive to believe.'[41] In this fashion, simply by practising the simplest arithmetic operations over and over again, children would learn about 'the three intellectual operations of which our mind is capable; *the formation of ideas, judgment, reasoning*'. The instructor must take care to choose examples that will show pupils that it is 'useful or pleasant' to perform calculations and to exercise them on so many particular examples that they would thereby become convinced of the 'exactitude' of the general method underlying the operations.[42] Elsewhere, in a lecture on adult education, Condorcet insisted that the teacher of mathematics should be less of a 'master than a guide', for reason could not be instilled by authority.[43]

Yet as in the case of all spiritual exercises, calculation was a regimen that demanded regular repetition if it was to mould the mind of the initiate. Calculation must become habitual, but not routinised, if it was to have this transformative effect. Hence the dangers of algebraic or logical formulas, which spared the mind a painstaking effort of attention, but at the price of letting the intellect go slack and sharp-edged ideas become

---

[41] M. J. A. N. Condorcet, *Élémens d'arithmétique et de géométrie* [1804], *Enfance* 4 (1989), 40–58, on 44.
[42] Condorcet, *Élémens*, pp. 45, 46, 56–7.
[43] M. J. A. N. Condorcet, *Discours sur les sciences mathématiques prononcé au Lycée le 15 février 1786* (Paris, 1812), p. 24.

blurry: 'One leaves the natural forces without exercise; one loses first their use, then the forces themselves.' The numbers from one to ten must never be memorised, but instead taught 'by intelligence and by reason; nothing is abandoned to routine'.[44] Children must be given small numbers with which to compute at first, so that the facility acquired by habit 'never separates itself from comprehension of the principles'.[45] Whenever these elements are manipulated in calculation, the mind must form anew a clear idea of their meaning as collections of units. In this way, Condorcet hoped, habit would not lead to mindless automatism.

Calculation had moral as well as intellectual resonances for Enlightenment philosophers. In a justly famous essay, Albert Hirschman documented the striking process by which the prudent and selfish interests were promoted first to lesser vices and then to lesser virtues in the writings of early modern moralists. By means of interests like greed, the still more dangerous passions like lust and ambition might be tamed.[46] Key to the moral re-evaluation of the interests was the belief that they involved self-disciplined as well as self-interested calculations and therefore resulted in reassuringly calculable conduct. Avarice might not be noble, but it was at least predictable and therefore reinforced the orderliness of the social order. In Samuel Johnson's novel *Rasselas*, for example, Lady Pekuah is relieved to discover that her Arab abductor loves gold, for 'avarice is a uniform and tractable vice: . . . bring money and nothing is denied.'[47] Condorcet, who laid great store by the moral sentiments of pity and sympathy, was not so tough-minded as Lady Pekuah, but he did assert that calculation could on occasion reinforce compassion.[48]

Yet if calculation simply confirms, as Condorcet never tired of repeating, the conclusions of reason and compassion, why calculate? The answer to this question goes to the heart of Condorcet's conception of *lumières* as a kind of inner illumination of the individual as well as outer enlightenment of society. 'Exactitude of the mind' demanded more than

---

[44] M. J. A. N. Condorcet, *Moyens d'apprendre à compter surement et avec facilité* (Paris, 1804), *Enfance* 4 (1989), 59–90, at 61–2.
[45] M. J. A. N. Condorcet, 'Seconde Mémoire. De l'instruction commune pour les enfants', in Condorcet, *Cinq mémoires sur l'instruction publique*, ed. Coutel and Kintzler, p. 97.
[46] Albert O, Hirschman, *The Passions and the Interests: Political Arguments for Capitalism before Its Triumph* (Princeton, 1977).
[47] Samuel Johnson, *The History of Rasselas, Prince of Abissinia* [1768], ed. J. P. Hardy (London, 1968), p. 93.
[48] M. J. A. N. Condorcet, 'Discours sur l'astronomie et le calcul des probabilités, lu au Lycée en 1787', in Arago and Condorcet-O'Connor (eds.), *Oeuvres de Condorcet*, 1. 482–503, at 502.

knowledge and reason, for knowledge and reason alone were too vague to solve many complex problems, particularly in the realm of politics, economics, and society. Writing on the optimal organisation of the judiciary, Condorcet acknowledged that unaided reason would lead to the conclusion that the greater the plurality of jurors required to condemn a defendant in a criminal case, the smaller the risk of subjecting an innocent person to torture or execution.[49] Naked reason could not, however, determine how large a plurality is necessary, no more than the naked eye could resolve the Milky Way into individual stars. Calculation was to reason what the telescope was to the eye. But the benefits of calculation extended beyond the instrumental for Condorcet. Only calculation, practised faithfully and mindfully, could create justified certainty, as opposed to the spurious certainty generated by mere reiteration of impressions. This effect is as much psychological as it is epistemological, simultaneously conviction and self-evidence. Calculation as a way of life steadied as well as clarified; it gave the timorous courage and rescued the sceptical from indifference. This is why habitual calculation displayed 'the price of *lumières*'.[50] Condorcet's own manuscripts are strewn with calculations, which for him were anything but cold and mechanical.

IV. Fear

Condorcet was hardly original in regarding fear as the most unphilosophical of the passions,[51] but he was unusual in enlisting calculation to fight it, and on two fronts: the practices of everyday life and the precepts of the life of the mind. In both cases, he paradoxically had recourse to probabilism in order to overcome paralysing uncertainty—or rather to calculated probabilities. Condorcet once defined the mathematical theory of probability as 'the art of conducting oneself in a certain manner in events subject to uncertainty'.[52] Dangers that had loomed large and dark, doubts that had gnawed silently and relentlessly were converted into quantified risks, and thereby psychologically shrunk. Once again, 'exactitude of ideas' served as a weapon, but this time sharpening the focus was not a means to an end, as it had been in Condorcet's computation of the

---

[49] Condorcet, *Essai*, p. v; cf. p. clxxxv.
[50] Ibid., p. clxxxvi.
[51] Rothschild, *Economic Sentiments*, pp. 12–14.
[52] Condorcet, *Discours sur les sciences mathématiques*, p. 18.

minimum plurality required to guarantee a fair jury trial, but an end in itself. Fear fed on the indistinct and the undefined; what could be more matter-of-factly distinct and defined than numbers?

Condorcet's projects for applying probability theory to everything from the design of tribunals to testing the efficacy of medical therapies to weighing the reliability of historical evidence are too numerous to review here. Instead, I shall restrict myself to two examples that were expressly designed to promote action by suppressing fear: the computation of the risks of commerce and of scientific generalisations. In the case of the former, Condorcet was concerned to encourage over-cautious merchants to invest in more venturesome undertakings. He drew a sharp distinction between the involuntary risks incurred in commerce as opposed to the voluntary risks incurred in gambling. No 'reasonable man' would indulge in cards or the lottery if his honour and family fortune were at stake; yet that is exactly what commerce demands of the merchant. Hence the merchant must be assured of two probabilities: first, of a 'sufficient' probability that losses will not drive him out of business; and second, of a 'very large and continually increasing probability' that his profits will repay his trouble the longer he persists in his enterprise. Condorcet believed that both probabilities could be ascertained for various trades by consulting the registers of maritime insurance companies.[53] For my purposes, what is noteworthy here is that the merchant is supposed to overcome his timidity neither by swashbuckling boldness or stoic indifference, but instead by a careful comparison made possible by the quantification of risk.

The dangers of trade on the high seas are easier to make vivid than doubts about the validity of scientific theories. Yet the latter were strong and consequential among mid-eighteenth century savants. The origins of modern philosophy, one might argue the origins of modern Western thought *tout court*, lie in a seventeenth-century diagnosis of pathological belief. The beliefs in question ranged from the theological to the astronomical to the geographical, from the anatomical to the natural philosophical: the voyages of discovery, the Reformation, the triumph of Copernican astronomy and Newtonian natural philosophy, the demonstration of the circulation of the blood—all confronted early modern

---

[53] M. J. A. N. Condorcet, 'Théorie mathématique des assurances', Bibliothèque de l'Institut, Paris, Manuscrit Condorcet 857, ff. 202–6. Condorcet's assumption that insurance companies kept such records may have been over sanguine; at least, it was rare for maritime insurance premiums to be set on the basis of statistics in the eighteenth century. Moreover, gambling and insurance were regularly conflated, both in legal theory and financial practice: Daston, *Classical Probability*, pp. 167–9.

thinkers with dramatic and disturbing examples of errors that had persisted for centuries on the authority of the very best minds. It is difficult to capture the enormity of this revelation of pervasive and enduring error for those who had been educated largely in the old systems of thought — the sickening realisation that so many respected authorities could have been so wrong for so long. Some of the most famous projects of the Enlightenment, such as the *Encyclopédie* of Denis Diderot and Jean d'Alembert, germinated in this overwhelming awareness of having only recently emerged from over a millennium of collective intellectual error: one of the avowed aims of the *Encyclopédie* was to serve as a kind of time capsule to preserve the new discoveries, should war and pestilence plunge Europe once again into darkness.

The search for an explanation and thereby an antidote to future intellectual disasters centred on the problem of excessive belief. This was regarded as an emotional, ethical, and even medical, as well as an intellectual malady, and one with potentially devastating consequences. Much blood as well as ink had been spilt in early modern religious controversies, and throughout the late seventeenth and eighteenth centuries 'enthusiasm' and 'superstition' were reviled as sources of ecclesiastical and civil unrest. Excessive belief stemmed from psychological and corporeal causes, both of which had to be strictly managed in the susceptible: too great an appetite for the wondrous (asserted to afflict the vulgar and unlettered), a too soft and therefore impressionable brain (as allegedly found in women and children), or too much black bile (the temperament of melancholics) might all cause credulity. The fact that excessive belief was understood at least partly in medical terms by no means exonerated sufferers from the moral responsibility of restraint; spiritual and bodily regimens must be rigorously followed in order to rein in such dangerous inclinations. Among philosophers, the responsibility was intellectual as well as ethical, e.g. Descartes' instructions to take inventory of all one's stock of beliefs and discard those with the least blemish of uncertainty, or Locke's insistence that belief be apportioned to evidence. These religious, philosophical, and theological programmes for disciplining belief not only raised the threshold of the credible; they also changed the nature of belief itself. Whereas belief had previously been conceived as an involuntary state and, in religious contexts, as a divine gift, by the late seventeenth century it had become a matter of voluntary assent, the 'will to believe' — or to disbelieve, had become possible.

The shock of the seventeenth-century encounter with past error left a lasting mark on philosophy, and, to a lesser extent, on science. Until the mid-seventeenth century, intellectuals in Latin Europe had generally worried about incredulity rather than credulity, about believing too little rather than too much. The avalanche of novelties—new flora and fauna, new continents, new planets, new peoples, new inventions, new religions, new sciences—that deluged early modern Europeans had initially worked to reinforce the prejudice against incredulity; it was a mark of provincialism and little learning to doubt reports of armadillos, Chinese paper money, or microscopic animals in a drop of water. But by the early eighteenth century, the pendulum had swung to the opposite extreme—to the point that scientific academies refused to credit reports of meteor showers as smacking of the prodigious—and stayed there. The insistence that belief be 'warranted' became and remains a philosophical dogma; according to the doctrine of warranted belief, the fact that a belief is true is by itself insufficient grounds for holding it without further explicit, reasoned justification. The emphasis upon warranted belief led to the spectacular rise of epistemology and the equally spectacular decline of metaphysics since the late seventeenth century.

Condorcet participated fully in this turn towards epistemology; he was well nigh obsessed with ascertaining the relationship between evidence and what he called the 'motive to believe [*motif de croire*]'. Yet he was also aware of excesses in the other direction, of excessive incredulity (the pathology of the learned) as well as of excessive credulity (the pathology of the ignorant). Both extremes were fuelled by fear, the epistemological fear of error in the one case and the superstitious fear of retribution in the other, and both led to paralysis, the inability to act. How to translate the 'motive to believe' into the 'motive to act'? Once again, Condorcet hoped that the calculation of probabilities would overcome scruples and caution. Inspired by the mathematical theorem of inverse probabilities independently proven by Thomas Bayes and Laplace, Condorcet set about calculating how many confirming observations were needed to guarantee what probability that putative cause and effect were necessarily rather than coincidentally conjoined in a natural law.[54] Even though certainty could never be obtained, doubts could be vanquished; modern natural philosophers need not succumb to the pyrrhonism and *ataraxia* of the ancients, to 'discouragement and indolence'. By determining the probabilities upon which our knowledge is based with 'a kind of exactitude', we will be able, Condorcet promised, to 'judge and conduct ourselves, no

---

[54] Condorcet, 'Mémoire sur le calcul des probabilités: Quatrième partie'; Daston, *Classical Probability*, pp. 253–84.

longer according to a vague and mechanical impression, but according to an impression subjected to calculation, whose relationship to other impressions of the same sort is known to us'.[55] We will have a motive to act in the world with confidence and conviction.

V. Enlightenment, enlightenment, and 0.999993

This promise returns us to the probability 0.999993, which Condorcet computed as the minimum probability a citizen in a just society must be guaranteed of not being falsely convicted of a crime. By itself, the figure is inert; it must be brought into relationship with other risks, also calculated so that they can be compared with one another. Ideally, Condorcet had wanted to use a risk small enough that anyone would take it without a second thought—e.g., taking the packet boat from Dover to Calais in calm weather on a seaworthy boat manned by a competent crew. Unfortunately, reliable statistics were not available for packet boat runs, so Condorcet turned to the one area where statistics had been gathered for almost a century, human mortality. He reckoned that the difference between dying in the next week between two closely spaced ages (say, age thirty-nine and forty) was comparably minute: that is where the fraction 144,767/144,768 (= 0.999993) comes from. Condorcet insisted that this must be a risk taken voluntarily and with eyes wide open, not a risk usually neglected because it is 'habitual and inevitable'.[56] The exercise also assumes that people be consistent about their risk-taking, always preferring a smaller to a larger risk and acting with equal nonchalance on equally small risks—an assumption that is anything but self-evident, as an enormous body of current psychological research on actual risk preferences (e.g. for automobile over airplane travel) demonstrates.

Condorcet was often and, in the end, tragically over-optimistic about human rationality, although he was not naïve about the psychological and political forces that subverted it and how the two worked hand-in-hand: uncertainty bred terror, which in turn bred subservience.[57] Uncertainty could never be overcome—like Locke, Condorcet believed we dwell in the twilight of probabilities—but it could be tamed: calcu-

---

[55] Condorcet, *Essai*, p. xciii.
[56] Ibid., pp. cvii–cxiv.
[57] M. J. A. N. Condorcet, 'Conseils d'un zélé républicain', Bibliothèque de l'Institut, Paris, at f. 362r, Manuscrit Condorcet 857, ff. 385–97.

lated, compared, faced up to with hope and consistency. There was nothing technocratic about Condorcet's vision of a future society based on science and technology:[58] all citizens, men and women, black and white, would be educated and politically enfranchised; all would be enlightened. That is what consistency demanded. Some of Condorcet's most daring predictions in his final philosophical testament—the remarkable increase in agricultural yields that would stave off starvation, the steady rise in human life expectancy, the spread of literacy and education—may also be seen as exercises in consistency, hopeful extrapolations of trends already underway. In this sense, his account of the progress of the human mind is very much history written by a mathematician, past, present, and future arranged in a convergent series.

But Condorcet's penchant for mathematics has been largely misunderstood, splintering his thought for post-Romantic readers who find him a jumble of contradictions: cold calculation and warm sentiment, technocrat and democrat, calm rationalist and fiery crusader, probabilist and dogmatist. Some, though not all, of these oppositions dissolve when Condorcet's well-known Enlightenment positions are infused with his forgotten enlightenment ethos. Calculation for Condorcet was not the grinding of machinery; it was a battering ram against fear and prejudice. Consistency for Condorcet was not the hobgoblin of little minds; it was a springboard into the future. Uniformity and universality did not bore Condorcet; exact minds delighted in them. The psychological colouring of these terms was essential for the progress of *lumières*: Condorcet, like Kant, was fully aware that reason alone was insufficient to bestir the will. When he wrote of the 'motive to believe' and the 'motive to act', the word 'motive'—not 'reason'—had been chosen advisedly. Enlightenment writ large was built upon enlightenment writ small.

In his capacity as Perpetual Secretary of the Académie Royale des Sciences, Condorcet was charged to write eulogies for deceased academicians, continuing the ancient genre, stretching back to Diogenes Laertius, of the lives and works of the philosophers. The eulogies reported on the character and manner of life, as well as the scientific contributions of the academicians, echoing the classical models eighteenth-century schoolboys had all read. Condorcet himself likened his own death to that of Socrates, a philosopher's death: 'I will perish like Socrates and Sidney for

---

[58] Condorcet, *Essai*, pp. 148–9.

having served [the liberty of my country] . . .'.[59] But in word and in deed, Condorcet had in fact exemplified a very different kind of philosophical vita. He had foresaken the *vita contemplativa* of the savant for the *vita activa* of the engaged intellectual—or rather, he had harnessed the *vita contemplativa* to the ends of the *vita activa*, mathematics in the service of social reform and individual renewal. Instead of defining independence as freedom from family ties,[60] he had viewed domestic life as the foundation of all virtues and political liberty as well.[61] And although his dramatic death was precisely the stuff of legend, a classical scene to be set down in a eulogy to gild Condorcet's own glory, he had already imagined a different kind of immortality for the disciples of *lumières*:

> If the indefinite perfectibility of our species is, as I believe, a general law of nature, man must no longer regard himself as a being limited to a passing and isolated existence, destined to vanish after an alternation of happiness and misfortune for himself. . .; he becomes an active part of the grand whole and a collaborator in an eternal work. In an existence of a moment at a point in space, he can, by his works, embrace all places, connect himself to all centuries, and still act long after his memory has disappeared from the earth.[62]

That was enlightenment, the enlightened sublime.

---

[59] Charles Coutel (ed.), *Politique de Condorcet* (Paris, 1996), p. 281. Algernon Sidney (1622–83), second son of the Earl of Leicester, famously defended the rights of parliament against executive oppression under both Cromwell and Charles II; he was executed for treason.

[60] Condorcet had rehearsed these traditional arguments against marriage in his 'Eloge de M. Du Hamel', *Histoire et mémoires de l'Académie royale des sciences. 1783* (Paris: Imprimerie Royale, 1785), pp. 131–55, at p. 151.

[61] M. J. A. N. Condorcet, 'Premier Mémoire. Nature et objet de l'instruction publique', in Condorcet, *Cinq mémoires sur l'instruction publique*, ed. Coutel and Kintzler (Paris, Librairie du bicentenaire de la Révolution Française, 1989), p. 53.

[62] Ibid., pp. 45–6.

ISAIAH BERLIN LECTURE

The Search for Perfection: Atlantic Dimensions

BERNARD BAILYN
Fellow of the Academy

I

IT IS AN HONOUR to address the Academy, especially in any association with Isaiah Berlin. I knew him only slightly, but recall vividly my first encounter with him. Students at Harvard in the late 1940s had been exposed to some remarkable lecturers from abroad: Joseph Schumpeter, Hans Kohn, Erwin Panofsky. But none of them prepared me for the experience of Isaiah Berlin's lectures. I do not have to describe to you how words, ideas, references, allusions came in floods. It was overwhelming. But I quickly realised, as I listened, that, while I was intensely interested in his announced subject, I had no idea what he was talking about—and would have none, until I drove my own intensity level to somewhere within his range. We listened to this Paganini of the platform, as Michael Oakeshott called him, and observed him, with awe.[1]

But at the same time, Berlin was listening to us and observing us, with something quite a bit less than awe. And upon his return to England he wrote a three-part commentary on his experiences at Harvard, and through Harvard with the American university world in general.

He liked the students, he said. They were 'more intellectually curious, more responsive to every influence, more deeply and immediately

---

Read at the Academy 11 October 2006.
[1] Michael A. Ignatieff, *Isaiah Berlin: A Life* (London, 1998), p. 205.

charmed by everything new . . . and above all, endowed with a quality of moral vitality unlike any I had found anywhere else'. But he had also to say that 'many of these excellent young people could not, as a general rule, either read or write, as these activities are understood in our best universities. That is to say, their thoughts came higglety-pigglety out of the big, buzzing, booming confusion of their minds, too many pouring out chaotically in the same instant.'

But there was a deeper problem. Harvard was an academic community, he wrote, 'painfully aware of the social and economic miseries of their society':

> A student or professor in this condition wonders whether it can be right for him to absorb himself in the study of, let us say, the early Greek epic at Harvard, while the poor of south Boston go hungry and unshod and negroes are denied fundamental rights.

He had suggested to his students that intellectual curiosity was not necessarily a form of sin, and that it was valid to pursue some branch of knowledge simply because one was interested in it. But that, they seemed to think, was a European point of view, rather exotic and perhaps slightly sinister. He had pondered all this and concluded that 'this naïve, sincere and touching morality, according to which . . . the primary duty of everyone is to help others . . . with no indication of what it is to help others to be or do' was leading to a view of the world as 'an enormous hospital of which all men are inmates, with the obligation of acting as nurses and physicians to one another'. How, in such a world, he asked, could disinterested study flourish and the potentialities of mind and sensibility unfold?[2]

---

[2] Isaiah Berlin, 'Notes on the Way', *Time and Tide* (12, 19, 26 Nov. 1949), quotations at 1133, 1157, 1158, 1188. Berlin's Harvard experience remained vivid in his memory. Thirty-five years later he recalled 'that when I was at Harvard—it was exhausting, but it obliged one to think more than anything at Oxford or Cambridge has in my day'. American students at Harvard and elsewhere, he wrote in 1987,

> believed that objective truth was discoverable; that the professor may well have possessed it; that with enough pressure he might reveal it; not much was understood of selective and critical reading. But I used to recommend bibliographies—and students used to ask which chapters, or even sections, of these books they were to read, as they read every word, without skipping, without the slightest sense of what was important and what was not. Their search for the truth, their belief that anything new, or even true, was worth earnest endeavours to extract from the professor, was touching—and for the professor often rather moving and flattering, after the biases of English students. But in the end it turned out to be a little too naïve—the graduates were sometimes very good at Harvard, the undergraduates seldom.

Berlin to Andrzej Walicki, 22 April 1985; 21 April 1987, *Dialogue and Universalism*, 9–10 (2005), 151, 155.

This was, and has been, the central paradox and energising dynamic of higher education and scholarship in America. Analysing the early Greek epic while attempting to improve the lives of the poor in south Boston—this duality of purpose has lain at the heart of the institutions of higher education in America from the beginning—from that critical, bitterly contested passage in the late seventeenth and early eighteenth centuries when Harvard College's self-governing Fellows, modelled on their counterparts in Trinity, Christ's, or Emmanuel, were transformed from an internal self-directing body of scholars and teachers to an external board of laymen whose charge it was to see that the College lived up to its public—social—responsibilities.[3] We were then, as institutions, and still are, devoted to both the welfare of the poor of south Boston and the subtleties of the early Greek epic: the duality arises from sources deep within American society—its pragmatism, its pluralism, its constant reinvention. It is a theme that echoes through three centuries of American history.

II

There are other themes of similar importance and antiquity in American history, some clearly recognised by other foreign observers—Tocqueville, James Bryce, Max Weber. Among them was a strange, though peculiarly perceptive, visitor, Charles Joseph Latrobe, who toured the United States in 1832–3 en route to his post as superintendent of the southern district of New South Wales. A curious amateur of science and music (he decided that the locusts and other insects in North America sing in the key of C sharp) Latrobe was the least provincial of British proconsuls, and his comments reflect his broad perspective.

Though the American people, he wrote, are separated from the Old World by a vast ocean,

> they are not without the influence of the vortex; every thing, their language, literature, necessities . . . all render them intimately connected with us. We whirl, they whirl too. Do we feel the revolution which is taking place in every thing— politics, religion, opinion, science—so must they. [But] there may be this difference, that as yet they have more room, the sweep is a wider one than ours, but they still obey the same law as ourselves.[4]

---

[3] Bernard Bailyn *et al., Glimpses of the Harvard Past* (Cambridge, MA, 1986), pp. 13–18.
[4] Charles J. Latrobe, *The Rambler in North America: MDCCCXXXII–MDCCCXXXIII* (London, 1835), 2. 96, 70. Latrobe's perceptions, at times strange, were often prescient: America,

A century and a half later this observation might stand as an epigraph to the burgeoning scholarship on Atlantic history.

This emerging perspective on aspects of early modern history has in recent years broadened the vision of historians writing on innumerable special subjects, spawned international seminars and conferences of exploration and elaboration, and reshaped aspects of university instruction. As the study of the common, interactive, and comparative experiences of the people in the lands surrounding the Atlantic basin, Atlantic history developed rapidly after the Second World War, stimulated in part by historians' awareness of, if not involvement in, the geo-politics of the Cold War, but propelled mainly by forces within scholarship itself—by the proliferation of monographic studies, by the vast increase in available documentation, by the continuous broadening of the units of inquiry (the Mediterranean world, the British archipelago, the Orient as opposed to the West), by the explanatory power of comparative analysis, and by the multiplying exchanges and increased mobility of scholars, especially the relocation of British historians in the major American research universities. As post-war historical scholarship fructified, important connections among distant places, people, and ideas could be seen, once obscure filiations traced, and latent structures revealed.[5] The Atlantic region could be seen as a distinctive historical entity, in the sense, David Eltis, a leading historian of the Atlantic slave trade, has written, that the values of the people within it were reshaped in some way by others living in different parts of the region. It was not a matter, the historical geographer D.W. Meinig noted, of the Old World impinging on the New but a 'sudden and harsh encounter between two old worlds that transformed both and integrated them into a single New World'.[6]

The early modern Atlantic world was immeasurably complex in its racial, political, economic, and cultural differences, and it was splintered by local, regional, and national conflicts. But there were centripetal forces as well, parallel developments and common themes which were neither

---

he wrote, was a land 'which no man can pass over from east to west, and from the north to the south, without bringing away the impression, that if on any part of His earthly creation, the finger of God has drawn characters which would seem to indicate the seat of empire,—surely it is there!' p. 71.

[5] On the origins and early history of the concept of Atlantic history: Bailyn, *Atlantic History, Concept and Contours* (Cambridge, MA, 2005), pp. 24–9.

[6] David Eltis, 'Atlantic History in Global Perspective', *Itinerario*, 23, no. 2 (1999), 141; D. W. Meinig, *The Shaping of America: A Geographical Perspective on 500 Years of History* I, *Atlantic America, 1492–1800* (New Haven, CT, 1986), p. 65.

wholly European, nor wholly African, nor wholly American.⁷ Impulses that stirred in the heart of Europe found expression in the trans-oceanic West, and none more constantly and significantly than the search for perfection.

III

This was a subject of great interest to Isaiah Berlin, for it went to the core of his defence of 'the liberal anticommunist position in the midst of the Cold War'.⁸ His comments on the dangers of perfectionism had begun with his discussion of positive liberty in his famous inaugural lecture, 'Two Concepts of Liberty', at Oxford in 1958. While at times, he then wrote, it might be justifiable 'to coerce men in the name of some goal (let us say, justice or public health) which they would, if they were more enlightened, themselves pursue', once one claims that one knows what others need better than they know it themselves, one is

> in a position to ignore the actual wishes of men or societies, to bully, oppress, torture them in the name, and on behalf, of their 'real' selves ... albeit often submerged and inarticulate.

It was a theme he came back to again and again, elaborately in 'The Decline of Utopian Ideas in the West' in 1978, eloquently in 'The Pursuit of the Ideal' in 1988. The pursuit of perfection, he then wrote—thirty years after 'Two Concepts'—was 'a recipe for bloodshed, no better even if it is demanded by the sincerest of idealists, the purest of heart'.⁹ The implications of this position were immense, and he was challenged from the ideological right and left, as well as from the philosophical centre. But the majority of informed opinion supported him in denouncing utopianism as the ideological source of modern totalitarianism and in describing the horrors that perfectionists of various kinds have wrought.¹⁰

---

⁷ John Elliott traces key differences and parallels between Britain's and Spain's Atlantic empires in his *Empires of the Atlantic World* (New Haven, CT, 2006), which came to hand after these pages were written.
⁸ Leo Strauss, *The Rebirth of Classical Political Rationalism*, ed. Thomas L. Pangle (Chicago, 1989), pp. xxviii, 16.
⁹ 'Two Concepts of Liberty' [1958] in *Four Essays on Liberty* (London, 1969), pp. 132–3, xliv, xlvii; 'The Decline of Utopian Ideas in the West' [1978], in *The Crooked Timber of Humanity* (New York, 1991), pp. 20–48, esp. pp. 45–7; 'The Pursuit of the Ideal', ibid., pp. 18–19.
¹⁰ Ignatieff, *Berlin*, pp. 234–6, 246–7, 253; Aurel Kolnai, *The Utopian Mind and Other Papers*, ed. Francis Dunlop (Atlantic Highlands, NJ, 1995), esp. pp. 39–46, 69–86; Judith N. Shklar, 'The

As he reached back through Western history to trace the origins and different formulations of the idea of perfection that had culminated in the crushing tyrannies of the twentieth century, Berlin thought, as always, in terms of formal discourses—texts worthy of logical analysis. For he was, in this as in all his major historical writing, a historian of ideas as only a philosopher, however non-practising, could be. It was the structure of ideas, their genealogies, and their implications and ramifications that chiefly interested him, not the details of historical circumstance. It was the master thinkers among the perfectionists who mattered, their cogent, fully developed texts that deserved analysis, not the often muddled and always eclectic derivatives that were part of everyday culture.

Yet it is perfectionism at that lower level—unoriginal, derivative, sometimes confused, often passionate, muddling together ostensibly compatible notions and attitudes to compose guides for action—that I wish to discuss, and to suggest that at that more colloquial level there lies an earlier history of perfectionism that reveals not sources of human devastation in the search for perfection, but hope and heightened aspirations—a pre-modern era in which, as Quentin Skinner wrote in the first of these lectures, positive liberty was 'a dream, not a nightmare'.[11] And further, I wish to suggest that the profound strain of perfectionism that runs through the culture of early modern Europe has a peculiar relationship to Atlantic history.

For it was in the seemingly unconstrained amplitudes of the Western Hemisphere where, as Latrobe observed, there was more room, the sweep was wider, the inhibitions fewer, the possibilities greater, and not in Europe's tightly meshed social environment where establishments ancient and modern forced the expression of such yearnings into narrow interstices, that the search for perfection could find practical fulfilment in shaping the lives of ordinary people. It was there that perfectionist

---

Political Theory of Utopia, from Melancholy to Nostalgia' and 'What is the Use of Utopia?' in Stanley Hoffmann (ed.), *Political Thought and Political Thinkers* (Chicago, 1998); George Kateb, comp., *Utopia* (New York, 1971); Melissa Lane, 'Plato, Popper, Strauss, and Utopianism', *History of Philosophy Quarterly*, 16 (1999), 119–42; essays in *Daedalus*, 94 (1965), No. 2 ('Utopia'). Ian Harris lists the voluminous criticisms of and commentaries on the full range of Berlin's ideas in 'Berlin and His Critics', Isaiah Berlin, *Liberty*, ed. Henry Hardy (Oxford, 2002), pp. [349]–366.

[11] Quentin Skinner, 'A Third Concept of Liberty', *Proceedings of the British Academy*, 117 (2002), 264.

aspirations could fully dilate, and expanded visions projected into what Keith Thomas has called 'action-oriented' utopias.[12]

IV

Perfectionist thinking is a subject of some complexity if only because it has taken so many forms. It includes humanistic literary utopianism, prophetic millenarianism, and mystical hermeticism. They are complex in themselves, and they are not wholly distinct. Nothing important in the culture of Christian Europe and America was solely secular. More's *Utopia* was fresh in most literate minds in the sixteenth and seventeenth centuries, but so too were the prophecies of Daniel and the dark complexities of the Book of Revelation. Keith Thomas lists eight forms of utopianism in seventeenth-century England but finds that they cannot be distinguished from the millenarian impulse 'which relied on divine intervention and envisaged a miraculous transformation of both man and nature . . . it was precisely when the millenarian current was running most strongly', he writes, 'that the utopian faith in human effort was most buoyant'. Seventeenth-century millenarianism and seventeenth-century utopianism, he concludes, 'were twins'.[13]

And so they were throughout the whole of early modern Europe, impelled by the great tectonic shifts of the Reformation and its Catholic response, and the vast efflorescence of knowledge in the Renaissance and beyond. Both created soaring hopes for the transcendence of life as it was

---

[12] Keith Thomas, 'The Utopian Impulse in Seventeenth-Century England', in Dominic Baker-Smith and C. C. Barfoot (eds.), *Between Dream and Nature: Essays on Utopia and Dystopia* (Amsterdam, 1987), pp. 43, 24.

Frank and Fritzi Manuel in their massive *Utopian Thought in the Western World* (Cambridge, MA, 1979), pp. 14–15, rule out any consideration of utopian ideas in the Americas because they were 'derivative', mere 'extensions of European idea systems', 'the pabulum of an age, the chewed cud of previous epochs'. Only in Europe, they write, were there 'significant innovations', 'new departures', 'the major constellations of utopian thought'. In what follows I concentrate on precisely the two aspects of Utopianism they dismiss: perfectionism in the Americas, including Spanish America, and the 'chewed cud' of derivative ideas. My purpose is to trace the implementation of some of these ideas in the real and uniquely favourable conditions of colonial America and to consider some of the consequences. On the feverish utopianism of England, 1640–60, ibid., ch. xiii, esp. p. 334.

[13] Ibid., 'Introduction: The Utopian Propensity'; Thomas, 'Utopian Impulse', pp. 24, 31, 32. J. C. Davis, in *Utopia and The Ideal Society . . . 1516–1700* (Cambridge, 1981), ch. i, distinguishes utopian societies from four other types of ideal communities.

known, ultimately for the possibility, if not of reaching perfection, then of approaching ideal goals.

England in the crisis years of the mid-seventeenth century was especially alight with projects for both mobilising secular knowledge in learned and benevolent societies, often in collaboration with the most imaginative scholars and scientists of Europe, and for advancing apocalyptic hopes. 'Virtually every sect', the Manuels write in their history of Utopian thought in Europe,

> carried its own utopia, and individuals moved easily from one circle into another, punctuating their advent and departure with an appropriate religious revelation. Men dropped in and out of groups, recanting previous errors, writing confessions and testimonials [as one radical sect sought] to distinguish itself from the teeming mass, and much energy was expended on touting the superiority of one future society over its rivals.

Some utopian designs were lofty abstractions, theoretical models of the ideal by which to measure the evils of the world and speculations on radical reform in all spheres of life. But others seemed to be within the reach of possibility. Most of these, on the Continent as in England, were the work of sects determined to recover a lost Christian perfection by drawing apart to live more perfect lives in some approximation to the assumed ways of the apostles.

Often the radical sectarians found the social atmosphere of their immediate localities too dense, the weight of traditional institutions and social controls too heavy to allow for local withdrawal. So they looked for refuge beyond their immediate horizons, some to distant trans-oceanic places, and in this they shared the visions of the humanist utopian theorists for whom imagined distances from the real world had always been a logical necessity, often involving fanciful ocean voyages to reach the perfectly imagined regime.[14]

For both, America's attraction was powerful. Not only would its limitless spaces and apparent lack of restrictive social pressures provide the ideal environment for the pursuit of perfectionist lives, but the existence of its vast population of pagans, descendants no doubt of the lost tribes of Israel, now Satan's captives, would provide the ultimate challenge for those who understood the stages of apocalyptic fulfilment. And so the perfectionist invasion began—by Catholics, regular and secular, by dissenting Anglicans, by German pietists, and by a range of radical

---

[14] Manuel, *Utopian Thought*, pp. 334, 21–3.

Protestants, from self-absorbed seekers to those wildly impatient Fifth Monarchy militants, led by a murderous New England 'fanatique', who stormed through Restoration London crying '*Live King Jesus!*' until rounded up and hanged.[15]

Utopian and perfectionist aspirations were an elemental part of the European invasion of the America. The conquest—by the British, Dutch, French, and Portuguese as well as by the Spanish—was barbarous for the conquerors, and for the natives catastrophic. Yet amid all the racist brutality, the loss of civility, and the remorseless, often bloody struggles to create new economic and social regimes, the search for perfection and for the fulfilment of apocalyptic prophecies—impulses that flowed from Europe's heartland—persisted. Certain passages in this complex multi-cultural history are particularly revealing. They exemplify something of the inner landscape of the European imagination and America's peculiar place within it.

V

For the early Franciscans, led by the ascetic Toribio Motolinía, who was convinced that America could be nothing less than the prime site of the millennial kingdom of Christ, the task was to help the natives recover the simplicity and innocence he believed they had lost in the Aztecs' conquest. Once, in earlier, pre-Aztec times, they had been free of luxury, greed, and the struggle for 'rank and honors'. If that pristine world could be revived, the Indians, in their innocence, would occupy 'a primordial, privileged role at the center itself of the future of humanity'. Motolinía lectured Charles V on the urgent need to 'hasten the hour of the Final Judgment', not by imposing modern Hispanic culture on the natives, as Las Casas and the crown counsellors urged, but by protecting them from all outside influences except Christian preaching, which could rightly be imposed by force. In his mind's eye there would be a world, a continent, of simple people, no longer corrupted, isolated in their own peculiar

---

[15] John L. Phelan, *The Millennial Kingdom of the Franciscans in the New World*... (Berkeley, CA, 1956), p. 73; Richard H. Popkin, 'Hartlib, Dury, and the Jews', in M. Greengrass, *et al.* (eds.), *Samuel Hartlib and Universal Reformation* (Cambridge, 1994), pp. 124–30; Champlin Burrage, 'The Fifth Monarchy Insurrections', *English Historical Review*, 25 (1910), 739–47 ('Fanatique' was Pepys's term); Philip F. Gura, *A Glimpse of Sion's Glory: Puritan Radicalism in New England, 1620–1660* (Middletown, CT, 1984), pp. 136–44.

Christian-Indian state, free, as once they had been, of property, guile, and the struggle for status, ready to receive the approaching dispensation.[16]

Though he wrote at length and with passion, Motolinía failed to convince the crown to protect the Indians' autochthonous cultures. So the aggressive Hispanisation proceeded, in innumerable missions, churches, and schools throughout the vice-royalties, creating in the process an auspicious background for specific utopian designs.

They appeared in different forms at different places. Some were newly invented, others drawn from classic sources. More's *Utopia*, published just before the major conquests of Mexico and Peru, was understood in humanist circles to be a learned, imaginative, and challenging commentary on Europe's ills; but in America it had practical consequences. For the *audiencia* judge and later bishop, Vasco de Quiroga, it provided a detailed model for the organisational structure and social discipline of the *pueblo*-hospitals he founded near Mexico City in the early 1530s. The specific provisions for these benevolent, perfectionist communities, built to shelter and care for the poor, vagrant, and dispossessed Indians, could not have been closer to the details of More's imaginative design. Property was owned in common, the basic social unit was the *familia*, urban and rural life alternated, work was limited to six hours a day, goods were distributed according to need, luxury and useless offices were eliminated, and judges were elected by families. Quiroga even considered a dress code based on *Utopia*, including clothes of fabrics specified by More. The organisation of More's *Utopia*, Quiroga wrote, should be the basis not only of his hospitals but of all Indian communities in America. But such was the all-absorbing power of millenarian aspirations that Quiroga conflated More's design with what he imagined the primitive church to have been. The barefooted, bareheaded, long haired natives went about, he believed, 'as [did] the Apostles'—appropriately for what he foresaw as 'the new primitive and reborn Church of the New World'.

More's utopian model had organised Quiroga's thoughts as he sought ways of bringing the pagan population towards Christian redemption, a stage in the universal ascent to the millennium. In the process a literary text had become 'a political program circulated across the Atlantic from a radical colonist to a monarch and used to initiate a social practice'.[17]

---

[16] Georges Baudot, *Utopia and History in Mexico ...(1520–1569)*, trans. Bernard R. and Thelma Ortiz de Montellano (Niwot, CO, 1995), chs. v, vi; quotations at pp. 87, xv, 310–13.

[17] Silvio Zavala, *Sir Thomas More in New Spain: A Utopian Adventure of the Renaissance* (*Diamante*, 3, London, 1955), p. 12; Zavala, 'The American Utopia of the Sixteenth Century',

For others, equally committed to ideal goals, there were no models, literary or other, and pragmatic solutions had to be found. So the Spanish Jesuits devised 'reductions' of the natives, in Paraguay most famously but elsewhere as well. They too were millenarian/utopian creations: gatherings of nomadic natives into disciplined urban communities where Christianity, hence civilisation, could be inculcated in people who would thereafter become productive members of the labour force and foot soldiers in the wars of imperial expansion.

Though few in number the Jesuits were driven by intense zeal to control the lives of the Indians who were drawn into their 'villages of perfect godliness'. And in many matters essential to their mission they succeeded, transforming these Tupi-Guarani-speaking peoples deep in the Amazon forests into Catholics living in perfected communities groomed for the coming of the Lord.

Yet the Guarani, and even more the Maranhese Indians the Portuguese Jesuits faced in Brazil and the Iroquois and Hurons the French Jesuits faced in New France, could not be forced, in Berlin's phrase, 'into neat uniforms demanded by the dogmatically believed-in schemes'. The indigenous cultures were too vibrant to be easily uprooted and the power of the invaders was too weak to force the natives into an ideal mould shaped by perfectionist visions. The Jesuits' wards, whether in New Spain, New France, or Brazil, never fully abandoned their native cultures. They absorbed the new regimes selectively, forcing their rulers, if only for the sake of stability, to accept major aspects of the indigenous organisations.[18]

The search for perfection in these forms, on the background of millenarian hopes for the redemption of the Western world, was an Atlantic phenomenon—a trans-oceanic projection of the apocalyptic prophecies

---

Huntington Library Quarterly, 4 (1947), 341, 344–7; Fintan B. Warren, *Vasco de Quiroga and his Pueblo-Hospitals of Santa Fe* (Washington, DC, 1963), pp. 4–5, 29, 32–5, 116–17. On Quiroga's larger scheme for congregating all Amerindians into *repúblicas de indios*, and the details of the regulations in his hospital-*pueblos*: Bernardino Verástique, *Muchoacán and Eden: Vasco de Quiroga and the Evangelization of Western Mexico* (Austin, TX, 2000), pp. 120–40; James Holstun, *A Rational Millennium: Puritan Utopias of Seventeenth-Century England and America* (New York, 1987), p. 14.

[18] Allan Greer and Kenneth Mills, 'A Catholic Atlantic', in Jorge Cañizares-Esguerra and Erik R. Seeman (eds.), *The Atlantic in Global History* (Upper Saddle River, NJ, 2006), p. 10. Barbara Ganson, *The Guaraní under Spanish Rule in the Rio de la Plata* (Stanford, CA, 2003), chs. ii, iii; José Gabriel Martínez-Serna, 'Instruments of Empire: Jesuit-Indian Encounters in the New World Borderlands' (Working Paper, Atlantic History Seminar, Harvard Univ., 2004), pp. 8–29; Philip Caraman, *The Lost Paradise: An Account of the Jesuits in Paraguay, 1607–1768* (London, 1975).

that gripped the European imagination and the associated yearnings for a return to the simplicity of the primitive church. As such it was not confined to the Iberian world and its empires abroad. In variant forms it was as much English, French, Dutch, and German as it was Spanish and Portuguese. These worlds too were inspired by apocalyptic prophecies and the longing for the simple purity of the apostles' church; and they too found the realisation of their vision in the transoceanic west.

There is no better illustration of the Atlantic dimensions of the search for perfection than the fortunes of the Puritans who, fleeing from ecclesiastical oppression at home, sought to establish in America a model of perfected Christianity. Everything seemed to favour their success. They had sufficient numbers and funds, administrative experience, and some of England's finest scholars and theologians who shared a passionate belief that they were building in Massachusetts God's 'new Jerusalem', laying 'one stone in the foundacion of this new Syon'. Those 'great persons', wrote Cotton Mather (the Puritans' over-learned encomiast), who like Guillaume Budé had 'mistook Sir Thomas Moor's UTOPIA for a country really existent, and stirr'd up some divines charitably to undertake a voyage thither, might now have certainly found a truth in their mistake; New England was a true Utopia'.[19]

But however utopian in aspiration, the Puritans did not have a unified belief in what the perfected church and society should be, and so, immediately upon landing, their community, boiling with perfectionist ambitions, exploded, 'hurling itself outward to its ultimate limits'. Perfectionist groups left and right fought for domination. Antinomians denounced the unconverted clergy as 'dead dogs' and tore the colony apart with their repudiation of ascetic discipline as they moved towards mystical union with God. Rationalist Socinians settled in villages a hundred miles inland declared that the Trinity, atonement, and the divinity of Christ were delusions and argued for religious toleration. And Anabaptists, scattered everywhere, insisted that infant baptism was a deadly corruption, to which conservatives replied by invoking memories of Münster where, a century earlier, zealous Anabaptists had been

---

[19] Theodore D. Bozeman, *To Live Ancient Lives* . . . (Chapel Hill, NC, 1988), ch. iii; W. Clark Gilpin, *The Millenarian Piety of Roger Williams* (Chicago, 1979), p. 14; Cotton Mather, *The Wonders of the Invisible World* . . . (Boston, 1692) p. 6. Mather was referring to, and misreading, Budé's letter to Thomas Lupset which first appeared as a Preface to More's *Utopia* in 1517.

slaughtered by the thousands by those, including Luther, who feared anarchic upheavals.[20]

But New England was no Münster. Its open spaces, social and geographical, invited the free, limitless expression of the many perfectionist impulses that lurked in the heart of Puritanism—not only antinomianism, socinianism, and anabaptism but familism, spiritism, and those nameless ecstatic urges that would become notorious and deadly when proclaimed by Ranters in London but that in Rhode Island, a colony the mainstream Puritans denounced as 'a cesspool of vile heresies and irreligion', found free institutional form. There, each of the various perfectionist villages, led by its own self-styled 'professor of the mysteries of Christ', was convinced of its purity and condemned its errant neighbours. All felt an irresistible pressure to press on through deepening stages to reach some ultimate, uncompromised, perfect resolution—a state of being that Roger Williams alone, finally, attained.[21]

Williams, the purest of Puritan perfectionists, began his career as a spiritual guide to Cromwell's aunt, the melancholic Lady Joan Barrington, whom he so berated for the unsatisfactory state of her soul that she banished him from her sight. The same 'unlambelike ... stiffnesse' led him to join the migration to Boston, and then to quit Boston after denouncing the Puritans' failure to separate fully from the corrupt Church of England, their union of church and state, the '*Soule-rape*' of their 'forcing of the *conscience* of any person', and their immoral seizing of Indian lands. Narrowly escaping deportation to England, he fled to the woods near Narragansett Bay where, with a small troop of followers, he formed his more perfect village.[22]

But not perfect enough. There was no stopping in his fiercely logical pursuit of the ultimate form of apostolic purity. Convinced that there could be no 'true Church until Christ himself reinstituted it at the end of time', he swept through and discarded layer after layer of recognised

---

[20] Edmund S. Morgan, *Roger Williams: The Church and the State* (New York, 1967), p. 4; Theodore D. Bozeman, *The Precisionist Strain* ... (Chapel Hill, NC, 2004), ch. ix, Part III. The most complete account of the great explosion of radical groups in early New England is Gura, *Sion's Glory*: on Münster and the Anabaptists, as 'incendiaries of commonwealths', pp. 93, 115, 128, 256. On the Antinomian turmoil: Michael P. Winship, *Making Heretics: Militant Protestantism and Free Grace in Massachusetts, 1636–1641* (Princeton, NJ, 2002).

[21] Sydney V. James, *Colonial Rhode Island: a History* (New York, 1975), p. 37.

[22] William Hunt, *The Puritan Moment: The Coming of the Revolution in an English County* (Cambridge, MA, 1983), pp. 222–3; John Cotton, *A Reply to Mr. Williams ...* in *The Bloudy Tenent, Washed and Made White ...* (London, 1647), p. 5; Arthur Searle, '"Overmuch Liberty": Roger Williams in Essex', *The Essex Journal*, 3 (1968), 85–92; Gura, *Sion's Glory*, p. 190.

doctrines until nothing was left but his own elemental convictions based on his millenarian view of Christian history. Since no post-apostolic church was true, no church should be joined, and so in the end Williams became a church unto himself, worshipping alone, or with his wife, in what he took to be the only true approximation of apostolic form, and sending back to England, from his Bay-side refuge, bulletins of his beliefs and blistering attacks on his enemies' and the world's corruptions.[23]

For Williams as for most of the Puritan divines, the search for perfection was part of the same apocalyptic design that dominated the minds of the Jesuits and Franciscans in Latin America. The precise interpretations differed, but the need to prepare for the approaching end by converting the American Indians and installing them in sanctified communities was as widely accepted by radical Puritans as by Tridentine Catholics.

The parallels between Motolinía's and Quiroga's efforts and those of the Puritans' chief apostle to the Indians, the Revd John Eliot, are striking. But it was Eliot, of all the millenarian missionaries, who drew the most radically utopian and elaborate prescriptions from the common, pan-European eschatological sources; it was Eliot who sought most efficiently to relate the conversion of the natives to the future of all mankind.

Eliot, not the most learned of the Puritan preachers, though he was said to have arrived in America with twenty-three barrels of books, had begun in the 1640s to reach out to the Indians to urge them to lead Christian lives and eventually to find true faith. Then two events coincided to elevate his mission to cosmic heights and to enclose within a single vision the perfectionist destinies of the Indians and the fulfilment of the millenarian prophecies.

In a series of lectures in the 1640s Boston's leading theologian, John Cotton, discoursed vividly on the twenty-two chapters of the Book of Revelation, leaving a searing impression on Eliot that the predestined end of history was approaching and that the entire drama of Christ's deliverance would soon be enacted, with all its momentous transformations. Then came the execution of Charles I, which could only be seen as the unmistakable first step in the prophesied destruction of all earthly monarchies and the presage of the rule of Christ. A new, millenarian polity was now required, and it would be extrapolated from the small-

---

[23] Gura, *Sion's Glory*, p. 217; Richard S. Dunn, *et al.* (eds.), *The Journal of John Winthrop 1630–1649* (Cambridge, MA, 1996), p. 300; on the maturing of Williams's beliefs and his 'obsession with personal and ecclesiastical purity', see Gilpin, *Millenarian Piety*, pp. 50 ff., and Morgan, *Williams*.

scale model that he, Eliot, would create among the Indians in New England. The Algonquians, like the Jesuits' Guaranis, would be 'reduced' to civility by being gathered from their wanderings into settled towns. There, governed by elected rulers of tens, of fifties, of hundreds, and of thousands as prescribed in Exodus 18, they would be able to lead perfected Christian lives within covenanted churches, in preparation for Christ's deliverance.[24]

For Eliot the praying Indian towns, of which fourteen were established by 1675, bore heavily on the destiny of mankind. 'I doubt not', he wrote to Cromwell, 'but it will be some comfort to your heart, to see the kingdom of Christ rising up in these western parts of the world, a blessed kingdom that will in time "fill all the earth"'. In his *Christian Commonwealth, or the Civil Polity of the Rising Kingdom of Jesus Christ*, written in 1651 at the height of his apocalyptic fervour, Eliot laid out the full vision of the 'Comenian pansophist project among the Indians' that gripped his imagination. With the praying towns epitomes of what could prevail in England—a nation, he believed, that was destined to be one of the two inaugural locations of the millennium (the other being New England)—and given the likelihood that the Indians, 'ripe for utopian molding', were descendants of the lost tribes of Israel, their conversion, followed by that of all gentiles would indicate that the kingdom of Christ was nigh.[25]

Everything pointed in that direction, not least the possibility that study of the Indians' speech would reveal elements of the 'universal language', which, as Comenius had made clear, expressed the inner, mystical nature of divinity. No effort could be spared. Eliot worked diligently with a bilingual Indian and an imported English printer to publish the entire Bible and several religious tracts in Algonquian translations, and to compose as well a grammar of that apparently Hebraic language,

---

[24] Richard W. Cogley, *John Eliot's Mission to the Indians before King Philip's War* (hereafter: *Eliot's Mission*) (Cambridge, MA, 1999), pp. 46, 251–2 (Cotton's lectures on Revelation); J. F. Maclear, 'New England and the Fifth Monarchy: The Quest for the Millennium in Early American Puritanism', *William and Mary Quarterly*, 3rd ser., 32 (1975), 225, 231–4, 255; James Holstun, 'John Eliot's Empirical Millenarianism', *Representations*, 4 (1983), 143, 145–6; Holstun, *Rational Millennium*, pp. 104–9, 113–14.

[25] Cogley, *Eliot's Mission*, pp. 92–3, 79–81, 88, 90; Maclear, 'New England and the Fifth Monarchy', pp. 254–5, 229, 244–7; Holstun, *Rational Millennium*, pp. 132, 115, 111–13 (on the relations of Eliot's utopianism to the classic utopias from Plato to Bacon and Comenius, pp. 132–3, 157–8). On the belief that the American Indians were Jews from the lost tribes, and its significance on the millenarian thought of the Hartlib circle in England, see Richard Popkin's essay in Greengrass *et al.* (eds.), *Hartlib and Universal Reformation*, ch. v.

which must have derived from the pristine era before the confusion of Babel.[26]

The whole programme was in its essence pan-Atlantic. Eliot sought to realise in utopian communities in America ideas drawn from common themes in European culture—both rationalist and millennialist—and then to transfer their embodied form back across the Atlantic to serve as templates for the radical transformation of England. But his message and the reports of his praying towns reached an England in turmoil over the proper form of republican government. His urgent advice was taken to mean that England should give up ransacking law, history, and constitutional theory to find proper forms of government and draw on scripture alone, for, he wrote, 'Christ is your King and Soveraign Lawgiver', 'the only right heir to the crown of England'. England's constitution should, like the Indians', consist of elected rulers of tens, fifties, hundreds, and thousands, with suffrage for all self-sufficient males. This, he wrote, is the form of government, infinitely expandable, 'by which Christ meaneth to rule all the nations on earth according to Scriptures'.[27]

It was a perfect scheme for a perfect Christian regime, but the world was not prepared for his perfection. Eliot's praying Indian towns were wiped out in the savage Indian war of 1675–6, their 1100 inhabitants exiled to a harbour island where many starved or died of disease. And his prophetic book, delayed in publication until the year before the Restoration, proved to be a deadly embarrassment to the Massachusetts authorities, promoting as it did Fifth Monarchy views that would surely bring down on the colony the wrath of the restored royal government. They forthwith collected and destroyed every copy of the book they could lay their hands on and forced Eliot to recant everything in it.[28]

As in some bewilderment he did so, perfectionist impulses were evolving elsewhere—in Holland and the scattered German states. One of the most fully developed schemes designed to begin the world's reformation emerged from Amsterdam, and specifically from the heated atmosphere of the poets and free thinkers who gathered at that city's Sweet Rest Tavern. It too would run its course through Atlantic networks.

---

[26] Sarah Rivett, 'Christian Translations: Indian Grammar and the Quest for a Universal Language in the British Atlantic World' (Working Paper, Atlantic History Seminar, Harvard University, 2006).
[27] Holstun, *Rational Millennium*, pp. 104, 131, 158; Holstun, 'Eliot's Empirical Millenarianism', pp. 131, 144, 147; Cogley, *Eliot's Mission*, p. 79.
[28] Ibid., pp. 165, 256–8, 114–16; Holstun, *Rational Millennium*, p. 159.

The designer and spiritual leader of this utopian programme was a visionary Dutchman, Pieter Cornelisz Plockhoy, who had been touched as a child in Zeeland by the fierce Biblicism and spirituality of the Mennonites and Anabaptists and as a young man had found inspiration among the Quaker-like 'Collegiant' philosophers in Amsterdam, devoted to absolute religious freedom and social justice. There he had begun his search for 'the ideal Christian commonwealth of love, equality, and freedom'. By the mid-1650s he had made contact with the famous German-Polish virtuoso of radical reform, Samuel Hartlib, then in London, and through him with the circle of erudite pansophists seeking to mobilise and employ all human knowledge to reform everything—from politics to agriculture, from employment to 'the spirits of men', and from commerce and poverty to law and the arts.[29]

For Plockhoy, the Hartlib circle, devoted to recovering 'man's lost dominion over nature' and to transforming life as it was known, was irresistible. Abandoning family and home, he joined Hartlib, and with his help gained access to Cromwell. The great man, Plockhoy said, listened 'several times with patience' to his ideas and proposals, which by then had taken elaborate form.[30]

Plockhoy knew exactly what the perfect world should be. It would have 'freedom of speech, absolute toleration, and a universal Christianity'. There would be no clergy, no ties of church to state, no tithes, and above all, no 'lording over consciences'. The thralldom brought on by malevolent governors, greedy merchants, and lazy ministers would be eliminated. Life's work would be shared in clear divisions of labour; specialisation would bring interdependence and mutual respect. There would be absolute equality of status; property would be held in common until divided by lot into private parcels. Above all it would be a full-employment welfare society in which the health and well-being of all people would be provided for. As to the controversial issue of equality, 'nobody will be so naïve', he wrote, 'much less malevolent, as to think ... that we are attempting to remove all differences among people'. The effect of the common rules would be to eliminate not natural human differences nor

---

[29] Leland Harder and Marvin Harder, *Plockhoy from Zurik-zee* (Newton, KS, 1952), ch. ii; Davis, *Utopia*, pp. 313–14, derived from Charles Webster's magisterial study of Hartlib and the world of utopian reform in all fields of learning, *The Great Instauration: Science, Medicine, and Reform 1626–1660* (London, 1975).

[30] Davis, *Utopia and the Ideal Society . . .1516–1700*, p. 313; Harder, *Plockhoy*, p. 28; Plockhoy to Cromwell, [1659?], ibid., pp. 120–30. Cf. Plockhoy to Cromwell, 4 June 1657, Hartlib Papers (Sheffield University Library), 54/23A–26B.

rewards for personal accomplishments but the differences created and maintained by force and intimidation, by the dead hand of custom, and by the coercive mandates of the princes of the church.[31]

Such was the programme Plockhoy presented to Cromwell, and after his death to the new Protector and to Parliament. Its aim, he said, was the true reformation of England as the first step in the rebirth of mankind. If in England complete religious freedom were created, he assured Cromwell, 'Holland, Denmark, Sweden, France and other kingdoms . . . will easily be brought to a firm bond of unity'. Notables were informed of his perfectionist plan: John Milton, some of whose views were not dissimilar to Plockhoy's; John Beale, scientist, theologian, and Christian humanist, a member of Hartlib's circle; and John Worthington, Master of Jesus College and prominent Platonist, with whom Hartlib discussed the similarities of Plockhoy's plans to those of the Hutterites.[32]

But while his proposals stirred up some writing and much talk there was little action. Plockhoy's thinking began to shift. In England, he wrote, it was becoming clear that he and his adherents might well prove to be 'insufferable to the world', and at the same time the world might be 'incorrigible or unbetterable as to us'. Therefore he and his people would have to establish their solidarity 'in such places as are separate from other men, where we may with less impediment or hindrance love one another and mind the wonders of God, eating the bread we shall earn with our own hands'.[33]

But where could such a refuge be found? The authorities in his native Holland turned him away, and he had no confidence in what he heard of a nobleman's sanctuary near Cologne. In the end, well aware that the Hartlib circle had talked of creating an ideal society ('Antilia', 'Macaria') in Virginia or Bermuda, he decided that his perfect society would only be safe, and fulfilled, in America. He knew about that distant land through his brother who had served the Dutch West India Company in New Netherland and from a member of the Parnassan Club who had lived

---

[31] Plockhoy, *Way to Peace* and his *A Way Propounded to Make the Poor . . . Happy . . .* (London, 1659), in Harder, *Plockhoy*, pp. 108 ff. and ch. vi.
[32] Plockhoy to Cromwell [1659] in Harder, *Plockhoy*, p. 124; Hartlib to John Worthington, 20 July 1659, in James Crossley, *et al.* (eds.), *Diary and Correspondence of James Worthington* (Manchester, 1847–86), 1. 156; Harder, *Plockhoy*, pp. 37–41.
[33] Ibid., pp. 31–2; Davis, *Utopia*, pp. 316, 338; Hartlib to Worthington, 20 July 1659, *Diary and Correspondence*, p. 156.

there for a decade and who celebrated its wonders in rhapsodic poems which he declaimed at length to his friends in the Sweet Rest Tavern.[34]

For this removal to their under-populated colony the Dutch West India Company and the Amsterdam authorities were happy to provide support. So on 28 July 1663 Plockhoy and forty-one adherents disembarked at an abandoned clearing on the Delaware River, to usher in a new era in human history.

What happened within Plockhoy's perfect world in the months that followed, how fully and in what detail he was able finally, on that distant shore, to realise his so carefully defined state of perfected being, is not known. What is known is that it ended swiftly. In August 1664 an overwhelming English force seized the Dutch colony and swept across Plockhoy's settlement like a whirlwind, stripping it bare and plundering it down 'to a very nail'. Plockhoy died in the attack or soon thereafter and his utopian flock scattered among the Finnish, Swedish, German, and English frontiersmen living in primitive settlements alongside the Lenape Indians. Only his blind son is known to have survived into the next century, the last remnant of the utopia that had once stirred the minds of aspiring intellectuals in Holland and learned pansophists in England and the German states.[35]

But if one utopian mission born in the heated atmosphere of European perfectionism failed on the banks of the Delaware River, others drawn from different sources in Continental Europe appeared nearby.

William Penn's private colony, founded in 1681 as a refuge for harassed Quakers committed to their own militant struggle for perfection, was open to people of all nations and (Protestant) creeds. It was quickly peopled not only by Welsh and English sectarians but also by German Protestants from the Rhineland and the Palatinate. Victims of

---

[34] Hartlib to Worthington, 15 Oct. 1660, ibid., p. 211; Harder, *Plockhoy*, pp. 36, 48; Davis, *Utopia*, pp. 313–14; Webster, *Instauration*, pp. 98, 368. References to Virginia as a possible site for a utopian settlement abound in the Hartlib Papers; cf. Catherine Armstrong, 'Antilia Revisited: Hartlib's Utopian Vision of America in Light of Recent Scholarship' (paper delivered at Birkbeck College conference, 'New Worlds Reflected: Representations of Utopia, the New World and Other Worlds (1500–1800)', Dec. 2005). Cf. Donald R. Dickson, *The Tessera of Antilia* (Leiden, 1998), pp. 118–25, 223–35, 251–6. The texts of Steendam's poems about New Netherland are in Henry C. Murphy, trans., *An Anthology of New Netherland . . .* (New York, 1865), pp. [37]–75. On Plockhoy's brother Harmen: Peter S. Craig, '1671 Census of the Delaware', *Pennsylvania Genealogical Magazine*, 40 (1998), 358–9.

[35] E. B. O'Callaghan, *et al.* (eds.), *Documents Relative to the Colonial History of the State of New-York* (Albany, NY, 1856–87), 2. 176; 3. 346.

the ravages of war and of religious persecution, most were members of established Lutheran and Reformed churches. But among them were small groups of radical perfectionists with different aims, disciples of the major figures in German Pietism: Spener, Boehme, and Francke. One such group, who called themselves the Chapter of Perfection, put together a programme drawn from cabbalist, Rosicrucian, and biblical sources that had allowed them to predict the arrival of Christ and the start of the millennium precisely in 1694. Confident of the accuracy of their textual analyses, their mathematical calculations, and the meaning of the revelations they had received, they were properly disposed, according to their androgynous theology, to accept in ecstasy the embrace of the Bridegroom when he arrived.[36]

So the Chapter of Perfection, under the leadership of Johannes Kelpius, both a Rosicrucian magus and a *magister* of the University of Altdorf, set out for Pennsylvania to prepare for the coming of the Lord and to seek that state of personal perfection that was free of all sensuous temptations and beyond all rational understanding. Quickly upon their arrival they built a log-walled monastery of perfect proportions: forty feet by forty feet. It had a common room for communal worship and also cells where the celibate brethren could search for personal perfection by contemplating their magic numbers and their esoteric symbols. In a primitive laboratory they conducted alchemical and pharmaceutical experiments aimed at eliminating disease and prolonging life indefinitely. And on the roof they placed a telescope, which they manned from dusk till dawn, so that in case the Bridegroom came in the middle of the night they would be prepared to receive him. But the heart of Kelpius's sect lay not in the common room, not in the cells, and not in the laboratory, but in a cave which the magus found in a nearby hillside and in which he spent most of the rest of his life pondering truths concealed to ordinary souls but revealed to him by signs, by symbols, by numbers, and by pure contemplation. Everything confirmed that it was here, in the Chapter of Perfection, that the 'dear Lord Jesus' would reveal himself and that all true Christians, while vigorously pursuing their own perfection, should await him and prepare for the heavenly feast.

---

[36] Elizabeth W. Fisher, '"Prophecies and Revelations": German Cabbalists in Early Pennsylvania', *Pennsylvania Magazine of History and Biography*, 109 (1985), 299–333, and more generally Jon Butler, 'Magic, Astrology, and the Early American Religious Heritage, 1600–1760', *American Historical Review*, 84 (1979), 317–46. Julius F. Sachse's antiquarian, anecdotal, rather chaotic *German Pietists of Provincial Pennsylvania* (Philadelphia, 1895), contains essential information.

When the year passed and the Bridegroom failed to appear, calculations were renewed, the contemplation of numbers and symbols was intensified, and trance-like states were repeated. But gradually the brethren's discipline weakened, their energy dissipated, and temptation drew them from their celibate state. Some defected to established churches, but others went off to more recent perfectionist sects that were multiplying across Penn's province. Few could tolerate the fierce self-mortifying discipline required in Johann Beissel's nearby Ephrata cloister, whose emaciated monks and nuns sought, through the demanding rites of the Rosicrucians, to achieve a higher, more perfect state of being.[37] More genial were the followers of Matthias Baumann, an ignorant labourer from Lambsheim, in the Palatinate, who believed that in the delirium of an illness he had been transported to heaven where, newborn, purged of all sin, he had attained perfection, and needed thereafter no intervention of church, sacraments, or any other means of grace. He was convinced that God dwelt in him as in Christ ('we are brothers', he said) and that he had become like Adam before the fall, incapable of sin—conditions he extended to his followers and which he urged the unregenerate to achieve. When some questioned the truth of his doctrine of perfection, he proposed to demonstrate his exalted state by walking across the surface of the Delaware River. And there was an array of semi-communistic Moravian settlements, fugitive groups of the Czech-Saxon *Unitas Fratrum*, which spawned dozens of obscure, short-lived utopias deep in Indian territory.[38]

VI

For two centuries perfectionist projects, plants of European origins, had blossomed in the open atmosphere of the Americas, had reached for the sun, and had faded and died. But they were not without lasting effect. Their creative influence can be found deep in the cultures of later times.

---

[37] Fisher, '"Prophecies and Revelations"', pp. 319–24; Ernst L. Lashlee, 'Johannes Kelpius and His Woman in the Wilderness', Gerhard Mueller and Winfried Zeller (eds.), *Glaube, Geist, Geschichte: Festschrift für Ernst Benz* (Leiden, 1967), pp. 327–31; Bernard Bailyn, *The Peopling of British North America* (New York, 1985), pp. 123–7.

[38] Julius F. Sachse, *The German Sectarians of Pennsylvania* (Philadelphia, 1899–1900), 1. 73–7; Philip C. Croll, *Annals of the Oley Valley* . . . (Reading, PA, 1926), ch. iii; Don Yoder (ed.), *Rhineland Emigrants* (Baltimore, MD, 1981), pp. 99; Gillian L. Gollin, *Moravians in Two Worlds* (New York, 1967).

How long Vasco de Quiroga's utopian *pueblo*-hospitals survived as model communities is not clear. But a century after their founding a visitor recorded that 'the Indians there were, up to a certain point, imitating the monks ... and devoting themselves to prayer and the pursuit of a more perfect life'. When in time Quiroga's perfectionist glow dimmed, an image, and a tradition, remained that would prove in later years to be as consistent with Marxist ideology as with Scholastic theology and that some would associate with social reform in modern Mexico. The Jesuits would be banished from America, but 'the Hispanic-Guarani-baroque towns in the subtropical forest' they created survived as 'unique syncretic societies', continuously changing and adapting as circumstances shifted. And the Jesuits' annual reports would survive as perceptive ethnographic studies, primary sources for social anthropologists.

New England Puritanism's once explosive radicalism was compromised into a sere orthodoxy, but Roger Williams's uncompromised perfectionism, feared and despised by his contemporaries, proved in the twentieth century to be an inspiration for advocates of religious freedom, human rights, and enlightened democracy. Eliot's passions were stifled and his efforts to convert and educate the natives and to modernise their way of life led to cultural deracination, but his translation of the Bible into Algonquian, 'the first printed in a non-European tongue, and the first printed for which an entire phonetic writing system was devised', together with his tracts in the natives' language and his *Indian Grammar*, contributed significantly to the development of Indian linguistics in the nineteenth and twentieth centuries.[39] Plockhoy's communal utopia was wiped out, but his ideas were not. Adopted by the Quaker political economist John Bellers later in the century, they were transmitted through him to Robert Owen, whose utopian hopes and radical social programmes they profoundly influenced; they were thereafter incorporated into Marx's labour theory of value, cited at length by Eduard Bernstein in his revisionist writings on social democracy, endorsed by the reformer Joshua Rowntree, and studied by modern full-employment economists. In 1968 all of Plockhoy's publications, Dutch and English, were translated into

---

[39] Zavala, *More in New Spain*, p. 19; Warren, *Quiroga*, pp. 118, 120–1; Ganson, *Guaraní Under Spanish Rule*, p. 84; Martínez-Serna, 'Jesuit-Indian Encounters', p. 8; Samuel H. Brockunier, *The Irrepressible Democrat, Roger Williams* (New York, 1940), pp. 283–9; Rivett, 'Christian Transformations', p. 11; Edward G. Gray, *New World Babel: Languages and Nations in Early America* (Princeton, NJ, 1999), ch. iii; Kenneth L. Miner, 'John Eliot of Massachusetts and the Beginnings of American Linguistics', *Historiographia Linguistica,* 1 (1974), 169–83; Stephen A. Guice, 'The Linguistic Work of John Eliot' (Ph.D. Diss., Michigan State University, 1990).

French as appendices to a treatise on Plockhoy's co-operative utopianism and Christian ecumenism published by the Ecole Pratique des Hautes Etudes.[40] And if Kelpius' Chapter of Perfection quickly disappeared, the spirit of German pietism did not, and produced enduring communities of Mennonites, Amish, Dunkards, and Schwenkfelders. Even Matthias Baumann's hallucinatory perfectionism had important consequences: it helped inspire the many 'holiness revivals' of the nineteenth century in both Europe and America and left traces in modern American evangelicalism.[41]

The search for perfection, generated in Europe's vortex, when played out in the spatial amplitudes of the West, was the source not of monstrous tyrannies but of spiritual and moral striving. It did not become the 'recipe for bloodshed' that Berlin so feared because everywhere it lacked the ultimate power to coerce. Utopianism, secular or religious, becomes a 'road to inhumanity' when it is enforced by a monopoly of power — ultimate, unconstrained power in whatever form it might appear: the repressive power of the Soviet state, the annihilatory power of the Nazi regime, the mind-blinding power of Maoist gangs, the suffocating power of Islamic fundamentalism, each of which emerged through distinctive historical circumstances, to seek by violence what could not be achieved by persuasion.

Did Berlin not know this? In some sense of course he did. 'Two Concepts' was formally cast as a discourse on the permissible limits of coercion; 'force' and 'constraint' are repeatedly referred to, and Berlin denied that all historical conflicts are reducible to conflicts of ideas. But

---

[40] Davis, *Utopia*, pp. 334–8; 'P.B.', ed., *Industry Brings Plenty. John Bellers' Scheme for a Colledge of Industry* (London, 1916); Tim Hitchcock, 'John Bellers', *Oxford Dictionary of National Biography* (Oxford, 2004); Robert Owen, *The Life of Robert Owen*... (London, 1857), p. 240; idem, *A Supplementary Appendix*... (London, 1858) reprints Bellers' *Colledge of Industry* and writes of Bellers: 'Whatever merit can be due to an individual for the original discovery of a plan that, in its consequences, is calculated to effect more substantial and permanent benefit to mankind than any ever yet perhaps contemplated by the human mind, it all belongs exclusively to John Bellers'; Eduard Bernstein, *Cromwell and Communism: Socialism and Democracy in the Great English Revolution* ([1895] trans. H. J. Stenning, London, 1930), ch. xv; Joshua Rowntree, *Social Service: Its Place in the Society of Friends* (London, 1913), pp. 48–54; J. K. Fuz, *Welfare Economics in English Utopias*... (The Hague, 1952), pp. 55–62; Jean Séguy, *Utopie Coopérative et Oecuménisme: Pieter Cornelisz Plockhoy van Zurick-Zee, 1620–1700* (Paris, La Haye, 1968).
[41] C. Lee Hopple, 'Spatial Development of the Southeastern Pennsylvania Plain Dutch...', *Pennsylvania Folklife*, 21 (1971–2), 18–20, 30–40; Yoder (ed.), *Rhineland Emigrants*, p. 99; Melvin E. Dieter, *The Holiness Revival of the Nineteenth Century* (Metuchen, NJ, 1980).

political concepts, he believed, when not subjected to rational criticism can 'acquire an unchecked momentum and an irresistible power over multitudes'.[42] From his embattled position in the defence of a liberal alternative to totalitarianism the enemy was ideological perfectionism, the passionate pursuit of which he took to be the driving force behind the twentieth century's tyrannies. No one knew better than Berlin or expressed more brilliantly the genealogy and structure of perfectionist ideas. But their threat to civilisation, in the most general terms, lay not in their intrinsic malevolence but in the brutality of those who implacably imposed them: the populist thugs, the fanatical monopolists of power— beings utterly alien to Berlin's sensibilities, incomprehensible to his humanely inquiring mind.

---

[42] Berlin, 'Two Concepts of Liberty', pp. 119–21, 132.

KEYNES LECTURE IN ECONOMICS

The Origins of Fair Play

KEN BINMORE
Fellow of the Academy

All animals are equal but some are more equal than others.

Orwell's *Animal Farm*

1. Introduction

THIS LECTURE IS A BRIEF OVERVIEW of an evolutionary theory of fairness. The ideas are fleshed out in a book *Natural Justice,* which is itself a condensed version of an earlier two-volume book *Game Theory and the Social Contract* (Binmore 2005, 1994, 1998).

2. How and why did fairness norms evolve?

My answer to the question *why?* is relatively uncontroversial among anthropologists. Sharing food makes good evolutionary sense, because animals who share food thereby insure themselves against hunger. It is for this reason that sharing food is thought to be so common in the natural world.

The vampire bat is a particularly exotic example of a food-sharing species. The bats roost in caves in large numbers during the day. At night, they forage for prey, from whom they suck blood if they can, but they are not always successful. If they fail to obtain blood for several successive nights, they die. The evolutionary pressure to share blood is therefore strong.

The biologist Wilkinson (1984) reports that a hungry bat begs for blood from a roostmate, who will sometimes respond by regurgitating some of the blood it is carrying in its own stomach. This is not too surprising when the roostmates are related, but the bats also share blood with roostmates who are not relatives. The behaviour is nevertheless evolutionarily stable, because the sharing is done on a *reciprocal* basis, which means that a bat is much more likely to help out a roostmate that has helped it out in the past. Bats that refuse to help out their fellows therefore risk not being helped out themselves in the future.

Vampire bats have their own way of sharing, and we have ours. We call our way of sharing 'fairness'. If the accidents of our evolutionary history had led to our sharing in some other way, it would not occur to us to attribute some special role to our current fairness norms. Whatever alternative norms we then found ourselves using would seem as solidly founded as those we find ourselves using today.

The *how?* questions are more troublesome. How do our current fairness norms work? How did they evolve? Both questions need to be addressed together, because each throws light on the other. In particular, I think that we need to be sceptical about answers to the first *how?* question that require our postulating 'hopeful monsters' when we seek to answer the second *how?* question. Richard Dawkins (1976) tirelessly explains how the eye might have evolved as the end-product of a process involving many small steps. We need to be able to do the same for the evolutionary processes that created our sense of fairness.

3. The Original Position

How do our fairness norms work? My thesis is that all the fairness norms that we actually use in daily life have a common deep structure that is captured in a stylised form by an idea that John Rawls (1972) called the device of the *original position* in his celebrated *Theory of Justice*.

Rawls—who is commonly said to be the leading moral philosopher of the last century—uses the original position as a hypothetical standpoint from which to make judgements about how a just society would be organised. Members of a society are asked to envisage the social contract to which they would agree *if* their current roles were concealed from them behind a 'veil of ignorance'. Behind this veil of ignorance, the distribution of advantage in the planned society would seem determined as though by a lottery. Devil take the hindmost then becomes an unattractive principle for those bargaining in the original position, since you yourself might end up with the lottery ticket that assigns you to the rear.

Rawls defends the device of the original position as an operationalisation of Immanuel Kant's categorical imperative, but I think this is just window-dressing. The idea certainly hits the spot with most people when they hear it for the first time, but I do not believe this is because they have a natural bent for metaphysics. I think it is because they recognise a principle that matches up with the fairness norms that they actually use every day in solving the equilibrium selection problem in the myriads of small coordination games of which daily life largely consists.

It is important to emphasise that I am not following Rawls here in talking about the major coordination problems faced by a nation state. Our sense of fairness did not evolve for use on such a grand scale. Nor am I talking about the artificial and unrealistic principles of justice promoted by self-appointed moral pundits, to which people commonly offer only lip service. Nor am I talking about the kind of moral pathology that led Osama bin Laden to believe that thousands of innocent New Yorkers should die to compensate for the humiliations that he thought Islam had received at the hands of the West. I am talking about the real principles that we actually use in solving everyday coordination problems.

The sort of coordination problems I have in mind are those that we commonly solve without thought or discussion, usually so smoothly and effortlessly that we do not even notice that there is a coordination problem to be solved. Who goes through that door first? How long does Adam get to speak before it is Eve's turn? Who moves how much in a narrow corridor when a fat lady burdened with shopping passes a teenage boy with a ring through his nose? Who should take how much of a popular dish of which there is not enough to go around? Who gives way to whom when cars are manoeuvring in heavy traffic? Who gets that parking space? Whose turn is it to wash the dishes tonight? These are picayune problems, but if conflict arose every time they needed to be solved, our societies would fall apart.

Most people are surprised at the suggestion that there might be something problematic about how two people pass each other in the corridor. When interacting with people from our own culture, we commonly solve such coordination problems so effortlessly that we do not even think of them as problems. Our fairness programme then runs well below the level of consciousness, like our internal routines for driving cars or tying shoelaces. As with Molière's Monsieur Jourdain, who was delighted to discover that he had been speaking prose all his life, we are moral in small-scale situations without knowing that we are moral.

Just as we only take note of a thumb when it is sore, we tend to notice moral rules only when attempts are made to apply them in situations for which they are ill-adapted. We are then in the same position as Konrad Lorenz (1997) when he observed a totally inexperienced baby jackdaw go through all the motions of taking a bath when placed on a marble-topped table. By triggering such instinctive behaviour under pathological circumstances, Lorenz learned a great deal about what is instinctive and what is not when a bird takes a bath. But this vital information is gained only by avoiding the mistake of supposing that bath-taking behaviour confers some evolutionary advantage on birds placed on marble-topped tables.

Similarly, one can learn a lot about the mechanics of moral algorithms by triggering them under pathological circumstances—but only if one does not make the mistake of supposing that the moral rules are adapted to the coordination problems they fail to solve. However, it is precisely from such sore-thumb situations that I think traditional moralists unconsciously distil their ethical principles. We discuss these and only these situations endlessly, because our failure to coordinate successfully brings them forcefully to our attention.

This is not to say that we should not talk about such games. On the contrary, it is partly because we need to extend the class of games that our social contract handles adequately that it is worth studying the problem at all. But we will not learn how natural morality works by confining our attention to situations where it does not.

4. Justice as fairness

John Rawls (1972) offers a theory that reduces our notions of justice to those of fairness. I think our traditonal personification of justice as a blindfolded maiden bearing a pair of scales in one hand and a sword in the other provides some support for this reduction. Her blindfold can be identified with Rawls's veil of ignorance. She needs her scales behind the veil of ignorance to weigh up the relative well-being of different people in different situations.

The issue of how interpersonal comparisons are to be made is often treated as a side issue of no great importance by tradititonal moral philosophers, but it is clearly necessary for people to be able to make such comparisons in order for it to be possible for them to use the original position to make fairness judgements. If we were not able to say whether we thought it preferable to be Adam in one situtation as opposed to being Eve in another situation, we would be helpless to say anything at all behind the veil of ignorance. Under mild conditions, John Harsanyi (1977) showed that such empathetic preferences—preferences requiring us to put ourselves in the position of another to see things from their point of view—can be summarised by naming a rate at which Adam's units of utility are to be traded off against Eve's units. But how do we acquire such standards of interpersonal comparison to which we implicitly appeal every time we make a fairness judgement?

Finally, attention needs to be drawn to the sword carried by our blindfolded maiden. The enforcement question is often neglected altogether by traditional moral philsophers, who commonly take for granted that fairness exists to trump the unbridled use of power that they think would otherwise reign supreme. However, I shall be arguing that fairness evolved as a means of *balancing* power rather than as a *substitute* for power. Without power being somehow exercised in her support, our blindfolded maiden would be no more than a utopian fancy. As Thomas Hobbes put it: 'Covenants without the sword are but words.'

5. Choosing between traditions

When I argue against traditional moral philosophers, I have in mind the metaphysical tradition that begins with Plato, and continues through Descartes and Kant to modern times, where it is firmly established as the reigning orthodoxy. Even John Harsanyi and John Rawls, from whom I draw much of my inspiration, regarded themselves as Kantians.

However, the naturalistic tradition is just as venerable. It begins with Aristotle, and continues through Epicurus, Hobbes and Hume, to the present day. Its leading modern exponent was John Mackie (1977), whose *Ethics: Inventing Right and Wrong* seems to me to offer a devastating critique of the orthodox view that morality somehow has an absolute status unconnected with the biological and social history of the human species. Instead of imagining that it is adequate in studying human morality to adopt the pose of Rodin's *Thinker* and await inspiration, he tells us to read the works of anthropologists and game theorists.

It is to this project that this paper and the books from which it is derived are devoted. It is particularly important to understand that the project requires disavowing Immanuel Kant on moral questions. If his categorical imperative implies anything specific, it surely calls for cooperation in the one-shot Prisoners' Dilemma, but his claim that such behaviour is *rational* seems absurd to game theorists. Our philosophical hero is David Hume, who was preaching our creed to an uncomprehending audience two hundred years before the first game theorist was born.

6. Pure foraging societies

There is no shortage of cultural differences between Kalahari bushmen, African pygmies, Andaman islanders, Greenland eskimos, Australian aborigines, Paraguayan Indians, and Siberian nomads, but the consensus is strong among modern anthropologists that these and other pure hunter-gatherer societies that survived into the twentieth century all operated social contracts without bosses or social distinctions in which food, especially meat, was shared on a markedly egalitarian basis.[1] Even Westermarck, a leading anthroplogist who was famous for his moral relativism, agreed that the Golden Rule—that we should do as we would be done by—was universally endorsed in such societies.

Two caveats are important here. The first is that it really matters that we are talking about *pure* foraging societies, in which the economic means of production remained the same as among our ancestors before the agricultural revolution of ten thousand or more years ago. The evidence is strong that a society's social contract evolves in tandem with its economy. I suspect that one would look in vain for universal principles underlying the social contracts that cultural history generated in different times and places after the agricultural revolution.

The second caveat is that one needs to put aside the idea that the egalitarianism of pure foraging societies makes them pastoral idylls, inhabited by noble savages filled with sweetness and light. Infanticide and murder are common. So is selfishness. Citizens of foraging societies do not honour their social contract because they like giving up food when they are

---

[1] See, for example, Bailey (1991), Damas (1972), Erdal and Whiten (1996), Evans-Pritchard (1940), Fürer-Haimendorf (1967), Gardner (1972), Hawkes *et al.* (1993), Helm (1972), Isaac (1978), Kaplan and Hill (1985), Knauft (1991), Lee (1979), Riches (1982), Tanaka (1980), Megarry (1995), Meggitt (1962), Rogers (1972), Sahlins (1974), Turnbull (1965).

hungry. They will therefore cheat on the social contract by secretly hoarding food if they think they can get away with it. The reason they comply with the norm most of the time is because their fellows will punish them if they do not.

Nor is there necessarily anything very nice about the way that food and other possessions are shared. In some societies, a fair allocation is achieved through 'tolerated stealing'. Eve may grab some of Adam's food because she thinks he has more than his fair share. If the rest of the group agree, Adam is helpless to resist. Even when possessions are voluntarily surrendered to others, the giver will sometimes explain that he or she is only complying with the norm to avoid being the object of the envy that precedes more serious sanctions. Indeed, we would find it unbearably stifling to live in some foraging societies because of the continual envious monitoring of who has what.

There is therefore squabbling and pettiness aplenty in pure foraging communities, but there is also laughter and good fellowship. In brief, human nature seems much the same in foraging societies as in our own. I therefore think the strong parallels that anthropologists have uncovered between the social contracts of geographically distant groups living in starkly different environments have important implications for us. If their nature includes an instinctive disposition to use fairness norms that all share the deep structure of the Rawlsian original position, is it not likely that the same disposition is built into our nature too?

7. Game theory

John Mackie invited us to look at both anthropology and game theory. The basic idea in game theory is that of a Nash equilibrium. John Nash was the subject of the movie *A Beautiful Mind,* but the writers of the movie got the idea hopelessly wrong in the scene where they tried to explain how Nash equilibria work. However, the idea is actually very simple.

A game is any situation in which people or animals interact. The plans of action of the players are called strategies. A Nash equilibrium is any profile of strategies—one for each player—in which each player's strategy is a best reply to the strategies of the other players.

Some simple examples appear in Figure 1. The game on the left is the famous Prisoners' Dilemma. The game on the right is the Stag Hunt, which game theorists use to illustrate a story of Jean-Jacques Rousseau.

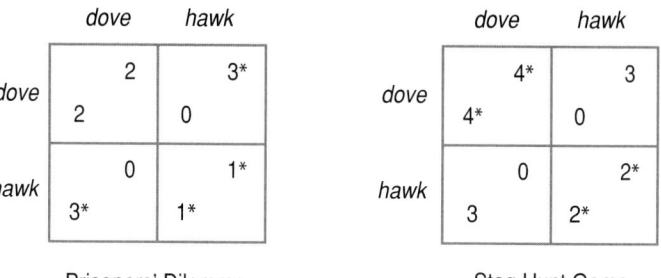

Figure 1. Two toy games.

Each of these toy games has two players, whom I call Adam and Eve. In both the Prisoners' Dilemma and the Stag Hunt, Adam has two strategies, *dove* and *hawk*, that are represented by the rows of the payoff table. Eve also has two strategies, *dove* and *hawk*, represented by the columns of the payoff table. The four cells of the payoff table correspond to the possible outcomes of the game. Each cell contains two numbers, one for Adam and one for Eve. The number in the south-west corner is Adam's payoff for the corresponding outcome of the game. The number in the north-east corner is Eve's payoff.

The payoffs will not usually correspond to money in the applications relevant in this lecture. Using the theory of revealed preference, economists have shown that *any* consistent behaviour whatever can be modelled by assuming that the players are behaving as though seeking to maximise the average value of *something*. This abstract something—which obviously varies with the context—is called utility. When assuming that a player is maximising his or her expected payoff in a game, we are therefore not taking for granted that people are selfish. In fact, we make no assumptions about their motivation except that the players pursue their goals—whatever they may be—in a consistent manner.

It would be easy for the players to maximise their expected payoffs if they knew what strategy their opponent was going to choose. For example, if Adam knew that Eve was going to choose *dove* in the Prisoners' Dilemma, he would maximise his payoff by choosing *hawk*. That is to say, *hawk* is Adam's best reply to Eve's choice of *dove*, a fact indicated in Figure 1 by starring Adam's payoff in the cell that results if the players choose the strategy profile (*hawk*, *dove*). However, the problem in game theory is that a player does not normally know in advance what strategy the other player will choose.

A Nash equilibrium is a strategy profile in which each player's strategy is a best reply to the strategies chosen by the other players. In the examples of Figure 1, a cell in which both payoffs are starred therefore corresponds to a Nash equilibrium.

Nash equilibria are of interest for two reasons. If it is possible to single out the rational solution of a game, it must be a Nash equilibrium. For example, if Adam knows that Eve is rational, he would be stupid not to make the best reply to what he knows is her rational choice. The second reason is even more important. An evolutionary process that adjusts the players' strategy choices in the direction of increasing payoffs can only stop when it reaches a Nash equilibrium.

Because evolution stops working at an equilibrium, biologists say that Nash equilibria are evolutionarily stable.[2] Each relevant locus on a chromosome is then occupied by the gene with maximal fitness. Since a gene is just a molecule, it cannot *choose* to maximise its fitness, but evolution makes it seem as though it had. This is a valuable insight, because it allows biologists to use the rational interpretation of an equilibrium to predict the outcome of an evolutionary process, without following each complicated twist and turn that the process might take.

The title of Richard Dawkins' (1976) *Selfish Gene* expresses the idea in a nutshell, but it also provokes a lot of criticism. It is easy to be tolerant of critics like the old lady I heard rebuking Dawkins for failing to see that a molecule can't possibly have free will, but tolerance is less easy in the case of critics like Lewontin or Gould, who chose to whip up public hostility against Edward Wilson and his followers on similar grounds. As Alcock's (2001) *Triumph of Sociobiology* documents, they wilfully pretended not to understand that sociobiologists seek explanations of biological phenomena in terms of *ultimate* causes rather than *proximate* causes.

Why, for example, do songbirds sing in the early spring? The proximate cause is long and difficult. This molecule knocked against that molecule. This chemical reaction is catalysed by that enzyme. But the ultimate cause is that the birds are signalling territorial claims to each other in order to avoid unnecessary conflict. They neither know nor care that this behaviour is rational. They just do what they do. But the net effect of an immensely complicated evolutionary process is that songbirds behave *as*

---

[2] John Maynard Smith (1982) defines an evolutionarily stable strategy (ESS) to be a best reply to itself that is a better reply to any alternative best reply than the alternative best reply is to itself, but biologists seldom worry about the small print involving alternative best replies.

though they had rationally chosen to maximise their fitness by operating a Nash equilibrium of their game of life.

The Prisoners' Dilemma is the most famous of all toy games. A whole generation of scholars swallowed the line that this trivial game embodies the essence of the problem of human cooperation. The reason is that its only Nash equilibrium calls for both Adam and Eve to play *hawk*, but they would both get more if they cooperated by both playing *dove* instead. The hopeless task that scholars set themselves was therefore to give reasons why game theory's resolution of this supposed 'paradox of rationality' is mistaken.

Game theorists think it just plain wrong to claim that the Prisoners' Dilemma embodies the essence of the problem of human cooperation. On the contrary, it represents a situation in which the dice are as loaded against the emergence of cooperation as they could possibly be. If the great game of life played by the human species were the Prisoners' Dilemma, we would not have evolved as social animals! We therefore see no more need to solve some invented paradox of rationality than to explain why strong swimmers drown when thrown in a lake with their feet encased in concrete. No paradox of rationality exists. Rational players do not cooperate in the Prisoners' Dilemma, because the conditions necessary for rational cooperation are absent in this game.

Fortunately the paradox-of-rationality phase in the history of game theory is just about over. Insofar as they are remembered, the many fallacies that were invented in hopeless attempts to show that it is rational to cooperate in the Prisoners' Dilemma are now mostly quoted as entertaining examples of what psychologists call magical reasoning, in which logic is twisted to secure some desired outcome. The leading example remains Kant's claim that rationality demands obeying his categorical imperative. In the Prisoners' Dilemma, rational players would then all choose *dove*, because this is the strategy that would be best if everybody chose it.

The following argument is a knock-down refutation of this nonsense. So as not to beg any questions, we begin by asking where the payoff table that represents the players' preferences in the Prisoners' Dilemma comes from. The economists' answer is that we discover the players' preferences by observing the choices they make (or would make) when solving one-person decision problems.

Writing a larger payoff for Adam in the bottom-left cell of the payoff table of the Prisoners' Dilemma than in the top-left cell therefore means that Adam would choose *hawk* in the one-person decision problem that he would face if he knew in advance that Eve had chosen *dove*. Similarly, writing a larger payoff in the bottom-right cell means that Adam would choose *hawk* when faced with the one-person decision problem in which he knew in advance that Eve had chosen *hawk*.

The very definition of the game therefore says that *hawk* is Adam's best reply when he knows that Eve's choice is *dove*, and also when he knows her choice is *hawk*. So he does not need to know anything about Eve's actual choice to know his best reply to it. It is rational for him to play *hawk* whatever strategy she is planning to choose. Nobody ever denies this utterly trivial argument. Instead, one is told that it cannot be relevant to anything real, because it reduces the analysis of the Prisoners' Dilemma to a tautology. But who would say the same of $2+2=4$?

In Rousseau's Stag Hunt story, Adam and Eve agree to cooperate in hunting a stag, but when they separate to put their plan into action, each may be tempted to abandon the joint enterprise by the prospect of bagging a hare for themselves. The starred payoffs in the payoff table show that there are two Nash equilibria in pure strategies, one in which the players cooperate by both playing *dove*, and one in which they defect by both playing *hawk*. We therefore have our first example of the equilibrium selection problem that will be our major preoccupation in the rest of this lecture.

If a society found itself at a social contract corresponding to the inefficient equilibrium in which everybody plays *hawk*, why would not they just agree to move to the efficient social contract in which everybody plays *dove*?

As the biologist Sewell-Wright explained, this may not be so easy if the task of moving from one equilibrium to another is left to evolution. But we are not animals who have to wait for the slow forces of evolution to take them to a new social contract. We can talk to each other and agree to alter the way we do things. But can we trust each other to keep any agreement we might make? The Stag Hunt is used by experts in international relations under the name of the Security Dilemma to draw attention to the problems that can arise even when the players are rational.

Suppose that Adam and Eve's current social contract in the Stag Hunt is the Nash equilibrium in which they both play *hawk*. However hard Adam seeks to persuade Eve that he plans to play *dove* in the future and so she should follow suit, she will remain unconvinced. The reason is that whatever Adam is actually planning to play, it is in his interests to persuade Eve to play *dove*. If he succeeds, he will get 4 rather than 0 if he is planning to play *dove*, and 3 rather than 2 if he is planning to play *hawk*. Rationality alone therefore does not allow Eve to deduce anything about his plan of action from what he says, because he is going to say the same thing no matter what his real plan may be! Adam may actually think that Eve is unlikely to be persuaded to switch from *hawk* and hence be planning to play *hawk* himself, yet still try to persuade her to play *dove*.

This Machiavellian story shows that attributing rationality to the players is not enough to resolve the equilibrium selection problem—even in a seemingly transparent case like the Stag Hunt. If Adam and Eve continue to play *hawk* in the Stag Hunt, they will regret their failure to coordinate on playing *dove*, but neither can be accused of being irrational, because both are doing as well as they can given the behaviour of their opponent.

The standard response is to ask why game theorists insist that it is irrational for people to trust one another. Would not Adam and Eve both be better off if both had more faith in each other's honesty? But nobody denies that Adam and Eve would be better off if they trusted each other, any more than anybody denies that they would be better off in the Prisoners' Dilemma if they were assigned new payoffs that made them care more about the welfare of their opponent. Nor do game theorists say it is irrational for people to trust each other. They only say that it is not rational to trust people without a good reason: that trust cannot be taken on trust. Who trusts a used-car dealer or a dean? What wife doesn't keep an eye on her husband? Who does not count their change?

The underlying point here is that those of us who would like society to move to what we think will be a better social contract just waste our time if we simply bleat that people should be more trusting or honest. We need to try and understand how and why it makes sense to be trusting or honest in some situations, but not in others. We can then hope to improve our social contract by doing what we can to promote the former situations at the expense of the latter.

8. Coordination Games

I think that fairness evolved as Nature's answer to the equilibrium selection problem in the human game of life. However, before I can elaborate on this idea, it is necessary to give examples of some toy games in which the equilibrium selection problem is even more pressing than in the Stag Hunt.

The game on the left of Figure 2 is a simplified version of the Driving Game that we play each morning when we get into our cars and drive to work. It does not matter on which of its two Nash equilibria a society coordinates, but it is obviously very important that we all coordinate on the same equilibrium. In Britain and Japan, the accidents of our social history have resulted in our all driving on the left. In the USA and France, everybody drives on the right. Culture can therefore be a significant factor in the way we solve an equilibrium selection problem. Indeed, it can be argued that a society's culture is nothing more than the set of conventions that it uses to solve equilibrium selection problems. A politically incorrect story accompanies the Battle of the Sexes on the right of Figure 2. Adam and Eve are on their honeymoon in New York City. At breakfast, they discussed whether to attend a boxing match or the ballet in the evening, but without reaching an agreement. During the day they got separated in the crowds, and they must now choose where to go in the evening independently.

The Battle of the Sexes has two Nash equilibria,[3] in one of which Adam and Eve both go to the boxing match, and one in which they both go the ballet. But, unlike the case of the Driving Game, it now matters to the players which equilibrium is chosen, because Adam prefers boxing to ballet, and Eve prefers ballet to boxing.

9. Reciprocity

I have already signalled my intention of modelling a social contract as the set of common understandings in a society that allows its citizens to coordinate on one of the many equilibria of their game of life. Game theorists think that only equilibria are viable in this role, because, when each citizen

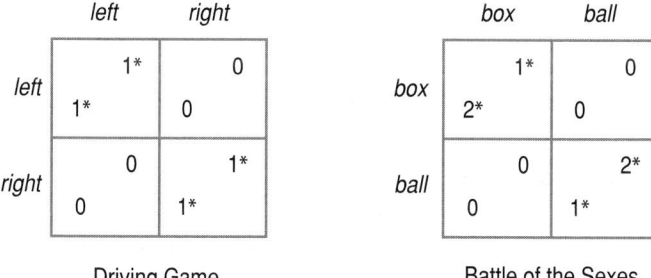

Figure 2. Coordination games.

---

[3] Only pure strategies are considered here.

has independent goals which sometimes conflict with each other, only equilibria can survive in the absence of an external enforcement agency. In brief, only equilibria are self-policing.

The suggestion that a social contract is no more than a set of common understandings among players acting in their own enlightened self interest commonly gets a sceptical reaction. How can anything very sturdy be erected on such a flimsy foundation? Surely a solidly built structure like the modern state must be firmly based on a rock of moral certitude, and only anarchy can result if everybody just does what takes his fancy? As Gauthier (1986: 1) expresses it in denying Hume (1975: 280): 'Were duty no more than interest, morals would be superfluous.'

I believe such objections to be misconceived. Firstly, there are no rock-like moral certitudes that exist prior to society. To adopt a metaphor that sees such moral certitudes as foundation stones is therefore to construct a castle in the air. Society is more usefully seen as a dynamic organism, and the moral codes that regulate its internal affairs are the conventional understandings which ensure that its constituent parts operate smoothly together when it is in good health. Moreover, the origin of these moral codes is to be looked for in historical theories of biological, social, and political evolution, and not in the works of abstract thinkers no matter how intoxicating the wisdom they distil. Nor is it correct to say that anarchy will necessarily result if everybody 'just' does what he wants. A person would be stupid in seeking to achieve a certain end if he ignored the fact that what other people are doing is relevant to the means for achieving that end. Intelligent people will *coordinate* their efforts to achieve their individual goals without necessarily being compelled or coerced by real or imaginary bogeymen.

The extent to which simple implicit agreements to coordinate on an equilibrium can generate high levels of cooperation among populations of egoists is not something that is easy to appreciate in the abstract. That *reciprocity* is the secret has been repeatedly discovered, most recently by the political scientist Axelrod (1984) in the eighties and the biologist Trivers (1971) in the seventies. However, David Hume (1978: 521) had already put his finger on the relevant mechanism some 230 years before:

> I learn to do service to another, without bearing him any real kindness: because I foresee, that he will return my service, in expectation of another of the same kind, and in order to maintain the same correspondence of good offices with me or others. And accordingly, after I have serv'd him and he is in possession of the advantage arising from my action, he is induc'd to perform his part, as foreseeing the consequences of his refusal.

In spite of all the eighteenth-century sweetness and light, one should take special note of what Hume says about foreseeing the consequences of refusal. The point is that a failure to carry out your side of the arrangement will result in your being *punished*. The punishment may consist of no more than a refusal by the other party to deal with you in future. Or it may be that the punishment consists of having to endure the disapproval of those whose respect is necessary if you are to maintain your current status level in the community. However, nothing excludes more active forms of punishment. In particular, the punishment might be administered by the judiciary, if the services in question are the subject of a legal contract.

At first sight, this last observation seems to contradict the requirement that the conventional arrangements under study be *self-policing*. The appearance of a contradiction arises because one tends to think of the apparatus of the state as somehow existing independently of the game of life that people play. But the laws that societies make are not part of the rules of this game. One *cannot* break the rules of the game of life, but one certainly can break the laws that man invents.

Legal rules are no more than particularly well-codified conventions. And policemen, judges and public executioners do not exist outside society. Those charged with the duty of enforcing the laws that a society formally enacts are themselves only players in the game of life. However high-minded a society's officials may believe themselves to be, the fact is that society would cease to work in the long run if the duties assigned to them were incompatible with their own incentives. I am talking now about corruption. And here I do not have so much in mind the conscious form of corruption in which officials take straight bribes for services rendered. I have in mind the long-term and seemingly inevitable process by means of which bureaucracies gradually cease to operate in the interests of those they were designed to serve, and instead end up serving the interests of the bureaucrats themselves.

10. The folk theorem

Game theorists rediscovered Hume's insight that reciprocity is the mainspring of human sociality in the early fifties when characterising the outcomes that can be supported as equilibria in a repeated game. The result is known as the *folk theorem,* since it was formulated independently by several game theorists in the early fifties (Aumann and Maschler 1995).

The theorem tells us that external enforcement is unnecessary to make a collection of Mr Hydes cooperate like Dr Jekylls. It is only necessary that the players be sufficiently patient and that they know they are to interact together for the foreseeable future. The rest can be left to their enlightened self-interest, provided that they can all monitor each other's behaviour without too much effort—as, for example, must have been the case when we were all members of small hunter-gatherer communities.

What outcomes can be sustained as Nash equilibria when a one-shot game is repeated indefinitely often? The answer provided by the folk theorem is very reassuring. Any outcome whatever of the one-shot game—including all the outcomes that are not Nash equilibria of the one-shot game—can be sustained as Nash equilibria of the *repeated* game, provided that they award each player a payoff that is at least as large as the player's minimax payoff in the one-shot game.

The idea of the proof is absurdly simple. We first determine how the players have to cooperate to obtain a particular outcome. For example, in the repeated Prisoners' Dilemma, Adam and Eve need only play *dove* at each repetition to obtain an average payoff of 2. In the repeated Battle of the Sexes, Adam and Eve can each get an average payoff of $1\frac{1}{2}$ if they attend the boxing match on odd days and the ballet on even days. To make such cooperative behaviour into a Nash equilibrium, it is necessary that a player who deviates be punished. This is where the players' minimax payoffs enter the picture. The worst punishment that Eve can inflict on Adam in the long run is to hold him to his minimax payoff, because when she acts to try and *minimise* his payoff, he will respond by playing whatever strategy *maximises* his payoff given her choice of punishment strategy. As long as the average payoff a player gets by cooperating exceeds his minimax payoff, the player can therefore be kept in line if he knows that his opponents will respond to any deviation on his part by holding him to his minimax strategy.

In the Prisoners' Dilemma, the minimax payoff for each player is 1, because the worst that one player can do to the other is play *hawk*, in which case the victim does best to respond by playing *hawk* as well. The folk theorem therefore tells us that we can sustain the outcome in which both players always play *dove* as a Nash equilibrium in the indefinitely repeated game. In the Battle of the Sexes, the minimax payoff for each player is also 1.[4] For example, the worst that Eve can do to Adam is play

---

[4] Provided that we neglect the possible use of mixed strategies.

ball, in which case he does best to respond by playing *ball* as well. The folk theorem therefore tells us that we can sustain the outcome in which both players alternate between attending the boxing match and the ballet as an equilibrium in the repeated game.

The kind of equilibrium strategy described above is often called the *grim* strategy, because the punishment that keeps potential deviants on the straight and narrow path is the worst possible punishment indefinitely prolonged. One sometimes sees this strategy in use in commercial contexts where maintaining trust is vital to the operation of a market. The Antwerp diamond market is a good example. Traders pass diamonds back and forward for examination without any writing of contracts or attempt to monitor those trusted with diamonds on approval. Why do not the traders cheat each other? Because any suspicion of misconduct will result in a trader being excluded from the market thereafter. To quote a trader in the similar New York antique market: 'Sure I trust him. You know the ones to trust in this business. The ones who betray you, bye-bye' (*New York Times,* 29 August 1991).

However, one seldom sees the grim strategy in use in games played among social insiders. The punishments are then typically minimal rather than maximal, because the deviant requiring punishment may then turn out to be yourself, or one of your friends or relations. Napoleon's exile in Elba is an extreme example. After all, any ruler may be overthrown. On the other hand, we bourgeois folk do not ever expect to steal a pizza, and hence the Californian doctrine of three strikes and you are out.

It is important to recognise that very few of the punishments that sustain a social contract are administered through the legal system. Indeed, nearly all punishments are adminstered without either the punishers or the victim being aware that a punishment has taken place. No stick is commonly flourished. What happens most of the time is that the carrot is withdrawn a tiny bit. Shoulders are turned slightly away. Greetings are imperceptibly gruffer. Eyes wander elsewhere. These are all warnings that your body ignores at its peril.

The accounts that anthropologists offer of the higher stages of punishment observed among pure hunter-gatherer societies are particularly telling, since they mirror so accurately similar phenomena that the academic world uses to keep rogue thinkers in line. First there is laughter. If this does not work—and who likes being laughed at—the next stage is boycotting. Nobody talks to the offending party, or refers to his research. Only the final stage is maximal: a persistent offender is expelled from the group, or is unable to get his work published.

Once the subtle nature of the web of reciprocal rewards and punishments that sustains a social contract has been appreciated, it becomes easier to understand why it is so hard to reform corrupt societies in which criminality has become socially acceptable. As the case of Prohibition shows, imposing the type of draconian penalty in which rednecks delight on the criminals unlucky enough to be caught is unlikely to be effective. The resulting disincentives will be almost certainly be inadequate, since the probability of any individual being unlucky is necessarily small when nearly everybody is guilty.

11. Selecting Equilibria

The study of Nash equilibria in repeated games offers us clues about how social contracts are sustained. I think that deontological philosophers derive their inspiration from focusing their attention largely on such stability questions. Conservative economists are led to similar positions by choosing to examine models that only have one equilibrium.

However, the folk theorem tells us that indefinitely repeated games—including those markets that are repeated on a daily basis—usually have very large numbers of equilibria amongst which a choice must somehow be made. The response that only efficient equilibria need be considered does not help with this equilibrium selection problem, because efficient equilibria are also usually present in large numbers.[5]

One way of selecting an equilibrium is to delegate the task to a leader or an elite, but our foraging ancestors had no leaders or elites. Some other equilibrium selection device was therefore necessary. Fairness is our name for the device that evolution came up with. Consequentialist philosophers commonly offer metaphysical explanations of why their own idiosyncratic theories of fairness should prevail, but the truth is simultaneously more complex and more prosaic. Our ancestors were fair for much the same reason that the French drive on the right and the Japanese on the left. Any solution to the equilibrium selection problem is better than none.

However, the consequentialists and the radical reformers of the left whom they inspire make a more serious mistake when they fail to appre-

---

[5] A (Pareto) efficient outcome is one on which no player can improve his payoff without making another player worse off. For example, the equilibria (*box, box*) and (*ball, ball*) are both efficient outcomes for the Battle of the Sexes.

ciate that fairness evolved to select among *equilibria*—that fairness norms that actually work are not substitutes for power, but merely help to determine how power is balanced. Deontologists and their conservative followers do not make this mistake. Instead, they close their eyes to the possibility of rational reform by failing to recognise that there may be alternative equilibria to those with which they familiar.

12. Deep structure of fairness

Recognition of the Golden Rule seems to be universal in human societies. Is there any reason why evolution should have written such a principle into our genes? Some equilibrium selection devices are obviously necessary for social life to be possible, but why should something like the Golden Rule have evolved?

If the Golden Rule is understood as a simplified version of the device of the original position, I think an answer to this question can be found by asking why social animals evolved in the first place. This is generally thought to have been because food-sharing has survival value.

The vampire bats of Section 2 provide an example. Unless a vampire bat can feed every sixty hours or so, it is likely to die. The advantages of sharing food among vampire bats are therefore strong—so strong that evolution has taught even unrelated bats to share blood on a reciprocal basis.

By sharing food, the bats are essentially *insuring* each other against hunger. Animals cannot write insurance contracts in the human manner, and even if they could, they would have no legal system to which to appeal if one animal were to hold up on his or her contractual obligation to the other. But the folk theorem tells us that evolution can get round the problem of external enforcement if the animals interact together on a *repeated* basis.

By coordinating on a suitable equilibrium in their repeated game of life, two animals who are able to monitor each other's behaviour sufficiently closely can achieve whatever could be achieved by negotiating a legally binding insurance contract. It will be easier for evolution to find its way to such an equilibrium if the animals are related, but the case of vampire bats shows that kinship is not necessary if the evolutionary pressures are sufficiently strong.

What considerations would Adam and Eve need to take into account when negotiating a similar mutual insurance pact?

Imagine a time before cooperative hunting had evolved, in which Adam and Eve foraged separately for food. Like vampire bats, they would sometimes come home lucky and sometimes unlucky. An insurance pact between them would specify how to share the available food on days when one was lucky and the other unlucky.

If Adam and Eve were rational players negotiating an insurance contract, they would not know in advance who was going to be lucky and who unlucky on any given day on which the contract would be invoked. To keep things simple, suppose that both possibilities are equally likely. Adam and Eve can then be seen as bargaining behind a *veil of uncertainty* that conceals who is going to turn out to be Ms Lucky or Mr Unlucky. Both players then bargain on the assumption that they are as likely to end up holding the share assigned to Mr Unlucky as they are to end up holding the share assigned to Ms Lucky.

I think the obvious parallel between bargaining over such mutual insurance pacts and bargaining in the original position is no accident. To nail the similarity down completely, we need only give Adam and Eve new names when they take their places behind Rawls's veil of ignorance. To honour the founders of game theory, Adam and Eve will be called John and Oskar.

Instead of Adam and Eve being uncertain about whether they will turn out to be Ms Lucky or Mr Unlucky, the new setup requires that John and Oskar pretend to be ignorant about whether they will turn out to be Adam or Eve. It then becomes clear that a move to the device of the original position requires only that the players imagine themselves in the shoes of somebody else—either Adam or Eve—rather than in the shoes of one of their own possible future selves.

If Nature wired us up to solve the simple insurance problems that arise in food-sharing, she therefore also simultaneously provided much of the wiring necessary to operate the original position.

Of course, in an insurance contract, the parties to the agreement do not have to *pretend* that they might end in somebody else's shoes. On the contrary, it is the reality of the prospect that they might turn out to be Ms Lucky or Mr Unlucky that motivates their writing a contract in the first place. But when the device of the original position is used to adjudicate fairness questions, then John knows perfectly well that he is actually Adam, and that it is physically impossible that he could become Eve. To use the device in the manner recommended by Rawls and Harsanyi, he therefore has to indulge in a counterfactual act of imagination. He cannot become Eve, but he must pretend that he could. How is this gap between reality and pretence to be bridged without violating the Linnaean dictum: *Natura non facit saltus*?

As argued earlier, I think that human ethics arose from Nature's attempt to solve certain equilibrium selection problems. But Nature does not jump from the simple to the complex in a single bound. She tinkers with existing structures rather than creating hopeful monsters. To make a naturalistic origin for the device of the original position plausible, it is therefore necessary to give some account of what tinkering she might have done.

In Peter Singer's *Expanding Circle* (1980), the circle that expands is the domain within which moral rules are understood to apply. For example, Jesus sought to expand the domain of the principle that you should love your neighbour by redefining a neighbour to be anyone at all. How might evolution expand the domain within which a moral rule operates?

My guess is that the domain of a moral rule sometimes expands when players misread signals from their environment, and so mistakenly apply a piece of behaviour or a way of thinking that has evolved for use within some inner circle to a larger set of people, or to a new game. When such a mistake is made, the players attempt to play their part in sustaining an equilibrium in the inner-circle game without fully appreciating that the outer-circle game has different rules. For example, Adam might treat Eve as a sibling even though they are unrelated. Or he might treat a one-shot game as though it were going to be repeated indefinitely often.

A strategy profile that is an equilibrium for an inner-circle game will not normally be an equilibrium for an outer-circle game. A rule that selects an equilibrium strategy in an inner-circle game will therefore normally be selected against if used in an outer-circle game. But there will be exceptions. When playing an outer-circle game as though it were an inner-circle game, the players will sometimes happen to coordinate on an equilibrium of the outer-circle game. The group will then have stumbled upon an equilibrium selection device for the outer-circle game. This device consists of the players behaving *as though* they were constrained by the rules of the inner-circle game, when the rules by which they are actually constrained are those of the outer-circle game.

I guess that nobody questions Aristotle's observation that the origins of moral behaviour are to be found in the family. A game theorist will offer the explanation that the equilibrium selection problem is easier for evolution to solve in such games. The reason why is to be found in Hamilton's (1963) rule, which explains that animals should be expected to care about a relative in proportion to their degree of relationship to the relative. For example, if Eve is Adam's full cousin, it makes evolutionary sense for him to count her fitness as worth one-eighth of his own fitness.[6] Family relationships therefore provide a natural basis for making the kind of interpersonal comparison of utility that is necessary to operate the device of the original position.

The circle was then ready to be expanded by including strangers in the game by treating them as honorary or fictive kinfolk, starting with outsiders adopted into the clan by marriage or cooption. Indeed, if you only interact on a regular basis with kinfolk, what other template for behaviour would be available?

The next step requires combining these two developments so that the original position gets to be used not just in situations in which Adam and Eve might turn out to be themselves in the role of Ms Lucky or Mr Unlucky, but in which they proceed as though it were possible for each of them to turn out to occupy the role of the other person. To accept that I may be unlucky may seem a long way from contemplating the possibility that I might become another person in another body, but is the difference really so great? After all, there is a sense in which none of us are the same person when comfortable and well fed as when tired and hungry. In different circumstances, we reveal different personalities and want different things.

To pursue this point, consider what is involved when rational players consider the various contingencies that may arise when planning ahead. To assess these, players compute their expected utility as a weighted average of the payoffs of all the future people—lucky or unlucky—that they might turn out to be after the dice has ceased to roll. When choosing a strategy in a family game, players similarly take their payoffs to be a weighted average of the fitnesses of everybody in their family.

In order to convert our ability to negotiate insurance contracts into a capacity for using fairness as a more general coordinating device in the game of life, all that is then needed is for us to hybridise these two processes by allowing players to replace one of the future persons that a roll of the dice might reveal them to be, by a person in another body. The empathetic preferences that are needed to assess this possibility require nothing more than that they treat this person in another body in much the same way that they treat their sisters, cousins or aunts.

---

[6] Because the probability that a newly mutated gene in his body responsible for modifying some relevant behaviour is also in her body is 1/8.

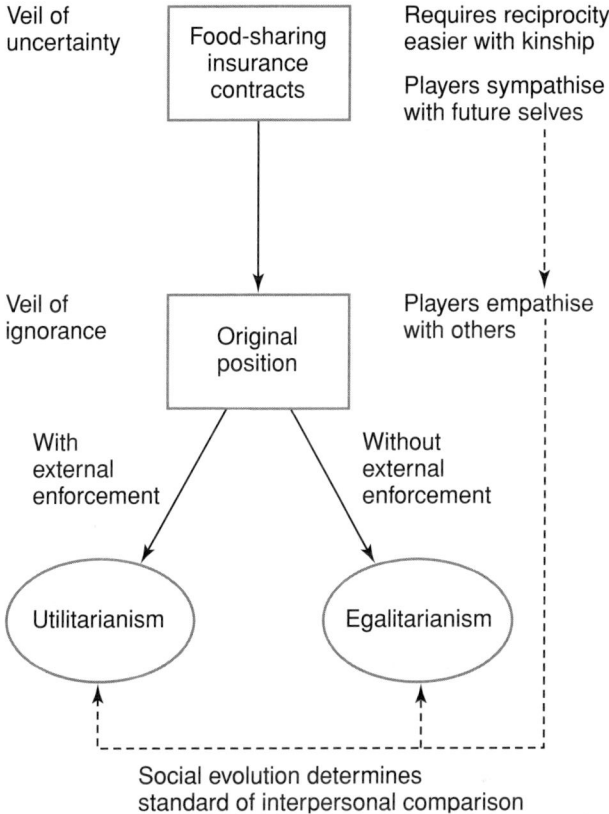

Figure 3. An evolutionary history of the original position?

Figure 3 illustrates the evolutionary history of the original position in the story told so far. It also draws attention to the need to consider the source of the standard of interpersonal comparison built into the empathetic preferences with which Adam and Eve enter the original position. I follow the psychology literature in specifying this standard by assigning positive numbers to Adam and Eve, but I refer to these positive numbers as social indices rather than worthiness coefficients.

The social indices we use when discounting the fitnesses of our partners in a family game are somehow obtained by estimating our degree of relationship to our kinfolk from the general dynamics of the family and our place in it. But where do we get the social indices with which to discount Adam and Eve's personal utils when constructing an empathetic utility function?

I do not think that we acquire the social indices we apply to different people at different times and in different contexts through any process of conscious reflection. Still less do we consult the works of moral philosophers. We pick up the appropriate social indices—in much the same way as we pick up most of our social behaviour—from unconsciously imitating the behaviour of those of our fellow citizens whom we admire or respect. That is to say, I attribute our standard of interpersonal comparison of utility in dealing with folk outside our intimate circle of family and friends to the workings of social or cultural evolution.

13. Enforcement

The previous section offers a putative evolutionary explanation for why we represent Justice as a blindfolded maiden bearing a pair of scales. But what of the sword that represents her powers of enforcement?

As Figure 3 indicates, this makes all the difference between whether the use of the original position leads to utilitarian or egalitarian conclusions. Space does not allow a review of the argument, but if we follow Harsanyi in assuming that the hypothetical deal reached in the original position is enforced by some outside agency, then the outcome will be utilitarian (Binmore 2005: chapter 10). On the other hand, if we admit no external enforcement at all, then the outcome is egalitarian (Binmore 2005: chapter 11).

Harsanyi (1977) invents an agency called 'moral commitment' that somehow enforces the hypothetical deal reached in the original position. Rawls (1972) similarly invents an agency called 'natural duty' for the same purpose. My own view is that we are not entitled to invent anything at all. If we treat the government of a modern state as an omnipotent but benign power whose function is to enforce the decisions made by the people under fair conditions, then Harsanyi's analysis provides a reason why the government should make decisions on a utilitarian basis. However, if there is no real (as opposed to invented) external enforcement agency, then Harsanyi's argument fails. In particular, it fails if the officers of a government are themselves treated as people with their own personal interests, just like any other citizen.

How come that Harsanyi is led to a utilitarian conclusion and Rawls to an egalitarian conclusion, given that they begin with the same assumptions? Game theorists trace the reason to Rawls's decision to deny orthodox decision theory. Without this iconoclastic expedient, he too would have been led to a utilitarian conclusion—although his *Theory of Justice* was explicitly written to provide a reasoned alternative to utilitarianism. My own view is that Rawls's purposes would have been better served if he had taken more seriously the concerns he refers to as the 'strains of commitment' in the third and longest part of his book. Taken to their logical extreme, these stability considerations require that everything involved in operating the original position must be self-policing. But then we are led to an egalitarian position not so very different from that he defends in his *Theory of Justice.*

There is, in fact, some empirical support for the kind of egalitarian sharing to which one is led by analysing the result of bargaining in the original position when all the arrangements must be self-policing.[7] As in Wilson (1983), the theory is usually called 'modern' equity theory, although it goes all the way back to Aristotle (1985), who observed that: 'What is just . . . is what is proportional.'

The theory says that people decide what is fair using the principle that each person's gain over the *status quo* should be proportional to the appropriate social index for that person in the relevant context. The fair outcome generated by such an egalitarian norm will generally be very different from the outcome generated by a utilitarian norm. The latter is determined by dividing each player's gain by the appropriate social index. The sum of these corrected payoffs is then maximised. Aside from other significant differences, a player gets more from the egalitarian norm if his social index is increased, but less from the utilitarian norm.

14. Moral relativism

Long ago, Xenophanes made an empirical observation which says everything that needs to be said about the supposedly universal character of the various supernatural entities that have been invented down the ages:

> The gods of the Ethiopians are black and flat-nosed, and the gods of the Thracians are red-haired and blue-eyed.

---

[7] See, for example, Adams *et al.* (1963, 1965, 1976), Austin and Hatfield (1980), Austin and Walster (1974), Baron (1993), Cohen and Greenberg (1982), Furby (1986), Homans (1961), Mellers (1982), Mellers and Baron (1993), Messick and Cook (1983), Pritchard (1969), Wagstaff *et al.* (1992, 1994, 2001), Walster *et al.* (1973, 1975, 1978).

However, the fact that we all belong to the same species implies that some of our natural properties must be universal.

I think that one of these universal natural properties is the deep structure of fairness. If I am right, then all the fairness norms we use successfully in solving the small-scale coordination problems of everyday life are rooted in Rawls' original position. Space precludes giving the arguments, but a testable consequence is that we should expect all fairness norms that are actually used in all well-established societies to respond in the same way to changes in contextual parameters like need, ability, effort, and social status (Binmore 2005: chapter 11).

Although I believe that the deep structure of fairness is probably universal in the human species, the same cannot be true of the standard of interpersonal comparison that is needed to operate the device of the original position. This must be expected to vary, not only between cultures, but between different contexts in the same culture. Otherwise it would not be possible to explain the substantial differences in what is regarded as fair in different places and times, as documented in books like Elster's *Local Justice* (1992).

If I am right, the analogy with language is therefore close. All our fairness norms share the same deep structure, but just as the actual language spoken varies between cultures and contexts, so does the standard of interpersonal comparison that determines who gets precisely how much of a surplus that is divided fairly. For example, my theory suggests that it will always be regarded as fair for a person with high social status to get a smaller share than a less exalted individual, but the exact amount by which their shares differ will depend on the cultural idiosyncracies of the society in which they live.

15. Reform

My theory of fairness is an attempt at a descriptive theory; it seeks to explain how and why fairness norms evolved. Karl Marx might respond that it is all very well seeking to understand society, but the point is to change it, and I do not disagree. I hope very much that the scientific study of how societies really work will eventually make the world a better place for our children's children to live in, by clarifying what kind of reforms are compatible with human nature, and which are doomed to fail because they are not.

As an example, consider the pragmatic suggestion that we might seek to adapt the fairness norms that we use on a daily basis for settling small-scale coordinating problems to large-scale problems of social reform. This is one of the few things I have to say that traditional moralists find half-way acceptable. But they want to run with this idea without first thinking hard about the realities of the way that fairness norms are actually used in solving small-scale problems. In particular, they are unwilling to face up to the fact that fairness norms did not evolve as a substitute for the exercise of power, but as a means of coordinating on one of the many ways of balancing power.

This refusal to engage with reality becomes manifest when traditionalists start telling everybody how they 'ought' to make interpersonal comparisons when employing the device of the original position. But if I am right that the standards of interpersonal comparison we actually use as inputs when making small-scale fairness judgements are culturally determined, then these attitudes will necessarily reflect the underlying power structure of a society. One might wish, for whatever reason, that these attitudes were different. But the peddling of metaphysical arguments about what would be regarded as fair in some invented ideal world can only muddy the waters for practical reformers who actually have some hope of reaching peoples' hearts. Nobody is going to consent to a reform on fairness grounds if the resulting distribution of costs and benefits seems to them unfair according to established habit and custom, whatever may be preached from the pulpit.

It is true that facing up to such facts requires recognising that it is sometimes pointless or counter-productive to urge reforms for which a society is not ready. What would anyone have gained by urging the abolition of slavery in classical times, when even Aristotle thought that barbarians were natural slaves? What of the emancipation of women at a time when even the saintly Spinoza took time out to expound on their natural inferiority? Instead of tilting at such windmills, I think reformers need to make a hard-nosed assessment of the nature of the current social contract, and all the possible social contracts into which it might conceivably be transformed by pushing on whatever levers of power are currently available. Only when one has seriously thought through this feasibility question is there any point in asking what is optimal.

This pragmatic attitude mystifies traditional moralists, who pretend not to understand how a naturalist like myself can talk about optimality at all. How do I know what is best for society? What is my source of authority? Where are my equivalents of the burning bush and the tablets of stone?

The answer is that I have no source of moral authority at all—but I think everyone else is in precisely the same boat. I know perfectly well that my aspirations for what seems a better society are just accidents of my personal history and that of the culture in which I grew up. If my life had gone differently or if I had been brought up in another culture, I would have had different aspirations. But I nevertheless have the aspirations that I have—and so does everyone else.

The only difference between naturalists and traditionalists on this score is that naturalists do not try to force their aspirations on others by appealing to some invented source of absolute authority. We do not need a source of authority to wish that society were organised differently. If there are enough people with similar aspirations sufficiently close to the levers of power, we can get together and shift the social contract just because that is what we want to do—and for no other reason.

Note. I am grateful to the Economic and Social Research Council and to the Leverhulme Foundation for funding this work through the Centre for Economic Learning and Social Evolution at University College London.

Discussion

Robert Sugden, *School of Economics, University of East Anglia*

Ken Binmore has had the difficult task of summarising, in a one-hour lecture to a non-specialist audience, a theory of natural justice which he first presented in a two-volume treatise, comprising almost a thousand pages of often technical argument. He has succeeded admirably: his lecture is characteristically thought-provoking and pugnacious, while being beautifully clear. My task, of delivering a short critical commentary on his argument, is hardly easier.[8] Where should I start?

Reading this theory of natural justice, I have the sense that it is the work of two different Binmores. Each has something important to say about justice and fairness, but I am not convinced that their respective ideas can be combined into a single theory.

The first Binmore is Binmore the homespun philosopher, the scourge of Platonists and Kantians, the disciple of David Hume. His position is summed up, with typical bluntness, on the first page of his book, *Natural*

[8] The ideas I present in this discussion are developed more fully in my article-length review of Binmore's treatise (Sugden, 2001).

Justice. He says that orthodox moral philosophy asks how we ought to live, but that is the wrong question. The authority of philosophers who claim insight into this question is 'conjured from nowhere'; they 'have no more access to some noumenal world of moral absolutes than the boy who delivers our newspapers' (2005: 1). The only source of what we call moral intuitions is our experience of the rules that in fact govern our moral behaviour. So, he says, we need to study the processes of biological and social evolution by which morality in fact evolves.

Binmore has made a lot of intellectual enemies by taking this position, especially by presenting himself as the boy who sees that the emperor has no clothes. Modern moral philosophers, of the kind that Binmore criticises, have found many sophisticated ways of engaging in non-naturalistic discussion about morality while denying they are claiming to have access to absolute moral truths. To such philosophers, Binmore is a bull in a china shop, an ignorant economist talking about things he does not understand. So it is with some nervousness that I declare that I think that Binmore the homespun philosopher is right.

The second Binmore is the Binmore that most economists know best, the master of mathematical game theory. In its original form, game theory was an analysis of the strategies that ideally rational agents would follow when playing games against one another (as in what chess players call 'chess theory'). Two of the high priests of this approach to game theory are John Nash and John Harsanyi. Over half a century ago, Nash (1950) asked the question: What would be the result of bargaining between two ideally rational agents? He constructed a very general model of a bargaining problem, defined in terms of the characteristics which (he claimed) were the only ones relevant for rational agents, and produced a beautiful proof that ideally rational bargainers would settle on a particular solution to this problem. A few years later, Harsanyi (1953) asked the question: What principles of morality would be accepted by ideally rational agents? His approach was similar to John Rawls's (1972) later 'original position', but presented in a more rationalistic and mathematical way. Each person's moral judgements correspond with what she would prefer in a hypothetical position in which she did not know her own identity. This approach transforms moral philosophy into rational choice under uncertainty. The second Binmore is a disciple of Nash and Harsanyi.

The substantive content of Binmore's theory of natural justice is an intricate blend of the ideas of Nash and Harsanyi, with an added dash of Rawls. Moral principles are derived by imagining an original position in which the contracting parties do not know who they will become: each party is equally likely to become any one of the real people in their society. So far, Binmore follows Harsanyi. But where Harsanyi assumes that all the contracting parties make the same interpersonal comparisons of utility, Binmore allows each party to make his or her own comparisons, so they need to resolve their disagreements by negotiation. This is where Nash's theory of rational bargaining is put to use. Binmore also differs from his predecessors in allowing each of his imaginary contracting parties the right to demand a re-run of the whole exercise if, after finding out who she has become, she does not like the result. But then Binmore proposes the empirical hypothesis that this elaborate edifice of rational choice theory is also the conception of fairness that in fact has evolved in human societies. Thus, Binmore the mathematical game theorist and Binmore the homespun philosopher converge on the same moral theory. I suggest that points of greatest tension in Binmore's analysis come at the joins between these two approaches—where he tries to convince us that the forces of social evolution have selected the Harsanyi–Nash theory.

On Binmore's account, moral theory is selected to resolve coordination problems: in the evolutionary sense of the word, resolving these problems is the *function* of moral theory. One of his examples of the kind of problem he has in mind is: 'Who gives way to whom when cars are manoeuvring in heavy traffic?' So let us think more about this problem.

Suppose that you and I are drivers approaching a crossroads from opposite directions. You want to go straight ahead; I want to turn right across your path. Who gives way to whom? Binmore's answer seems to be that when I am deciding whether to give way to you, I imagine a hypothetical original position and reconstruct a rational bargain between you and me, taking account of my own judgements about interpersonal comparisons of utility between you and me, and of what I think your interpersonal comparisons are. If we succeed in coordinating, it is because our simulations of this hypothetical bargain lead to the same conclusion.

But can this really be how drivers decide whether to give way? In my experience of the crossroads problem, the driver who is first to reach the junction has priority; when there are queues on both roads, this results in the drivers on the two roads taking turns. I certainly follow this rule. Why? Because I have learned to expect other drivers to do so. Given this expectation, it is normally in my interest to follow the rule. Further, because I have come to expect the rule to be followed, and because I have good reason to believe that other drivers have the same expectation, attempts to seek advantage by deviating from the rule appear to me as unfair. In order to explain why I give way when I do, there is no need to consider hypothetical contracts; I am simply following the convention that has already evolved. In order to explain why I perceive breaches of this convention as unfair, there is no need to show that the convention would have been chosen in some idealised bargaining position; it is sufficient to recognise that the convention is generally followed, and that given that this is the case, each of us is harmed if the other breaches it.

That still leaves the question of how that convention has evolved. The answer, I suggest, is that it has evolved through the combined effects, over a long period, of people reasoning in just the way I do at the crossroads, each trying to do the best he can, given the behaviour of other drivers. Why the particular convention of priority to the first arrival? Probably because it's easy to learn, simple to use, applicable in a wide range of situations, and so capable of spreading from one situation to another by analogy. Such equilibrium selection mechanisms have very little to do with Nash bargaining theory, interpersonal comparisons of utility or original positions. They have very little to do with morality, as that has been understood by moral philosophers. But they can still generate rules that we come to regard as fair.[9]

My diagnosis is that Binmore is looking at morality from the perspective of a game theorist, imbued with the rationality-based traditions of that theory, rather than from the perspective of an empirical social scientist, trying to explain the facts on the ground. What he is trying to naturalise is not the collection of norms which we in fact find in human societies, but a form of morality which derives from an analysis of a world of ideally rational agents. Binmore the homespun philosopher is too much under the influence of the Binmore the mathematical game theorist. Dare I say that Binmore is too Kantian to be a true disciple of Hume? He has shaken off the myth of the truly good, but he is still in thrall to the myth of the truly rational. He has not accepted the full implications of a proposition to which his naturalism commits him: that even the greatest game theorists, even Nash and Harsanyi, have no more access to the concept of what is truly rational than the boy who delivers the newspapers.

---

[9] In my book, *The Economics of Rights, Cooperation and Welfare*, I argue that many conventions and norms have evolved in this kind of way (Sugden, 2004).

Ken Binmore, *Reply to Robert Sugden*

The first edition of Bob Sugden's *Economics of Rights, Cooperation and Welfare* (Sugden 2004) was one of the books that inspired my work on the evolution of fairness norms, and so it is comforting that his criticism of my approach seems to have softened since he last commented on my theory (Sugden 2001). I continue to believe that we are actually singing from the same hymn sheet, but there is space here only to consider two of the differences between us that he identifies in his commentary and elsewhere.

Sugden defends the Humean view that social norms are usually established gradually over time by a hard-to-model process of cultural evolution. I also believe this to be the case. Where we differ is in his belief is that there is nothing special about fairness norms. Brian Skyrms holds a similar view (Skyrms 1996, 2003). On this subject, their philosophy is more homespun than mine, because I believe that the Kantians John Rawls (Rawls 1972) and John Harsanyi (Harsanyi 1977) put their fingers on something real about how human fairness norms work when they independently formulated the idea of the original position.

As Sugden comments, I make intellectual enemies by stoutly denying Kant's metaphysics when it might be wiser to remain silent, but I hope he will find few takers for the idea that I come in two contradictory varieties: a homespun Binmore and a quasi-metaphysical Binmore who abandons evolution for neoclassical economics when it suits his purpose. What he fails to see is that there are not two Binmores, but two ways of interpreting Nash equilibria: a rational interpretation and an evolutionary interpretation. It is because one can sometimes pass back and forward between these two interpretations that I think game theory has proved so successful in both economics and biology.

A pair of strategies is a Nash equilibrum in a game if each is a best reply to the other. The rational reason for caring about Nash equilibria can be expressed in terms of what should be written in an authoritative book on how games should best be played. Such a book cannot recommend something other than a Nash equilibrium as the rational solution of a game, because at least one player would then have a reason for not following the book's advice. However, a book cannot be authoritative on what is rational if rational people do not play as it recommends.

The evolutionary reason for caring about Nash equilibria arises when the payoffs in a game correspond to how fit the players are. An adjustment process that favours the more fit at the expense of the less fit will stop working when we get to a Nash equilibrium, because all the survivors will then be as fit as it is possible to be in the circumstances. This is why the requirements for a Nash equilibrium are built into the formal definition of evolutionary stability used by biologists (Maynard Smith 1982).

I share Sugden's distaste for the arrogance of certain neo-classical economists. I agree that a methodology which exploits the dual interpretation of Nash equilibria deserves to be classed as speculative. But there is a baby in the bathwater that we cannot afford to throw away.

References

Adams, J. (1963), 'Towards an understanding of inequity', *Journal of Abnormal and Social Psychology*, 67: 422–36.
Adams, J. (1965), 'Inequity in social exchange'. In L. Berkowitz (ed.), *Advances in Experimental Social Science*, 2 (New York).
Adams, J. and Freedman, S. (1976), 'Equity theory revisited: Comments and annotated bibliography'. In L. Berkowitz (ed.), *Advances in Experimental Social Science*, 9 (New York).
Alcock, J. (2001), *The Triumph of Sociobiology* (New York).
Aristotle (1985), *Nicomachean Ethics*. Trans. T. Irwin (Indianapolis).
Aumann, R. and Maschler, M. (1995), *Repeated Games with Incomplete Information* (Cambridge, MA).
Austin, W. and Hatfield, E. (1980), 'Equity theory, power and social justice'. In G. Mikula (ed.), *Justice and Social Interaction* (New York).
Austin, W. and Walster, E. (1974), 'Reactions to confirmations and disconfirmations of expectancies of equity and inequity', *Journal of Personality and Social Psychology*, 30: 208–16.
Axelrod, R. (1984), *The Evolution of Cooperation* (New York).
Bailey, R. (1991), 'The behavioral ecology of Efe pygmy men in the Atari Forest, Zaire', Technical Report Anthropological Paper 86, University of Michigan Museum of Anthropology.
Baron, J. (1993), 'Heuristics and biases in equity judgments: A utilitarian approach'. In B. Mellors and J. Baron (eds.), *Psychological Perspectives on Justice: Theory and Applications* (Cambridge).
Binmore, K. (1994), *Playing Fair: Game Theory and the Social Contract, I* (Cambridge, MA).
Binmore, K. (1998), *Just Playing: Game Theory and the Social Contract, II* (Cambridge, MA).
Binmore, K. (2005), *Natural Justice* (New York).
Cohen, R. and Greenberg, J. (1982), 'The justice concept in social psychology'. In R. Cohen and J. Greenberg (eds.), *Equity and Justice in Social Behavior* (New York).
Damas, D. (1972), 'The Copper Eskimo'. In M. Bicchieri (ed.), *Hunters and Gatherers Today* (New York).
Dawkins, R. (1976), *The Selfish Gene* (Oxford).

Elster, J. (1992), *Local Justice: How Institutions Allocate Scarce Goods and Necessary Burdens* (New York).
Erdal, D. and Whiten, A. (1996), 'Egalitarianism and Machiavellian intelligence in human evolution'. In P. Mellars and K. Gibson (eds.), *Modelling the Early Human Mind* (Oxford).
Evans-Pritchard, E. (1940), *The Nuer* (Oxford).
Furby, L. (1986), 'Psychology and justice'. In R. Cohen (ed.), *Justice: Views from the Social Sciences* (Cambridge, MA).
Fürer-Haimendorf, C. (1967), *Morals and Merit* (London).
Gardner, P. (1972), 'The Paliyans'. In M. Bicchieri (ed.), *Hunters and Gatherers Today* (New York).
Gauthier, D. (1986), *Morals by Agreement* (Oxford).
Hamilton, W. (1963), 'The evolution of altruistic behavior', *American Naturalist*, 97: 354–6.
Harsanyi, J. (1953), 'Cardinal utility in welfare economics and in the theory of risk-taking', *Journal of Political Economy*, 61: 434–5.
Harsanyi, J. (1977), *Rational Behavior and Bargaining Equilibrium in Games and Social Situations* (Cambridge).
Hawkes, K., O'Connell, J., and Burton-Jones, N. (1993), 'Hunting income patterns among the Hadza'. In A. Whitten and E. Widdowson (eds.), *Foraging Strategies and Natural Diet of Monkeys, Apes and Humans* (Oxford).
Helm, J. (1972), 'The Dogrib Indians'. In M. Bicchieri (ed.), *Hunters and Gatherers Today* (New York).
Homans, G. (1961), *Social Behavior: Its Elementary Forms* (New York).
Hume, D. (1975 [1777]) *Enquiries Concerning Human Understanding and Concerning the Principles of Morals*, 3rd edn., ed. L. A. Selby-Bigge, rev. P. Nidditch (Oxford),
Hume, D. (1978 [1739]), *A Treatise of Human Nature*, 2nd edn., ed. L. A. Selby-Bigge, rev. P. Nidditch (Oxford).
Isaac, G. (1978), 'The food-sharing behavior of protohuman hominids', *Scientific American*, 238: 90–108.
Kaplan, H. and Hill, K. (1985), 'Food sharing among Ache foragers: Tests of explanatory hypotheses', *Current Anthropology*, 26: 223–45.
Knauft, B. (1991), 'Violence and sociality in human evolution', *Current Anthropology*, 32: 223–45.
Lee, R. (1979), *The !Kung San: Men, Women and Work in a Foraging Society* (Cambridge).
Lorenz, K. (1997), *King Solomon's Ring* (New York).
Mackie, J. (1977), *Ethics, Inventing Right and Wrong* (London).
Maynard Smith, J. (1982), *Evolution and the Theory of Games* (Cambridge).
Megarry, T. (1995), *Society in Prehistory: The Origins of Human Culture* (London).
Meggitt, M. (1962), *Desert People: A Study of the Walbiri Aborigines of Central Australia* (Chicago).
Mellers, B. (1982), 'Equity judgment: A revision of Aristotelian views', *Journal of Experimental Biology*, 111: 242–70.
Mellers, B. and Baron, J. (1993), *Psychological Perspectives on Justice: Theory and Applications* (Cambridge).

Messick, D. and Cook, K. (1983), *Equity Theory: Psychological and Sociological Perspectives* (New York).
Nash, J. (1950), 'The bargaining problem', *Econometrica*, 18: 155–62.
Pritchard, R. (1969), 'Equity theory; A review and critique', *Organizational Behavior and Human Performance*, 4: 176–211.
Rawls, J. (1972), *A Theory of Justice* (Oxford).
Riches, D. (1982), 'Hunting, herding and potlatching: Toward a sociological account of prestige', *Man*, 19: 234–51.
Rogers, E. (1972), 'The Mistassini Cree'. In M. Bicchieri (ed.), *Hunters and Gatherers Today* (New York).
Sahlins, M. (1974), *Stone Age Economics* (London).
Singer, P. (1980), *The Expanding Circle: Ethics and Sociobiology* (New York).
Skyrms, B. (1996), *Evolution of the Social Contract* (Cambridge).
Skyrms, B. (2003), *The Stag Hunt and the Evolution of the Social Structure* (Cambridge).
Sugden, R. (2001), 'Ken Binmore's evolutionary social theory', *Economic Journal*, 111: F213–48.
Sugden, R. (2004 [1986]), *The Economics of Rights, Cooperation and Welfare*, 2nd edn. (Basingstoke).
Tanaka, J. (1980), *The San Hunter-Gatherers of the Kalahari Desert: A Study of Ecological Anthropology* (Tokyo).
Trivers, R. (1971), 'The evolution of reciprocal altruism', *Quarterly Review of Biology*, 46: 35–56.
Turnbull, C. (1965), *Wayward Servants* (London).
Wagstaff, G. (1994), 'Equity, equality and need: Three principles of justice or one?', *Current Psychology: Research and Reviews*, 13: 138–52.
Wagstaff, G. (2001), *An Integrated Psychological and Philosophical Approach to Justice* (Lampeter).
Wagstaff, G., Huggins, J., and Perfect, T. (1996), 'Equal ratio equity, general linear equity and framing effects in judgments of allocation divisions', *European Journal of Social Psychology*, 26: 29–41.
Wagstaff, G. and Perfect, T. (1992), 'On the definition of perfect equity and the prediction of inequity', *British Journal of Social Psychology*, 31: 69–77.
Walster, E., Berscheid, E. and Walster, G. (1973), 'New directions in equity research', *Journal of Personality and Social Psychology*, 25: 151–76.
Walster, E. and Walster, G. (1975), 'Equity and social justice', *Journal of Social Issues*, 31: 21–43.
Walster, E., Walster, G., and Berscheid, E. (1978), *Equity: Theory and Research* (London).
Wilkinson, G. (1984), 'Reciprocal food-sharing in the vampire bat', *Nature*, 308: 181–4.
Wilson, J. (1993), *The Moral Sense* (New York).

BRITISH ACADEMY LAW LECTURE

Judicial Independence: Who Cares?

NEIL MacCORMICK
Fellow of the Academy

I. Introduction

EPIMENIDES THE CRETAN, whom I briefly encountered in Princes Street last week, assured me that contemporary Cretans have the most scrupulous possible regard for truthfulness. He went on to explain that he was momentarily at an acute pecuniary disadvantage, having forgotten his PIN number, despite having a very substantial surplus in his Euro account with the Bank of Knossos. He asked if I could lend him £100 so as to let him catch a train to London where he had a prepaid onward connection to Crete. He assured me that he would instruct his bank to make an equivalent transfer to my account (if I would just kindly give him necessary IBAN number and other details). . . .

Well, there would be a nice inversion of the liar paradox. Hitherto Epimenides' line has been that all Cretans are liars—but, if so, could we believe what he said? Suppose he now starts assuring us that they all tell the truth always. What then? This is on its face as self-referential as the liar paradox, and it seems almost as fishy but in a different way. There is something pretty questionable about someone who assures us that all he says is true. It is the all-but-invariable opening gambit of every confidence trickster. It seeks to divert attention from obvious grounds for mistrust. Ordinary truthful people simply let their yea be yea and their nay be nay, say what they have to say, and let us take it at face value without further

Read at the Academy 24 October 2006.

Proceedings of the British Academy **151**, 195–211. © The British Academy 2007.

self-certification of its truthfulness. If it is true, self-certification adds nothing; if not, it is doubly worthless.

One may in similar vein remark that it is only when some value has become in some way problematic that people normally resort to making an explicit rule aimed at upholding it.[1] What goes without saying needs no rule. Moreover, what can be done by establishing a rule can be undone by repealing it. In that sense, making a rule may express a problem as much as a solution, showing that a principle or value hitherto taken-for-granted has somehow come into question.

Has this a message for us in relation to the subject of my lecture, the Independence of the Judiciary? Perhaps there are grounds for unease. Let us remember the grand flourish with which the Constitutional Reform Act 2005 commences:

1. This Act does not adversely affect—
    (a) the existing constitutional principle of the rule of law, or
    (b) the Lord Chancellor's existing constitutional role in relation to that principle. . . .

3. (1) The Lord Chancellor, other Ministers of the Crown and all with responsibility for matters relating to the judiciary or otherwise to the administration of justice must uphold the continued independence of the judiciary.

Meanwhile in Scotland the Minister of Justice and the Lord Advocate, acting together on behalf of the Scottish Executive, earlier this year put in train a consultation about 'Strengthening Judicial Independence in a Modern Scotland'.[2] Their prefatory remarks to the consultation include this: 'We are strongly committed to the independence of the judiciary, and we propose to make a statutory statement of this commitment.' Following this, they sketch out quite firm general outlines of the statutory provisions they mean to bring forward, and they append many questions as elements of their public consultation. These invite comment on their own proposed scheme, rather than having a more open-ended character that would encourage broader reflection on the prerequisites of judicial independence in contemporary Scotland.

---

[1] I owe this insight to Professor Walter Weyrauch of the University of Florida. See 'The "Basic Law" or "Constitution of a Small Group"', *Journal of Social Issues*, 27 (1971), 49 and I gratefully acknowledge helpful correspondence with him about this paper and other related writings of his.
[2] *Strengthening Judicial Independence in a Modern Scotland* (Edinburgh, Consultation paper, Scottish Executive 2006) <http://www.scotland.gov.uk/Publications/2006/01/30154152/0>.

These Scottish proposals address among other things a perceived need to put Scotland on an equal footing with, or a footing similar to, that recently established in England and Wales, where a whole new order of judicial organisation has emerged through the aforementioned Constitutional Reform Act 2005.[3] It is worth remembering how that came about.

The office of Lord Chancellor was pronounced abolished in June 2003, following the dismissal from office of Lord Irvine of Lairg on 12 June.[4] This abolition proved premature, so many were the statutory and other functions exercisable only by the Lord Chancellor. Nevertheless, the abolition of the office was driven forward by the then Prime Minister's determination to reshape the three branches of government and sharpen the differentiation of the judicial function. There was to be a new United Kingdom Supreme Court[5] in place of the House of Lords (and the Privy Council, in those of its judicial functions pertaining to the United Kingdom). There was need for a new speakership of the House of Lords, and a new Department of Constitutional Affairs in place of the Lord Chancellor's Department of old. This all took some time to emerge clearly into view, but always it was being relentlessly pushed forward by the government, by the executive branch of the state.

For England and Wales, there also came sharply into focus the need for a new definition of the role of head of the judiciary and guarantor of its independence. The former role and a share of the latter was to be exercised thenceforward by the Lord Chief Justice, with consequential changes affecting other senior judicial posts. Inside government, the now purely executive office of Lord Chancellor would continue (as noted) to carry the duty of special vigilance for judicial independence.[6]

---

[3] Information that came my way under the 'Chatham House Rule' subsequently to my lecture leads me to believe that in fact the first moves in relation to the Scottish position and the need to consider possible parallels with new developments in England and Wales may have originated among the judiciary. It would be wrong to portray the Scottish Executive as having taken up the subject out of the blue, though it remains an open question how satisfactory the Executive approach has been.

[4] See K. Malleson 'Modernizing the Constitution; Completing the Unfinished Business' in G. Canivet, M. Andenas and D. Fairgrieve (eds.) *Independence, Accountability, and the Judiciary* (London: British Institute of International and Comparative Law, 2006), pp. 145–62 at pp. 148–50.

[5] This development was under discussion for several years before. See Lord Steyn, 'The Case for a Supreme Court', *Law Quarterly Review*, 118 (1999), 382.

[6] See Lord Bingham of Cornhill, 'The Old Order Changeth', *Law Quarterly Review*, 122 (2006), 211–23 at 222.

New arrangements by way of a Judicial Appointments Commission were to take effect in respect of appointing judges. In addition, there were to be elaborately balanced powers of appointment to, or recommendation for appointment to, the new United Kingdom Supreme Court. These reflect the asymmetrical constitutional schema of the United Kingdom, and respond to the historic guarantees of the independence and integrity of the Scottish Legal System.[7] The whole idea might however turn out still to be open to challenge. For it is not clear that any appeal to anything other than the Parliament (or one of its houses) is legitimate under the Articles of Union—the United Kingdom Supreme Court has a distinct look of a 'Court in Westminster-hall' or at least a 'Court of like nature'.[8]

That gives in very brief summary the comparative background to the Scottish Executive's proposal about judicial independence in Scotland. The main idea is that the Lord President of the Court of Session should, by a development parallel to that taking place under the Constitutional Reform Act, become the Head of the Scottish Judiciary. The Lord President should thus acquire responsibilities encompassing not only the Court of Session and the High Court of Justiciary as at present, but extending also to all sheriffs principal and sheriffs and district judges. It is not a proposal that has itself been rendered necessary because of the demise of the Lord Chancellor's role as head of the judiciary and guardian of its independence. For the Lord Chancellor never had either of these roles in Scotland. Given the spectacularly variable constitutional geometry to which we are growing accustomed, the urgency of achieving symmetry in this respect between Scotland and the southern neighbours seems open to doubt.

---

[7] These are, of course, enshrined in the 1707 Treaty of Union, as that was put in force by the enabling legislation of the two parliaments that were predecessors to that of Great Britain. Scottish legal distinctiveness nowadays additionally falls to be considered in the light of the re-establishment of a Scottish Parliament under the devolutionary legislation. See N. MacCormick, 'The English Constitution, the British State, and the Scottish Anomaly', *Proceedings of the British Academy*, 101 (1998), 298–306.

[8] Article 19 of the Treaty of Union provides *inter alia* that 'no Causes in Scotland be cognoscible by the Courts of Chancery, Queen's Bench, Common Pleas, or any other Court in Westminster-hall; And that the said Courts, or any other of like nature after the Union, shall have no power to Cognosce, Review or Alter the Acts or Sentences of the Judicatures within Scotland, or stop the Execution of the same;' (Cited from T. B. Smith, *A Short Commentary on the Law of Scotland* (Edinburgh, 1962) p. 878). For extended discussion of the question whether the Constitutional Reform Act violates this provision, see N. MacCormick 'Doubts about "The Supreme Court" and Reflections on *MacCormick v Lord Advocate*', *Juridical Review* (2004), 236–50 esp. at 242–50.

It has to be said, moreover, that the proposals themselves, and the manner of pressing forward with them—legislation was originally promised during the present Parliament, with an election due in May 2007—have given rise to some disquiet in legal and, notably, high judicial circles in Scotland, as well as among serious newspaper columnists.[9] The ancient office of Lord President may find itself yet more radically reconfigured than that of the Lord Chief Justice. Without other visible gains, this could wreak severe detriment to the established working usages of the Court of Session and High Court of Justiciary. In the absence of a radical re-think of responsibility for the Scottish Court Service, and its relation to the Scottish Courts Administration, which is a department of the Scottish Executive under the Justice Minister, the authority of the Lord President will be somewhat confined and his or her capability actively to champion judicial independence may be cramped and confined.

The establishment of a very substantial purely Court-dedicated civil service, with strong senior management responsible to the Lord President in consultation with other senior judges, could make a real difference.[10] In its absence, the proposed new model for the Lord Presidency will fail to achieve the purpose for which it is designed. To the extent that it would be workable, it would be a poor guarantee of real continuing judicial independence. For without some radical redesign, achieved after careful comparative study in the European Union and with similar sized jurisdictions elsewhere,[11] the pre-eminence of the Lord President as a judge rather than as a kind of CEO of the whole judiciary of Scotland would become a thing of the past. What is more, the independence of the judiciary conceived as the independence of every judge may be compromised if 'independence' is defined primarily as a quality of the whole corps of judges under direction of a new-model Lord President.

---

[9] See *Copies of responses received for the consultation paper entitled 'Strengthening Judicial Independence in a Modern Scotland'* web publication, 13 June 2006, <http://www.scotland.gov.uk/Publications/2006/06/13143517/0>. The website includes twenty submissions from representative bodies, including one from the Scottish judges collectively, and seventeen from individuals, including the present Lord President, Lord Hamilton, and two of his predecessors, Lords Hope and Cullen.

[10] Compare the statement by Lord Hamilton, cited above, n. 9.

[11] The Scottish Judges, in their submission cited above, n. 5, and also Sir David Edward in his submission, cite Ireland as a relevant comparator in the light of recent reforms to the Irish Courts system.

On the other hand various aspects of accountability,[12] so far as this is a proper counterbalance to independence, and a safeguard against its abuse, might indeed be more easily worked into a new statutory framework than into present structures. The risk of Executive over-dominance of the bench might also be further warded off under a statutory version of the current Scottish Judicial Appointments Board, with special arrangements concerning appointment to the offices of Lord President and Lord Justice Clerk. The proposals of the Executive point in this direction, hence in these respects deserve more than a merely tepid response.

It would not be appropriate to the present occasion to go into much greater detail about the Scottish proposals and responses to them. Suffice it to say that we cannot wholly assure ourselves of a clean difference between Epimenides the truth-teller and the Scottish Executive. 'We are strongly committed to the independence of the judiciary, and we propose to make a statutory statement of this commitment.' Is there a rat here to be smelled?

In the same suspicious frame of mind, I am bound to ask: Does section 3 of the Constitutional Reform Act quell all possible concerns about judicial independence in England and Wales? 'The Lord Chancellor, other Ministers of the Crown and all with responsibility for matters relating to the judiciary or otherwise to the administration of justice must uphold the continued independence of the judiciary.' Well, that's all right then—or is it really?

These may seem mean-minded doubts, but there is ground for them. If judicial independence matters, it matters most highly in respect of the interface between the executive and the judicial branch of government. In the present circumstance of party government, tough-minded political leaders in executive office can very frequently have their will done by means of the legislation a parliamentary majority can be persuaded to enact. In deep constitutional questions, this approach to law-making can be very disturbing. For the executive takes upon itself the task of deciding the lines of change to be pushed through, and only then does consultation in parliament and outside it commence. Sometimes, very often, perhaps, this consultation process does result in valuable modification of what was originally proposed. But the process and the upshot do not much

---

[12] See Andrew Le Sueur, 'Developing Mechanisms for Judicial Accountability in the UK', in Canivet, Andenas and Fairgrieve (eds.), *Independence, Accountability, and the Judiciary*, pp. 49–76.

resemble the kind of calm reflection that a constitutional convention or even a royal commission might produce.

The on-the-hoof or off-the-sofa approach to redrafting the basic elements of a constitution, especially but not only affecting England and Wales, that followed the announced abolition of the Chancellorship (old style) was an instructive example of how not to do it. One cannot quite equiparate this with the Red King's 'verdict first, evidence afterwards', but it went a bit down that line. Save for long and arduous debates and committee work in Parliament's upper house, the result would have been greatly worse than it turned out. The constitution does not belong to the executive of the moment. Although governments have indeed the right to legislative initiative, and are entitled to achieve programmes of reform for which they have a reasonable electoral mandate, there should be considerable caution and a wider view when it comes to revising constitutional fundamentals. A mature and wide-ranging exchange of views ought to be included in, and perhaps to precede, any strong taking of position by the executive. Parliaments have a much larger part to play in deliberation upon possibilities than current practice seems to allow them.

In Scotland, the single-chamber character of our Parliament makes the more urgent a highly prudent and discursive approach to projects for reform of constitutional fundamentals. This was not initially conspicuous in respect of the 'judicial independence' proposals and consultation, though the responses received and the public controversy surrounding them have led to the adoption of wiser counsels. In both England and Wales and Scotland, the executive branch of government, in the act of proclaiming unshakable adherence to the principle of judicial independence, has acted in ways that suggest it is itself entitled to a privileged part in re-shaping that other branch of government whose independence it proclaims. Surely, that will not do.

II. Judicial independence: why valued?

A lecture such as the biennial Law Lecture of the British Academy affords an opportunity to underline the importance of things that in fortunate times are simply taken-for-granted features of our civil and constitutional scenery. We live, by contrast, in interesting times. Lurid organs of the tabloid press frequently pillory judges on the basis of very partial reporting of decisions in individual cases. Two Home Secretaries have apparently added their voices to the virulent critique of particular judicial decisions, and a third has sought a private audience with the law lords to discuss the sound balancing of priorities among human rights, and been rebuffed.[13] The Prime Minister, Mr Blair, was sufficiently discontented with the response of the judiciary to anti-terrorist measures that he sought parliamentary authority for detention of terrorist suspects up to ninety days. 'The rules have changed', he proleptically announced, while making preparation to have them changed.[14] There is a tension in the air between executive and judiciary. On each side, the one is considered insufficiently sensitive to the proper, legitimate, and deep concerns of the other during dangerous times.

Judicial Independence—Who Cares? Indeed, why should anyone care? We must at least nod in passing to first principles. Judicial independence is one essential corollary of the yet more fundamental principle of separation of powers. That itself, however, is by no means undisputed as to its meaning or its value. Admittedly, since at least the writings of John Locke, and all the more those of Montesquieu, it has been a kind of byword that free government—free government as distinct from despotism or tyranny—requires such things as the following. Those who make the laws should themselves be subject to governance under the laws they make, along with fellow citizens and other subjects of the law. Hence holders of the highest executive power should not themselves be able to determine the content of the legislation whose execution it falls to them to progress—their task is pursuit of the common good under the law, not to exercise domination over it. The administration and application of the law in individual cases, whether in its criminal aspects, in respect of private citizens in controversy with public authorities, or in respect of private persons litigating among themselves, must be entrusted to a quite separate corps of judges. These must be outside the executive and the legislature, and must not be exposed to undue or improper influence by these institutions or any of their individual members. This absence of improper influence is quite as important as both the actuality, and the clear appearance, of absence of any undue friendship or favouritism towards or financial dependency on, persons outside government. Judicial independence and impartiality so understood are indeed cornerstones of

---

[13] See <http://www.downingstreetsays.org/archives/002913.html>. *The Times*, 14 June 2006 (Rt. Hon. John Reid); <http://www.irr.org.uk/2003/march/ak000010.html> (Rt. Hon. David Blunkett); *New Statesman*, 26 Sept. 2005 (Mary Riddell, Interview with Charles Clarke).

[14] Prime Minister's press conference 5 Aug. 2005 <http://www.number10.gov.uk/output/Page8041.asp>.

liberty under the rule of law,[15] and essential to free government in a free society. This is part of the rule of law and the separation of powers as we know them.[16]

Not everyone agrees about the separation of powers. Some think that Montesquieu simply misunderstood the British Constitution, with mischievous effects for those in America, France and other places who tried to guarantee liberty by making constitutional provisions for strict separation of powers—though doing so in decidedly different ways in their different countries.[17] All along there was never a clean separation of powers in any of England, Great Britain, the United Kingdom, each in succession to its predecessor. Still, one should surely acknowledge that differentiation of constitutional functions, and especially a jealous regard for judicial independence has long been a standing feature of our constitutional practice. Much has depended on convention and usage and the self-policing of elite institutions (the conduct of the Court of Session and Faculty of Advocates, and the special position of the Lord Advocate, hitherto afforded one telling example, pertinent to the opening section of this lecture).

Everything is now changing. Adjudication is to be moved out of the House of Lords and re-established in a Supreme Court elsewhere in Westminster. The dismemberment of the Lord Chancellor's office, though happily not of either the former or the current holder of the office, and other current developments, represent a cleaner separation than heretofore of executive power both from judicial and from legislative power. If the theory of separation of powers was a mistake, the United Kingdom is now committing that very mistake two centuries after everyone else.

It was not a mistake, however, as I argue elsewhere.[18] Any person of generous spirit ought to welcome this as an attempt to catch up and to put the constitutional house in order. Mr Blair's government showed due mindfulness of the imperatives of the Human Rights Convention. It showed a proper willingness to amend the curious example the United

---

[15] Compare Lord Irvine of Lairg, *Human Rights, Constitutional Law, and the Development of the English Legal System* (Oxford, 2003), pp. 201–8 (chap. on 'Judicial Independence and the British Constitution').

[16] This paragraph summarises points argued at greater length in N. MacCormick, *Institutions of Law: An Essay in Legal Theory* (Oxford, 2007), pp. 43–8, to which I refer the reader in preference to overloading the text of this lecture with excess of footnotes.

[17] See, e.g., I. Claus, 'Montesquieu's Mistakes and the True Idea of Separation', *Oxford Journal of Legal Studies*, 25 (2005), 419–52.

[18] *Institutions of Law*, see above, n. 16.

Kingdom has hitherto presented to the former Communist states that the European Council, United Kingdom included, exhorted to get their constitutions in better shape as regards the separation of powers and the rule of law. Having been somewhat critical of the methods adopted by governments in the opening section of this lecture, surely I must in concluding this section acknowledge that Mr Blair's was the government that 'brought rights home'.[19] This was the government that worked into the tapestry[20] of our law the Convention Rights—the rights asserted by ourselves and most other Europeans in the European Human Rights Convention. Faced with the question 'Judicial Independence: Who Cares?' one can properly answer: 'Everyone who takes seriously human rights as these have been codified in the post-1945 period does and must take seriously the issue of judicial independence.' The right to a fair trial before an independent tribunal[21] is one of the foundational rights of the human condition as the international community now conceives this.

Certainly, in the light of intellectual and political commitments formed over many years, I for one am bound to salute the wisdom and courage of a government that did 'bring rights back home'. In time to come, this will surely be seen as one of the greater politico-legal achievements of the closing years of the twentieth century in this country. This will be so long after momentary conflicts and frustrations between ministers and judges over the correct interpretation and balancing of rights in difficult cases has passed out of public memory. So the doubts I expressed in my opening section about the approach of the United Kingdom Government and the Scottish Executive to the issue of judicial independence need to be put more fairly in context. The situation is one in which the greatest obstacles to hasty and perhaps ill-considered ministerial action under pressure of emergency situations are constituted by legislation originally promoted by the self-same government. If ministers have fallen into a trap, it is one they set and baited themselves. It should be seen, however, not as a trap, but as a safety net, situated very fortunately well in place when it was needed at a difficult time.

---

[19] The White Paper *Rights Brought Home: the Human Rights Bill* (1997 Cm. 3782) preceded and laid the ground for the Human Rights Act 1998.
[20] I borrow this phrase from Elspeth Attwooll's *The Tapestry of the Law: Scotland, legal culture and legal theory* (Dordrecht, 1997). MacCormick, *Rhetoric and the Rule of Law*, chap. 13. But contrast, for example, J. Balkin 'Ideological drift and the Struggle over Meaning', *Connecticut Law Review*, 25 (1993) 869.
[21] See Article 6 of the European Convention for the Protection of Human Rights and Fundamental Freedoms.

III. Judicial Independence—a Pious Fraud after all?

Ministerial concern about judicial interference in political issues is matched by legal concerns that the domestication of the Convention Rights has led to enhanced judicial activism, giving the judges an openly political role in deciding priorities among legally recognised values. This comes on top of the substantial growth of judicial review of administrative and governmental action during the Thatcher and Major years. As Home Secretary, Michael Howard set the precedent followed by subsequent Labour Home Secretaries when he complained of judges usurping domains of ministerial discretion and overruling ministers on essentially political questions.[22]

More generally, it is a widely held view that judges are simply a different kind of lawmakers from parliamentarians and ministers, but are lawmakers just the same. 'The day is long gone', say Chris Himsworth and Alan Paterson, 'when the Law Lords could credibly deny that lawmaking is part of their role. As Lord Reid of Drem observed . . . over thirty years ago, "we do not believe in fairy tales any more"'.[23] We can add that general view of the judicial function to more specific and recent complaints about judicial intrusion into the political realm. We may then end up with enhanced scepticism about the very idea of a separation of powers. It seems yet another fairy tale that it is possible to draw any clean or clear line between judicial and legislative functions. One contemporary critic of the Montesquieu theory indeed includes the judiciary, in the USA in particular but also in the United Kingdom, as participants in the legislative power.[24] The declaratory theory of judicial interpretation, though it may have some life left in it, seems most prominently asserted in the recent *Kleinwort Benson* case in which the Law Lords apparently re-wrote the English law concerning the recoverability of money paid under a mistake of law.[25] 'Some declaration of pre-existing law that was!' an objector might say.[26]

---

[22] See D. Woodhouse, 'Judicial Independence and Accountability within the United Kingdom's New Constitutional Settlement', in Canivet, Andenas and Fairgrieve (eds.) *Independence, Accountability, and the Judiciary*, pp. 121–44 at p. 127.

[23] Chris Himsworth and Alan Paterson, 'A Supreme Court for the United Kingdom' in Canivet, Andenas and Fairgrieve (eds.) *Independence, Accountability, and the Judiciary*, pp. 99–120 at p. 112, quoting Lord Reid, 'The Judge as Law Maker' in *Journal of the Society of Public Teachers of Law* (NS), 12 (1972), 22.

[24] I. Claus, cited above, n. 10.

[25] *Kleinwort Benson v Lincoln City Council* [1999] 2 AC 417.

[26] But see the discussion in N. MacCormick, *Rhetoric and the Rule of Law* (Oxford, 2005), pp. 256–6.

Moving to more recent controversy, over the permissibility of detaining terrorist suspects without trial, or about what is to be deemed torture, or inhuman or degrading treatment of such suspects, one may ask: 'What is the key issue when the matter comes before the law courts? Is it what the law is, or is it what the law shall be?' If it is the former, no doubt the judges are the most competent decision makers. But if it is the latter, why should judges have the final say, not elected politicians holding office in a democratically accountable government? Really, the one question is: 'Who should make that law, and be final arbiter of its meaning? Parliament and ministers answerable to it? Or judges answerable to no one?' (It is usual, in such talk, to add 'unelected' before 'judges'.)

Legal neo-realists, many traditional positivists and most if not all exponents of Critical Legal Studies can more or less join hands on this issue. Whether it is politicians or judges who take the final decisions about matters of this kind, the decisions are ineluctably political ones.

Hence this line of thought raises a crucial point material to the judicial independence debate. If judges are simply another set of political actors alongside of ministers, MPs and senior civil servants, by what right do they have the final say? What is their independence other than a kind of designed-in unaccountability for the political content of inevitably political decisions (albeit they may be in various ways accountable in respect of other aspects of their conduct)? It can be argued that all the stuff I put forward in my introduction about present-day problems in Scotland and other parts of the United Kingdom merely amounts to a kind of complicity in pious fraud. Judges are not decision-makers of a cleanly different kind from ministers or legislators. They are as much political actors as anyone else. Political decision-making is a seamless web, and the distribution of decision-making power among different institutions or persons is largely arbitrary, or, at any rate, highly pliable. The case for a specially protected judicial sphere depends on a false view about the possibility of differentiating what is strictly juridical from what is strictly political. In that case, however many people proclaim their deep concern for judicial independence, they may simply be victims of a dominant ideology.

I disagree strongly with this line of objection. It seems to me to be based on a faulty analysis or understanding of the possibility of applying practical reason of a specifically juristic kind even to the solution of controversial and politically sensitive questions of law, such as those posed in nearly every case involving application of the Human Rights Act. The same practical reason comes to bear on these politically salient issues as in others of equal difficulty but less political sensitivity.

Most often, statute law, probably quite recent statute law, is at the heart of the kinds of controversy that most concern us. Any statute, for example one or another Prevention of Terrorism Act, represents a new input into an already ongoing legal system. The legal system has already deep-seated principles about personal liberty built into it. Added to that are competing recent statutory obligations to apply Convention Rights as domestic rights. The restrictions on liberty imposed by the new Act take effect in that context. To make sense of this newly enacted law one has to read it in the light of the existing legal system to see what changes it brings about, and how best to make sense of newly enacted rules in the whole context of the amended but continuing legal system.

It will not be remarkable if a judge or an advocate forms an understanding of the whole meaning and impact of the enacted law that does not perfectly match that of the politicians who participated in enacting it as law. It will certainly be formed in a different general context, based on awareness of the law more than on attention to a particular political programme or a particular security emergency. The longer legislation sits in the statute book unamended, the more must this be the case. Many statutes fall to be applied long after the particular lawmakers who promoted them or enacted them have moved on to different concerns, suffered electoral defeat, even retired altogether, or died.

In just such settings, respect for the Rule of Law imperatively requires insulating the courts and the judiciary from improper political pressures by members of the executive and the legislature. This is a cornerstone of all the most authoritative human rights declarations, charters and conventions currently in force in Europe and around the world. Even a politician who is understandably surprised, disappointed or even outraged by the interpretation a judge or bench of judges has given to recently enacted law has to beware of undermining the rule of law on which her or his own position also in the end depends. Politicians ought not to interfere with or put pressure on judges to take a particular political line in legal interpretation, except by the weight and quality of the interpretative arguments their own advocates advance in open court. The law once enacted, it is the courts that have the last word in ascribing authoritative meaning to it in any case of controversy.

When parliamentarians or ministers are dissatisfied with the results, their legitimate recourse is that of a return to the legislative drafting board with a view to producing a new version of the law that will be yet clearer in pointing the way to the desired outcome. The sequence of re-enactments of legislation amending quite recent statute law about terrorism affords an object lesson in this.

It is trivially true that the law is always a target for political action. All political parties with any kind of reforming programme, whether of the left or of the right or of the ever-more-crowded centre, or of an ecological or a consumer-protectionist or trade union sympathetic cast of mind, need to change the law. Parties elected on a reform ticket need to carry out their reforms. Political reforms need legal enactment. New ministers with reforms to bring forward need legislative time, and legislative draftsmen, and ways to translate political principles into workable laws. What makes the laws workable, however, is their subsequent implementation through judicial decisions on the basis of interpretations that may have to be refined and then refined again through the stages and processes of appeal. This cannot but involve both putting it in the context of a coherent overall conception of the legal system, and also implementing the values implicit in the legislation, those very values that have been argued out in the political process.[27]

Recently, the search for overall coherence has become both acute and yet acutely difficult in areas concerning liberty and security, where important human rights commitments and new restrictive laws have to be read together as a coherent whole. I know of no more powerful example of painstaking and careful legal-coherentist reasoning than that expounded by Lord Bingham in his leading speech in the first of the *A v Home Secretary* terrorist suspects cases.[28]

It is no part of my argument that judges are infallible or always wiser than other mortals. Unfortunate judicial embroilment in politics can occur otherwise than by some actual or attempted exercise of improper influence by ministers or other politicians—or, indeed, agents of big business. Judges who resist or denature political reforms that have been successfully embodied in legislation run a similar risk, and do so more culpably. Some thinkers of the Critical Legal Studies (CLS) movement indeed go so far as simply to deny the existence of any gap at all between law and politics, precisely because of the role the courts play in implementing the law. 'Critical' theorists point out that judges are always having to choose whether to pursue values akin to those that currently prevail

---

[27] This is substantiated in MacCormick, *Rhetoric and the Rule of Law*, pp. 139–41.
[28] *A (FC) and others v Secretary of State for Home Affairs* [2005] 2 AC 68 at 90–129.

in legislative programmes, or values opposed to them.[29] In a curious way, their most dire opponent, Ronald Dworkin, himself also elides any real differentiation between the deepest legal questions and those of political and moral philosophy.[30]

It took me a whole book—my recent *Rhetoric and the Rule of Law*—to argue this matter to a conclusion that seemed to me satisfactory. The 'critical' thesis about law-application is grossly overstated when it denies that there really can be objective legal arguments that give better or worse interpretations regardless of personal preferences among judges. On this Dworkin and I are in agreement, and he saw this light long before I did. Objective grounds of legal preference do indeed exist, though of course there is frequent and honest subjective disagreement about these. Judges can make mistakes, and of course they sometimes do, even if there can be no correcting the mistakes of final appellate tribunals save through subsequent scholarly and journalistic critique and eventual judicial response to that, if it has been well and convincingly stated. Judges can also take sides in an improper way, and sometimes do. One very distinguished judge once confessed that there was a time when, in respect of trade union law, the judiciary seemed generally to act on the basis of a probably unconscious kind of class bias.[31] They can surely be biased on other grounds—look at the language in some of the nineteenth-century cases about women's right to vote or to undertake medical education.[32] There must be present-day parallels, though it would not serve my present purpose to dig them up.

Errors that are possible are not inevitable, nor are they universal. Judges can indeed, and by my impressionistic judgement most of them do, steer well clear of any kind of political partisanship in fulfilling the duties of their office. Thus do they keep well out of politics in any crude sense.[33] Common sense confirms the main thrust of the sociological case Niklas Luhmann advances in his 'system theory' of law, concerning the

---

[29] Compare generally D. Kennedy, *A Critique of Adjudication* (Cambridge, MA, 1997); A. Norrie (ed.), *Closure or Critique* (Edinburgh, 1993), esp. chap. 7 (P. Goodrich, 'Fate as Seduction').

[30] R. Dworkin, 'Hart's Postscript and the Character of Political Philosophy', *Oxford Journal of Legal Studies*, 24 (2004), 1–37.

[31] Compare Lord Justice Scrutton, 'The Work of the Commercial Court', *Cambridge Law Journal*, 1 (1921–3), 6–20 at 8.

[32] See A. Sachs and J. H. Wilson, *Sexism and the Law* (London, 1978).

[33] MacCormick, *Rhetoric and the Rule of Law*, chap. 13. But contrast, for example, J. Balkin, 'Ideological drift and the Struggle over Meaning', *Connecticut Law Review*, 25 (1993), 369.

distance that can be maintained, and that perhaps has to exist, between the political and the legal.[34]

Taking politics in a larger view, however, as concerning whatever is for the common good of a polity and its citizens, the non-partisanship of the judiciary, coupled with their institutional and individual independence, is itself a precious political achievement. If there really can be states that live by the Rule of Law as a genuine achievement, not an ideological smokescreen, it does depend on a successful, if not necessarily a formal and absolute, separation of powers. Such a separation ensures that different functions are carried out by different agencies each of which reasonably trusts the others to keep to their own patch according to local constitutional understandings.

It is not then the case that judges and courts are in every sense non-political—of course they ought to be non-partisan, refraining from taking sides overtly in matters of inter-party dispute in the ongoing political struggles of the day. But achieving non-partisan impartiality is itself a particular political role, one of inestimable value in securing constitutional balance. It is by participating in this way that judges contribute most to sustaining the common good of the polity. There is no single constitutional blueprint for free government, nor any one-size-fits-all version of the separation of powers. Judicial independence comes with quite acceptable local variations in different constitutional traditions and structures. Some forms of 'judicial activism' are tolerated and tolerable in one kind of liberal state that would seem intolerable in another.

In both England and Wales and in Scotland we are in a period of transition. Established and unwritten, perhaps even hitherto unspoken, norms that have supported judicial independence and facilitated mutually respectful distance between the judicial and the other branches of government are changing and require new articulation. To do this well calls for much careful reflection about the process whereby it is done as well as about outcomes that may be desirable. In the opening section of the paper I expressed concern that the executive has tended to take too much of a directing role in what needs to be a conversation with several parties. For one arm of state to take too strong a lead in setting the balance between it and the others cannot be healthy. This does not undermine proper deference to the democratic will that is expressed in parliamentary legis-

---

[34] N. Luhmann, *Law as a Social System*, trans. K. Ziegert, ed. D. Nobles and others (Oxford, 2004), chaps. 9 and 10, esp. at pp. 408–9; for constructively critical discussion, see MacCormick, *Institutions of Law*, chap. 10.

lation. It concerns how we should collectively come to the moment of legislative decision on deep constitutional issues.

Note. Thanks are due for comment and advice on this text to: Sir David Edward, KCMG, the Hon. Lord Hodge, Professor Alan Paterson, and Professor Zenon Bankowski, none of whom is either to blame for any flaws it contains or subject to the imputation of supporting the views stated in it.

ELIE KEDOURIE MEMORIAL LECTURE

Nation and Covenant
The Contribution of Ancient Israel to Modern Nationalism

ANTHONY D. SMITH
London School of Economics

I AM GRATEFUL TO THE BRITISH ACADEMY and to Mrs Sylvia Kedourie for their invitation to give this Memorial Lecture in honour of her husband, the late Professor Elie Kedourie. It affords me an opportunity to acknowledge the eminence of a scholar who, among his many achievements, was one of the seminal contributors to the great debate about the origins and nature of nationalism, that central phenomenon of the modern world. Professor Kedourie's work in this field continues to exert a wide influence, and his trenchant critique remains the most forceful and concise statement of the argument against nationalism and all its works.

Of course, not all those who subscribe to his critique have been convinced by Professor Kedourie's positive theses. But my purpose here is not to engage in a general survey of the field, much less of a critique of it. Instead, I wish to put forward a specific argument about a crucial aspect of modern nationalism—which, for want of a better term, I shall call 'covenantal'. To support this argument, I shall need to turn back to two of Professor Kedourie's most important theses: the secular nature of modern nationalism, and what we might term its religious lineage. By building on his theses, I hope to be able to acknowledge and demonstrate my continuing debt to Elie Kedourie's powerful insights into the nature of nationalism.[1]

Read at the Academy 4 May 2006.
[1] For Kedourie's influence, see the essays in Sylvia Kedourie (1998).

My overall aim is twofold. First, I shall try to show some cultural affinities between the covenantal and prophetic ideals of ancient Israel, as revealed in the Hebrew Bible, and some of the main themes and goals of modern nationalism. Second, I hope to suggest possible causal links between the two in certain political frameworks and Christian traditions, notably through the post-Reformation return to the Old Testament, which helped to shape what I regard as the earliest form of nationalism, a 'covenantal' form, in early modern Western Europe.

I: Nationalism and the Hebrew Bible

It may be helpful to start with definitions of some vexed but indispensable terms in this field of study. Accordingly, I define *nationalism* as an ideological movement for attaining and maintaining autonomy, unity and identity on behalf of a human population some of whose members deem it to constitute an actual or potential 'nation'; *nation* as a named and self-defining human population whose members cultivate shared symbols, memories, myths and values, inhabit an historic homeland, disseminate a distinctive public culture, and observe common laws and customs; and *national identity* as the continuous reproduction and reinterpretations of the pattern of values, symbols, myths and memories that compose the distinctive heritage of nations, and the identification of individuals with that heritage.[2]

A secular doctrine

In the well-known first sentence of his celebrated book on *Nationalism*, Professor Kedourie claimed that 'Nationalism was a doctrine invented in Europe at the beginning of the nineteenth century.' (Kedourie, 1960: 1). He went on to argue that, despite the legend of the French Revolution, the first full exposition of the doctrine of nationalism was that of Johann Gottlob Fichte in his *Addresses to the German Nation* of 1807–8, in which he set out his programme for a truly German national education by, in Kedourie's words, 'fashioning in man a stable and infallible good will'. (Kedourie, 1960: 83) Here, Fichte was only following through to its political conclusion the teaching of his master, Immanuel Kant, that 'the good

---

[2] For definitions of these terms, see especially Deutsch (1966: chap. 1); Connor (1994: chap. 4); and A. D. Smith (1973: section 1) and (2002).

will, which is the free will, is also the autonomous will', that is, one that obeys only the laws of morality within the human soul, as opposed to the laws of God or nature (Kedourie, 1960: 24). By extension, nationalism for Fichte is, in Kedourie's words, 'a method of teaching the right determination of the will', and hence of national self-determination. (Kedourie, 1960: 81) It is in this radical sense that nationalism is revealed as a thoroughly secular doctrine.

It would, of course, be possible to adduce an earlier statement of an exemplary political nationalism during the French Revolution. Professor Kedourie admitted that its celebrated declaration that 'The principle of sovereignty resides essentially in the Nation' is 'one prerequisite without which a doctrine such as nationalism is not conceivable'. (Kedourie, 1960: 12–13) And we could go further, and argue that in documents such as Rousseau's *Considérations sur le Gouvernement de Pologne* of 1772 (admittedly unpublished at the time) there is not only a foretaste of Fichte's passion for the moulding power of national education, but a consuming ardour for the nation and its distinctive character. Thus, in the section on Education, Rousseau writes:

> It is education that must give souls a national formation, and direct their opinions and tastes in such a way that they will be patriotic by inclination, by passion, by necessity . . .

> This love is his whole existence; he sees nothing but the fatherland, he lives for it alone; when he is solitary, he is nothing; when he has ceased to have a fatherland, he no longer exists; and if he is not dead, he is worse than dead. National education is proper only to free men; it is they only who enjoy a collective existence and are truly bound by law. . . .

And, after condemning the uniform slavery of modern Europeans, Rousseau urged the Poles: 'At twenty a Pole ought not to be a man of any other sort; he ought to be a Pole' (Watkins, 1953: 176).[3] But, in a sense, this only serves to confirm Kedourie's basic contention, that nationalism is a thoroughly secular doctrine, in which humanity, not the divine, is the measure of all things. This is, if anything, underlined by Rousseau's

---

[3] For Rousseau's definition of 'civil religion' in his *Du Contrat Social*, IV, chap. VIII, see Watkins 1953: 142–55, especially 147–8, where we read:

> The second [sc.species of religion], limited to a single country only, gives that country its special patrons and tutelary deities. Its dogmas, its rites and its external cult are prescribed by law; outside of the single nation which follows it, it regards everything as infidel, foreign and barbarous; it extends the rights and duties of man no farther than its altars.

eulogy of the work of three ancient legislators—Moses, Lycurgus and Numa Pompilius—in which he contrasts the petty egotism of modern European nations with the heroic souls of the ancients. Here I am concerned only with his description of the work of Moses:

> The first [sc. Moses] conceived and executed the astonishing project of creating a nation out of a swarm of wretched fugitives, ... who were wandering as a horde of strangers over the face of the earth without a single inch of ground to call their own. Out of this wandering and servile horde Moses had the audacity to create a body politic, a free people; ...
>
> To prevent his people from melting away among foreign peoples, he gave them customs and usages incompatible with those of the other nations; he overburdened them with peculiar rites and ceremonies; he inconvenienced them in a thousand ways in order to keep them constantly on the alert and to make them forever strangers among other men; and all the fraternal bonds with which he drew together the members of his republic were as many barriers keeping them separate from their neighbours and preventing them from mingling with them. That is how this peculiar nation, so often subjugated, so often dispersed and apparently destroyed, but always fanatical in its devotion to its Law, has nevertheless maintained itself to the present day, scattered among but never intermingled with the rest; and that is why its customs, laws and rites subsist, and will endure to the end of time, in spite of the hatred and persecution of the rest of the human race.   (Watkins, 1953: 163–4)

Leaving aside the exaggerations of this passage, it is clear that Rousseau is intent on presenting a purely secular version of the sacred history of the Jews. It is no longer the Covenant with the Lord that has formed the children of Israel into a nation, and Moses is no longer the servant of the Lord, not even the greatest of the prophets, as he is called in the last chapter of the book of Deuteronomy. He has become a national hero, a nation-builder, and the nation, as David Bell points out, is envisaged as a construct (Bell, 2001: 39). This, then, is an early example of what Professor Kedourie called the 'transformation of religion into nationalist ideology', many examples of which he then went on to describe and deplore (Kedourie, 1960: 76).[4]

---

[4] To create his subversive secular narrative, Rousseau has exaggerated the plight of the Jews after the Exodus, as well as their degree of separation and devotion to the Law thereafter; on which, see Bell (2001: chap. 1). Baron (1960: chap. 2) and Cohler (1970) discuss Rousseau's views on nationalism.

The religion of nationalism

And yet, this is only one aspect of nationalism. Nationalism may be a secular ideology, both in its German Romantic and its French republican varieties, but it is at the same time a special form of religion. This is already manifest in Rousseau's advice to the Poles to keep alive and nurture their national spirit through collective activities like festivals, games and schooling, as it is in his obvious admiration for the devotion to the Law and the longevity of the Jewish people, as well as the importance which he and later nationalists ascribe to rituals and ceremonies in national perpetuation. For Kedourie, too, secular nationalism can annex and use the powerful and tenacious loyalties of a long-held faith, and in this connection he cites the modern Egyptian, pan-Arab, Armenian and Greek cases. But I think we can go further. Nationalism, as he also concedes, may act as a substitute for traditional religion. But it can do so, only because it constitutes itself as a form of religion. A religion of this world, certainly, and in that original sense of the term, secular; but a religion with a divinity of its own, the nation, a separation of the elect, the members of the nation, a distinction between sacred national and profane objects and symbols, a strong emphasis on national ritual and self-sacrifice, and a powerful belief in national history, destiny and posterity. As the Petition of the Agitators of 1792 put it: 'The image of the *patrie* is the sole divinity whom it is permissible to worship.'

This form of religion clearly differs from the traditional soteriological kind analysed by Max Weber in his multi-volume *Religionssoziologie*, in which human salvation is sought from a source external to the phenomenal world, a transcendent cosmic power that guides and shapes our world. Rather the religious aspect of nationalism resembles the kind of societal religion defined and treated so extensively by Emile Durkheim in his *Elementary Forms of the Religious Life* (1915). Here Durkheim emphasises the role of religion, in accordance with the word's etymology, in binding together a group of people into a moral community by means of beliefs and rituals relating to the distinction between sacred and profane things. In fact, Durkheim's analysis fits the religion of nationalism rather more closely than it does the totemism of the Australian tribes. Nationalism, as an ideology, is self-reflexive; its object of worship is the community defined as a nation, and the worshippers of that community form a sacred communion of believers ready to sacrifice themselves on the altar of the nation for the sake of national defence and regeneration. Moreover, the communal religion of nationalism elevates the people, this particular people, and identifies them closely with a specific ancestral territory and its distinctive landscapes. This it does, not because this happens to be the spot where the community dwells, an accident of nature, but because in the nationalist vision homeland and people belong together and endow each other with genuineness, originality, and 'authenticity'. Here is the heart of the inner-worldly religion of nationalism: a world of autonomous, unified and exclusive peoples drawing sustenance from their intimate ancestral landscapes and regenerating themselves through the rediscovery and dissemination of their authentic cultures.[5]

It should be clear from the foregoing that I am not using the term 'religion of nationalism' in the sense in which several scholars describe the contemporary manifestations of 'religious nationalism', notably in the Islamic, Hindu and Buddhist traditions, but also of the Christian revival in America. These manifestations are, to my mind, more reminiscent of what Professor Kedourie terms the use of religion by a nationalism, which seeks to harmonise traditional religious beliefs and precepts with its own postulates, so as to intensify and extend itself among traditional believers. In this sense, traditional religions, suitably emended, may act as 'carriers' of collective sentiments and activities, redirected of course to new political ends, as Tilak used the cult of the dread goddess Kali in India for anti-British political ends. Nationalism may need these carriers if it is to extend its hold among traditional believers, but it does not require them for its own formation; and it is with that formation that I am chiefly concerned here.[6]

Religious origins of nationalism

Since the Second World War, if not earlier, the scholarly consensus has come to regard both nations and national*ism*, the ideology and movement, as modern—that is, chronologically recent and structurally novel. For many scholars, the ideology dates from the late eighteenth-century Western revolutions, with most nations seen as creations of a modern nationalism. In this perspective, both nations and nationalism are regarded as products of the 'modernisation' of society and the revolution

---

[5] For Weber's *Religionssoziologie*, see Weber (1965); and for Durkheim's theory, see Durkheim (1915). Though Durkheim wrote very little on nations and nationalism, much of his thought presupposes the nation as the form of modern society and nationalism as its cohesive force; on which, see Mitchell (1931); also Llobera (1994).

[6] On contemporary 'religious nationalisms' in Islam, Hinduism, Judaism and Christianity, see especially Juergensmeyer (1993), Van der Veer (1994) and Kepel (1995).

of thought known as the Enlightenment. There is much to commend in this view. Without doubt, it represents a major advance on its predecessor, the perennialist perspective which defined as nations most pre-modern named political and ethnic communities. Clearly, many nations *have* been formed in the last two hundred years, and in many cases the nationalist movements of their intelligentsias have indeed helped to shape and direct them.[7]

Many nations, but not all of them. Even some of the champions of the modernist orthodoxy had their doubts, most notably with regard to England. Thus, in a footnote to his *Nations and Nationalism*, Ernest Gellner puzzles over 'the early emergence of national sentiment in England' centuries before the coming of the industrial order, which may be due, he thinks, to the rise of an individualist, mobile spirit (Gellner, 1983: 91, footnote 1). And in his *Nations and Nationalism since 1780*, Eric Hobsbawm speaks of membership of an historic state acting directly 'upon the consciousness of the common people to produce proto-nationalism—or perhaps even, in the case of Tudor England, something close to modern patriotism' (Hobsbawm, 1990: 75). But suppose this early patriotism is due neither to individualism nor to an historic state inducing this common consciousness, what other grounds might we invoke that makes England such a challenge to modernist orthodoxy? And are there other cases which cast doubt on the dominant paradigm?

I think there are such cases, and that we may even speak of a form of national*ism*, the ideology and movement, *avant la lettre*. Nationalism, after all, appears in different historical forms, and the modern Western secular form is but one of these, albeit the best-known. Here I am aligning myself with a growing number of historians for whom the modernist perspective is too restrictive, both because it dismisses the possibility of cases of pre-modern nations, and because it rules out a priori the possibility of a pre-modern form of national*ism*. In its largely secular form nationalism may have emerged in the late eighteenth-century West, but this should not make us frame our definition and our account of it in narrowly ethnocentric terms.[8]

---

[7] There is a large literature on modernist theories of nationalism. The key works here are Kedourie (1960) and (1971); Gellner (1964: chap. 7) and (1983); Nairn (1977); Breuilly (1982/1993); Hobsbawm (1990); and Anderson (1983/1991). For a critical review, see A. D. Smith (1998).

[8] Here I include Susan Reynolds (1984: chap. 8), John Gillingham (1992), Patrick Wormald (1984) and Adrian Hastings (1997). See also Len Scales (2000), and some of the essays in Zimmer and Scales (2005), especially by Susan Reynolds, Patrick Wormald and Sarah Foot; see also Hutchinson (2000).

This, I believe, is where the second of Professor Kedourie's theses, about the religious origins of nationalism, can help us. On the one hand, as we saw, nationalism is a form of secular, that is, inner-worldly religion, and as such opposed to the traditional kind of transcendental religions, even when it forms alliances with them. On the other hand, the religion of nationalism draws on many of the motifs, beliefs and rituals of traditional religions and uses them for its own political purposes; and these essentially pre-modern traditions have remained relevant in the forging of nations and the formation of nationalisms. For example, in 1817, German student and gymnastic organisations garlanded themselves with oak-leaves and marched up to the Wartburg Castle, by torchlight, lit fires, burned 'un-German' books, listened to sermons, and with joined hands, to the tolling bells of the nearby church of Eisenach, swore to uphold their Bund. Their model for this display of nationalist exaltation was the Lutheran liturgy and service, including the singing of various Protestant hymns. In the same spirit, at the ruins of the castle of Devin in 1836, where the Moravian king Svatopluk had resided in the ninth century, a Slovak students' festival celebrated with popular songs the memory of an obscure nobleman named Pribina who ruled the city of Neutra around 830. And, lest we should be misled into thinking these fantasies were simply effusions of the spirit of Romanticism, we can observe similar borrowings and models at various points in the French Revolution where, for all its anti-clerical fervour, Catholic motifs were interwoven with secular patriotic messages; examples include the staging at Notre-Dame of the semi-sacred cantata, *Prise de la Bastille*, based in part on the apocryphal book of *Judith*, during the great *Fête de la Fédération* in July 1790, the liturgy for the funeral of Marat in 1793, where the procession accompanying his body sang 'O coeur de Jesus, coeur de Marat', and the celebration of the feast of the Supreme Being in 1794, which saw Robespierre descend from a cardboard and plaster mountain topped with a tree of liberty.[9]

Of course, as these examples indicate, nationalism has been shaped by more than one cultural tradition. But, if we focus specifically on its religious aspect, that is, nationalism as an inner-worldly religion of the people, where should we go to seek its source and formative process? Professor Kedourie himself was minded to discover it in the drive for

---

[9] On the Slovak festival, see Kohn (1960: 15–16), and for the *fêtes* of Revolutionary France, Kohn (1967: Part I) and Schama (1989: 491–513). For the artistic dimensions of these festivals, see Herbert (1972). Marat's death and David's painting of *Marat Assassiné* (1793) are discussed in the essays in Vaughan and Weston (2000). For Germany, see Mosse (1975: chap. 3).

religious uniformity in Europe from the time of the later Roman empire, and in the later millennial tradition of antinomian heterodox Christian sects like the Franciscan Spirituals and the Anabaptists. Other scholars like Adrian Hastings have looked to Christianity's sanctioning of vernacular worship and Bible translation, and its adoption of the national political ideal of ancient Israel as recorded in the Old Testament which the Church had taken over and reinterpreted. For Hastings, therefore, nations and nationalism were at root Christian phenomena, products of a vernacularising Judeo-Christian tradition.[10]

It is true that Christian millennialism draws on the messianic idea of ancient Israel; and that messianism, in one form or another, has played an important, if variable, part in modern nationalisms—in some cases more than others. But the messianic age and the coming of the Messiah can also impede the rise of nationalism, which depends on autoemancipation and human political engagement. This applies even more to millennialist beliefs, which often reject this world and in any case depend on divine intervention rather than self-help. As for Christianity's vernacularising tendency, this did not preclude the dominance of certain transterritorial (and transethnic) languages. But the fundamental difficulty with these accounts is that Christianity, for all its territorial and ethnic compromises on the ground, is a universalist, and universalising, world religion which for much of its history has been purveyed through clerisies, liturgies and languages which were transterritorial and supranational in both the Greek East and the Latin West. Nations and nationalism, on the other hand, are founded on principles of cultural diversity and uniqueness, and contain strong ethnic, ethnopolitical and territorial components. This means that we need to look for a source and a model of cultural individuality, ethnic specificity and territorial attachment, beyond a universalising Christianity, both in historical time and in ideological scope; and that, as a number of scholars from Hans Kohn to Liah Greenfeld and David Aberbach have argued, brings us back to the Jewish root of the Christian tradition in the Hebrew Bible, to the Prophets, the Psalms, and above all, the Pentateuch and its Torah.[11]

---

[10] See Kedourie (1971: Introduction); and Hastings (1997: esp. chaps. 1–2, 8). Hastings (1999) presents his views on chosen peoples; and see the symposium on his contribution in *Nations and Nationalism* (2003).

[11] For some earlier analyses of the general influence of the Old Testament on nationalism, especially in England, see Kohn (1944: chaps. 1 and 4), Greenfeld (1992: chap.1) and Aberbach (2005), the latter also highlighting the importance of biblical poetry for national sentiment.

The Biblical Covenant

Central to the laws and narratives of the Pentateuch is the ideal of the Covenant between God and His people, seen as a specific cultural community of descent. This Covenant took two forms: on the one hand, God's unconditional promise to Noah not to bring another flood to destroy humanity and His choice of Abraham's seed and His grant of the land of Canaan to his descendants, and on the other hand a *conditional* grant of election of the whole people of Israel in the Covenant given to Moses on Mount Sinai. Whereas the focus of the first is on a land and an ethnic community seen as an extended family, the later covenant is directed to the Torah and the creation of a 'kingdom of priests, and an holy nation' (Exodus, 19:6). God has chosen a particular people because of the love He bore them and their ancestors, the Patriarchs, and He will bless them *on condition that* they obey his laws and keep his commandments. As Moses reminds his people:

> The Lord did not set his love upon you, nor choose you, because ye were more in number than any other people; for ye were the fewest of all people; But because the Lord loved you, and because he would keep the oath which he had sworn unto your fathers, hath the Lord brought you out with a mighty hand, and redeemed you out of the house of bondmen, from the hand of Pharoah king of Egypt. (Deut.7:6–8)

This latter Covenant has a number of aspects. Conceived as a partnership between God and his people, but not as a contract for personal advantage, the Covenant is prior to all other pacts, open-ended and intergenerational. For the children of Israel, choosing to enter into the Covenant meant being intimate and at one with God through the collective observance of His righteous statutes and judgements. It also meant being His 'witnesses' and a 'servant whom I have chosen' (Isaiah 43:10). On the other hand, this elevated status brought with it much greater divine scrutiny and judgement. As the prophet Amos reminded the people: 'You only have I known of all the families of the earth: therefore I will punish you for all your iniquities' (Amos 3:2).

Exactly here lies the coiled spring of the ideal of covenantal ethnic election, which was to prove so energising for so many peoples. For election depends entirely on performance, the continuing conduct of the community in executing God's laws. This dynamic was reinforced by another antinomy: separation and engagement. On the one hand, the Covenant involved a quest for holiness through the separation of the chosen people from all other peoples; on the other hand, it contained a promise of blessings on all peoples through the example, light and message of a righteous Israel. In the words of Isaiah: 'I the Lord have called thee in righteousness, and will hold thy hand, and will keep thee, and give thee for a covenant of the people, for a light of the Gentiles' (Isaiah 42:6–7).

Where the Psalms plumb the depths of individual intimacy and redemption by a compassionate God, the Prophets both expand upon the covenantal ideal, and relate it to divine promises of collective deliverance and restoration. Jeremiah tells us that the Lord will bring the people back from the north country, 'and with them the blind and the lame'; He will bring them again to their land, where they will all know the Lord (Jeremiah 31:8, 34). Amos promises a restoration of the 'tabernacle of David that is fallen' and a rebuilding of 'the waste cities' and a replanting of the vineyards (Amos 9:11, 14), while the post-Exilic Prophets, Haggai and Zechariah, speak of the return of the exiles from Babylon to Jerusalem and rebuilding of its Temple, destroyed by the Babylonians. Each of them recalls an earlier deliverance, the model of divine power and justice, the Exodus from Egypt and the redemption from slavery and Pharaonic oppression; in Haggai's words: 'According to the word that I covenanted with you when ye came out of Egypt, so my spirit remaineth among you: fear not' (Haggai 2:5).[12]

Cultural affinities with nationalism

While we may recognise the ancient Jewish roots of the Christian traditions, what relevance, we may ask, can they have to a modern ideology like nationalism? How can we conceivably span an interval of some three thousand years, with all its vast intervening economic, social and political changes across Europe and the Middle East? Here I shall attempt to answer these questions by following a modified version of the method advocated by Max Weber, namely of establishing a *cultural affinity* between two disparate phenomena, in this case biblical Israel and modern nationalism, and then supporting it, as far as the historical data will allow, by a *causal explanation* which, in the nature of things, can only be partial.

---

[12] For the ancient Jewish Covenant in its biblical and post-biblical settings, see Nicholson (1988) and Novak (1995); Walzer (1985) gives an original account of the energising role of Exodus politics. More theological accounts are provided in Gillman (1992) and Sacks (2002). Covenanted peoples and their histories, with special reference to the Ulster-Scots, Afrikaners and Zionists, are analysed by Akenson (1992); and on myths of ethnic election, see A. D. Smith (2003: chaps. 3–5) and the essays in Hutchinson and Lehmann (1994).

In attempting this, I am all too conscious of the many lacunae in the historical records which permit of only the sketchiest of reconstructions.[13]

Two words of caution are in order. Inevitably, the burden of any explanation in such a case falls, as Professor Kedourie recognised, on continuities and changes in cultural traditions, and these are open to misinterpretation, especially by those of us who are not specialists in particular historical periods. Yet, that is not, I think, sufficient reason for not attempting to put forward generalisations and explanatory models, even where this involves a considerable degree of speculation. We are dealing here with religious traditions that were widely accepted in medieval and early modern Europe, at least by the educated classes, however much they were reinterpreted; and, as Edward Shils reminds us, 'tradition, when it is accepted, is as vivid and as vital to those who accept it as any other part of their action or belief. It is the past in the present but it is as much part of the present as any very recent innovation' (Shils, 1981: 12).

Second, in treating of the ideals of 'ancient Israel', I shall sidestep the vigorous current debates between conservatives and revisionists on the dating of different parts of the Hebrew Bible and the degree of historical accuracy that they convey. Here I am concerned solely with 'biblical Israel', a construct not of the Higher Biblical Criticism, but a living tradition of various Jewish and Christian communities from the onset of the Middle Ages to the Reformation and beyond. Hence, this is a picture of ancient Israel shorn, for example, of the much later insights of archaeology and epigraphy, but it is one that lived in the consciousness and memory of countless generations of Jews and Christians in Europe.[14]

Let me start with the argument from cultural affinity. At the outset, I defined nationalism as an ideological movement for attaining and maintaining autonomy, unity and identity for a human population some of whose members deem it to constitute an actual or potential 'nation'. Specifically, the core doctrine of nationalism holds that humanity is divided into nations, each with its own character, history and destiny; that the nation is the source of political power; that to be free, human beings

---

[13] Weber (1965) uses the concept of an 'elective affinity' between certain ideals and their 'bearer' strata in his sociology of religion. Here I use a modified version, to signal a *cultural* affinity (without any element of choice) between separate sets of ideas and practices in different epochs and geocultural areas.

[14] For the debate with the biblical 'revisionists', who regard the composition of the Pentateuch as post-Exilic, and even of Hellenistic date, see the essays in Day (2004); see also Ahlstrom (1986) and Davies (1995). The revisionist archaeological evidence is presented in Finkelstein and Silberman (2001); for a detailed critique, see Dever (2003).

must belong to and give their first loyalty to a nation; that nations must seek maximum autonomy and self-expression; and that a world of peace and justice can only be founded on a plurality of free nations (See A. D. Smith, 1973: section 1).

Put like this, it is obvious that no legislator and no prophet in ancient Israel, or anywhere else, conceived of his people, let alone of humanity, in these abstract ideological terms. But, if we move to the concrete level of specific nationalisms, we find significant cultural affinities between some of the key concepts employed by these nationalisms, and the covenantal and prophetic ideals of ancient Israel as purveyed in the Hebrew Bible. Perhaps the most obvious of these is the long perceived parallel between the Exodus narrative of the departure of the Israelites from Pharaonic Egypt and their liberation from slavery and oppression, and the many modern ideologies and movements of national liberation from foreign oppression. But this affinity has recently been examined by Michael Walzer, Simon Schama and others, and here I want to focus specifically on the ideals of the Covenant itself, although it will be necessary later to link these to the Exodus narrative from time to time (Walzer 1985; Schama, 1987: ch. 2).

The covenantal ideals in question include the strong belief in Israel's conditional election; second, its fervent attachment to the Promised Land; third, its continual urge for a spiritual and political unity that so often eluded it; and finally, its promise of collective redemption and restoration to the Land of Israel.

Undoubtedly, the most potent of these ideals was the biblical belief in *ethnic election* contained in the Covenant. Its counterpart in modern nationalism is the aspiration for national individuality and uniqueness, entailing a special status and mission among the nations. Here the *locus classicus* is Herder, who called on his fellow-Germans, along with many East European ethnic communities, to cultivate their own languages and cultures, in order to rediscover their true identities, for 'Each nationality contains its centre of happiness within itself, as a bullet the centre of gravity.' Inveighing against Enlightenment cosmopolitanism, Herder invoked the divine plan, claiming that: 'God did not permit Himself such an amalgamation; therefore he has instructed each national group after its own manner' (Ergang, 1976) [1931]: 84, 97, citing Herder, J. G., *Sammtliche Werke*, ed. B. Suphan, E. Redlich *et al.* (Berlin, 1877–1913), 17, 59; 18, 206). He therefore went on to exhort his fellow-Germans: 'Let us follow our own path . . . let all men speak well or ill of our nation, our language, our literature: they are ours, they are ourselves, and let that be enough' (Berlin, 1976: 182, citing Herder, *Werke*, 18, 206).

For Schleiermacher, too, each nation is unique and has its own mission, because this is part of God's plan:

> Each nationality is destined through its peculiar organisation and its place in the world to represent a certain side of the divine image ... For it is God alone who directly assigns to each nationality its definite task on earth and inspires it with a definite spirit in order to glorify himself through each one in a peculiar manner. (Cited in Ergang, 1976: 250)

These ideals of chosenness and mission were expressed in a heroic past of unity and simplicity, which would guide Germany's rebirth. For Herder himself, German regeneration had to be sought in the poetry of the 'crude songs' that 'are the mirror of the ancient German soul and of the simplicity of their character'. For others like Friedrich Schlegel this required recapturing in colourful prose political memories of

> Germany in early times when its liberty and its original character were untrammelled, as well as its cultural development in the Middle Ages. This meant that I had to pay especial attention to the medieval state, to the unity of Christianity, to the Holy Roman Empire, and to the spirit of knighthood. (Friedrich Schlegel, *Lectures of 1812*, cited in Kohn, 1965: 61)

The Germans were by no means unique in these respects. Even earlier, English authors like Richard Hurd, John Brown and Tobias Smollett, as Gerald Newman has demonstrated, pointed to the honesty, purity and sincerity of the English, which can be related to the Protestant heritage of a chosen island people, who owed their free institutions to their 'Saxon ancestors'. *Per contra*, their counterparts across the Channel prized the sociability and refinement of the French national character, but, as in Germany, also lamented its decline into effeminacy. As antidote, artists and writers began to seek out golden ages of French greatness in the Middle Ages or the Renaissance, exhorting the French to return to the virtues of their ancestors, like Bayard, St Louis and Du Guesclin, or even Clovis's Franks. In this latter vein, Ange Pithou, in *Le triomphe des parisiens*, published shortly after the fall of the Bastille, called on his countrymen:

> Frenchmen, you have reconquered your liberty, that liberty of which the first Franks, your ancestors, were jealous; you will again become like them, strong and healthy; like them you will let your beards grow, and you will wear the long hair that they favoured. (Quoted in Bell, 2001: 153)

Such expressions of French heroic mission became ever more insistent in the next century, as during the Syrian crisis of 1840, when *Le National* exhorted its countrymen:

France, noble France, awake! ... resume your task, the task of 89 and 1830, and since you are forced to draw the sword of Fribourg and Marengo, draw the sword! The time has come. Think of supreme mission and the grandeur of your destiny. (*Le National*, 4, 7, 8 October 1840, cited in Gildea, 1994: 116)[15]

Such instances could be multiplied many times over. Belief in a national mission and destiny, coupled with a desire for national regeneration and unity, has become a staple of every nationalism across the globe. I am not arguing that these ideals are simply updated equivalents of the Covenant with ancient Israel. That would be both anachronistic and reductive, collapsing 'nationalism' into 'religion'. Rather, I seek to establish a cultural affinity between different phenomena, far removed in time and place, but nevertheless interrelated through living cultural traditions.

For it is, in fact, possible to demonstrate that these biblical motifs of chosenness, homeland, unity and ethnic regeneration find strong parallels in modern European nationalisms. Take the second ideal of the Promised Land. Ancient Jewish attachment to the Land of Israel finds its counterpart in the nationalist ideal of the homeland and of ancestral poetic landscapes.

Thus, one of the founders of the Swiss Helvetic Society, Franz Urs Balthazar, declared in 1763 that 'the character of the Swiss nation found its complete expression in its untamed Alpine landscape'; and a few years later, Johann Caspar Lavater in his *Schweizerlieder* urged Switzerland to '... hold fast with constant hand the newly tied bond of unity, because in this world there is no country like you, you Fatherland of Heroes' (Lavater, *Schweizerlieder*, 1767, cited in Kohn, 1944: 383; Zimmer, 1998: 647).

The links between Swiss chosenness, Alpine Confederation and unity were actually conceived in biblical terms by the historian Johannes von Muller, in his *History of the Swiss Confederation* of 1786, when he wrote:

> It is strange how the Bible seems to fit no other people better than you. What was originally a community of free shepherds grew into a Confederation of as many cantons as there were tribes in biblical times. This Confederation received three laws from God. If you keep them faithfully, you are invincible: to remain always, in war and peace, closely united by your patriotic habits and the joy of common festivities, one nation like one family; not to think of commercial

---

[15] On the rise of English nationalism, see Newman (1987) and for Britishness, Colley (1992). See also Trumpener (1997). For a general historical sociology of English identity, see Kumar (2003). Among many works on French nationalism, see Herbert (1972), Best (1989, especially the essays by Conor Cruise O'Brien and Hew Strachan), Gildea (1994) and Bell (2001); and especially the essays in Nora (1997–8). On German nationalist ideology, apart from Kohn (1965), see the works by Mosse (1963 and 1975) and James (2000).

> profits as Tyre did, nor of conquest, but to dwell on your inherited lands with your herds in innocence and freedom; to regard the imitation of foreign principles and habits as the end of your constitution. (Johannes von Muller, *Sammtliche Werke*, ed. Johannes Georg Muller, 40 parts in 7 vols. (Stuttgart: Cotta, 1831–5), 7, Pt. 1, p. XXXIII, cited in Kohn, 1957: 28–9)

Nor were such ideas confined to the neo-classical and Romantic eras. In the late nineteenth century, as Oliver Zimmer has pointed out, Swiss distinctiveness was increasingly tied to its Alpine habitat, so it is no surprise to find Ernest Bovet, a professor of French at Zurich University, writing in 1909 of an almost mystical link between them:

> A mysterious force has kept us together for 600 years and has given us our democratic institutions. A good spirit watches our liberty. A spirit fills our souls, directs our actions and creates a hymn on the one ideal out of our different languages. It is the spirit that blows from the summits, the Alps and the glaciers. (Ernest Bovet, 'Nationalité', *Wissen und Leben*, 21 (1909), 431–5, cited in Zimmer 1998: 652)[16]

Similar sentiments can be found in Greek nationalism, especially after the turn towards Byzantium from the mid-nineteenth century. The Greeks, of course, were doubly chosen: by the golden age of Athens and the sacred realm of Constantinople, as the fount of democracy and the sole bearer of Orthodox Christianity.

For the first, we may cite Adamantios Korais' belief in innate Greek superiority, despite the Greeks' current lamentable backwardness. In the Report which he delivered in 1803 to a French audience in Paris, and which Professor Kedourie included in his anthology of nationalist writings, we read that:

> The Greeks, proud of their origins, far from shutting their eyes to European enlightenment, never considered the Europeans as other than debtors who were repaying with substantial interest the capital which they had received from their own ancestors. (Adamantios Korais, *Lettres inédites de Coray à Chardon de la Rochette* (Paris, 1877): 451–90, cited in Kedourie, 1971: 158–9)

For the second myth of ethnic election, we must look to the potent prophetic tradition that kept alive the belief in a Byzantine imperial restoration, to the propagation of the *Megali Idea* after 1844, and to the

---

[16] On Swiss nationalism, see Kohn (1957) and Steinberg (1976). The growth of the *Eidgenossenschaft* is described by Im Hof (1991: chap. 1) and the Helvetic Society and the development of modern Swiss nationalism are analysed by Zimmer (2003). On the Alpine dimension, see Schama (1995: 479–81, 490–3) and Charlton (1984: 45–9); for its links with Swiss national identity, see Zimmer (1998).

five-volume *History of the Greek Nation* penned by Konstantinos Paparrigopoulos from 1860–77. Here the historian seeks to integrate 'our medieval Empire' and 'our medieval forefathers' into the history of a Greek nation that has been active over a period of three thousand years, and thereby to fuse the nation with its Orthodox heritage and its continuity of faith and ritual. The implication was clear: the Greeks would realise their mission and destiny by uniting all Greek-speakers outside Greece within the new Greek state and by restoring their homeland. In line with the ancient prophetic hope of redemption through territorial restoration, many Greeks came to believe that national regeneration could only be achieved through restoration of the empire and the reconquest of the Byzantine imperial capital.[17]

In Catholic Poland, likewise, a heightened sense of chosenness raised messianic expectations and the hope of redemption through the restoration of their state. This was particularly true of the Polish exiles in Paris and other cities after 1830. Already in the Warsaw of the 1831 revolt, Kazimierz Brodzinski declared:

> God wished to have the nations as separate individualties, like human beings, in order that they might be his instruments to influence the whole of mankind and to establish the necessary harmony of the world. The Polish nation, I declare, is through an inspiration from Heaven the philosopher, the Copernicus of the moral world. Misunderstood, persecuted, the Polish nation will continue its existence, it will find men who will profess its faith, and its crown of thorns will be changed into a crown of victory and national glory . . . Its mission has been to stand guard in the midst of storms on the frontier which divides barbarism and civilisation. (Cited in Kohn, 1960: 39–40)

But, nowhere was this messianic theme of chosenness for suffering and ultimate triumph more poignantly expressed than in the poems and writings of Adam Mickiewicz. In *Forefathers' Eve*, he expressed it succinctly: 'Now is my nation on the Martyr's throne'. In *The Books of the Polish Nation and of the Polish Pilgrims*, he spoke in prophetic terms of the resurrection of the Polish nation, which will cause all the wars in Christendom to cease, and he likened the Pole to a pilgrim who has made a vow to journey to the holy land. Speaking of the Poles in particular, Mickiewicz averred that 'The Slav nationality has received a special mission; through

---

[17] Korais' Report is translated in Kedourie (1971: 153–88). For the Greek Enlightenment and neo-classicism, see especially Campbell and Sherrard (1968: chap. 1) and Kitromilides (1979) and (1989). The Byzantine ideal is assessed by Kitromilides (1998); cf. the sociological analysis in Roudometof (2001: chaps. 1, 2, 4).

it, it exercises a magic influence on the souls and draws them towards truth and towards God' (Kohn, 1960: 42, 50).

These mystical outpourings must, of course, be seen in the context of a people which had lost its independent kingdom, whose homeland had been partitioned, and whose hopes of political salvation were repeatedly dashed; its nationalism, perhaps for that very reason, was all the more imbued with biblical and Christian motifs and imagery.[18]

What of the Jews themselves, whose ancestors had entered into the original Covenant and bequeathed its model to so many after them? Though, after the devastation of the First Crusade in 1099, there had been a trickle of returnees to Zion in the Middle Ages, notably Yehudah Halevi and much later Isaac Luria and his followers in Safed and elsewhere, calls for national restoration of the Jews to Israel were rare indeed until the mid-nineteenth century. Then, under the impulse of the Greek, Serb, Polish and German movements, rabbis Yehudah Alkalai and Zvi Kalisher, and the ethical socialist Moses Hess, began to urge their fellow-Jews to enter what Hess called the 'Sabbath of History' by returning to the land of their forefathers and foremothers. In their writings and those of their immediate successors, Peretz Smolenskin and Moshe Leib Lilienblum, the nationalist message has clear covenantal overtones. Thus Moses Hess writes: 'Each people must become, like the Jewish people, a people of God', thereby exemplifying just that nationalist transformation of religious beliefs which Professor Kedourie castigated (Hess, 1862/1958: 50, 74).

For Smolenskin, too, the Jews

> ... have always been a spiritual nation, because one whose Torah was the foundation of its statehood. From the start our people has believed that its Torah took precedence over its land and over its political identity.... (Peretz Smolenskin, *Maamarim* (Jerusalem, 1875–77/1925–26), cited in Hertzberg, 1960: 147).

For Eliezer Ben-Yehudah, on the other hand, the unique creativity of the Jewish people could not be severed from the homeland: 'The nation cannot live except on its own soil; only on this soil can it revive and bear magnificent fruit, as in days of old!' (Eliezer Ben-Yehudah, *HaShahar* x, 145 (Vienna, 1885), cited in Hertzberg, 1960: 165).

---

[18] The basic work on Polish history is Davies (1981, esp. Vol. II, I, chap. 1 for the growth of a Polish nation). For the Romantics and Pan-Slavists in Poland, see Kohn (1960: Part I, chap. 2); see also Peter Brock 'Polish nationalism' in Sugar and Lederer (1969: 310–72).

Here we already have a new covenant, not one between man and God, but between humanity and the land, one which entails the radical disruption of the *Galut* (exile) and an end to homelessness. This meant a new set of values, more concrete and physical, centred on human labour and nature, but still inspired by a powerful ethical imperative stemming from the Covenant and the Prophets. Thus, in Herderian vein Micha Berdichevski called on the Jews: 'Let us sing our song of life in our own way, and so achieve our essence, our immediacy': 'The wholeness of heart, man's purity, is the ultimate end.' But he went on to insist that a holy people must live on its own soil: '. . . a beaten, tortured and persecuted people is unable to be holy' (Micha Berdichevsky, *Ba-Derekh*: ii, 47, cited in Hertzberg, 1960: 299, 301).

If we recall that holiness in the Torah requires separation from other peoples, and that nationalism translates holiness into authenticity and uniqueness, then we have in these prophetic utterances of the early Zionists the clearest expression of cultural affinities with the covenantal ideal of the Torah. But they are not alone in this. For later socialist Zionists, from Aaron David Gordon and David Ben-Gurion to Berl Katznelson, the Bible, the Land, its heroes and the prophecies of national restoration remained the bedrock and spring of their thought and actions.[19]

II: Reformation and Nationalism

Ethnic election in medieval Christian traditions

Even if we were to concede the striking affinities between ancient biblical myths and ideals, and those of modern nationalisms, what possible historical links could there be between two such temporally distant cultural phenomena? Is there any evidence that these affinities were anything more than the expression of nationalists who had been steeped in biblical religion, and who sought, more or less consciously, to harmonise the two and fit their nationalism into a biblical mould? Of course, such a possibility begs the question of why they should try to do so, and why biblical ideals

---

[19] On early Zionism, see Vital (1980). Zionism and Judaism are discussed in Luz (1988) and Mendes-Flohr, 'In pursuit of normalcy: Zionism's ambivalence towards Israel's election' in Hutchinson and Lehmann (1994: 203–29); also the controversial account in Sternhell (1998). For a key early text, see Hess (1958) [1862]. On Berdichevski, see Ohana (1995) and for Ben-Gurion's practical messianism, see Tsahor (1995). The best Reader on Zionism remains Hertzberg (1960). For Zionism as a form of diaspora nationalism, see A. D. Smith (1999a: chap. 8).

should continue to matter so much to secular nationalists. For, undoubtedly, as we saw, there were powerful instances of nationalists seeking to ground their secular ideals on biblical foundations, both of the Old Testament and the New. In fact, by the eighteenth century, there was already a long tradition of returning to the Hebrew Bible and to ancient Jewish beliefs for illumination and legitimation, for what Colin Kidd has termed 'Mosaic history' and its 'ethnic theology' (Kidd, 1999: chap. 2).

We can, I think, go further and specify linkages between biblical ideals and modern nationalism, both general and specific. The more general linkages find their expression in the beliefs and practices of medieval Roman Catholic and Orthodox Christianity that preserved some of the traditions of biblical Israel. I am thinking in the first place of the tradition of sacred kingdoms and sacred kingship, highlighted by the practice of anointing with oil, such as was used in the ampulla for the kings of France crowned at Rheims, and of the many sculptured and stained glass images of sacred kingship exemplified by Israel's kings, David and Solomon, in churches, abbeys and cathedrals across Europe; and of the many Christian sovereigns who like Alfred and Henry VIII sought in David and Solomon, Hezekiah and Josiah, models of virtue and sanctity. Of course, this is a different, even a counterposed tradition, to that of the popular covenant, and it was sometimes denounced by prophets like Hosea for whom the sole king of Israel was the Almighty Himself: 'I gave thee a king in my anger, and took him away in my wrath' (Hosea 13:11).[20]

But what of those biblical motifs that spring from the covenantal tradition itself—motifs of election, homeland, unity and regeneration—that I have identified as having close parallels in modern nationalism? Can these too be found in the various traditions of medieval Christianity? To a certain extent I think they can, but their significance before the Reformation is often unclear. For example, a tradition of holy lands modelled on the Holy Land of Israel can be found in several parts of medieval Europe—in Hungary, Russia, Bohemia, France and Spain. Increasingly, this betokened a growing, if uneven, attachment to one part of medieval Christendom above others, an allegiance to the territorial kingdom identified with a dynasty and a people. Yet this was rarely accompanied by any drive for ethnic and territorial unity in a feudal Europe that, after the dis-

---

[20] Sacred kingship in western Europe, notably France and England, is analysed and illustrated by Strayer (1971: chap. l6), Beaune (1985), Guenée (1985: I, chap. 4) and John Guy, 'Monarchy and counsel: models of the state', in Collinson (2002: 113–42). On kingship in ancient Israel, see Talmon (1986: section 1).

integration of the Carolingian and Ottonian empires and the reduction of Byzantine territories, remained a patchwork of overlapping loyalties. Only towards the end of the medieval period, in the Spanish, French, Scottish and English kingdoms, was there any discernible movement towards territorial, if not yet social, unification. As for the biblical ideals of redemption and restoration, these tended to be spiritualised and translated into an otherworldly setting. Redemption of souls took the place of restoration of land and rebirth of community.[21]

However, what does retain its hold over the hearts and minds of many people in medieval Christian Europe is the myth of ethnic election, of the chosenness of a kingdom and its people. It was particularly marked in France from the thirteenth century onwards. Thus in his papal bull *Rex glorie* of 1311, Clement V claimed that God had divided the world into political territories based on language and ethnic descent, and that among these the kingdom of France held a special place:

> In the same way that the Israelites are known to have been granted the Lord's inheritance by the choice of Heaven, to carry out the hidden wishes of God, so the kingdom of France has been selected as the Lord's special people, marked with signs of honour, and chosen to carry out God's commands. (*Regestum Clementis* V, ed. cura et studio monarchorum Ordinis S. Benedicti, 8 vols. (Rome, 1885–92), no. 7501 cited in Housley, 2000: 235)

France's holiness was the result of the exemplary faith of its people and its 'most Christian king', but also of the virtue of its ancestors, the quality of its saints, especially St Denis and St Louis, the number of its holy relics and its vast array of great abbeys and cathedrals (See Beaune, 1985; Strayer, 1971: chap. 16).

Similar beliefs could be found across the Channel. In 1377, Adam Houghton, Edward III's Chancellor, claimed before Parliament that England was favoured by God, and that the English were the new Israelites and their kingdom the *heritage de Dieu*. His vision presented the Englishman of the fourteenth century (in the words of M. Wilks cited by Norman Housley) as a '*piers plowman*, the tiller of the soil of a landed church, a co-worker with Christ in the green fields of England', in analogy with the ancient Israelite in occupation of his sacred soil (cited in Housley, 2000: 238). This kind of English 'territorial patriotism' was particularly marked in the reigns of Richard II and Henry V, especially in the

---

[21] On the Holy Land and holy lands in medieval and early modern Europe, see the essays in Swanson (2000), especially that of Housley; for interpretations of the role of sacred territories, see Hastings (2003) and A. D. Smith (1999*b*).

celebrations after Agincourt—though only a few years later it was to be matched by Joan of Arc's belief that an attack on the 'saint royaume de France' was an affront to God Himself (Housley, 2000: 236, 238).

Far away at the other end of Europe, in the reign of Ivan III, the Great, in the latter half of the fifteenth century, Muscovite Russia, its ruler, its land and its people, became the focus of an increasingly fervent belief in divine election. The belief itself went back to Kievan Rus, indeed to not long after Vladimir's conversion to Christianity. But it was only several centuries later, after the fall of Constantinople in 1453, that it became the fulcrum of an elite national identity that saw in the Muscovite Russian kingdom the last bastion of Orthodox Christianity, the only truly Christian state. This in turn engendered the notion of Tsarist Russia as the Third Rome, an ideal most clearly formulated in the epistle of Philotheos, Abbot of Pskov, to Vasilii III at the beginning of the sixteenth century, when he wrote of the Russian kingdom and Church: 'Two Romes are fallen, but the third stands fast; a fourth there cannot be. Thy Christian kingdom shall not be given to another' (cited in Zernov, 1978: 49).

It was in this spirit that Ivan IV Grozny used Byzantinesque ritual for his coronation as Tsar in 1547, and launched a crusade against the Muslim Khanate of Kazan in the name of Christian Orthodoxy; and in this same spirit that Church Councils in 1547 and 1549 canonised many Russian holy men and national heroes. In the succeeding Times of Troubles, from 1598 to 1613, the concept of 'Holy Russia', recorded in song and legend, took root among the people, and began to be applied to the whole land and people, not just the monarch, forming one basis for the defence of Russia against the invading Poles in 1610. At the same time, the myth of Holy Russia as the Third Rome under the Tsar as 'father of his people' signalled the predominance of a dynastic myth of election and mission at the expense of a truly covenantal ideal of the whole Russian community tested by God.[22]

Reformation and covenant

It was the Reformation that began to change all this, and which provides a more specific link between biblical Israel and nationalism. It turned what till then had been a mainly descriptive myth of ethnic election into

---

[22] On the Russian sense of ethnic election going back to Kievan Rus, see Milner-Gulland (1999); for the Muscovite period and the ideal of the Third Rome, see M. Cherniavsky: 'Russia', in Ranum (1975: 118–43), Crummey (1987), and Hosking (1997: 6–8, 47–56).

a prescriptive and active ideal. It reconnected that ideal to its original Old Testament covenantal framework. And, by injecting a new popular fervour, it began a shift from a more or less exclusively dynastic myth to a communal ideal, in which a whole people or nation could become the elect—in theory, if not yet always in practice—or at least, could be seen as *an* elect nation, in virtue of its possessing a reformed church and godly members.

Two immediate objections to this argument need to be considered. The first is that the Reformation was a European, not a national, movement, and it had been preceded by various attempts at reform within the Catholic Church, not to mention Lollardy in England and the more radical Hussites in Bohemia, the latter indeed coupled with a strong assertion of a Czech national identity. Foxe's *Actes and Monuments*, first published in 1560, which used to be read as a tract of English nationalism, was in point of fact concerned with all those reformers in Europe who were suffering at the hands of the Catholic powers, and envisaged the end of Days in the battle against the anti-Christ. On the other hand, insofar as his 'Book of Martyrs' was particularly concerned with the origins and plight of *English* Protestants and was the product of the *English* Marian exiles, Foxe's focus was inevitably on England as *an* hoped-for elect nation and on the sufferings of its English martyrs. In its effects, too, its English dimension was unmistakable, and it soon became for later generations of Protestants the major English religious text after the vernacular Bible. More generally, despite their pan-European dimensions, the various magisterial reformations and especially the Reformed churches in each state soon became embedded in different ethno-linguistic cultures and modified by varied political traditions and circumstances (Loades, 1982; MacCulloch, 2004).

There is a second, perhaps more fundamental objection, namely, that the rise of both nations and nationalisms from the sixteenth century can be explained in political and economic terms as the long-term outcome of the consolidation of a network of competing and exploitative territorial states in western Europe, as aristocratic fragmentation was gradually replaced by centralised monarchies and bureaucracies in Spain, France, England, Denmark and Sweden, supported by a growing commerical bourgeoisie. There is much truth in this view. Not only did these political trends fracture the unity of Christendom, even before the onset of the Reformation. They also helped to bring into the political community the upper middle strata of merchants and traders on whose support so many monarchs relied, notably for financing their wars. It is also true that in several cases, such as England, Denmark and Sweden, Protestant Reformation was carried out under the auspices of a centralising state and monarchy, though there was often a tension between the assertion of royal Supremacy and the evangelical drive of the godly. At any rate, as we saw, there was here a markedly greater recourse to the ideal of sacred kingship, ultimately derived from the biblical kings and their anointed status; both Henry VIII and Elizabeth I of England consciously looked to these role models as the source of their *imperium*.[23]

In the same vein, Anthony Marx has gone so far as to credit centralising states with the formation of both nations and an exclusionary nationalism. To bolster their position against rival aristocrats and clergy, he claims that state elites used a strategy of mobilising the masses into a homogenous political community or nation, by persecuting and excluding religious minorities like the Catholics, Protestants, Jews and Moors. As a result, he places the origins of nationalism further back than modernists allow, namely to the late sixteenth century, especially in England and France. But, quite apart from the fact that religious exclusion was nothing new, as heretics and Jews knew only too well, Marx's analysis, and more broadly the political perspective, leaves out a vital element. Nationalism is a dynamic ideological movement, and national identities are often vivid, albeit changing, assertions of a distinctive sense of national community. These facets cannot easily be accounted for by the slow, uneven growth of centralised states, the victory of their elites over rivals, and the gradual religious homogenisation of the masses. The latter provide the base, not the coiled spring, of the ideology and the movement of nationalism. For that we need to look elsewhere.[24]

My suggestion is that we look for the breakthrough to the later development of the Reformation, as it turned increasingly from its early evangelical, Lutheran phase to a Reformed, especially Calvinist and Zwinglian, Old Testament and covenantal outlook. Of course, concern with human sinfulness—the legacy of St Augustine to all the reformers—humanity's predestined status, justification by faith and individual

---

[23] On this political theory of nationalism, with special emphasis on the links between the state and warfare, see Tilly (1975, Introduction, and essay by Finer). For the example of England, see Collinson (2002); also Marshall (2003: chap. 5).

[24] Marx (2003) concentrates on Spain, France and England. But Spain became a counter-case, a failed nationalism, because there was no need to mobilise the people after the expulsion of the Jews and Moors. In France, national*ism* was delayed by the Religious Wars and the suppression of the Calvinists, despite the presence of much national sentiment among the elites. For a critique, see A. D. Smith (2005).

salvation through God's Grace, were always paramount for the godly, as they sought some assurance that they might escape perpetual damnation. Nevertheless, a much greater emphasis on the discipline of the Puritan community and its elders living under the rule of law and the Ten Commandments, widespread translation and more intensive study of the Old Testament, a belief in God's providence, the salvation of the elect and the priesthood of all believers, prepared the way for a return to, and identification with, the Israelite model of covenantal election. And it was not long before not just churches and small communities, but whole peoples were identified as the special recipients of God's Grace, provided that they repented of their sins and sought to fulfil the divine precepts, as foreshadowed in the Covenant with Israel.

Three Elect Nations

We see this particularly clearly in the later evolution of Protestant ideals of national election in England, especially during the Civil War. Protestants may have been in a minority at first, but their experience of Marian persecution predisposed them to identify their own sense of election with that of a beleaguered England. Already in 1554, one pamphleteer had prayed: 'O lord, defend thy elect people of Inglond from the handes and force of thy enemies the Papistes' (cited in Loades, 1982: 304). This same sense of insular identity, coupled with consciousness of England's unique institutional and legal continuity, also encouraged a certain religious self-confidence which found early expression in the future Bishop of London, John Aylmer's, marginal exclamation of 1559 that 'God is English' (cited in Williamson, 1979: 5).

The growing Anglican conformism which followed the Elizabethan Settlement of 1559, punctured periodically by a series of Catholic plots and fed by growing anti-Papist and anti-Spanish sentiment in the 1580s and 1590s, helped to create a favourable national environment for the Puritan minority and their sense of special election. But, as Christopher Hill demonstrates, the idea of the election of all the English people was a recurring theme. It reappeared in John Field's *A godly Exhortation* of 1583: 'God hath given himself unto us'; and Thomas Cartwright's *An Answere unto a letter of Master Harrisons* tells us that 'The Lord is in covenant to that people to whom he giveth the seals [i.e. sacraments] of his covenant', as 'he doth to our assemblies in England'. This was echoed in 1591 by George Gifford: 'God hath put his covenant of mercy in England' (all cited in Hill, 1994: 267).

By the 1620s, this sense of identity between fervent Protestant religion and an English elect began to pervade the gentry, partly as a result of the 'Arminian' policies pursued by Charles I's government, which were seen as a Trojan horse 'ready to open the gates to Romish tyranny and Spanish monarchy'. By 1642, this close identification of English nationhood with Puritan destiny had become widespread in Parliament; according to Anthony Fletcher, 'Civil war was a forcing house of national identity' (Fletcher, 1982: 315–16).

What of national*ism*? Can we discern a movement for autonomy, unity and identity for an actual or potential nation in this period? If there is such a movement, it is to be found among the godly Puritans in Cromwell's New Model Army and in the Commonwealth that was inaugurated after Charles's execution. It is to be discovered in the fervour of the Cromwellian wars prosecuted against England's enemies, notably in Ireland, in the dual cause of God's England and England's God. As Cromwell himself put it in 1653 to Parliament: 'Truly you are called by God as Judah was, to rule with Him, and for Him . . .' (cited in Kohn, 1944: 176). For Cromwell, the interests of Christians and those of the Nation were one and the same, 'the two greatest concernments that God hath in the world' (cited in Greenfeld, 1992: 75).

Milton, for all his pan-European Protestantism, went even further. In *Areopagitica*, he exclaims:

> Consider what Nation it is whereof ye are, and whereof ye are the governours: a Nation not slow and dull, but of a quick, ingenious and piercing spirit . . . this Nation chos'n before any other . . . [When] God is decreeing some new and great period . . . What does he then but reveal Himself . . . as his manner is, first to his English-men? (John Milton, *Areopagitica*, IV, 339–40, cited in Greenfeld, 1992: 76)

This was in great part a nationalism inspired by Old Testament ideals of covenantal election. Cromwell's soldiers went to war to 'fight the Lord's battles' with psalms on their lips, and with bibles consisting of mainly Old Testament quotations on war and soldiering, but God's battles were England's wars, as they had been Israel's long ago, serving the unity and godly superiority of England's commonwealth. Milton interpreted English covenantal election and the unity it inspired in almost mystical and prophetic terms. Describing England as a 'Nation of Prophets, of Sages, and of Worthies', he exclaimed:

> For now the time seems come, wherein Moses the great Prophet may sit in heaven rejoicing to see that memorable and glorious wish of his fulfilled, when

not only our seventy elders, but all the Lord's people are become Prophets. (John Milton *Prose Works* (London, 1884–89), 3. 315, cited in Kohn, 1944: 171).[25]

But England was not alone in drawing so deeply from the well of biblical covenantalism. It found a spiritual companion and rival across the sea in the United Provinces. If anything, the earlier Dutch revolt against the repressive Catholic Habsburg armies, had set the goals and tone of a covenantal nationalism. Already in the 1570s, the 'beggars' songs' (*Geuzenliederen*) compared William of Orange to Moses and David, and the king of Spain to Pharoah; while the Dutch people were described as 'God's elect' or 'God's people', in opposition to the arrogant and cruel 'foreign nation' of the Spaniards. The *biddagsbrieven* of the same period, the official proclamations of prayer and fast days, were also saturated with biblical imagery, and the God they addressed was that of the Old Testament. Philip Gorski cites the example of one such proclamation in 1575 by William of Orange:

> His Excellency, following in the footsteps of Christian Princes, who, in times of danger and distress have sought refuge in the Almighty God, and, together with their people, have humbled themselves before His almighty hand and have repented and turned away from their previous and sinful lives ... [knowing that] God has never left his people in their moment of need, but has always stood by them and delivered them. (Cited in Gorski, 2000: 1441–2)

Another *biddagsbrief* of 1580 drew on the Exodus saga to beg God to

> turn away the horrible plagues, the great destruction and the long-lasting war from these lands ... and liberate these lands and their good inhabitants from all which leads to their ruin and from this accursed and eternal slavery. (Cited in Gorski, 2000: 1442)

However, it was somewhat later, after the first truce of 1609–21, that the full force of Dutch covenantal nationalism became apparent. This was largely, but not only, the work of Calvinists, supported by the House of Orange in their struggle with the Arminians and Remonstrants. Their goals were to impose religious conformity and unity, along with strict moral discipline, including sumptuary laws and compulsory observance

---

[25] For the lively debates about a Puritan nationalism in England, see Kohn (1940) and (1944: chap. 4); Hill (1977); the essays by David Loades and Anthony Fletcher in Mews (1982); and more recently, especially Greenfeld (1992: chap. 1) and the vigorous critique in Kumar (2003: chap. 5). For a vivid analysis of the role of the Bible in the seventeenth-century English Civil War, see Hill (1994); for Cromwell's Soldiers' Bible, see Calamy (1997). Milton's statement about Moses refers to the Book of Numbers (chap. 11), where Eldad and Medad prophesy in the camp and Moses wishes that all the Lord's people were prophets.

of the Sabbath, and to create an autonomous Church and strong government committed to carrying on the war with Spain, a programme that Gorski argues is derived from the Pentateuch (Gorski, 2000: 1445; Green, 1964: 325–8).

Even more striking is the use of the Exodus and Mosaic motifs by so many Dutch rhetoricians, preachers, writers and artists of the early to mid-seventeenth century. The biblical narrative possessed an added poignancy for the many Dutch Protestants who had fled Alva's persecution in the southern Netherlands and crossed the water barriers to the free lands of the north—hence the peculiar importance of the parallel with the departure of the Jews from Egypt. In 1612, Joost van den Vondel published his play *Passcha ofte De Verlossinge Israels uit Egypten*, in which he compared William of Orange to Moses:

> O wondrous fate that joins Moses to Orange
> The one fights for the law, the other beats the drum
> And with his own arm, frees the Evangelium
> The one leads the Hebrews through the Red Sea flood
> The other guides his people through a sea ... of tears and blood.
> (Vondel, *Passcha*: 58, cited in Schama, 1987: 113)

The Exodus narrative, and its leader Moses, also figured in several Dutch paintings—by artists like Hendrik Goltzius, Abraham Bloemart, Cornelis van Harlem, Ferdinand Bol, and Rembrandt. For, as Simon Schama points out, just as the Jewish slaves in Egypt had been liberated, separated and reshaped by Moses in the wilderness, so the Dutch had been moulded and separated as a people by the brutality and Catholic fanaticism of Alva and Philip II and by the long years of hardship and war. Little wonder that the narrative of ancient Israel's Torah appeared to so many Dutch to fit and explain their own predicament.[26]

Perhaps the most vivid expression of this covenantal message is to be found in the history compilation entitled the *Nederlantsche Gedenck-Clanck* (The Netherlands Anthem of Commemoration) composed by the Zeelander Adriaan Valerius in 1626, part of whose closing prayer reads:

> ... O Lord when all was ill with us You brought us up into a land wherein we were enriched by trade and commerce and have dealt kindly with us, even as you led the Children of Israel from their Babylonian prison; the waters receded before us and you brought us dry-footed even as the people of yore, with Moses

---

[26] On the Dutch revolt, see Parker (1985); also MacCulloch (2004: 309–13, 367–78) and Green (1964: chap. 14). On Calvin, see Rublack (2005: chap. 3), and Green (1964: chap. 10). For Dutch national identity and Dutch art, see Schama (1987: 106–17), and Westermann (1996: chap. 5)

and with Joshua, were brought to their Promised Land. O Lord, you have performed wondrous things for us. And when we have not heeded you, you have punished us with hard but Fatherly force so that your visitations have always been meted out to us as a children's punishment. You have not counted the sins of your people against them but have freed us from the yoke of the Moabites even as it was with Deborah and with Barach whose power went before us in the field and that of stout-hearted Gideon who fought against the violence of the Midianites. (Cited in Schama, 1987: 98)

An accompanying engraving shows the seven sister-provinces and the princes of Orange-Nassau kneeling in prayer before the Dutch hat of liberty on a pole beneath a banner inscribed with the biblical holy tetragrammaton in a cloud of glory (ibid.: 98–9, with illustration). This close patriotic analogy of 'Netherlands–Israel' became a standard motif in Dutch political life throughout the seventeenth century, widely assimilated by the public through cheap pamphlets and prints. At the same time, the programme of the Calvinists turned it into a veritable covenantal movement on behalf of the Netherlandish nation aimed at cleansing the republic of enemies within and fighting those without, whether they be Catholic Spain or Protestant England or Indians overseas (Gorski, 2000: 1446–7; Green, 1964: 325–8).

Scotland provides yet a further example of a 'covenantal' type of nationalism. Starting with the formation of the first Covenant in late 1557, the Scots Reformation of 1559–60 adopted the Calvinist Confession of Faith and the Book of Discipline in a revolution against an absentee Queen Mary who was a Catholic. In the 1560s, in his *History of the Reformation in Scotland*, John Knox claimed 'the Scottish church to be the purest and best reformed of any Protestant church'. At the same time, he drew upon the analogy of the decline of ancient Israel which fell apart into two kingdoms, Israel and Judah, to bemoan the failure of Protestant England and Scotland to unite under a godly prince like King David (Williamson, 1979: 4).

But Covenant theology really came into its own only in the 1580s and 1590s in the politically oriented writings of Robert Bruce and John Davidson and in the theological idea of a 'covenant of works' advanced by Robert Rollock, principal of Edinburgh University. This was also the period when the covenant, renewed in 1580–1, 1590 and 1596, began to be seen as a symbol of national unity against the threat to the Kirk from Scottish sovereigns, and became a regular feature in Scots politics (Williamson, 1979: ch. 3; Hill, 1994: 274–7).

The best-known of these renewals was that of 1638, in response to Charles I's attempt to harmonise religion in both his domains, when an oath was sworn to stand to the defence of the King 'in the defence and preservation of the aforesaid true religion, liberties and laws of the kingdom . . .'; likewise, each was to behave 'as beseemeth Christians who have renewed their covenant with God' (cited in Mackie, 1976: 206). It was renewed yet again in 1643 during the English Civil War by a treaty with the English Parliament which took the form of 'The Solemn League and Covenant', to preserve the reformed religion 'according to the Word of God and the example of the best-reformed Churches', to extirpate Popery and Prelacy, and preserve peace between England and Scotland, the parties 'acknowledging their own short-comings and professing their desire to amend their own lives'. (ibid.: 212–13). Certainly, the idea of a double Covenant between God and people, and king and people, on the ancient Jewish model, had become by the seventeenth century, as in the Netherlands, a staple of political argument (Williamson, 1979: ch. 3).[27]

There were, of course, other examples of covenantal nationalisms, notably those of the Ulster-Scots, the Puritan settlements in the northern United States, and much later, the Afrikaners. In the major cities of Switzerland, too, the Reformation led by Huldrych Zwingli and Heinrich Bullinger in Zurich, struck deep roots, embracing the concept of the Covenant of ancient Israel as firmly as the Scots. In other cases, such as parts of Bohemia, Hungary and Poland, there were strong Calvinist churches and widespread support, but here covenantalism was confined to large enclaves or what Schama calls 'conventicles'; it failed to feed or take over a whole society or state, and in some cases the Protestants were suppressed in bloody religious wars such as those of France and Bohemia (Schama, 1987: 96).[28]

---

[27] On Scots national identity, apart from Williamson (1979), see Webster (1997) for the medieval period, and for the early modern period, Kidd (1993), Keith Brown, 'Scottish identity in the seventeenth century', in Bradshaw and Roberts (1998: 236–58), and MacCulloch (2004: 291–5, 378–82).

[28] On the Ulster-Scots and the Afrikaners, see Akenson (1992); also Bruce Cauthen, 'The myth of divine election and Afrikaner ethnogenesis', in Hosking and Schöpflin (1997: 107–31). On Hungary, especially Calvinist Transylvania, see Graeme Murdock, 'Magyar Judah: constructing a new Canaan in Eastern Europe', in Housley (2000: 263–74); for the religious wars in France, see Briggs (1998: 10–32), MacCulloch (2004: 306–9, 337–40) and Marx (2003: chaps. 2–3); on Switzerland, see MacCulloch (2004: 137–50, 172–9) and Im Hof (1991); and on Bohemia and the Hussites, see Joseph Zacek, 'Nationalism in Czechoslovakia', in Sugar and Lederer (1969: 166–206). For Calvinism, generally, see Rublack (2005: chap. 3) and MacCulloch (2004: 194–7, 237–52).

On the other hand, in cases where the Reformation was state sponsored and encompassed the whole community, the type of reformed religion tended to be less covenantal. The form that took hold in Denmark and Sweden from the 1530s, for example, was Lutheran and evangelical; it was centred on the more apolitical New Testament and did not turn to the political activism which, given the right circumstances, could be triggered by the covenantal ideal, although the Old Testament and the general parallel with ancient Israel were frequently invoked, especially in Sweden well into the eighteenth century (see Ihalainen, 2005: ch. 3).

In Denmark, Frederick II (1523–33) and Christian III (1536–59) were concerned, as in England, with the royal supremacy and the expropriation of Church lands, and the same was true of Gustav Vasa (reigned 1523–60) and his successors in Sweden. But their political revolutions were accompanied by more grassroots religious reform. In Sweden, this was a rather uneven process, largely inspired by the educational work of a few preachers. Pre-eminent among these was Olaus Petri, whose handbook of 1529 and other writings, coupled with the church ordinances in 1562 and 1571 of Laurentius Petri, helped to ensure widespread acceptance of evangelical doctrine and organisation at the general Church Council of 1593, which finally ratified Lutheranism as the national religion of Sweden. In Denmark, influenced by northern German Lutheranism, doctrinal reform was taken up much more enthusiastically, given the popular response to the Lutheran idea of the equality of all believers, and it was equally swiftly confirmed by Christian III's firm declaration in 1536 for a princely Lutheran church, and his sponsorship of a translation of the Bible into Danish in 1550. And yet, it was really only as late as the early nineteenth century, under the impulse of a more popular form of Pietism, that the Lutheran reform became linked to a truly nationalist ideology, that associated with the *folkelighed* mass movement of Nicolai Grundtvig (1783–1871) and his popular Folk High Schools of the 1840s.[29]

The character of 'covenantal' nationalism

Despite gaps in the chain of evidence, I think a fair *prima facie* case can be made for the existence in the seventeenth century of what I have called

---

[29] On Denmark and its princely Lutheran Reformation since the 1530s, see Jesperson (2004: especially chap. 5 on the Church); also Oakley (1972: chap. 7). For the state-sponsored Lutheran Reformation in Sweden, see Scott (1977: 124–30, 153–6); and for the later monarchy, Ihalainen (2005: esp. chap. 3).

'covenantal nationalism'. We need to recall that nationalisms, though united around a core doctrine of national autonomy, unity and identity, take different forms in different periods and culture areas. As I argued earlier, the covenantal kind of nationalism takes a different form to both the civic-republican nationalisms of the French Revolution and its successors, and to the ethnic nationalisms of Germany and Eastern Europe, and much of Asia. It was, first of all, avowedly religious, not just in the generic and functional sense of nationalism as a this-worldly 'religion of the people', but in the substantive sense of a transcendental religion of salvation from the beyond, that is, through God's free gift of grace, as the various forms of Protestantism undoubtedly were. This meant that for Protestants, God, not the nation, was sovereign. At the same time, providence required nations: God worked His plan, above all through covenants with elect communities and nations, a doctrine proclaimed by some Puritan divines, and embraced, as we saw, by Herder and the Romantics. Second, the Protestant concept of equality was also religious: the priesthood of all believers and the primacy of the Bible reader in a community of the faithful, took the place of the citizen of the republic, or rather defined that citizenship of the commonwealth and its attendant duties.

Third, while all those who belonged to the ethnocultural community were seen as potential priests and members of the elect, not all of them were likely to achieve this status. Members of a nation possessed what Calvin termed 'general election'; a more limited, secondary election was reserved for the godly. The nation might well become *an* elect nation, but only the godly among them were eligible to constitute *the* elect. But, then, had not the ancient Jewish Prophets distinguished the righteous remnant of Israel who would be restored to their land from the mass of backsliding sinners who would perish in exile? And is not the same logic in evidence in many a modern nationalism, where the activist cadres of the movement have often seen themselves, or 'their' idealised peasants, as more 'authentic' and more 'truly national' than the rest of their co-cultural kinsmen?

There is another respect in which covenantal nationalisms differ from many of the later, more secular nationalisms. They build on, and depend upon, a pre-existing national community-in-the-making, and often a burgeoning sense of national identity, at least among the elites. This was true of England, Scotland and, by the 1560s, the United Provinces, for all their particularism and divisions. In contrast, though modernists often exaggerate the role of secular nationalisms, in many cases, particularly in Eastern Europe, they *have* helped to turn passive *ethnies* into active nations, while in the ex-colonial territorial states of Africa and Asia today, nationalists continue to try to create nations out of often heterogenous populations.[30]

On the other hand, the similarity in *social* composition is rather greater than expected. In terms of size, the contrast that is often drawn between narrowly elite pre-modern movements and sentiments and modern mass nationalisms, is in this case hard to sustain. As W. J. Argyle demonstrated, most nineteenth-century European nationalisms outside France had very small active constituencies; those who manned the barricades in the 1848 revolts numbered in each case a few hundreds. These numbers were certainly exceeded by the armies fielded by the Puritan and Calvinist godly in the Netherlands in the 1570s to 1600s and 1620s to 1640s, or in Scotland and England in the 1640s. As for their social background, while the middle strata were certainly well represented in both covenantal and secular nationalisms, we know that Protestantism had a wide cross-class appeal. For example, in the case of the Netherlands, Geoffrey Parker cites figures of detected heretics in the province of Flanders from 1521 to 1565 for whom their social background is known, and these reveal that nearly half of the Reformed heretics came from the lower classes (Argyle, 1976; Parker, 1985: 60).

Nor is there any doubt about the *political* content of these covenantal nationalisms, which match in intensity and scope the political goals of modern nationalisms. While evangelical Lutheranism tended towards a more apolitical stance, dependent as it was upon a regnant prince, as in Denmark or large parts of Germany, the other Reformed Churches, and notably Calvinism and the Swiss reformers, always suspicious of princes, were ready to enter the political fray and seek political power wherever they could. Their religion of 'inner-worldly asceticism', to use Max Weber's phrase, had a clear social message and, where circumstances permitted, concrete political goals. Above all, it required freedom from external authority, except that of God. The Reformers' demands, as we saw, were for both internal reform and moral discipline of a society, and for the extension of that reformation to others, if necessary by force. Hence they sought a much greater degree of unity and organisation under

---

[30] For nationalism 'inventing' nations, see Gellner (1983) and Hobsbawm (1990); for a critique, see A. D. Smith (1991). For the growth of Netherlands unity in the mid-sixteenth century, prior to a Dutch nationalism, see Parker (1985: chap. 1). For Scots unity, forged by war, see Webster (1997); and for medieval England, see Davies (2000: chap. 2).

the law, a definite arena or territory in which to build their Reformed churches, and the restoration of the true church in place of the anti-Christ, the corrupt Roman church, in order to create the conditions for that assurance that they might be part of the elect that constituted their ultimate goal. It is exactly these ideological features that enabled the Reformed churches to galvanise peoples and societies, whose elites already possessed some sense of national identity, with a promise of much greater autonomy, unity and sense of identity, turning them into elect nations in covenant with God.

This is where the Pentateuchal model of biblical Israel was so relevant, and where the more intensive return to the study of the Old Testament in this period proved so fruitful. Here, if anywhere, was to be found the prototype of God's chosen people and the record of the Almighty's dealings with those He had chosen to follow His Torah. Its stories of exemplary heroes and heroines, and its emphasis upon holiness through separation and communal right conduct seemed especially relevant to often persecuted, but activist, churches of the godly seeking freedom from prince and Pope. It was not in the disputes over the Eucharist, nor in the doctrine of justification by faith, nor even in the more general attack on Papist abuses, but in the return to reading the Old Testament as a separate testament of God's will, and acting in its spirit, that the long-standing beliefs in covenant and ethnic election gained new dynamism and concreteness. Contrasting the 'wholly sacred' character of the New Testament with the 'this worldly' character of the Old Testament in the eyes of Calvinists and other Reformed churches concerned with right conduct, Simon Schama commented:

> The result of all this was to rescue the Old Testament from its position in Catholic theology as a necessary preface, a 'second stage' in the teleology of original sin and eventual redemption, and to restore to the relation between the two books a kind of complementary symmetry. In the world view of Catholics, the exemplary nature of Old Testament stories was overshadowed by the distinction between Christians and, as it were, incipiently deicidal Jews. In the Calvinist mentality, the eventual Messianic chronicle *could only* be comprehended by the history of the Jews, through whom the Almighty had worked his will. (Schama, 1987: 94–5, italics in original)

Indeed, ancient Israel came to have great significance for Calvin, both as a mixed church and as a covenanted people; while the Covenant, as we saw, was particularly important to the Swiss Reformers like Zwingli and Heinrich Bullinger.

Not, I hasten to add, that this return to the Old Testament boded any greater toleration, let alone compassion, for the descendants of God's chosen in the reformers' midst. Not all the reformers were as vituperative in their condemnation of the Jews as the later Martin Luther. But they all operated within the old medieval Catholic framework whose goal was to preserve the Jews in their separate and inferior status as a witness to their perverse 'blindness', until they too would ultimately be converted to the true faith. Even Calvin, whose interest in and use of biblical Israel and the Mosaic Law in Geneva is well-documented, did not depart from the traditional Christian view of the Jews as collectively guilty of deicide. On the other hand, in several passages, he evinced a greater sympathy with Biblical Jews, insofar as he endowed his own followers with a providential role in history similar to that of ancient Israel. Commenting on a bleak chapter of Jeremiah, he ruminated:

> When we see that we are like the Jews, we have a mirror in which to know our rebellion against God ... Thus ... let us learn not to condemn the Jews at all, but ourselves, and to know that we are not worth any more, and that if there was such brutality then that the word of God served for nothing, that today there is just as much [brutality] or more. (Jean Calvin, *Sermons on Jeremiah 16*, cited in Edwards, 1988: 63).[31]

Here, *in nuce*, Calvin exposes the coiled spring of covenantal election, which, in the more providential vein that Calvin evinced in his plans and actions, was to generate the energy and dynamism of a disciplined and regulated church and help to create unified godly communities and ultimately elect nations. For, while the sombre doctrine of double predestination might seem to breed a sense of passive acceptance, it also left open the hope, if not the assurance, of escape from damnation through election by God's grace, especially as Calvin always stressed God's providence. For the Swiss Reformers, even more, their emphasis on the Covenant showed that God had given his people the hope, and the means, of election.

To be sure, the Calvinist and Reformist sense of 'election' possessed rather different theological and social meanings from those of biblical chosenness. It stemmed from the need for 'justification' by faith through God's Grace, stressed by both St Paul and St Augustine, and it was originally oriented to individual rather than communal salvation. Yet this is

---

[31] On the Jews and the Reformation, see Edwards (1988: chaps. 2 and 4). On medieval Jewry under Catholic Christendom, see Stow (1992), and on their legal status in medieval Europe, see Cohen (1994: chap. 3). For a sociological thesis about the decline of the position of the Jews, along with that of heretics and lepers, in the eleventh and twelfth centuries, see Moore (1987).

only part of the story. It overlooks the religious and political context of the Reformist doctrine, not to mention the long history of 'missionary' election before the Reformation (A. D. Smith, 2003: ch. 5).

Theologically, for Calvin and the Swiss Reformers, justification by faith meant faith in the Word of God, and the Word of God was to be found solely in the Bible, the Old Testament as well as the New. Besides, an individual who believed himself of the saved would perform good works in gratitude and for the love of God. That way, the problem of 'antinomianism' could be avoided. An even surer way was for the godly to seek election through faith in God's Grace by re-entering the Covenant in a Reformed church, as the Swiss Reformers had recommended; there they might succeed where ancient Israel had failed. In this respect, the this-worldly separation of the godly from sinners was not in principle different from Israel's quest for holiness and intimacy with God through separation from idolators. Nor, for that matter, was the origin of election in both cases: God's absolute choice and His free gift of grace.

Politically, moreover, the persecution and travail in which so many of the reformers and their conventicles so often found themselves appeared strikingly similar to the plight of the Jews under Pharoah and their subsequent wanderings in the wilderness. As a result, their identification with ancient Israel and its sacred history from slavery in Egypt to freedom in the Promised Land of Israel, seems hardly surprising. Hence, too, the shift towards understanding individual salvation of the godly in collective, and even national terms, became increasingly common. In this connection, Michael Walzer has highlighted the pivotal role of an energising 'Exodus politics' in the English and American revolutions. But, as Simon Schama points out, the role of the Exodus and Covenant ideals in stimulating godly nationalism was just as great and more immediate.[32]

Yet, for all the radicalism of the later Reformation, we should not forget that the return to ancient Israel and its Covenant, was hardly novel. Not only was the biblical tradition of sacred kingship widely drawn upon in the Middle Ages; so was the idea of divine election of kingdoms and even of peoples. It was within these long-standing Catholic Christian traditions which went back to the Old Testament that the post-Reformation return to a more intensive study of the Hebrew Bible and a

---

[32] Though we should add that 'election' in both biblical Israel and Calvinism was founded on God's unfettered choice, rather than humanity's assent; see Patrick Collinson, 'The late medieval church and its reformation (1400–1600)', in McManners (2002: 243–76, esp. 272). See Walzer (1985); and Schama (1987: 104). On 'missionary' election, see A. D. Smith (2003: chap. 5).

closer and more personal identification with ancient Israel and its Covenant must be located. Together, the older traditions and the post-Reformation innovations go a long way to accounting for the sacred, covenantal character of the first great outbursts of nationalism in Europe, which occurred over a century before the French Revolution; and perhaps more fundamentally, for the sacred elements in nationalism as a political 'religion of the people' (A. D. Smith, 2000, and 2003: ch. 2).

Conclusion

My argument here has been threefold. First, I have tried to demonstrate the cultural affinities between biblical Israel and its covenant, and the main themes of modern nationalisms. Second, I have suggested that the links between them are to be found in certain Christian cultural traditions, and more especially in the post-Reformation return to the Old Testament for study and guidance. Third, and as a result, I have argued that, in the context of competing territorial states, what I term 'covenantal' nationalism in certain early modern societies has proved to be the first kind of nationalism, to be followed over a century later by secularising nationalisms, both civic-territorial and ethnic-romantic in kind.

I am not, of course, arguing that the character of later secular nationalisms stems wholly from this covenantal nationalism, nor indeed from the covenantal tradition within Judaism and Christianity. Other cultural traditions have exercised considerable influence in shaping the tone and content of different kinds of secular nationalisms; and these traditions can in turn be traced back to alternative legacies from antiquity. What I am claiming is that the covenantal form of nationalism was the first type to appear, and that as a consequence, we find, as one might expect, biblical and covenantal elements in many subsequent nationalisms across Europe and America.

Nor am I claiming that the covenantal tradition provides a sufficient explanation for the incidence and timing of particular nationalisms. For this, we need to look at broader political factors, such as the fragmentation of Christendom consequent on the rise of a network of territorial states based on dominant *ethnies* in the later Middle Ages and early

Renaissance. Clearly, it was only in *this* particular social and political setting, which had already given rise to a sense of national identity among certain elites in a few such states, that the post-Reformation breakthrough to an intense biblical covenantalism could engender a dynamic sacred nationalism of the godly and elect. In other words, it was only under these political and social conditions that we could witness a fusion of a heightened sense of national identity with a dynamic covenantal ideal, of 'nation' with 'covenant'.

That the result gives rise to a mixed form of nationalism, combining the ideals of nation and biblical covenant, should not surprise us, nor cause us to reject the nationalist designation. There are few forms of nationalism that come unalloyed and pure. We habitually encounter liberal and fascist, conservative and socialist, romantic and pragmatic nationalisms; why not, then, religious forms of nationalism such as the covenantal? And if it be objected that they place God before the nation, the same can be said of socialist or indeed liberal nationalism, in that they see the ideal nation as a vehicle and example of human brotherhood or of freedom. And, as I said earlier, what could be more obvious and 'natural' than for the Protestant godly to think of their political lot in terms of the original people of God who saw themselves as an elect nation surrounded by idolators from whom they desired to separate in order to devote themselves to the worship of the one true God? Fleeing their own Pharoahs, whether Popes or Habsburgs, the Protestant godly saw in the biblical narrative of God's dealings with the children of Israel the image of their own travails and hopes of ultimate salvation as an elect nation of God-fearing souls. In making these equations between political *ethnies* and covenanted communities of believers, the Protestant godly provided a political model and a set of cultural themes which would help to energise and fertilise subsequent nationalisms. As a result, the Exodus and the Covenant of ancient Israel would turn out to possess much greater long-term significance for the shaping of nations and nationalism than anyone could have expected at the time.

References

Aberbach, David (2005), 'Nationalism and the Hebrew Bible', *Nations and Nationalism*, 11, 2: 223–42.
Ahlstrom, Gosta (1986), *Who were the Israelites?* (Winona Lake, IN).
Akenson, Donald (1992), *God's Peoples: Covenant and Land in South Africa, Israel and Ulster* (Ithaca, NY).

Anderson, Benedict (1991), *Imagined Communities: Reflections on the Origins and Spread of Nationalism*, 2nd edn. (London).
Argyle, W. J. (1976), 'Size and scale as factors in the development of nationalist movements', in A. D. Smith (1976).
Baron, Salo (1960), *Modern Nationalism and Religion* (New York).
Beaune, Colette (1985), *Naissance de la nation France* (Paris).
Bell, David (2001), *The Cult of the Nation in France, 1680–1800* (Cambridge, MA).
Berlin, Isaiah (1976), *Vico and Herder* (London).
Best, Geoffrey (ed.) (1989), *The Permanent Revolution: The French Revolution and Its Legacy, 1789–1989* (London).
Bradshaw, Brendan and Roberts, Peter (eds.) (1998), *British Consciousness and Identity: The Making of Britain, 1533–1707* (Cambridge).
Breuilly, John (1993), *Nationalism and the State*, 2nd edn. (Manchester).
Briggs, Robin (1998), *Early Modern France, 1560–1715* 2nd edn. (Oxford and New York).
Calamy, Edward (1997 [1643]), *Cromwell's Soldier's Bible*, facsim. repr. (Whitstable, Walsall and Winchester).
Campbell, John and Sherrard, Philip (1968), *Modern Greece* (London).
Charlton, D. G. (1984), *New Images of the Natural in France* (Cambridge).
Cohen, Mark (1994), *Under Crescent and Cross: The Jews in the Middle Ages* (Princeton).
Cohler, Anne (1970), *Rousseau and Nationalism* (New York).
Colley, Linda (1992), *Britons: Forging the Nation, 1707–1837* (New Haven, CT).
Collinson, Patrick (ed.) (2002), *The Sixteenth Century, 1485–1603* (Oxford and New York).
Connor, Walker (1994), *Ethno-Nationalism: The Quest for Understanding* (Princeton).
Crummey, Ian (1987), *The Formation of Muscovy, 1304–1613* (London and New York).
Davies, Norman (1981), *God's Playground: A History of Poland*, 2 vols. (Oxford).
Davies, Philip (1995), *In Search of 'Ancient Israel'* (Sheffield).
Davies, Rees (2000), *The First English Empire: Power and Identities in the British Isles, 1093–1343* (Oxford and New York).
Day, John (ed.) (2004), *In Search of Pre-Exilic Israel* (London and New York).
Deutsch, Karl (1966), *Nationalism and Social Communication*, 2nd edn. (New York).
Dever, William (2003), *Who Were the Early Israelites and Where Did They Come From?* (Grand Rapids, MI and Cambridge).
Durkheim, Emile (1915), *The Elementary Forms of the Religious Life*, trans. J. Swain (London).
Edwards, John (1988), *The Jews in Christian Europe, 1400–1700* (London and New York).
Ergang, Robert (1976), *Herder and the Foundations of German Nationalism* (New York).
Finkelstein, Israel and Silberman, Neil (2001), *The Bible Unearthed: Archaeology's New Vision of Ancient Israel and the Origin of its Sacred Texts* (New York).
Fletcher, Anthony (1982), 'The first century of English Protestantism and the growth of national identity', in Mews (1982: pp. 309–17).
Gellner, Ernest (1964), *Thought and Change* (London).
Gellner, Ernest (1983), *Nations and Nationalism* (Oxford).

Gildea, Robert (1994), *The Past in French History* (New Haven).
Gillingham, John (1992), 'The beginnings of English imperialism', *Journal of Historical Sociology*, 5: 392–409.
Gillman, Neil (1992), *Sacred Fragments: Recovering Theology for the Modern Jew* (Philadelphia).
Gorski, Philip (2000), 'The Mosaic moment: an early modernist critique of modernist theories of nationalism', *American Journal of Sociology*, 105, 5: 1428–68.
Green, V. H. H. (1964), *Renaissance and Reformation: A Survey of European History between 1450 and 1660* (London).
Greenfeld, Liah (1992), *Nationalism: Five Roads to Modernity* (Cambridge, MA).
Guenée, Bernard (1985), *States and Rulers in Later Medieval Europe*, trans. Juliet Vale (Oxford).
Haller, William (1963), *Foxe's Book of Martyrs and the Elect Nation* (London).
Hastings, Adrian (1997), *The Construction of Nationhood: Ethnicity, Religion and Nationalism* (Cambridge).
Hastings, Adrian (1999), 'Special peoples', *Nations and Nationalism*, 5, 3: 381–96.
Hastings, Adrian (2003), 'Sacred homelands', *Nations and Nationalism*, 9, 1: 25–54.
Herbert, Robert (1972), *David, Voltaire, Brutus and the French Revolution* (London).
Hertzberg, Arthur (ed.) (1960), *The Zionist Idea, A Reader* (New York).
Hess, Moses (1958) [1862], *Rome and Jerusalem*, trans. Maurice J. Bloom (New York).
Hill, Christopher (1977), *Milton and the English Revolution* (London).
Hill, Christopher (1994), *The English Bible and the Seventeenth-Century Revolution* (London).
Hobsbawm, Eric (1990), *Nations and Nationalism since 1780* (Cambridge).
Hosking, Geoffrey (1997), *Russia: People and Empire, 1552–1917* (London).
Hosking, Geoffrey and Schöpflin, George (eds.) (1997), *Myths and Nationhood* (London).
Housley, Norman (2000), 'Holy Land or holy lands? Palestine and the Catholic West in the late Middle Ages and Renaissance', in Swanson (2000): pp. 228–49.
Hutchinson, John (2000), 'Ethnicity and modern nations', *Ethnic and Racial Studies*, 23, 4: 651–9.
Hutchinson, William and Lehmann, Hartmut (eds.) (1994), *Many Are Chosen: Divine Election and Western Nationalism* (Minneapolis).
Ihalainen, Pasi (2005), *Protestant Nations Redefined: Changing Perceptions of National Identity in the Rhetoric of the English, Dutch and Swedish Public Churches, 1685–1772* (Leiden and Boston).
Im Hof, Ulrich (1991), *Mythos Schweiz: Identität-Nation-Geschichte, 1291–1991* (Zürich).
James, Harold (2000), *A German Identity, 1770 to the Present Day* (London).
Jesperson, Knud (2004), *A History of Denmark*, trans. Ivan Hill (Houndmills, Basingstoke).
Juergensmeyer, Mark (1993), *The New Cold War? Religious Nationalism Confronts the Secular State* (Berkeley and Los Angeles, CA).
Kedourie, Elie (1960), *Nationalism* (London).
Kedourie, Elie (ed.) (1971), *Nationalism in Asia and Africa* (London).

Kedourie, Sylvia (ed.) (1998), *Elie Kedourie, CBE, FBA, 1926–1992: History, Philosophy, Politics* (London and Portland, OR).
Kepel, Gilles (1995), *The Revenge of God* (Cambridge).
Kidd, Colin (1993), *Subverting Scotland's Past: Scottish Whig Historians and the Creation of an Anglo-British Identity, 1689–c.1830* (Cambridge).
Kidd, Colin (1999), *British Identities before Nationalism: Ethnicity and Nationhood in the Atlantic World, 1600–1800* (Cambridge).
Kitromilides, Paschalis (1979), 'The dialectic of intolerance: ideological dimensions of ethnic conflict', *Journal of the Hellenic Diaspora*, 6, 4: 5–30.
Kitromilides, Paschalis (1989), '"Imagined communities" and the origins of the national question in the Balkans', *European History Quarterly*, 19, 2: 149–92.
Kitromilides, Paschalis (1998), 'On the intellectual content of Greek nationalism: Paparrigopoulos, Byzantium and the Great Idea', in David Ricks and Paul Magdalino (eds.), *Byzantium and Modern Greek Identity* (Centre for Hellenic Studies, King's College, Aldershot).
Kohn, Hans (1940), 'The origins of English nationalism', *Journal of the History of Ideas*, 1: 69–94.
Kohn, Hans (1944), *The Idea of Nationalism* (New York).
Kohn, Hans (1957), *Nationalism and Liberty: The Swiss Example* (London).
Kohn, Hans (1960), *Pan-Slavism, Its History and Ideology*, 2nd edn. (revised) (New York).
Kohn, Hans (1965), *The Mind of Germany* (London).
Kohn, Hans (1967), *Prelude to Nation-States: The French and German Experience, 1789–1815* (New York).
Kumar, Krishan (2003), *The Making of English National Identity* (Cambridge).
Llobera, Josep (1994), *The God of Modernity: The Development of Nationalism in Western Europe* (Oxford).
Loades, David (1982), 'The origins of English Protestant Nationalism', in Mews (1982): pp. 297–307.
Luz, Efraim (1988), *Parallels Meet: Religion and Nationalism in the Early Zionist Movement*, trans. Len J. Schramm (Philadelphia).
MacCulloch, Diarmaid (2004), *Reformation: Europe's House Divided, 1490–1700* (London).
Mackie, John D. (1976), *A History of Scotland* (Harmondsworth).
McManners, John (ed.) (2002), *The Oxford History of Christianity* (Oxford and New York).
Marshall, Peter (2003), *Reformation England, 1480–1642* (London).
Marx, Anthony (2003), *Faith in Nation: Exclusionary Origins of Nationalism* (Oxford and New York).
Mews, Stuart (ed.) (1982), *Religion and National Identity* (Oxford).
Mitchell, Marion (1931), 'Emile Durkheim and the philosophy of nationalism', *Political Science Quarterly*, 45: 87–106.
Milner-Gulland, Robin (1999), *The Russians* (Oxford).
Moore, R. I. (1987), *The Formation of a Persecuting Society: Power and Deviance in Western Europe, 950–1250* (Oxford).
Mosse, George (1964), *The Crisis of German Ideology* (New York).

Mosse, George (1975), *The Nationalisation of the Masses: Political Symbolism and Mass Movements in Germany from the Napoleonic Wars through the Third Reich* (Ithaca, NY).
Nairn, Tom (1977), *The Break-up of Britain: Crisis and Neo-Nationalism* (London).
Nations and Nationalism (2003), 'Religion and nationalism: Symposium in honour of Professor Adrian Hastings', 9, 1: 5–28.
Newman, Gerald (1987), *The Rise of English Nationalism: A Cultural History, 1740–1830* (London).
Nicholson, Ernest (1988), *God and His People: Covenant and Theology in the Old Testament* (Oxford).
Nora, Pierre (ed.) (1997–8), *Realms of Memory: The Construction of the French Past*, English edn., ed. Lawrence Kritzman, 3 vols. (New York).
Novak, David (1995), *The Election of Israel: The Idea of the Chosen People* (Cambridge).
Oakley, Stewart (1972), *The Story of Denmark* (London).
Ohana, David (1995), 'Zarathustra in Jerusalem: Nietzsche and the "New Hebrews"', *Israel Affairs*, 1, 3: 38–60.
Parker, Geoffrey (1985), *The Dutch Revolt*, revised edn. (Harmondsworth).
Ranum, Orest (ed.) (1975), *National Consciousness, History and Political Culture in Early-Modern Europe* (Baltimore, MD).
Reynolds, Susan (1984), *Kingdoms and Communities in Western Europe, 900–1300* (Oxford).
Roudometof, Victor (2001), *Nationalism, Globalisation and Orthodoxy: The Social Origins of Ethnic Conflict in the Balkans* (Westport, CT).
Rublack, Ulinka (2005), *Reformation Europe* (Cambridge).
Sacks, Jonathan (2002), *The Dignity of Difference: How we avoid the Clash of Civilisation* (London).
Scales, Leonard (2000), 'Identifying "France" and "Germany": medieval nation-making in some recent publications', *Bulletin of International Medieval Research*, 6: 26–43.
Schama, Simon (1987), *The Embarrassment of Riches: An Interpretation of Dutch Culture in the Golden Age* (London).
Schama, Simon (1989), *Citizens: A Chronicle of the French Revolution* (New York).
Schama, Simon (1995), *Landscape and Memory* (London).
Scott, Franklin D. (1977), *Sweden: The Nation's History* (Minneapolis).
Shils, Edward (1981), *Tradition* (Chicago).
Smith, Anthony D. (1973), 'Nationalism, A Trend Report and Annotated Bibliography', *Current Sociology*, 21, 3: 1–178 (The Hague).
Smith, Anthony D. (ed.) (1976), *Nationalist Movements* (London).
Smith, Anthony D. (1991), 'The nation: imagined, invented, reconstructed?', *Millennium, Journal of International Studies*, 20, 3: 353–68.
Smith, Anthony D. (1998), *Nationalism and Modernism: A Critical Survey of Recent Theories of Nations and Nationalism* (London).
Smith, Anthony D. (1999*a*), *Myths and Memories of the Nation* (Oxford and New York).
Smith, Anthony D. (1999*b*), 'Sacred territories and national conflict', *Israel Affairs*, 5, 4: 13–31.

Smith, Anthony D. (2000), 'The "sacred" dimension of national identity', *Millennium, Journal of International Studies*, 29, 3: 791–814.
Smith, Anthony D. (2002), 'When is a nation?', *Geopolitics*, 7, 2: 5–32.
Smith, Anthony D. (2003), *Chosen Peoples: Sacred Sources of National Identity* (Oxford and New York).
Smith, Anthony D. (2005), 'Nationalism in early modern Europe', *History and Theory*, 44: 404–15.
Steinberg, Jonathan (1976), *Why Switzerland?* (Cambridge).
Sternhell, Zeev (1998), *The Founding Myths of Israel: Nationalism, Socialism and the Making of the Jewish State*, trans. David Maisel (Princeton, NJ).
Stow, Kenneth (1992), *Alienated Minority: The Jews of Medieval Latin Europe* (Cambridge, MA).
Strayer, Joseph (1971), *Medieval Statecraft and the Perspectives of History* (Princeton, NJ).
Sugar, Peter and Lederer, Ivo (eds.) (1969), *Nationalism in Eastern Europe* (Seattle and London).
Swanson, Robert (ed.) (2000), *The Holy Land, Holy Lands and Christian History* (Woodbridge).
Talmon, Shmaryahu (1986), *King, Cult and Calendar in Ancient Israel* (Jerusalem).
Tilly, Charles (ed.) (1975), *The Formation of National States in Western Europe* (Princeton, NJ).
Trumpener, Katie (1997), *Bardic Nationalism: The Romantic Novel and the British Empire* (Princeton, NJ).
Tsahor, Ze'ev (1995), 'Ben Gurion's mythopoetics', *Israel Affairs*, 1, 3: 61–84.
Van der Veer, Peter (1994), *Religious Nationalism: Hindus and Muslims in India* (Berkeley and Los Angeles, CA).
Vaughan, William and Weston, Helen (eds.) (2000), *David's The Death of Marat* (Cambridge).
Vital, David (1980), *The Origins of Zionism* (Oxford).
Walzer, Michael (1985), *Exodus and Revolution* (New York).
Watkins, Frederick (1953), *Rousseau: Political Writings* (Edinburgh).
Weber, Max (1965), *The Sociology of Religion*, trans. Efraim Fischoff (London).
Webster, Bruce (1997), *Medieval Scotland: The Making of an Identity* (Basingstoke).
Westermann, Mariet (1996), *The Art of the Dutch Republic, 1585–1717* (London).
Williamson, Arthur (1979), *Scottish National Consciousness in the Age of James VI* (Edinburgh).
Wormald, Patrick (1984), 'The emergence of Anglo-Saxon kingdoms', in Lesley Smith (ed.), *The Making of Britain: The Dark Ages* (Basingstoke).
Zernov, Nikolai (1978), *Eastern Christendom: A Study of the Origin and Development of the Eastern Orthodox Church* (London).
Zimmer, Oliver (1998), 'In search of natural identity: Alpine landscape and the reconstruction of the Swiss nation', *Comparative Studies in Society and History*, 40, 4: 637–65.
Zimmer, Oliver (2003), *A Contested Nation: History, Memory and Nationalism in Switzerland, 1761–1891* (Cambridge).
Zimmer, Oliver and Scales, Leonard (eds.) (2005), *Power and the Nation in European History* (Cambridge).

SIR ISRAEL GOLLANCZ MEMORIAL LECTURE

Bonjour Paresse: Literary Waste and Recycling in Book 4 of Gower's *Confessio Amantis*

JAMES SIMPSON
Harvard University

WASTE DEFINITION IS AN INEVITABLE function of cultural history. We routinely underline the value of studying the past, but if we think about it, we know that we are going to have to jettison a good part of any past. Reading takes time and requires energy, which are irreducible elements in the economy of scholarship. C. S. Lewis wrote this in the *Allegory of Love*: 'Humanity does not pass through phases as a train passes through stations: being alive, it has the privilege of always moving yet never leaving anything behind.'[1] The paucity of footnotes in that book offers some clue as to how Lewis had the confidence to make this erroneous statement. Not leaving anything behind might be a potential privilege, but none of us can enjoy it, since none of us has world enough and time. The entire system of book preservation and retrieval, including anthologies, indices, encyclopaedias, and libraries might be designed to stay the inevitable tendency to leave books behind, but that system equally satisfies our secret desire for dereliction: the anthology selects; the index allows us to pick; the encyclopaedia gives us the facts neatly wrapped and summarised; and the library is a tomb of books, a place for relieving a bad conscience as much as giving readerly access: we know the book is there, even as we also know that we will never read it.

Read at the Academy 30 March 2006.
[1] C. S. Lewis, *The Allegory of Love: A Study in Medieval Traditions* (London, 1972; first published 1936), p. 1.

Indeed, each hugely successful pedagogic movement knows that it must legitimate short cuts and must actively define waste material that a student need not, or, better, should not read. Built secretly into the programme of such pedagogies is a shrewd appreciation of human limitations. To look no further than the relatively recent English past, one of the secrets of Leavisite success was the permission it gave *not* to read whole libraries of books. Donald Davie recorded the pleasure of a Leavisite education thus:

> Every issue of the magazine [i.e. *Scrutiny*] made me a present of perhaps a dozen authors or books or whole periods and genres of literature which I not only *need* not read, but *should not*. To be spared so much of literature, and at the same time earn moral credit by the exemption—no wonder that I loved *Scrutiny,* and Leavis's *Revaluation* and his *New Bearings in English Poetry*.[2]

The public face of Leavisism may have been stringently rigorous, but one secret of its success was permission to skip.

These pedagogic movements are, predictably, very alluring in revolutionary periods, precisely because what drives the entire revolutionary moment is a desire to jettison the burdens of history, which requires new definitions of waste. Moments of cultural revolution take a certain pleasure in trashing what has been newly defined as cultural waste, as in Augustine's *City of God,* where Augustine gleefully reduces pagan cultic practice to a kind of rubble. Moments of cultural revolution can even go so far as to destroy books, as in Mao's China, for example. In sixteenth-century England libraries were also destroyed, and that destruction was in part underwritten by alluring and brilliantly successful new pedagogies. Those were either Humanism, which (in its early phases) mocked scholasticism as cultural rubbish, or evangelical religion, which insisted that only one book was necessary. All others, and in particular 'poetry', were dismissed as idle distraction, or, worse, as muddy pools or even vomit, a kind of literary sewage. John Bale reports on the treatment of monastic books as waste matter after the dissolution of the monasteries: the new owners of the books 'reserved of those lybrarye bokes, some to serve theyr iakes, some to scoure theyr candel styckes, and some to rubbe their bootes'. At the service of both these pedagogies was the new philology, whose sophisticated techniques were in part designed to define what books need *not* be read. The philological project is driven by an economy of sorts: one

---

[2] Cited in Muriel Bradbrook, '"Nor Shall My Sword": The Leavises' Mythology', in Denys Thompson (ed.), *The Leavises: Recollections and Impressions* (Cambridge, 1984), pp. 29–43 (at p. 36).

recovers literary value by scraping away the accreted, accidental waste of history. Cultural history is in part driven by the need to minimise exhaustion, and so needs actively to *define* waste.

Anxiety about waste in the sixteenth century was also accentuated by new theological pressures on the very notion of productive works. The importation of Lutheran theology into England in the 1520s brought with it a radical devaluation of human works, since, by the terms of this theology, only God's unmerited grace could save (and work). Irredeemable human sinfulness, and God's predestination of souls, introduced a short circuit into the economy of works, since human works became genuine, unrecyclable waste before God. Suddenly evangelicals found themselves surrounded and swamped by waste, by a once-numinous world that was now mere matter. Bunyan's list of what is on sale at Vanity Fair unsettlingly lumps evident waste with just about everything else: all that is civil and social is included in the list of vanities: 'as houses, lands, trades, places, honours, preferments, titles, countries, kingdoms, lusts, pleasures; and delights of all sorts, such as whores, bawds, wives, husbands, children, masters, servants, lives, blood, bodies, souls, silver, gold, pearls, precious stones, and what not'.[3] The abject uselessness of works reduces everything to vanity, in which case one can only rely on predestination. And predestination changes the function of works: works no longer operate in an economy of salvation, but serve instead as *signs* of divine approbation, or otherwise. Works, despite their uselessness as currency, become valuable as signs of a gift already bestowed. It is perhaps no accident that the most haunting images of despair derive from a post-Lutheran Northern Europe, as in Dürer's *Melancholia* (1514) or Bruegel's *Desidia* (*c.*1557). If Protestants did indeed work harder and idealise work, it was because works had become a semiotic field one must scrutinise for signs of divine approval. The uncertainty and necessity of the search produced the neurotic commitment to keep working until such a sign demonstrably appeared.[4]

Many of us are the living heirs of Protestant anxiety regarding work and waste. We find it difficult to recover the charisma of idleness of any kind, be it religious or aristocratic. Even if most of the seven deadly sins

---

[3] John Bunyan, *Grace Abounding to the Chief of Sinners and Pilgrim's Progress*, ed. Roger Sharrock (London, 1966), p. 211.

[4] For the paradox of Protestant dismissal of and commitment to works, see Max Weber, *The Protestant Ethic and the Spirit of Capitalism*, translated by Talcott Parsons (New York, 1958; first published 1904), p. 112.

are often treated in secular society as virtues of a kind, or at worst as forgivable foibles, sloth is the one sin whose status as sin remains non-negotiable. Professional university literary readers are in particular vulnerable to charges of idleness. The carapace of protocols governing our productivity, and our own eagerness to demonstrate the intensity of our labour, disguise but cannot conceal that literary reading is non-utilitarian; it can very easily be described as wasting time, as conspicuous and unproductive consumption. We have a long and embarrassing tradition behind us, after all, of our own kind dismissing reading as a waste of time. Coleridge, for example, refused to dignify 'the *pass-time*, or rather *kill-time*' of reading 'novels and tales of chivalry in prose or rhyme' with the name of reading:

> Call it rather a sort of beggarly day-dreaming, during which the mind of the dreamer furnishes for itself nothing but laziness and a little mawkish sensibility; while the whole *materiel* and imagery of the doze is supplied *ab extra* by a sort of mental *camera obscura* manufactured at the printing office, which *pro tempore* fixes, reflects and transmits the moving phantasms of one man's delirium, so as to people the barrenness of an hundred other brains afflicted with the same trance or suspension of all common sense and all definite purpose.

Reading of this kind satisfies the simultaneous 'indulgence of sloth, and hatred of vacancy'; it should be classed along with 'gaming, swinging, or swaying on a chair or gate; spitting over a bridge; smoking; snuff-taking; tête-à-tête quarrels after dinner between husband and wife'.[5]

In this essay I want to get behind that durable hostility to idleness, and in particular to apparently wasted, idle reading. My larger claim is that late medieval, pre-Reformation textual practice is not driven by a need to define and expel cultural waste; on the contrary, idle reading is an essential part of a cultural economy. More specifically, *otium* and idle reading are an essential part of a psychic economy. That is an important argument for all literary study, since if it is not true then the study of literature per se looks otiose in the negative sense (literary reading takes time, and has no utilitarian purpose).[6]

---

[5] Samuel Taylor Coleridge, *Biographia Literaria*, ed. James Engell and W. Jackson Bate 2 vols. (Princeton, 1983), vol. 1, chap. 3, n. 2, pp. 48–9. I am grateful to my colleague Leah Price for alerting me to this delightful citation. One might add Pope's comment, in the Preface to 1717 *Works*: 'Poetry and Criticism being by no means the universal concern of the world, but only the affair of idle men who write in their closets, and idle men who read there'. See *The Poems of Alexander Pope*, ed. John Butt (London, 1963), p. xxv.
[6] For the Roman ideal of otium, see Jean-Marie André, *L'Otium dans la vie morale et intellectuelle romaine, des origines à l'époque augustiéenne* (Paris, 1966). For the ambivalence towards

The case is generated from consideration of Book 4 of Gower's *Confessio Amantis* (1390–2). There it is a kind of hardest case, since Amans' literary education in that book looks like nothing so much as a plain waste of time idly frittered. The text as a whole, further, seems unworried about idling away in archives of old texts.

I

It would, of course, be possible if paradoxical to generate a whole branch of Idleness Studies in Middle English. We cannot do that in one essay, but we can make a start at the most delightful point of entry, into erotic and literary idleness. I suggest we enter the Garden of Love, whose porteress is the gloriously insouciant Oiseuse, who 'porter of the gate is of delices', and who, by her own account, worries about nothing 'but to my joye and my pleying'.[7] The *Confessio* is a dialogue between Amans, the lover, and his confessor, Genius, whose role it is to offer Amans therapy for his hopeless love longing. Each book of the poem works within one of the seven deadly sins of which the lover may be guilty. Book 4 of the *Confessio* broaches the sin of Sloth in its various branches: unpunctuality (lachesse), pusillanimity, forgetfulness, negligence, idleness, somnolence, and despair (tristesse).

The enterprise of Amans' encounter with Genius is of course a therapeutic one, the apparent aim of which is to move Amans on from debilitating psychic stasis as a lover. That psychic stasis is most fully on show in the discussion of Sloth. Strikingly, nothing much moves at all in Book 4. Both Amans and Genius occupy roughly the same position for a good deal of the book, and both positions can plausibly be described as wholly unproductive. I deal in this section with Amans the idle lover and in the next with Genius the idle literary teacher.

Amans denies that he is slothful under some of the pertinent heads. He has never missed a lover's appointment, not least because he has never been given one. Neither has he been idle: 'toward love, as be mi wit, | Al ydel

---

otium in the Renaissance, see Brian Vickers, 'Leisure and Idleness in the Renaissance: the Ambivalence of *otium*', *Renaissance Studies*, 4 (1990), 1–37, 107–54.
[7] Chaucer, *The Romaunt of the Rose*, in *The Riverside Chaucer,* ed. Larry D. Benson (Oxford, 1987), line 598.

was I nevere yit' (4. 1115–16).⁸ Certainly he has procrastinated, and he has also been a coward; yes, he has forgotten his lines, and he is subject to the 'sin' of what he calls 'tristesce'. Often as not, though, he is 'innocent' of sloth. The more he insists on just how busy he is as a lover, however, the more he fills out the very image of an entirely inactive, idle and profitless life. The amusing Ovidian conceit of accounting for sloth as busyness runs as a comic leitmotif throughout the book.⁹ Thus in Amans' denial of idleness, he insists that he is busy as a bee: whatever his lady bids him do, it is done; should she call him, he is there; if she sits, then he is on his knees nearby, but if she stands, then so does he; he intently examines her graceful fingers as she does embroidery; he arranges his countenance to look just right; sometimes he plays with the puppies on the bed, sometimes on the ground. Sometimes, for a change, he plays with the caged birdies, or with servants, and so on, 'to dreche forth the long dai' (4. 1185). This catalogue of entirely idle pursuits is itemised so as to demonstrate just how busy a man can be: 'Thus mowe ye sen mi besi whiel, | That goth noght ydeliche aboute' (4. 1196–7).

Amans' predicament throughout the book conforms to a formula along the lines of 'the more I do, the less I do'. He articulates that formula in a variety of ways: 'The more besinesse I leie . . . The more I am refused ofte' (4. 1747–50); 'thogh my besinesse laste, | Al is bot ydel ate laste' (4. 1757–8); in his dreams, the somnolent man 'clymbeth up the banckes | And falleth into slades depe' (4. 2726–7). It is also found within narratives: concerning Araxarathen, Genius says that 'the more he preide, | The lesse love on him sche leide' (4. 3527–8). And it is found at the very beginning of the book, as a headline to Sloth: the person who keeps postponing duties will never conclude: '. . . whan he weneth have an ende, | Thanne is he ferthest to beginne' (4. 12–13). Given his commitment to idleness, in short, everything Amans says about activity is unwittingly ironic: 'Al ydel was I nevere yit' means 'I have always (in this affair at any rate) been entirely idle.'¹⁰ Even Amans becomes revealingly confused

---

⁸ All citations of Gower's *Confessio Amantis* are taken from *The English Works of John Gower*, ed. G. C. Macaulay, 2 vols., EETS, es 81, 82 (1900–1901; rpt. Oxford, 1979). Further references will be made in the body of the text, and will cite the poem by book and line number.

⁹ For the Ovidian tactic of describing the otiose life of the lover in the terms of public service, see Joseph B. Solodow, 'Ovid's *Ars Amatoria*: the Lover as Cultural Ideal', *Wiener Studien*, NS 11 (1977), 106–27. Ovid's *Ars* is presented as a treatise on the 'labour' of gaining a lover: see especially *Ars Amatoria*, I. 35–40.

¹⁰ For a well informed account of Amans' sloth within an Ovidian tradition, see Gregory M. Sadlek, *Idleness Working: The Discourse of Love's Labour from Ovid through Chaucer and Gower*

about the definition of idleness: 'For when theffect is ydelnes, | I not what thing is busyness' (4. 1759–60).

II

That Amans should consistently deny that he is idle as a lover, only to insist on his total oisivity, is perhaps unsurprising. He is in denial, and that is part of his problem. The disparity between the negligible, often pathetic quality of Amans' situation and that of the frequently tragic figures in the tales narrated by Genius is a consistent source of comedy in Book 4, as it is throughout the entire *Confessio*. To compare Amans to Aeneas (4. 77–137), Ulysses (4. 147–233), Achilles (4. 1693–1701), and, not least, Hercules (2045–134) has to provoke a quiet mirth.

Comic it might be, but if the *Confessio* were designed to produce only gentle Ovidian mockery, then we might dismiss the poem as otiose, offering no more than subtly amusing satire of an ineffectual lover. Before we took that route, we should of course consider the work's further reach through the action of Amans' therapist Genius. In my view Genius is a faculty of the psyche of which Amans is himself a part: Amans is the will, or desire, while Genius represents his imaginative faculty or *ingenium*.[11] The reach of this exceptionally rich faculty is wide in the psyche: situated between the common sense on the one side and abstract reason on the

---

(Washington, DC, 2004), pp. 167–207. Sadlek does not register Genius' participation in Amans' sloth at all.

[11] For the larger history of the concept of Genius and its later medieval reflexes, see Jane Chance Nitzsche, *The Genius Figure in Antiquity and the Middle Ages* (New York, 1975). For the late medieval poetic reflexes specifically, see Winthrop Wetherbee, 'The Theme of Imagination in Medieval Poetry and the Allegorical Figure Genius', *Medievalia et Humanistica*, NS 7 (1976–7), 45–64. For the overlapping medieval concepts of the imagination, see Alastair Minnis, 'Medieval Imagination and Memory', in Alastair Minnis and Ian Johnson (eds.), *The Cambridge History of Literary Criticism*, vol. 2, *The Middle Ages* (Cambridge, 2005), pp. 239–74. For the figure of Genius in the *Confessio Amantis*, see James Simpson, *Sciences and the Self in Medieval Poetry: Alan of Lille's 'Anticlaudianus' and John Gower's 'Confessio Amantis'* (Cambridge, 1995), pp. 167–97, and Kurt Olsson, *John Gower and the Structures of Conversion: a Reading of the Confessio Amantis* (Cambridge, 1992), pp. 52–62. For the larger tradition of late medieval philosophical *involucra*, see the indispensable studies of Winthrop Wetherbee, *Platonism and Poetry in the Twelfth Century: the Literary Influence of the School of Chartres* (Princeton, 1972), and Kathryn L. Lynch, *The High Medieval Dream Vision: Poetry, Philosophy, and Literary Form* (Stanford, CA, 1988).

other,[12] *ingenium* is capable both of genial sympathy with sensual desire and of a kind of practical, psychic engineering, in which reason is informed by imaginative apprehension. Genius is the perfect therapist, precisely because he is in touch with both psychic parties at war with each other, sensual desire and abstract reason.

If Genius serves these psychological functions, then he is also by the same token a literary instructor. Just as the *ingenium* mediates between sensual desire and abstract reason, so too does Genius draw on literary texts to mediate between the sensual body of literary narrative and the abstract, rational understanding of those texts. Genius as reader has access to all literature, classical, Biblical and medieval. As a natural faculty, Genius' understanding of texts is primarily ethical; he draws, accordingly, primarily on classical sources.[13] *Poetria* as a science is valuable precisely because it has the power to inform the reason through imaginative apprehension.[14] The most persuasive ethical defence of poetry as a discipline derives from its power to apprehend the particularities of sensual pain and pleasure in narrative.[15] The tyrannical severities of abstract reason are humanised by commerce with the body of the text, via the imagination.

In short Genius is, among other things, a literary teacher or *grammaticus*.[16] The imagination is a treasure house of remembered images,

---

[12] For a visual image of the imagination placed between the common sense and the reason, see James Simpson, 'The Rule of Medieval Imagination', in Jeremy Dimmick, James Simpson and Nicolette Zeeman (eds.), *Images, Idolatry and Iconoclasm in Late Medieval England* (Oxford, 2002), pp. 4–24, fig. 1.

[13] For the medieval reception of the classical poetic tradition within which Genius works, see the fine chapters by Winthrop Wetherbee, 'The Study of Classical Authors: From Late Antiquity to the Twelfth Century', and Vincent Gillespie, 'The Study of Classical Authors: from the Twelfth Century to c.1450', both in Minnis and Johnson (eds.), *The Cambridge History of Literary Criticism*, vol. 2, 99–144, and 145–236 respectively.

[14] For the classification of poetry in medieval pedagogy under Ethics, see Gillespie, 'The Study of Classical Authors: from the Twelfth Century to c.1450', in Minnis and Johnson (eds.), *The Cambridge History of Literary Criticism*, vol. 2, 160–78, and further references.

[15] For theorisations of this tradition, see especially Kathy Eden, *Poetic and Legal Fiction in the Aristotelian Tradition* (Princeton, 1986); Wesley Trimpi, *Muses of One Mind: The Literary Analysis of Experience and its Continuity* (Princeton, 1983), chap. 10; and Martha Nussbaum, *Love's Knowledge: Essays on Philosophy and Literature* (New York and Oxford, 1990). For the applications of this tradition to Gower's *Confessio Amantis*, see Charles Runacres, 'Art and Ethics in the 'Exempla' of *Confessio Amantis*', in A. J. Minnis (ed.), *Gower's 'Confessio Amantis': Responses and Reassessments* (Cambridge, 1983), pp. 106–34; Simpson, *Sciences and the Self*, pp. 167–97, and 252–71; and Wetherbee, 'The Theme of Imagination in Medieval Poetry'.

[16] For the broad tradition of grammatical education, see Martin Irvine and David Thompson, '*Grammatica* and Literary Theory', in Minnis and Johnson (eds.), *The Cambridge History of Literary Criticism*, 2, *The Middle Ages*, 15–41. For practical application, see Wetherbee, 'The

drawn from ever-fresh literary narrative. Genius himself defends this kind of literary remembrance from within the current of Book 4, which is what we would expect, precisely given that this book is in part about forgetting. The forgetful person is such that he 'lost hath his memorial, | So that he can no wit withholde' (4. 532–4). That rememorative failure is specifically linked to verbal, and perhaps literary remembrance, since the forgetful person

> ... in the tellinge of his tale
> Nomore his herte thane his male
> Hath remembrance of thilke forme,
> Whereof he scholde his wit enforme
> As thanne, and yit ne wot he why.
> (4. 545–9)

Later in the book, in the explicit discussion of human labour and sciences, Genius elevates the writing, understanding and transmission of books to the highest form of human work:

> Of every wisdom the parfit
> The hyhe god of his spirit
> Yaf to the men in erthe hiere
> Upon the forme and the matiere
> Of that he wolde make hem wise:
> And thus cam in the ferste apprise
> Of bokes and of alle goode
> Thurgh hem that whilom understode
> The lore which to hem was yive,
> Wherof these other, that now live,
> Ben every day to lerne newe.
> (4. 2363–73)

Genius, then, offers ample theorisation from within Book 4 of his own customary practice in that book and in the *Confessio* more generally: profound value derives from philosophical meditation on books, intuiting form in matter. Just as Genius defends the information of 'wit' through imaginative remembrance of tales in theory, so too does he draw on literary remembrance in practice: he routinely sees, or so it would appear, the 'form', or animating idea within the 'matiere' of texts he draws from 'Poesie' (4. 2668), texts he even goes so far to call 'my wrytinges' (4. 2924).

Study of Classical Authors: From Late Antiquity to the Twelfth Century', and Gillespie, 'The Study of Classical Authors: from the Twelfth Century to *c.*1450', pp. 150–60.

Genius is nothing if not a literary exegete, working within a long tradition that prescribes reading as an antidote to idleness.[17]

In Book 4, though, is he a successful interpreter of texts? The theory might sound impressively subtle as an account of how poetic impressions inform the soul, but Book 4 offers ample evidence that it does not happen in practice this way at all. In the very defence of the writing, understanding and transmission of literary understanding to which I have just alluded, Genius ends with praise of Grammar and Rhetoric. He underlines the achievements of the Latins in the making of books and 'Poesie', and makes especial reference to Ovid as the writer to whom the passionate lover should turn for understanding of how love might be cooled (4. 2668–71). Amans' response does not inspire confidence in the power either of Genius or the educative power of literary books:

> My fader, if thei mihte spede
> Mi love, I wolde his bokes rede;
> And if thei techen to restreigne
> Mi love, it were an ydel peine
> To lerne a thing which mai noght be.
> (4. 2675–9)

Books are a waste of time unless they advance Amans' love: 'There is', he concludes, 'bot only to poursuie | Mi love, and ydelschipe eschuie' (4. 2685–6). There is, in short, nothing for it in the matter of books but to eschew idleness, which, coming from Amans, means precisely the opposite: that there is nothing for it in the matter of books but to waste time.

This, needless to say, does not of itself mean that Genius will be a poor transmitter of literary knowledge. There is no shortage of evidence from within Book 4, however, to suggest exactly that. Neither is there shortage of evidence to suggest that literary education can very easily run into the sands of waste. I deal first with the suggestions from within Book 4 to suggest that literary education can be a waste of time, before turning to Genius' own, spectacularly poor interpretations in this book.

Amans wants to learn, but he is only interested in learning the successful art of love. He is 'curious | Of hem that conne best enforme | To knowe and witen al the forme, | What falleth unto unto loves craft' (4. 922–5), but somehow has not yet heard anyone give the surefire recipe for

---

[17] The *Rule of St Benedict* requires scriptural reading as an antidote to idleness: 'ociositas inimica est animae; et ideo certis temporibus occupari debent fratres . . . in lectione divina'. See *The Rule of St Benedict*, ed. and trans. Justin McCann (London, 1952), pp. 110–11.

success.[18] While he waits for the right moment, he idly listens to tales: in admitting to procrastination, for example, Amans says that whenever he thinks to speak to his lover, Lachesce bids him wait: 'Thus with his tales to and fro | Mi time in tariinge he drowh' (4. 34–5). Tales, perhaps even the tales narrated by Genius, can very easily serve not to inform but rather to neutralise action, by feeding pathological desire. The soporific dangers of poetry are underlined, too, in the narrative of Argus, in which Mercury sends the hundred-eyed Argus to sleep, having first 'affaited | His lusty tales', and 'in his pipinge evere among | He told him such a lusty song, | That he the fol hath broght aslepe' (4. 3337–47). All this, of course, before Mercury decapitates the sleeping Argus; by this account, poetry can kill you if you are not careful. Given Amans' habitual listening practice, all the books adduced by Genius can serve no purpose whatsoever, and might be positively dangerous. Book 4 potentially presents the spectacle of books being remembered only to be forgotten, being read only to be unwritten. This literary nightmare finds explicit utterance in Amans' account of forgetfulness. Like Troilus at the beginning of Book 3 of *Troilus and Criseyde*, Amans 'records' all his lines to his lover before he meets her. Once in her presence, however, they all vanish: he acts as if he had seen a ghost, and entirely forgets his text:

> Lich to the bok in which is rased
> The letter, and mai nothing be rad,
> So ben my wittes overlad,
> That what as evere I thoughte have spoken,
> It is out fro my herte stoken.
> (4. 580–4)

There are, then, plenty of meta-narrative suggestions in Book 4 that the literary education offered Amans in this very book is less an antidote to the sin of Sloth than an example of that very sin. Book 4 might be offering the spectacle of literary erasure, of texts being adduced only to be idly unwritten before our eyes. One of the ways that Amans says he idly fills in time with his lady, as an alternative to dice, or dancing, or discussing *demandes d'amour*, is none other than literary, 'to rede and here of Troilus' (4. 2795). Literature might be on a level with dicing, or 'swinging on a gate'.

This is, in fact, exactly what happens in Genius' interpretations in Book 4, which are spectacularly ill-judged. As I suggested above, Genius

---

[18] For Gower's conscious and philosophical use of the terms 'form' and 'information', see Simpson, *Sciences and the Self*, pp. 168–79.

has a wide range of psychic potential, capable as he is of sympathy with sensual desire on the one hand and with abstract reason on the other. This psychic range explains his instability, or at least his flexibility, as an interpreter. An earlier view had it that Genius as priest of Venus serves rather the same functions as a Christian priest, and that lovers' sins are Christian sins.[19] Once we recognise Genius' psychic mobility, however, we can account for his interpretative moves that seem wholly consistent with Amans' erotic passion. In Book 4, however, he makes more such moves than in any other book; in Book 4 literary interpretation and education threaten, that is, to exemplify rather than resist the psycho-pathology of sloth.

Gower headlines the sheer wrong-headedness of Genius' interpretations from the very start of Book 4, beginning with Aeneas and Dido. For later medieval readers the *Aeneid* was the secular literary narrative *par excellence*. A long and living tradition of exegesis interpreted Virgil's poem as a *Bildungsroman*, according to which the first six books at any rate were an allegory of (male) ethical development.[20] In that powerful tradition Dido personifies lust, whose powerful attractions Aeneas must overcome before he can descend to the underworld and achieve full philosophical understanding.[21] An alternative tradition, derived from Ovid's *Heroides* 7, aligns itself wholly with Dido.[22] Ovid's Dido works into the

---

[19] For this critical tradition, see, in order, C. S. Lewis, 'Gower', in Peter Nicholson (ed.), *Gower's 'Confessio Amantis:' A Critical Anthology* (Woodbridge, Suffolk, 1991), pp. 15–39 (first published 1936); J. A. W. Bennett, 'Gower's 'Honeste Love', in ibid., pp. 49–61 (first published 1966); and A. J. Minnis, 'John Gower, Sapiens in Ethics and Politics', in ibid., pp. 158–80 (first published 1980). For revisions to that position, which first stressed the incongruences in the *Confessio*, see James Simpson, 'Ironic Incongruence in the Prologue and Book I of Gower's *Confessio Amantis*', *Neophilologus*, 72 (1988), 617–32; and A. J. Minnis, '*De Vulgari Auctoritate*: Chaucer, Gower and the Men of Great Authority', in R. F. Yeager (ed.), *Chaucer and Gower: Difference, Mutuality, Exchange* (Victoria, BC, 1991), pp. 36–74.

[20] For the three principal classical traditions of Dido (i.e., the Virgilian Dido, the 'historical Dido', and the Ovidian Dido), each alive in the later medieval and early modern periods, see Marilynn Desmond, *Reading Dido: Gender, Textuality and the Medieval 'Aeneid'* (Minneapolis, 1994), pp. 23–73. For the tradition of allegorical interpretation of the *Aeneid*, see Christopher Baswell, *Virgil in Medieval England: Figuring the 'Aeneid' from the Twelfth Century to Chaucer* (Cambridge, 1995), pp. 84–135.

[21] For an example of such a reading, see the commentary attributed to Bernard Sylvestris, *The Commentary on the First Six Books of the 'Aeneid' Commonly Attributed to Bernard Sylvestris*, eds. Julian Ward Jones and Elizabeth Frances Jones (Lincoln, NB, 1977), pp. 23–5.

[22] For this tradition, see especially Desmond, *Reading Dido*; Peter Dronke, 'Dido's Lament: From Medieval Latin Lyric to Chaucer', in Ulrich Justus Stache, Wolfgang Maaz, and Fritz Wagner (eds.), *Kontinuität und Wandel: Lateinische Poesie von Naerius bis Baudelaire* (Hildesheim, 1986), pp. 364–90; and James Simpson, 'Subjects of Triumph and Literary History:

chink in Aeneas's reputation as a faithless lover in the *Aeneid*, and exposes a large area for reinterpretation. The voice of a single, suffering woman of labile memory pits itself, not unsuccessfully, against the voice of Virgil's divine Muses. She watches Aeneas sail away from Carthage, pleading with him to return as she knows he will not. The reader is encouraged to identify with the voice of female, lyric suffering against the epic of male proto-imperialism.

How does Genius interpret Aeneas and Dido? Aeneas arrives in Carthage; Dido falls in love with him; Aeneas leaves, and Dido writes her letter saying that she will commit suicide should he delay his return. When he delays, she criticises his slothful tardiness ('. . . who fond evere such a lak | Of slowthe in eny worthi knight?' (4. 128–9)), before committing suicide. Genius concludes by commenting that 'tariinge upon the need | In loves cause is forto drede' (4. 139–40).

This is an extraordinary under-reading, which, while obviously ignoring the moral reading of the *Aeneid*, also fails to capture the pathos of Dido in the *Heroides*: this Dido expects Aeneas to return, and this Aeneas is criticised for not doing so. Either way, Genius' reading is strikingly superficial. The imperial narrative of the *Aeneid* is implicitly dismissed: all Aeneas needed to have done was to keep his appointment (which appointment?); and the Ovidian story is also derailed, by focusing less on Dido's pathos and more on Aeneas' 'tarrying'. Not keeping an appointment was never an imaginable charge against him in either the Virgilian or Ovidian tradition. The narrative of the *Aeneid* need not have happened, and Dido's suicide could have been avoided, if only Aeneas had been better at keeping time. This interpretation is driven less by imaginative remembrance and more by the fantasy that Aeneas and Dido could have shared erotic happiness were it not for an unfortunate delay. The superficiality of this reading is underlined later in the book, when Genius praises none other than Aeneas as an active lover in gaining the hand of Lavinia; here the slothful Aeneas becomes the energetic Aeneas, who is 'bold | And dar travaile and undertake | The cause of love' (4. 2183–219). Medieval exemplary readings are more opportunistic, and less beholden to interpretative consistency than post-Renaissance reading protocols, but inconsistency at this level beggars both interpretations of Aeneas advanced in Book 4. After such spectacular inconsistency, one wants simply to begin again.

Dido and Petrarch in Petrarch's *Africa* and *Trionfi*', *Journal of Medieval and Early Modern Studies*, 35 (2005), 489–508.

The narratives of Dido and Aeneas, in both principal classical traditions, along with their attendant interpretative traditions, are the highest profile literary sources available to Gower. Genius' under-reading of these traditions at the very beginning of Book 4 can only be described as remarkable. Many interpretations that follow run equally counter to plausible and meditated readings of well-known narratives. Some narratives run counter to well-known versions of a story. The very next story Genius tells, again about delay, is a positive exemplum of not delaying: once Ulysses reads Penelope's letter, he thinks of his wife, and rushes home as soon as Troy is destroyed:

> He made non delaiement,
> Bot goth him home in alle hihe,
> Wher that he fond tofore his yhe
> His worthy wif in good astat.
> (4. 226–9)

The near-infinite delay of Ulysses' homeward journey may not have been as well known in all its details as Virgil's poem was to Gower, although Gower certainly did know of its difficulty and length.[23] Genius' reading of the Homeric story is a massive collapsing of the long-drawn narrative of desire-deferred into a single, four-line narrative of rapid erotic fulfilment.[24]

Genius narrates a number of stories concerning female virgins in Book 4, in each one of which his interpretation is weighted, sometimes very strangely indeed, more towards grief for the loss of a virgin body than towards grief for a life lost. He passes quickly over the five foolish Biblical virgins whose lamps were unfilled (4. 250–60). That Genius should interpret a Biblical story (Matthew 25: 1–13) from a strictly tropological perspective is wholly in keeping with his standard practice, since he nowhere engages in other levels of Biblical allegory.[25] That his single other large Biblical narrative should also concern a virgin girl is, however, significant.

---

[23] See, for example, Book 6, lines 1391–1788, the opening of which makes reference to the 'see divers', the 'many a wyndi storm revers', and 'many a gret peril' from which Ulysses escaped on his way home from Troy (6. 1415–21).

[24] Gower enjoys radically abbreviating long narratives. He also does it with Chaucer's *Troilus and Criseyde* at *Confessio Amantis*, 5. 7597–602.

[25] For Gower's familiarity with the tradition of the moralised Ovid, but his consistent resistance to any but tropological, or ethical readings, see C. Mainzer, 'John Gower's Use of the "Mediaeval Ovid" in the *Confessio Amantis*', *Medium Aevum*, 41 (1972), 215–29.

Genius insists to Amans that a girl should not delay her marriage, since by doing so she might lose up to three crucial years 'Whil sche the charge myghte bere | Of children', without which the world cannot survive (4. 1488–1501). By way of exemplifying this notion, Genius tells the story of Jephtha's daughter (4. 1505–95; cf. Judges, 11: 33–5). This child is sacrificed in the name of an appallingly dangerous and finally savage oath by her father, to the effect that he will sacrifice the first creature he sees on return if he is victorious in battle. In Gower's narrative it is the child's very anxiety to see her father again that ensures that she is 'tofore | Al othre' at the gate to meet her victorious father and her dreadful death. So far from recoiling in horror from the fulfilment of this oath, as other late medieval writers did,[26] Genius lays the weight differently, on the daughter's 'failure' to have married earlier and produced children. The child accepts her dreadful fate, but regrets that 'sche hir time hath lore so' (4. 1573); the most she begs is a respite, that she might have time with her friends to lament the loss 'That sche no children hadde bore' (4. 1587). The powerful narrative of Jephtha's daughter is, in short, seen wholly from the drives of a Genius like that in Jean de Meun's *Roman de la Rose*, interested only in procreation.[27] All other concerns are ruthlessly suppressed, even the 'kynde' love between father and daughter.

The other large scale narrative of virginity 'slothfully' prolonged is that of Rosiphelee (4. 1245–1446), who, slow to love, is granted a vision of beautiful women riding on splendid horses, followed at a distance by a woman on a poor horse, carrying about her dozens of halters. Asked why she is behind and in the position of servant, the woman replies that, a princess in life, she was 'slow in loves lore, | When I was able forto lere, | And wolde noght the tales hiere | Of them that couthen love teche' (4. 1402–5). The one splendid bridle she has, worn by her horse, marks a love unconsummated before her own sudden death, which failure she must now regret in the afterlife. The dead princess concludes to the living Rosiphelee that she must be 'noght ydel' in love (4. 1433).

The dead princess' failure to listen to 'tales' by those who 'couthen love teche' refracts back onto the position of Amans himself: is Amans the positive type of the princess' negative, since he is only too keen to

---

[26] See, for example, Dante's response to the dreadful execution of Jephtha's stupid vow: *Paradiso*, 5. 64–8.

[27] For Jean de Meun's Genius, see especially George D. Economou, 'The Character Genius in Alan de Lille, Jean de Meun, and John Gower', in Nicholson (ed.), *Gower's 'Confessio Amantis:' A Critical Anthology*, pp. 109–16 (first published 1970), and Denise N. Baker, 'The Priesthood of Genius: A Study of the Medieval Tradition', in ibid., pp. 143–57 (first published 1976).

listen to those who tell tales regarding love's lore? Or is it rather the case that this tale of idleness reveals that Genius' own pedagogic programme is itself idle, since all it does is to provide a story that satisfies Amans' own wish fulfilment? The tale itself reveals that Rosiphelee sees an image of herself in her vision, since the woman whose sad story she learns is, like Rosiphelee herself, a 'slow' princess, not wishing 'to love obeie' (4. 1388–9). That dreamers and readers see only themselves might be pertinent to Genius' story as told to Amans too, since this story encourages women not to be slow in returning love to petitioning men. As a narrative it has nothing to offer Amans but encouragement, and a certain *Schadenfreude* with regard to Amans' own, unfailingly cold lover: the woman who resists love will be punished in the afterlife.

Genius gives odd inflexions to other stories concerning virgins: he tells the story of Penthesilea, which becomes instead the story of Philemenis, the king of Patagonia, who takes the dead body of Penthesilea and gives it proper burial, for which respect he is offered three Amazonian virgins each year as a tribute payment. Genius praises this 'success' as exemplary of energetically seeking fortune through military success. Nothing is made of Penthesilea's commitment to feminine isolationism; nor is anything made of the horrible resonances of her death at the hands of Phyrrus, son of Achilles (4. 2161–4), who also murdered the innocent virgin Polyxena. Genius ignores Amazonian feminist ethos, just as he ignores the exploitation of young women in war. Instead, he focuses on male military success, and blithely defines the annual tribute of three virgins as success.

Genius, then, seems focused on tales that promote sexual activity at all costs, even when those tales run counter to both natural claims (in the case of Jephtha's daughter), and to personal claims (in the case of Rosiphelee). Those stories would tend to suggest that Genius serves, rather than redirects or re-educates, Amans' desire. They therefore also suggest that Genius' literary education is devoted to nothing so much as idle fantasy. Perhaps the most striking narrative of art serving erotic desire is that of Pygmaleon and his statue (4. 371–450). The narrative is well known and simply told: Pygmaleon the sculptor fashions the statue of a woman; falls in love with it; and prays to Venus, until finally 'The colde ymage he fieleth warm' (4. 422). They have a son, Paphos. Even if simply told, such emphases as the tale is given are rich in meta-narrative implications, pertinent both to Amans and to Genius. The object of Amans' hopeless love is nothing if not stony: never throughout the *Confessio* is there the remotest suggestion that she encourages Amans in any way. Despite that, Amans idolises and fetishises her, subjecting himself to a grinding discipline of self-deception and humiliation, 'drecch[ing] forth the longe dai' (4. 1185). So too Pygmaleon:

> His love upon this faire ymage
> He sette, and hire of love preide;
> Bot sche no worde ayeinward seide.
> The longe day, what thing he dede,
> This ymage in the same stede
> Was evere bi.
> (4. 392–7)

He feeds her, lays her in his bed, kisses her, whispers in her ear, lays his arm across her 'as he hir wolde embrace' (4. 409). And, as with Amans, Venus hears Pygmaleon's prayer (4. 415–19). In short, like Amans, Pygmaleon is obsessed with a hopeless and self-destructive love.

The hypothetical status of Pygmaleon's actions, serving his stony image as if she were alive, evokes Amans' subjection to the seductive stories of Genius. For Pygmaleon, like Amans, is subject to his imagination. From the imagination's capacity to manufacture images derives art's power to create hypothetical realities, whether those realities save or damn. Pygmaleon 'himself beguileth', as he looks on the erotic statue, 'So that thurgh pure impression | Of his ymaginacion | With al the herte of his corage | His love upon this faire ymage | He sette' (4. 389–93). This evokes Amans' own subjection to his imagination, which he articulates later in Book 4: he says that he sometimes spots the chance of leading his lover to mass, though it grieves him when her arm is clothed:

> ... afterward it doth me harm
> Of pure ymaginacioun;
> For thane this collacioun
> I make unto miselven ofte,
> And seie, 'Ha, lord, hou sche is softe,
> How sche is round, hou sche is small!
> Now wolde god I hadde hire al
> Withoute danger at my wille!'
> (4. 1141–8)

Just as Pygmaleon is subject to his imagination, so too is Amans subject to his, in the figure of Genius (and vice-versa). This narrative is especially attractive to Genius, since, like Pygmaleon, his role is also to fashion images. Both are artist figures, and both become potential idolaters.[28] For this narrative obviously evokes the possibility of artistic idolatry, for it

---

[28] For Genius as artistic maker in the *Confessio*, see Simpson, *Sciences and the Self*, pp. 252–71. For Genius and Pygmaleon as potentially idolatrous makers in the *Romance of the Rose*, see

invests the shaped artistic object with the emotional fullness of humanity; as Genius himself says in his discussion of idolatry in Book 5, the 'worchipe of ydolatrie | Drowh forth upon the fantasie | Of hem that weren thane blinde' (5. 1587–89). Oblivious to that danger, both artists Pygmaleon and Genius praise the astonishing, miraculous power of the image to come to life. Pygmaleon's erotic fantasy of fashioning a wholly subservient woman comes to fruition: 'Lo, thus he wan a lusti wif, | Which obeisant was at his wille' (4. 424–5). If Pygmaleon shapes a statue, Genius shapes a tale: he shapes the image of a desirable woman in Amans' imagination, and nourishes the idea that she, too, will come to life. He encourages Amans to be like Pygmaleon:

> Bi this ensaumple thou miht finde
> That word mai worche above kinde.
> Forthi, my sone, if that thou spare
> To speke, lost is al thi fare,
> For slowthe bringeth in alle wo.
> (4. 437–41)

Genius encourages the idea that more talk will bring the lady to life, and that such talk (Genius' talk, of the kind exemplified by this very tale), is a way of avoiding sloth. Once again, though most powerfully, the story told has bearings on the story telling in the *Confessio* more generally. And both suggest that this particular combination of psychic desire and literary education leads backwards into a finally self-destructive idleness, even as they pretend to lead out of it. Like Ovid's *Remedia amoris*, the story telling exemplifies the 'sin' rather than offering a remedy for it.[29] It is a book that goes backwards even as it pretends to proceed. Book 4 of the *Confessio* would seem also to be following the traces of the *Roman de la Rose*, whose lover enters the Garden of Pleasure only via the gate whose porteress is Idleness.

Further narratives give extra colouring to the idea of Genius as an *ingenium* wholly subject to the sensual will. The very next story concerns the girl Iphis who, disguised as a boy of necessity, is betrothed to the girl Ianthe (4. 451–515). Placed in bed together, 'sche and sche', their intense

---

Nicolette Zeeman, 'The Idol of the Text', in Dimmick, Simpson and Zeeman (eds.), *Images, Idolatry and Iconoclasm in Late Medieval England*, pp. 43–62. For images of both artists at work and idolatrous prayer, see figs. 3–5.

[29] For Gower's subtle relations with Ovid's *Remedia amoris*, see Simpson, *Sciences and the Self*, pp. 198–203.

sexual desire is answered by Cupid, who transforms Iphis into a male.[30] This story of miraculous transformations answering to sexual desire caps and confirms the preceding story of Pygmaleon in obvious ways. Here, though, transformation goes one step further, since the very concept of nature is transformed. Cupid is said, out of pity for the two feminine lovers, to 'let do set kinde above, | So that his lawe mai ben used, | And thei upon here lust excused' (4. 489–92). Gender as an expression of 'kinde' is here subjected to a novel and higher definition of what constitutes nature, in this case sexual desire itself. Erotic desire by this argument is alone the measure of the natural; both gender (in Iphis and Ianthe) and materiality itself (in Pygmaleon) concede the force of this newly devised natural law, since both are transformed so as to serve it.

In sum, Genius serves Amans' erotic passion in Book 4. It is true that he does this in various ways across the first six books of the *Confessio*, and, given his place and function in the psyche, we would expect him to do precisely this. This genial sympathy with desire is the very quality that could make him a subtle, homoepathic therapist, offering more of the disease in order to cure its pathological effects. And, as the imagination, literary texts are his medicine. He is simultaneously *grammaticus* and therapist. We would, as I say, expect him to act like this in part, but in Book 4, the book of Sloth, much more so than in any other book, Genius offers the sympathy but not the therapy. While apparently leading the way out of idleness, Genius fosters that very pathology, encouraging Amans in an 'ydel thoght' of erotic fantasy that clearly has nowhere to go but into destructive psychological sands.[31] Genius might cite the paired exempla of Phaeton and Icarus as classic stories of negligence (4. 979–1034, and 4. 1035–71 respectively): neither listens to paternal counsel, and both are destroyed as a result. But whereas Phaeton, for example, allows the horses of his chariot to go 'as hem liketh wantounly' (4. 1017) against his father's advice, Amans seems headed for catastrophe precisely *on* the advice of 'fader Genius' (4. 2771). Not only is Amans in danger in Book 4, but literary education itself looks to be failing on its pedagogic promise.

---

[30] For discussion of the Iphis and Ianthe narrative, see Diane Watt, *Amoral Gower: Language, Sex, and Politics* (Minneapolis, 2003), pp. 73–6.
[31] The citation is from Chaucer, *Book of the Duchess*, line 4, in *The Riverside Chaucer*, 3rd edn., general ed. Larry D. Benson (Oxford, 1987).

III

What, then, is going on in Book 4? Both Amans and Genius seem to occupy rather the same position for a good part of the book, and those positions are self-supporting constructions of idle fantasy: Amans draws Genius forth to tell exactly the kind of story that he wants to hear, and Genius complies. The penitential frame of the dialogue offers a camouflage of therapy, but the actual content of that therapy serves only to aggravate the pathology to which it is ostensibly directed. Talk ostensibly designed to cure idleness, that is, turns out to promote idleness. The strategy of Book 4 seems to be modelled on Ovid's *Remedia amoris*, a book to which Genius explicitly directs Amans for sound advice on how to fool oneself out of love (4. 2668–71). Just as the *Remedia* turns out playfully to offer a good deal more erotic fantasy even as it pretends to wean the lover from desire, so too, it seems, does Book 4 feed the fantasy it pretends to retrain.

As Thorstein Veblen argued so suggestively in 1899, doing nothing is hard work.[32] Humans are inescapably economic creatures, and everything they do, even doing nothing, contributes productively to one economy or another. In this final section I offer three ways of accounting for what is going on productively in Book 4. I begin with the reader; I then turn to ways in which the interaction of Genius and Amans turns out to be productive; finally I address the grave and moving account of suicidal despair at the end of the book. My argument across each of these brief *essais* is that Book 4 does offer a regeneration of sorts, and that that regeneration can only derive from the apparently idle, static play of fantasy. The psyche has its own economy, by this poem's account. Idleness is part of that economy, but the psyche cannot rest idle; idleness generates its own antidote.

The reader: the very fact that I have generated the reading of Book 4 so far advanced implies that the poem's own stasis *can* provoke movement of a kind in its readers. Medieval poems are less well-wrought urns than interactive games; even if literature unwrites its force in the represented action of the poem, that does not mean that the poem itself is without force. The reader, that is, can be provoked *by* the text to reinstate a literary education that is being undone *in* the text.[33] The text's illocutionary

---

[32] Thorstein Veblen, *The Theory of the Leisure Class* (London, 1994; first pub. 1899), pp. 68–101. Veblen anticipates Bourdieu's idea of cultural capital.
[33] For the reader as the point to which the *Confessio is* directed, see Simpson, *Sciences and the Self*, pp. 263–71.

force is different from its perlocutionary force.[34] Not only that: if the reader is doing hermeneutic work left undone in the poem's represented action, then the reader is also rethinking the nature of hermeneutics itself. The literary pedagogue Genius within the text acts as if literary texts had an extractable, exemplary meaning, whereas Gower's reader witnesses in Amans as reader the undoing of that simplistic hermeneusis. Amans only sees himself in narrative, and he only wants narrative to confirm and encourage his own position: this is exactly what he says when he avers that he will read books 'if thei mihte spede | Mi love;' but if 'thei techen to restreigne | Mi love, it were an ydel peine' (4. 2675–7). The poem's reader, then, is provoked to recognise that reading depends not only on books but also on their readers: a readerly disposition to read books profoundly, and to be changed by them, is the precondition of literary education.[35] The real target of the *Confessio* is less the decoy Amans and more the poem's own reader.

Reading *of* the poem, then, turns out to be potentially different from reading *in* the poem. Book 4's representation of readerly sloth turns out to provoke unslothful readings. But before we entirely dismiss the represented action of Book 4 as one of idle reading, we should also consider the interaction of Genius and Amans. Even if both separately maintain idle positions pretty steadily, what about their interaction?

Book 4 produces interesting and productive conflicts between Amans and Genius, particularly concerning violence and love. Idleness is to be shunned, says Genius after his telling of the story of Rosiphelee, from which point he generalises to say that 'Among the gentil nacion | Love is an occupacion, | Which forto kepe hise lustes save | Scholde every gentil herte have' (4. 1451–4). This might seem uncontentious in a late medieval text, expressing as it does the fundamental premise of *fin amour*: that nobly born lovers should actively devote themselves to the pursuit of a single erotic passion. The restrictive definition of 'gentle' implied here might, however, surprise, coming as it does from Genius.[36] Genius is a

---

[34] These terms are drawn especially from Quentin Skinner, 'Motives, Intentions, and the Interpretation of Texts', *New Literary History*, 3 (1971–2), 393–408; the terms derive from J. L. Austin, *How to Do Things with Words* (Oxford, 1962).

[35] For medieval literary theory on readerly disposition, see Gillespie, 'The Study of Classical Authors: from the Twelfth Century to *c.*1450', pp. 160–78.

[36] Note this comment by Winthrop Wetherbee: 'Chivalry is in effect the villain of the *Confessio*, at odds with Genius's teaching in virtually every area', in his 'John Gower', in David Wallace (ed.), *The Cambridge History of Medieval English Literature* (Cambridge, 1999), pp. 589–609 (at p. 602); see also Winthrop Wetherbee, 'Classical and Boethian Tradition in the *Confessio Amantis*', in Siân Echard (ed.), *A Companion to Gower* (Cambridge, 2004), pp. 181–96 (at 192–4).

figure of the natural self and a literary maker; one might expect him to participate in the long tradition of humanist opposition to an aristocratic, restrictive definition of nobility.[37] The side note at this point also strikes a warning note: 'Non quia sic se habet veritas, set opinio Amantum', which is the only marginal note in the entire *Confessio* that explicitly disagrees with Genius.[38] The immediately following tale of Jephtha's daughter, while not underwriting any doctrine of courtly love, does produce, as we have already seen, a frankly peculiar reading from Genius. And immediately after that story, Genius introduces an explicit defence of militarist pursuit of amatory success:

> Forthi who secheth loves grace,
> Wher that these worthi wommen are,
> He mai noght thanne himselve spare
> Upon his travail forto serve,
> Wherof that he mai thonk deserve,
> There as these men of armes be.
> (4. 1620–5)

Asked if he has been militarily active on behalf of his lady, Amans replies both comically and seriously. Comically, he rapidly denies any military involvement whatsoever: every man must have been more aggressive militarily than he has been. He would rather win his love than Cairo and all its treasure (4. 1648–58). The comic, Ovidian defence of non-military action itself produces, however, a serious objection to Genius: Amans persuasively argues that he cannot see what good will derive from the shedding of non-Christian blood. And besides, he goes on forcefully, Christ forbad killing; and those who actively promote the crusades themselves remain at home comfortably enjoying an easy and sinful life. He concludes his attack on complacent ecclesiastical preachers:

> Bot hierof have I gret mervaile,
> Hou thei wol bidde me travaile:
> A Sarazin if I sle schal,
> I sle the soule forth withal,
> And that was nevere Cristes lore.
> Bot nou ho ther, I seie nomore.
> (4. 1677–82)

---

[37] For the late medieval tradition of nobility of soul, see A. J. Minnis, 'From Medieval to Renaissance?: Chaucer's Position on Past Gentility', *Proceedings of the British Academy*, 72 (1986), 205–46.
[38] 'Not because the truth has it thus, but the opinion of lovers'.

Out of the apparently irresponsible and self-serving Ovidian excuse for lack of public service, Amans generates a sharply topical attack on the immorality of crusading, whose topical danger he underlines by his abrupt halt to further critique.[39] Activated in this way, Amans the slothful lover becomes Amans the active literary reader: he recalls a text in which a hero did all he could to avoid military involvement in the name of erotic passion: he remembers Achilles, who temporarily withdrew from the Trojan War out of love for Polyxena.

In defending militarist action in the name of love, Genius seems to me to dig himself in deeper with his counter examples. He begins with the story of Ulysses, who tried to avoid the Trojan War because he preferred to stay at home with his wife (4. 1815–1900). Genius argues that Ulysses finally recognised that it is better to win honour than love, which goes very close to contradicting the earlier narrative of Ulysses hurrying home from the war to his wife. We then hear the story of Protesilaus, who rejects his wife's pleas to avoid the Trojan War and stay at home, and goes instead to war, preferring to die 'as a knyht' than live in dishonour (4. 1901–34). The barely relevant story of Saul follows (4. 1935–62), in which Saul, ignoring the prophecy that he will die in battle, goes to battle and dies, preferring 'worschipe.' After that narrative, we hear that as a child Achilles was taught to kill or wound at least once a day, which 'proves' that knightly courage is superior to all other amatory endowments (4. 1963–2019); Genius does not pause once to consider the terrible effects of Achilles' violence in love or otherwise. Neither does he pause to consider the disasters consequent on the love aggressively pursued by Lancelot (4. 2029–39). Hercules, we are told, successfully gained the love of Deianira (4. 2045–2134), but we are not told of the disastrous finale to that story.[40] Finally, after telling the story of Philemenis, whose very questionable conclusion I considered above, Genius blithely concludes all these narratives by saying that they all demonstrate how women admire military courage, especially among the 'gentles' (4. 2190–2219).

Amans, then, activates an anti-war position that is more persuasive than Genius' own defence of an aristocratic erotic-militarism. True, it is Amans' self-serving defence of his own idleness that moves him to argue against the ethos of chivalric love, but the interaction produced leads in

---

[39] For Lollard opposition to the Dispenser Crusade of 1383, see Anne Hudson, *The Premature Reformation: Wycliffite Texts and Lollard History* (Oxford, 1988), pp. 368–70.
[40] For the Ovidian-derived Gowerian tactic of referring to amatory stories without taking their disastrous consequences into account, see Simpson, *Sciences and the Self*, pp. 134–66.

productive directions. That interaction produces further interest in the question Amans now poses: what is true nobility? In direct opposition to the idea of nobility as restrictive and aristocratic, Genius now adopts an opposed position: he defines nobility as nobility of soul, so that, he insists, 'of generacion | To make a declaracion, | Ther mai no gentilesce be' (4. 2227–9). Whoever pursues virtue out of a 'resonable entencion' is 'a verrai gentil man' (4. 2270–7).

It seems to me that Amans and Genius are interacting here so as to produce more profound and civilised accounts of action in each other.[41] While Amans defends his own idleness, he attacks the unchristian bloodshed of the crusades, so unthinkingly defended by Genius. And if Genius provisionally approves a specifically aristocratic ethos of militarist eroticism, Amans produces in him a deeper commitment to an alternative, ethical definition of true nobility. And as Genius produces that more civilised definition, so too is he moved to articulate the origins and uses of practical and intellectual arts and sciences, which is the one large inset disquisition in Book 4 (4. 2363–2700). If true nobility is achieved through cultivation of the soul, then Genius provides a map of skills and sciences by which humans can practise that cultivation. Genius knows these sciences, from the art of writing to cookery and alchemy, since Genius is the psychological faculty that produced them in the first place. The women who invented linen 'were of grete engyn' (4. 2438), Carmente invented 'of hire engin' the first Latin alphabet (4. 2637); those who fail to practise the arts are 'otios[i] ... qui excellentis prudencie ingenium habentes absque fructu operum torpescunt'.[42]

So Genius begins with praise of a restrictive, aristocratic version of nobility and its ethos of passionate love; he moves, however, through an unpredictable yet productive psychological interaction, to a 'clerical' account of nobility, an account of nobility of soul achieved through cultivation of arts and sciences. Some invented the practical sciences, while others began to 'studie and muse' (4. 2385) in the writing of books, among which literate sciences are included Grammar, Rhetoric and 'Poesie' (4. 2632–71). It seems to me that the very process by which Genius arrives at this account of nobility achieved through active pursuit

---

[41] The situation is similar to that at the end of Book 6, when Amans is exhausted by discussing love, and wants to change the subject; he asks for political instruction, which in fact turns out to be exceptionally productive; see Simpson, *Sciences and the Self*, pp. 205–7.

[42] 'Idle, who, while possessing an imagination of excellent wit, lie supine without the fruit of works'.

of the sciences, including the sciences of letters, itself prompts us to reflect on the process of literary knowledge in this very poem. The model of knowledge here is not authoritarian, deriving from one, stable figure or from one simple hermeneutic process. Instead it derives from the interaction of different faculties of the psyche, each unpredictably provoking the other to a deeper perception, and each working, I think, by an inherently productive and optimistic economy of soul. Of course, as we have seen, this schema of the sciences ends without much uptake: the very last reference in Genius' disquisition is to Ovid's *Remedia amoris*; and, as we have seen, Amans remains uninterested in remedies to love. Something, however, has happened here: the very operations of idle fantasy have, without outside or aggressive intervention, pointed a way out of idleness and into the ennobling labour, including the ennobling but unpredictable labour of reading.

Both the reader's engagement with the poem, and aspects of the poem's represented interaction do, then, generate antidotes to idleness. By way of ending, I propose one further argument that Book 4 works its own way out of the dead-end of static, obsessive, repetitive readerly sloth. I focus on the final two sequences of the book, devoted respectively to somnolence and despondency, which include grave and moving stories. These final stories have their own persuasive power to retrieve human sense and purposiveness from waste, forgetfulness and negligence.

Aspects of Book 4 are comic, particularly when Amans' 'sins' are the kind he wishes he had had the chance to commit, or when the contrast between Amans and the protagonists of Genius' stories is especially wide and improbable. Thus Amans denies ever having been late for an assignation with his lover, mainly because he has never had an assignation (4. 270–80). And the comparison between Achilles' training in blood savagery as an incitement to Amans to be more active as a lover (4. 1963–2022) can only strike the reader as comically implausible, not least because it is followed by a narrative concerning the bravery of Hercules. Amans is no Achilles or Hercules.

Discussion of the final 'sins' is, however, no joke. These final sequences are focused less on avoidable ethical failings than on troubling and disabling states of depression and listlessness; as with much of the ethical reflection in the *Confessio*, Gower liberates the 'sins' from their penitential limitations; he uses the sins as material to reflect in more complex ways about the needs of the psyche and the polis. He does this especially with states of melancholy, in ways that the standard scholarly treatments resolutely refuse to recognise, reserving as they do creative melancholy for the Renaissance.[43] I briefly discuss these two sustained narratives, of Alceone and of Iphis and Araxarathen.

Amans' account of the grinding cycle of despair led, and repetitively betrayed, by faint hope, introduces the narrative of Alceone. Like the narrator of Chaucer's *Book of the Duchess*, Amans cannot sleep; when he finally goes to bed, before sleep itself, he is wholly vulnerable to the image of his lover:

> Into hire bedd min herte goth,
> And softly takth hire in his arm
> And fieleth hou that sche is warm,
> And wissheth that his body were
> To fiele that he fieleth there.
> And thus miselven I tormente,
> Til that the dede slep me hente.
> (4. 2884–90)

This, though, is the prelude to further torment: in his dreams he keeps winning only to keep losing his love; the intense joy of meeting her, alone and in freedom from 'danger', leads directly to a waking despair that is itself victim to an insuppressible desire to continue the dream. This moving pathology recalls the 'sorwful ymaginacion' of the *Book of the Duchess* narrator, who is also incapable of sleeping, obsessed as he is by 'ydel thought', until he reads the narrative of Ceys and Alceone. This same story follows the same psychic pathology in the *Confessio*. As in the Chaucerian text, so too in the *Confessio*: Juno sends Iris to engage Morpheus in order to reveal the truth to the anxious Alceone. Morpheus' cavern of sleepy forgetfulness, by which runs the river of Lethe, is the very image of sloth; interestingly, nonetheless, from this very place of total stasis and oblivion, Morpheus resuscitates images to tell the tragic truth, and so restore a transformed Alceone to a kind of happiness.[44]

The images of oblivious, slothful sleep, in this powerful story at any rate, turn out to be productive and finally transformative. That may not

---

[43] Thus Raymond Klibansky, Erwin Panofsky and Fritz Saxl, *Saturn and Melancholy: Studies in the History of Natural Philosophy, Religion, and Art* (New York, 1964). For a vigorous and persuasive rebuttal of this chronological restriction, see Giorgio Agamben, 'The Noonday Demon', in *Stanzas: Word and Phantasm in Western Culture*, translated by Ronald L. Martinez (Minneapolis, 1993), pp. 3–15.

[44] For late medieval and early modern imitations of Ovid's Morpheus, see Colin Burrow, '"Full of the Maker's Guile": Ovid on Imitating and on the Imitation of Ovid', in Philip Hardie, Alessandro Barchiesi, and Stephen Hinds (eds.), *Transformations: Essays on Ovid's Metamorphoses and Its Reception* (Cambridge, 1999), pp. 271–87.

be irrelevant to the images produced by Genius for the sick and tired Amans. Psychic waste can, that is, generate profitable images. Certainly the last image produced in these stories, that of Iphis and Araxarathen, delivers a powerful and memorably imagistic shock to the despairing lover. Amans' state of mind, as expressed at the beginning of this tale, is no joke:

> For be my trouthe I schal noght lie,
> Of pure sorwe, which I drye
> For that sche seith sche wol me noght,
> With drecchinge of myn oghne thought
> In such wanhope I am falle,
> That I ne can unethes calle,
> As forto speke of eny grace,
> Mi ladi merci to pourchace.
> (4. 3473–80)

The story told by Genius answers directly and seriously to this state of mind. Iphis the prince falls in love with Araxarathen, who rebuffs his insistent approaches so forcefully that he succumbs to despair. After a long and articulate lament outside the house of Araxarathen, he hangs himself. Araxarathen, in turn, blames herself for the suicide, and is transformed into a stone statue, a petrified and perfect image of herself. The body of the male suicide and the stone image of the female are taken to the temple of Venus, where the statue is memorably set above the tomb of the dead prince.

It is true that the female suffers the vengeance of the gods in this story, as in earlier narratives of hard-hearted girls in Book 4. But this story offers no consolation or hope to the male lover who will not give up; on the contrary, Genius' final tale serves as a riposte to earlier, wish-fulfilment stories. Here the boy Iphis dies as a suicide, whereas the earlier Iphis story in Book 4 has the protagonist transform into a man so as to satisfy sexual desire. And this story also responds to the narrative paired with the earlier Iphis tale, that of Pygmaleon. For the Pygmaleon myth satisfies fantasist dreams of both sexual desire and idolatrous love of art, in having the beautiful statue come to warm and sexually pliant life. Here, by contrast, the metamorphosis is the other way around: through the unrelenting burden of suffering the human is petrified, and the verisimilar art object serves the function of visible and minatory remembrance, placed as it is in Venus' temple. And whereas Pygmaleon's prayer to Venus is answered, Iphis' is not. Genius tells the story, indeed, precisely by way of underlining the fact that such a sore is incurable, and that the 'goddes ben vengable' (4. 3509–10). Late medieval Christian penitential manuals were confident to warn against despair, by affirming God's ever-readiness to accept the penitent sinner,[45] but Genius knows that psychic forces are less forgiving.

In conclusion, we can concede that a literary education can easily feed the psyche's capacity for delusive satisfaction. That said, we have seen various ways in which Gower recognises the value of *otium*; there are some states of soul that cannot be broached directly, and that require homeopathic therapy that pretends to feed pathological desire even as it begins the cure. And that homeopathic psychic treatment involves a cultural commitment to idle, apparently wasted reading: like many other Middle English works that recycle prior texts, the *Confessio* demonstrates no desire to define books and libraries as waste. It offers instead a model of recreative relaxedness among many books; books will respond creatively to the big questions, but only if we allow them to do their own work on us. Even in the depths of despair, a new rewriting may be going on in the soul's deepest powers, as it is in Dürer's *Melancholia*.[46] The recycling of old texts in the *Confessio* is less a matter of humble obeisance to older, higher literary authority, and more a matter of understanding how texts and traditions are creatively recycled through the complex operations of idle reading.

Note. I thank the anonymous readers of this essay. I altered the essay in the light of their forceful comments wherever I agreed with them. At some points (particularly with regard to the *Confessio Amantis*) I hold by, and build on, ground work laid in my *Sciences and the Self: Alan of Lille's 'Anticlaudianus' and John Gower's 'Confessio Amantis'* (Cambridge, 1995).

---

[45] For penitential accounts of sloth, see Siegfried Wenzel, *The Sin of Sloth: Acedia in Medieval Thought and Literature* (Chapel Hill, NC, 1960).
[46] Note the busily writing putto to the right of Melancholia.

BRITISH ACADEMY LECTURE

Kinds of People: Moving Targets

IAN HACKING
Fellow of the Academy

I HAVE LONG BEEN INTERESTED in classifications of people, in how they affect the people classified, and how the effects on the people in turn change the classifications. Since 1983 that has led me to undertake an unending series of studies: two books, one about 1980s multiple personality and one about 1890s dissociative fugue;[1] articles about old criminology, about contemporary child abuse, and a study of the very idea of the poverty line.[2] There were detailed unpublished talks on genius and on suicide, plus some lectures, on-line in French, about autism and obesity.[3] I coined two slogans. The first one, 'making up people', referred to the ways in which a new scientific classification may bring into being a new kind of person, conceived of and experienced as a way to be a person.[4] The second,

---

Read at the Academy 11 April 2006.
[1] *Rewriting the Soul: Multiple Personality and the Sciences of Memory* (Princeton, 1995). *Mad Travelers: Reflections on the Reality of Transient Mental Illnesses* (Charlottesville, VA, 1998; Cambridge, MA, 2002).
[2] One example of each topic: 'Criminal behavior, degeneracy and looping', David T. Wasserman and R. T. Wachbroit (eds.), *Genetics and Criminal Behavior* (Cambridge, 2001), pp. 141–67. 'The Making and Molding of Child Abuse', *Critical Inquiry*, 17 (1991), 253–88. 'Façonner les gens : le seuil de pauvreté', J.-P. Beaud and J.-G. Prévost (eds.), *L'ère du chiffre: Systèmes statistiques et traditions nationales* (Québec, 2000), pp. 17–36.
[3] In the lectures for 2004–5 at <www.college-de-france.fr/site/phi_his>. I intend to publish some of this material in English, under the titles, 'Where did the BMI come from?' and 'The many faces of Autism'.
[4] 'Making Up People', T. Heller *et al.* (ed.), *Reconstructing Individualism* (Stanford, CA, 1986), pp. 222–36. This talk, given at Stanford in the fall of 1983, is reprinted in my *Historical Ontology* (Cambridge, MA, 2002), pp. 99–114.

the 'looping effect', referred to the way in which a classification may interact with the people classified.⁵ Right from the start, I said that there is 'no reason to suppose that we shall ever tell two identical stories of two different instances of making up people'.⁶ But some generalisations are possible. I shall now propose a framework within which to think about making up people and the looping effect.

Many kinds of people fit into this framework, but I shall not be concerned with every kind. This is because I am especially interested in the ways in which the social, medical and biological sciences create new classifications and new knowledge. Many of the kinds of people I want to discuss are new kinds, or kinds that may bear old names but have acquired new meanings in the light of new knowledge. Some kinds have been with us always. Sex, race and gender: these categories have been intensely examined these many years, especially in the light of gender studies and post-colonial histories. Since I shall say little about them here, I should explain why not.

Some kinds of people that I shall not discuss

I do not want, for example, to examine the various classifications that at present we politely call 'ethnic'. A good old word taken from the Greek, betokening other kinds of people, nations, or, in New Testament Greek, gentiles or heathen, the matching concept for the Hebrew goyim; in short, the others. *Others* have been alongside us always. Human beings are said to be social animals. A society includes—and excludes. Societies imply other people, the excluded. The speculations of evolutionary psychology or the more systematic studies of comparative anthropology confirm that, but history as written down suffices. Amidst the ruins of the ancient city of Persepolis there still stand the real-life sentiments of Shelley's imagined Ozymandias. Proclamations in three languages abound, in Old Persian, Elamite, and Babylonian. My guide book translates one sentence as: 'I am Xerxes the great King, King of Kings, King of the countries having many kinds of people.'⁷ Twenty-three of these kinds of people are

---

⁵ 'The Looping Effects of Human Kinds', D. Sperber, D. Premack and A. Premack (eds.), *Causal Cognition. An Interdisciplinary Debate* (Oxford, 1995), pp. 351–83.

⁶ 'Making up People', p. 223; reprint, p. 114.

⁷ Ali Sami, *Persepolis* (*Takht-i-Jamshid*), trans. R. Sharp, 9th edn. (Shiraz, 1977), p. 35; for almost identical sentences found in other parts of the city, see pp. 21, 51. For full texts and the standard scholarly translations, see the microfiche edition, *Persepolis and Ancient Iran*, compiled

illustrated by carvings on the Great Staircase, beginning with the Medes and ending with the Ethiopians.[8] A carved stereotype of each kind is shown, one or more men bearing or leading their characteristic tribute of wares, foodstuffs, or animals.

Xerxes ruled the Persian Empire at its apogee and on its way out, but in this respect it was no different from any other. A recent exhibition at the Royal Academy in London displayed a scroll, 'Qing Imperial Illustration of Tributaries', namely, 'Minorities from Yunnan, Guizhou, Guangxi'. Sixteen metres of beautifully drawn examples of subject peoples were on display.[9]

The conceptions of Christians were the cruellest. At Vézelay in Burgundy is a Romanesque cathedral from which two world wars were launched, the second and third crusades. It has a great porch where the pilgrims were received. There is a prodigious sculpture in the tympanum on the nave side of the narthex, said to represent the holy spirit flowing from Christ, first to the Apostles but in due course even to the unconverted gentiles. Once again there is a sculpted procession of these others. To cite another guide book, 'the little personalities sculpted on the lintel are from the pagan peoples (men whose heads are dogs' heads, or with enormous ears, pygmies, etc.) walking towards Christ in a movement that represents their conversion'.[10]

It has been said that 'the category of race—denoting primarily skin colour—was first employed as a means of classifying human bodies by François Bernier, a French physician, in 1684'.[11] Perhaps Europeans did not get their colour-coded geographically based concept of race until the great voyages, but racial classification, more generally understood, has been with us always. Classifying kinds of subject people is an imperial imperative. How else did the science of anthropology begin, than as the science of European powers that studied tributary peoples?

---

by Ursula Schneider (Chicago, 1976). An excellent on-line version is readily available. I use my guidebook rather than the best scholarship because it is in itself a splendid multi-imperial artefact. Its publication date is given as 2535 Shahanshahee, and the translator is identified as 'The Reverend R. Sharp, M.A., Cantab'.

[8] Ibid., pp. 31–3. A tablet listing 29 provinces ruled by Xerxes, overlapping with the kinds of people, is given on pp. 66ff. Photographs of the carvings are found in the University of Chicago publication.

[9] E. S. Rawski and J. Rawson, (eds.), *China, the Three Emperors, 1662–1795* (London, 2006), plate 77. Original in the Palace Museum, Beijing, Gu 6306.

[10] *France*, Guides Bleus (Paris, 1990), p. 299.

[11] Cornel West, 'A Genealogy of Modern Racism', *Prophesy Deliverance! An Afro-American Revolutionary Christianity* (Philadelphia, 1982), pp. 47–65, on p. 55.

The idea that peoples just separate naturally into overarching racial, ethnic, or linguistic groups is largely a product of a recent invention, the nation state. In a vast region such as Mesopotamia, the site of invasion, conquest and trade from time immemorial, people do not simply come sorted. Families, tribes and local regimes are what count, a human eye's view of the population rather than the vision of a hegemonic power. Xerxes's father Darius imposed a structure of satrapies on the empire created by Cyrus. The peoples, that is, the different classes of inhabitants of these administrative districts, were exactly what the Greeks referred to as the different 'ethnos' of the Persian Empire.

All of this suggests a model for 'making up people'. We can well imagine that Darius's captains chose to categorise his subjects for the convenience of administration. The subjects were not classified in exactly this way before they were conquered. Geography, language, allegiances, previous social cohesion, bodily structure, and skin colour would all have been grounds for forming classifications, and in some cases, those kinds of people would not have existed, *as a kind of people*, until they had been so classified, organised and taxed. Others were cemented as kinds of people by classification and administration, and also by revolt, for a people has to solidify in order to throw off the imperial yoke.

The framework of such a story has five primary aspects. There is (*a*) the *classification* into kinds of people. Classification is usually within a category, a most general principle of classification. Here the category is subject peoples of the Persian Empire. There are *classes* that fall under this category, here called Armenians, Bactrians, and so on. These are the many kinds of people of which Xerxes boasts.

There are (*b*) the *individuals* and *peoples* in the various classes. In traditional logic, they are in the extensions of the classes defined in (*a*). In real life they are the flesh and blood individual men, women and children, or socially cohesive groups of them. There will be many borderline cases, individuals or smaller groups who are not so clearly of the main ethnicities such as 'Pointed-capped Sythians' or 'Somali'. With the course of empire the individuals will increasingly be filed in one class or another and, for at least some purposes, they will self-identify in that way.

There are (*c*) the *institutions*, for example those that manage tribute, taxation and recruitment. They firm up the classifications. The tax collectors and recruitment officers work within structured bureaucracies. By institutions I chiefly mean established organisations, rather than matters of practice or custom, although of course organisations have their own practices and affect the habits of people with whom they interact.

Most institutions that matter on a day-to-day basis are not exactly imposed from the top down. Empires can succeed only if they foster quasi-autonomous local administrations that are run by the peoples themselves.

A fourth primary aspect of the framework is (*d*) *knowledge* about the kind of people in question, their characteristics, fierce or docile, artistic or warlike, skilled artisans or able hunters. Some of this knowledge will be precise matters of detail known to (*e*) *experts* in the administration, local officers on the ground, their regional allies, collaborating Scythians or Somalis. Some of the knowledge will consist of more traditional facts well known to the classified people themselves. Some will be imperial myths that over the years become concretised facts.

Classification tends to invite *stereotypes*, handily illustrated by the images sculpted on the frieze on the staircase, in which each people brings its most desired produce, be it materials, animals, or craftsmanship. My guidebook tells us what has always been the official story, which we now read with irony:

> The offering of the best produce and works of art of each country to the Court, and the presentation of these gifts to the King was not only a ceremonial act, but was beneficial in stimulating the products of each land and developing its arts and crafts. Every year the craftsmen tried to prepare and present to the King articles that were finer and more beautiful than in previous years.[12]

Moreover the artisans modify their wares, and that alters their stereotype. Were the Ethiopians who are shown bringing tusks and giraffes about to present elegantly carved tusks and even more exotic species? This is a benign example of the looping effect: the classified people enhance and adjust what is true of them. (Think of recent Inuit soapstone carving, and present aboriginal Australian art. These combine traditional practices and shrewd marketing by art dealers. They are changing conceptions of who the peoples are, both for 'us' and for 'them'.)

We have become all too aware of the evil effects of stereotypes. The stereotypes of American slaves became essential properties not only in the eyes of the masters, but also were experienced by the victims as true of themselves. When there is revolt and black power, a new self-conception is fostered, and there is an attempt at looping, in order not only to

---

[12] Sami, *Persepolis*, n. 1, p. 35. I do not know if the notes were written by the author or the translator.

upgrade self-conceptions and raise consciousness, but also to change the knowledge of the powerful about the oppressed.

All that provides many tidy illustrations for my slogans, making up people and the looping effect. Despite the way they fit my framework, ethnicity and its kin are not my topic here. The imperial organisation of kinds of people is in the end very much a matter of brute power, which, in the present context does not concern me. I am interested in the classifications that are studied in the sciences, where the knowledge is not simply instrumental. Michel Foucault has led many of his readers to think of the power-effects of seemingly innocent or inevitable scientific classifications. That is not the path I shall take in this lecture, although it has by now been so well trodden that readers will not fail to notice it.

But was there not explicit race science that I should take into account, just as there is a welter of sex sciences practised around us right now? Yes, there was. Race science began at the dawn of the nineteenth century. It is one of the first sciences of man, the one that Steven Jay Gould called *The Mismeasure of Man*. The doctrine that there are exactly five races became fixed in the 1790s. It was fostered by Kant's friend Johann Friedrich Blumenbach, once thought of as the first comparative anthropologist, thanks to his meticulous measurements of sixty human crania from around the world. Kant himself was publishing his *Anthropologie* and had introduced the question, *What is Man?* into his annual logic lectures about that time. That is also when sociology begin to stir. The collection of statistics of suicide, crime, and many other deviations was the beginning of numerical sociology. Counting, and making the numbers public, began in earnest after 1815; serious correlating began about 1870. One fruit was Durkheim's 1897 *Suicide*, the culmination of eighty years of reflections on new knowledge about suicide.[13] Francis Galton's type of race science, which he called eugenics, gave us the foundational ideas for modern statistical inference, namely correlation and regression. Race science has thus been historically connected, in an intimate way, to topics that I shall address later. But ideas of race and of 'others' began long before the sciences of race, and will probably outlast them. They have a life of their own (as do ideas of sex), that is far more entrenched than any science, and hence they are not my immediate topic.

---

[13] I. Hacking, 'How Numerical Sociology Began by Counting Suicides: From Medical Pathology to Social Pathology', I. B. Cohen (ed.), *The Natural and the Social Sciences* (Dordrecht, 1993), pp. 101–33. For a more extensive treatment of such topics, see my *The Taming of Chance* (Cambridge, 1990).

I do not say so because of the comfortable doctrine that there is no such thing as race—and hence that there cannot be a viable race science. That is not my reason for wanting to exclude race from these studies. Indeed I believe that legitimate sciences of race are evolving right now. The complacent denial of race as a scientific concept is outmoded.[14] Developments in epidemiology and genetics lead to what the anthropologist Paul Rabinow has called biosociality, which in turn leads to biosocial identities, the linear descendant of racial identity.[15] There we have some kind of making up of identities in abundance, but I still do not want the category of race, simply because it has, like sex, been with us humans since the beginning. Race science itself is tangential to the formation of conceptions of race and 'the other', a mere moment in an unending history.

Human kinds (not)

When I started this work long ago, I used a horrible label to characterise my subject: 'Human kinds'. That matched the natural-kind concept that English philosophers derived from John Stuart Mill.[16] Thanks to Saul Kripke and Hilary Putnam, there was an explosion of interest in natural kinds during the 1970s and later. It took me all too long to realise that my notion of a human kind was totally confused. I was helped in jettisoning the term by the collapse of the idea of natural kinds itself.[17]

---

[14] One of the themes of my, 'Why race still matters', *Daedelus*, 134 (2005), 102–16.

[15] P. Rabinow, 'Artificiality and Enlightenment: From Sociobiology to Biosociality', in Jonathan Crary and Sanford Kwinter (eds.), *Incorporations* (New York, 1992); reprinted in his *Essays on the Anthropology of Reason* (Princeton, 1996), pp. 91–111. I. Hacking, 'Genetics, Biosocial Groups, and the Future of Identity', *Daedalus*, 135 (Fall, 2006), 81–95.

[16] Thus I so used the label in print in 'A Tradition of Natural Kinds', *Philosophical Studies*, 61 (1991), 106–26. It was taken up by other writers after my, 'The Looping Effects of Human Kinds', a talk given in 1993 and published in 1995. I do not recall when I started talking about 'human kinds': I gave a talk at MIT with that title in 1979.

[17] I. Hacking, 'Natural Kinds: Rosy Dawn, Scholastic Twilight', A. O'Hear (ed.), *Philosophy of Science* (Cambridge, 2007), 203–39. A simple deduction: there is no such thing as a natural kind, *a fortiori*, there is no such thing as a human kind. Rachel Cooper in my opinion did not get to the root of the evil in her astute paper, 'Why Hacking is Wrong about Human Kinds', *British Journal for the Philosophy of Science*, 55 (2004), 73–85. She opposes what she calls my 'central claim that human kinds and natural kinds are fundamentally distinct'. In fact, there do not exist two classes (of the sort indicated) that can be defined sufficiently clearly to be either distinct or not distinct.

The philosopher of biology John Dupré also used 'Human Kinds', but only for the title of a paper, and not in the paper itself.[18] The label has, however, turned out to be useful to other writers, for exactly what I did not intend. Lawrence Hirschfeld, an anthropologist steeped in developmental cognitive psychology, used it for racial classifications.[19] This little meme, 'human kinds', has recently been absorbed in a most interesting book written by David Berreby for a popular audience. He chose the telling title, *Us and Them*.

> Categories like Americans and Iranians, Muslims and Christians, blacks and whites, men and women, southerners and northerners, doctors and lawyers, gays and straights, soccer moms and NASCAR dads, outgoing people and shy types, smart ones and lucky ones. Those—and all the other labels that define more than one person but fewer than all—are what I (following the philosopher Ian Hacking and the psychological anthropologist Lawrence Hirschfeld), call "human kinds".[20]

The listed labels all have standard uses as Us-and-Them epithets.

I am glad that my (former) term 'human kinds' has become a tool with which to analyse the Us-and-Them use of names for groups of people. It takes us back to the beginning, to the *other*, to the Greek word from which hails our tight-lipped 'ethnic'. But it is a not a term that I myself will continue to use.

Human sciences

We think of many kinds of people as objects of scientific inquiry. We do so sometimes to control them, as with prostitutes, and sometimes to help them, for example to stop potential suicides. Sometimes the aim is to organise and to help, but at the same time to keep society safe, as when prosperous people or the state aid the poor or the homeless. Sometimes

---

[18] J. Dupré, 'Human Kinds', J. Dupré, *The Latest on the Best* (Boston, MA, 1987), pp. 327–48; reprinted in J. Dupré, *Humans and Other Animals* (Oxford, 2002), pp. 127–50. Dupré was studying what, if anything, evolutionary psychology might teach about cultural characterisations of groups of people. (Short answer: nothing.) His usage of 'human kind', to refer to human groups picked out by social characteristics, is not so far from the us-and-them use about to be mentioned.

[19] L. A. Hirschfeld, *Race in the Making: Cognition, Culture, and the Child's Conception of Human Kinds* (Boston, MA, 1996). Hirschfeld was present at the Paris conference where I presented 'Looping Effects' in 1993.

[20] D. Berreby, *Us and Them: Understanding your Tribal Mind* (New York, 2005), pp. 14ff.

we try to change others for what is deemed to be for their own good: the obese furnish an example that I shall use later. Sometimes we study a kind of person just to admire, to understand, to encourage and perhaps even to emulate, as (sometimes) with genius. We think of these kinds of people as given, as definite classes defined by definite properties. As we get to know more about these properties, we will able to control, to help, to change, or to emulate them better. But it is not quite like that. They are moving targets because our investigations interact with the targets themselves, and change them. And since they are changed, they are not quite the same kind of people as before. The target has moved. That is the looping effect. Sometimes our sciences create kinds of people that in a certain sense did not exist before. That is making up people.[21]

All this may seem closer to sociology than to philosophy, and indeed I have a sociological hero, Erving Goffman, whom I invoke from time to time, but not here.[22] I am concerned with the sciences of man, but not in the style of the sociologist. My target is broader then the social and the human sciences, for I count psychiatry and much of clinical medicine among the sciences of man. What shall we call this family of sciences without sounding sexist? 'Sciences of human beings' is pedantic and ugly. I shall call them the human sciences: for although that label has a fairly clear denotation in French, it is not systematically used in English. The human sciences, thus understood, include many social sciences, psychology, psychiatry, and a good deal of clinical medicine. The 'kinds of people' of my title are those studied by the human sciences. I am only pointing, for not only is my definition vague, but specific sciences should never be defined except for administrative and educational purposes. Living sciences are always crossing borders and borrowing from each other.

I shall later list some of the engines used in these sciences. They are engines of discovery, which have side-effects that are seldom noticed: for they are also engines for making up people. Statistical analysis of classes

---

[21] After giving up on the notion of a 'human kind', I still accepted some idea of a natural kind, and thus clung to the idea that there was a definite class of 'kinds' which I called 'interactive kinds', as opposed to 'indifferent kinds'. See my *The Social Construction of **What**?* (Cambridge, MA, 1999), chap. 4. Interactions among classifications, people, institutions, knowledge and experts are essential to the explanation of the looping effect and making up people, but there is no well-defined type of classification of people worth calling interactive or human kinds. Interaction, yes, but interactive kinds as a distinct class, no.

[22] 'Between Michel Foucault and Erving Goffman: Between discourse in the abstract and face-to-face interaction', *Economy and Society*, 33 (2004), 277–302.

of people is a fundamental engine. Likewise we constantly try to medicalise: doctors attempted to medicalise suicide as early as the 1830s. The brains of suicides were dissected to find the hidden cause.[23] More generally, we try to biologise, to recognise a biological foundation for the problems that beset some class of people. More recently, we hope to geneticise as much as possible. Thus obesity, once regarded as a problem of incontinence, or weakness of the will, became the province of medicine, then of biology, and at present the search is on for inherited tendencies to become very fat. A similar story can be told of the search for the criminal personality.

Nominalism

Is this philosophy? Yes it is. These reflections on the classification of people are a species of nominalism. I would love to place them in the grand tradition of British nominalism, of Ockham, of Hobbes, of Locke, of Mill, of Russell, of Austin. But traditional nominalism is wholly static. Mine is dynamic, for I am interested in how names interact with the named.

For precedents we have to move to the Continent. The first dynamic nominalist may have been Friedrich Nietzsche. An aphorism in *The Gay Science* begins, 'There is something that causes me the greatest difficulty, and continues to do so without relief: unspeakably more depends on *what things are called* than on what they are.' It ends, '... creating new names and assessments and apparent truths is enough to create new "things"'. This section is headed *Only as creators,* the point being that we can undo a named idea only by creating some positive concept. Deconstruction for its own sake is self-indulgent play. 'Only a fool', Nietzsche continues, 'would think it was enough to point to this misty mantle of illusion in order to *destroy* the world that counts as essential ...'[24] Making up people is a special case of Nietzsche's phenomenon. My concern is less sweeping than his but it has caused me the greatest difficulty these twenty years.

I do not believe that 'more depends on what things are called than on what they are'. My sense of reality is too strong to go down the road

---

[23] See my *Taming of Chance,* chap. 8.
[24] Friedrich Nietzsche, *The Gay Science: with a Prelude in Rhymes and an Appendix of Songs,* translated by Walter Kaufmann from the 2nd edn. (1887), (New York, 1964), § 58.

towards linguistic idealism. And there is something else wrong with Nietzsche's text, because it sounds as if names work their magic by themselves. As Nietzsche well knew but did not bother saying, names are only one part of the dynamics. In the case of kinds of people, there are not only the names of the classifications, but also the *people* classified, the *experts* who classify, study and help them, the *institutions* within which the experts and their subjects interact, and through which authorities control. There is the evolving body of *knowledge* about the people in question—both expert knowledge and popular science. Here I repeat the framework of five interacting aspects of making up people mentioned in connection with race.

Michel Foucault was a more recent practitioner of dynamic nominalism. Only very recently did I notice this passage, found in his review, in a daily newspaper, of Kenneth Dover's well known book about Greek homosexuality.

> Dover clears away a cluttered conceptual countryside. You still find pleasant people who think that, all in all, homosexuality has always existed. They cite in evidence Cambacérès, the Duke of Crequi, Michelangelo or Timarchus. Dover offers such naïfs an excellent lesson in historical nominalism. Relations between two persons of the same sex are one thing. But to love someone of the same sex for himself, to take pleasure with him, is something else, a whole other experience, with its own objects and their values, together with the way of being a subject and the awareness that he has of himself.[25]

Homosexuality, as understood by Foucault, is a way of being, of experiencing, a very specific way to be a person. 'The homosexual' is a kind of person that exists only in a particular historical and social setting, for example now, but not in ancient Athens. The homosexual 'as a kind of person' did not exist then, although there were plenty of same-sex acts with complex codes about which acts were right and which were wrong.

Historical nominalism is only half the cake. My nominalism is historical, but it is also Nietzschian; it is dynamic; it is about the interaction between names and things, or rather names and people. I learned that way of thinking from Michel Foucault, even if he did not in fact propose my name for this philosophy.

---

[25] Michel Foucault, review of John Dover, *Homosexualité grecque*, the translation of *Greek Homosexuality*, in *Libération*, 1 June 1982. Reprinted in *Dits et Écrits*, 4 vols. (Paris, 1994), 4. 315–16. (No. 314.)

An easy example

It is essential to have examples in mind, to put flesh on abstract statements. I should briefly mention my first example of making up people and the looping effect, multiple personality. It is written up in *Rewriting the Soul*. It seemed misleadingly easy. Around 1970 there arose a few sensational paradigm cases of strange behaviour similar to phenomena discussed a century earlier and largely forgotten. A few psychiatrists began to diagnose multiple personality. It was rather sensational. More and more unhappy people started manifesting these symptoms. At first they had the symptoms they were expected to have. But then they became more and more bizarre. First a person had two or three personalities. Within a decade the mean number was seventeen. This fed back into the diagnoses, and entered the standard set of symptoms. It became part of the therapy to elicit more and more alters. The psychiatrists cast around for causes, and created a primitive, easily understood pseudo-Freudian aetiology of early sexual abuse, coupled with repressed memories. Knowing this was the cause, the patients obligingly retrieved the memories. More than that: this became a way to be a person. In 1983 I confidently said that there could never be split bars, analogous to gay bars. In 1991 I went to my first split bar.

A framework for analysis

These events can be placed in the same five-aspect framework of interacting elements that has been mentioned twice already. We have (*a*) a *classification*, multiple personality, associated with what at the time was called a 'disorder', Multiple Personality Disorder. This is the *kind* of person that is a moving target. We have (*b*) the *people*, those people I refer to as unhappy, unable to cope. We have (*c*) *institutions*, which include clinics and the International Society for the Study of Multiple Personality and Dissociation. Afternoon talk shows on American television are another type of institution: Oprah Winfrey and Geraldo Rivaldo made a big thing of multiples, once upon a time. I attended some weekend training programmes for therapists, in order to study yet another type of institution. As usual, when I speak of institutions, I mean deliberately organised and structured entities, not mere practice and custom.

There is what is commonly (but not by most analytic philosophers) called (*d*) *knowledge*. I do not mean justified true belief, but something more like Popper's sense of conjectural knowledge. More specifically, there are the presumptions that are taught, disseminated, refined and applied within the context of the institutions. Especially there are what are presented as the basic facts, for example that multiple personality is caused by early sexual abuse, that five per cent of the population suffer from multiple personality, and the like. Basic assumptions that we later regard as ghastly mistakes interact with people and classifications just as much as the facts that we hold to be stable, true, and beyond controversy. Knowledge, or at any rate what is experienced as knowledge at some time, is of two kinds that shade into each other. There is expert knowledge, the knowledge of the professionals, and there is popular knowledge that is shared by a significant part of the interested population. Some expert knowledge is always esoteric, but in the more flagrant cases of making up people, the expert quickly becomes exoteric. There was a time, partly thanks to those talk shows and other media, when 'everyone' believed that multiple personality was caused by early child abuse.

Finally there are (*e*) the *experts* or professionals who generate or legitimate the knowledge (*d*), judge its validity, and use it in their practice. They work within (*c*) institutions that guarantee their legitimacy, authenticity, and status as experts. They study, try to help, or advise on the control, of the (*b*) people who are (*a*) classified as of a given kind.

This is a truly banal framework of five elements. Their roles and weights will be different in every case. There is 'no reason to suppose that we shall ever tell two identical stories of two different instances of making up people'. This trite framework discourages an excess of philosophy. Serious students of society need no such structural reminders, but philosophers, including both Nietzsche and myself, do. We tend to pay too much attention to words and things—to write as if the interactions involve only the names and the people named, or the classification and the people classified. This is not so. Names of classes, and the people who fall under them, interact through larger interactions in the thriving world of institutions, experts, and their knowledge (as well as much else). One of the many things we learned from Michel Foucault is the capital role that knowledge itself plays in this process.

There are many complications. For example, there are competing schools of thought. In the case of MPD, there was the multiple movement, a loose alliance of patients, therapists and psychiatric theorists on the one hand, who believed in this diagnosis and in a certain kind of person, the multiple. There was the larger psychiatric establishment that rejected the diagnosis altogether. I recall a doctor in Ontario who, when a patient arrived announcing she had multiple personality, demanded to be shown her Ontario Health Insurance card (which has a photograph and a name on it). '*This* is the person I am treating, nobody else.' Thus there are rival frameworks. Hence reactions and counter-actions between the two frameworks further contribute to the working out of this kind of person, the multiple personality. If my sceptical colleague convinces his potential patient, she will very probably become a very different kind of person than if she had been treated for multiple personality by a believer.

Here, to repeat, are the interactive elements of my framework. All five of the elements listed—and more—are players, usually key players, in looping effects and making up people:

(*a*) classification
(*b*) people
(*c*) institutions
(*d*) knowledge
(*e*) experts.

As usual the choice of a framework represents a decision. One could add Nicholas Jardine's questions, or perhaps even replace knowledge by questions.[26] Jardine defined inquiries by the questions that make sense. Others, taking Foucault at his word, would prefer to emphasise the questions that are actually asked. It might be wise to replace 'experts' by Ludwik Fleck's *thought collective*, and the 'knowledge' by his *thought styles*.[27] One virtue of (*a*)–(*e*) is, nevertheless, that it is a nicely positivist list. Any diligent empirical study will show who the experts are, which institutions are important in which ways, and what counts as knowledge, either among experts or in larger publics.

Making up

A wholly new kind of person came into being, the multiple, with a set of memories and a set of behaviours. She is reminiscent of previous ways of

---

[26] Nicholas Jardine, *The Scenes of Inquiry: On the Reality of Questions in the Sciences* (Oxford, 1991).
[27] Ludwik Fleck, *Entstehung und Entwicklung einer wissenschaftlichen Tatsache. Einführung in die Lehre vom Denkstil und Denkkollectiv* (Basel, 1935; Frankfurt, 1980). Translated as *Genesis and Development of a Scientific Fact* (Chicago, 1979).

being a person. There was double consciousness in the 1880s.[28] Some compare multiple personality to trance or to possession. Notice a certain kind of rhetoric. When we maintain that many people of long ago and in different places are of the kind that interests us, it makes our kind seem more genuine. The search for earlier manifestations of multiplicity was a way to legitimate a contested classification.

The multiple personality of the 1980s was, in my judgement, a kind of person unknown in the history of the human race. That is not an idea that we can comfortably express. It is familiar enough to novelists and to social historians, but careful philosophical language is not prepared for it. Pedantry is in order. Distinguish two sentences:

> (A) There were no multiple personalities in 1955; there were many in 1985.
>
> (B) In 1955 this was not a way to be a person, people did not experience themselves in this way, they did not interact with their friends, their families, their employers, their counsellors, in this way; but in 1985 this was a way to be a person, to experience oneself, to live in society.

In my opinion, both are true, but A is too brief and contentious. Our topic is B.

To see that A and B are different, an *enthusiast* for what is now called Dissociative Identity Disorder will say that A is false, because people with several 'alter personalities' undoubtedly existed in 1955, but were not diagnosed. A *sceptic* will also say that A is false, but for exactly the opposite reason: multiple personality has always been a specious diagnosis, and there were no real multiples in 1985 either. The first statement, A, leads immediately to heated but pointless debates about the reality of multiple personality, on which I have spilt too much ink and to which I shall never again return. But open-minded opponents could peacefully agree to B. When I speak of making up people, it is B that I have in mind, and it is through B that the looping effect occurs.

---

[28] Curious phenomena such as double consciousness were sensational at the end of the nineteenth century. William James was fascinated by them. I wrote about this as a historical problem, before I realised that an epidemic of multiple personality was under way under my nose. 'The Invention of Split Personalities', A. Donegan *et al.*, (eds.), *Human Nature and Social Knowledge* (Dordrecht, 1986), pp. 63–85.

Harder cases

Multiple personality was renamed Dissociative Identity Disorder. That was no mere change in name, no mere act of diagnostic house-cleaning. Symptoms evolve, patients are no longer expected to come with a roster of altogether distinct personalities, and they no longer do. This disorder is an example of what in a second book, *Mad Travelers*, I called a transient mental illness: transient not in the sense of affecting a single person for a while and then going away, but in the sense of existing only at a time and at a place. I offered an analysis of transient mental illnesses in terms of ecological niches in which they can appear and thrive. Transient mental illnesses are easy cases for making up people, precisely because their very transience leads outsiders to suspect they are not really real, and so could plausibly be said to be made up.

Now turn to less transient problems. I work with two sorts of examples. There are the old ones, wholly closed, apparently finished history, such as fugue, the fancy name for mad travelling. All the facts are in: you can get as good a grip on the totality of events as the archive can provide. Then there are the current ones, very live examples that are under intense discussion, both popular and scientific, right now. Multiple personality was such an example when I started on the topic, with new events coming in almost every week. I turned to child abuse early in my game when I asked a distinguished feminist sociologist, Dorothy Smith, for an example of a kind of person who is changing before our eyes. 'Child abuse' was her slow and weighty answer.

It is important to have different types of illustrations, so as not to suffer from the vice of too slender a diet of examples, as Wittgenstein put it. Let us choose autism as the primary example and let obesity be a contrast case. These two examples are obviously current, obviously different. We now read of an autism epidemic and an obesity epidemic, just as we used to read about the multiple personality epidemic and an epidemic of child abuse. I am an unhappy Midas; as soon as I touch a topic it turns into an epidemic. I shall say a few words about autism.

Autism

The conception of autism has evolved. Dictionaries are not very good at keeping up. Their stately attention to change in meaning, always behind the times, is a dignified reflection of what has already happened. One large reliable desktop dictionary that tries to keep in touch is *The American Heritage Dictionary of the English Language*. In 1992 it defined autism as:

> 1. *Abnormal introversion and egocentricity; acceptance of fantasy rather than reality.* 2. Psychology: *Infantile autism.*

In 2000 it gave:

> *A psychiatric disorder of childhood characterized by marked deficits in communication and social interaction, preoccupation with fantasy, language impairment and abnormal behavior, usually associated with intellectual impairment.*

Something has happened to prompt so radical a change in definition. The word 'autism' was invented by the great Swiss psychiatrist Eugen Bleuler in 1908. He meant the 1992 dictionary's first sense of abnormal introversion (and self-absorption). It was one type of behaviour associated with the group of schizophrenias, another word Bleuler introduced at about the same time. The second 1992 sense, infantile autism, was a transfer from the first sense. It was introduced in 1943.

The 2000 definition is about as good as you can do with so small a number of words. It could have added the obsession with literalness, the obsession with order and keeping things the same, the terrible tantrums, biting and hitting that follow when things cease to be the same. Since dictionaries of any size provide masses of empirical as opposed to semantic information, it could have added that most people with autism are male, in a ratio of 4 out of 5. It could have added the habit of echoing what has been said, rather than speaking. In short it could have added lots more, but the definition, in so small a number of words, is not bad.

The one thing that is certainly wrong in the definition is that autism is not just a childhood disorder. Autism is almost always for life. It is a developmental disorder that can be recognised very early, usually no later than 30 months, for which there is no known cause and for which there is no known cure. At most, it is widely believed, a child can learn to compensate for the deficits, although there are some remarkable recoveries. Another aspect of the definition at which many would protest, is regarding autism as a 'disorder', now the standard euphemism for mental illness. Many advocates for autism insist that it is neither a disorder nor an illness but a disability.

One could add more. The problem is almost certainly some combination of neurological, biological, and genetic abnormality. Unfortunately, for all the hype one reads from time to time, we have no idea what. One could add that the only treatments that are known systematically to help a child to compensate for autism are behavioural. They are the purest operant conditioning, B. F. Skinner in action, except that they work best in an environment of loving care.[29]

In 1943, indeed in 1973, autism was a rare developmental disorder with a quite definite, narrowly characterised stereotype. A figure of 4.5 children per ten thousand was derived from school and social services in Camberwell, London. But this proportion has been growing rapidly in recent years. Prevalence rates of ten times as many are now cited. There are doubtless many reasons for this. One is that schools, social workers and health services have been alerted to symptoms of autism. We are noticing a change in *reporting*. Another reason is that we have moved from a conception of core symptoms, used in such early surveys, to the 'autistic spectrum'. This is a change in *criteria*. Thus we now have high-functioning people with autism. We have Asperger's. This name was introduced into English in 1981 by the British child psychiatrist, Lorna Wing. It is adapted from a diagnosis made in 1944 in Vienna by Hans Asperger, a distinguished paediatrician in the German-speaking world, whom Wing made prominent in English. It now tends to refer to people with autistic symptoms who had few difficulties acquiring language, but have all the other problems. It is often loosely synonymous with high-functioning autism.

Let us return to making up people. Consider a certain kind of teenager or adult, the high-functioning autist. I shall leave Asperger out of it. The typical case is someone who grew from an autistic child into an adult with full or almost full possession of language, and some residual eccentricities of an autistic sort, some of which are socially disadvantageous, some possibly advantageous. Temple Grandin is the most famous example. She emphasises her empathy with animals, urging that her way of seeing the world is closer to animals than to most humans. She has had a significant effect on American slaughterhouse techniques.[30] Many read-

---

[29] One excellent guide to autism states that: 'Today the treatment of choice is that based on the behavioral model. In fact, behavioral treatment is the only treatment that has been empirically demonstrated for children with autism.' Laura Schreibman, *The Science and Fiction of Autism* (Cambridge, MA, 2005), p. 133. See Lovaas, note 40, for the classic operant conditioning method.

[30] Temple Grandin, *Emergence, labeled autistic* (New York, 1986). *Thinking in pictures: and other reports from my life with autism* (New York, 1995). *Animals in translation: using the mysteries of autism to decode animal behavior* (New York, 2005). I much like Donna Williams, *Nobody nowhere: the extraordinary autobiography of an autistic child* (New York, 1990);

ers will know the hero of the novel *The Curious Incident of the Dog in the Night-Time.*[31] High-functioning autists are beginning to crop up in thrillers and cheap novels, much as multiple personalities did twenty years ago. (Thank goodness they have exited.) Some high-functioning autistic people talk of forming an autism liberation front. Stop trying to make us like you. We do some things better than you, and you do some things better than us, so leave us be.

Now consider A and B again, this time for autism:

(A) There were no high-functioning autists in 1950; there were many in 2000.

(B) In 1950 this was not a way to be a person, people did not experience themselves in this way, they did not interact with their friends, their families, their employers, their counsellors, in this way; but in 2000 this was a way to be a person, to experience oneself, to live in society.

I said that in my opinion, A is *true* for multiple personality: it is a transient mental illness, after all. Multiple personality advocates will have disagreed with me. My opinion about A for high-functioning autism is quite different: it is absolutely false. It is almost as absurd as saying that infantile autism did not exist before 1943, when Kanner introduced the name. But B is plausible enough. Before 1950, maybe even before 1975, high-functioning autism was not a way to be a person. There probably were a few individuals who were regarded as retarded and worse, who recovered, retaining the kinds of foibles that high-functioning autistic people have today. But people did not experience themselves in this way, they did not interact with their friends, their families, their employers, their counsellors, in the way they do now. Later this did become a way to be a person, to experience oneself, to live in society.

It is easy to see why there could not have been high-functioning people with autism, in the sense of B, until some time after autism itself had been diagnosed. That was simply not a way to be a person. The first such individuals to be aware of themselves in that way had first to be diagnosed as autistic—impossible before 1943—and then somewhat mysteriously to 'recover'. They had to grow out of it, to acquire social skills, to be able to understand what other people are thinking and feeling, to overcome, or at any rate to live unproblematically with, the obsessive need for

---

Somebody somewhere: breaking free from the world of autism (New York, 1994). The latest autistic autobiography is Kamran Nazeer, *Send in the Idiots: Or how we grew to understand the world* (London, 2006). See my review essay in the *London Review of Books*, 11 May 2006, 3–7.

[31] Mark Haddon *The Curious Incident of the Dog in the Night-Time* (London, 2003).

literalness. This was a looping effect: a few of those diagnosed with autism developed in such a way as to change the very concept of autism. They brought into being the idea of a high-functioning autistic person.

Once there were such 'recovered' autists, it was possible for other adults, who had never been diagnosed as autistic, to be seen as having similar difficulties, even if their childhood was not as bad. They could see themselves in that way: 'That's me!' A wholly new way of experiencing oneself came into being. Hence the class of high-functioning autists rapidly expanded. Some such individuals will have strengths in one direction, some strengths in another.

The conceptual evolution of the high-functioning autist thus arises from interactions among the five elements in our framework. We have (*a*) a new classification, a new kind of person whom it is possible to be. (*b*) Individual people themselves change, as they are recognised to be of that type, or see themselves as high-functioning autists. (*c*) All of this requires institutions, including schools, social and health services, which disseminate and revise the current (*d*) knowledge. And there are the (*e*) experts, including Lorna Wing. The institutions are vastly more ramified and the experts from more diverse fields than was the case with multiple personality.

What about A and B for autism itself? Statement (A) would assert that there were no autistic children before 1943, the year that Kanner introduced the diagnosis of infantile autism. That is plainly false.[32] Of course there were autistic children before Kanner singled them out. Nevertheless, I urge you to reflect on B: before Kanner, autism was not a way to be a person. But if, as is widely supposed, autism is a congenital neurological deficit, then there were certainly autistic children who were dismissed as retarded, feeble-mind, and so on, a long previous litany of dismissive epithets.

---

[32] But there is still the rhetorical need, mentioned above in connection with MPD, to ask: Where were all the autists before 1943? One of the leading British autism researchers, Uta Frith, addresses the problem squarely. She has suggested that autistic children were put out in woods and fields to fend for themselves. Most died. The numerous 'wild children' are, then, the lucky ones who survived. Uta Frith, *Autism: Explaining the Enigma* (Oxford, 1989). She also diagnoses historical figures as autistic, e.g. R. A. Houston and Uta Frith, *Autism in History: The Case of Hugh Blair of Borgue* (Oxford, 2000). The hypothesis of feral children is attractive until seen in the wider context of the uses that have been made of them. See Adriana S. Benzaquén, *Encounters with Wild Children: Temptation and Disappointment in the Study of Human Nature* (Montreal and Kingston, 2006).

Engines of discovery

How does making up people take place? That is a question for psychology and sociology, but a first answer has to be, in many ways. Long ago 'hip' and 'square' became common names in white middle-class culture. By a parody of Nietzsche, two new kinds of people came into being, the hip and the square. In this case, more does depend on what those people are called than on what they are! The truly square did not care much, but those at risk of being called square did their best to be hip, while the hip moved on, leaving hip to the square. As is the way of slang imported from another social class, both kinds had short built-in shelf lives, but there is certainly a social history to be told of the ways in which these kinds of people were made up, and how the looping effects led these categories to self-destruct. Systematic knowledge of the sort we call scientific had no part to play in this story.

The kinds of people that concern us are those who are studied in the human sciences, from sociology to medicine. Here knowledge, one aspect of my five-part framework, plays a central role, along with the experts who generate it and the institutions within which it is produced and applied. There has been making up of people in all times and places, but only in the past two hundred years have the sciences been so central to the human understanding of who we are. We make ourselves in our own scientific image of the kinds of people it is possible to be. But science is not one thing, nor is scientific method. The human sciences have been driven by several engines of discovery. These are thought of as finding out the facts, but they are also engines for making up people. Here are seven of them, ordered roughly according to the times at which they became effective. Thus we classified and counted different kinds of people (Engine 1) long before we were able to look for genetic markers (Engine 7).

I present these engines as imperatives for those who want to find out. It is taken for granted within the human sciences that to understand some kind of person, one must first classify. That is a sort of prior imperative. After that, almost the first step is to count people of the relevant kinds. The most recent imperative is genetic, so that today, if you want to understand autism or obesity, you must search for genetic correlates of these abnormalities. The most striking and most general of the scientific imperatives are:

1. Count!
2. Quantify!
3. Create Norms!

4. Correlate!
5. Medicalise!
6. Biologise!
7. Geneticise!

These seven engines of discovery are not the only engines that drive both knowledge and the making up of people. Here are three more that I shall presently explain. The eighth is an engine of organisation and control. The ninth is an engine of administration. They are often what readers of Foucault have in mind when they talk about the power effects of knowledge. The tenth engine has been increasingly powerful of late. It involves resistance by the known to the knowers, and it has become the source of many looping effects.

8. Normalise!
9. Bureaucratise!
10. Reclaim our identity!

The seven engines at work

The success of the seven engines of discovery has been astonishing. Nor is it any criticism to say that they have side effects, so that they sometimes bring new kinds of people into being, in the modest sense of propositions of type B. Nor is it any criticism to say that they affect the kinds of people they study, affect both the 'kinds' and the 'people', that is, (*a*) the classifications themselves and (*b*) the individuals and groups that are studied. How the engines can achieve these effects prompts many questions. They have to be fuelled by talent, which we hope the (*e*) experts will possess, and by money. A modicum of popular support is needed to keep the (*d*) institutions running. How the fuel of talent and wealth is consumed, is a proper topic of the sociology of scientific knowledge.

Here I strive, once again, for the banal, for reminders about engines of discovery. Again the question, why go for the obvious? The answer is, in order to assert what is seldom noticed, that the engines of discovery are also engines for making up people. It is thanks to the success of these engines that the rate of interaction among the five elements of our framework has accelerated to its present breakneck pace.

Here are some brief remarks suggesting what each of the seven engines involves. Autism and obesity furnish convenient contrasting illustrations for all seven. Often the way in which an engine has led to interactions involving autism is very different from the way it has worked on obesity. With these two very different examples as models, it becomes easier to carry on in depth with other examples.

1. Counting

People have long been counted for purposes of taxation and recruitment. There are five biblical references, ranging from Exodus 38:26 to Luke 2:2.[33] But counting kinds of people for other purposes is mostly post-Napoleonic, part of what I call the avalanche of printed numbers.[34] The first attempts to count autistic children gave rates, as we have seen, of about 4.5 per 10,000. There are now about eighty published countings, and growing, as is the proportion of autism which some find as high as six per 1000. A report by the US Center for Disease Control led the media to state in headlines that autism is now 'common' among American children between the ages of 4 and 18.[35]

We have all heard the horror figures for obesity rates. The rate really has increased all over the world in the past two decades. Autism is a contrast. There we debate whether the swollen figures for autism show that the prevalence of autism is increasing, or only that we have expanded definitions and are more alert for possible diagnoses. That type of debate is not on the cards for obesity: however we define obesity, there are more obese people in the world than there ever were before, and this is as true of poor and under-developed regions as it is true of the rich and prosperous ones.

---

[33] The census has always been part of imperial administration—The New Testament teaches that Jesus was born in Bethlehem when his parents were complying with the rules for a census. (The higher criticism is sceptical about the history here.) In the modern period, the first censuses were in the colonies—Quebec, Peru, Virginia, Iceland. When the census and related tabulations start enumerating new kinds of people or their characteristics, they may inaugurate a new kind of person that had not been self-conscious before. Ian Hacking, 'Biopower and the Avalanche of Printed Numbers', *Culture and History*, 4 (1983), 279–95. For a sustained study of the interaction of the census with kinds of people, see Alain Desrosières, *The Politics of Large Numbers* (Cambridge, MA, 1998). This book is an insider job, for Desrosières has a senior post at INSEE, the main French agency for demographic and economic analysis.

[34] See my *Taming of Chance*, chap. 4.

[35] The *Morbidity and Mortality Weekly Report* of the Center for Disease Control, 4 May 2006. The media seldom mentioned the question which led to this statistic. A great many parents were asked, 'Has a doctor or health care provider ever told you that [your child named so and so] has autism?'

2. Quantity

In the case of obesity, quantity is built in. We have our bathroom scales. In 1903 the Society of Actuaries and the Association of Life Insurance Medical Directors of America defined 'overweight' as weighing more than the average for insured people of one's own age, height, and sex. At that time, they said that, 'Obesity is defined as an excessive accumulation of body fat'. Thus at the beginning of the last century, fat was already being distinguished into a lesser and a greater evil, overweight and obesity. During the 1970s the Body Mass Index took hold, a quantity defined as the ratio of the weight of a person in kilograms divided by the square of the height in metres. Only in 1998 (!) did the World Health Organization, in company with numerous national bodies, define overweight as a BMI of over 25, and obesity as a BMI of over 30. Thus quantification has an intrinsic tendency to generate new classifications of people. For a sense of what these numbers mean, James Joyce's Bloom had a BMI of 23.8. Marylyn Monroe varied between 21 and 24. 'Underweight' is defined as below 18.5. During the past twenty years models in *Playboy* have gone down from 19 to 16.5. Fauja Singh, the British marathon man, aged 94, fastest man on earth over 90 years of age, has a BMI of 15.4.

Autism resists quantity. There are many diagnostic questionnaires, but it is hard to quantify deficits. Nevertheless we now speak of the autistic spectrum, with the implication of a quantitative range of disabilities.

3. Norms

Quantitative norms followed Adolphe Quetelet's *homme moyen* in midcentury. Georges Canguilhem's classic study of the normal and the pathological showed how medicine acquired the concept of normalcy not long after 1800.[36] We have 'the normal range' for the Body Mass Index, 20 to 25. Many of our examples are deviations from the norm, for better—genius—or worse—obesity. Canguilhem addressed the question, which comes first, normalcy or deviance? There is no general answer. Sometimes one, sometimes the other, often hand in hand. Canguilhem favoured the idea that pathology tends to define good health. But the diagnosis of

---

[36] Georges Canguilhem, *Le Normal et le pathologique* (Paris, 1966). *On the Normal and the Pathological* (Dordrecht, 1978). For my own account, which starts with Canguilhem, see I. Hacking, 'Normal People', D. R. Olsen and R. Torrance (eds.), *Modes of Thought* (Cambridge, 1996), pp. 59–71, and *The Taming of Chance*, chap. 19.

infantile autism in 1943 followed the growing emphasis, during the 1920s, on normal development for children.

4. Correlation

This is the fundamental engine of the social sciences. It began around 1870 when Francis Galton devised the correlation coefficient. Quetelet had the mean, but Galton made deviation from the mean the core of his social philosophy, and so devised the correlation coefficient. The rest is history.

We try to correlate autism with everything, not excluding the relative lengths of the mother's fingers and testosterone in the foetus.[37] The less we know, the more we search for correlations in the hope that they will direct us to something important. Some correlations need no statistical theory or analysis: four out of five children with autism are male. On the other hand, excess weight needs subtle statistics. A Body Mass Index between 25 and 30—which now defines 'overweight'—is said to be bad for you because of significant correlation with numerous risk factors, which are themselves statistical entities. It is a strange situation. Being overweight, unlike being obese (BMI > 30), does not importantly affect your life expectancy, although unless you are a body builder or rugby forward, it will make you less attractive in current society, less physically active and so forth. Unlike obesity, being overweight correlates with risk factors, not with death rates. These really are two kinds of people, the obese and the overweight, defined in the first instance by the imperative to quantify.

5. Clinical medicine

We medicalise kinds of deviant people relentlessly, not always with success. The modern concept of child abuse was introduced by doctors around 1960, but there have been substantial battles over the so-called 'medical model' ever since.

There have always been fat people, some of them ill. But stout, plump persons have often been in fashion, as the works of Rubens or Renoir attest. 'Let me have men about me that are fat, sleek-headed men and such as sleep o' nights.' Today we treat the stout as having medical problems, and the obese as sorely needing medical instruction. A new generation of

---

[37] S. Lutchmaya, S. Baron-Cohen, P. Raggatt and J. T. Manning, 'Maternal 2nd to 4th digit ratios and foetal testosterone', *Early Human Development*, 77 (2004), 23–8.

anti-craving medicines is about to make a fortune.[38] Autism was regarded as a diagnosis made by a child psychiatrist, and so it is filed as a mental disorder and hence in the end as a medical problem. But if activists succeed in turning it from a disorder into a disability, it may seem less and less medical.

6. Biology including neurology

Autism almost certainly has biological causes, specifically neurobiological. One of the great moral benefits of biologising what used to be a vice is that it relieves a person of responsibility. Overeating attributed to chemical imbalance ceases to be a moral defect. A retarded child is a liability and a shame for the family. Today an autistic child is a human being somewhat different from most, but a person to understand, love, and help.

7. Genetics

There is now is a steady drive to trace the medical to the biological, and the biological to the genetic. There is a vast research programme to find the genetic causes for autism—it is almost an act of faith in the research community that there must be one. A less extensive programme tries to discover kinds of obesity that are genetic. This confidence in the heritability of deviance is not new. A century ago there was a great push to discover the genetic origins of criminal behaviour and 'the criminal personality'. This programme has returned today in more cautious forms.[39]

Control, bureaucracy and resistance

The engines of discovery are of a piece. Counting is ancient, genetics is recent, but all seven engines aim at the production of knowledge, understanding, and the potential for improving or controlling deviant human beings. We turn finally to three engines of a different sort, each deriving

---

[38] For Sanofi-Aventis, which is now the third largest drug multinational. It was formed to market Accomplia, an anti-eating, anti-smoking product. The French Sanofi had the chemical know-how and the German Aventis had the American marketing clout, so they merged.

[39] The current drive to criminal genetics curiously recapitulates, on what is thought to be a sound scientific basis, the doctrine current at the end of the nineteenth century, according to which criminal and other undesirable behaviour, such as alcoholism, were forms of inherited degeneracy. See Hacking, 'Criminal behavior, degeneracy and looping'.

from the engines of discovery and the knowledge that they produce, but each acting in its own specific way.

8. Normalisation

In many cases, we try to make unfavourable deviants as close to normal as possible. That is the point of the behavioural therapies for autism; that is the point of anti-craving drugs for obesity. A perspective different from mine would emphasise that this is where all the action is. It is not ideas that change people, but treatments, be they behavioural or pharmaceutical.

9. Bureaucracy

Some schools of thought speak of bureaucratic power as if that were always a bad thing. So let us emphasise the positive. Most prosperous nations have quite complex bureaucracies that pick out children with developmental problems in the early years of schooling, and assign them to special services. The system sees itself as an objective way to determine who needs help, but the relation is reciprocal. The criteria used by the system in turn define what it is to fall under various categories such as autistic. This is an ongoing feedback effect. Autism is among other things a bureaucratic concept, used in the administration and management of awkward schoolchildren.

Once again obesity is a contrast case, for it has not been much bureaucratised. But let us not forget that it was penalised by bureaucracies in the form of life insurance companies. That goes back to the dawn of the twentieth century. The insurers defined the first standards because they were convinced that fat people were bad risks.

10. Resistance

Kinds of people who are medicalised, normalised, and administered, increasingly try to take back control from the experts and the institutions, sometimes by creating new experts, new institutions. The famous case is homosexuality, so highly medicalised from the time of Krafft-Ebing late in the nineteenth century. That was the very period in which legal institutions became active in punishing it. Gay pride and its predecessors restored to homosexuals control of the classifications into which they fall. There are always twists and turns in the tales of making up people, few more striking than the attempts to geneticise male homosexuality, to find the gay gene.

I mentioned moves towards an 'autism liberation front', something that would make high-functioning autistic people the experts on their condition. There are a number of organisations of overweight and obese people trying to re-install pride and dignity in heavy bodies. I like, both for its acronym and its activities, a rather modest and cautious French organisation: Groupe de Réflexion sur l'Obésité et le Surpoids, or GROS.

Moving targets

All ten engines produce effects on the kinds of people to whom they are applied. They change the boundaries. They change the characteristics. This in no way detracts from the fact that seven of these are engines of discovery. Conjectures about causes, treatments, and cures, both for obesity and autism, abound. Fortunately there is competition. Different groups have different guesses about which one will be corroborated. We might find that there is no genetic basis for autism, and none for all but a small proportion of obese persons. Or we might find that most obesity and all autism is linked to a certain organisation of genetic anomalies. It is important to know. We try to find out by using all seven listed scientific engines. I observe that we tend to think of them as directed at fixed targets. I suggest that the engines modify the targets. This in no way queries their objectivity.

Kinds of people

I have rejected the idea that there is a distinct and definable class of 'human kinds' or 'interactive kinds'. But we do certainly have the idea of different kinds of people. Some of these kinds are Us-and-Them kinds, as when Xerxes boasted of ruling the different kinds of people. Talk of 'the Negro sense of rhythm' or 'the Arab mind' have become absolutely insupportable. But when we turn to the kinds of people investigated by the human sciences we are rather ready to go into the species mode, 'the X person', as in 'the autistic child'. There are book titles, *The Autistic Child*, and *The Obese Child*.[40] Grammatically speaking, this is the construction we use when speaking of species, the whale is a mammal.

---

[40] Thus we have titles, Igor Lovaaas, *The Autistic Child: Language Development through Behavior Modification* (New York, 1977); I. N. Kugelmas, *The Autistic Child* (Springfield, 1970); Milada

Some autism advocates strongly object to 'the autistic child' and prefer, 'children with autism', and one can sense what they are opposing.[41] To speak in the species mode about people is to depersonalise them, to turn them into objects for scientific inquiry. For other thoughtful people, 'autistic child' is right. For example a parent who founded the Autism Society of America, and wrote one of the first books about the topic, does so because, 'Autism is who his son is, not just a characteristic'.[42] Many philosophers would say that autism is an essential property of his son. It is part of his nature to be autistic.

Except in very rare cases, I am disinclined to say the same thing of an obese person, but the sixth and seventh engines of discovery may be driving us in that direction. There are, it is argued, people whose nature or essence it is to be obese, thanks to their genetic inheritance. This is an important theme now being argued by 'resisters', obesity activists who are trying to remove the stigma attached to the condition. We can almost hear, 'Obesity is who I am!'

In the case of overweight, as opposed to obesity, so many people are overweight—as defined in terms of BMI in 1998 by the World Health Organization—that such a move is less plausible. Being overweight but not obese is usually just a characteristic of a person. Overweight is almost never who the stout man is, it is just one of his enduring, and maybe endearing, properties.

John Stuart Mill, progenitor of the doctrine of natural kinds, left us a possible way to distinguish autism and obesity, on the one hand, from overweight on the other, in this respect.[43] He thought that there are endless characteristics that are associated with some classifications—he gave *horse* and *phosphorus* as examples. Horses and phosphorus have innumerable features in common, in addition to their being horses or phosphorus. White things, in contrast, have nothing much in common except that they are white. He said that *Horse* was a 'real Kind' (of animal), what

---

Havelkova, *The Autistic Child: A Guide for Parents* (Toronto, 1994); P. L. Girogi, R. M. Suskind, and C. Catassi, *The Obese Child* (New York, 1992).

[41] Laura Schreibman notes and explains this in her preface, and opts for both expressions indifferently: *The Science and Fiction of Autism*, p. 5.

[42] Schreibman, ibid., speaking of Bernard Rimland, author of virtually the first book about autism, namely *Infantile Autism: The Syndrome and its Implications for a Neural Theory of Autism* (New York, 1964).

[43] J. S. Mill, *A System of Logic, Ratiocinative and Inductive: Being a Connected View of the Principles of Evidence and the Methods of Scientific Investigation*, 1st edn. (London, 1843); vols. VII and VIII of J. Robson (ed.), *Collected Works of John Stuart Mill*, 28 vols. (Toronto, 1965–83), book I. chap. vii, § 4.

philosophers later came to call a natural kind. 'White' was a merely finite kind. He worried about whether the races and sexes were real or finite Kinds. That was a matter to be decided by scientific inquiry, mostly biological. But he expected that the members of a given race would have little in common except the superficial features that were the marks of their race: just as Christians have nothing in common but their faith. The races—and, he thought, the sexes—would therefore turn out not to be real Kinds.

Mill's distinction well expresses the idea I quoted, that 'autism is who my son is, not just a characteristic'—without committing us to any sort of essentialism.[44] Autistic children have a wide range of characteristics in common, distributed on a spectrum, or, I would prefer to say, in a space that is at least three-dimensional—language problems, social problems, and obsession with order and literalness. Some of these types of features are what we look for on diagnostic interview schedules. Many others are unknown, and are thus far hidden in bio-neuro-genetic space. Essentialism leads to all sorts of harmful stereotyping. Yet the insistence by the father I have quoted, that the autism is no mere characteristic, may be captured by Mill's nominalist and empiricist account of 'real Kinds', without the noxious connotation of essences.

In contrast to autistic people, overweight people have nothing much in common except that they are rather plump. Obese people may, however, have more in common than that they are fat—they tend to have shorter lives, to have diabetes, and the like. There *may* be subclasses of obese people who have a distinct biological cause for their having a Body Mass Index in the very high range. Whatever that is, it may be part of their nature, and may bring in a host of other characteristics. Such a subclass would come close to being what Mill called a real Kind. That is a way of saying that obesity may be more than a mere characteristic of a person, without the stereotyping implications of essence.

---

[44] Mill's distinction now seems rather simplistic, but I think it does the job here while the battery of different theories of natural kinds now in competition leads both to excess sophistication and conceptual confusion. My doubts about present conceptions on natural kinds are to be found in 'Natural Kinds: Rosy Dawn, Scholastic Twilight'.

In brief: the poverty line

My probes pay more attention to the rich detail of examples than is the wont of most analytic philosophers. They are nonetheless driven by general speculation, even if the chosen topics do not lend themselves to generalisations. Every case is different, but certain phrases fit, for example, the changing faces of autism, the changing faces of obesity, the changing faces of suicide and even of poverty. The poor have been with us always, but the introduction of the poverty line in the 1890s, later used to define the poor, has made a difference.[45] We use 'the poor' in the species sense; we have the working poor. In France there is a guaranteed minimum income, the *revenus minimum d'insertion* or RMI (ehr-em-ee). The French love acronyms, so now there is a new kind of person, the *rmiste* (ehr-em-eest), an expression regularly used by the media and in conversation. That is no more a real Kind, in Mill's sense, than the overweight, but we do have a tendency to stereotype, and to treat them as 'real'.

In brief: suicide

It is part of our scientific attitude that what we find out about people using any of the seven engines of discovery, and more, is a fixed target that we hit. Of course we hit! And what we find out is for the most part true, or not far from the truth. Yet the target is often where it is because of the interaction between our five elements, ranging from classifications through people to experts. These interactions are driven by the seven engines of discovery and hence by the growth of knowledge. Sometimes this breeds conceptual confusion. There may be no better example than the changing faces of suicide.

Suicide is now tied to depression. 'An attempted suicide is a cry for help.' Nothing is more shattering than the suicide of a friend. Nothing more smashes the spirit of a psychiatrist than the suicide of a patient. Nothing seems more awful than for young people to kill themselves. When a wave of suicides passes through an adolescent cohort in a native village in northern Canada, the entire nation is steeped in shame and guilt. This wholly modern feel to suicide, and the gamut of associated meanings, is a product of interaction with statistical and medical sciences,

---

[45] See Hacking, 'Façonner les gens : le seuil de pauvreté'.

a family of interactions that began around 1825. This modern arrangement of intense feelings and meanings makes us totally confused when we think about either euthanasia or the suicide weapon.

The latter is a ruthless and terrifying weapon that is often callously exploited by older men who have no intention of killing themselves. It is nevertheless a remarkable response of angry impotent Muslims when faced by omnipotent hegemony. It can be used by anyone: the Tamil Tigers developed much of the early technology. The suicide weapon is the polar opposite of the invincible nuclear weapon. But they are an exact match, equally indifferent to the people whom they kill.

We have great difficulty thinking about the suicide weapon because of our established scientific knowledge about suicide. That knowledge is true knowledge about the people among us, the suicides and those who meditate self-destruction. They have grown through their lives to conform to the meanings and the stereotypes that the knowledge teaches. But what we know about suicide is not a human universal; it is something that has become true of Westerners rather recently.

In brief: genius

I should end on a more cheerful note. Genius has put on an amazing number of masks since the very word was used with such effect in antiquity, notably in Athens. The word—I hardly dare to say the concept, but perhaps one could say cluster of associated ideas—maps the fantasies of the age—be it Athens in its prime, Elizabethan England, Romantic Germany, *fin-de-siècle* (the nineteenth century) France, Wittgenstein and 'the duty of genius'.[46] But genius is not a serious concept in our day. It has quite lost the allure of the Romantic era. That is because we now measure it, and genius of its nature abhors a measure.

Starting with Galton's *Hereditary Genius*, we have gradually made intelligence statistical, with norms. Indeed the usual IQ tests are so statistical that the questions are designed so that a curve of scores forms a normal distribution with a mean of 100. When the tests were first applied to women, they scored higher than men, with a mean of about 105, so the questions had to be modified to make them harder for women. They were adjusted until the mean score for females was also 100.

---

[46] The title of Ray Monk's biography, *Wittgenstein, the Duty of Genius* (London, 1990).

IQ tests are excellent at evaluating the ability of a child to prosper in our times, numerate, technical, and with a new kind of literacy. At the top end, genius is forced on to a linear scale and hence off the map. There are batteries of tests that make more delicate distinctions among people who score highly on a standard test, and the numbers can be read off as near-genius, genius, and their ilk.

Galton aimed at measuring genius but in fact he expelled it from our culture. In the United States the MacArthur Foundation awards annual prizes for outstanding non-standard contributors to the collective artistic, intellectual, scientific and social good. But they are not simply for success: in principle they are given to those who are, or who began, on untrodden tracks and who had personal or social hurdles to overcome. The press call the MacArthur prizes the genius prizes. I recently had the privilege of being asked to evaluate two nominees. They are truly exceptional, very different in style and demeanour, as well as in their contributions. I suspect neither has ever been called a genius, and both would shudder at the idea.

It is part of the deep, ultimately Socratic, notion of genius, that when genius is measured on scales that stem from Galton, and were refined in 1917 by the United States army for evaluating recruits, true genius—I do not hesitate to use that phrase—will be living somewhere else. Rejecting classification, it will blithely refuse to interact with questionnaires, institutions, experts and knowledge. Ah—I have just bought into the romantic face of genius.

SHAKESPEARE LECTURE

Shakespeare, Jonson, and the Invention of the Author

IAN DONALDSON
Fellow of the Academy

THE LIVES AND CAREERS OF SHAKESPEARE and Ben Jonson, the two supreme writers of early modern England, were intricately and curiously interwoven. Eight years Shakespeare's junior, Jonson emerged in the late 1590s as a writer of remarkable gifts, and Shakespeare's greatest theatrical rival since the death of Christopher Marlowe. Shakespeare played a leading role in the comedy that first brought Jonson to public prominence, *Every Man In His Humour*, having earlier decisively intervened—so his eighteenth-century editor, Nicholas Rowe, relates—to ensure that the play was performed by the Lord Chamberlain's Men, who had initially rejected the manuscript.[1] Shakespeare's name appears alongside that of Richard Burbage in the list of 'principal tragedians' from the same company who performed in Jonson's *Sejanus* in 1603, and it has been conjectured that he and Jonson may even have written this play together.[2] During the years of their maturity, the two men continued to observe

---

Read at the Academy 25 April 2006.

[1] *The Works of Mr William Shakespeare*, ed. Nicholas Rowe, 6 vols. (London, printed for Jacob Tonson, 1709), I, pp. xii–xiii. On the reliability of Rowe's testimony, see Samuel Schoenbaum, *Shakespeare's Lives* (Oxford, 1970), pp. 19–35.

[2] The list is appended to the folio text of the play, published in 1616. For the suggestion that Shakespeare worked with Jonson on the composition of *Sejanus*, see Anne Barton, *Ben Jonson: Dramatist* (Cambridge, 1984), pp. 93–4. Scholarly opinion continues to favour George Chapman as the 'second pen' who assisted Jonson with this play. Rudyard Kipling attractively imagines Shakespeare and Jonson together translating a chapter of Isaiah for the King James Bible: 'Proofs of Holy Writ', *The Sussex Edition of the Complete Works in Prose and Verse of Rudyard Kipling*, 35 vols. (London, 1937–9), vol. 30, *Uncollected Prose* (1938), 2, first published in *The Strand Magazine*, April 1934.

each other's practice with sharp attention, as the evidence of echoing words, phrases, and structural devices throughout their work attests.[3] Though their professional pathways, like their styles of writerly self-presentation, diverged in ways I want now to describe, the two men clearly continued to act, each to the other, as a powerful creative stimulant, irritant, and example.

Shakespeare stands as the archetypal model of what the American critic Hugh Kenner, speaking of T. S. Eliot, was to term 'the invisible poet'. He is the *deus absconditus* of his own creative world, whose seemingly mysterious and illegible personality has prompted centuries of ingenious speculation; whose very identity is still vigorously disputed in monographs bearing such titles as *The Shakespeare Enigma*; *The Shakespeare Conspiracy*; *Shakespeare, Thy Name is Marlowe*; *Was Shakespeare Shakespeare? A Lawyer Reviews the Evidence.* He is the writer who seems, in the suggestive title of Jorge Luis Borges's haunting fable, *everything and nothing*, his personal identity so widely dispersed throughout—so fully projected into—the characters who inhabit his imaginative world that it is seemingly nowhere ultimately to be found.[4]

Jonson is a writer of a quite different kind, who manifests himself (or so it seems) throughout his work, forever creating and presenting versions and portraits of himself. He is, one might say, the visible poet, whose writings pronounce his personal opinions, his literary ambitions, his material needs, his physical appearance, his very name; who incorporates and instantiates himself within the literary text:

---

[3] See S. Musgrove, *Shakespeare and Jonson*, The Macmillan Brown Lectures 1957 (Folcroft, PA, 1975); Ian Donaldson, 'Looking Sideways: Jonson, Shakespeare, and the Myths of Envy', in Takashi Kozuka and J. R. Mulryne (eds.), *Shakespeare, Marlowe, Jonson: New Directions in Biography* (Aldershot, 2006), pp. 241–57.

[4] Hugh Kenner, *The Invisible Poet: T. S. Eliot* (London, 1960), Peter Dawkins, *The Shakespeare Enigma* (London, 2004); Graham Phillips and Martin Keatman, *The Shakespeare Conspiracy* (Post Falls, ID, 1994); David Rhys Williams, *Shakespeare, Thy Name is Marlowe* (New York, Philosophical Library, 1966); Milward W. Martin, *Was Shakespeare Shakespeare? A Lawyer Reviews the Evidence* (New York, 1965); Jorge Luis Borges, 'Everything and Nothing' in Donald A. Yates and James E. Irby (eds.), *Labyrinths: Selected Stories and Other Writings* (Harmondsworth, 1970), pp. 284–5.

> ... being a tardy, cold,
> Unprofitable chattel, fat and old,
> Laden with belly, and doth hardly approach
> His friends, but to break chairs or crack a coach.
> (*The Underwood*, 56. 7–10)

> Rest in soft peace, and, asked, say here doth lie
> Ben Jonson his best piece of poetry ...
> (*Epigrams*, 45. 9–10)

> Father John Burgess
> Necessity urges
> My woeful cry,
> To Sir Robert Pye;
> And that he will venture
> To send my debenture.
> Tell him his Ben
> Knew the time, when
> He loved the muses;
> Though now he refuses
> To take apprehension
> Of a year's pension,
> And more is behind...
> (*The Underwood*, 57. 1–13)[5]

It is hard to think of another poet writing in English—not even John Skelton, whose skittish measures Jonson follows in the lines just quoted, or Yeats, who studied Jonson's verse with such attention—who so frequently offers himself as the object or subject of his own poetic scrutiny.[6]

This contrast between the two writers—the one, seemingly absent from the text; the other, seemingly immanent; more pressingly, more personally, at our side—assumes a particular interest in relation to the central question I want to pursue in this lecture: the emergence of an early modern concept of authorship. Shakespeare significantly uses the word

---

[5] All quotations from Jonson are given in modernised form (as they will appear in the forthcoming *Cambridge Edition of the Works of Ben Jonson*, ed. David Bevington, Martin Butler, and Ian Donaldson: 25 vols., Cambridge, 2008) but linked for ease of reference to the old-spelling edition of C. H. Herford and Percy and Evelyn Simpson, *Ben Jonson*, 11 vols. (Oxford, 1925–52).

[6] Jonson introduces John Skelton as a character in his 1624 masque, *The Fortunate Isles*, where he again adopts Skeltonic verse forms. Yeats immersed himself in Jonson's work in 1905/6 (R. F. Foster, *W. B. Yeats: A Life, 1: The Apprentice Mage 1865–1914* (Oxford, 1997), pp. 337, 345 and n.) and his verse frequently echoes Jonsonian lines and phrases: e.g. 'dull ass's hoof' ('While I, from that reed-throated whisperer', line 5, W. B. Yeats, *Collected Poems* (London, 1963), p. 143, from *Poetaster*, Apologetical Dialogue, 238–9 and *The Underwood*, 23. 35–6); 'household spies' ('Parting', line 3, Yeats, *Collected Poems*, p. 311, from *Volpone*, 3. 7. 177 and *The Forest*, 5. 12).

'author' self-referentially on only two occasions in the entire canon, and then with an air of mild self-deprecation. 'One word more, I beseech you', says the speaker of the Epilogue of *2 Henry IV*, 'If you be not too much cloy'd with fat meat, our humble author will continue the story, with Sir John in it, and make you merry with fair Katherine of France; where (for anything I know) Falstaff shall die of a sweat, unless already a be kill'd with your hard opinions' (lines 26–31). The word emerges again in the final Chorus to *Henry V*:

> Thus far, with rough and all unable pen
> Our bending author hath pursu'd the story,
> In little room confining mighty men,
> Mangling by starts the full course of their glory.   (1–4)[7]

This author seems to apologise humbly, bendingly, through his actors, not just (in time-honoured style) for a lack of personal talent, but—one might almost say—for the very genre in which he dares to write; for the physical limitations of the playhouse in which he works, and the dubious status of his chosen literary vehicle: the drama. Such diffidence speaks to an age in which plays, in the scale of literary creation, were not highly regarded; in which Sir Thomas Bodley, with fatal lack of speculative instinct, famously instructed his librarian not to bother collecting mere playbooks for his grand new repository in Oxford; in which dramatic composition was still largely a backroom and anonymous affair.[8] The actual identity of the humble author of *2 Henry IV*, the bending author of *Henry V*, would probably have been unknown to the majority of play-goers in the 1590s. Nowhere in the theatre of this time was the author's name displayed or evident. Theatre programmes did not yet exist, and while theatrical playbills advertising the pieces to be performed might include the titles of the works in question and the names of one or two

---

[7] See Mark Rose's lively study, *Authors and Owners: The Invention of Copyright* (Cambridge, MA, 1993), p. 26. Quotations from *The Riverside Shakespeare*, ed. Harry Levin and others (Boston, etc., 1974).

[8] *Letters of Sir Thomas Bodley to Thomas James, Keeper of the Bodleian Library*, ed. G. W. Wheeler (Oxford, 1926), pp. 219–20; G. E. Bentley, *The Profession of Dramatist in Shakespeare's Time, 1590–1642* (Princeton, NJ, 1971), chap. 2, 'Status of Dramatists'. As Heidi Brayman Hackel has shown, Bodley's disapproval of playbooks was not widely shared amongst private collectors, but may have reflected particular views about the composition of a university collection, and the disproportionate space such items might occupy: '"Rowme" of Its Own: Printed Drama in Early Libraries', chap. 7 in John D. Cox and David Scott Kastan (eds.), *A New History of Early English Drama* (New York, 1997), pp. 113–30. Bequests to the Bodleian Library from collectors of drama such as Robert Burton were soon to erode the founder's original policy: see Ian Philip, *The Bodleian Library in the Seventeenth and Eighteenth Centuries* (Oxford, 1983).

principal actors—who were often well known to the play-going public—the authors' names were not thought worthy of mention in playbills until the final years of the seventeenth century, when their public accreditation attracted comment as something of a novelty.[9] So far from constituting an 'enigma' or a 'conspiracy', Shakespeare's relative invisibility as a writer of plays was an unsurprising consequence of the working conditions of the theatre of his time. Like the musical composer (a word first recorded in the late 1590s) the dramatic author, as an accredited professional category and a person worthy of public notice, did not yet fully exist.[10]

There was not even yet a settled term to describe such a person. The words most commonly used in modern times to denote a writer of plays, *dramatist* and *playwright*, did not appear until after the Restoration, if the *Oxford English Dictionary* is to be trusted, and seem to have been slow even then to move into popular currency. 'Playwright', as it happens—the *OED* has missed these examples—is a word that is actually found in three epigrams written by Ben Jonson before 1612, where it is used as a term of unmitigated contempt. The word may perhaps be Jonson's invention.[11] Here is one of the epigrams, 'To Playwright'.

---

[9] Commenting on a playbill accompanying a revival of *The Double Dealer* that bore the words, 'Written by Mr Congreve; with Severall Expressions omitted', John Dryden wrote to Mrs Steward (4 Mar. 1698/9) that 'the printing of an Authours name in a Play bill, is a new manner of proceeding, at least in England': Charles E. Ward (ed.), *The Letters of John Dryden With Letters Addressed to Him* (Durham, NC, 1942), letter 59, pp. 112–13; cit. Bentley, *The Profession of Dramatist*, pp. 60–1. Some awareness of the identity of the author must nevertheless be assumed in plays such as Dekker's *Satiromastix*, which tauntingly refers to Jonson's physical appearance and personal characteristics.

[10] *OED*'s first example of 'composer' in its musical sense is from Thomas Morley's *A plaine and easie introduction to practicall musicke*, 1597. The word was also commonly used at this time in relation to a writer of literary works. On the nineteenth-century development of the concept of the musical composer (and the variety of terms preceding its establishment), see Lydia Goehr, *The Imaginary Museum of Musical Works* (Oxford, 1992).

[11] Another early occurrence of the word is to be found in the commendatory verses of 'Cygnus'—probably Jonson's friend, Hugh Holland—prefixed to the quarto edition of *Sejanus* in 1605, that distinguish, in Jonsonian style, the work of 'the deserving Author', from that of 'the crew | Of common playwrights' (*Ben Jonson*, ed. Herford and Simpson, 11. 314). In 1617 Henry Fitzgeffrey fleered at 'Crabbed (*Websterio*) The *Play-wright, Cart-wright*' ('Notes from Black-fryers', in *Satyres and Satyricall Epigrams*, Stationers' Register, 9 Oct. 1617). The dramatist John Webster ('Websterio') appears to have worked with his father in the family business in Cow Lane, building and hiring out coaches: see David Gunby, 'John Webster', *Oxford Dictionary of National Biography* (Oxford, 2004). The gibe again demeaningly associates dramatic composition with manual labour.

> Playwright me reads, and still my verses damns:
> He says I want the tongue of epigrams;
> I have no salt: no bawdry, he doth mean;
> For witty, in his language, is obscene.
> Playwright, I loathe to have thy manners known
> In my chaste book: profess them in thine own.
>
> *Epigrams*, 49

This *playwright* presumptuously dares to pass judgement on a traditional poetic form, the epigram, of which, as a mere theatrical hack, he has no knowledge or understanding. From the second epigram addressed to the same figure, it is possible to deduce that the hack in question may have been John Marston, who did in fact write poetry as well as plays, though Jonson's neologism witheringly confines him to the theatre.[12] 'Stage-wright' is another, equally hostile Jonsonian term to describe the same kind of theatrical drudge.[13] The suffix reveals Jonson's own valuation of much dramatic work in his day as menial labour, and also perhaps a lingering sensitivity about the trade he himself had not entirely yet abandoned. After leaving Westminster School, William Drummond of Hawthornden noted, Jonson 'was put to another craft (I think was to be a wright or bricklayer) which he could not endure'. Bricklaying was a craft to which, after various theatrical disasters, Jonson's critics were accustomed to suggest he might usefully return.[14]

Both Shakespeare and Jonson entered the theatre as actors, and moved into writing only by degrees. In the first unmistakable reference to Shakespeare after his arrival in London from the provinces, Robert Greene in 1592 famously describes him as a bombastic player and would-be writer, a stealer of the ideas of others, an 'upstart crow', 'beautified with our feathers'. He is (Greene goes on) 'an absolute *Johannes Factotem*'—a do-all, a Jack of all trades.[15] *Factotem* here is an obvious term of abuse, and yet it would also in the years to come have reflected with increasing accuracy the sheer range of Shakespeare's professional

---

[12] 'Playwright, convict of public wrongs to men, | Takes private beatings, and begins again', etc. (*Epigrams*, 68. 1–2); Jonson told William Drummond of Hawthornden that 'He beat Marston, and took his pistol from him', *Conversations with Drummond*, line 125. 'Playwright' appears once more in *Epigrams*, 100.

[13] 'Ode. To Himself' (on *The New Inn*), line 35; *OED*'s only example of the word.

[14] *Conversations with Drummond*, lines 196–7. Taunts about his work as a bricklayer dogged Jonson from early in his career (*The Return from Parnassus*, Part 2, lines 293–8, in *Three Parnassus Plays*, ed. J. B. Leishman (London, 1949)) until late in life: see Alexander Gill's verses, line 52, on *The Magnetic Lady*, ed. Peter Happé (Manchester and New York, 2000), p. 217.

[15] Robert Greene, *Groats-worth of witte, bought with a million of Repentance* (1592), sig. F1ᵛ.

duties in the Lord Chamberlain's company, as player and shareholder, overseeing the hiring and payment of musicians and scribes and tiremen and stagehands and casual actors, the payment of rent, the division of income. Like Molière later in France, like Garrick and Sheridan later in England, Shakespeare led a busy and versatile professional life, in the midst of which, miraculously, he found time also to write his plays. Years later Ben Jonson was to find a similarly abusive term to describe his colleague Inigo Jones, who tried busily to commandeer all professional roles when staging their masques at court: *Dominus Do-All*.[16]

Jonson's own early work in the theatre had itself been various. Henslowe had soon begun to give him additional work, patching and mending old plays for revival, and working collaboratively with Thomas Dekker, Henry Chettle, Henry Porter, and others in his team on plays that Jonson chose significantly not to include amongst his later published work, and that are known today chiefly by their titles: *Hot Anger Soon Cold, Page of Plymouth, Robert II, The King of the Scots' Tragedy*. With such jointly written plays, it might often have been difficult to say precisely where responsibility for particular scenes, lines, and episodes finally lay. When Jonson and two fellow-actors from Pembroke's company, Robert Shaa and Gabriel Spencer, were incarcerated in Marshalsea Prison in 1597 following the performance of the notorious, now-lost satirical piece, *The Isle of Dogs*—co-written by Jonson and Thomas Nashe (who had prudently fled to the safety of Great Yarmouth)—all those concerned, including the actors, who may have added their own improvised material, seem sturdily to have denied responsibility for whatever it was that had caused the offence. This pattern was later repeated when Jonson and one of his two co-authors, George Chapman, were arrested following performances of another play which angered those in authority, *Eastward Ho!* In such contexts as these, the very notion of authorship seemed as elusive as some of the authors themselves (John Marston, the third collaborator on *Eastward Ho!*, having this time seemingly slipped through the net).

Yet as Jonson's career advanced from the late 1590s he began increasingly to create and assert an authorial identity, a dramatic character resembling and representing himself, a figure who hovers generally just out of sight, almost within earshot, at the very borders of the dramatic action: 'he do not hear me I hope', says Carlo Buffone in *Every Man Out*

---

[16] 'An Expostulation with Inigo Jones', *Ungathered Verse*, 34. 59–65.

of His Humour (Grex before Act 1, 342); 'I am looking, lest the poet hear me', says the Stage-Keeper in the Induction to *Bartholomew Fair* (7–8). This figure of The Author sends his agents and emissaries occasionally forward to speak on his behalf in prologues and epilogues, inductions and choruses, and threatens at times to intervene directly, to walk if need be straight on to the stage, to set matters right. Ben Jonson seems, like Bernard Shaw after him, to have been a disconcertingly close and demanding observer of his own plays in performance, to judge from Sir Vaughan's rebuke to the character of Horace—a thinly disguised representation of Jonson—in Dekker's satirical comedy *Satiromastix* in 1601:

> you shall not sit in a gallery, when your comedies and interludes have entered their actions, and there make vile and bad faces at every line, to make sentlemen have a eye to you, and to make players afraid to take your part.   (5. 2. 298–301)[17]

In the Induction to Jonson's own comedy, *Cynthia's Revels*, one of the three child actors (who are struggling between themselves as to who is to speak the prologue) asks where the author of the play may be at this moment. One of his companions insists that he is nowhere near at hand; for this author, unlike other authors, always keeps his distance, always behaves decorously behind the scenes:

> We are not so officiously befriended by him, as to have his presence in the tiring house, to prompt us aloud, stamp at the book-holder, swear for our properties, curse the poor tire-man, rail the music out of tune, and sweat for every venial trespass we commit, as some author would . . .   (160–5)

This elaborate denial, markedly at odds with other evidence of Jonson's behaviour in the playhouse, may well have prompted a smile amongst members of the company. Gossip Mirth in Jonson's later comedy, *The Staple of News*, has glimpsed the author in another mood, 'rolling himself up and down like a tun' in sweaty agitation as he issues last-minute directions to the actors in the tiring-room.

> . . . never did vessel of wort or wine work so! His sweating put me in mind of a good Shroving-dish (and I believe would be taken up for a service of state somewhere, an't were known)—a stewed poet! He doth sit like an unbraced drum with one of his heads beaten out. For that you must note, a poet hath two heads as a drum hath. One for making, the other repeating; and his repeating head is all to pieces . . .   (Induction, 62–70)

---

[17] *Satiromastix*, in *The Dramatic Works of Thomas Dekker*, ed. Fredson Bowers, 4 vols. (Cambridge, 1953–61), 1. 382; text modernised.

Earlier in his career, at the start of his satirical comedy, *Poetaster*, Jonson had famously presented a Prologue clad in full armour, who speaks in robust defence of the play's author, and explains his dress as follows:

> If any muse why I salute the stage
> An armed Prologue, know, 'tis a dangerous age,
> Wherein who writes had need present his scenes
> Forty-fold proof against the conjuring means
> Of base detractors and illiterate apes . . . (5–9)

In a wry rejoinder to this flamboyant gesture, Shakespeare begins *Troilus and Cressida* with another Prologue who enters clad in full armour

> . . . but not in confidence
> Of author's pen or actor's voice, but suited
> In like condition as our argument. (23–50)

'Suited': with this gentle play on words, Shakespeare insinuates his own sense of what may or may not be appropriate to the nature of theatrical representation.[18] While there is no clear evidence about the way these prologues were originally presented in the theatre, it is tempting to ask if Jonson may not have been inside that suit of armour at the opening of *Poetaster*, speaking in his own voice about the perils and pains of authorship. Might not Shakespeare, indeed, in answering fashion, have donned that other suit of armour in order to utter the prologue to *Troilus and Cressida*? This would certainly have been an apt and appropriate piece of company casting.[19] It is equally possible that Jonson appeared in his own person at the end of *Poetaster*, in a highly unusual and complementary scene, the so-called Apologetical Dialogue, that was performed only once in the theatre before being (in the words of the quarto text) 'restrained . . . by Authority'.[20] Here the figure of The Author is discovered in his study, lamenting the ignorance of his audiences and his critics, declaring at some length his total indifference to their opinions, and—in a wonderfully tormented moment of simultaneous self-exposure and retreat—his wish to be left alone.

---

[18] Despite Jonson's seeming hesitations in the epilogue to *Cynthia's Revels* over the appropriate tone to adopt in an authorial address ('I neither must be faint, remiss, nor sorry, | Sour, serious, confident, nor peremptory, | But betwixt these': 9–11), the epilogue's climatic line—'By (—) 'tis good, and if you like't, you may'—had already attracted mockery. Jonson worries over the line's reception in *Poetaster*, prologue, 15–20.

[19] I owe the latter suggestion to Professor Jonathan Bate.

[20] 'To the Reader' (Quarto text). The suggestion that Jonson may have played this role is made by A. W. Ward, *English Dramatic Literature to the Death of Queen Anne* (London, 1899), 2. 360.

> Leave me. There's something come into my thought
> That must and shall be sung, high and aloof,
> Safe from the wolf's black jaw and the dull ass's hoof. (237–9)

Though such a personal appearance by a dramatic author was (to the best of my knowledge) without precedent on the English stage, a similar defence of the authority of the author was a familiar feature of Greek Old Comedy, as Jonson would have known, when the leader of the chorus, in a movement known as *parabasis*, would come forward (turning aside from the dramatic action) and address the audience directly on behalf of the poet, speaking in his name, praising his work, denigrating the work of rivals, and exhorting the audience to pay attention.[21] In the Apologetical Dialogue to *Poetaster* Jonson imports into the English theatre, and aligns himself with, a model of authorship derived partly from the example of Aristophanes and his contemporaries and partly also from 'those great master spirits', the poets of Augustan Rome—Virgil, Horace, Ovid—who are central characters in the action of his own comedy just ended, *Poetaster*.

Jonson scatters these small self-portraits throughout his plays in almost Hitchcockian style as a kind of personal signature, a reminder of human agency, of the tenuous but enduring link between artist and artefact. Viewed in one light, they could be seen as a means of maintaining vestigial control over the work which the author has entrusted to the skills of the players and the critical judgement of the play-going public. Viewed another way, they seem to acknowledge, often with some humour, the author's impotence, his inability any longer wholly to direct or possess the work he has brought into being.

> When we do give, Alfonso, to the light
> A work of ours, we part with our own right;
> For then all mouths will judge, and their own way;
> The learned have no more privilege than the lay.
> *Epigrams*, 131. 1–4

Jonson wrote these lines to his friend Alfonso Ferrabosco—composer, violist, lutanist, and musical instructor to Prince Henry—on the publication of his musical *Lessons* in 1609, adding some words of classical con-

---

[21] See Victor Ehrenberg, *The People of Aristophanes: A Sociology of Old Attic Comedy* (London and New York, 1943), pp. 32–7; A. M. Bowie, *Aristophanes: Myth, Ritual, and Comedy* (Cambridge, 1993); Coburn Gum, *The Aristophanic Comedies of Ben Jonson: A Comparative Study of Jonson and Aristophanes* (The Hague, 1969); Jonson, *Poetaster*, ed. Tom Cain, Revels Plays (Manchester and New York, 1995), p. 261.

solation, taken from the writings of Horace and Persius, urging authors to pay no heed to anyone's judgement other than their own.[22] Giving a creative work 'to the light', whether through publication or performance, parting with the authorial 'right'—a word of great resonance in his work, anticipating in a moral, if not yet strictly legal sense, the modern notion of intellectual property, of copy*right*—was always for Jonson a painful if not traumatic act, which he negotiates at times philosophically, at times with sardonic humour. 'When I suffered [the work] to go abroad', Jonson writes of *The Masque of Queens*, 'I departed with my right; and now, so secure an interpreter I am of my chance, that neither praise nor dispraise shall affect me'.[23] 'It is further agreed', says the Scrivener in the Induction to *Bartholomew Fair*, reading out Articles of Agreement with the Author, which purportedly bind the spectators at the Hope Theatre to behave themselves with good sense and decorum,

> It is further agreed that every person here have his or their free-will of censure, to like or dislike at their own charge; the author having now departed with his right, it shall be lawful for any man to judge his six penn'orth, his twelve penn'orth, so to his eighteen pence, two shillings, half a crown, to the value of his place—provided always his place get not above his wit. (85–91)[24]

The author: such repeated references—even in humorous contexts such as this—bring into prominence, and confer new status upon, the hitherto obscure writer of the dramatic work. Jonson, one might say, *invents* the idea of the author—not in the same manner that he may invent such words as 'playwright', 'stage-wright', 'poetaster', terms not hitherto known in English, but as Renaissance rhetoricians understood invention, *inventio*, as a happy discovery of an already existing term or subject which could be manipulated in a novel way.[25] The word 'author' was as old as creation itself, its dignity deriving from its evident association with the godhead, 'the author of eternal salvation', 'the author . . . of peace', 'the author and finisher of our faith', as the King James Bible has it; 'the author both of life and light', as Jonson himself writes in his

---

[22] Horace, *Epistles*, I. 20. 6; Persius, *Satires*, 1. 7.

[23] This sentence does not appear in the holograph, but is inserted significantly in the published texts, quarto and folio, after line 679.

[24] Cf. Jonson's Fitzdottrel in *The Devil is an Ass*, as he allows Wittipol to speak without interruption to his wife, Frances Fitzdottrel, for a fixed period of time: 'Speak what you list, that time is yours; my right | I have departed with. But not beyond | A minute or a second look for' (1. 4. 82–4).

[25] The *OED*'s first recorded instance of word 'poetaster' is from *Cynthia's Revels*, 2. 4. 11. Jonson discusses *inventio* in *Discoveries*, 2161–91; cf. *The Underwood*, 25. 2

'Hymn On the Nativity of My Saviour'.[26] In this regard it resembles those etymologically related terms so favoured by Jonson, 'poet' and 'maker', whose significance Sir Philip Sidney—'God-like Sidney', as Jonson knowingly calls him (*The Forest*, 12. 91)—had ringingly defended in his *Apology for Poetry*:

> Neither let it be deemed too saucy a comparison to balance the highest point of man's wit with the efficacy of Nature; but rather give right honour to the heavenly Maker of that maker, who having made man to His own likeness, set him beyond and over all the works of that second nature: which in nothing he showeth so much as in Poetry, when with the force of a divine breath he bringeth things forth far surpassing her doings, with no small argument to the incredulous of that first accursed fall of Adam: since our erected wit maketh us know what perfection is, and yet our infected will keepeth us from reaching it. But these arguments will by few be understood, and by fewer granted. Thus much (I hope) will be given me, that the Greeks with some probability of reason gave him the name above all names of learning.[27]

Sidney's *Apology* focuses closely on the etymology and inherited significance of the terms associated with poetic activity.

> Among the Romans a poet was called *vates*, which is as much as a diviner, foreseer, or prophet, as by his conjoined words *vaticinium* and *vaticinari* is manifest: so heavenly a title did that excellent people bestow upon this heart-ravishing knowledge.[28]

'A Poet is as much to say as a maker', declares George Puttenham in similar fashion at the outset of *The Arte of English Poesie* in 1589,

> And our English name well conformes with the Greeke word: for of *poiein* to make, they call a maker *Poeta*. Such as (by way of resemblance and reverently) we may say of God: who without any travell to his divine imagination, made all the world of nought. . . .[29]

Jonson inherits this Sidneyan view of the writer's god-like role, whose value was mysteriously expressed through, and vested in, the terminology

---

[26] Hebrews, 5:9; 1 Corinthians, 14:33; Hebrews, 12:1–2; *The Underwood*, 1. 3. 1–2. With this last example, cf. Campion's 'Author of light, revive my dying spright', *The Works of Thomas Campion*, ed. Walter R. Davis (New York, 1970), p. 59.

[27] Sir Philip Sidney, *An Apology for Poetry*, ed. Geoffrey Shepherd (London, 1965), p. 101.

[28] Sidney, *An Apology*, ed. Shepherd, p. 98. Jonson similarly sees poets as *vates* ('priests and poets', *The Underwood*, 70. 82). Cf. Sir John Harington: 'Prophets and Poets have been thought to have a great affinitie, as the name *Vates* in Latin doth testifie', *A Preface, or rather a Briefe Apologie of Poetrie, and of the Author and Translator* prefixed to *Orlando Furioso* (1591), in G. Gregory Smith (ed.), *Elizabethan Critical Essays*, 2 vols. (Oxford, 1904), 2. 205.

[29] George Puttenham, *The Arte of English Poesie* (1589), in Smith (ed.), *Elizabethan Critical Essays*, 2. 3.

with which it was traditionally associated. At a time when many of the terms used in relation to literary activity and to the professions more generally in early modern England were still quite fluid and unstable, Jonson's own usage remained remarkably precise and consistent. He distinguished sharply between poets (or makers), on the one hand, and mere versifiers (or rhymers), on the other: 'A rhymer and a poet are two things', as he remarks tartly in *Discoveries* (lines 2448–9). Samuel Daniel would pass as a rhymer, but not as a poet.[30] In the Epistle Dedicatory to *Volpone* Jonson notes that nothing nowadays remains 'of the dignity of poet but the abused name, which every scribe usurps' (lines 34–5), and attempts to set out the true significance of that term.[31] Jonson described himself at times as a 'maker', but more regularly as a 'poet'. 'In his merry humour he was wont to name himself The Poet', noted Drummond wryly.[32]

'Author' is a word that Jonson employed with a similar care and consciousness of its traditional signification. The Latin root-word, *auctor*, carried a range of senses ('promoter', 'producer', 'father', 'progenitor', 'originator', 'performer', 'authority', 'teacher', 'counsellor', 'advisor', etc.) as well as the sense that has come to dominate its modern English derivative: 'writer'. In Renaissance usage, the words *auctor* and 'author' might signify the patron or enabler of an artistic work, as well as the actual artist. Thus Lorenzo de' Medici (for example) was described as the *auctor*, the author, of the church of San Gallo in Florence; a usage which, as F. W. Kent observes, 'may imply that Lorenzo was both entrepreneurially and creatively involved in its construction', though 'architectural historians almost unanimously attribute its design to Giuliano da Sangallo.'[33] In a similar fashion the Venetian ambassador who witnessed a performance at court of Jonson's *Masque of Beauty* described Queen Anne, who commissioned and danced in the masque, as 'the authoress of

---

[30] Jonson told William Drummond of Hawthornden that 'Samuel Daniel was a good honest man, had no children, but no poet' (*Conversations with Drummond*, lines 23–4). Earlier he had written that the Countess of Bedford, in giving her patronage to Daniel, was thought to have 'a better verser got | (Or "poet", in the court account) than I . . .' (*The Forest*, 12. 68–9). Mercury remarks of Hedon in *Cynthia's Revels* (Q), 2. 1. 45–9 that 'he loves to have a fencer, a pedant, and a musician seen in his lodging a-mornings'. Cupid: 'And not a poet?' Mercury: 'Fie, no; himself is a rhymer, and that's a thought better than a poet.'

[31] *Discoveries*, 2346 ff., *Epigrams*, 10, *Every Man Out of His Humour*, 3. 6. 209, *The Staple of News*, Prologue for the Stage, 5.

[32] *Conversations*, line 636. The term jocularly recalled the familiar styling of Aristotle as 'The Philosopher'.

[33] F. W. Kent, *Lorenzo de' Medici and the Art of Magnificence* (Baltimore and London, 2004), p. 98.

the whole'.[34] Jonson himself used the word in relation to non-textual, as well as textual artistry: 'The author was Master Thomas Giles', he writes, when describing the intricate dances devised for *The Masque of Queens* (line 638).[35]

Significantly, however, Jonson chose never to use the term 'author' in relation to his colleague, Inigo Jones, despite the two men's close and brilliant collaborations at court. When In-and-In Medlay in Jonson's late comedy, *A Tale of a Tub*—a character obviously representing Inigo Jones—claims he is the 'author' of a village puppet-show, he is sharply contradicted by his companion Squire Tub, who tells him he is merely the 'workman' or 'artificer' (*A Tale of a Tub*, 5. 7. 22–3). The comic dispute about the nature of authorship in this comedy mirrors the real life dispute between Jonson and Jones as to which of them was the true or primary 'inventor' of the masques which they collaboratively brought into being (Medlay in *A Tale of a Tub* 'must be sole inventor', grumbles the 'great writer', D'ogenes Scriben, 5. 2. 37).[36] Jonson was equally reserved about Jones's adoption of the term 'architect' to designate his profession. Like 'author', 'poet', 'maker', the word *architect* seemed to carry—presumptuously, in Jonson's view—a suggestion of divine power, for God himself was known as 'the great architect', as Raphael was to call him in *Paradise Lost* (8. 72). Even in non-Christian contexts, the word 'architecture' and its cognates had developed special connotations. *Architectonike* was the term used by Aristotle to describe the ultimate end to which all knowledge was directed and subordinate, namely, virtuous action. Jones's 'Almighty architecture', on the other hand, was for Jonson not simply

---

[34] *Calendar of State Papers (Venetian) 1607–10*, p. 86. I am grateful to Professor Martin Butler for this reference. With a playful consciousness of the family's literary reputation, Jonson similarly describes the Sidneys as 'authors of the feast' designed to celebrate the twenty-first birthday of Sir William Sidney: *The Forest*, 14. 10.

[35] Describing the dances in *Hymenaei*, Jonson writes: 'Here they danced forth a most neat and curious measure, full of subtlety and device, which was so excellently performed as it seemed to take away that spirit from the invention, which the invention gave to it; and left it doubtful whether the forms flowed more perfectly from the author's brain or their feet' (310–14). Here Jonson's prose leaves it equally and appropriately doubtful whether 'the author' on this occasion is Jonson himself or his choreographer.

[36] Jones had objected to his name appearing after Jonson's on the title-page of *Love's Triumph Through Callipolis* in 1631 ('The Inventors, Ben Jonson, Inigo Jones'). Jonson responded by omitting Jones's name altogether from the title-page of *Chloridia*, and by writing 'An Expostulation with Inigo Jones' and two other satirical poems about his collaborator. On the intellectual background to the dispute, see D. J. Gordon, 'Poet and Architect: The Intellectual Setting of the Quarrel between Ben Jonson and Inigo Jones', in Stephen Orgel (ed.), *The Renaissance Imagination* (Berkeley, Los Angeles, and London, 1975).

devoid of ethical content; it was mere technical work, a kind of trade dangerously close to bricklaying.³⁷

The precise meaning of the word *author* continued to attract discussion during Jonson's lifetime. In Thomas Hobbes's account 'Of Persons, Authors, and things personated' in chapter 16 of *Leviathan* the author is seen as the ultimate owner and authoriser of words or actions that might however be spoken or negotiated or personated on his behalf by someone else, who is variously described by Hobbes as a *persona*, a person, an actor.

> The word Person is latine; instead whereof the Greeks have *prosopon*, which signifies the *Face*, as *Persona* in latine signifies the *disguise*, or *outward appearance* of a man, counterfeited on the Stage; and sometimes more particularly that part of it, which disguiseth the face, as a Mask or Visard: And from the Stage, hath been translated to any Representer of speech and action, as well in Tribunalls, as Theaters.³⁸

Hobbes is here exploring a question that lay at the very heart of contemporary political and religious debate: where civil authority ultimately lay. Quentin Skinner, in an acute analysis of this section of *Leviathan*, points to a curious oddity in Hobbes's use of the theatrical analogy, for in the theatre of Hobbes's time ultimate authority lay not with the author but with the regulating officer, acting on the monarch's behalf, who licensed plays for theatrical performance: the Master of the Revels.³⁹ Jonson, oddly enough, had been granted the reversion of this post in 1621; while he never finally inherited this position, he was well acquainted with its mode of operation, and with the conflicting kinds of 'authority' (legal, authorial, popular, etc.) that vied for supremacy within the theatre of his time.⁴⁰ According to John Aubrey, Jonson was Hobbes's 'loving and familiar friend and acquaintance' and closely associated with him and his

---

³⁷ 'An Expostulation with Inigo Jones', lines 10, 92. Jonson's references to architects and architecture are generally disparaging: cf. *The Underwood*, 77. 25; *The Staple of News*, 4. 2. 35–7; *Discoveries*, 1135. See also A. W. Johnson, *Ben Jonson: Poetry and Architecture* (Oxford, 1994).
³⁸ Thomas Hobbes, *Leviathan*, ed. Richard Tuck (Cambridge, 1991).
³⁹ Quentin Skinner, 'Hobbes and the Purely Artificial Person of the State', in *Visions of Politics*, vol. 3, *Hobbes and Civil Science* (Cambridge, 2002), 177–208. I am grateful to Professor Skinner for guidance on this passage. See also Christopher Pye, 'The Sovereign, the Theater, and the Kingdome of Darknesse: Hobbes and the Spectacle of Power' in Stephen Greenblatt (ed.), *Representing the English Renaissance* (Berkeley, Los Angeles, and London, 1988), pp. 279–301; and David Runciman, *Pluralism and the Personality of the State* (Cambridge, 1997), chaps. 2, 11.
⁴⁰ See Richard Dutton, *Mastering the Revels: The Regulation and Censorship of English Renaissance Drama* (Houndmills, Basingstoke, 1991); Richard Burt, *Licensed by Authority: Ben Jonson and the Discourses of Censorship* (Ithaca and London, 1993).

intellectual circle during the 1620s and 1630s.[41] It is tempting to wonder if Hobbes's thinking on the question of authorship may not have been stimulated by his familiarity with Jonson's own dramatic practice, and even conceivably through conversations with Jonson himself. A comedy such as *Bartholomew Fair* explores the very terrain of chapter 16 of *Leviathan*, asking where authority finally rests both within the theatre and in society at large, presenting an array of petty officials who serve as agents or deputies—*persons*, in Hobbes's terminology—who act on delegated authority, claiming, in a wild collision of conflicting interests, licence or warrant for their actions. The authority they claim derives variously from the Judge of Pie Powders, from a guardian, from a husband, from the king, from the commonwealth, from scripture, from the Master of the Revels. 'Sir, I present nothing but what is licensed by authority', protests the puppeteer, Lantern Leatherhead, as the Puritan Zeal-of-the-Land Busy angrily demolishes his show. 'Thou art all licence, even licentiousness itself, Shimei!', exclaims Busy. 'I have the Master of the Revels' hand for't, sir', responds Leatherhead. 'The Master of Rebels' hand, thou hast', says Busy: 'Satan's' (5. 5. 14–20). In an epilogue written for performance of the play at Court, Jonson makes it clear that final authority, the ultimate licence or warrant for what is allowed in the kingdom, is firmly vested in King James himself.[42]

When *Bartholomew Fair* was performed before King James in 1614, Shakespeare had already retired to Stratford upon Avon, having made, in what must seem to modern eyes an astonishing act of neglect or renunciation, no apparent effort to bring his works together in collected form, to present a Shakespearian canon to the world. Jonson's attitude to publication differed from that of Shakespeare in a number of obvious ways. From his earliest professional years Jonson had methodically prepared quarto editions of his individual plays—including, defiantly, those which had not succeeded in the theatre, and those over which he had, legally speaking (as Joseph Lowenstein has shown in remarkable detail) no formal rights of ownership—confidently proclaiming his authorship on the title pages.[43] The traditional belief that Shakespeare and the theatrical

---

[41] *Aubrey's 'Brief Lives'*, ed. A. Clark, 2 vols. (Oxford, 1898), 1. 365.

[42] Jonson's use of authorial delegates—characters who speak on the author's behalf—closely anticipates the role that Hobbes attributes to the *persona*: 'if you please to confer with our author by attorney, you may sir', comments one of the boys in the Induction to *Cynthia's Revels* (136–7), 'our proper self here stands for him'. Cf. *The Magnetic Lady*, Induction, 14–16.

[43] Joseph Loewenstein, *Jonson and Possessive Authorship* (Cambridge, 2002); 'The Script in the Marketplace', in Greenblatt (ed.), *Representing the English Renaissance*, pp. 265–78; and *The*

company for which he worked were, by way of contrast, wholly indifferent or opposed to publication of play texts has been sharply challenged in recent years. During the early part at least of Shakespeare's career—as Lukas Erne has persuasively argued in an important revisionist study—Shakespeare and the Lord Chamberlain's Men seem to have regarded the publication of his plays in quarto format as conducive to their commercial success in the playhouse, rather than prejudicial. While the company normally left an interval of about two years between first performance of a play and its entry in the Stationers' Register, it seems to have found publication a useful means of reviving theatrical interest in plays that were no longer entirely new in performance. Of the first dozen or so plays that Shakespeare wrote for the Chamberlain's Men, as Erne points out, 'not a single one that could legally have been printed remained unprinted by 1602'. Many of these quartos carried the author's name, as Jonson's did.[44] Yet the evidence for Shakespeare's continuing interest in the publication of plays during the latter part of his career (post-1602) is less coherent and less compelling; and the notion that he may have begun to prepare a collected edition of his writings during his final years in Stratford remains entirely speculative, and based in part on dubious anecdote. If Shakespeare, early in his career, shrewdly perceived that publication of his plays might be of practical advantage to his company, it is none the less difficult to see him as driven by the same authorial imperative, the same systematic recourse to the medium of print, that Jonson's lifelong record of publishing seems to imply.[45]

In 1616, the year of Shakespeare's death, the printer and bookseller William Stansby produced under Jonson's watchful eye a folio collection

---

Author's Due: Printing and the Prehistory of Copyright (Chicago, 2002). See also Douglas A. Brooks, *From Playhouse to Printing House: Drama and Authorship in Early Modern England* (Cambridge, 2000).

[44] Lukas Erne, *Shakespeare as Literary Dramatist* (Cambridge, 2003); the passage quoted is from p. 86. Erne (chap. 2) corrects Douglas Brooks's mistaken assertion (*From Playhouse to Printing House*, pp. 71 and passim) that the quarto title-page of *2 Henry IV* in 1600 was the first to attribute authorship to Shakespeare: it was in fact the sixth such attribution. Peter W. M. Blayney speculates that peaks in publication of playbooks between December 1593 and May 1595 and May 1600 to October 1601 may suggest a deliberate strategy of 'publicity' or 'advertising' of plays for the theatre: 'The Publication of Playbooks', chap. 21 in John D. Cox and David Scott Kastan (eds.), *A New History of Early English Drama* (New York, 1997), pp. 383–422, at p. 386.

[45] Jonson was none the less sharply ambivalent in relation to the print culture of his day: see Ian Donaldson, 'Jonson's Poetry', in *The Cambridge Companion to Ben Jonson* (Cambridge, 2000), chap. 9, esp. pp. 120–3, and the revealing analysis of manuscript circulation offered by Colin Burrow in his forthcoming edition of the poems in *The Cambridge Edition of the Works of Ben Jonson*.

of *The Works of Benjamin Jonson*: a volume comprising more than a dozen Court masques, a handful of entertainments, a panegyrical address to King James on his entry to the first session of parliament in 1604, two substantial collections of verse, and—most controversially—a group of nine plays, a kind of writing seldom before included in England in any volume bearing the serious title *Works*. 'Pray tell me, *Ben*', wrote one wag later, 'where doth the mystery lurk, | What others call a play you call a worke'.[46] Yet through the 1616 folio, modelled as it was in part on Renaissance editions of classical authors, and in part on the great folio edition of King James's works published earlier that same year, Jonson was signalling his wish to elevate drama to a more serious literary status, and to present himself as no mere playwright, but as an *author* of classical range, dignity, and proportion.

This annual lecture recognises Shakespeare's undisputed genius, his unrivalled standing in the field of English literature. That modern consensus is in no way diminished if we recall that during the century or so following his death it was not William Shakespeare but Ben Jonson who was reckoned by many good judges to have been the greatest writer England had ever produced.[47] Such a verdict, however fantastical it may appear to later generations, was perhaps in part encouraged by Jonson's more forward style of self-presentation, which I have tried to illustrate here; and validated in part by Jonson's sheer versatility and ambition as a writer, venturing as he did into so many branches of humanistic learning: as poet, as deviser of Court and civic entertainments, as dramatist, as historian, philologist, rhetorician, as writer on statecraft, social conduct, theology, as England's first literary critic worthy of the name. Jonson too in his own fashion was a great factotum, a Dominus Do-All, but he found a more flattering name to describe his chosen role, and that name was *Author*.

When in the early 1620s members of Shakespeare's old company, heading off a venture from a rival bookseller, began to prepare for publi-

---

[46] *Wit's Recreation* (1640). Plays by both Gascoigne and Daniel had previously appeared in volumes entitled 'Works': Erne, *Shakespeare as Literary Dramatist*, p. 45. See also Ian Donaldson, 'Collecting Ben Jonson' in Andrew Nash (ed.), *The Culture of Collected Editions* (Houndmills, Basingstoke, 2003), pp. 19–31; and *Ben Jonson's 1616 Folio*, ed. Jennifer Brady and W. H. Herendeen (Newark, London, and Toronto, 1991), which includes Sara van den Berg's 'Ben Jonson and the Ideology of Authorship', pp. 111–37.

[47] G. E. Bentley, *Shakespeare and Jonson: Their Reputations in the Seventeenth Century Compared*, 2 vols. (Chicago, 1945). Bentley's methodology has been questioned, most notably by David L. Frost in *The School of Shakespeare* (Cambridge, 1968), but the evidence he assembles still supports this general conclusion.

cation a collected folio edition of his dramatic works, they were assisted by Jonson himself, who prepared two poems which stand at the head of the 1623 First Folio. He may also—as numerous small stylistic touches suggest—have drafted the famous address 'To the great Variety of Readers' that is signed by the players John Heminge and Henry Condell:[48]

> It had bene a thing, we confesse, worthie to have bene wished, that the Author himselfe had liu'd to set forth, and ouerseen his owne writings; But since it hath bin ordain'd otherwise, and he by death departed from that right, we pray you do not envie his Friends, the office of their care, and paine, to haue collected & publish'd them . . .

'The Author himselfe': Shakespeare here is dignified with the styling that, throughout his lifetime, he was generally reluctant to adopt, but that is now emphatically accorded to him by his friends, to whom the 'right' of publication has passed.

That styling is repeated in the title of Jonson's poem 'To the Memory of My Beloved, The Author, Mr William Shakespeare, and What He Hath Left Us', in which those words, THE AUTHOR, are significantly emphasised in large-sized upper-case typography. Jonson's poem places Shakespeare above all other English writers for the stage, alongside the greatest dramatic authors of antiquity, Aeschylus, Euripides, Sophocles, Seneca; hailing him as a 'Starre of Poets', now standing high in the heavens, visible and illuminating to all. The dramatic author is no longer an anonymous backroom boy, but has become at last a star. In another brief poem accompanying Martin Droeshout's famous engraving of Shakespeare, Jonson vouches for the likeness of the portrait, but urges the reader to study not Shakespeare's picture but his book, through which his personality is expressed, and his life continues. Jonson's two poems at the head of the 1623 folio have proved over the years to be the most formidable barrier to those wishing to prove that Shakespeare was not Shakespeare, but somebody else; to assert that no real evidence exists to link the player from Stratford to the works attributed to him. A not uncritical appraiser of his greatest colleague's writings, Jonson could scarcely have expressed himself more clearly or unambiguously than he does on this occasion, affirming that this man, known and beloved by him, pictured in the accompanying illustration, was indeed 'THE AUTHOR' of the works this volume contains.

---

[48] For a more detailed discussion of this possibility (first proposed by George Steevens) see Ian Donaldson, *Jonson's Magic Houses* (Oxford, 1997), p. 19 and n. 34.

In death as in life, Ben Jonson and William Shakespeare are intimately linked through these verses in the opening pages of the 1623 Folio; a book which, together with Jonson's own 1616 Folio, was to become a foundational volume in the history of collected editions in England, much imitated and emulated in the years to come, and in the establishment of Shakespeare's own reputation as a writer, in Jonson's own phrase—astonishingly predictive in 1623—'not of an age, but for all time'. The volume may also be seen as a landmark in the history of authorship itself; as what one might term, in homage to Roland Barthes, Michel Foucault, and much vexed textual argumentation still to come, the birth of the author.[49]

Note. I am most grateful to Professors Martin Butler and Quentin Skinner for stimulating help and advice during the preparation of this lecture.

[49] See Richard Dutton, 'The Birth of the Author' in R. B. Parker and S. P. Zitner (eds.), *Elizabethan Theater: Essays in Honor of S. Schoenbaum* (Newark and London, 1996), pp. 71–92.

WARTON LECTURE ON ENGLISH POETRY

'Now Shall I Make My Soul': Approaching Death in Yeats's Life and Work

R. F. FOSTER
Fellow of the Academy

IT IS A DAUNTING VENTURE to give the Warton Lecture on English Poetry when one is actually an Irish historian. But the founder, Mrs Frida Mond, wanted Warton to be commemorated as the 'first *historian* of English poetry', which of course he was—as well as Professor of Poetry at Oxford (like his father), a notable commentator on Spenser and Milton, and a much-derided Poet Laureate. Further, he was at one point elected Camden Professor of History at Oxford. My more substantial rationale must be that I am Yeats's biographer as well as a historian and I want to consider work and life, in a way that biographers dangerously do—while remembering throughout that Yeats's creative writing is not autobiography, even if his autobiography is often creative writing. My subject is in fact *death* and work, death being a perhaps peculiarly Irish subject. Lady Morgan remarked in *The Wild Irish Girl*, published two hundred years ago, 'With respect to the attendant ceremonies of death, I know of no country which the Irish at present resemble but the modern Greeks'.[1] Her fictional narrator put this similarity down to their shared sense of the immediacy of another world. The resemblance has been noted by other commentaries on Irish funerary culture, one of which is actually called

---

Read at the Academy 6 December 2006.
[1] Sydney Owenson, Lady Morgan, *The Wild Irish Girl: a national tale*, ed. Claire Connolly and Stephen Copley (London, 2000), pp. 178–9.

Proceedings of the British Academy **151**, 339–360. © The British Academy 2007.

Talking to the Dead;[2] both in traditional Irish folklore, and in the tradition of Irish supernatural writing, the veil between the living and the dead is often presented as a very insubstantial matter indeed.

Yeats is in this very Irish. He famously wrote to Olivia Shakespear in 1927 that only two subjects could be of the least interest to a serious and studious mind, sex and the dead.[3] Addressing such a remark to one's long-ago first lover, as both of you contemplate old age, may have a special appropriateness, but he certainly lived up to it. For Yeats, his preoccupation with death was by no means a gloomy predilection: one of my themes will be the way that he uses death as an affirmation of life. 'We begin to live', he famously wrote, 'when we have conceived life as tragedy.'[4] Sometimes he sees death, and its attendant excitements, as a more engrossing, and a more serious business, than the everyday world: even, *pace* his remark to Olivia, than sex. When he went to see Villiers de l'Isle Adam's symbolist play *Axel*, as a very young man, one phrase from it resounded in his head afterwards: 'As for living, our servants will do that for us.' This alluring prospect is presented, when read in context, as part of a suggested suicide pact, which takes the form of a seduction—a seduction into the virginal grave rather than the consummated bed. It is not a *liebestod* in the classic sense, but a kind of avoidance. And this too had resonances for the youthful—and sexually evasive—Yeats.[5]

Several critics have noted this death-preoccupation, though there are surprisingly few detailed treatments of it.[6] The way that critics approach Yeats and death often says as much about them as about him. Hugh Kenner went so far as to claim that Yeats wrote three 'deaths' into his creative life, as part of a deliberate freeing of his imagination, but also as a way of dictating the shape in which his work would be received: first, in producing his *Collected Works* in 1908, when aged only 43, as a way of

---

[2] Nina Witoszek and Pat Sheeran, *Talking to the Dead: a study of the Irish funeary tradition* (Amsterdam, 1988); see also Fiona Mackintosh, *Dying Acts: death in ancient Greek and modern Irish tragic drama* (Cork, 1994).
[3] *The Collected Letters of W. B. Yeats* (Oxford University Press, InteLex Electronic edn., 2002), Accession no. 5034. Also in Allan Wade (ed.), *The Letters of W. B. Yeats* (London, 1954), p. 730.
[4] *Autobiographies* (London, 1955), p. 189.
[5] For Yeats and *Axel* see my *W. B. Yeats, A Life, I: The Apprentice Mage, 1865–1914* (Oxford, 1997), pp. 139–41.
[6] Distinguished exceptions are Jahan Ramazani, *Yeats and the Poetry of Death: elegy, self-elegy and the sublime* (London, 1990), Seamus Heaney, 'Joy or Night: last things in the poetry of W. B. Yeats and Philip Larkin' in *The Redress of Poetry: Oxford Lectures* (London, 1995), pp. 146–63 and T. R. Henn, 'The Property of the Dead', in *Last Essays* (Gerrards Cross, 1976), pp. 221–39.

liberating himself for a departure into new style; second, in *The Tower*, where he declared it was time for him to make his soul, and nominated his heirs; and thirdly, in his *Last Poems*. The scheme fits with Kenner's preoccupation with Yeats as a maker of books and self-canoniser, though I think there are problems here too.[7] Seamus Deane has rather censoriously seen Yeats's preoccupation with death as a way of distinguishing himself from the common mob.[8] Several others have applied to Yeats the Freudian interpretation of the creative instinct as a flight from the fear of death;[9] Harold Bloom, in his endlessly influential *Anxiety of Influence*, generalises this insight: 'Every poet begins (however "unconsciously") by rebelling more strongly against the consciousness of death's necessity than all other men and women do.'[10] But I think this is not quite right for Yeats, for whom death's 'necessity' was an *enabling* realisation. I should like to connect this to his sense of religion, and of supernaturalism, to the idea of 'late style', recently intriguingly defined by Edward Said in some of his own last writings, and to Yeats's own gathering sense of 'making his soul' as his end neared.

The idea of death as opening a door, which he approaches 'Dreading and hoping all', comes from a short poem he placed second in his collection *The Winding Stair*: called, appositely, 'Death', it reflects all these themes.

> Nor dread nor hope attend
> A dying animal;
> A man awaits his end
> Dreading and hoping all;
> Many times he died,
> Many times rose again.
> A great man in his pride
> Confronting murderous men
> Casts derision upon
> Supersession of breath;
> He knows death to the bone—
> Man has created death.[11]

---

[7] Hugh Kenner, 'The Three Deaths of Yeats' in *Yeats: an annual of critical and textual studies*, 5 (1987), 87–92. Also see the Introduction to *W. B. Yeats, Last Poems: manuscript materials*, ed. James Pethica (Ithaca, 1997), especially pp. xxiii–xxx.
[8] *Celtic Revivals: essays in modern Irish literature 1880–1980* (London, 1985), pp. 41–4.
[9] See Joseph Hassett, *Yeats and the Poetics of Hate* (Dublin, 1986), p. 68.
[10] *The Anxiety of Influence: a theory of poetry* (Oxford, 1973), p. 10. See Ramazani, *Yeats and the Poetry of Death*, pp. 9–13 for an astute general treatment of the theme.
[11] Peter Allt and Russell K. Alspach (eds.), *The Variorum Edition of the Poems of W. B. Yeats* (2nd edn., New York, 1966), p. 476.

Unlike the 'dying animal' (a phrase which also occurs in 'Sailing to Byzantium'), this suggests man's—or Yeats's—ability to arrange a posthumous existence for himself, by dictating the shape of his life from beyond the grave, as he effectively would do in *Last Poems*. His post-mortem energy is astounding and continues to produce some strange special effects. One of the oddest books written about him is apparently constructed around what Yeats would have done, or thought, or felt, during the Second World War, which actually broke out eight months after his death. Thus he is endowed with an active after-life (and incidentally convicted, more or less, as a committed Nazi).[12] This peculiar project, however off-beam in other directions, bears eccentric witness to the ability of the poet, somehow, to survive death.

It is tempting, as Jahan Ramazani has done, to identify very many of Yeats's poems as forms of elegy. The death-images come up from the very beginning. He seems sometimes to be afflicted by the delusion called 'Cotard's Syndrome', a *'délire des négations'* where the sufferer thinks that he has died and become a ghost. If we are to trust Yeats's memories of his youth, he was preoccupied by death, dreamt of it, fantasised it, was surrounded by it; he was even, with his sallow colouring and jet black hair, christened 'King Death' by his schoolmates. More often noted are the images of death in his early poetry, from the very beginning in 'Time and the Witch Vivien' through to the poems to Maud Gonne and Olivia Shakespear in the 1890s. An early poem to Gonne fantasised that she died while abroad in a strange land, and was nailed into her coffin; he thoughtfully sent it to her in France, where she was in fact perfectly well, but recovering from an 'illness' which was probably a pregnancy. She found this kind of solicitude very funny. Still, the titles of the poems in his first collections show a decided death-fixation.[13] Another poem of this period was titled 'He Wishes That His Beloved Were Dead'. Frivolously, this might be seen as a reflection of the uncomfortable fact that, as Yeats himself put it on another occasion, 'There is always something in our enemy that we like and something in our sweet-heart that we dislike.'[14] But more profoundly, this is in a tradition very much of its time—the personae of Yeats's love-poems of the 1890s suggest Pelleas and Melisande or Tristan and Isolde, or indeed Axel and Sara rather than the more robust *alter egos* whom he would later choose. For these images, death is a central part of

---

[12] W. J. Mc Cormack, *Blood Kindred: W. B. Yeats, the life, the death, the politics* (London, 2005).
[13] As pointed out by Ramazani, *Yeats and the Poetry of Death*, pp. 19–20.
[14] W. B. Yeats, *Mythologies*, ed. Warwick Gould and Deirdre Toomey (London, 2005), p. 51.

their love. He reports with satisfaction in *The Celtic Twilight*: 'It is said that no-one that has a song made about them will ever live long'.[15] Love-poems are proleptic epitaphs. Freud's belief that 'the aim of all life is death' is oddly close to Yeats's early linkage of love and death. 'All our lives long, as da Vinci says, we long, thinking it is but the moon that we long [for], for our destruction, and how, when we meet [it] in the shape of a most fair woman, can we do less than leave all others for her? Do we not seek our dissolution upon her lips?'[16] 'Leaving all others' is not just abandonment here, and dissolution is not just the little death. It means embracing the void, and leaving the servants to get on with the messy business of living. Yeats would leave this phase behind him decisively (think of Crazy Jane); but many of the poems in his canonical collection of 1899, *The Wind Among the Reeds*, identify love with the sacrifice of death, embellished with a heavy-breathing Christological imagery which sometimes suggests Wilde or Simeon Solomon.

> When the flaming lute-thronged angelic door is wide;
> When an immortal passion breathes in mortal clay;
> Our hearts endure the scourge, the plaited thorns, the way
> Crowded with bitter faces, the wounds in palm and side,
> The vinegar-heavy sponge, the flowers by Kedron stream;
> We will bend down and loosen our hair over you,
> That it may drop faint perfume, and be heavy with dew,
> Lilies of death-pale hope, roses of passionate dream.[17]

Death and resurrection is not just a Christian framework. It is a recurrent theme in Fraser's *The Golden Bough*, a key book for Yeats, where death is often linked to rituals of power—a theme Yeats explored to ringing effect in 'Parnell's Funeral'. But the death-trope in the early poems is also coming more immediately from Yeats's immersion in the Young Ireland poets of the 1830s and 1840s, to whose work John and Ellen O'Leary had introduced him, notably Thomas Davis and James Clarence Mangan. Death keeps coming up in Davis's poetry: in the sense of dying for Ireland, in lamentations for the death of others, and finally in previsions of his own death, which he referred to as 'a very comfortable sort of phantasy and sweet dream'. His first published poem was called 'My Grave'. Mangan is even more preoccupied with spectral visions and the

---

[15] Ibid., p. 17: Yeats related this to Raftery and Mary Hynes.
[16] W. B. Yeats, *Memoirs: Autobiography—First Draft; Journal*, ed. Denis Donoghue (London, 1972), p. 88. This goes back to a much earlier invocation in 'The Tables of the Law': see *Mythologies* (2005), pp. 197, 416 (n. 20).
[17] 'The Travail of Passion', *Variorum Poems*, p, 172.

morbid necessity of death: the presence of the pale companion is a necessary proof both of poetic credibility and nationalist commitment. Yeats's poetry of the 1890s is similarly nationalist in tone to these avatars. But there is a difference. When he writes perhaps his most fervent nationalist poem 'To Ireland in the Coming Times' (and places it as the *envoi* to his first collection), it is not about dying for Ireland. It is, in a sense, written from beyond the grave—not only in the sense that the poet is calling to the future, from a point when he will arguably be no more—but also in the sense that he is claiming a fusion between nationalism, poetic art (as specifically represented by Davis and Mangan), and the supernatural sphere. We must accept that this dimension matters for Yeats. The mysteries of magic are invoked as well as the sacred traditions. What is striking in 'To Ireland in the Coming Times' is its energetic forward drive—very different from the narcoleptic atmosphere of some of his other-worldly poems of the same period. What he is beginning to eradicate, even this early, is the sense of pathos which he would come to dislike in much Romantic poetry.

Still, several of Yeats's best-known poems are formal elegies, and much attention has been paid to his use of the elegy form—which is, in the work of some critics, interpreted with a reckless inclusiveness.[18] The genesis of these elegies is very often closely linked to dislocations in his life, such as the slow decline of his old friend Mabel Beardsley from cancer. Yeats's visits to her bedside in Hampstead are the subject of his series 'On A Dying Lady', tactfully withheld from publication until she actually did finally die. Death here appears inconsistently—sometimes the 'Great Enemy', sometimes a parent calling a child in from a half-finished game. The death of Synge provoked a great prose elegy, and constant references in poems; the death of Robert Gregory brought forth an unambiguous instruction from his mother Augusta Gregory to write one, which took several stabs to get right. (Some of Yeats's elegies are, in fact, among his least successful published poems: 'In Memory of Alfred Pollexfen', and his first effort for Robert Gregory, 'Shepherd and Goatherd' are poems so constrained and forced that it is hard to read them without wincing.)

Yeats was also much inclined towards the anticipatory elegy.[19] One of the strangest aspects of his relationship with Augusta Gregory was the way that, in his poetry, he 'aged' her before her time. As early as 1923, in

---

[18] As in Helen Vendler, 'Four Elegies' in A. N. Jeffares (ed.), *Yeats, Sligo and Ireland: essays to mark the 21st Yeats International Summer School* (Gerrard's Cross, 1980), pp. 216–33.

[19] Ramazani uses the phrase 'pre-mortem elegies': *Yeats and the Poetry of Death*, p. 50.

his speech receiving the Nobel Prize at Stockholm, he described her, to her fury, as 'sinking into the infirmity of old age', and had to change it. In 1929, three years before her death, he wrote 'Coole Park, 1929', clearly anticipating her death and the death of the house; 'Coole Park and Ballylee, 1931' reads in a similar way. This may have been a function of his fear of her actual death; when it came, in May 1932, it caused a major creative block and he wrote no poetry for months.[20] But he did write a great prose elegy for her, which is one of his most moving compositions. In a sense, ever since those early poems imagining Maud Gonne's death, he had been practising elegies; and though Gonne would outlive him by many years, his chilling late poem 'A Bronze Head' is a last proleptic elegy to the other enduring female relationship founded in his youth. Jon Stallworthy calls it 'a poem about Maud Gonne alive and dead and alive-in-death'.[21] If Yeats is placing Gonne at the entrance to the tomb, long before her time, he had been doing something like this ever since he met her.

Yeats's belief in supernaturalism was one of the ways that allowed death to be incorporated—even welcomed—into his work. This too is deeply woven into his background and early life. Fairies are, as Andrew Lang had established to his and many people's satisfaction, ghosts of the dead and Yeats's longstanding interest in them is linked to his belief in more abstruse and demanding theories of supernatural survival.[22] I have written before of the attraction felt by Irish Protestants to super-naturalism and Philippe Ariès, the pioneer chronicler of death, has made the same observation about the Protestant subculture in France.[23] Yeats's attitude to formal religion is complex and in its way very Irish—particularly his feelings towards Catholicism (attraction, resistance, respect, repulsion, fascination). When seriously ill, he told his great friend Dorothy Wellesley, he tended to become Christian 'and that is abominable'; though she, sharp for her purposes, told him that several of his pronouncements about Purgatory and the journey of the soul would

---

[20] See my article 'Yeats and the Death of Lady Gregory' in *Irish University Review*, 34 no. 1 (Spring/Summer 2004) (a special issue on Lady Gregory, ed. Anne Fogarty), 109–21.
[21] Jon Stallworthy, *Between the Lines: W. B. Yeats's poetry in the making* (Oxford, 1963), p. 221.
[22] See Kathleen Raine, 'Hades Wrapped in Cloud' in George Mills Harper (ed.), *Yeats and the Occult* (London, 1975), especially pp. 86–107.
[23] See my Chattterton lecture 'Protestant Magic: W. B. Yeats and the Spell of Irish History', *Proccedings of the British Academy*, 75 (1989), pp. 243–66 reprinted in my *Paddy and Mr Punch: connections in Irish and English history* (London, 1993), pp. 212–32; and Philippe Ariès, *The Hour of Our Death*, trans. Helen Weaver (New York, 1982), p. 462.

'hurry us back into the great arms of the Roman Catholic Church'. ('His only retort was his splendid laugh.')[24] But having in his youth, as he himself said, a religious temperament but no religion, his ventures into the Order of the Golden Dawn and other occult involvements is not a surprise. And here too, death is a central part; indeed, a ritual death and resurrection was part of the initiation rites of the Order, which Yeats both underwent—at Clipstone Street, in January 1893—and conducted others through. The idea of death as a two-way door, through which one could pass and return if initiated to the necessary degree (like the mirrors in Cocteau's *Orphée*), would recur in his mind and his work (the liminal position of Cuchulain in *The Only Jealousy of Emer* is just one example).

Again, *The Golden Bough* is important here. The idea of death as a process, and quite a lengthy one, is central to the Greek dramatic imagination, and much of Yeats's work rediscovers it, from *The Wanderings of Oisin* and *The Celtic Twilight* through to *Purgatory*.[25] But it is, for him, not just a question of an aesthetically useful exercise or technique: it is a matter of belief. Supernatural belief and occult practice accompanied Yeats throughout his life, and any understanding of his work has to accept this. (It is why some critics remain so deaf to him.) He himself wrote about this in an essay—haunting, in every sense—called 'Swedenborg, Mediums and the Desolate Places'. This defends (among much else) his interest in attending seances. 'That is an absorbing drama, though if my readers begin to seek it they will spoil it, for its gravity and simplicity depend on all, or all but all, believing that the dead are near.'[26] He was writing this long essay in 1914–15, when sharing a cottage with Ezra Pound, and both poets were deep in the study of ghosts, especially in Japanese literature and the classics. Pound suggested a ringing phrase from the *Odyssey* (where Odysseus meets his mother in the Shades): 'The departing soul hovers about "as a dream"'. Though Yeats chose alternative Homeric lines, ghosts and dreams pervade not only Pound's 'Three Cantos' but Yeats's Swedenborg essay and the marvellous meditation, *Per Amica Silentia Lunae*, which followed it.[27] ('Ghosts and Dreams' was, in fact, the title of a controversial lecture Yeats gave on All Hallows Eve 1913 in Dublin and reprised in London the next year: in it he endorsed

---

[24] Dorothy Wellesley (ed.), *Letters on Poetry from W. B. Yeats to Dorothy Wellesley* (Oxford, 1940), p. 195.
[25] Mackintosh, *Dying Acts*, pp. 19 ff.
[26] W. B. Yeats, *Explorations* (London, 1962), pp. 30–1.
[27] See James Longenbach, *Stone Cottage: Pound, Yeats and Modernism* (Oxford, 1988), p. 245.

'spiritism' rather than telepathy or 'subliminal memory' as the origin of psychic manifestations.)[28] In his youth Yeats discovered—via Blake—the eighteenth-century seer Emanuel Swedenborg, who remained an inspiration (and may have influenced Yeats's later interest in Tantric sex). He also, with his image of simultaneous worlds, the sense of death moving all around us, and the divine union of angels, provided Yeats with a sense in which ghosts were very real presences, especially at times of dislocation.[29] This could be after a personal catharsis, as in 'The Cold Heaven':

> Suddenly I saw the cold and rook-delighting heaven
> That seemed as though ice burned and was but the more ice,
> And thereupon imagination and heart were driven
> So wild that every casual thought of that and this
> Vanished, and left but memories that should be out of season
> With the hot blood of youth, of love crossed long ago;
> And I took all the blame out of all sense and reason,
> Until I cried and trembled and rocked to and fro,
> Riddled with light. Ah! When the ghost begins to quicken,
> Confusion of the death-bed over, is it sent
> Out naked on the roads, as the books say, and stricken
> By the injustice of the skies for punishment?[30]

Times of astrological conjunction, like Samhain, the Celtic festival that coincides with All Souls Night, preoccupied Yeats: the point when the boundaries dissolve between the Otherworld and this.[31] But it is clear that historical crisis also thinned the membrane between the living and the dead. This is a powerful theme in 'Meditations in Time of Civil War', and perhaps still more in 'Nineteen Hundred and Nineteen'. The idea inspired another Irish writer with a taste for the supernatural and a sense of history, Louis MacNeice, who conjures up an army of ghosts in 'Autumn Journal'. Elizabeth Bowen, would repeat exactly this theme in her novel about the London Blitz, *The Heat of the Day*, where the living

---

[28] Peter Kuch, '"Laying the Ghosts"?—W. B. Yeats's lecture on Ghosts and Dreams' in W. Gould (ed.), *Yeats Annual*, no. 5 (London, 1987), pp. 114–38.
[29] *Explorations*, pp. 32 ff. deals with Swedenborg; also see Marsha Keith Schuchard, *Why Mrs Blake Cried: William Blake and the sexual basis of spiritual vision* (London, 2006), especially chaps. 5, 6 and 9.
[30] *Variorum Poems*, p. 316. Heaney judges that 'The Cold Heaven' suggests that there is an overarching purpose to life, by its 'poetic action' as well as its content: 'Joy or Night', p. 149.
[31] Paul Muldoon relates this concept to 'All Souls' Night', using James McKillop's commentary, in *The End of the Poem: Oxford Lectures on Poetry* (London, 2006), p. 13. For further Yeatsian references to Samhain, see *Mythologies* (2005), pp. 81–2, 141–2.

walking down the newly bombed streets rub shoulders with the recently dead. 'Uncounted, [the dead] continued to move in shoals through the city day, pervading everything to be seen or heard or felt with their torn-off senses, drawing on this tomorrow they had expected—for death cannot be so sudden as all that.'[32]

Yeats would have agreed: famously, when asked in the Senate during a particularly tactless speech to 'leave the dead alone', he indignantly replied 'I would hate to leave the dead alone'. That was not what they were there for. And they were, of course, there. Ghosts inhabit his work with an odd persistence: whether lurching in unbidden like Robert Artisson in 'Nineteen Hundred and Nineteen' or summoned with full ritual, like the presences in 'All Souls Night'. His political poetry after the Rising also uses ghosts with dramatic immediacy, in 'The Rose Tree', the play *The Dreaming of the Bones*, and above all 'Sixteen Dead Men', where the dead 'converse bone to bone'.

> O but we talked at large before
> The sixteen men were shot,
> But who can talk of give and take,
> What should be and what not
> While those dead men are loitering there
> To stir the boiling pot?
>
> You say that we should still the land
> Till Germany's overcome;
> But who is there to argue that
> Now Pearse is deaf and dumb?
> And is their logic to outweigh
> MacDonagh's bony thumb?
>
> How could you dream they'd listen
> That have an ear alone
> For those new comrades they have found,
> Lord Edward and Wolfe Tone,
> Or meddle with our give and take
> That converse bone to bone?[33]

Later, in the 1930s, the ghost of Roger Casement would come beating at the door, like the Commendatore in 'Don Giovanni'. Other late poems, like 'The Municipal Gallery Revisited', obsessively call up the dead, and even interrogate them.

---

[32] Elizabeth Bowen, *The Heat of the Day* (London, 1949), pp. 86–7.
[33] *Variorum Poems*, p. 395.

By the last decade of his life, death was a constant presence in Yeats's life; he had faced it down twice by 1930, and it would recurrently threaten him. And from this time too, we find a preoccupation with an ancient phrase, which opens the great closing section of 'The Tower': 'Now shall I make my soul'.[34] The phrase deserves some attention: Yeats had an affection for it and it has a peculiarly Irish provenance. Dineen's great Irish dictionary gives it as a usage of the word 'anam', soul: 'ag deanamh a anma , making his peace with God, preparing for eternity'. Yeats's relationship with God was chequered, but he had a strong sense of eternity. And for him 'making one's soul' had a parallel meaning: creating one's consciousness.

> Now shall I make my soul,
> Compelling it to study
> In a learned school
> Till the wreck of body,
> Slow decay of blood,
> Testy delirium
> Or dull decrepitude,
> Or what worse evil come—
> The death of friends, or death
> Of every brilliant eye
> That made a catch in the breath—
> Seem but the clouds of the sky
> When the horizon fades;
> Or a bird's sleepy cry
> Among the deepening shades.[35]

We will hear that bird's cry again.

As Yeats journeyed towards death he 'made his soul' in a very deliberate way. Those serious illnesses in 1924, 1927–8 and 1929–30 produced a very distinct creative reaction. As he noted himself, the experience brought on a sort of euphoria.[36] He finished *A Vision*, his extraordinary philosophy-cum-psychic handbook, while convalescing in Italy; he warmed himself into life in 1927 after very nearly dying at Rapallo by writing 'Byzantium' and finding a new inspiration in Jonathan Swift

---

[34] Thomas R. Whitaker, *Swan and Shadow: Yeats's dialogue with history* (2nd edn., Washington, DC, 1989), p. 202, interprets it as a reference to artistic creativity only, but the colloquial Irish usage is clearly central to Yeats's theme. See also A. N. Jeffares, *A New Commentary on the Poems of W. B. Yeats* (London, 1984), p. 117, glossing the poem 'Beggar to Beggar Cried', where the phrase also occurs.
[35] *Variorum Poems*, p. 416.
[36] Vividly expressed in a letter of 29 Nov. 1927 to Olivia Shakespear: Wade, *Letters*, pp. 732–3.

(whose ghost would take a starring role in one of Yeats's best plays about the continuance of life after death). Death and enlightenment had always been linked in his mind; long before, in *The Hour Glass*, the Wise Man proclaims

> I can explain all now
> Only when our hold on life is troubled,
> Only in spiritual terror can the Truth
> Come through the broken mind.[37]

The insights conferred when approaching the end might be seen as consolation; but it should also be remembered that for Yeats, the end was not the end. Time and again, he had — so he thought — held in his hand the proofs of a continued existence after death. His searches in the rituals of the Golden Dawn, his communion with occultist circles in Paris, his determined pursuit of mediums, are all closely recorded in his own writings, often in the most matter-of-fact manner. In 1903 he encountered the psychologist, philosopher and psychic researcher William James in Boston; Yeats had been taken to see James by a young academic, Fritz Robinson, who wrote down his recollection much later.

> Yeats withdrew with James to a table in a distant corner of the library, and they had a tete-a-tete which lasted throughout the call. As we left the house he said to me, 'Well, Robinson, this afternoon has been highly profitable. I have a magical formula which I have confided to the one man in the world who will be best able to use it.' [Robinson added:] I never heard of it again. I have sometimes regretted that I never asked James about it. But I had a feeling that I should be intruding on a solemn secret.[38]

What had they talked about? It was their only meeting. There is no account of it in James's twelve-volume correspondence. But Yeats, in his notes on Augusta Gregory's *Visions and Beliefs in the West of Ireland*, did mention that he had discussed with James accessing the world of the dead (as in the celebrated time-travelling account, *An Adventure*) and the idea of intersections between individual and subliminal memory.[39] The Otherworld was a preoccupation of James's as much as of Yeats's:

---

[37] Russell K. Alspach and Catherine C. Alspach (eds.), *The Variorum Edition of the Plays of W. B. Yeats* (London, 1966), p. 625.

[38] F. N. Robinson to Frank Hatch, 2 May 1965, in the possession of the late Professor F. S. Stewart. See John Kelly and Ronald Schuchard (eds.), *The Collected Letters of W. B. Yeats Volume III, 1901–1904* (Oxford, 1994), p. 509 for a useful note on Robinson and James.

[39] *Visions and Beliefs in the West of Ireland, collected and arranged by Lady Gregory, with two essays and notes by W. B. Yeats* (London, 1920), p. 351; Anne Moberley and Eleanor Jourdain, *An Adventure* (London, 1911).

just at this time he was much absorbed in the reactions to Frederic Myers's *Human Personality and its Survival of Bodily Death*.[40] James was a more sceptical psychic researcher than Yeats, for whom the dead obligingly continued to come through at seances, including his father and his uncle George Pollexfen. In 1913, he owed to a medium the welcome news that his girlfriend Mabel Dickinson was not—as she claimed—pregnant. The psychic wireless-machine of David Wilson had briefly convinced Yeats in 1917 that he had found irrefutable proof of continued existence across the Styx. Above all, the voices mediated by his wife's automatic writing had brought wisdom from the land of the dead.[41] Death was very clearly not the end. This could intersect with certain aspects of Christian belief. In the middle of an interminable philosophical correspondence with his friend Thomas Sturge Moore in 1928, he was capable of tartly remarking: 'By the bye, please don't quote your brother [G. E. Moore the philosopher] again till you have asked him this question: "How do you account for the fact that when the tomb of St Teresa was opened her body exuded miraculous oil and smelt of violets?" If he cannot account for such primary facts he knows nothing.'[42] But the 'primary facts' and wisdoms that came from mediums, the Golden Dawn, and Swedenborg were more convincing still. And this continued throughout his life (just as his membership of, and preoccupation with, the Golden Dawn lasted much longer than used to be thought).

From the early 1930s, his sense of death was intensified by the deaths of so many friends and collaborators—George Moore, AE, above all Augusta Gregory. Significantly, his evocation of her in *Dramatis Personae*, where he compares her integrity and nobility of spirit to George Moore's frivolity and malice, draws upon a powerful imagery of ghosts, and incidentally starts with a generalisation very relevant to my subject:

> A writer must die every day he lives, be reborn as it is said in the Burial Service, an incorruptible self, that self opposite of all that he has named 'himself'.

---

[40] See Ignas K. Skrupselis and Elizabeth M. Berkeley (eds.), *The Correspondence of William James* (Charlottesville, VA, 1992–2004), vol. 10 (1902–5), p. 326.
[41] See my *Apprentice Mage*, pp 488–9; my *W. B. Yeats, A Life: II, The Arch-Poet, 1915–1939* (Oxford, 2003), pp 80–1, and chap. 3; also Yeats, *Autobiographies*, p. 124. Yeats's report on David Wilson's psychic wireless-machine is published in Christopher Blake's edited text in 'Ghosts in the Machine: Yeats and the Metallic Homunculus with transcripts of reports by W. B. Yeats and Edmund Dulac' (*Yeats's Collaborations: Yeats Annual No. 15: a Special Number* 2002, pp. 69–101.
[42] Ursula Bridge (ed.), *W. B. Yeats and T. Sturge Moore: their correspondence 1901–1937* (London, 1953), pp. 121–2. This preoccupation recurs in poems such as 'Oil and Blood' and 'Vacillation', *Variorum Poems*, 483, 499.

> George Moore, dreading the annihilation of an impersonal bleak realism, used life like a medieval ghost making a body for itself out of the drifting dust and vapour; and have I not sung in describing guests at Coole—'There one that ruffled in a manly pose, For all his timid heart'- that one myself? Synge was a sick man picturing energy, a doomed man picturing gaiety; Lady Gregory, in her life much artifice, in her nature much pride, was born to see the glory of the world in a peasant mirror.[43]

By the time he wrote this great reflection on the way that artistic genius meets its other self, the writer's block imposed by Gregory's death had been cleared and the poems he was producing were astonishing in many ways. They reflect the way that an artist and his Daimon are halves of the same whole, a thought which also lies behind his judgement of Gregory, and recalls the philosophies of Swedenborg and Blake.

Yeats's late poems also raise the question I mentioned earlier: the issue penetratingly addressed by Edward Said as 'late style'. In this last book, Said advances some fascinating ideas about how an artist towards the end of his or her life often moves into a radical phase. Ibsen is instanced, in a way that can only make one think of Yeats; Ibsen's final works, Said says,

> tear apart the career and the artist's craft and reopen the questions of meaning, success and progress that the artist's late period is supposed to move beyond. Far from resolution, then, Ibsen's last plays suggest an angry and disturbed artist for whom the medium of drama provides an occasion to stir up more anxiety, tamper irrevocably with the possibility of closure, and leave the audience more perplexed and unsettled than before.[44]

In his consideration of late style Said never mentions Yeats, which seems an oversight, though we should realise that this is unfinished work—dictated, in fact, in a sense from beyond the grave. (Another surprising omission is Philip Roth, whose own late style is such a compelling departure, and whose recent books are studded with references to Yeats.) But one reason for the omission of these and other writers is that what Said in fact wanted to write about is music. Here too, the assonance with Yeats is irresistible, especially when Said quotes Adorno on Beethoven's late works—the deliberate waywardness, the discontinuities, the dislocated modernity (if one can use the word) of the last piano sonatas, for instance. As Adorno puts it, 'The maturity of the late works does not resemble the kind one finds in fruit. They are . . . not round, but furrowed,

---

[43] *Autobiographies*, p. 457.
[44] Edward Said, *On Late Style: music and literature against the grain* (London, 2006), p. 7.

even ravaged. Devoid of sweetness, bitter and spiny, they do not surrender themselves to mere delectation.'[45] The analysis is arresting: partly because of another effect of those late sonatas. Alfred Brendel, one of the supreme interpreters of these works, said once that the achievement of the 'Hammerklavier' sonata was the quality of the silence it created when the last note had died away. That deliberate sense of creating the receptive silence that follows is inseparable from Yeats's very late works: works written, in fact, on his deathbed.

Yeats's deathbed was a very active and indeed public place. Woody Allen once said that he wasn't afraid of dying, he just didn't want to be there when it happened. Yeats would have profoundly disagreed with this—as also with a rather different thinker, Ludwig Wittgenstein, who declared that death was 'not an event of life, not something lived through'.[46] Yeats's death was very much lived through, recorded, written about in parallel by himself, controlled. Long before he had written about the death of Synge: 'It was as though we and the things about us died away from him, and not he from us.'[47] He ensured the same kind of continuing presence for himself.

It has been established that the inspiration (or at least jumping-off point) for Yeats's own epitaph-poem, 'Under Ben Bulben', was an essay on Rilke's ideas about death. These revolved around finality and annihilation—wood consumed by flame—and anger at the process. Yeats found this unsympathetic, as he would probably have found Dylan Thomas's injunction to 'rage against the dying of the light', or the unrelenting grimness of Larkin's 'Aubade'—which Seamus Heaney has brilliantly set in counterpoint to Yeats's 'The Man and the Echo'.[48] Paul Muldoon has recently written about the 'end of the poem' but the ends of poets provide an engrossing subject in themselves—especially for those whose work constantly anticipates it, like Shelley, or compulsively joke about it, like Emily Dickinson. Biographers should approach the deaths of their subjects with great care: Hermione Lee has written a brilliantly admonitory essay on the assumptions and manipulations that the

---

[45] Ibid., p. 12.
[46] Quoted by Ramazani, *Yeats and the Poetry of Death*, p. 1.
[47] *Autobiographies*, p. 511.
[48] Heaney, 'Joy or Night', pp. 153–63. For Yeats and Rilke see Yeats to Dorothy Wellesley, 15 Aug. [1938], *Collected Letters* (InteLex version), Accession no. 7790: partly in Wade (ed.), *Letters*, p. 913. See also Jon Stallworthy, *Vision and Revision in Yeats's Last Poems* (Oxford, 1969), pp. 148–9.

death-bed scene involves.[49] But sometimes poets' deaths seem almost unbearably apposite to the circumstances that inspired them in life: Robert Lowell's heart-attack in the back of a taxi at Kennedy Airport, returning to his first wife Elizabeth Hardwick, the suicides of Berryman and Plath, the 'torn-off' endings of Randall Jarrell, under a bus, or Theodore Roethke in a swimming-pool, or Chatterton as imagined by Watts. There are also the deaths in far-flung places of Byron, Rimbaud and Brooke, oddly conflating exoticism, idealism and mundaneness (rather like their poetry). Yeats's death also took place far from home, on the French Riviera. But he made it the site of an exploration back into his beginnings, writing in those final weeks a series of works which interrogated the origins of his inspiration, right back to Ireland in the heroic age. One thinks again of that quotation from Homer which Pound gave to Yeats, 'the departing soul hovers like a dream'; and we remember, as Yeats himself had put it in a key passage of *A Vision*, that leaving life involves a re-visioning of all that has made us what we are.

> In the *Dreaming Back* the *Spirit* is compelled to live over and over again the events that had most moved it; there can be nothing new, but the old events stand forth in a light which is dim or bright according to the intensity of the passion that accompanied them. They occur in the order of their intensity or luminosity, the more intense first, and the painful are commonly the more intense, and repeat themselves again and again. In the *Return*, upon the other hand, the *Spirit* must live through past events in the order of their occurrence, because it is compelled by the *Celestial Body* to trace every passionate event to its cause until all are related and understood, turned into knowledge, made a part of itself. All that keeps the *Spirit* from its freedom may be compared to a knot that has to be untied or to an oscillation or a violence that must end in a return to equilibrium.[50]

The notion of re-living the key moments of one's life in reverse order at the moment of death has been exploited by countless biographers since Lytton Strachey's flowery conclusion to *Queen Victoria*.[51] More profoundly, these ideas about the spirit slowly detaching itself from life had been addressed in several of Yeats's works—obviously *Purgatory*, but perhaps more relevantly *The Only Jealousy of Emer*, a play written when he was himself being torn between his competing relationships with three women. Here he places his *alter ego* Cuchulain in a liminal state between

---

[49] 'How to End It All' in *Body Parts: essays on life-writing* (London, 2005), pp. 200–18.
[50] W. B. Yeats, *A Vision* [1937 version] (London, 1962), p. 226.
[51] Hermione Lee, 'How to End It All', pp. 207–9, deals with maladroit versions by John Halperin (for Jane Austen), D. J. Taylor (for George Orwell) and Peter Ackroyd (for Charles Dickens).

the next world and this one, called back into life by a woman's sacrifice—death and resurrection once again. And on his deathbed he chose to return to Cuchulain and finish his story. In his play 'The Death of Cuchulain' and his nearly-last poem, 'Cuchulain Comforted', both completed at Roquebrune in the last weeks of his life, he explored the hero's leavetaking of life and anticipated his reception into the Shades. To make Cuchulain more emphatically his *alter ego*, he ages him (the Cuchulain of mythology dies young) and presents his death as the necessary fate for a man out of joint with his times, and the decadent culture which has invaded the world. Much in this short play (especially its jarring prologue) echoes the uncomfortable reflections which Yeats has just committed to *On the Boiler*. *The Death of Cuchulain*, in fact, presents a classic 'late style' conundrum: critics like Vendler, Kermode and others disagree radically on how to evaluate it.[52] (His wife, a sensible woman and a good critic, just thought it 'a bad play'.) But for our purposes, the circumstances of the play's conception are what matter. Long before, in *Per Amica Silentia Lunae*, he had written of heroes who claim their deaths as essentially their own, to be lived (or died) on their own terms, and had written—with eerie prescience—that perhaps the deaths of such heroes 'will, it may be, haunt me on my own death-bed'.[53] Twenty years after writing this, he made it come true.

The way he approached this is of a piece with his belief in tragic joy and the need to meet death with dignity rather than excessive emotion, much less sentimentality. (This was connected with his firm decision not to have a large-scale ceremonial leavetaking in Dublin: 'I write my poems for the Irish people but I am damned if I will have them at my funeral'.)[54] Tragedy, Augusta Gregory had told him long before, must be a joy to the man who dies. Yeats himself thought it must break down the dykes that separate man from man.[55]

---

[52] Frank Kermode considered it 'perhaps Yeats's finest play': *Romantic Images*, 2nd edn. (London, 1961), p. 82. On the other hand, Helen Vendler finds it 'disconnected and jerky', the end-product of Yeats's effort to make plays for a 'coterie theatre', and incapable of achieving 'tragic joy': *Yeats's 'Vision' and the Later Plays* (Oxford, 1963), pp. 236–46.

[53] *Explorations*, 416

[54] To Dorothy Wellesley, 7 Sept. 1938 Harry Ransom Humanities Research Center, University of Texas at Austin; see *Collected Letters* (Intellex), Accession no. 7300.

[55] 'The heroes of Shakespeare convey to us through their looks, or through the metaphorical patterns of their speech, the sudden enlargement of their vision, their ecstasy at the approach of death, "She should have died hereafter", "Of many million kisses, the poor last", "Absent thee from felicity awhile"; they have become God or Mother Goddess, the pelican, "My baby at my breast", but all must be cold; no actress has ever sobbed when she played Cleopatra, even the

But there is, of course, another dimension to all this. As he grew older, the dead were all around him; he wrote in the Introduction to the *Oxford Book of Modern Verse* in 1937 'we find it more and more difficult to separate ourselves from the dead when we commit them to the grave'.[56] The Swedenborgian idea of love beyond the grave, and the intercourse of angels, added to the interest, and is dealt with in Yeats's poem 'Ribh at the Tomb of Baile and Ailinn'.[57] (Sex and the dead, again.) It is important to remember that Yeats's death was the death of someone who believed in psychic survival. The deaths of believers in spiritualism are not, apparently, all approached in the same way. Yeats's old friend and fellow-occultist Florence Farr, approaching death from cancer twenty-odd years before, had written to him at great length of Hindu beliefs about the journey of the soul out of life, and the possibilities of liberation at the moment of death; but as her own death approached she wrote jauntily to her other old lover, GBS, that her own awaited liberation had got rid of 'my secret horror of death, I mean of the death-bed scene—I have been through with it once or twice & it's nothing at all'.[58] (Yeats wrote of her death in 'All Souls Night'.) The death of another prominent psychic researcher, Arthur Conan Doyle, was considered by his spiritualist family as an incident of very little significance; at a great memorial service in the Albert Hall, his wife and children sat smiling on the platform beside an (apparently) empty chair which they were quite convinced held his liberated spirit. Rosamond Lehmann spent her last days astrally travelling from her bed, convinced (inaccurately) that she was going to live for an extremely long time. Yeats himself had written 'It is even possible that being is only possessed completely by the dead',[59] and the notion that death was actually a non-event is perhaps the crudest reduction of spiritualism.

---

shallow brain of a producer has never thought of such a thing. The supernatural is present, cold winds blow across our hands, upon our faces, the thermometer falls, and because of that cold we are hated by journalists and groundlings. There may be in this or that detail painful tragedy, but in the whole work none. I have heard Lady Gregory say, rejecting some play in the modern manner sent to the Abbey Theatre, "Tragedy must be a joy to the man who dies"'. See also *Essays and Introductions* (London, 1961), pp. 522, 241.

[56] *The Oxford Book of Modern Verse 1892–1935, Chosen by W. B. Yeats* (Oxford, 1936), p. xx.
[57] See also *Explorations*, p. 34, for Swedenborg's version of the post-death state.
[58] Josephine Johnson (ed.), 'Florence Farr's Letters to W. B. Yeats 1912–1917' in Deirdre Toomey (ed.), *Yeats and Women: Yeats Annual No. 9, a special number* (London, 1992), pp. 241–2, 249.
[59] *Essays and Introductions*, p. 226.

But Yeats's own approach was not of this kind. Leaving life would be a process of considered detachment, as with the ancient Greeks.[60] His withdrawal to the Riviera, where he arranged to be surrounded by the women closest to him and to 'make his soul', is a moving and appropriate final act in the great drama of his life. William James once wrote that people who had devoted themselves to psychic research, like Myers and Hodgson, grew happier, stronger in personality, and handsomer as they approached death.[61] Yeats himself, in an unpublished draft for *A Vision*, wrote that Asiatic philosophy combined with psychic research prepared people to 'face death without flinching, perhaps even with joy'.[62] But at the very end the way he choreographed it did not depend upon the insights of the mediums and mystics whom he had pursued in Boston suburbs or up Soho staircases and defended in essays such as 'Swedenborg, Mediums and the Desolate Places'. Ideas of reincarnation, which were much tangled up in the arcane theories of after-life shared with him by Farr and others, are notable by their absence. In fact, though Yeats's anticipatory epitaph for himself, 'Under Ben Bulben', contains some implications about reincarnation, it is notable that this reassuring theory features very little in his elegies and his writings about death—with the possible exception of 'News for the Delphic Oracle'. But an aspect of 'Under Ben Bulben' that has not been remarked is that it returns to and reworks that early invocation of Irish nationalism, 'To Ireland in the Coming Times'—in metre, language and theme.

As the end approached, the presence invoked in poems like 'Cuchulain Comforted' is Dante (also chosen as a guide into the Shades by poets as diverse as Pound, Eliot, Lowell and Heaney). Until late in life Yeats invoked Dante carefully, but sparingly, and mostly in his prose.[63] Pound, however, had been influential here as elsewhere. In the end, Yeats's

---

[60] Mackintosh, *Dying Acts*, pp. 20 ff.
[61] *Memories and Studies* (London, 1911), p. 194. Cf 'The Apparitions', *Variorum Poems*, p. 624.
>When a man grows old his joy
>Grows more deep day after day,
>His empty heart is full at length,
>But he has need of all that strength
>Because of the increasing night
>That opens her mystery and fright.
>*Fifteen apparitions have I seen;*
>*The worst a coat upon a coat-hanger.*

[62] Hazard Adams, *Blake and Yeats: the contrary vision* (Ithaca, 1955), p. 302.
[63] See Stephen Paul Ellis, 'Yeats and Dante', *Comparative Literature*, 33, no. 1 (Winter 1981), 1–17.

own continued existence was to be dictated by his poetic masters and his own creative bedrock of inspiration. This is the recurring message of 'Last Poems'. By this I do not mean everything comprehensively gathered into the section of *Collected Poems* called by that name, but the nineteen literally last poems which he himself saw as an entity and whose arrangement preoccupied him on his deathbed. It is a remarkable list: 'Under Ben Bulben', 'Three Songs to One Burden', 'The Black Tower', 'Cuchulain Comforted', 'Three Marching Songs', 'In Tara's Halls', 'The Statues', 'News for the Delphic Oracle', 'Long-legged Fly', 'A Bronze Head', 'A Stick of Incense', 'Hound Voice', 'John Kinsella's Lament for Mrs Mary Moore', 'High Talk', 'The Apparitions', 'A Nativity', 'Man and the Echo', 'The Circus Animals' Desertion', and 'Politics'. To which can be added the poems from *On the Boiler*: 'Why Should Old Men Not Be Mad?', 'Crazy Jane on the Mountain' and 'Avalon'.

These works have been marvellously clarified by the work of scholars such as Jon Stallworthy and James Pethica. Their order, partially dictated by Yeats in perhaps one of his last conscious acts before slipping into a coma, has been much argued about, as has their varying states of accomplishment. Not all are as achieved and successful as 'Long-legged Fly' or 'The Circus Animals' Desertion'. It is the affirmation of their message that counts, and the eerie way that they arc back to his early inspirations, and even ballad forms, while simultaneously asserting that edge of dislocation, that bracing jolt, that deceptive simplicity of language, which Adorno identifies with Beethoven's late style, or Said with Ibsen's. As in Yeats's first work, inspired by Celtic mythology, horsemen ride out of the sides of mountains, revelation is at hand, and the dead are all around us—as 'buried men' thrust back into life. The old inspiration of Hindu mysticism recurs too, eclectically combined with Zen Buddhism. Above all, the prophecy of 'The Tower' is coming true. At the end of *The Death of Cuchulain*, Cuchulain's wife Emer pauses at the end of her mourning dance and there are heard a few faint bird cries: a sign that her hero–husband has passed into the shades. The poem 'Cuchulain Comforted' follows him there and we leave the hero joining the world of shrouds in Dante's wood of the dead: among a company of outcasts who 'had changed their throats and had the throats of birds'. He died days after completing the poem.

Yeats's death is in its own way an extraordinary achievement, for which some at least of his obituarists could not forgive him; several of his death notices implicitly censure him for not dying in a state of abject repentance. Much of the material of the late poems was deemed offensive, as was his own supernaturalist faith. While this attitude moderated in Ireland by the time of his reburial in 1948, some of his admirers continued to fret: W. H. Auden's marvellous elegy fixed in print the idea of Yeats's genius competing with his 'silliness'. It could be argued, however, that Yeats's esoteric beliefs equipped him both for life and for death in unexpected ways; and his method of 'making his soul' had assonances not only with the Christianity of his childhood, but with the classical virtues which inform his work throughout. This is echoed in the great late poem 'The Man and the Echo'. It is set in the Sligo landscape of his youth, with a man (called in the first draft 'Poet') 'shouting a secret to the stone' in a hidden chasm on Knocknarea. It might be claimed as Yeats's quintessential death-poem and the concluding section runs:

> While man can still his body keep
> Wine or love drug him to sleep,
> Waking he thanks the Lord that he
> Has body and its stupidity,
> But body gone he sleeps no more
> And till his intellect grows sure
> That all's arranged in one clear view
> Pursues the thoughts that I pursue,
> Then stands in judgement on his soul,
> And, all work done, dismisses all
> Out of intellect and sight
> And sinks at last into the night.
>
> *Echo.* Into the night.

Most poets would end it there. But in a characteristic 'late style' swerve Yeats gives to the man's voice a closing note of concreteness which establishes what he called elsewhere 'the desolation of reality'. The man replies to the Echo:

> O Rocky Voice
> Shall we in that great night rejoice?
> What do we know but that we face
> One another in this place?
> But hush, for I have lost the theme,
> Its joy or night seem but a dream;
> Up there some hawk or owl has struck,
> Dropping out of sky or rock,
> A stricken rabbit is crying out,
> And its cry distracts my thought.[64]

---

[64] *Variorum Poems*, pp. 632–3.

That audacious note of uncertainty makes this a masterpiece of Yeats's late style. The same tone comes through a fragment from a letter he wrote to his friend Elizabeth Pelham about three weeks before he died.

> I know for certain my time will not be long. I have put away everything that can be put away that I may speak what I have to speak, & I find my expression is a part of 'study'. In two or three weeks—I am now idle that I may rest after writing much verse—I will begin to write my most fundamental thoughts & the arrangement of thought which I am convinced will complete my studies. I am happy and I think full of energy, of an energy I had despaired of. It seems to me that I have found what I wanted. When I try to put all into a phrase I say, 'man can embody truth but he cannot know it.' I must embody it in the completion of my life. The abstract is not life and everywhere draws out its contradictions. You can refute Hegel but not the Saint or the song of sixpence.[65]

It is beautifully of a piece with all he was writing as he headed into the shades. The 'Song of Sixpence' also features in an abandoned epilogue to 'The Death of Cuchulain'. (The note reads: 'Four and Twenty blackbirds—the pie—the sixpence—the ry [sic] & the pocket—nothing to do with each other—an untrue story and yet immortal.')[66] We long to know more, but the letter quoted above is a fragment—which has only survived because its recipient quoted it in a letter to Yeats's widow. Elizabeth Pelham was one of Yeats's great confidantes in his last years; endearingly eccentric to the end, she died in a crowded London flat in 1975. 'She kept everything', her nephew told me, 'tons of letters and papers. They filled a whole skip in Mecklenburgh Square.' The biographer winces in agony at the thought of the rest of *that* letter, and so much else, blowing around the streets of Bloomsbury. But Yeats would have felt it hardly mattered: creatively speaking, he had made his soul. Long before his death, prophetic as ever, he remarked 'If you don't express yourself you walk after you're dead. The great thing is to go empty to the grave.'[67]

---

[65] 4 Jan. 1939: Wade, *Letters*, p. 922.
[66] W. B. Yeats, *The Death of Cuchulain: Manuscript Materials, including the author's final text*, edited by Phillip L. Marcus (Ithaca, 1982), pp. 8–9.
[67] An interview with Louise Morgan in June 1931: Louise Morgan, *Writers at Work* (London, 1931), pp. 1–9, and E. H. Mikhail, *Interviews and Recollections* (London, 1977), 2. 199–204 at p. 203. My thanks to Warwick Gould for pointing out that this remark can be read as a gloss on 'Crazy Jane and the Journeyman' (*Variorum Poems*, p. 511).

ALBERT RECKITT ARCHAEOLOGICAL LECTURE

Recovering Maya Civilisation

NORMAN HAMMOND
Fellow of the Academy

THE MAYA CREATED one of the most notable and surprising civilisations of the ancient world, in what are now the Yucatan Peninsula of southern Mexico and the adjacent countries of Guatemala, Belize, and the western fringes of Honduras and El Salvador. Best known from great cities such as Tikal, Copan, Palenque and Chichén Itzá, which were first explored in the nineteenth century by scholars including John Lloyd Stephens, Alfred Maudslay and Teobert Maler, the Maya reached their apogee in the Classic Period of *c.* AD 250–900, when a multiplicity of small polities ruled by divine kings flourished and fought across this part of tropical Central America (Hammond 2000; Martin and Grube 2000; Sharer 2006; Fig. 1). This was followed by the Postclassic, ending with the Spanish conquest of the mid-sixteenth century, and preceded by a Preclassic (or Formative) period extending back to the beginnings of settled farming villages in the second millennium BC. In this lecture I discuss three successive themes: the origins of a settled society; the emergence of a complex literate civilisation in the latter part of the first millennium BC in the Maya Lowlands; and the wider understanding of that culture's apogee in the middle centuries of the following millennium, before its demise in the tenth century AD.

The Maya area has three major regions: the volcanic and metamorphic highlands of Chiapas and southern Guatemala, extending down to the narrow Pacific coastal plain and dominated by a chain of dormant and still-active volcanoes up to 4,265 m in elevation; the flat, arid limestone platform of the northern Yucatan Peninsula, where annual rainfall

---

Read at the Academy 15 November 2006.

Proceedings of the British Academy **151**, 361–385. © The British Academy 2007.

Figure 1. The Maya Area, with the locations of important sites (from Sharer 2006).

rarely exceeds 500 mm, supporting a low scrub forest, and where the karstic landscape allows access to water only through sinkholes (*cenotes*) and caves reaching the subterranean water table; and the central region of Belize, the Petén of northern Guatemala, and northern Chiapas. In this area of hilly limestone ranges there is abundant rainfall (up to 4,000 mm), mainly in the June–November wet season, large permanent rivers such as the Usumacinta, the Río Hondo, and the Belize River, and a tropical rain forest vegetation with a canopy up to 40 m above the forest floor (Hammond 1982: 67–90).

Initial human penetration of the region occurred around 10,000 years ago, marked by scattered finds of Clovis-style spear-points (Hester *et al.* 1981; Gruhn and Bryan 1977; Zeitlin and Zeitlin 2000). Archaic hunter-collectors in later millennia were detected by MacNeish (Zeitlin and Zeitlin 2000) and subsequently by Rosenswig and Masson (2001) and Lohse *et al.* (2006) in Belize, and documented stratigraphically in Pacific Chiapas by Voorhies (2004). The first forest clearance by maize farmers occurred around 3500 BC on the Pacific coast and 2500 BC in Belize, documented by pollen cores but not so far by settlement sites.

Agriculture began late in Mesoamerica compared with the Old World: the single cereal staple, maize (*Zea mays*), was domesticated from *teosinte* (*Zea mexicana*) in central Mexico, and cultivated by around 5300 BC in Tabasco (Pohl *et al.* 2007), prior to 4000 BC in Oaxaca (Piperno and Flannery 2001) and in the high, dry Tehuacan Valley by 3600 BC, appearing in the humid tropical lowlands of the Maya area shortly thereafter, where farming necessitated forest clearance. Neff and colleagues (2006), coring along the lower Río Naranjo on the Pacific coast of Guatemala have found *landnám* events with dramatic vegetation changes beginning around 3500 BC, and becoming permanent around 1800–1500 BC as settled village culture began, in an era of drier climate. Investigations at Paso de la Amada in coastal Chiapas have documented this process, including early ceramics of the Barra complex, marked by highly decorated jars and bowls, perhaps used for brewing and consuming maize beer (*chicha*) in rites of social solidarity or competitive generosity (Clark and Blake 1994). Blake and Clark (1999) argue that the initial emergence of social inequality is a by-product of powerful men trying to increase their prestige vis-à-vis their local rivals, using material inducements such as feasting to acquire adherents and instil a sense of obligation (the 'big men' of Melanesia and the potlatchers of the Pacific Northwest are noted ethnographic examples, while the social mechanism involved applies almost universally). For such inequality to become hereditary, overcoming the homœostatic mechanisms that preserve egalitarian societies, symbolic alliances with potential rivals, a reliable surplus to fund continued loyalty, and a move to descent-based vertical, not horizontal association, are needed.

Structures at Paso de la Amada included a large apsidal house platform (Mound 6) with multiple construction phases supporting a timber-framed and palm-thatched superstructure, arguably a chiefly residence rather than a communal building. Lesure and Blake (2002: 21) argue, however, that the status differences indicated by house sizes are 'not linked to the sort of economic powers and privileges with which we might normally expect such a degree of differentiation to appear: the high-status inhabitants of platform buildings did not constitute a fully formed, coercive class'. A large ball court dating to $c.1400$ BC, the construction of which was certainly the result of directed collective action, suggests the emergence of factional and perhaps inter-community competition.

In the Maya Lowlands to the north, this process of settlement seems to have begun around a millennium later: Pohl et al. (1996) at Cob Swamp and Pulltrouser Swamp in northern Belize, and Wahl et al. (2006) in the Mirador Basin of northern Petén both see a *landnám* horizon around 2600–2500 BC, in which forest disturbance and the pollen of cultigens such as maize and manioc (*Manihot esculenta*) suggest human presence. The Cob-3 pollen core (Pohl et al. 1996: fig. 4) shows a dramatic coincident rise in particulate charcoal, diminution of tree pollen, rise in weed pollen and appearance of cultigens around this time: a single grain of manioc pollen at $c.3500$ BC may indicate earlier forest horticulture. A core from Lake Salpetén in the central Petén documents forest loss and soil erosion from 1700 BC onwards (Rosenmeier et al. 2002), but for much of the second millennium BC the environmental evidence for Maya occupation, forest clearance and agriculture is not matched by known settlement sites, except for Puerto Escondido on the eastern margin of the Maya area in Honduras, which may be as early as 1600 BC (Joyce and Henderson 2001).

Such villages in the central zone are present by 1200 BC. Cuello in northern Belize remains the earliest so far discovered (Hammond 1991a, 2005), although earlier sites undoubtedly exist in the region: Cuello was set in an already open and disturbed agricultural landscape, and its people used pottery in an established and distinctive ceramic tradition (Kosakowsky and Pring 1998) which developed and diversified in similar settlements across northern Belize, such as K'axob (McAnany 2004). Both Blackwater Eddy and Cahal Pech in the Belize River valley have yielded radiocarbon dates in the same late second/early first millennium

BC span, associated with the newly documented Cunil ceramic complex (Garber 2004). A suite of regional pottery styles appears across the Petén and Belize, including the Swasey and Bladen in northern Belize, Cunil on the Belize River, Eb in the northeastern Petén around Tikal, and Xe on the Río de la Pasión at Altar de Sacrificios and Seibal. Yucatán seems to lack village settlements until later in the first millennium BC, but the density and complexity of settlement, with public architecture including many ballcourts, from 700 BC onwards are striking (Andrews and Robles 2004: 8–9).

Cuello, excavated between 1975 and 2002 (Hammond 1991*a*, 2005), documents the development of domestic architecture (Gerhardt 1988), stone-tool technology, pottery (Kosakowsky and Pring 1998), and a subsistence economy based on maize, root crops (Hather and Hammond 1994), deer hunting and domesticated dog (Clutton-Brock and Hammond 1994), in a Middle Preclassic tradition clearly antecedent to the more complex societies of the Late Preclassic and Classic periods. The presence of roller-stamps bearing abstract designs and what may be early forms of notation suggest the emergence of forms of symbolic expression by 900 BC, while the coeval use of bark-beaters indicates the possibility of bark paper as a vehicle for such symbols (Hammond 2006): bark-paper codices are attested from at least the Early Classic period, although the only surviving examples are of Postclassic date, and were used as almanacs and planetary tables; ethnohistoric evidence suggests a wider range of subjects including historical chronicles. The first special-purpose buildings also appeared at Cuello around 900 BC, notably a sweatbath similar to that of some 1500 years later at Cerén in El Salvador, well-preserved under the volcanic ash of an eruption around AD 590 (Hammond and Bauer 2001; Sheets 2006: figs 6–7, 6–8). Such sauna-like structures continued throughout the prehispanic period across Mesoamerica—the Aztec *temezcal* was used for both practical and ritual cleansing, as the earlier Maya examples probably had been also—and are still built today in the highlands of Guatemala. The pattern of village life observed at Middle and Late Preclassic Cuello is one which persisted for more than two millennia and is still visible in many essentials today.

The conflicts of the 1980s over whether the ancient Maya had intensive agriculture have died down, leaving a consensus that shifting slash-and-burn (*milpa*) farming as practised historically was a major subsistence method, albeit with shorter-term fallow and more labour investment per unit area. Maize was the one cereal staple, but so genetically plastic as to allow rapid enhancement of kernel and cob size and overall yield: the development of the Nal-Tel and Chapalote strains in the Late Preclassic allowed the emergence of larger and more densely populated Maya communities. Although the thesis that breadnut (*ramón*; *Brosimum alicastrum*) was another staple, harvested from urban orchards, has failed from lack of evidence—it seems to have been a famine food at best—root crops were a source of carbohydrates undervalued by scholars because of the difficulty of recovering macroscopic remains, given the loose fibrous structure of the tubers and the traditional methods of preparing and cooking them. Innovative recovery methods developed by Jon Hather led to the recognition of manioc and malanga (*Xanthosoma* sp.), and possibly sweet potato (*Ipomoea batatas*) at Cuello, with the former being present from the early first millennium BC onwards (Hather and Hammond 1994). Beans (*Phaseolus vulgaris*), long assumed to have been of equally early importance from their prominence in the historic Mesoamerican diet, seem to have been a relatively late component, perhaps only from the late first millennium BC (Kaplan and Lynch 1999): their cultivation alongside, and nutritional complementarity with, maize may have been a synergistic development providing enhanced productivity that underpinned the social developments of the Late Preclassic.

The construction of hillside terraces to provide additional planting platforms and impede soil erosion in a clear-cut landscape, proposed by Turner (1974), has proved to be less important than initially thought because of the limited areas in which such terracing was created. The concurrent debate about whether some Maya lowland drained-field complexes (known from at least the sixth century BC) along the edges of rivers and swamps were constructed using transported fill to create island fields capable of perennial cultivation, rather than simply canalised to remove water from wetland margins more swiftly to facilitate seasonal recessional farming, remains unresolved, although the economic and symbolic importance of water management has received increasing attention (Lucero and Fash 2006). Berry's (2008) examination of the Pulltrouser Swamp field systems adjacent to the Late Preclassic site of K'axob in northern Belize now suggests, however, 'that channelising and raising seem to have been practised: a buried canal in the middle of an island field indicates that such islands were reworked and that modification included the transport of fill' (personal communication, 2007). Such artificial econiches contributed to, but turned out in no way to resolve, the provision of sufficient foodstuffs for the expanding Maya populace of the Late Preclassic and subsequent periods. Stable-isotope (SI) analyses of human skeletons from Cuello spanning the period from ~1200 BC to AD 300 by Van de Merwe *et al.* (2000: 29; see also Tykot *et al.* (1996)) show that maize may have provided only a third of the Preclassic diet, the remainder coming from root and tree crops and from animal protein.

The question of protein procurement has been little discussed recently: while white-tailed deer (*Odocoileus virginianus*) remain by far the single most important source of animal protein, measured by both bone frequency, MNI and implied meat weight, suggestions of loose-herding, semi-domestication or any other man : animal relationship closer than opportunistic hunting have received no support. Other animals, including peccary and agouti, were casual and minor contributions to the diet, but Fradkin and Carr (2003) have shown that at Cuello exploitation of nearby wetland environments including marshes and shallow ponds yielded both turtles (notably *Kinosternon* spp.) and freshwater fish such as swamp eel (*Synbranchus marmoratus*) and cichlids (cf. *Cichlasoma* spp.), perhaps collected on a seasonal basis. Coyston (2002) has shown that such freshwater fish, cooked with a root crop such as manioc, may have made an underestimated dietary contribution, detectable by SI analysis of residues on pottery even when the fragile bones do not survive. Estuarine and marine fish were probably not important except near the coasts, although the likelihood of their being traded as dried or salted fillets (thus also providing necessary salt to inland peoples) makes this difficult to assess: a range of species represented by a few individuals each have been identified well inland in both the Preclassic at Cuello and in the Late Classic at Lubaantun, in southern Belize. Wild birds, both forest species and occasional aquatic birds from the wetlands, were hunted; the domestic turkey does not seem to have arrived in the Maya area until the end of the Classic. The importance of domesticated dog (*Canis familiaris*) as a protein source has been demonstrated for the Preclassic by Clutton-Brock and Hammond (1994) and the Postclassic by Hamblin (1984): production was controlled and reliable, with most puppies being killed at the end of their first-year growth spurt.

One noted delicacy of ritual importance that has received renewed attention is cacao (*Theobroma cacao*: Maya *ka-ka-wa*), remarked by the Spanish conquistadors as the source from which a drink reserved for Aztec nobility (Nahuatl *chocolatl*) was made. Classic period Maya use of cacao, and the location of the site of Lubaantun in proximity to a large tract of high-quality cacao-growing soils were noted by Hammond (1975: figs. 8 and 147), and more recently a lock-lid vessel from Tomb 19 at Río Azul in Guatemala was found to have contained a chocolate drink as well as having hieroglyphs spelling out *ka-ka-wa* on its exterior (Adams 1999:

97–8, plate 5). Late Preclassic use was demonstrated at Cuello, Belize (Hammond and Miksicek 1981), and this was pushed back to the Middle Preclassic, c.600 BC, by residue analysis of spouted 'chocolate pot' vessels from burials at Colha, also in northern Belize (Hurst *et al.* 2002; Powis *et al.* 2002). It seems likely to have been used, perhaps already a sumptuary divider, from as early as the lowland Maya had ranked societies. Recent dedicated studies have included fieldwork in the modern cacao-growing area of the upper Xibun basin in central Belize (McAnany and Murata 2006) and McNeil (2006) draws together the many strands of current research on cacao in Mesoamerica.

It seems clear that from at least the Middle Preclassic around 600 BC, the Maya subsistence economy was both established and sophisticated in its utilisation of natural resources complemented by cultural enhancement that included landscape engineering. Such complexity existed in the exchange economy also, where procurement of jade from distant sources in the Motagua Valley occurred from c.650 BC onwards. Blue as well as green jade was exploited in the Middle Preclassic, and the source of the former was located by Gendron (2002) in 1996 and subsequently explored by Seitz *et al.* (2001). The forms of some early blue jades at Cuello suggest that the raw material was on occasion mediated through craft centres such as La Venta in the Olmec region of the Gulf Coast to the west (Hammond 1991*a*: fig. 9.8n; 1999: fig. 1). Obsidian, initially from the San Martín Jilotepeque (Río Pixcaya) outcrops near Chimaltenango in the Guatemalan highlands, appeared in the Maya lowlands at least this early also, apparently a rarity (an early fragment from Cuello having ended up worked into an ornament—rather like iron when it first appeared in the west Asian bronze age)—but by the Late Preclassic a new and better source, in terms of accessibility and workability of the obsidian nodules, had came on stream at El Chayal to the east, some 25 km north of Guatemala City. These shifts in social and economic patterns suggest that my prediction that 'what happened in the late Middle Preclassic [from 700 to 400 BC], and why, is one of the most crucial research topics in Maya archaeology today: here lies the key to the genesis of Maya civilisation' (Hammond 1986: 402) has been more than borne out by the discoveries of the past two decades, including most recently in the area east of Tikal, where work at Cival and other sites in the overall Holmul region (Estrada-Belli *et al.* 2006) has documented substantial architectural construction of later Middle Preclassic date, including the formal building ensemble known as an 'E-Group' (matched also at this period in the Mundo Perdido group of Tikal), with a square pyramidal western and an elongated eastern structure; whether such groups had any practical function as solar observatories, the received wisdom for some decades although cogently challenged some years ago, is less relevant than their consistent plan and location in Middle Preclassic ceremonial precincts, where their function was clearly of general and not local significance. Cival has also yielded a formally arranged cruciform cache including numerous blue jade axes and pebbles (Bauer 2005), and, like the Late Preclassic stela dedicated on the same axis a few metres away and a few centuries later, may show influence from the Olmec area of the Gulf Coast, several hundred kilometres to the west: Mesoamerica in the middle centuries of the first millennium BC was already an emergent *oikumene*.

At the beginning of the 1980s it was already clear 'that to talk of "Preclassic Maya civilisation" is no longer a contradiction in terms: the outward and visible signs of Classic civilisation emerge from an already complex society' (Hammond 1980: 189). This was as apparent at small sites such as Cuello as at larger centres in the Petén, where truly astounding discoveries had been made. Although Coe (1965) had already made the case for a substantial Preclassic architecture underlying the Great Plaza and North Acropolis of Tikal, and Smith (1982) had by 1968 documented impressive coeval construction at Seibal, it was revelations from the Mirador Basin in the far north of Petén that caused the most surprise. Initial reports by Matheny (1980) and others on the colossal site of El Mirador have been followed by large-scale investigations there (Hansen 1998) and at neighbouring Nakbe that have documented the largest structures ever raised in the Maya area, with the Danta pyramid at El Mirador reaching a height of 72 m and with a footprint that would engulf the entire Great Plaza area of Tikal or the whole central precinct of Late Classic Copán. By the second century BC there were monumental centres as grand as or grander than those in any Classic-period city.

This was a society that clearly commanded enormous and disciplined human and material resources, but its rulers were apparently anonymous: no dated texts were known prior to Tikal Stela 29 (AD 292), and the few undated ones were on portable objects assigned to the Late Preclassic on stylistic grounds only. The art of the Late Preclassic had public, visible portrayal of gods on the broad façades of temples, which at El Mirador and Nakbe bore impressive and enormous masks of avian deities, but the explicit and human portrayals that might give some understanding of how Late Preclassic Maya rulers thought and acted were lacking. All that changed in 2001, with the discovery of San Bartolo.

This relatively small site, located in the northeastern Petén near the much larger Classic city of Xultún, was discovered in 2001, when William Saturno noted polychrome mural paintings exposed in the wall of a looters' trench cut into the tall temple pyramid now dubbed Pinturas, at the centre of the site but east of the main plaza with its palace and other Preclassic ceremonial buildings. The murals formed the interior frieze of a low, rectangular structure (Pinturas Sub-1) some nine by four metres in size, butted on to the back of the main pyramid in the first century BC, then largely demolished and buried beneath one of the later phases (Saturno *et al.* 2005). The north wall, the first area to be uncovered, shows an immense plumed serpent emerging from a mountain (*witz*) cave in the form of a monster maw with a stalactite fang; on the serpent's back seven human figures cluster round the Maize God (some of his features clearly derived from Olmec art). Three are kneeling women, naked to the waist, three are men with elaborate body decoration bringing offerings, one of them already kneeling, and the last is a striding figure which may be a corn goddess (Saturno *et al.* 2005: fig. 26). Behind the mountain a second scene has an elaborately decorated and accoutred supernatural confronting a cleft gourd which expels five infants, their umbilical cords still attached. While the significance of this scene remains unclear, some reference to the four world directions and centre, a staple of Mesoamerican iconography, is possible (Saturno *et al.* 2005: 12–13): quadripartition, perhaps associated with directional colours, may be as early as 600 BC on the evidence of the cruciform cache from Cival in the Holmul site complex (Bauer 2006).

More recently the west wall has been uncovered (the south and east walls were demolished, but substantial areas of their friezes have been recovered in fragments from the building infill and await analysis). It has a series of scenes, in each of which a male (deity?) performs penis bloodletting with a long perforator, in front of an offering and a tree in which sits the Principal Bird Deity seen also on the temple masks of Nakbe and El Mirador. The figures are in water, on land, and in the air, and their offerings also vary, from a fish to a deer to a turkey to perfumed flowers: the domains of the waters, earth, sky and heavens may be intended, and the ceremonies match to a surprising degree those depicted in the Dresden Codex some seventeen centuries later.

At the north end of the wall is an enthronement scene, in which a ruler seated on a raised throne reached by a ladder is presented with a diadem by an elaborately dressed man: this, together with the standing ruler on Cival Stela 1, is among the earliest examples of explicit royal iconography in lowland Maya art; a short text includes the glyph for *ahaw*, 'ruler'. Recently a similar but much earlier text also including the *ahaw* sign has been found on a plastered block reused in the construction fill of an antecedent phase of the Pinturas pyramid: dating to the third century BC, its script is already distinctively formed, and suggests that the origins of Maya writing lie in the Middle Preclassic period, and may well be independent of the genesis of writing in other parts of Mesoamerica such as Oaxaca and the Gulf Coast.

The San Bartolo murals, some nine centuries older than those of Bonampak but in a style almost as naturalistic, show that Preclassic Maya art was much more sophisticated than we thought, and with symbolism of an arcane complexity that reflects a well-developed cosmology unsuspected a generation ago, but now increasingly revealed to us in excavations at Calakmul and Uaxactun as well as in the Mirador Basin (Hansen 1998; Valdés *et al.* 1999). What that cosmology and its iconography lacked was any central focus on the figure of the ruler: at San Bartolo the enthronement scene is tucked into one corner of the frieze, the ruler almost the least noticeable figure in the entire panorama: only with the institution of stela dedication towards the end of the Preclassic, in which carved and inscribed stone pillars were set up in public locales, did the ruler's image become as apparent as the political and economic exercise of his power.

Doubts had been expressed as to whether the dynasts of the Early Classic were real rulers, or the retrospectively promoted humbler ancestors of Late Classic kings: at Copan, Altar Q, dedicated by Yax Pasaj in AD 776 (Sharer 2006: fig. 7.21; Schele and Freidel 1990: fig. 8.3) shows fifteen generations of precursors, few of them until recently otherwise documented. The first of these, Yax K'uk' Mo', is shown handing a sceptre to Yax Pasaj, legitimating the latter's rulership as the sixteenth in the dynasty, while the inscription on top of Altar Q documents Yax K'uk' Mo's arrival and foundation of the dynasty (probably replacing an existing ruling house) in AD 426. Extensive tunnelling into the Copan Acropolis, notably below the focal Temple 16, and below Temple 26 and the Hieroglyphic Stairway just to the north, has revealed some four centuries of continuous buildup (Bell *et al.* 2004; Andrews and Fash 2005) during which separate foci of residential and ritual action fused to create a single massive architectural ensemble. Here I note only three of the numerous important discoveries: first, the eighth-century Temple 16 of Yax Pasaj enshrined a carefully interred sixth-century precursor nicknamed 'Rosalila', its spectacular polychrome stucco decoration making it the best-preserved Early Classic temple we are ever likely to see (and the full-scale replica in the new Copan Sculpture Museum makes it possible to appreciate the sheer exuberant inventiveness of its creators). Conceived as a smoking censer-mountain, Rosalila commemorates in lavish detail the institutionalised cult of the dynastic founder Yax K'uk' Mo' found also on the effigy censers from the tomb of the twelfth ruler and on Altar Q.

The reason why became apparent as excavations below Rosalila revealed a succession of older and smaller buildings containing tombs. One, dubbed 'Margarita', contained the jade-draped body of a woman of local origin, accompanied by pottery vessels originating from as far away as the central highlands of Mexico, and suggested as having been Yax K'uk' Mo's widow. Below, in the 'Hunal' tomb set inside a small building with central Mexican architectural motifs, was the burial of a middle-aged man plausibly identified as Yax K'uk' Mo' himself (Sharer 2006: figs 7.23, 7.25–7.27). Bone chemistry shows him to have been a 'stranger king', by conquest or recruitment, who had grown up in the region of Tikal in the northern Petén; this origin, perhaps also that of any followers who helped him to establish himself at Copan (and possibly Quirigua as a strategic outpost down in the Motagua Valley) may explain the Petén-like features of both sites' plans and some of their architecture (Ashmore 1991).

Yax K'uk' Mo' appears again in the third discovery, the raised, carved and inscribed stone disc known as the 'Motmot Stone' (Sharer 2006: fig. 7.24) which was dedicated to commemorate the 'Maya millennium' of 9.0.0.0.0. in the Long Count in AD 435. The founder sits opposite his son and eventual successor, with a double column of glyphs between them celebrating this important event. The stone sealed a cylindrical shaft tomb holding the seated skeleton of a young woman whose accoutrements suggest that she was a day-keeper, a calendar priest of a type still surviving in highland Guatemala. She was accompanied by a puma skeleton, probably her *way* or familiar, and when the tomb was reopened for a purificatory fire ceremony—something reflected in the ritual phrase 'the fire enters his house' often found in Classic texts—a deer skull and a decapitated human head with vertebrae attached were added to its contents. When the stone was later buried under new construction, it was capped with an astonishing layered offering including pigments, feathers, marine *Spondylus* shells and jade earflares. The ceremonial world of Copan's early kings was as complex in its intellectual structure as that adumbrated on the San Bartolo murals half a millennium earlier.

Much of Early Classic Copan is buried under later construction, as is that of Tikal (summarised in Sabloff 2003), but the village of Cerén under its blanket of volcanic ash preserves features not surviving elsewhere, while the small northeastern Petén city of Rio Azul presents an Early Classic cityscape relatively unencumbered by Late Classic buildings (Adams 1999), as does the trading community of Chunchucmil in Yucatan which lies exposed by the sparse vegetation of this arid zone. While Chunchucmil had Preclassic origins, its major florescence was after AD 300, when an extraordinarily dense community with a population estimated at 39,000 flourished; the central 9.4 km^2 mapped in detail had an estimated population of 25,000 (Hutson *et al.* 2006). Surface visibility has revealed numerous élite residential quadrangles, walled houselots, and the dendritic *albarrada* road network that linked them. The largest quadrangles clustered near the centre, although no civic core of public buildings is apparent. Each had a prime residence, ancillary structures, and an eastern pyramidal shrine, the latter a feature found also in the much more numerous house compounds. Most of these enclosures were between 700m^2 and 10,000m^2 in area, averaging 4,000m^2 apart from eight exceptionally large examples. Each household had one cooking area, documented by phosphorus analysis of occupation soils, suggesting a tightly knit family structure: involvement in the salt trade based on the nearby coastal *salinas* seems a likely source of Chunchucmil's prosperity and lack of élite public buildings. The Puuc city of Oxkintok, to which Chunchucmil perhaps owed allegiance, was the principal Early Classic and early Late Classic polity in the region, and shows the presence of southern lowland characteristics such as Long Count monuments from at least AD 475. Recent work at other Early Classic sites in Yucatan, including Acanceh, Aké and Izamal, is beginning to put our knowledge of this under-investigated period on a par with that current in the southern lowlands. In the latter region there is also a continuing debate as to why so many prosperous Late Preclassic sites, such as Seibal, Cerros and Nohmul, underwent quasi- or total abandonment early in the Classic: it is not a point I will pursue here, beyond noting that climatic change, and specifically drought, is one strongly asserted explanation, as it is for the end of Late Classic civilisation six centuries later, something I discuss below.

Before that, however, I want to discuss briefly recent developments in the study of Maya hieroglyphic writing. As I noted above, the short texts on the San Bartolo murals document the public use of script (its private use on personal possessions comes rather later) from the fourth or third century BC onwards, and in the highlands the dedication of inscribed stelae dates from at least the late first century BC. In the lowland zone the oldest firmly dated monument is still, after half a century of further exploration, Tikal Stela 29 at AD 292, although Late Preclassic monuments are known from Nakbe, El Mirador, Tintal, Polol, Cuello, and probably Actuncan and Blackman Eddy in the Belize Valley. While increasing numbers of Early Classic stelae are coming to light, the overwhelming majority of monumental texts date to the Late Classic after AD 600, and appear in a wide variety of contexts that includes not only stelae and their accompanying altars, but also hieroglyphic stairways, wall panels, less accessible places such as lintels over temple doorways, and totally concealed locations such as the sarcophagus of K'inich Janab Pakal (reigned AD 615–83: recent studies of Pakal's skeleton have confirmed his age at death as being 80, as specified in the sarcophagus text (Greene Robertson 1983; Tiesler and Cucina 2006)) in its vault below the Temple of the Inscriptions at Palenque. Some monuments were for overt public perusal, image and text complementing each other in proclaiming the triumphs and virtues of the reigning king and his ancestors, while others were archives for the ages.

Decipherment has progressed with increasing rapidity: in AD 1800 only a few glyphs had been drawn by early explorers, and none published. By 1900 the working structure of the Maya Long Count had been elucidated by Ernst Förstemann and others, and the Maya calendar correlated with the Christian by Joseph T. Goodman. After half a century of frustrating attempts to understand non-calendric hieroglyphs, notably by J. E. S. Thompson (1950), three breakthroughs in the 1950s transformed our understanding: Yuri Knorosov showed that the Maya script had a large phonetic and syllabic component, Heinrich Berlin's identification of the Emblem Glyph as a placename or polity identifier showed that texts dealt with places in the real world and not the heavens, and Tatiana Proskouriakoff's recognition of historical patterning in the inscriptions of Piedras Negras showed that they also recorded the actions of real people in real time, not the stately movements of the cosmos (see Coe 1982 for a useful though partial summary; Houston *et al.* 2001 reprint many of the crucial studies for these and later developments). By 1960 we had the beginnings of a Maya political history and historical geography, and by the mid-1970s detailed dynastic structures for a number of Maya polities, notably Palenque and Tikal but also including Yaxchilan and Quirigua. Numerous other dynasties have been elucidated since then, including those of Palenque's rival Tonina and Tikal's great nemesis Calakmul, together with its allies at Dos Pilas and Caracol: we have now reached a stage, at least in the southern lowlands where both monuments and the use of Emblem Glyphs are prolific, where we can chart both the trajectories of individual Classic polities and the complex interactions between them (Martin and Grube 2000: 21), a fruitful combination of history and process.

At the same time, the linguistic understanding of Maya hieroglyphic writing has progressed at an encouraging rate: landmark publications during the 'great boom in phonetic decipherment' (Wichmann 2006: 290) include Justeson and Campbell (1984), which signalled the broad acceptance, after two decades, of Knorosov's ideas, Bricker (1986), which codified then existing knowledge, and Stuart (1987), described by Wichmann (2006: 293) as 'containing some of the most beautiful demonstrations of decipherment methodology ever published'. These were followed by interpretive works such as Houston and Stuart (1989), which elucidated an entire new category of Maya supernatural beings as 'co-essences' or 'familiars' of living individuals, and Stuart and Houston (1994), which established local toponymy and showed that individual buildings, even individual monuments, had proper names. Establishment of the language of the glyphs as a form of Ch'olan (Houston *et al.* 2000; Lacadena and Wichmann 2002), possibly a prestige language retaining archaic features no longer in vernacular use, has been an important recent advance, while the fusion of linguistic with iconographic studies, bringing text and image into a synergistic understanding of how the Maya perceived themselves, is analysed in Houston *et al.* (2006). A case study of this, Stuart's (2005) examination of the newly discovered reliefs of Palenque Temple XIX, with their intense naturalism, brings the hitherto little-known ruler K'inich Ahkal Mo' Nahb, (reigned AD 721–*c*.737), grandson of the famed K'inich Janab Pakal, and members of his court into sharp focus, and adumbrates royal rituals previously unknown such as Salaj Bolon's engagement in a 'rope-taking' ceremony.

Maya royal courts, based in sprawling palace complexes such as Palenque's or Cancuen's and Tikal's Central Acropolis, and portrayed in the Bonampak murals and other media, have been the subject of widespread recent attention (Inomata and Houston 2001), and the origins of Maya royal palaces in the Preclassic are being investigated at San Bartolo, Holmul, and elsewhere. Varied and informative scenes of courtly life such as those illustrated by Reents-Budet (1994) and Kerr (2000), for example, on Late Classic polychrome vases are, unfortunately, almost all on looted vessels, not only lacking provenance but with the attendant risk of falsification: sufficient evidence can however be extracted from *in situ* sculpture and architecture to construct a scenario of the royal palace as a machine for rulership, which can be compared with the better-documented courts of other pre-industrial societies, in medieval and Renaissance Europe (Steane 2001) and western Asia, to reach a deeper understanding of how the divine kings of the Maya governed the secular state. We have in recent years gone from a static to a dynamic vision of Maya polities, their functioning and their interactions, which is based largely on advances in hieroglyphic decipherment and iconographic analysis, but which has also begun to illuminate the beginnings of the Maya state in the text-deficient period of the Preclassic.

At the other end of the social and architectural scale from the royal courts in the polity capitals, settlement archaeology, the mainstay of Maya research in the latter part of the last century, has continued with numerous surveys: at a few sites, exceptional circumstances of history and preservation have resulted in unexpectedly illuminating snapshots of Classic Maya society. At Cerén in El Salvador, close to the southeastern limit of Maya culture, a small village overwhelmed by volcanic eruption in the seventh century AD was preserved by ashfall: dishes of food ready to serve, young corn plants growing beside the houses, and both domestic and ritual utensils stored inside them have been recovered; among the most interesting structures was a domed sweatbath built from adobe and latticed branches (Sheets 2006: 96–100). Little of this would have survived under normal circumstances. The small lowland city of Aguateca was stormed and burned by enemies around AD 800. while the ruling élite had time to conceal ritually important objects in a sealed niche and flee, probably with personal jewellery, the rest of their moveable property was found in place on the floors or fallen from shelves in the palace and adjacent buildings (Inomata 1997; Inomata *et al.* 2002).

A different kind of visibility has allowed extensive settlement research in Yucatán, where the paucity of rainfall and vegetation results in even low walls being easily visible and mappable: aerial photography and more recently satellite imagery have considerably aided in this, in a way difficult in the rainforest zone to the south (although extensive mapping of Palenque by Ed Barnhart has shown what can be accomplished by traditional methods using EDM technology (Sharer 2006: fig. 8.35)). A systematic survey southwest of Mérida by Andrews and Robles (2004) revealed an unexpected density and complexity of early settlement dating to the Middle Preclassic period, including a large number of ball-courts. Understanding of the distribution, density, internal structure and historical trajectory of ancient Maya settlement in northwestern Yucatán has undergone drastic change in recent years, and there is no reason to suppose that similar work across the north and northeast of the peninsula will not improve our knowledge commensurately. Of the many architecturally notable Classic Maya centres in Yucatán, only the surrounding settlements of Sayil (Sabloff and Tourtellot 1991) and more recently parts of Chichén Itzá (Cobos 2003) have been analysed, together with some smaller sites such as Xculoc (Michelet *et al.* 2000), although new maps have been made of Oxkintok, Uxmal and other sites. Kepecs (2005: 115–20) notes the complexity of the prehispanic Maya economy in Yucatán, an area of investigation that has lagged behind studies of architecture and material culture but which is now receiving new attention. As can be seen from these few examples, the Late Classic remains for good reason a focus of much Maya research, with dozens of new sites and important monuments being recorded in regions such as northwestern Belize and southern Campeche (Šprajc 2004) in the past decade alone.

The notorious 'collapse' of the Classic Maya in the ninth and tenth centuries has remained a similarly perennial subject of interest (reviewed most recently by Webster 2002), with some scholars attempting to substitute a terminology of 'transformation' for the more dramatic 'collapse' to mark the fact that substantial, although less urban, populations remained in parts of the southern lowlands, and that the polities of Yucatan continued to flourish into the early second millennium AD and were still functioning in some form at the time of the Spanish conquest, albeit from different capitals and with a less complex political structure.

The great cities of the tropical forest were, whatever terminology is applied, abandoned in the ninth century: construction of public buildings including palaces and temples, patronage art on both the communal and personal scale, and dedication of dated monuments bearing the images and deeds of divine kings all ceased: few cities have Long Count dates after 10.3.0.0.0. (AD 889). Explanations range from the political—invasion, insurrection, internecine warfare and social decay—to the natural, the latter including soil exhaustion and crop failure; combination theories include larger, and more closely packed cities overstretching both the productive capacity of the landscape and the managerial capacity of the Maya political structure to deliver enough sustenance to increasingly stressed urban populations.

A group of theories that have received renewed attention and some cautious acceptance as at least partial explanation involve climate change, especially severe episodic drought leading to subsistence failure. The notion of catastrophic climate change as a salient cause of the Maya collapse had been mooted earlier, but discounted: Maya historical records had indeed complained of episodic droughts and crop failure, but the

Maya had survived to tell the tale. Then, a decade ago, oxygen-isotope data from cores in Lake Chichankanab in Yucatan suggested a two-century drought from AD 800–1000, the period of the collapse (Hodell *et al.* 1995; Gill 2000). There was one major problem, however: this was just when cities such as Uxmal and Chichén Itzá in the driest part of the Maya area reached their apogee. How could these disparate data be reconciled, if at all?

The alternating seasons of the Maya year are governed by the migration of the meteorological equator, when the tropical trade winds shift north and south, giving a dry season from January to May and a wet one from June to December, with as much as 90 per cent of the rainfall within a three-month period of that. The effect of this has been documented in a recent 170 m core from the Cariaco basin off Venezuela, where anoxia has left the thin laminae of annual deposits undisturbed by burrowing marine organisms (Haug *et al.* 2003; Peterson and Haug 2005). Shifts in titanium and iron levels stand proxy for the amount of seasonal runoff— effectively an ancient rain gauge. The Cariaco core showed a broad band of low rainfall over the AD 800–1000 period, but also four short periods of intense drought within that, each lasting five to six years and separated by around half a century; Hodell *et al.* (2005), working with further data from Lake Chichankanab, have refined their thesis of a decade earlier to suggest two major droughts, one from AD 770–870 with two half-century cycles, the second from AD 920–1100 in four similar cycles, separated by a moister interval. During these intense droughts, groundwater sources would have been vital for community survival, since reservoirs could not have been replenished. In the wetter southern part of the Maya lowlands, where the great cities were abandoned earliest, the water table lies deeply buried. Only in Yucatan does it come close enough to the surface to be accessible through caves and cenotes, which might explain the continued existence (though not the evident prosperity) of the Puuc cities and Chichén Itzá.

Gill's (2000) model of these phases of collapse, based on the latest dated monuments at sites, fits quite well into this more precise model, with its drought maxima around AD 760, 810, 860, and 910. The first of these coincides with the estimated maximum Maya population, when more people were crammed into more and larger cities, more closely packed into the landscape than ever before and competing more ferociously for resources of land and labour. The failure of crops may have been seen as a failure of the divine kingship to protect the people from the malignity of personified nature. People voting with their feet—moving out to find subsistence in the countryside—would rapidly remove the underpinnings of élite urban culture. Construction of temples and dedication of monuments would cease before actual abandonment and appear more precipitate, as we have found at La Milpa in northwestern Belize, where several major royal construction projects including enlargement of the palace and a new temple-pyramid were left uncompleted with apparent, but perhaps deceptive, suddenness (Hammond *et al.* 1998). The evidence for climatic as well as demographic and political causes for the end of Classic Maya civilisation gives a new dynamic to our research and leads us to seek similar environmental factors behind earlier cultural perturbations, as has been suggested by Hodell *et al.* (2007).

Maya civilisation began to emerge, we now know, as far back as the seventh century BC, when the differentiation of an élite became marked by access to exotic goods such as jade and in burial practices—a layering of Maya society into strata which became increasingly rigidly divided by ascription instead of achievement (Rathje 1970; Hammond 1991*b*: 267–72). Shortly after this, special-purpose public buildings rapidly became the vehicles for large-scale sculpture encoding the iconography of the ruling ideology. Hieroglyphic writing to facilitate rulership and government existed by at least the third century BC, more than a millennium before the Classic apogee: the transparency that many Classic texts have now achieved has revolutionised our understanding of Maya society, while at the latter end of the Maya cultural tradition there is striking continuity through the Classic collapse into the contact and colonial periods. In the sacrifices of the fifteenth-century Dresden Codex we can see reflected the rituals used at San Bartolo seventeen centuries before; in traditional Maya dwellings we see the same environmentally adapted technology and materials that were used at Cuello three thousand years ago; and the Maya people today have preserved many of the concepts that guided the first Maya farmers, artists, and priests. Prehispanic Maya culture lasted for more than two millennia—less, perhaps, than in Egypt, Mesopotamia, or China, but still giving the lie to notions of New World civilisations as short-lived and less complex than those of Eurasia. We still see the ancient Maya through a glass darkly, but we see them more clearly, much more clearly, than we did before.

Note. My title is both 're-covering Maya civilisation', in that the only previous treatment of this at the British Academy has been in William R. Coe's (unpublished) Reckitt Lecture of 1973, and 'recovering' in the sense of reporting on some aspects of recent Maya research. I am grateful to several colleagues for the provision of unpublished data, and especially to William Saturno for the use of unpublished images from San Bartolo in my lecture. Many topics had to remain unremarked both there and here, but the abundant literature on Maya archaeology is sampled in the excellent bibliographic summaries and bibliography of Robert J. Sharer's *The Ancient Maya* (6th edn., 2006: 785–888), which also has numerous useful illustrations: Figure 1 is reproduced from it, with grateful acknowledgement. The principal journals covering the field and reporting recent research include *Ancient Mesoamerica, Estudios de Cultura Maya, Latin American Antiquity*, and *Mexicon*, while recent survey articles with extensive bibliographies include Love (2007) and Marcus (2003). Current research is reported with admirable despatch in the annual volumes of the *Simposio de Investigaciones Arqueológicas en Guatemala*, for Mexico in the annual *Investigadores de la Cultura Maya* (Universidad Autónoma de Campeche) and the slightly less frequent *Memorias del Congreso Internacional de Mayistas*, and for Belize by the annual *Research Reports in Belizean Archaeology*.

References

Adams, R. E. W. (1999), *Río Azul: An Ancient Maya City* (Norman, OK).

Andrews, A. P. and Robles Castellanos, F. (2004), 'An Archaeological survey of Northwest Yucatan, Mexico', *Mexicon*, 26: 714.

Andrews, E. W. and Fash, W. L. (eds.) (2005), *Copán: The History of an Ancient Maya Kingdom* (Santa Fe, NM).

Ashmore, W. (1991), 'Site-Planning Principles and Concepts of Directionality among the Ancient Maya', *Latin American Antiquity*, 2: 199–226.

Bauer, J. R. (2005), 'Between Heaven and Earth: the Cival Cache and the Creation of the Mesoamerican Cosmos', in V. M. Fields and D. Reents-Budet (eds.), *Lords of Creation: The Origins of Sacred Maya Kingship* (Los Angeles, Los Angeles County Museum of Art), 28–9.

Bell, E. E., Canuto, M. A., and Sharer, R. J. (eds.) (2004), *Understanding Early Classic Copan* (Philadelphia).

Berry, K. (2008), 'Farming the Scales of the Crocodile: Cultural and Geoarchaeological Evidence for Ancient Maya Wetland Reclamation at K'axob, Belize'. Ph.D. thesis, Boston University.

Blake, M. and Clark, J. E. (1999), 'The Emergence of Hereditary Inequality: the Case of Pacific Coastal Chiapas, Mexico', in M. Blake (ed.), *Pacific Latin America in Prehistory: The Evolution of Archaic and Formative Cultures* (Pullman, WA), 55–73.

Bricker, V. R. (1986), *A Grammar of Mayan Hieroglyphs* (Publication 56; New Orleans, Middle American Research Institute, Tulane University).

Clark, J. E. and Blake, M. (1994), 'The Power of Prestige: Competitive Generosity and the Emergence of Rank Societies in Lowland Mesoamerica', in E. Brumfiel and J. Fox (eds.), *Factional Competition and Political Development in the New World* (Cambridge), 17–30.

Clutton-Brock, J. and Hammond, N. (1994), 'Hot dogs: comestible canids in Preclassic Maya culture at Cuello, Belize', *Journal of Archaeological Science*, 21: 819–26.

Cobos, R. (2003), 'The Settlement Patterns of Chichén Itzá, Yucatan, Mexico'. Ph.D. thesis, Tulane University.
Coe, M. D. (1982), *Breaking the Maya Code* (London).
Coe, W. R. (1965), 'Tikal, Guatemala, and emergent Maya Civilization', *Science*, 147: 1401–19.
Coyston, S. (2002), 'Noble chemists and archaeologists: chemical analyses of food residues from ancient Maya vessels'. Ph.D. thesis, McMaster University.
Estrada Belli, F., Bauer, J., Callaghan, M., Neivens, N., Velásquez, A., and Calvo, J. (2006), 'Las épocas tempranas en el área de Holmul, Petén', in J. P. Laporte, B. Arroyo and H. E. Mejía (eds.) *XIX Simposio de Investigaciones Arqueológicas en Guatemala*, 2005 (Guatemala, Ministerio de Cultura y Deportes & Instituto de Antropología e Historia): 639–47.
Fradkin, A. and Carr, H. S. (2003), 'Middle Preclassic Landscapes and Aquatic Resource Use at Cuello, Belize', *Bulletin of the Florida Museum of Natural History*, 44: 35–42.
Garber, J. F. (ed.) (2004), *The Ancient Maya of the Belize Valley*. (Gainesville, FL).
Gendron, F. (2002), 'Discovery of Jadeite-Jade in Guatemala Confirmed by Non-Destructive Raman Microscopy', *Journal of Archaeological Science*, 29: 837–51.
Gerhardt, J. C. (1988), *Preclassic Maya Architecture at Cuello, Belize* (International Series 464; Oxford, BAR).
Gill, R. B. (2000), *The Great Maya Droughts: Water, Life, and Death* (Albuquerque, NM).
Greene Robertson, M. (1983), *The Sculpture of Palenque, Volume 1: The Temple of the Inscriptions* (Princeton).
Gruhn, R. and Bryan, A. L. (1977), 'Los Tapiales: A Paleo-Indian Campsite in the Guatemalan Highlands', *Proceedings of the American Philosophical Society*, 121: 235–73.
Hamblin, N. L. (1984), *Animal Use by the Cozumel Maya* (Tucson AZ).
Hammond, N. (1975), *Lubaantun: a Classic Maya realm* (Monograph 2; Cambridge, MA, Peabody Museum of Archaeology and Ethnology, Harvard University).
Hammond, N. (1980), 'Early Maya ceremonial at Cuello, Belize', *Antiquity*, 54: 176–90.
Hammond, N. (1982), *Ancient Maya Civilization* (Cambridge).
Hammond, N. (1986), 'New light on the most ancient Maya', *Man*, NS, 21: 398–412.
Hammond, N. (ed.) (1991a), *Cuello: an early Maya community in Belize* (Cambridge).
Hammond, N. (1991b), 'Inside the black box: defining Maya polity', in T. P. Culbert (ed.), *Classic Maya Political History* (Cambridge), 253–84.
Hammond, N. (1999), 'The Genesis of Hierarchy: Mortuary and Offertory Ritual in the Pre-Classic at Cuello, Belize', in D. C. Grove and R. A. Joyce (eds.), *Social Patterns in Pre-Classic Mesoamerica* (Washington, Dumbarton Oaks Research Library and Collections), 49–66.
Hammond, N. (2000), *The Maya* (London).
Hammond, N. (2005), 'The Dawn and the Dusk: Beginning and Ending a Long-Term Research Program at the Preclassic Maya Site of Cuello, Belize', in I. Šprajc (ed.), *Contributions to Maya Archaeology* (Anthropological Notebooks, 11; Ljubljana, Slovene Anthropological Society), 45–60.

Hammond, N. (2006), 'Early Symbolic Expression in the Maya Lowlands', *Mexicon*, 28: 25–8.

Hammond, N. and Bauer, J. R. (2001), 'A Preclassic Maya sweathouse at Cuello, Belize', *Antiquity*, 75: 683–4.

Hammond, N. and Miksicek, C. H. (1981), 'Ecology and Economy of a Formative Maya site at Cuello, Belize', *Journal of Field Archaeology*, 8: 259–69.

Hammond, N., Tourtellot, G., Donaghey, S. and Clarke, A. (1998), 'No slow dusk: Maya urban development and decline at La Milpa, Belize', *Antiquity*, 72: 831–7.

Hansen, R. L. (1998), 'Continuity and Disjunction: The Pre-Classic Antecedents of Classic Maya Architecture', in S. Houston (ed.), *Function and Meaning in Classic Maya Architecture* (Washington, Dumbarton Oaks Research Library and Collections), 49–122.

Hather, J. G. and Hammond, N. (1994), 'Ancient Maya subsistence diversity: root and tuber remains from Cuello, Belize', *Antiquity*, 68: 330–5, 487–8.

Haug, G. H., Gunther, D., Peterson, L. C., Sigman, D. M., Hughen, K. A., and Aeschlimann, B. (2003), 'Climate and the collapse of Maya civilization', *Science*, 299: 1731–5.

Hester, T. R., Kelly, T. C., and Ligabue, G. (1981), *A Fluted Paleo-Indian Projectile Point from Belize, Central America* (Working Papers of the Colha Project No. 1; San Antonio, Center for Archaeological Research, University of Texas).

Hodell, D. A., Curtis, J. H., and Brenner, M. (1995), 'Possible Role of Climate in the Collapse of Classic Maya Civilization', *Nature*, 375: 391–4.

Hodell, D. A., Brenner, M., and Curtis, J. H. (2005), 'Terminal Classic drought in the northern Maya lowlands inferred from multiple sediment cores in Lake Chichancanab (Mexico)', *Quaternary Science Reviews*, 24: 1413–27.

Hodell, D. A., Brenner, M., and Curtis, J. H. (2007), 'Climate and cultural history of the Northeastern Yucatan Peninsula, Quintana Roo, Mexico', *Climatic Change*, 83: 215–40.

Houston, S. and Stuart, D. (1989), *The Way Glyph: Evidence for 'Co-Essences' among the Classic Maya* (Research Reports on Ancient Maya Writing 30; Washington, Center for Maya Research).

Houston, S., Chinchilla Mazariega, O., and Stuart, D. (eds.) (2001), *The Decipherment of Ancient Maya Writing* (Norman, OK).

Houston, S., Robertson, J., and Stuart, D. (2000), 'The language of Classic Maya inscriptions', *Current Anthropology*, 41: 321–56.

Houston, S., Stuart, D., and Taube, K. (2006), *The Memory of Bones: Body, Being, and Experience among the Classic Maya* (Austin, TX).

Hurst, W. J., Tarka, S. M., Powis, T. G., Valdez, F., Jr., and Hester, T. R. (2002), 'Cacao Usage by the Earliest Maya Civilization', *Nature*, 418: 289–90.

Hutson, S. R., Magnoni, A., Mazeau, D. E., and Stanton, T. W. (2006), 'The Archaeology of Urban Houselots at Chunchucmil, Yucatan, Mexico', in J. P. Mathews and B. A. Morrison (eds.), *Lifeways in the Northern Lowlands: New Approaches to Maya Archaeology* (Tucson, AZ), 77–92.

Inomata, T. (1997), 'The last day of a fortified Classic Maya center: archaeological investigations at Aguateca, Guatemala', *Ancient Mesoamerica*, 8: 337–51.

Inomata, T. and Houston, S. (eds.) (2001), *Royal Courts of the Ancient Maya*, Vol. 1, *Theory, Comparison, and Synthesis*. Vol. 2, *Data and Case Studies* (Boulder, CO).

Inomata, T., Triadan, D., Ponciano, E., Pinto, E., Terry, R. E., and Eberl, M. (2002), 'Domestic and politicial lives of Classic Maya elites: the excavation of rapidly abandoned structures at Aguateca, Guatemala', *Latin American Antiquity*, 13: 305–30.

Joyce, R. A. and Henderson, J. S. (2001), 'Beginnings of Village Life in Eastern Mesoamerica', *Latin American Antiquity*, 12: 5–23.

Justeson, J. S. and Campbell, L. R. (eds.) (1984), *Phoneticism in Maya Hieroglyphic Writing* (Albany, State University of New York, Institute of Mesoamerican Studies).

Kaplan, L. and Lynch, T. F. (1999), '*Phaseolus* (Fabaceae) in Archaeology: AMS Radiocarbon Dates and Their Significance for Pre-Columbian Agriculture', *Economic Botany*, 53: 261–72.

Kepecs, S. (2005), 'Mayas, Spaniards, and Salt: World systems shifts in Sixteenth-Century Yucatán', in S. Kepecs and R. T. Alexander (eds.), *The Postclassic to Spanish-Era Transition in Mesoamerica* (Albuquerque, NM), 117–37.

Kerr, J. (2000), *The Maya Vase Book*, Vol. 6. (New York).

Kosakowsky, L. J. and Pring, D. C. (1998), 'The Ceramics of Cuello, Belize: A New Evaluation', *Ancient Mesoamerica*, 9: 55–66.

Lacadena, A. and Wichmann, S. (2002), 'The distribution of Lowland Maya languages in the Classic period', in V. Tiesler, R. Cobos and M. Greene Robertson (eds.), *La Organización Social Entre los Mayas: Memoria de la Tercera Mesa Redonda de Palenque* II (Mexico, Instituto Nacional de Antropología e Historia), 275–314.

Lesure, R. G. and Blake, M. (2002), 'Interpretive Challenges in the Study of Early Complexity: Economy, Ritual, and Architecture at Paso de la Amada, Mexico', *Journal of Anthropological Archaeology*, 21: 1–24.

Lohse, J. C., Awe, J., Griffith, C., Rosenswig, R. M., and Valdez, F., Jr. (2006), 'Preceramic Occupations in Belize: Updating the Paleoindian and Archaic Record', *Latin American Antiquity*, 17: 209–26.

Love, M. (2007), 'Recent Research in the Southern Highlands and Pacific Coast of Mesoamerica', *Journal of Archaeological Research*, 15: 275–328.

Lucero, L. J. and Fash, B. W. (eds.) (2006), *Precolumbian Water Management: Ideology, Ritual, and Power* (Tucson, AZ).

McAnany, P. A. (ed.) (2004), *K'axob: Ritual, Work and Family in an Ancient Maya Village*. (Los Angeles, UCLA, Cotsen Institute of Archaeology).

McAnany, P. A. and Murata, S. (2006), 'From Chocolate Pots to Maya Gold: Belizean Cacao Farmers through the Ages', in C. McNeil (ed.), *Chocolate in Mesoamerica: A Cultural History of Cacao* (Gainesville, FL), 429–50.

McNeil, C. (ed.) (2006), *Chocolate in Mesoamerica: A Cultural History of Cacao* (Gainesville, FL).

Marcus, J. (2003), 'Recent Advances in Maya Archaeology', *Journal of Archaeological Research*, 11: 71–148.

Martin, S. and Grube, N. (2000), *Chronicle of the Maya Kings and Queens* (London).

Matheny, R. T. (ed.) (1980), *El Mirador, Petén, Guatemala: An Interim Report* (Papers of the New World Archaeological Foundation 45: Provo, New World Archaeological Foundation).

Michelet, D., Becquelin, P., and Arnauld, M.-C. (2000), *Mayas del Puuc: Arqueología de la Región de Xculoc, Campeche* (Mexico, Centre Français D'Études Mexicaines et Centreaméricaines).

Neff, H., Pearsall, D. M., Jones, J. G., Arroyo, B., Collins, S. K., and Freidel, D. E. (2006), 'Early Maya Adaptive Patterns: Mid-Late Holocene Paleoenvironmental Evidence from Pacific Guatemala', *Latin American Antiquity*, 17: 287–315.

Peterson, L. C. and Haug, G. H. (2005), 'Climate and the Collapse of Maya Civilization', *American Scientist*, 93: 322–9.

Piperno, D. R. and Flannery, K. V. (2001), 'The Earliest Archaeological Maize (*Zea mays* L.) from Highland Mexico: New Accelerator Mass Spectrometry Dates and Their Implications', *Proceedings of the National Academy of Sciences of the USA*, 98: 2101–3.

Pohl, M. D., Pope, K. O., Jones, J. G., Jacob, J. S., Piperno, D. R., DeFrance, S. D., Lentz, D. L., Gifford, J. A., Danforth, M. E., and Josserand, J. K. (1996), 'Early Agriculture in the Maya Lowlands', *Latin American Antiquity*, 7: 355–72.

Pohl, M. E. D., Piperno, D. R., Pope, K. O., and Jones, J. G. (2007), 'Microfossil evidence for pre-Columbian maize dispersals in the neotropics from San Andrés, Tabasco, Mexico', *Proceedings of the National Academy of Sciences of the USA*, 104: 6870–5.

Powis, T. G., Valdez, F., Jr., Hester, T. R., Hurst, W. J., and Tarka, S. M. (2002), 'Spouted Vessels and Cacao Use among the Preclassic Maya', *Latin American Antiquity*, 13: 85–106.

Rathje, W. L. (1970), 'Socio-Political Implications of Lowland Maya Burials: Methodology and Tentative Hypotheses', *World Archaeology*, 1: 359–74.

Reents-Budet, D. (1994), *Painting the Maya Universe. Royal Ceramics of the Classic Period* (Durham, NC).

Rosenmeier, M. F., Hodell, D. A., Brenner, M., and Curtis, J. H. (2002), 'A 4000-year Lacustrine Record of Environmental Change in the southern Maya Lowlands, Petén, Guatemala', *Quaternary Research*, 57: 183–90.

Rosenswig, R. M. and Masson, M. A. (2001), 'Seven new Preceramic sites documented in northern Belize', *Mexicon*, 23: 138–40.

Sabloff, J. A. (ed.) (2003), *Tikal: Dynasties, Foreigners, and Affairs of State: Advancing Maya Archaeology* (Santa Fe, NM).

Sabloff, J. A. and Tourtellot, G. (1991), *The Ancient Maya City of Sayil: The Mapping of a Puuc Regional Center* (Publication 60; New Orleans, Middle American Research Institute, Tulane University).

Saturno, W. A., Taube, K., and Stuart, D. (2005), *The Murals of San Bartolo, El Petén, Guatemala. Part 1: the North Wall* (*Ancient America* 7; Barnardsville, Center for Ancient American Studies).

Schele, L. and Freidel, D. (1990), *A Forest of Kings: The Untold Story of the Ancient Maya* (New York).

Seitz, R., Harlow, G. E., Sisson, V. B., and Taube, K. (2001), '"Olmec Blue" and Formative jade sources: new discoveries in Guatemala', *Antiquity*, 75: 687–8.

Sharer, R. J. (2006), *The Ancient Maya* (Sixth edn. (with L. P. Traxler) of (orig.) S. G. Morley, 1946, *The Ancient Maya*) (Stanford).

Sheets, P. D. (2006), *The Ceren Site: An Ancient Village Buried by Volcanic Ash in Central America*, 2nd edn. (Belmont).

Smith, A. L. (1982), 'Major architecture and caches', in G. R.Willey (ed.), *Excavations at Seibal, Department of Petén, Guatemala* (Memoirs of the Peabody Museum of Archaeology and Ethnology, Harvard University, 15 (1); Cambridge, MA, Peabody Museum).
Šprajc, I. (2004), 'Maya sites and Monuments in SE Campeche, Mexico', *Journal of Field Archaeology*, 29: 385–407.
Steane, J. M. (2001), *The Archaeology of Power* (Stroud).
Stuart, D. (1987), *Ten Phonetic Syllables* (Research Reports on Ancient Maya Writing 14; Washington, Center for Maya Research).
Stuart, D. (2005), *The Inscriptions from Temple XIX at Palenque* (San Francisco, Pre-Columbian Art Research Institute).
Stuart, D. and Houston, S. (1994), *Classic Maya Place Names* (Dumbarton Oaks Studies in Pre-Columbian Art and Archaeology 33) (Washington, Dumbarton Oaks Research Library and Collections).
Thompson, J. E. S. (1950), *Maya Hieroglyphic Writing: Introduction* (Publication 589; Washington, Carnegie Institution).
Tiesler, V. and Cucina, A. (eds.) (2006), *Janaab' Pakal of Palenque: Reconstructing the Life and Death of a Maya Ruler* (Tucson, AZ).
Turner, B. L., II. (1974), 'Prehistoric Intensive Agriculture in the Maya Lowlands', *Science*, 185: 118–24.
Tykot, R. H., Van der Merwe, N. J., and Hammond, N. (1996), 'Stable isotope analysis of bone collagen, bone apatite, and tooth enamel in the reconstruction of human diet: A case study from Cuello, Belize', in M. V. Orna (ed.), *Archaeological Chemistry* V (Washington, American Chemical Society), 355–65.
Valdés, J. A., Fahsen, F., and Escobedo, H. L. (1999), *Reyes, tumbas y palacios: la historia dinástica de Uaxactun* (Mexico, Universidad Nacional Autónoma de México).
Van der Merwe, N. J., Tykot, R. H., Hammond N., and Oakberg, K. (2000), 'Diet and animal husbandry of the Preclassic Maya at Cuello, Belize: Isotopic and zoo-archaeological evidence', in S. H. Ambrose and M. A. Katzenberg (eds.), *Biogeochemical Approaches to Paleodietary Analysis* (New York), 23–38.
Voorhies, B. (2004), *Coastal Collectors in the Holocene: The Chantuto People of Southwest Mexico* (Gainesville, FL).
Wahl, D., Byrne, R., Schreiner, T., and Hansen, R. (2006), 'Holocene vegetation change in the northern Petén and its implications for Maya prehistory', *Quaternary Research*, 65: 380–9.
Webster, D. (2002), *The Fall of the Ancient Maya: Solving the Mystery of the Maya Collapse* (London).
Wichmann, S. (2006), 'Mayan Historical Linguistics and Epigraphy: A New Synthesis', *Annual Review of Anthropology*, 35: 279–94.
Zeitlin, R. N. and Zeitlin, J. F. (2000), 'The Palaeoindian and Archaic cultures of Mesoamerica', in. R. E. W. Adams and M. J. McLeod (eds.), *The Cambridge History of the Native Peoples of the Americas, Vol. II, Mesoamerica* (Cambridge), 45–121.

2007 BRITISH ACADEMY LECTURE

The Devil in the Holy Water: Political Libel in Eighteenth-Century France

ROBERT DARNTON
Fellow of the Academy

WHY TAKE SLANDER SERIOUSLY? It has infected politics and dogged politicians since antiquity, but it could be dismissed as 'noise'—the inevitable by-product of friction in any political system. Whether directed against a Roman emperor or an American president, it seems to have a sameness that deters historical analysis. The head of state has a scandalous private life: so what? *Plus ça change, plus c'est la même chose.*

I would like to argue for the historicity of slander—that is, for its character as a cultural phenomenon peculiar to a time and place, in this case eighteenth-century France. Similar arguments can be applied to seventeenth-century England[1] and to other regimes threatened with revolution. But France developed a particularly rich vein of slanderous literature, which calls for special attention.

In a previous study, I tried to determine which books actually reached readers through the vast sector of the illegal book trade during the twenty

---

Read at the Academy 22 February 2007.
[1] As examples of recent literature on scandal and libel in England, see Alastair Bellany, *The Politics of Court Scandal in Early Modern England: News Culture and the Overbury Affair, 1603–1660* (Cambridge, 2002) and John Brewer, 'Personal Scandal and Politics in Eighteenth-Century England: Secrecy, Intimacy and the Interior Self in the Public Sphere' in Marie-Christine Skuncke (ed.), *Media and Political Culture in the Eighteenth Century* (Stockholm, 2005). For a rich corpus of texts that can be consulted on the Web, see Alastair Bellany and Andrew McRae (eds.), *Early Stuart Libels: An Edition of Poetry from Manuscript Sources* <http://purl.oclc.org/emls/texts/libels>.

years before the French Revolution.² To my surprise, I found that along with the works of Voltaire and Rousseau, the French bought an enormous number of books known as *libelles* (libels), a general term for scandalous attacks on the private lives of public figures. Libels took many forms. They could be biographies (often indicated by a title that began with 'Vie privée' or 'Vie secrète' such as *Vie privée de Louis XV* (1781)), *chroniques scandaleuses* (journalistic compilations derived from manuscript newsletters such as *Correspondance politique, civile et littéraire pour servir à l'histoire du XVIII siècle* (1783)), full-scale histories (sometimes set in exotic places so that they had the allure of a *roman à clé*, for example, *Mémoires secrets pour servir à l'histoire de Perse* (1745)) or pamphlets (sometimes short enough to read like the *pièces de circonstance* that circulated in manuscript, thus *Les Amours de Charlot et Toinette* (1779), a poem about the supposed cuckolding of Louis XVI by his brother, the comte d'Artois).

Libel literature was so varied and extensive that one cannot do justice to it in a single essay.³ Instead of attempting to survey it all, I propose to discuss four representative libels. By concentrating on their textual and paratextual qualities, I hope to show how they were designed to appeal to a particular reading public. They also refer to one another; so by following their intertextual links, I will try to trace a story. The story is worth telling in itself, but it is especially important, I believe, because it illustrates the changing character of political polemics from the reign of Louis XV to the Terror. It shows how an underground literature from the *Ancien Régime* surfaced in the power struggles of the Revolution.

As its title announced, the first libel, *Le Gazetier cuirassé, ou anecdotes scandaleuses de la cour de France* (1771), contained plenty of salacious material about the behaviour of the great (*les grands*) in Versailles (Fig. 1). The false address on the title page served both as a provocation and an invitation to the reader: 'printed at a hundred leagues from the Bastille, at the sign of liberty'. Enough readers responded for the book to

---

² Robert Darnton, *The Forbidden Best-Sellers of Pre-Revolutionary France* (New York, 1995) and the supplementary volume with statistics and bibliography: *The Corpus of Clandestine Literature in France* (New York, 1995).

³ This lecture summarises some of the material I have discussed in a forthcoming book, *Slander: the Art of Libel in Eighteenth-Century France*. After writing this lecture, I received a copy of Simon Burrows, *Blackmail, Scandal, and Revolution. London's French Libellistes, 1758–92* (Manchester, 2006), which also discusses the libellers of London and contests some of the views that I advanced about them in my earlier work, notably the essays collected in *The Literary Underground of the Old Regime* (Cambridge, MA, 1982).

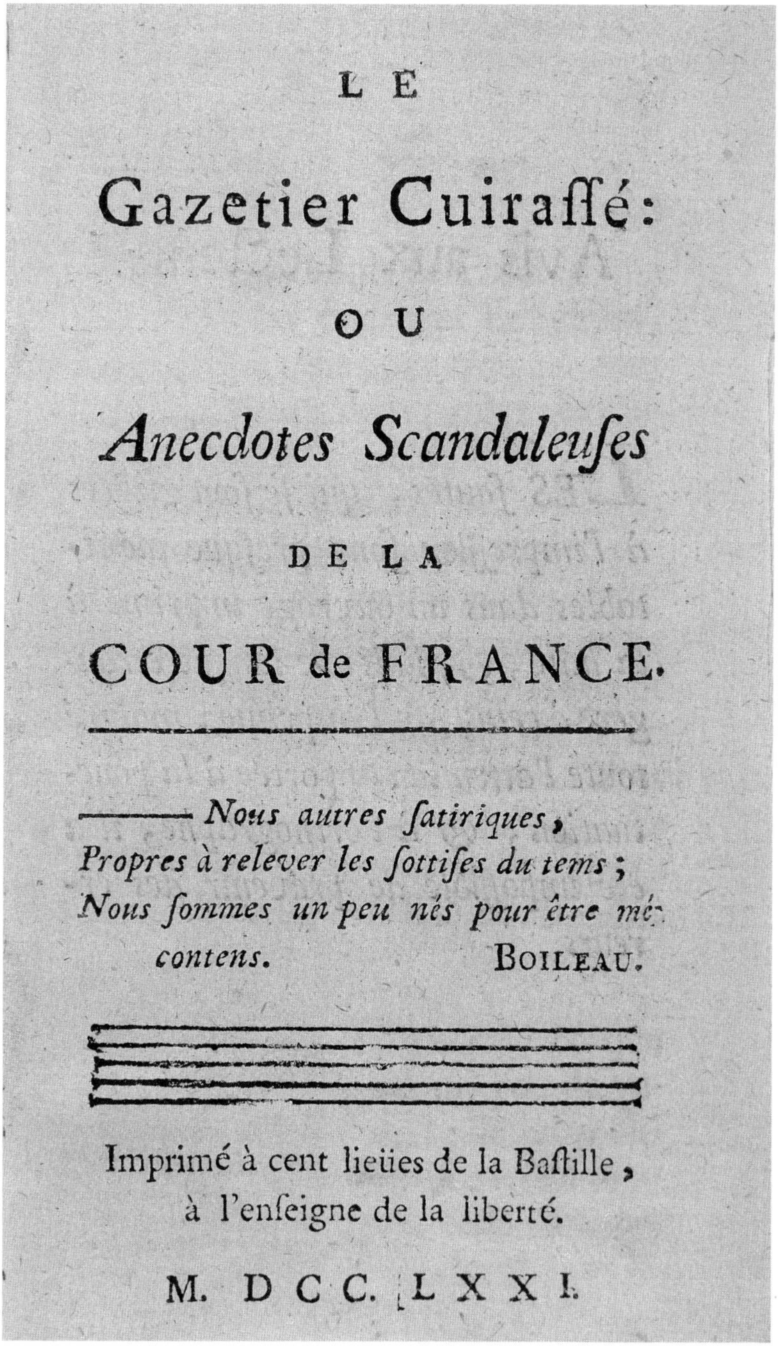

LE

Gazetier Cuirassé:

OU

Anecdotes Scandaleuses

DE LA

COUR de FRANCE.

───── *Nous autres satiriques,*
Propres à relever les sottises du tems;
Nous sommes un peu nés pour être mé-
  contens.   BOILEAU.

Imprimé à cent lieües de la Bastille,
à l'enseigne de la liberté.

M. DCC. LXXI.

Figure 1. *Le Gazetier cuirassé*, title page, 1771.

enjoy a *succès de scandale*.⁴ It stood out as one of the most notorious attacks on the government during the crisis of 1771–4, when the chancellor René Nicolas de Maupeou restructured the judicial system of the kingdom in such a way as to destroy the power of the parlements to resist the authority of the crown. A second edition appeared on the heels of the first in 1771, this time with an elaborate frontispiece, and at least three more editions followed during the next fourteen years. The edition of 1777 carried a long subtitle, which emphasised the book's character as a *chronique scandaleuse* by promising to regale the reader with all kinds of 'news' (*nouvelles*)—news that would be 'political' but also 'apocryphal', 'secret', 'extraordinary', and especially bawdy, for it would include plenty of anecdotes about women of small virtue (Fig 2).

The text of the this edition remained unchanged, but its meaning had shifted, because by 1777 the context had changed. As the Maupeou government had disappeared at the accession of Louis XVI in 1774, the book now read as an indictment of despotism during the previous reign. Yet the title page of 1777 also offered new revelations about the 'inquisition' that continued to threaten the French, and the new edition contained an extensive supplement about the nature of that threat: 'Remarques historiques et anecdotes sur le château de la Bastille et l'Inquisition de France'. By detailed descriptions of the fetid cells and brutal treatment of the prisoners, the supplement reinforced a political myth: the Bastille stood as testimony to the growing tyranny of Versailles. Instead of striking a note of righteous indignation, however, the subtitle maintained a strangely jocular tone. Along with the revelations about the Bastille, *Le Gazetier cuirassé* would offer a 'confused miscellany about clear subjects' ('mélanges confuses sur des matières fort claires'). Readers could expect to be amused as well as shocked.

The frontispiece was stranger still. It showed how the anonymous author chose to represent himself (Fig. 3). In conformity with the book's

---

⁴ I have identified five editions between 1771 and 1789, but there probably were more, because scandalous 'nouveautés' were widely pirated. The French foreign ministry tried to repress a pirated edition produced in Geneva in mid-1771: see Voltaire to Gabriel Cramer, *c*. 25 Dec. 1771 in Theodore Besterman (ed.), *The Complete Works of Voltaire: Correspondence and Related Documents*, 38 (Oxford, The Voltaire Foundation, 1975), 197. In sampling the demand for illegal literature among French booksellers, I found that *Le Gazetier cuirassé* ranked fifty-third among 720 works: Darnton, *The Corpus of Clandestine Literature*, p. 196. For reports on the scandal produced by the book, see *Mémoires secrets pour servir à l'histoire de la république des lettres en France, depuis 1762 jusqu'à nos jours ou journal d'un observateur par feu M. de Bachaumont*, 21 (London, 1777–1789), entries for 10 Aug. 1771, 15 Aug. 1771, and 1 Sept. 1771.

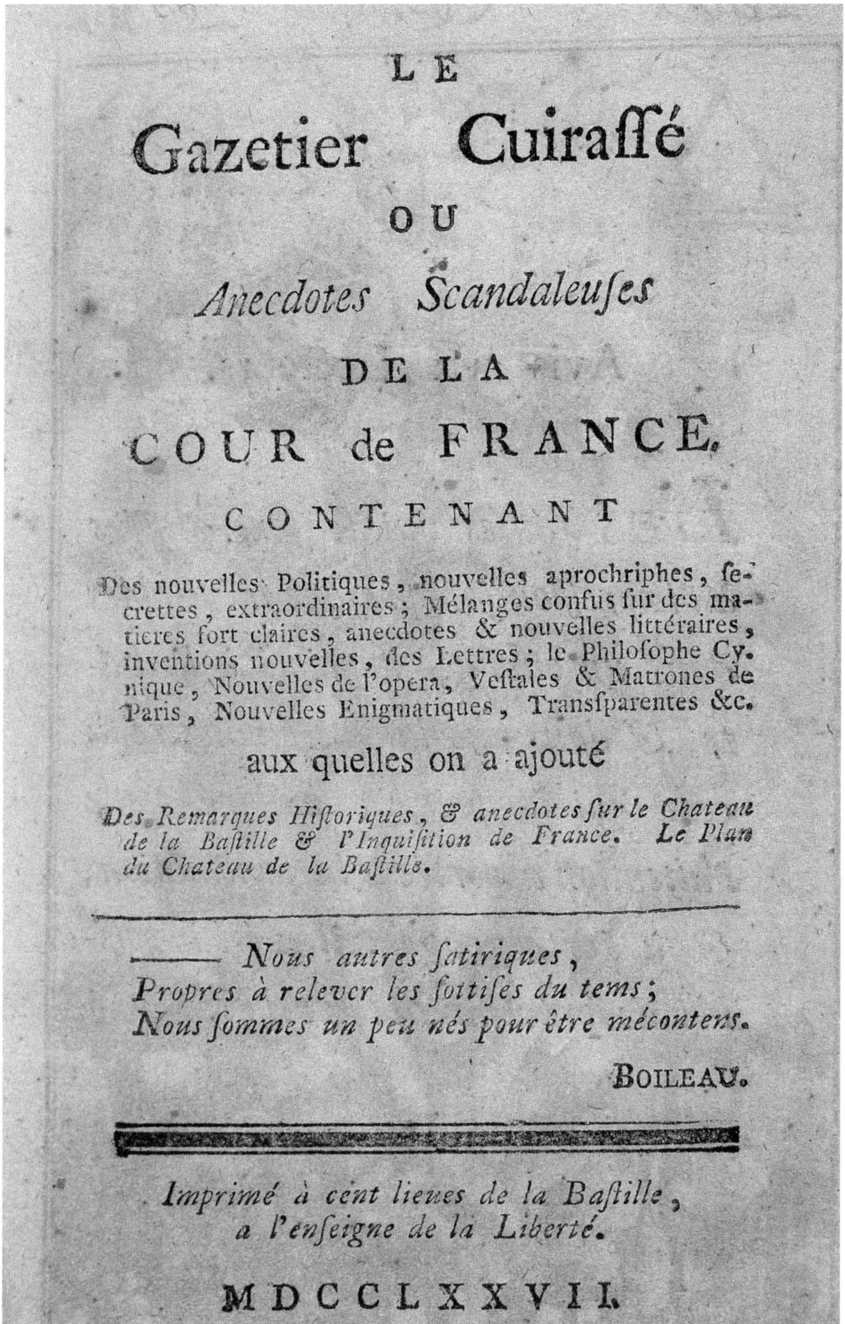

LE
Gazetier Cuiraſſé

OU

Anecdotes Scandaleuſes

DE LA

COUR de FRANCE,

CONTENANT

Des nouvelles Politiques, nouvelles aprochriphes, ſecrettes, extraordinaires; Mélanges confus ſur des matieres fort claires, anecdotes & nouvelles littéraires, inventions nouvelles, des Lettres; le Philoſophe Cynique, Nouvelles de l'opera, Veſtales & Matrones de Paris, Nouvelles Enigmatiques, Transparentes &c.

aux quelles on a ajouté

Des Remarques Hiſtoriques, & anecdotes ſur le Chateau de la Baſtille & l'Inquiſition de France. Le Plan du Chateau de la Baſtille.

———— *Nous autres ſatiriques,*
Propres à relever les ſottiſes du tems;
Nous ſommes un peu nés pour être mécontens.

BOILEAU.

Imprimé à cent lieues de la Baſtille,
a l'enſeigne de la Liberté.

MDCCLXXVII.

Figure 2. *Le Gazetier cuirassé*, title page, 1777.

Figure 3. *Le Gazetier cuirassé*, frontispiece.

title, he struck the pose of an iron-plated gazetteer, a heroic knight in armour who fired off cannonades in all directions, despite the bolts of lightning that threatened to destroy him. That much was clear, but the gazetteer was also surrounded by odd images and inscriptions, which the reader had to puzzle out and which the researcher can use to decipher some of the mysteries inherent in the history of reading. The Latin caption at the bottom reads like a riddle:

> Etna provides these weapons for the stalwart man,
> Etna which will defeat the mad fury of the giants.

To make sense of it, the reader would have to know the ancient myth about the titan Typhon who tried to storm the kingdom of Zeus by hurling Mount Etna at the heavens. Zeus fired back thunderbolts, which pinned Typhon under Etna, where he remains to this day, belching smoke and lava. Evidently the gazetteer identified himself with Typhon in a battle against the giants. He was the stalwart man shooting grapeshot at *les grands* above.

Who were the giants? The initials at the top of the frontispiece—intricately inscribed but legible enough to be deciphered—helped to identify them, provided that the reader's glance moved vertically to the images below. Underneath the 'DB' at the upper left, a barrel served as a rebus that evoked one of the anecdotes in the text: 'The equestrian statue of one of our kings was found covered with filth from a barrel, which had been overturned on top of it and covered it down to its shoulders.'[5] In 1763 a statue of Louis XV had been erected in the centre of the new Place de Louis XV (today Place de la Concorde). *Baril* in the eighteenth century was pronounced without enunciating the final *l*.[6] So the frontispiece said that Mme du Barry had defecated all over the French monarchy.

The 'SF' after the 'DB' stood for Louis Phélypeaux, comte de Saint Florentin, the minister of the king's household who was responsible for the administration of the Bastille. He countersigned all *lettres de cachet* beneath the signature of the king. So the Medusa or Gorgon head (a symbol of tyranny) beneath the 'SF' spits out thunderbolts carrying *lettres de cachet* stamped with oval seals (the *cachets*) and bearing the formulaic

---

[5] *Le Gazetier cuirassé ou anecdotes scandaleuses de la cour de France* (1777), p. 54. The edition of 1771 contains an 'Explication du frontispiece' on the reverse side of the title page, although the explanation does not go into great detail.

[6] 'Baril' in *Le Grand Vocabulaire français*, 1 (Paris, 1768), p. 147: 'Le l final est muet devant une consonne; mais il se fait sentir devant une voyelle.' See also André Martinet and Henriette Walter, *Dictionnaire de la prononciation française dans son usage réel* (Paris, 1973), p. 129.

inscription 'et plus bas Phélypeaux' ('and, lower, Phélypeaux'). At the upper right, 'DM' denoted the chancellor de Maupeou, who also spits out thunderbolts (but without *lettres de cachet*, as they did not come under his jurisdiction) intended to *foudroyer* or strike down his enemies. But the iron-plated gazetteer fires back his salvoes, undeterred and protected by clouds of smoke.

The imagery and allusions were aimed at readers knowledgeable enough to understand Latin, to connect the caption with the myth of Typhon, and to decipher all the other clues scattered across the frontispiece. The book's preface also indicates the kind of audience to which it was directed and the way it was meant to be read:

> I must warn the public that some of the news items that I present to it as true are at most likely and that they include some that are obviously false. I have not taken it upon myself to disentangle them. It is up to people in high society who know how to distinguish truth from lies (by their frequent usage of both) to judge and choose.[7]

The preface cast the readers in the role of worldly sophisticates who could sift through gossipy news items in order to extract nuggets of truth. It operated as an inducement to play a game or to solve a puzzle—for the sheer fun of it, as in the case of the word games featured in nearly all the literary reviews of the time. Every issue of *Le Mercure de France*, the most widely read periodical in the kingdom, contained *énigmes*, *charades*, and *logogryphes*, which the reader had to puzzle out. The answers always appeared in the subsequent issue along with a new set of brain teasers. 'Find the word of the enigma' (*trouver le mot de l'énigme*) was a common expression, meaning to find the key to a riddle or mystery. *Le Gazetier cuirassé* drew on this convention in a section entitled 'enigmatic news' (*nouvelles énigmatiques*). One *énigme* challenged the reader to identify a person with the following characteristics: he was '... a little mad, very cheeky, horribly false, an absolute blackguard, a villain perfidious beyond all limits, who plays an important role and passes himself off as an enlightened genius'.[8] The answer, which appeared in a 'key' at the end of the section—or, in some editions, in a footnote at the bottom of the page—was: Maupeou.

Reading as puzzle solving also characterised another popular genre, the *roman à clé*. In order to understand the hidden message of a novel,

---

[7] *Le Gazetier cuirassé*, p. v.
[8] Ibid., p. 155. See also the similar enigma on p. 151.

readers had to identify the real persons disguised behind the fictitious characters. If a key was not printed at the back of the volume, they made one of their own or bought one from the pedlars and book dealers who sold them separately.[9] *Le Gazetier cuirassé* never named its villains. It merely gave the first letters or syllables of their names and then provided a key so that its readers could verify the accuracy of their guesses. Some identifications were so obvious that they did not require keys:

> The Chancel... [Chancellor Maupeou] and the duc d'Aiguil... [d'Aiguillon, the foreign minister] have so much mastery over the k... [king] that they only leave him the freedom to sleep with his mistress, to pet his dogs, and to sign marriage contracts.[10]

But others required considerable skill and familiarity with gossip about the great. What reader would be able to identify the relatively obscure 'comtesse de la Mar...', who, 'seeing the impossibility of making a prince, decided to make a little bishop'? Answer: the comtesse de la Marck, who took up with the archbishop of Reims in order to procure an heir to her impotent husband.[11]

These items took the form of anecdotes, as announced in the book's subtitle, 'scandalous anecdotes from the court of France'. 'Anecdote' in the eighteenth century meant nearly the opposite of what it means today. As defined in contemporary dictionaries and the *Encyclopédie*, it designated a 'secret history' of the kind originally developed by Procopius in the sixth century AD—that is, an account of something that had actually happened but remained excluded from official versions of the past.[12] Anecdotes might be exaggerated, but they always contained a kernel of truth; so they, too, had to be deciphered. *Le Gazetier cuirassé* played with

---

[9] On *romans à clé* and political attacks on Louis XV, his mistresses, and ministers, see my 'Mlle Bonafon et la vie privée de Louis XV', *Dix-huitième siècle*, no. 35 (2003), 369–91.
[10] *Le Gazetier cuirassé*, p. 31.
[11] Ibid., p. 49.
[12] See, for example, 'Anecdote' in *Dictionnaire de l'Académie française* (1762 edition): 'Particularité secrète d'histoire, qui avait été omise ou supprimée par les historiens précédents. *Anecdote curieuse. Les anecdotes sont ordinairement satyriques.* Il s'emploie aussi adjectivement. *L'Histoire anecdote de Procope'*. In contrast to the negative connotations of the word today, as in 'anecdotal evidence' meaning something of dubious veracity, the article 'Anecdotes' in the *Encyclopédie* of Diderot and d'Alembert also conveyed the notion of something true but hidden: 'Anecdotes, nom que les Grecs donnaient aux choses qu'on faisait connaître pour la première fois au public.... Ce mot est en usage dans la littérature pour signifier des histoires secrètes de faits qui se sont passées dans l'intérieur du cabinet ou des cours des princes et dans les mystères de leur politique.... Procope a intitulé *Anecdotes* un livre dans lequel il peint avec des couleurs odieuses l'Empereur Justinien et Théodore, épouse de ce prince.'

the reader by attaching tantalising footnotes to its anecdotes. One footnote merely stated, 'Half of this article is true.'[13] Which half? It was up to the reader to guess. Another read, 'This adventure may well not be true, but we can be sure that it is not completely false.'[14]

Anecdotes were the building blocks from which libels were composed. They usually took the form of a paragraph, which could be combined with other paragraphs and cemented together by some transitional phrasing to make a narrative. In the case of *chroniques scandaleuses* like the *Gazetier cuirassé*, the paragraphs simply followed one another without connecting links or any general structure, like the items in contemporary newspapers provided by 'paragraph men'—and even the news 'flashes' in some forms of journalism today.[15] Libellers often lifted anecdotes from one another's texts and rearranged them to suit their own purposes. They also inflated them by making small incidents look like major scandals—a technique known as 'piping' among modern reporters. But they always selected stories that had a grain of truth. The game would not work if it involved nothing more than fiction.

Where did the iron-plated gazetteer get his information? He did not reveal his sources, although he hinted that he had secret informants in Versailles. A later pamphlet identified one of them as 'une dame de Courcelles', who relayed gossip to him by means of a clandestine correspondence.[16] The text that he cobbled together contained enough accurate information to horrify contemporaries. Voltaire, an expert on such matters, testified to its power as a vehicle for shocking readers: 'A satanic work has just appeared where everyone, from the monarch to the last

---

[13] *Le Gazetier cuirassé*, p. 34.
[14] Ibid., p. 44.
[15] The Revd Henry Bate (Dudley), known as 'the Reverend Bruiser', and the Revd William Jackson, known as 'Doctor Viper', exemplified the scandal-mongering developed by 'paragraph men' in the London press of the 1770s. A contemporary described Jackson, editor of the *Morning Post*, as follows: 'His great *forte* discovered itself in that species of writing known by the name of paragraphs, which he had the happy knack of giving more *point* to than any of his contemporaries. The acrimony of his pen soon rendered him conspicuous to the public, but the extreme and unexampled virulence of his invectives . . . only served to expose him to the resentment of Government': quoted in Lucyle Werkmeister, *The London Daily Press 1772–1792* (Lincoln, NB, 1963), p. 80. See also John Brewer, *A Sentimental Murder. Love and Madness in the Eighteenth Century* (New York, 2004), pp. 40–2. Most of the items in clandestine newsletters such as the *Mémoires secrets* consisted of a single paragraph and often were designated as anecdotes.
[16] *Le Diable dans un bénitier, et la métamorphose du Gazetier cuirassé en mouche, ou tentative du sieur Receveur, inspecteur de la police de Paris, chevalier de St. Louis, pour établir à Londres une police à l'instar de celle de Paris*, (1784), pp. 36 and 79.

citizen, is insulted with fury, where the most atrocious and absurd calumny distills a hideous poison on everything that one respects and loves.'[17]

Who was this gazetteer? He identified himself, though without breaking out of his anonymity, in the dedication of the book. It provides another example of paratextual parody, in this case a lampoon of fulsome dedications to literary patrons:[18]

Dedicatory Epistle

to ME

My dear Person,
    Enjoy your glory without concern for any danger. You will be exposed to it, of course, because of all the enemies of your fatherland. You will sharpen their fury and double their ferocity. But you should know, my dear person, that in revealing their iniquitous mysteries . . . you avenge the innocent. . . . Make them tremble, those cruel monsters whose existence is so odious and so harmful to humanity. . . .
    I know you too well to fear any slackening of your principles. Your resolve is a guarantee that you will never deviate from them. In this opinion, I am, my dear person,

your most humble and obedient servant.

Myself

Beneath the burlesque rhetoric, the author dramatised himself as a hero who battled despotism single-handedly through the power of the press. He fired off copies of his book like the cannonballs aimed at the evil powers in the frontispiece. But who was he? The answer to that puzzle appeared in the second of the four libels I would like to discuss.

Le Diable dans un bénitier (1783) also had a complex title page that required a great deal of decoding (Fig. 4). The main title played with a colloquial expression—to thrash about like a devil in a baptismal font—which referred to frantic and ineffective agitation.[19] It enticed the reader with a hint about a book full of devilry, and it left an implicit question dangling: who was this devil? The other elements of the title page also operated as bait to attract the reader's attention, because, as a trained eye

---

[17] Voltaire, 'Quisquis' in his *Questions sur l'Encyclopédie par des amateurs*, 6 (no place of publication, 1775), p. 278.
[18] *Le Gazetier cuirassé*, pp. vii–viii.
[19] According to the *Grand Dictionnaire universel du XIXe siècle* (Paris, 1866–70), the expression was picked up and popularised by Jean-Baptiste-Louis Gresset in *Ver-Vert* (1734): 'Bien vite il sut jurer et maugréer | Mieux qu'un vieux diable au fond d'un bénitier.'

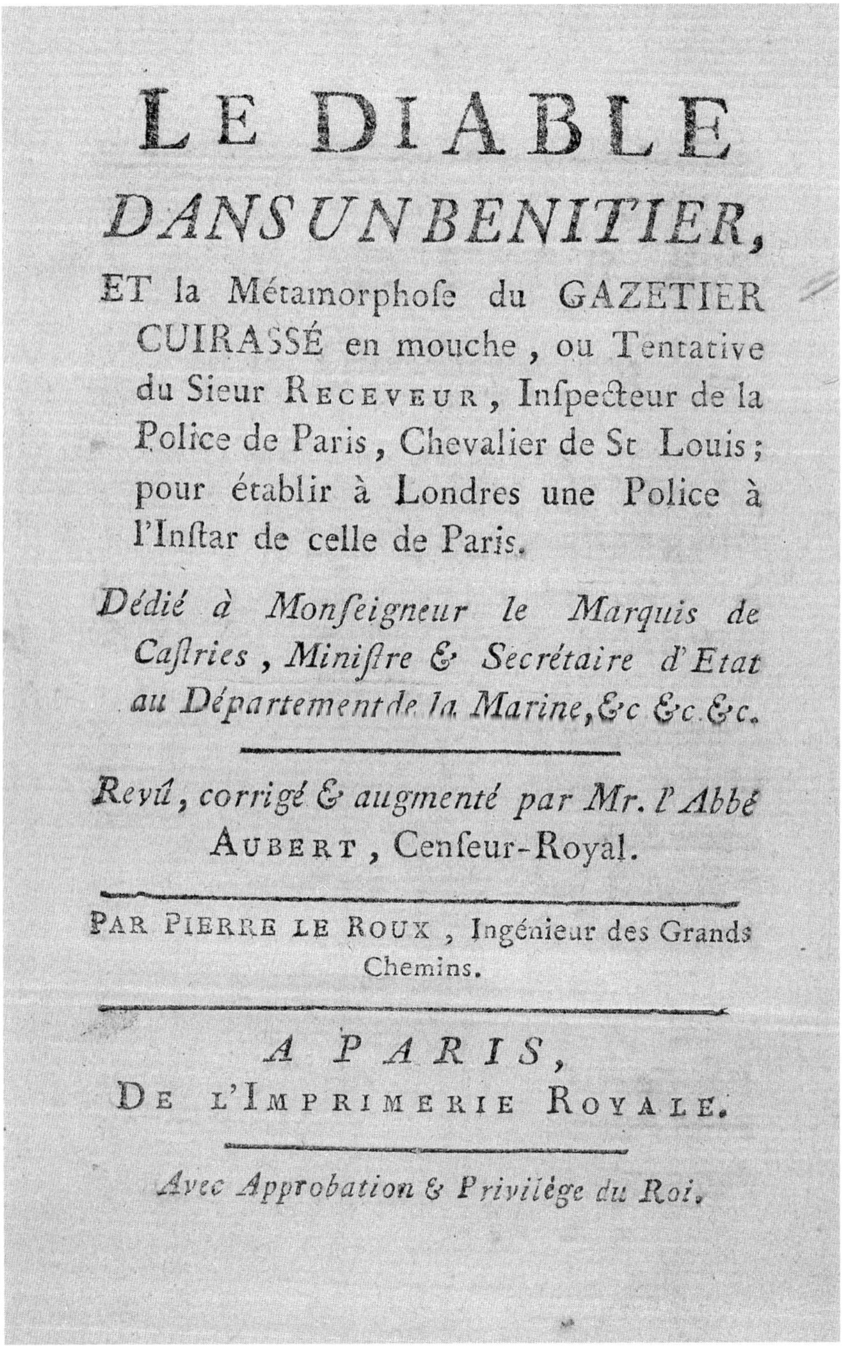

LE DIABLE
DANS UN BENITIER,

ET la Métamorphose du GAZETIER CUIRASSÉ en mouche, ou Tentative du Sieur Receveur, Inspecteur de la Police de Paris, Chevalier de St Louis; pour établir à Londres une Police à l'Instar de celle de Paris.

Dédié à Monseigneur le Marquis de Castries, Ministre & Secrétaire d'Etat au Département de la Marine, &c &c &c.

Revû, corrigé & augmenté par Mr. l'Abbé Aubert, Censeur-Royal.

Par Pierre le Roux, Ingénieur des Grands Chemins.

A PARIS,
De l'Imprimerie Royale.

Avec Approbation & Privilège du Roi.

Figure 4. *Le Diable dans un bénitier*, title page.

could easily see, they parodied all the signs of legality in a book that had been cleared through the censorship. They included a fake notice of an approbation and privilege; a fake, super-legal address (the royal printing shop); a fake author (Pierre Leroux; I have not been able to identify him); a fake editor (the abbé Jean Louis Aubert, editor of the orthodox *Gazette de France* and censor of the unorthodox *Courier de l'Europe*, a journal produced by French expatriates in London); and a fake dedication (to the marquis de Castries, minister of the navy and a main target of the slander in the text.) The long subtitle summarised the book's plot. Far from being a hero, the iron-plated gazetteer had turned coat as a 'mouche' or police spy, and he had sold out to an inspector who was trying to establish a secret branch of the Parisian police in London.

The frontispiece added new pieces to the puzzle (Fig. 5). Using ellipsis dots to disguise the names, its caption read: 'The plenipot . . . [plenipotentiary] receives the abjuration of Charlot and R . . . . . . r [Receveur] gives him the cross of Saint Andrew.' What was this devilry all about? By working through the text, the reader soon discovered the identity of the iron-plated gazetteer: he was 'Charlot' or Charles Théveneau de Morande, the most notorious libeller in the colony of French expatriates in London. Receveur was the police inspector who had arrived in London on a secret mission to exterminate the libellers. The anonymous author of *Le Diable dans un bénitier* cast these two as the villains of his narrative; and in its climactic scene, he described a burlesque ritual: Receveur inducted Morande into a Masonic-like secret society of the Parisian police. The cross on Receveur's jacket was the insignia of the order, a cross of Saint Andrew—that is, a representation of two boards attached together in the shape of an X, which the police supposedly used to hold down their victims during torture sessions in the Bastille. Around his neck, Receveur wears the order's medal, a miniature of a wheel on which prisoners were broken. He carries handcuffs in his pocket, and he dubs Morande with another symbol of despotism, tongs used to hold hot coals to prisoners' feet in order to extract confessions. By joining the secret society, Morande renounced his past as a libeller and agreed to collaborate in the repression of his former colleagues. The comte de Moustier, France's chargé d'affaires in London in 1783, presides over the scene against a background of a curtain decorated with the Bourbon fleurs de lys. On the far left, Ange Goudar, another libeller turned police spy, carries a box of opium pills, which Morande is to take in order to forget his past. Goudar accompanied Receveur to London, serving as his interpreter and guide to the literary underworld, which Goudar knew well,

Figure 5. *Le Diable dans un bénitier*, frontispiece.

having inhabited it for years. The title of his best-known *chronique scandaleuse*, *L'Espion chinois*, dangles from his pocket. And with his left arm he offers Morande the medal of the society, which will seal the satanic pact being enacted through the initiation rite.[20]

After deciphering as much as possible of the title page and frontispiece, the readers were expected to continue to play the guessing game as they made their way through the text. They had to identify the characters whose names were hidden behind ellipsis dots. One copy of the book contains a key which an eighteenth-century reader wrote on a blank sheet at the end of the volume, just as readers often did while perusing *romans à clé* (Fig. 6). It gets most of the identifications right, but it contains a few mistakes—an indication that reading really did involve puzzle solving and that the puzzles could be difficult, even for seemingly well-informed contemporaries.[21] But there was no mistaking the libellous character of the text. It slandered the most powerful men in France, from ministers down to their subordinates in the police force, and it treated the entire system as a noxious form of despotism, which it contrasted with England, a regime where the liberty of the press and other fundamental rights were respected. Curiously, however, this radical political message was embedded in a story that was designed to entertain its readers. Libelling in 1783 appealed to *homo ludens*; it had a play-element to it.

The narrative recounts Receveur's efforts, aided by Morande, to destroy the colony of French libellers, and in doing so it includes a short and slanderous biography of each man—in effect, libels within the libel. It describes Morande as the depraved son of a corrupt attorney in Burgundy, whose career combined writing with crime. After enlisting in a cavalry regiment, he deserted, drifted into the underworld of gambling dens and brothels in Paris, and landed in the infamous prison of Bicêtre. Upon his release, he emigrated to London, where he lived by pimping for homosexuals and blackmailing them. The success of *Le Gazetier cuirassé* convinced him that he could do better by blackmailing the greatest figures

---

[20] This scene is described in the text: *Le Diable dans un bénitier*, pp. 84–5. It was not meant to be taken literally but rather to express Morande's defection to the police.

[21] On the left side of the page, the key gives the number of the page on which a name first appears. The next column gives the disguised versions of the names as they were printed, with dashes to conceal their full identity. The column on the right gives the identifications worked out by the reader. He or she wrongly identified 'le Gazetier cuirassé' as Beamarchais and 'M. De la F—' as a 'M. de la Fare'. In fact, De la F—stood for la Fite de Pelleport—or so I have concluded after a close reading of the text and a study of Pelleport's career. The key is in a copy that I possess.

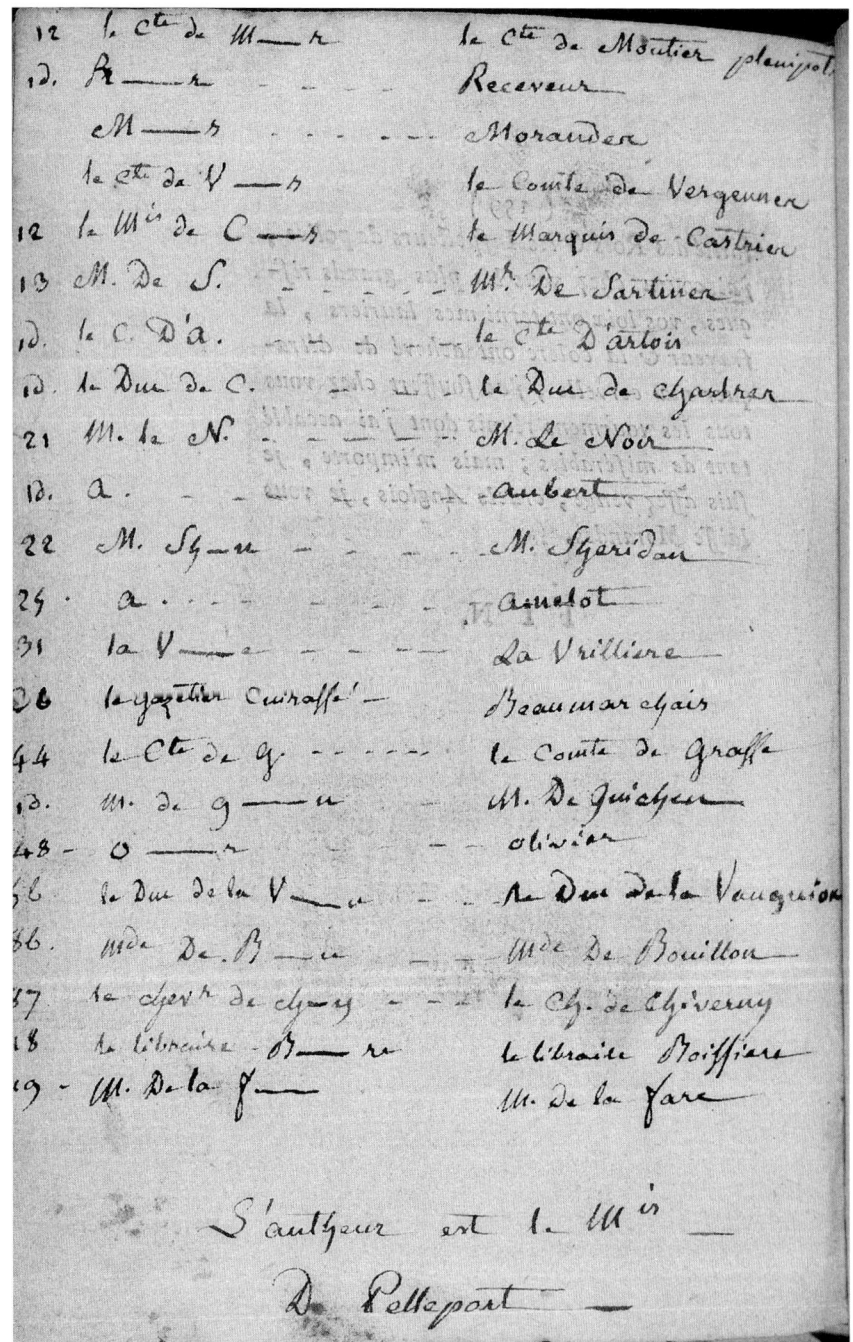

Figure 6. *Le Diable dans un bénitier*, manuscript key by an eighteenth-century reader.

in the French court. He therefore threatened to publish a sequel to it, *Mémoires secrets d'une femme publique*, which would relate the inside story of Mme du Barry's ignominious origins and her ascension from a brothel to the throne. In order to prevent such horrors from circulating in print, the French government dispatched Beaumarchais to buy Morande off: a matter of 32,000 livres and an annuity of 4,000 livres. From then on, Morande renounced libelling and collaborated with the attempts of the French authorities to repress the libellers who followed in his footsteps.

As described in *Le Diable dans un bénitier*, Receveur outdid Morande in villainy, for he was the actual devil in the holy water. Born with a penchant for cruelty—as a child he trotted after inspectors hauling off victims to torture chambers and as an adolescent he aspired to marry the daughter of the public executioner—he became a police agent who specialised in kidnapping exiled writers and torturing them in the Bastille. In fact, as *Le Diable dans un bénitier* revealed, he was the last in a series of secret agents sent to murder, abduct, or buy off the libellers in London. After Beaumarchais moved on to other adventures, the government commissioned Louis Valentin Goezman, Beaumarchais's opponent in a famous court case that compromised the Maupeou judiciary in 1773–4, to prevent the publication of a libel against Marie-Antoinette. Disguised as an Alsatian 'baron de Thurne', Goezman purchased the (purportedly) entire edition of *Les Amours de Charlot et Toinette*—an obscene poem-pamphlet about the supposed impotence of Louis XVI and the queen's supposed orgies with his younger brother, the comte d'Artois—for 17,400 livres. Then he warned that more books on the same subject were in press; and having run up a suspiciously high expense account, he kept repeating the same refrain: send money.

Instead, *Le Diable dans un bénitier* recounted, the French authorities sent another agent, Alexis d'Anouilh, a police spy attached to the naval ministry who knew nothing about England, except that it rained a great deal there. He therefore set off for London disguised as an umbrella merchant. Gravitating to taverns and gambling dens, he, too, accumulated huge expenses. Eventually he made contact with Richard Sheridan, the playwright who had become an undersecretary for foreign affairs in 1782. With Sheridan's help, he hoped to get Parliament to pass a bill that would make it a crime to libel non-British subjects living abroad—such as the queen of France. To round up the necessary votes in the House, Sheridan would have to pay out vast sums in bribes. So d'Anouilh returned to Versailles for consultations and a bigger expense account. After hearing him out, the naval minister, the marquis de Castries, promptly sent him to the Bastille. Receveur, who delivered the *lettre de cachet*, eventually tortured d'Anouilh into revealing how he had misspent the king's money. But then the government needed to find another agent.

At this point, faute de mieux, it fell back on Receveur himself. It dispatched him to London disguised as a 'baron de Livermont'. Admittedly (all this according to *Le Diable dans un bénitier*) he had a defect: boneheadedness. He was so stupid that he could barely read and write. But at least he could be trusted. After setting up headquarters in Jermyn Street with a staff of hit men and intermediaries, he attempted to flush the libellers from their hiding places and favourite haunts, notably the French bookshop of Boissière in St James Street. As *Le Diable* recounted it, Receveur's efforts at detective work turned into a comedy of errors. Unable to speak a word of English and baffled by the customs of the natives—strange prejudices like habeas corpus, trial by jury, and the liberty of the press—he tripped over his own feet and got nowhere.

At first he tried kidnapping. He had arrived with a full kit of handcuffs, chains, and all the paraphernalia of despotism, including a carriage with a secret compartment big enough to contain a trussed-up victim, who could be smuggled back to Paris and tortured in the Bastille so that the police could unravel the whole network of authors, printers, and clandestine pedlars. But *force majeure* failed, because the libellers got wind of the plot and exposed it in a broadside, which called upon all brave Britons to stand up against a gang of perfidious Frenchmen who were threatening British liberty (Fig. 7). In 1783 London was still seething with the anti-French mania stirred up by the American War and memories of the Gordon Riots. A crowd had set upon an earlier contingent of police agents who had attempted to kidnap Morande in order to prevent the publication of *Mémoires secrets d'une femme publique*. Receveur therefore changed his strategy and attempted to revive the plan to bribe Parliament. But he lacked the skill to negotiate with Sheridan, so he finally attempted to engage in *pourparlers* over blackmail payments, using Boissière as a middleman. His goal was to suppress three works announced by the libellers: *Les Passe-temps d'Antoinette*, another exposé of the queen's sex life; *Les Amours du vizir de Vergennes*, an attack on the foreign minister; and *Les Petits Soupers de l'Hôtel de Bouillon*, an account of orgies by the princesse de Bouillon and the marquis de Castries. The bidding got up to 150 louis (3,600 livres), which Receveur was willing to pay, but the hidden libeller demanded 175 louis (4,200 livres), which was more than Receveur had been authorised to spend. In the end, therefore,

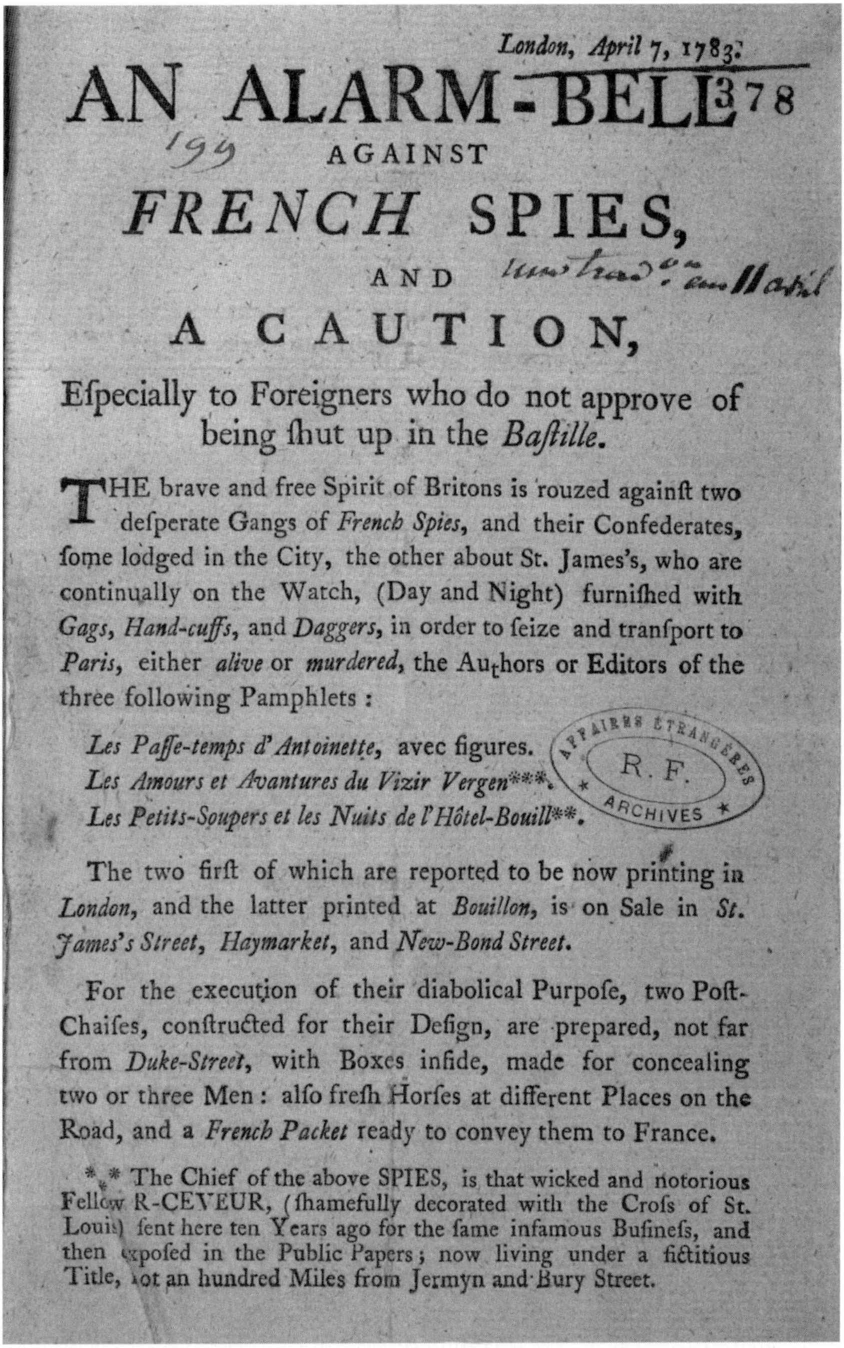

London, April 7, 1783.

AN ALARM-BELL
AGAINST
FRENCH SPIES,
AND
A CAUTION,

Especially to Foreigners who do not approve of being shut up in the *Bastille*.

THE brave and free Spirit of Britons is rouzed against two desperate Gangs of *French Spies*, and their Confederates, some lodged in the City, the other about St. James's, who are continually on the Watch, (Day and Night) furnished with *Gags, Hand-cuffs,* and *Daggers,* in order to seize and transport to *Paris,* either *alive* or *murdered,* the Authors or Editors of the three following Pamphlets:

Les Passe-temps d'Antoinette, avec figures.
Les Amours et Avantures du Vizir Vergen***.
Les Petits-Soupers et les Nuits de l'Hôtel-Bouill**.

The two first of which are reported to be now printing in *London,* and the latter printed at *Bouillon,* is on Sale in *St. James's Street, Haymarket,* and *New-Bond Street.*

For the execution of their diabolical Purpose, two Post-Chaises, constructed for their Design, are prepared, not far from *Duke-Street,* with Boxes inside, made for concealing two or three Men: also fresh Horses at different Places on the Road, and a *French Packet* ready to convey them to France.

*** The Chief of the above SPIES, is that wicked and notorious Fellow R-CEVEUR, (shamefully decorated with the Cross of St. Louis) sent here ten Years ago for the same infamous Business, and then exposed in the Public Papers; now living under a fictitious Title, not an hundred Miles from Jermyn and Bury Street.

Figure 7. A broadside alerting Londoners to Receveur's mission in 1783.

the negotiations broke down, Receveur returned to Paris, and the libeller took revenge by exposing the whole business in *Le Diable dans un bénitier*, a libel about libelling, which took Morande, the police, and their superiors in Versailles as its target.

The libellers, by contrast, appeared as the heroes of the story. Unlike Morande, they defied the police and continued to attack French despotism, undeterred by the danger and glorying in the freedom of the press guaranteed by the British constitution. The author did not mention them by name, of course. In fact, he hinted in places that they were a rum lot, as they resorted to blackmailing their enemies. But the narrative skirted round that awkward point by concentrating on the ineptitude of their persecutors. Despite its denunciations of the French police state and its uninhibited radicalism, it read like a burlesque farce—an account of failed hugger-mugger on the part of a bunch of clowns decked out in absurd disguises who believed they could plant the seeds of despotism in the unfavourable climate of England. *Le Diable dans un bénitier* was just as irreverent as *Le Gazetier cuirassé* but much wittier and better written. So the question inevitably arises: who wrote it?

The answer is to be found in the third libel, *La Police de Paris dévoilée* (Fig. 8). Here, however, we are faced with a work that appears to belong to another order of literature. We are in 1790, the 'second year of liberty', as the book proclaims on its title page. It carries an honest, straightforward address, 'chez J. B. Garnery, rue Serpente, no. 17', and its title is short and clear, set off by a classical page design, which contrasts with the baroque title pages of the previous two libels and their long, satirical wording. We have moved into a new era, when the dominant metaphors take the form of unveiling and unmasking. As the epigraph makes clear and the text reiterates, 'publicité'—transparency in public affairs guaranteed by the liberty of the press—is the basic condition of a healthy political system.

La Police de Paris dévoilée presented itself as a manifestation of patriotism, and its author, Pierre Manuel, assumed the role of a selfless patriot. He placed his name prominently, in capital letters, on the title page. He dedicated the book to the members of the Jacobin Club, and he explained in the dedication that he wrote in his capacity as an administrator of the Paris Commune, where he had assumed the duty of overseeing the policing of the book trade. Unlike his predecessors under the *Ancien Régime*, he did not confiscate books but instead intervened to prevent their confiscation. He revered the liberty of the press as his highest principle. Indeed, he took advantage of his access to the papers of the

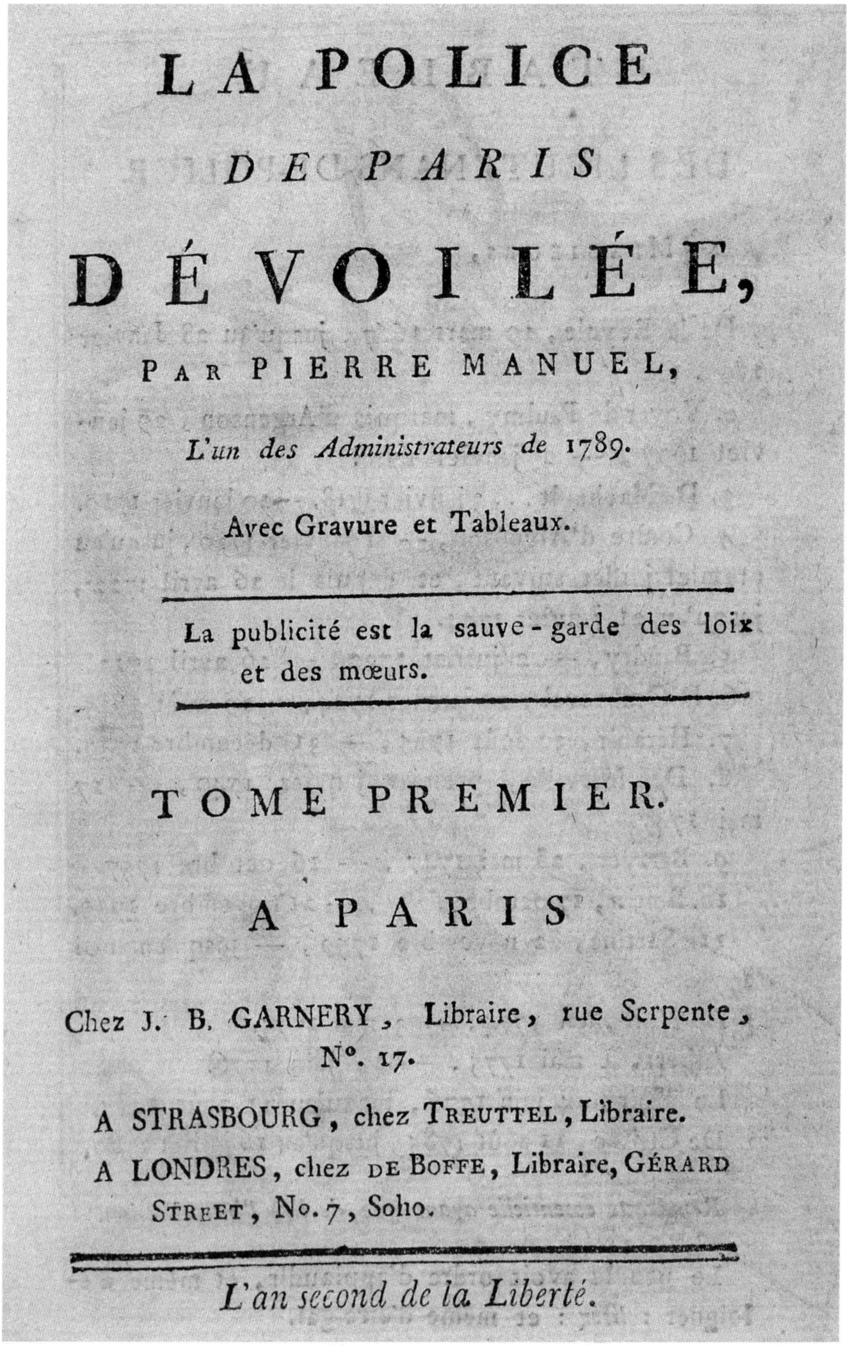

LA POLICE
DE PARIS
DÉVOILÉE,

PAR PIERRE MANUEL,

L'un des Administrateurs de 1789.

Avec Gravure et Tableaux.

La publicité est la sauve-garde des loix et des mœurs.

TOME PREMIER.

A PARIS

Chez J. B. GARNERY, Libraire, rue Serpente, N°. 17.

A STRASBOURG, chez TREUTTEL, Libraire.
A LONDRES, chez DE BOFFE, Libraire, GÉRARD STREET, No. 7, Soho.

L'an second de la Liberté.

Figure 8. *La Police de Paris dévoilée*, title page.

police in order to expose their abuses: hence this volume, which every citizen should read as evidence of the despotism that had stifled free expression before 1789 and as a summons to be on guard against future threats to liberty.

The frontispiece provides an iconographic version of the theme of unveiling (Fig. 9). It shows the Bastille in the background, where two police agents are hauling off a victim in handcuffs. In the foreground, two figures in antique costumes convey a symbolic message: Innocence or Truth lies chained on a bed of straw as if in a cell of the Bastille, while Perfidy or Tyranny, unmasked and with a another Medusa-like head, prepares to plunge a dagger into the victim's breast. Above this scene, a winged figure, possibly meant to be Chronos, pulls back a curtain revealing these evil deeds, and at the same time he spreads light from a torch held high. Manuel seemed to identify himself with this figure, because he placed his name under it and, in the dedication, proclaimed his role as an investigator who would uncover the crimes of the police under the *Ancien Régime*, exposing them to the light of 'publicité'.

The text consisted of two volumes of extracts from the police archives recovered after the storming of the Bastille. Manuel guaranteed their accuracy and said that he had deposited them at the Parisian Lycée, a patriotic club where any citizen could inspect them in order to verify their content. But he also edited them, eliminating some things and featuring others. A great deal of the text looks like scandal published for its own sake. Whole sections were devoted to the adventures of priests in brothels (30 pages), prostitution in general (48 pages), gambling dens (14 pages), and assorted vice (144 pages, mainly about incidents involving depraved aristocrats and dancing girls). The entire book has a sensational character reinforced by the editing, which separates the episodes into anecdotes, usually a paragraph in length. Thus a typical item about venereal disease among the great:

> The prince de Conti was wounded by a young girl known as the little f . . . . . . He is furious at Guerin, his surgeon.[22]

The unveiling, however true, reads like the scandalous 'news' dished out in pre-revolutionary *chroniques scandaleuses*, *nouvelles à la main*, and manuscript police gazettes. Manuel exposed shocking behaviour under the reign of Louis XVI just as the libellers from that era pulled the veil off

---

[22] Pierre Manuel, *La Police de Paris dévoilée* 1 (Paris, 1790), p. 91.

Figure 9. *La Police de Paris dévoilée*, frontispiece.

scandal that had occurred under Louis XV.[23] Retrospective libel was an old technique, but *La Police de Paris dévoilée* represented a new, revolutionary version of it. The book belonged to a series of exposés, all of them drawn from the police archives and edited, at least in part, by Manuel: *La Bastille dévoilée* (1789), *La Chasteté du clergé dévoilée* (1790), and *Lettres originales de Mirabeau, écrites du donjon de Vincennes* (1792). It also contained material that was recycled later in a work whose title conveyed the flavour of the genre, *La Chronique scandaleuse ou mémoires pour servir à l'histoire de la génération présente, contenant les anecdotes & les pièces fugitives les plus piquantes que l'histoire secrète des sociétés a offertes pendant ces dernières années* (Paris, 'dans un coin d'où l'on voit tout', 1791)—and that had originally appeared in 1783.[24]

One of the principal scandals exposed in *La Police de Paris dévoilée* was the story behind *Le Diable dans un bénitier*. In fact, *La Police de Paris dévoilée* contained so much material about the attempts of the police to eradicate the London libellers that it can be read, at least in part, as a sequel to *Le Diable dans un bénitier*, which it quoted at length. Manuel confirmed the accuracy of the narrative in the earlier book; he recounted its dénouement, and he revealed the name of its author: Anne-Gédéon Lafite, marquis de Pelleport.

The entries on Pelleport in *La Police dévoilée* provide a brief biography of his 'private life,' revealing a Grub Street existence similar to Morande's. Pelleport was a nobleman and a déclassé who had been discharged from two regiments and imprisoned several times at the request of his family 'for atrocities against honour'.[25] He took up hack writing, drifted to Geneva and Neuchâtel, married a chambermaid, and fathered several children while working as a private teacher. In 1783 he abandoned his family in order to seek his fortune in London, where he lived by tutoring, writing libels, and using the libels to blackmail eminent people in

---

[23] Although a great deal of 'Maupeouana' (pamphlets against the Maupeou government) circulated under the cloak in 1771–4, some of the most widely diffused attacks on Louis XV and his ministers appeared after the king's death on 10 May 1774. They include *Anecdotes sur Mme la comtesse du Barry* (1775), *Mémoires de l'abbé Terray, contrôleur général, contenant sa vie, son administration, ses intrigues et sa chute* (1776), and *L'Observateur anglais, ou correspondance secrète entre Milord All'Eye et Milord All'Ear* also known as *L'Espion anglais* (1777–8).

[24] *La Chronique scandaleuse* originally appeared in one volume in 1783. By 1791, it had grown to five volumes, which included a great deal of material lifted from other sources. In volume I, 29–31 it recounted Receveur's mission in a manner close to that in *Le Diable dans un bénitier*, and it reworked material from *La Police de Paris dévoilée* in volume V, pp. 143–75. See also the preface and introduction to volume V. Plagiarism of this kind was typical of libel literature.

[25] *La Police de Paris dévoilée*, II, 235. See also II, 28.

France. The last attempt at blackmail failed, exactly as related in *Le Diable dans un bénitier*. After its publication, Morande captured some page proofs with corrections in Pelleport's handwriting. He forwarded them to the Paris police; they lured Pelleport to Boulogne-sur-mer and locked him up in the Bastille on 11 July 1784. He stayed there for more than four years and was released only because his nemesis, the foreign minister Vergennes, had died and the new ministers were more concerned with the preparations for the Estates General than with a genre of polemics that went back to the reign of Louis XV. But the genre took on new life after 1789, thanks in large part to the unveiling and unmasking done by writers like Pierre Manuel. So we face a final question: who was he?

He appears on the frontispiece of the fourth and last libel in the series, *Vie secrète de Pierre Manuel* (1793) (Fig. 10).

The image provides a straightforward view of Manuel looking out at the reader in a dignified pose, the sash of a deputy to the Convention around his shoulder. But the caption conveys the secret hidden behind the picture:

> I was not born with a delicate disposition,
> My soul is sordid and vulgar,
> I have pillaged altars and betrayed the state
> In order to increase my fortune.

The contrast between the undoctored image and the tendentious caption is typical of all the 'private lives' or slanderous biographies from the Old Regime and the Revolution. Here, for example, is the frontispiece of *Anecdotes sur Mme la comtesse du Barry* (1776), one of the best-selling libels of the pre-revolutionary period (Fig. 11).

Despite the strong elements of continuity from the libel literature of the *Ancien Régime*, the revolutionary libels adopted a fundamentally new tone. As one can see at a glance from their frontispieces and title pages, they do not try to attract the reader with the prospect of games to play. They offer nothing to decipher, no jokes to get, no ambiguity, no humour. Instead, they employ a rhetoric aimed at a different audience: the common people or sans-culottes. They also utilise a popular variety of imagery, one that did not assume any sophistication on the part of the public. To illustrate that point, I would like to make a quick detour into revolutionary iconography.

After 14 July 1789, the streets of Paris were flooded with images — caricatures, broadsides, canards, posters, portraits, engravings about current events. They were churned out by craftsmen in the rue Saint Jacques,

Figure 10. *Vie secrète de Pierre Manuel*, print serving as a frontispiece.

Sans esprit, sans talens, du sein de l'infamie
  Jusques au trône on la porta :
  Contre une Cabale ennemie
  Jamais elle ne complotta :
Et de l'ambition ignorant les allarmes,
Jouet des intriguans, regna par ses seuls charmes.

Figure 11. *Anecdotes sur Mme la comtesse du Barry*, frontispiece.

hung up for sale in book shops everywhere, and peddled through the streets. A public hungry for information of all kinds wanted to know what the new race of politicians looked like and what kind of lives they had led. A popular print went perfectly with a 'private' or 'secret' life.[26]

Vie secrète de Pierre Manuel belonged to this street literature. The portrait probably was not intended as a frontispiece. It was glued like a cancel between the last two leaves of the first gathering—that is, between pages six and seven. The book or pamphlet—sixty-three pages in length—is a crude piece of work: an octavo in half sheets, or eight gatherings of cheap, flimsy paper stitched together without any extraneous material—except the print of Manuel.

The print probably belonged to the series of engravings of deputies to the National Convention that were hawked in the streets after the collapse of the monarchy on 10 August 1792. Hundreds of these prints can be studied in the collections of the Bibliothèque nationale de France. I have located eight of Manuel, all slightly different but apparently derived from the same source: a painting of Manuel by Joseph Ducreux now in the museum of Versailles. Ducreux belonged to the circle of David; Manuel belonged to the Jacobin Club. They made a likely pair, especially during the hottest months in 1792, when Manuel gained notoriety as the public prosecutor of the Commune and as an official active during the journée of 10 August and the massacres of 2–6 September. When he took his seat in the Convention on 21 September 1792, Manuel stood out as one of the best known radicals in the Parisian delegation. Although he has been pretty well forgotten today (there is no biography of him), he was someone worthy of figuring in the Revolution's gallery of patriots and rogues.[27]

This print, a rather flattering portrait of Manuel without anything negative in its caption, probably dates from August or September, 1792 (Fig. 12). It bears an address that shows its origins in the heart of the print-making area of Paris: 'chez Basset, at the rue St Jacques at the

---

[26] On popular prints and the French Revolution, see Antoine de Baecque, *La Caricature révolutionnaire* (Paris, 1988); Klaus Harding and Rolf Reichardt, *Die Bildpublizistik der Französischen Revolution* (Frankfurt am Main, 1989); and *French Caricature and the French Revolution* (Los Angeles), a catalogue of an exhibition held in 1988 at the Grunwald Center for the Graphic Arts, Wright Art Gallery, University of California, Los Angeles.

[27] Much of Manuel's biography can be pieced together from his numerous publications, his speeches in the Jacobin Club and in the Convention, and the dossier of his arrest in 1786 for involvement with a pamphlet on the Diamond Necklace Affair: Archives Nationales W 295, no. 246. Brief biographical sketches of Manuel appear under his name in Auguste Kuscinski, *Dictionnaire des conventionnels* (Paris, 1916–19) and Louis Gabriel Michaud, *Biographie universelle ancienne et moderne* (Paris, 1843–65).

Figure 12. Print of Manuel, 1792.

corner of the [rue] des Mathurins'. Paul-André Basset was the most important producer and dealer of prints during the Revolution.[28] He made a fortune and hewed to the dominant political line, from the early enthusiasm for Louis XVI through the Terror to the Empire. In 1790, he sold this print, a bawdy commentary on the secularising of the monasteries, which shows his shop, located at the juncture of the rue St Jacques and the rue des Mathurins at the image of a basset hound (Fig. 13). In the background, one can see a saleswoman sitting behind the counter with prints piled in front of her and displayed outside the door. A pedlar walks out of the shop, setting forth to hawk his wares in the street. On his pack one can make out one of the most popular prints of 1789: a bent-over peasant carrying a priest and a nobleman on his back and lamenting, 'One must hope that this game will finish soon.'

This royalist print from December 1792 shows Manuel in the company of the radical republicans who had led the attacks on Louis XVI (Fig. 14). While a motley crew of agitators tries to save the nation—represented as an ice sculpture that is melting under rays from a Bourbon sun—he flounders ignominiously on a manure pile accompanied by a notorious open letter to the king that he had published a month after assuming the office of public prosecutor of the Commune on 2 December 1791. It began with a phrase that made him famous: 'Sire, I do not like kings.'[29] By the time he entered the Convention, Manuel had acquired the reputation of a left-wing Jacobin and champion of the sans-culottes. The engraving in *Vie secrète de Pierre Manuel* was typical of the prints that proliferated in the wake of a revolutionary's rise to power. It belonged to the imagery visible everywhere in the streets of Paris (Fig. 15).

The layout of the text also suggests a work that was meant to be hawked in the streets. The title page is the simplest in the family of four libels. It consists of nothing more than a short title plus an epigraph and an address but no author's name. We are back where we began, with anonymous slandering. By revealing Manuel's secret life, the libeller stripped away the mask of patriotism that disguised his sordid self-interest. In contrast to the unmasking that took place in the pre-revolutionary libels, however, the text contains no allusions to be puzzled out, no games to be played. It is deadly serious. A note at the end of the last page says that Manuel has just been arrested: 'May he serve as an example for

---

[28] Maxime Préaud, Pierre Casselle, Marianne Grivel, Cormine Le Bitouzé, *Dictionnaire des éditeurs d'estampes sous l'Ancien Régime* (Paris, 1987).
[29] Kuscinski, *Dictionnaire des Conventionnels*, article 'Manuel'.

Figure 13. A satirical print of 1790 showing Basset's shop (detail).

Figure 14. A royalist print of 1792 satirising Manuel and other leaders of the left.

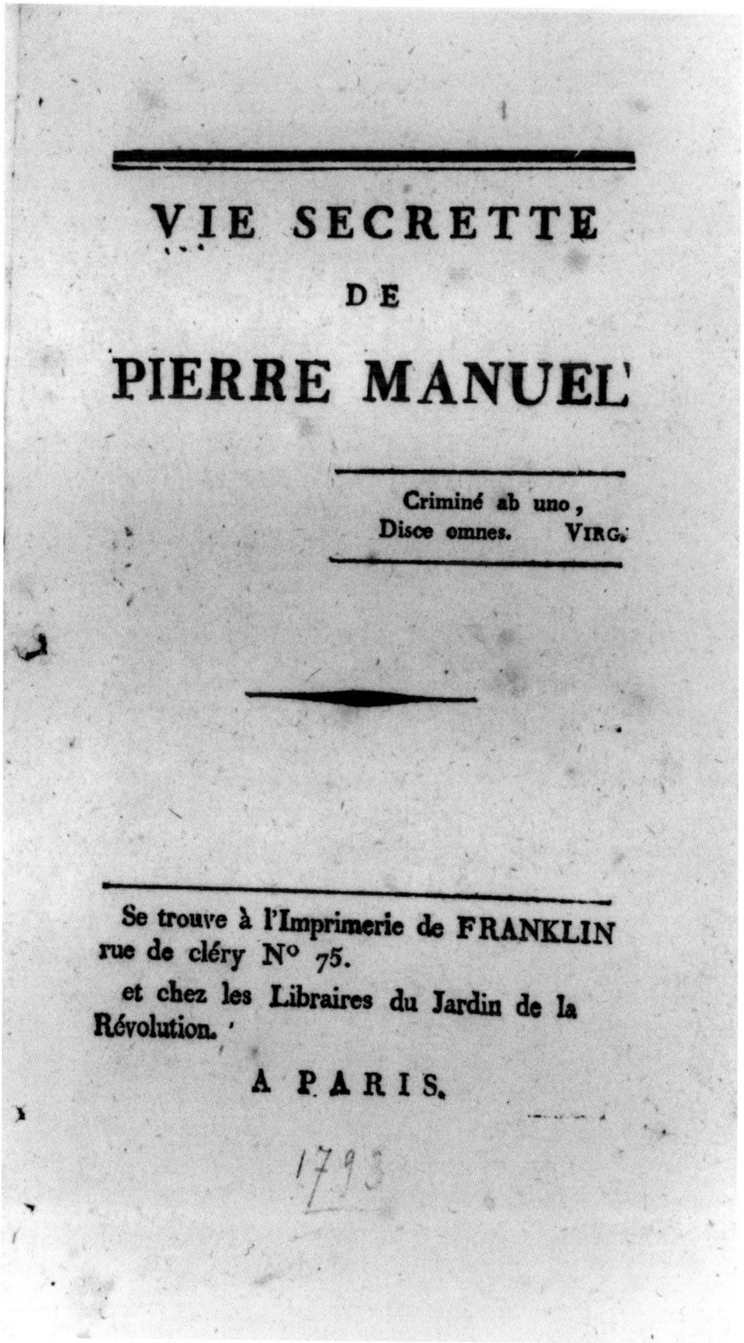

VIE SECRETTE

DE

PIERRE MANUEL

Criminé ab uno,
Disce omnes. VIRG.

Se trouve à l'Imprimerie de FRANKLIN rue de cléry N° 75.
et chez les Libraires du Jardin de la Révolution.

A PARIS.

1793

Figure 15. *Vie secrète de Pierre Manuel*, title page.

anyone audacious enough to imitate him.'[30] The arrest occurred on 20 August 1793. Manuel was tried by the Revolutionary Tribunal on 12 November and executed on 14 November.

Vie secrète de Pierre Manuel was Jacobin propaganda, a crude call for the guillotine. In order to expose the private life hidden behind Manuel's public career, it took the form of a slanderous biography. Manuel was the son of a poor haberdasher in Montargis, it explained. He did so well in school that his parents sent him to a seminary, hoping he would become a priest. Instead, he became a Voltairean, drifted to Paris, sank into poverty, and survived by expedients, including a tract on the Diamond Necklace Affair that led to a stint in the Bastille. By 1789, he had moved into a room in the printing shop of Garnery in the rue Serpente, the bookseller who later published *La Police de Paris dévoilée*. In exchange for his lodging, Manuel corrected proofs, wrote the occasional libel, and distributed material to pedlars. Thanks to his good relations with the pedlars, who supported his campaign to be elected to the Commune as a representative of his district, he gained a foothold in local politics and wormed his way into the office under the mayor that supervised the policing of the book trade.

Once installed in power, Manuel began to make money. Instead of using his authority to confiscate libels, he wrote them. He culled through the police archives in order to extract 'libertine anecdotes',[31] which he published under the pretence of revealing abuses from the *Ancien Régime*. In fact, his publications only had a negative effect: they corrupted the morals of revolutionary youths while fattening Manuel's purse. He made still more money by blackmailing people such as Champion de Cicé, the archbishop of Bordeaux, who paid 3,000 livres to keep his dossier out of print. Mirabeau's letters, which Manuel published with Garnery in January 1792, made him both rich and famous, because they led to a highly publicised trial engineered by the royalist authorities of the Department of Paris. They accused him of pilfering the letters from the archives and suspended him as the Commune's prosecuting attorney. Manuel rebutted the charges in a burst of patriotic oratory which made him a hero to the public. Reinstalled in office, he helped himself to the property that he confiscated from counter-revolutionaries, and he reinforced his cover as a champion of the people by radical speeches in the Jacobin Club. During the overthrow of the monarchy and the September

---

[30] *Vie secrète de Pierre Manuel*, p. 63.
[31] Ibid., p. 48.

Massacres, he appeared at the side of the sans-culotte leaders. But the contradiction between his public and private lives surfaced as soon as he became embroiled in the politics of the Convention. He sat with the Girondins, voted against the death of the king, and then retired to Montargis in the hope of enjoying his ill-gotten gains in obscurity. In the end, as in the case of all false patriots, the Revolution caught up with him. His life illustrated the greatest danger facing the republic in 1793: vice disguised as virtue.

Everything about *Vie secrète de Pierre Manuel*, its slipshod style as well as its crude printing, suggests that it was a hack work put out at great haste by the propaganda machine of Robespierre and the Committee of Public Safety. It belonged to a series of similar libels, all of them anonymous, produced in the Year II (1793–4) with the same address, 'à l'Imprimerie de Franklin, rue de Cléry no. 75'. They included *Vie secrète et politique de Brissot, Vie de Capet, ci-devant duc d'Orléans, Vie privée et politique de J.-R. Hébert*, and *Vie politique de Jérôme Pétion* (this last libel actually had no address). The Robespierrists needed to win over public opinion in 1793–4, just as Maupeou did in 1771, but they dealt with a different public, one that responded to denunciation and moral indignation, not wit and word games.

The succession of 'private lives' actually extended through the entire Revolution. I have found thirty-eight of them published between 1789 and 1800—or forty-two, if one counts short biographies grouped together in a single volume. Most of the revolutionary leaders were slandered in this fashion, from Lafayette and Mirabeau to Marat, Robespierre, and the top figures of the Directory. The line also extends far back into the *Ancien Régime*. *Vie privée de Louis XV, Mémoires de Mme la marquise de Pompadour*, and *Anecdotes sur Mme la comtesse du Barry* made most of the century look like a continuous *chronique scandaleuse*. Moreover, those works derived from varieties of slander that went back to the Huguenot attacks on Louis XIV, the Fronde, the religious wars, and the power struggles in the Renaissance courts of Italy. Libelling of this sort still exists today. *Primary Colors*, an anonymous *roman à clé* about the private life of Bill Clinton, shows that the tradition has life in it yet.

But the long-term continuities should not obscure the differences that stand out if one examines libel literature up close during a particular era. The four works that I have discussed represent successive stages of libelling as it evolved from the France of Louis XV to that of Louis XVI, the early Revolution and the Terror. By studying the common qualities of the libels, one can see the basic continuity in their character while distinguishing changes in their content and style.

The most important change was a shift from the seditious but playful and sophisticated slander of 1771 to the crude denunciation of 1793. Change also can be pinpointed by studying the self-referential nature of the libels. Each linked up with its predecessors to form an intertextual narrative about slander, blackmail, and political conflict. Nearly every detail in that story can be confirmed by documents in the French ministry of foreign affairs and the police archives. But instead of drawing on those sources in order to relate the story in a conventional manner, I have tried to tell it from the texts themselves, at a level that Roland Barthes has defined as 'mythologique'.[32] I also have attempted to show how the intertextual connections made by means of words, pictures, and typography expressed complex views of authorship, from Morande's dramatisation of himself as the intrepid gazetteer to Pelleport's mockery of the police from the perspective of their enemies and Manuel's self-glorification as the patriot who unmasked the whole business—only to be unmasked himself in the deadliest of the 'private lives'. The interlinked story about literary low-life may not be edifying, but I hope it opens up the possibility of pursuing book history into Grub Streets, both in Paris and in London, and from there to the battle of books at the heart of the French Revolution.

---

[32] Roland Barthes, *Mythologies* (Paris, 1957). My forthcoming *Slander: the Art of Libel in Eighteenth-Century France* includes an account of the attempts to repress libels as seen from the archives in the Quai d'Orsay and the papers of the Bastille.

2005 MASTER-MIND LECTURE

Einstein

JOHN STACHEL
Boston University

Henrietta Hertz and the Master-Mind Lectures

MISS HENRIETTE HERTZ, the Maecenas of these lectures, died in 1913.[1] She bequeathed the *Palazzo Zuccari* in Rome, which she had reconstructed, to the *Kaiser-Wilhelm-Gesellschaft*[2] in Berlin: 'With the aim that, in accord with its tradition, it shall serve the lasting cultivation of art and science.'[3] In that same year, Albert Einstein was offered a position as a Permanent Member of the Prussian *Akademie der Wissenschaften*, with the promise of heading the Physics Institute of the *Kaiser-Wilhelm-Gesellschaft*. He moved to Berlin in 1914 and, had Miss Hertz lived, it is not improbable that the two would have met there.

Earlier, Miss Hertz had provided for the endowment at the British Academy of three lecture series.[4] One of these is the Master-Mind lectures, in each of which:

Read at the Academy 19 July 2005.
[1] For her biography, see Julia Laura Rischbieter, *Henriette Hertz Mäzenin und Gründerin der Bibliotheca Hertziana in Rom* (Stuttgart, 2004).
[2] In 1948, it was re-founded as the *Max-Planck-Gesellschaft*.
[3] 'In der Absicht, daß dieselben ihrer Tradition gemäß dauernd der Pflege von Kunst und Wissenschaft dienen sollen'. See ibid., p. 169. Her will adds: 'Zu diesem Zweck ist in den unteren Räumen, die von Federico Zaccari selbst ausgemahlt wurden, eine kunst-historische Bibliothek eingerichtet worden, die unter den Namen "Bibliotheca Hertziana" dort für immer ihre Heimstätte finden soll.' [For this purpose, in the rooms of the lower floor, decorated by Federico Zaccari himself, a Library of Art History shall be installed, which, under the name Bibliotheca Herziana, shall find its home there in perpetuity.]
[4] See Rischbieter, *Henrietta Hertz*, p. 107. Her niece Alide's husband, Sir Israel Gollancz, was a founding member and first Secretary of the British Academy from 1902 until his death in 1930.

Figure 1. Albert Einstein in 1916. © Hulton-Deutsch Collection/CORBIS.

some Master-Mind [is] considered individually with reference to his life and work especially in order to appraise the essential elements of his Genius: the subject to be chosen from the great Philosophers, Artists, Poets, Musicians.

The first lecture was given in 1916, the year in which Einstein published the definitive account of the general theory of relativity.[5] He considered general relativity to be his greatest accomplishment and it certainly manifested 'the essential elements of his Genius'.

Scientists were not included in Miss Hertz's pool of candidates, and in the sixty-two previous Master-Mind lectures, only *three* natural scientists have been chosen as subjects: Sir Isaac Newton (1927 lecture by C. D. Broad); Charles Darwin (1959 lecture by Gavin de Beer); and Eratosthenes (1970 lecture by P. M. Fraser).[6] I am a bit perplexed about the subject of the 2002 lecture, Sigmund Freud: should he be included among the natural scientists? But discussion of that question is best reserved for my own psychoanalysis.

Of course, Einstein has been justly characterised as a 'philosopher-scientist',[7] so perhaps he can be slipped in under that rubric. And indeed, in trying to fulfil Miss Hertz's behest, in addition to science I shall invoke some philosophy as well as considerable psychology,[8] not a little poetry; several works of art; and even one reference to music. But before turning to the topic proper of this lecture, I shall discuss a major obstacle to an appraisal of 'the essential elements of his Genius': the widespread image of Einstein as *Magus*.

The scientist as Magus

Tony Rothman recently has summarised the problem:

> Strangely, the festivities embody a paradox, perhaps a double paradox: On the one hand, more has been written about Einstein than any scientist who ever lived, and to say anything fresh is almost impossible. The superfluity can only cause problems for publishers and conference organizers wishing to be original. On the other hand, Princeton's publication of the *Collected Papers* as well as

---

[5] 'Die Grundlage der allgemeinen Relativitätstheorie', *Annalen der Physik*, 49 (1916), 769–822.
[6] Fraser starts by remarking: 'I am not convinced that Eratosthenes qualifies for discussion as a Master Mind', so perhaps one should say only *two* scientists have been justly honoured.
[7] The volume dedicated to him in the *Library of Living Philosophers* is entitled *Albert Einstein: Philosopher-Scientist* (La Salle, IL, 1949).
[8] In 1913 psychology was still in the process of separating itself as a discipline from philosophy.

diligent sleuthing by historians have allowed a more nuanced view of Einstein to emerge. Any subtleties are so utterly defeated by the public mythology surrounding the man, however, that the traditional incantations continue to be repeated by journalists and scientists alike.[9]

In other words, Einstein has become a Magus. I am referring not to John Fowles well-known novel *The Magus*,[10] but to a homonymous work by Francis Barrett,[11] the full title of which constitutes a précis of its contents.[12] It has been described as:

> one of the primary sources for the study of ceremonial magic, and for a long time... one of the rarest and most sought after of the 19th century grimoires. Barrett's magnum opus embodies deep knowledge of Alchemy, Astrology, and the Kabbalah.... Written in 1801 in the middle of the 'Age of Reason', sandwiched between Newton and Darwin, this was possibly the last epoch that a

---

[9] 'What Einstein Knew: One Year and Five Papers That Changed Physics Forever', *The American Scholar*, 74 (2005), 127.

[10] *The Magus* (New York, 1965); rev. edn. (London, 1977). I have been a fan of the book since its publication.

[11] 'Barrett, an Englishman, claimed himself to be a student of chemistry, metaphysics, and natural occult philosophy. He was an extreme eccentric who gave lessons in the magical arts in his apartment and fastidiously translating the Kabbalah and other ancient texts into English. ... Barrett's belief in magical power might be summed up this way: The magical power is in the inward or inner man. A certain proportion of the inner man longs for the external in all things. When the person is in the appropriate disposition an appropriate [sic] between man and object can be attained. The Magus also served as an advertizing tool. In it Barrett sought interested people wanting to help form his magic circle. It is uncertain whether he accomplished this goal, but the British historian Montague Summers claims Barrett did, and turned Cambridge into a center for magic.' Alan G. Hefner, article on 'Francis Barrett' in *The MYSTICA/An on-line encyclopedia of the occult, mysticism, magic, paranormal and more* <www.themystica.com/mystica>.

[12] *The Magus, Or Celestial Intelligencer, Being A Complete System of Occult Philosophy in Three Books, Containing the Antient and Modern Practice of the Cabalistic Art, Natural and Celestial Magic, &c.; shewing the wonderful Effects that may be performed by a Knowledge of The Celestial Influences, the occult Properties of Metals, Herbs, and Stones, and the Application of Active to Passive Principles. Exhibiting the Sciences of Natural Magic; Alchymy, or Hermetic Philosophy; Also The Nature, Creation and Fall of Man, His natural and supernatural Gifts; the magical Power inherent in the Soul, &c.; with a great Variety of rare Experiments in Natural Magic. The Constellatory Practice, or Talismanic Magic; The Nature of the Elements. Stars, Planets, Signs, &c.; the Construction and Composition of all Sorts of Magic Seals, Images, Rings, Glasses, &c.; The Virtue and Efficacy of Numbers, Characters, and Figures, of good and evil Spirits. Magnetism, and Cabalistic or Ceremonial Magic; In which, the secret Mysteries of the Cabala are explained; the Operations of good and evil Spirits; all Kinds of Cabalistic Figures, Tables, Seals, and Names, with their Use, &c. The Times, Bonds, Offices and Conjuration of Spirits. To Which is Added Biographia Antiqua, or the Lives of the most eminent Philosophers, Magi, &c. The Whole illustrated with a great Variety of Curious Engravings, Magical and Cabbalistic Figures, &c.* (London, 1801).

work like this could be composed[13] see <www.sacred-texts.com/grim/magus/>).

Einstein is not the first savant whose public image has blended with that of such Magi, possessed of occult powers. The Magus *par excellence* of the West-European tradition undoubtedly is Dr Johannes Faustus, whose image has inspired countless work of art—to say nothing for the moment of literature—from the most banal to the most sublime.

Learned Faustus was a medical doctor, and we shall return to him in due course. Coming closer to our subject, who does not recall Alexander Pope's lines?

> Nature and Nature's Laws lay hid in night;
> God said, Let Newton be!—And all was light.

These lines pale—if not as poetry, then as praise—in comparison with Edmund Halley's *Ode* to Newton's *Principia*:

> Mortals arise, put aside earthly cares,
> And from this treatise discern the powers of a mind sprung from heaven,
> Far removed from the life of beasts, He who commanded us by written tablets to abstain from murder,
> Thefts, adultery, and the crime of bearing false witness,
> Or he who taught nomadic peoples to build walled cities, or he who enriched the nations with the gift of Ceres,
> Or he who pressed from the grape solace for cares,
> Or he who with a reed from the Nile showed how to join together
> Pictured sounds and to set spoken words before the eyes,
> Exalted the human lot less, inasmuch as he was concerned with only a few comforts of a wretched life,
> And thus did less than our author for the condition of mankind.
> But we are now admitted to the banquet of the gods,
> We may deal with the laws of heaven above; and we now have
> The secret keys to unlock the obscure earth; and we know the immovable order of the world
> And the things that were concealed from the generations of the past.
> O you who rejoice in feeding on the nectar of the gods in heaven,
> Join me in singing the praises of Newton, who reveals all this,
> Who opens the treasure chest of hidden truth,
> Newton, dear to the Muses,

---

[13] Given the current fervent interest in witchcraft, astrology and anti-rational credos in general—curiously combined as it is with an equally fervent worship of the latest technology (get your horoscope on the internet)—I consider the last statement wildly optimistic.

> The one in whose pure heart Phoebus Apollo dwells and whose mind he
> has filled with all his divine power;
> No closer to the gods can any mortal rise.[14]

Turning from poetry to art, there is William Blake's curiously ambiguous image of Newton, which has been interpreted variously as praising, mocking, or decrying Newton (Fig. 2).[15]

Einstein has inspired similar flights of ambiguous imagination. The attempt to characterise his sober scientific work as exotic esoteric lore started early, with the 1920s legend that only three other people could understand his theory of relativity. It would need a separate lecture to give even a brief history of the Einstein legend; so I confine myself to citing the names of a few books in English that make Einstein the universal Magus.

In 1930, George Bernard Shaw described Einstein as a 'maker of universes' and H. Gordon Garbedian echoed the phrase in the title of his book *Einstein: Maker of Universes* (New York and London, 1939). This was followed by: Lincoln Barnett's *The Universe and Dr. Einstein* (New York, 1946)—at least the universe comes first!—Nigel Calder's *Einstein's Universe* (New York, 1979), Michio Kaku's *Einstein's Cosmos* (New York, 2004)—presumably 'cosmos' was used because 'universe' was already taken, and J. Richard Gott's *Time Travel in Einstein's Universe* (New York, 2001). The Berlin Exhibition on the centenary of Einstein's *Annus Mirabilis* was more modestly entitled: *Albert Einstein: Chief Engineer of the Universe*.[16]

When Princeton University Press kindly suggested that I edit an annotated English translation of Einstein's 1905 papers, they suggested the title *Einstein's Miraculous Year: Five Papers That Changed the Universe*. I was able to persuade them to change it to *Five Papers That Changed the Face of Physics*.

Nor did the muse of poetry flag when confronted with Einstein:[17] Archibald MacLeish's 'Einstein' describes not the man but the Magus:

---

[14] *Ode on This Splendid Ornament of Our Time and Our Nation, the Mathematical-Physical Treatise by the Eminent Isaac Newton.* Cited from I. Bernard Cohen and Ann Whitman (eds.), *The Principia: A New Translation and Guide* (Berkeley, Los Angeles, London, 1999), p. 380.
[15] See Donald D. Ault, *Visionary Physics: Blake's Response to Newton* (Chicago and London, 1974).
[16] See the catalogue: Jürgen Renn (ed.), *Albert Einstein—Chief Engineer of the Universe: Documents of a Life's Pathway* (Weinheim, 2006).
[17] See Alan J. Friedman and Carol C. Donley, *Einstein as Myth and Muse* (Cambridge, 1985).

Figure 2. Newton, William Blake (1795). © Tate, London 2007.

> Nor could Jehovah and the million stars
> Staring with their multitude of light,
> Nor all night's constellations be contained
> Between his boundaries . . .
> He lies upon his bed
> Exerting on Arcturus and the moon
> Forces proportional inversely to
> The squares of their remoteness and conceives
> The Universe.
>   Atomic.
>   He can count
> Oceans in atoms and weigh out the air
> In multiples of one and subdivide
> Light into numbers.
>   If they will not speak
> Let them be silent in their particles.
> Let them be dead and he will lie among
> Their dust and cipher them—undo the signs
> Of their unreal identities and free
> The pure and single factor of all sum—
> Solve them unity.[18]

I believe that we shall better understand the public impact of semi-mythical figures such as Newton and Einstein—and Moses, Jesus, Muhammad and Buddha, for that matter—if we realise that, to the broad public, they are not mere men but Magi—figures who stand in some unique relation to the cosmos and whatever mysterious forces guide its destiny.[19] If they cannot create universes (as Shaw would have it), at least they have some mystical connection with our universe that enables them to penetrate its deepest secrets, unveil its hidden depths, engineer its destiny. This power may be exerted for good or for ill, for there is always some moral ambiguity associated with the image of the Magus. The popular—but mythic—image of Einstein as father of the atomic bomb, embodies that ambiguity.

Of course, when associated with the supposed incomprehensibility of his ideas, this oracular aspect can be put to humorous use, as in this cartoon from the *New Yorker* (Fig. 3):

---

[18] Written in 1926, cited from Friedman and Donley op. cit., p. 72.
[19] I recently secured a copy of the book that convinced me as a child that I wanted to study science, Norton Wagner's *Unveiling the Universe: Where We Are and What We Are as Told by the Telescope and Spectroscope* (Scranton, PA, 1936): If astronomy could unveil the universe, I wanted to be in on its secrets; and I am sure that I am not alone in having been so motivated to a career in science.

'People slowly accustomed themselves to the idea that physical states of space itself were the final physical reality.'

Professor Albert Einstein

Figure 3. Drawing by Rae Irvin from *The New Yorker*.

The grain of truth

As is usually the case for such widespread myths, there is an important grain of truth hidden in this storehouse of shamanism. If they do not create an *external* world, these larger-than-life figures do create an *inner* world. Of course, they do not create it out of whole cloth, and—most importantly—this world does not remain purely internal. Each manages somehow to impose at least a part of his or her inner world on the appropriate community (or communities) in the outer world. The larger this community, the wider the impact of their ideas, the more likely it is that their 'creator' will be elevated to the status of Magus.

This phenomenon has not gone unnoted by psychologists. Freud suggests that the creation of such an inner world begins in childhood:[20]

> Should we not look for the first traces of imaginative activity as early as in childhood? The child's best-loved and most intense occupation is with his play or games. Might we not say that every child at play behaves like a creative writer, in that he creates a world of his own, or, rather, rearranges the things of his world in a new way which pleases him? It would be wrong to think he does not take the world seriously; on the contrary he takes his play very seriously and he expends large amounts of emotion on it. The opposite of play is not what is serious but what is real. In spite of all the emotion with which he cathects his world of play, the child distinguishes it quite well from reality; and he likes to link his imagined objects and situations to the tangible and visible things of the real world. This linking is all that differentiates the child's 'play' from 'phantasying'.[21]

---

[20] 'Sollen wir die ersten Spuren dichterischer Betätigung nicht schon beim Kinde suchen? Die liebste und intensivste Beschäftigung des Kindes ist Spiel. Vielleicht dürfen wir sagen: Jedes spielende Kind benimmt sich wie ein Dichter, indem es sich eine eigene Welt erschafft oder, richtiger gesagt, die Dinge seiner Welt in eine neue, ihm gefällige Ordnung versetzt. Es wäre dann Unrecht zu meinen, es nähme diese Welt nicht ernst; im Gegenteil, es nimmt sein Spiel sehr ernst, es verwendet große Affektbeiträge darauf. Der Gegensatz zu Spiel ist nicht Ernst, sondern—Wirklichkeit. Das Kind unterscheidet seine Spielwelt sehr wohl, trotz ihre Affektbesetzung, von der Wirklichkeit und lehnt seine imaginierten Objekte und Verhältnisse gerne an greifbare und sichtbare Dinge der wirklichen Welt an. Nichts anderes als diese Anlehnung unterscheidet das "Spielen" des Kindes noch vom "Phantasieren".' Cited from 'Der Dichter und das Phantasieren', in *Gesammelte Werke, Chronologisch Geordnet*, vol. 7, *Werke aus den Jahren 1906–1909* (London, 1940), p. 214.

[21] Cited from 'Creative Writers and Day-Dreaming', in *The Standard Edition of the Complete Psychological Works of Sigmund Freud, Volume IX (1906–1908) Jensen's 'Gradiva' and Other Works* (London, 1986), pp. 143–4.

I remind you that the book[22] that includes Erik Erikson's seminal essay on Einstein[23] bears the following epigraph by William Blake:

> The Child's Toys and the Old Man's Reasons
> Are the Fruits of the Two Seasons.[24]

There is some evidence of Einstein's youthful interest in patient play with toys that involved delicate, hands-on construction; and of his mastery of how new-fangled technical devices, such as the telephone, worked. His sister Maja reports that, before the age of ten, his games—which were 'very indicative of his natural aptitudes'—included 'work with the fretsaw and the erection of complicated structures with the well-known "*Anker*" building sets, but best of all the construction of many-storied houses of cards.'[25]

A fellow student at the Luitpold Gymnasium, the prestigious Munich secondary school he attended, recalled Einstein explaining to him the principles of the telephone. And no wonder. While he was growing up his uncle Jakob, a trained engineer, and Einstein's father Hermann, a business man, were partners in the first Munich electrical engineering firm. Jakob had dabbled (unsuccessfully) in marketing an early model of the telephone and, at a time when they were still scarce, there was one in the Einsteins' Munich home; so one may surmise that his knowledge of its workings was acquired by 'hands on' methods. A few years later, Uncle Jakob remarked to one of the workmen in his factory:

> Do you know, it is really fabulous with my nephew. Whereas my assistant engineer and I broke our heads a whole day long [on a technical problem], the young lad worked out the whole story in a mere quarter of an hour. Something more will come of him![26]

---

[22] Erik H. Erikson, 'Einstein's Puzzles', in *Toys and Reasons* (New York, 1977). Peter Carruthers discusses 'Human Creativity: its cognitive basis, its evolution and its connections with childhood pretence' (*British Journal for the Philosophy of Science*, 53 (2002), 225–49) without mentioning either Freud or Erikson.
[23] In his essay, Erikson—following the lead of Gerald Holton, draws attention to the significance of *Anschauung* (visual imagery) in Einstein's mode of thought as child and adult, a topic discussed below.
[24] From 'Auguries of Innocence'.
[25] Maja Winteler-Einstein, 'Albert Einstein—Beitrag für sein Lebensbild [hereafter cited as 'Beitrag'], cited from John Stachel *et al.* (eds.), *The Collected Papers of Albert Einstein* (Princeton) [hereafter cited as *Collected Papers*], vol. 1 (1987), p. lix.
[26] Otto Neustätter, letter to Albert Einstein, 12 Mar. 1928. Translation cited from John Stachel, 'Introduction to the Centenary Edition' [hereafter cited as 'Introduction'] in John Stachel (ed.), *Einstein's Miraculous Year: Five Papers That Changed the Face of Physics* (Princeton, 2005) [hereafter cited as *Einstein's Miraculous Year*], p. xxx.

Einstein's first (1905) relativity paper shows that he was familiar with the then still-intense debate among physicists about the nature of unipolar induction,[27] a debate closely connected with practical engineering problems of electric dynamos,[28] the design and construction of which had been a major activity of the Einstein firm. Uncle Jakob actually held patents on a dynamo design; so again it is a fair surmise that young Albert first learned about the debate in its engineering context. In an authorised biography of Einstein, his son-in-law Rudolf Kayser wrote: 'As a result of his father's calling and his own mathematical ability, the position of technician and engineer was the first to be thought of [for Einstein].'[29] A letter written in 1918 confirms this:[30] 'I was also originally supposed to be a technical worker. But the thought of having to expend my inventive power on things, which would only make workaday life more complicated with the goal of dreary oppression by capital, was unbearable to me.'[31] Let us play out for a moment what might have happened to someone endowed with strong visual and tactile mental faculties (more about this later) that, in his family milieu, were easily channelled into an inclination towards technology, if—instead of failing—the family business had prospered and grown into a major force in the German electrical industry. Instead of the burden of debts his father left behind, suppose Einstein had faced the prospect of inheriting a vast and growing technical-industrial empire. Was it foreordained that, like Jesus in the Wilderness, he would reject all worldly temptations in favour of the pursuit of pure science?

---

[27] Albert Einstein, 'Zur Elektrodynamik bewegter Körper', *Annalen der Physik*, 17 (1905), 891–921, cited from the reproduction in *Collected Papers*, 2 (1989), 276–306. Unipolar induction is mentioned on p. 295, in which it is shown that the problem disappears in the relativistic framework.

[28] See Arthur I. Miller, 'Unipolar Induction: A Case Study of the Interaction between Science and Technology', *Annals of Science*, 38 (1981), 155–89, reprinted in *idem, Frontiers of Physics: 1900–1911: Selected Essays* (Boston, Basel, Stuttgart, 1986), pp. 153–89.

[29] Published only in English under the pseudonym Anton Reiser [Rudolf Kayser], *Albert Einstein: A Biographical Portrait* (New York, 1930), p. 42.

[30] 'Ich sollte ursprünglich auch Techniker werden. Aber das Gedanke, die Erfindungskraft auf Dinge verwenden zu sollen, welche das werktägliche Leben noch raffinierter machen, mit dem Ziel öder Kapitalschinderei, war mir unerträglich.' Albert Einstein to Heinrich Zangger, before 11 Aug. 1918, *Collected Papers*, 8B (1998), 850.

[31] Translation from 'New Introduction' to *Einstein's Miraculous Year*, p. xxxiii. Kayser adds: 'The choice of profession, however, had other implications: it made necessary a relationship with society and with a mechanical life constantly controlled by end-in-view and utilitarian purposes. Nothing seemed more frightful to young Albert Einstein. Moreover he was not ambitious: he wanted neither fame nor success. These mundane ideas were repugnant to him' (Resier [Kayser] *Albert Einstein*, p. 42).

The case of Walther Rathenau, who confronted just such a life-situation as I have described, suggests that it was not foreordained.[32] Scion of Emil Rathenau, who rose from obscurity to preside over the giant German electrical firm, the *AEG,* Walther also came from a middle-class Jewish background. He too combined a technical bent with a profound intellectual curiosity, and after Einstein moved to Berlin the two became good friends, sharing many intellectual interests and social concerns.

A decade older than Einstein, Rathenau had studied chemistry, physics and philosophy, culminating in a thesis on 'The Absorption of Light by Metals'. Going into the family business, he went on to become industrial czar of Germany during the First World War and then Foreign Minister during the Weimar Republic—a reminder that it was quite possible in early twentieth-century Germany to combine a career at the centre of power with a profound inner intellectual and spiritual life.[33] His career was cut short in 1922 by an assassin's machine gun, part of a wave of anti-Semitic attacks that led to serious concern for Einstein's life, a foretaste of what was in store for all of Germany a decade later.

Rather than regarding it as the external unfolding of some pre-existing inner pattern of development (I call this viewpoint 'the homunculus theory of personality'), I suggest we view the adolescent Einstein's turn away from his expected career in commerce[34] as a reaction to what he had seen first as excessive greed, and then inability to accept financial failure,[35] do to his family: his father, whose health deteriorated

---

[32] For a biographical study by Count Kessler, who knew both Rathenau and Einstein, see Harry Kessler, *Walther Rathenau: His Life and Work* (New York, 1969).

[33] 'The British politician Robert Boothby wrote of him: "He was something that only a German Jew could simultaneously be: a prophet, a philosopher, a mystic, a writer, a statesman, an industrial magnate of the highest and greatest order, and the pioneer of what has become known as "industrial rationalization"' (*Wikipedia* article 'Walther Rathenau').

[34] A turn that was more gradual than he depicted it in retrospect, and less complete: he did take out a number of patents over his lifetime, on at least one of which he collected royalties, and served as a technical expert witness in several financially important cases involving patent infringements.

[35] Maja Einstein wrote:

> Not only were the assets of Albert Einstein's mother lost at this time, but significant contributions from relatives as well. The family had hardly anything left. . . . In contrast [to uncle Jakob], Albert Einstein's father could not bring himself to take the same step [becoming an employee] and relinquish his professional independence. In particular, he did not want to bring suffering on his wife, who would have had great difficulty in accommodating herself to a lower standing in the social scale. Against the perceptive advice of his still quite young son, he founded a third electrical firm in Milan. ('Beitrag', translation cited from 'New Introduction' to *Einstein's Miraculous Year*, pp. xxviii–xxix).

rapidly under the influence of these blows, died in debt in 1902 at the age of 55; and his mother, brought up in wealth and used to servants, was left penniless and forced to take work as a housekeeper.

One possible reaction to the suggestion that, had circumstances been different, Einstein might have pursued a practical career is that of Helen Dukas. His secretary and later housekeeper for over twenty-five years, and the keeper of his flame for another quarter century after his death, she recounted her reply to an Einstein scholar who dared to suggest the crucial role of some external influences on his life: 'If Professor Einstein had been born at the North Pole and grown up among the polar bears, he still would have been Professor Einstein!' Some may laugh at these words, but still regard such external factors as at most exerting a facilitating or hindering influence on the unfolding of a creative talent such as Einstein's. This raises the question: 'What is creativity?'

The Transformative Question and the Question of Transformational Creativity[36]

But is this the right question to ask? As Eugene Ionescu observed, 'It is not the answer that enlightens, but the question.' Mihalyi Czikszentmihalyi has suggested that, rather than '*What* is creativity?' one should ask '*Where* is Creativity?' [37] First of all, he distinguishes between 'creativity with a small "c"' and 'creativity with a big "C"'.

> The definition that most people usually agree on is that creativity is a new idea or product which is socially acceptable, and which is brought to fruition. That's creativity with a big 'C', creativity that changes the culture. Then we can talk also about creativity which is a more personal experience, which affects the way one experiences life, with originality, openness, and freshness. That is something different, though the two overlap. Creativity with a small 'c', the personal creativity, is what makes life enjoyable, but it does not necessarily result in renown or success.

---

[36] From this point on I shall eschew use of 'genius' in favour of a discussion of 'transformational creativity'.

[37] Mihalyi Czikszentmihalyi, *Creativity: Flow in the Psychology of Discovery and Invention* (New York, 1996). See also *idem*, 'Society, culture, and person: a systems view of creativity', in Robert J. Sternberg (ed.), *The Nature of Creativity: Contemporary Psychological Perspectives* (New York, 1988).

With Einstein, we are dealing with 'creativity with a big "C"', which Czikszentmihalyi also calls 'transformational creativity'; so that is what we must analyse; and from now on the term 'creativity' will be used in this sense. Elsewhere, Czikszentmihalyi offered this short definition: 'Creativity is a new idea or product [of the individual], which is socially acceptable [to the field] and which is brought to fruition [in the domain]'. He distinguishes three elements that are involved in any creative process:

1 The Domain: e.g., mathematics or biology 'consists of a set of symbols, rules and procedures'.

2 The Field: 'the individuals who act as gatekeepers to the domain ... [they] decide whether a new idea, performance, or product should be included'.

3 The Individual: creativity is 'when a person ... has a new idea or sees a new pattern, and when this novelty is selected by the appropriate field for inclusion in the relevant domain.'[38] (Fig. 4.)

The psychologist Howard Gardner, who has done so much to popularise and develop Czikszentmihalyi's approach, emphasises:

> In Czikszenmihalyi's persuasive account, creativity does not inhere in any single node, nor, indeed, in any pair of nodes. Rather, creativity is best viewed as a dialectical or interactive process, in which all three of these elements participate.[39]

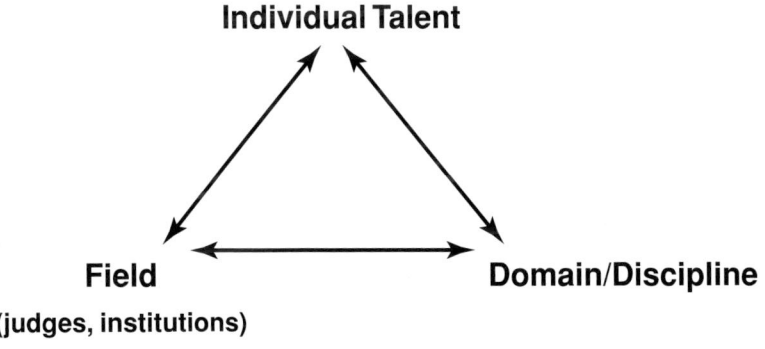

Figure 4. Mihalyi Czikszentmihalyi's triangle.

---

[38] 'The Well of Creativity', a conversation with Mihalyi Czikszentmihalyi by Michael Toms [hereafter cited as 'Toms Interview'], <www.newdimensions.org/online-journal/ articles/well-of-creativity.html>.

[39] Howard Gardner, *Creating Minds* (New York, 1993), p. 38.

So a discussion of transformational creativity takes one beyond the Individual to a consideration of the Domain and the Field. But I shall begin with the Individual.

Complexity of the Personality: Polarities

When asked, 'is there a creative personality with recognisable characteristics?', Czikszentmihalyi answered:

> People who are able to transform the domain in which they work do have certain similarities in the way their personality is put together. I call this the complexity of the personality.
>
> Each of us has several possible options for personality. We can either be extroverted and enjoy people but then feel a bit anxious when we are alone, or we can be introverted, which means that we like solitude but can't handle people. We are either masculine or feminine,[40] or cooperative or competitive, *et cetera*.
>
> Creative people, however, have the ability to use the full range of these separate dimensions, so that they have, for example, both masculine and feminine traits—both men and women have some of the strengths of the opposite gender.[41] They can be introverted when they have to be. When they have to work, they love being alone and working. But they also love being with people when that helps their work, so that they can get information, to know what other people are thinking and doing. The complexity of personality, that ability to unite the parts of the opposite traits of what normally are polarized personality traits, is common in creative people. . . .
>
> [T]hey are playful and responsible at the same time. The popular wisdom about these people is that they are very rebellious and iconoclastic; they like to break the rules; they like to break tradition. And that's true. But on the other hand, they are also very traditional, because they know that they are standing on the shoulders of giants, as Newton said. Whatever they accomplish is based on the accomplishments of previous generations. They take very seriously those accomplishments, and at the same time they are willing to go beyond and break the limits of what has been done or known in the past. All of these polarities are somehow integrated in their work.[42]

---

[40] I can make sense of theses words only if they are taken in the sense of a distinction of gender (which is socially constructed) rather than of sex (which is biologically determined).
[41] I would also purge this account of its sexist overtones.
[42] 'Toms Interview'.

This list of inseparable, opposing, but complementary traits consists of examples of what, following Karl Marx, I call *polarities* (Fig. 5).[43]

Elsewhere,[44] following the lead of Gerald Holton,[45] I have discussed some striking polarities characterising the development of Einstein's personality that are closely related to items on Czikszentmihalyi's list. Here I shall simply mention three of them:

1 His striving for recognition and approval from elders in positions of authority versus his need to maintain his independence of, and sometimes even to show defiance of, such authority figures,[46] in order to pursue his own goals. No better example of this youthful polarity can be found than a letter to his fiancée, written in 1901 when he was jobless. Having found what he thought to be some errors in an article by Paul Drude, an eminent physicist whose work Einstein valued highly, he wrote to Drude eagerly, hoping to establish contact with him and perhaps

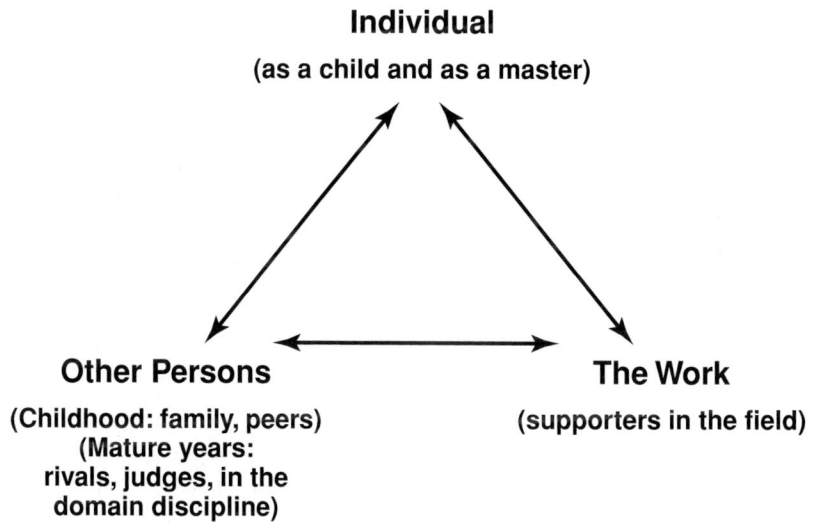

Figure 5. Howard Gardner's elucidation of Czikszentmihalyi's Triangle.

---

[43] In contradistinction to Czikszentmihalyi's usage, it is inherent in such polarities that both poles be present and interact dynamically. See John Stachel, 'The Concept of Polar Opposition in Marx's *Capital*', to appear in *idem*, *Going Critical*, vol. 2, *The Practice of Marxism*.

[44] John Stachel, 'New Introduction' to *Einstein's Miraculous Year, Centenary Edition*.

[45] Gerald Holton, 'On Trying to Understand Scientific Genius', in *idem*, *Thematic Origins of Scientific Thought*, rev. edn. (Cambridge, MA, 1988), pp. 371–98.

[46] 'Long live impudence! It is my guardian angel in this world!' Albert Einstein to Mileva Marić, 12 Dec. 1901 (*Collected Papers*, 1. 323).

obtain his help in finding an academic position, which Einstein needed desperately. But Drude's reply dashed his hopes as he told Marić:

> I just got home . . . and found this letter from Drude. It is such manifest proof of the wretchedness of its author that no further comment by me is necessary. From now on I'll no longer turn to such people, and will instead attack them mercilessly in the journals, as they deserve. No wonder little by little one becomes a misanthrope.[47]

Fortunately (for him), he never carried out this threat, and later on Drude was one of the first physicists to acknowledge Einstein's work on relativity.

2 His longing for close companionship and an intimate human relationship versus his need for solitude.[48] As we shall see below, he needed solitude to develop his intellectual 'inventions': the first stage of his thought process, being entirely non-verbal, required solitude; while the second stage, involving translation of the results of the first stage into words, depended on communication with others.

3 His attraction by the technical side of the family electrical engineering business, to which he even contributed from time to time, versus his repulsion by its commercial aspects, which had led to continual disappointment of his father's hopes for success and finally just for financial independence.

Erikson has discussed the defiant element in Einstein's personality and how it served him well in the course of his education:

> Were the boy's symptoms [beginning with his comparatively late start in speech] due to an outright *defect* or to a systematic *difference* in development; or were they also reinforced by a mighty *diffidence*—or, eventually, even some *defiance*? . . . [L]ittle Albert had it in him to object to having to learn anything in any but his own way. In his early childhood this could be expressed in a sudden rage (against a private teacher, for example) that was attributed to a disposition inherited from his maternal grandfather. Later, the resistance against enforced instruction, far from ever being 'broken', became a deep and basic character trait that permitted the child and the youth to remain free in learning, no matter how slowly or by what sensory or cognitive steps he accomplished it. (pp. 152–3)[49]

---

[47] Albert Einstein to Mileva Marić, 7? July 1901 (*Collected Papers*, 1. 308).
[48] 'I seek solitude, only then silently to lament it', Albert Einstein to Pauline ('Mama') Winteler, 21 May 1897 (*Collected Papers*, 5 [1993]. 3).
[49] 'Psychoanalytic Reflections on Einstein's Centenary', in Gerald Holton and Yehuda Elkana (eds.), *Albert Einstein: Historical and Cultural Perspectives* (Princeton, 1982), pp. 151–73.

The dialectical interplay of individual, others, and work

Czikszentmihalyi was asked, 'We have the myth of single individual out there being creative, but there's something else involved, right?' He replied:

> Yes, luck was the most often-mentioned reason for successful creativity that these creative and well known people gave—people like Jonas Salk ... and Linus Pauling, who won two Nobel prizes... By that they meant several things. They meant, as Pauling said, good genes are luck. Having a background that allows you to focus on a particular domain of knowledge, that is partly luck. Being in the right time and right place is luck.... In many ways luck does play a big role in transforming creativity with a small 'c' into creativity with a capital 'C'.[50]

So one must pass beyond the individual, to what Gardner called the 'dialectical or interactive process', between an Individual, others in the Field and the work contributed to the Domain. First of all, one must learn to relate individual and social psychology.

If I may be permitted a personal note, sixty years ago, I took Gardner Murphy's course on 'The Theory of Personality'.[51] From him I learned the concept of the *canalisation* of human drives:[52] that the individual, biological aspects of these drives cannot be separated from their culturally shaped expression in the developing personality. This approach helped me avoid the then common—and still not uncommon—discussion of human behaviour in terms of innate human instincts,[53] which are either facilitated or inhibited by society,[54] an approach leading to the still familiar dilemma of nature versus nurture with its deterministic overtones.

---

[50] 'Toms Interview' (see above, n. 38).
[51] See Gardner Murphy, *Personality: A Biosocial Approach to Origins and Structure* (New York and London, 1947), 2nd edn. (New York, 1966).
[52] Murphy pointed out that the term 'canalisation' was introduced by the nineteenth-century French psychologist Pierre Janet.
[53] It is still popular among evolutionary psychologists: 'what is special about the human mind is not that it gave up "instinct" in order to become more flexible, but that it proliferated "instincts"—that is content-specific problem-solving specializations' (J. Tooby and L. Cosmides, 'The psychological foundations of culture', in J. H. Barkow *et al.* (eds.), *The Adapted Mind* (New York, 1992), pp. 19–136. I shall present a critique of evolutionary psychology in the last section.
[54] My reading of the then practically unknown Erik Homberger Erikson, in particular 'Problems of infancy and early childhood', in *Encyclopedia of Medicine, Surgery and Specialties* (Philadelphia, 1940), pp. 714–30, also helped me to see the possibility of a less strict interpretation of Freud than orthodox psychoanalysis provided. In 1979 I was privileged to meet Erikson and discuss Einstein with him at length.

Gardner Murphy, then a renowned social psychologist, appears to have been forgotten,[55] but his biosocial approach to personality is alive and well today—perhaps more so than it was when I was a student. Witness for example, the work of Jaan Valsiner, who warns that 'The glory of the person becomes a myth that overrides the person's linkages with the social world',[56] a danger that one must be especially on guard against in approaching Einstein. This is so not only because of the aura of popular myths that surrounds his name, but because of the need to re-examine many scholarly myths about Einstein in the light of the dialectic between individual talent, domain and discipline.[57]

Einstein himself started spreading such myths even as he was shaping himself as an adolescent. In 1897, aged 18, he wrote to Pauline 'Mama' Winteler,[58] declining an invitation to spend the Easter holidays with the Winteler family:

> It would be more than shameful if I were to buy a couple of days of pleasure at the price of the pain, much too much of which I have already caused the dear child through my fault. It fills me with a sort of strange satisfaction to have to experience now a part of the pain that my thoughtlessness and ignorance have caused such a delicate nature as that of the dear girl. Strenuous intellectual work and the contemplation of God-given Nature are the angels that will guide me—reconciled, fortified, and yet inexorably strong—through all the turmoil of this life. . . . One thus creates for himself a small world—however pitifully insignificant it may be compared to the eternally changing greatness of true existence—and yet feels wonder himself at how great and important it is, just like for example the mole in the hole that he has excavated for himself.[59]

This credo simultaneously reveals and conceals a great deal about himself. It is interesting to compare this statement, evidently written in large part as self-justification for his emotional withdrawal from a youthful affair, with another that he wrote twenty years later as a mature scientist:

---

[55] I take this opportunity to belatedly acknowledge that taking his course was an unforgettable experience.
[56] See Jaan Valsiner, *The Guided Mind: A Sociogenetic Approach to Personality* (Cambridge, MA, 1998), p. 1; see also Jaan Valsiner and René van der Veer, *The Social Mind: Construction of an Idea* (Cambridge, 2000).
[57] I do not exempt my own work from this stricture.
[58] She was the wife of Jost Winteler, a teacher at the Aargau Kantonsschule. Einstein boarded with the Winteler family while attending the school and grew quite fond of 'Papa' and 'Mama' Winteler. He had a brief but apparently chaste affair with Marie, one of the Winteler daughters.
[59] Albert Einstein to Pauline Winteler, May 1897, *Collected Papers*, 1. 55–6.

> [O]ne of the strongest motives that leads to art and science is escape from everyday life with its painful crudity and bleak aridity, from the fetters of ever-changing personal desires. . . . Each human being tries to make for himself in the fashion that suits him best a simplified and intelligible picture [*Bild*] of the world and thus to overcome the world of experience, by trying to some extent to substitute for it this picture of his own. . . . He displaces the center of gravity of his emotional life to this picture and its shaping in order to seek the repose and solidity that he cannot find in the all-too-narrow sphere of the maelstrom of personal experience.[60]

Erik Erikson, after discussing the child's development of 'the rudiments of sense of guilt' and 'the awareness of some sinful curiosity', goes on:

> I shall not, and could not, specify the fate of such early conflicts in Einstein's childhood. I can only conclude that when he made the statement of his turn from 'I' and 'We' to 'It', he was aware of some of the interpersonal conflicts that he thus learned to avoid and yet also to sublimate in his concentration on the phenomenal.[61]

Nor shall I pursue this topic any further, except to remark that the emotional detachment, with which the older Einstein increasingly portrayed the younger—no doubt in all sincerity—was the terminus and not a starting point of his development.

Creation, discovery, or invention?

Before going further, let us pause to consider the proper word to characterise Einstein's individual contribution to the process of scientific creativity. He preferred 'invention',[62] and I think 'invention' is a good choice. I suggest that three words—creation, discovery and invention—as applied to individuals be used to describe different processes. These

---

[60] Albert Einstein, 'Motive des Forschens' ['Motives for Research'], speech given in 1918 at a meeting in honor of Max Planck's sixtieth birthday, *Collected Papers*, 7 (2002), 55–8. English translation: 'Principles of Research', in Albert Einstein, *Ideas and Opinions* (New York, 1954), p. 225; the translation has been modified.
[61] 'Psychoanalytic Reflections on Einstein's Centenary', in Gerald Holton and Yehuda Elkana (eds.), *Albert Einstein: Historical and Cultural Perspectives* (Princeton, 1982), p. 152.
[62] See his comments on this question in Alexander Moszkowski, *Einstein: Einbicke in seine Gedankenwelt* (Hamburg and Berlin, 1921). Einstein once wrote about the philosopher Ernst Mach: 'Mach's weakness [was that he thought] theories . . . arise [from] discovery and not [from] invention.'

processes are distinguished by two factors: the source of the goal of the process and the source of the constraints on it (Fig. 6).

Creation, as in the phrase 'Lev Tolstoi created Anna Karenina', combines an internally set goal with internal constraints. The urge to portray a certain woman in a certain social milieu and how this milieu ultimately drove her to suicide came from no external compulsion. And (however much advice he may have received) the judgements about how to go about writing her story and when he had finished were ultimately his own. The term creation seems generally more appropriate in the arts than in the sciences.

Discovery, as in the phrase 'Columbus discovered the West Indies' (for white Europeans, I hasten to add), combines an externally set goal with external constraints on it. The goal of Columbus was to reach the East Indies, but a rather large external constraint—the Americas—prevented him from reaching that goal, and so he reached the West Indies instead. The term discovery seems to fit much experimental work in science,[63] and perhaps even some theoretical work; but hardly the kind of grand theoretical enterprises that characterised Einstein's life work (discussed below).

Invention, as in 'Einstein invented general relativity', combines the right mixture of internally set goals and externally imposed constraints. In 1907, Einstein set out to include gravitation within the scope of the 1905 theory of relativity (which we now call 'special relativity'), but an external constraint on his search—the equality of gravitational and inertial mass—soon led him to conclude that he would have to pass beyond

Invention
(Internal Impulse
Plus External Constraints)

Discovery
(External Impulse,
External Constraints)

Creation
(Internal Impulse,
Internal Constraints)

Figure 6. Invention, Discovery and Creation.

---

[63] As in 'The Curies discovered radium', or 'Pluto was discovered by Lowell' (I do not want to get into controversies about who discovered Neptune).

the special theory to reach his goal. And another external constraint—the challenge of explaining the anomalous motion of the perihelion of Mercury—drove him onwards until his final triumph in November 1915. The term invention seems to well characterise the level at which a Newton, a Darwin, a Freud, operated, to mention only other scientists treated in Master-Mind lectures.[64]

Einstein's inventiveness

We can learn a great deal about Einstein from his younger collaborators and assistants, several of whom I shall cite. Peter Bergmann, his assistant from 1936 to 1941, recalled:

> [W]hat impressed me most after I had gotten to know Einstein and his style ... was his tremendous persistence. Once having perceived the really important problems, he would not let go. He might let go temporarily if a road seemed to be completely blocked, but he would pick up the problem again a few weeks later—in the meantime having worked on another, equally interesting problem.[65]

Elsewhere Bergmann reminisced:

> A second thing that impressed me—and remember that I was very young and that Einstein was in his late fifties—was his tremendous creativity, even on the small, day-to-day difficulties, his sheer inventiveness of new approaches, of new mathematical tricks. I think what made Einstein extraordinary (a common characteristic is that many creative persons are very uncritical toward their own ideas; they may be critical toward the ideas of others) was that he could work up tremendous enthusiasm for a new unitary field theory—and during the five years I was in Princeton certainly there was a large number of new unitary field theories—but there would always come the moment of truth. Einstein would discover the fatal flaw in what he himself had initiated and ruthlessly cut off that attempt, only to take on a new idea for work usually within a few days.[66]

Early in his career, Einstein was aware of his ability to single out significant problems in physics:

---

[64] I shall 'bracket' the question of Eratosthenes and the nature of mathematics. Clearly a Platonist and a constructivist will differ completely on how to characterise mathematical research.
[65] 'Reminiscences', in Holton and Elkana (eds.), *Albert Einstein*, p. 398.
[66] 'Working with Einstein', in Harry Woolf (ed.), *Some Strangeness in the Proportion: A Centennial Symposium to Celebrate the Achievements of Albert Einstein* (Reading, MA, 1980), p. 479.

> The fact that I neglected mathematics to a certain extent had its cause not merely in my stronger interest in the natural sciences ... but also in the following peculiar [*eigentümlich*] experience. I saw that mathematics was split into numerous specialties, each of which could absorb the short lifetime granted to us ... [M]y intuition was not strong enough in the field of mathematics to differentiate clearly the fundamentally important ... from the rest of the more or less dispensable erudition ... [P]hysics also was divided into separate fields, each of which was capable of devouring a short lifetime of work without having satisfied the hunger for deeper knowledge. The mass of insufficiently connected experimental data was overwhelming here also. *In this field, however, I soon learned to scent out that which might lead to fundamentals, and turn aside from everything else*, from the multitude of things that clutter up the mind and divert it from the essentials.[67]

Ernst Straus, Einstein's next assistant, cited Goethe's *Faust* to describe Einstein's goal.[68] Einstein revered Goethe as one of the rare creative figures at the highest level: 'It is only men who are free, who create the inventions and intellectual works which to us moderns make life worthwhile.'[69] And with Faust, we return to the Magus *par excellence* of Western European civilisation—the man who sold his soul to the devil for knowledge of and power over the universe (Fig. 7). Einstein once commented to the novelist Hermann Broch about Broch's novel *Virgil*: 'The book shows me clearly what I fled from when I devoted myself body and soul to science—the flight from the I and from the We to the It.'[70] And since becoming associated with the development of the atomic bomb (for whatever good or bad reasons), the mythic Einstein of the popular imagination has taken on much of the moral ambiguity of the mythic Faust.

Returning to Straus, he cites two passages from *Faust* for aptness in characterising Einstein. The first passage he cites reads:

> *um zu verstehen was die Welt*
> *in Innersten zusammen hält.*

---

[67] Albert Einstein, 'Autobiographical Notes' (1949), cited from *idem, Autobiographical Notes* (LaSalle, IL, 1979), pp. 15 and 17, emphasis added.
[68] 'Working with Einstein', in Harry Woolf (ed.), *Some Strangeness in the Proportion*, p. 482.
[69] Albert Einstein, 'Science and Civilization' in *Out of My Later Years* (Secaucus, NJ, 1956), pp. 148–51.
[70] 'Es zeigt mir das Buch deutlich, vor was ich geflohen bin, als ich mich mit Haut und Haar der Wissenschaft verschrieb: Flucht vom Ich und vom Wir in das Es', Albert Einstein to Hermann Broch, 1945, cited from Banesh Hoffmann and Helen Dukas, *Albert Einstein Creator and Rebel* (New York, 1972), p. 254. German text cited from the German edition, *Einstein: Schöpfer und Rebell Die Biographie* (Zürich 1976), p. 298.

Figure 7. Rembrandt, *Faust*, c.1652. © Rijksmuseum, Amsterdam.

Straus's translation of this text is 'to understand what holds the world together at its core'. But the text he cites is incorrect! In all versions of *Faust*,[71] it actually reads:

> *Daß ich erkenne, was die Welt*
> *Im Innersten zusammen hält*

---

[71] That is, *Urfaust, Faust Ein Fragment*, and the final version. Both this and the following quotation are from 'Nacht', the first scene of the drama.

Erkennen is more intuitive than *verstehen*, so the translation should run something like:

> That I recognise what holds the world
> together in its innermost parts.

This is reminiscent of Einstein's words: 'Invention appears here as a constructive activity. So what constitutes the originality of the matter essentially does not consist of this ... The really valuable thing is basically intuition.'[72] Going back to the correct passage from *Faust* and considering its applicability to Einstein, it continues in a quite striking way:

> *Schau alle Wirkenskraft und Samen,*[73]
> *Und tu nicht mehr in Worten kramen*
>
> Behold all active forces and seminal elements,
> And stop rummaging about with words.

As will soon be seen, Einstein reported that his primary thinking process did not involve 'rummaging about with words', bur rather with visual and tactile images.

Straus cites a second passage from *Faust* as follows:

> *und was sie [Natur] deinem Geist nicht offenbart,*
> *das zwingst du ihr nicht ab mit Hebel und Schrauben*
>
> and what she [nature] won't reveal to your spirit,
> you won't force from her with levers and screws.
> (Straus's translation)

Again, this passage is not accurately cited. The full, correct German text reads

> *Läßt sich Natur des Schleiers nicht berauben,*
> *Und was sie deinem Geist nicht offenbaren mag,*
> *Das zwingst du ihr nicht ab mit Hebeln und mit Schrauben.*
>
> Do not rob nature of her veils,
> And what she does not want to reveal to your spirit
> You cannot force from her with levers and with screws.

---

[72] 'Das Erfinden tritt hier als eine konstruierende Tätigkeit auf. Hierin also liegt nicht das, was die Originalität der Sache im wesentlichen ausmacht ... das eigentlich Wertvolle ist im Grunde die Intuition.' Reported in Alexander Moszkowski, *Einstein: Einbicke in seine Gedankenwelt* (Hamburg and Berlin, 1921), p. 111.

[73] Samen, literally 'semen' or 'seeds', is an alchemical term for 'the primordial substances ... out of which all things have grown' (*Goethe's Faust—Part I*, ed. Calvin Thomas (Boston, 1892), p. 256).

I have presented both Straus's and Goethe's versions because the obvious difference between them leads straight to Einstein's view of the difference between Art and Science. After stating what they have in common: 'When the world ceases to be the scene of our personal hopes and wishes, where we face it as free beings admiring, asking, and observing, there we enter the realm of Art and Science', he states the distinction:

> If what is seen and experienced is portrayed in the language of logic, we are engaged in science. If it is communicated through forms whose connections are not accessible to the conscious mind but are recognized intuitively as meaningful, then we are engaged in art.

Finally, he returns to the common theme: 'Common to both is the loving devotion to that which transcends personal concerns and volition.'[74] So, in the Sciences, Einstein evidently sides with Straus's version of the text. In the Arts (here we finally come to Music), Einstein sides rather with Goethe's original: 'This is what I have to say about Bach's life work: listen, play, love, revere—and keep your trap shut!' [*das Maul halten!*] 'As to Schubert, I have only this to say: play the music, love—and shut your trap' [*Maulhalten*].[75]

Now I shall 'shut my trap' about the arts and return to science.

Banesh Hoffmann, an Einstein collaborator from the 1930s, reports Einstein's view of scientific theories:

> I asked him once about a theory, and he said, 'When I am evaluating a theory, I ask myself, if I were God, would I have made the universe that way.' If the theory did not have the sort of simple beauty that would be demanded of a God, then the theory was at best only provisional.[76]

Einstein on his 'proper life's work'

What were the 'really important problems,' that 'inner core' for which Einstein was searching? In 1932 he wrote:

> The goal of my research has always been the simplification and unification of the system of theoretical physics. I attained this goal satisfactorily for macroscopic phenomena, but not for the phenomena of quanta and atomic structure. I believe that, despite considerable success, the modern quantum theory is also still far from a satisfactory solution of the latter group of problems.[77]

---

[74] Albert Einstein, 'What Artistic and Scientific Experience Have in Common' (1921), cited from Helen Dukas and Banesh Hoffmann (eds.), *Albert Einstein: The Human Side* (Princeton 1979), pp. 37–8.
[75] Both citations are from *The Human Side*, p. 75.
[76] 'Working with Einstein', in Harry Woolf (ed.), *Some Strangeness in the Proportion*, p. 476.
[77] *The Human Side*, p. 12.

I do not believe that anything that happened in the remaining twenty-three years of his life would have led Einstein to modify these judgements. In the same year he wrote to a psychologist enquiring about the motivation of his scientific work:

> It was always the striving for a logically simple interpretation of empirically known connections, supported by the conviction of the existence of a logically simple interpretation.[78]

Einstein once listed three key questions that he had posed to himself in the course of his work in physics, the pursuit of which he characterised as follows: 'These three questions characterize my own proper life's work.' The first question was:

> How does the representation of a light ray depend on the state of motion of the coordinate system, with respect to which it is referred?

About ten years of work on this question led to the special theory of relativity. Einstein summarised this work as follows:

> I will give you as an example the situation that led to the setting up [*Aufstellung*] of the special theory of relativity. Mechanically all inertial systems are equivalent. Experience shows that this equivalence also extends to optics and electrodynamics. But this equivalence appeared unattainable in the theory of the latter. Early on I came to the conviction that this had its basis in a deep incompleteness of the theoretical system. The desire to discover and remove this generated a state of physical tension in me that was resolved after seven years of vain searching by the relativising of the concepts of time and length.[79]

The result, special relativity, is certainly an example of transformational creativity. And one may say that, in the main, its effects in transforming the domain of physics have been completed.[80]

The second key question was:

> What is the basis for the equality of the gravitational and inertial mass of bodies?

Work on this question for about eight years led to the general theory of relativity, after ninety years still the best theory of gravitation that we have. In this case, I do not believe that the transformational effects on the domain of physics have been completed. As I have discussed in detail else-

---

[78] Einstein to Erika Oppenheimer, 13 Sept. 1932. See Erika Fromm, 'Lost and Found Half a Century Later: Letters by Freud and Einstein', *American Psychologist*, 53 (1998), 1195–8.
[79] Ibid.
[80] I qualify this statement a bit, because many textbooks still present accounts of the special theory that are based more on Lorentz's pre-relativistic dynamical interpretation of the Lorentz transformations than on the kinematical interpretation of them that Einstein gave.

where,[81] all previous physical theories including the special theory, have been based on the existence of a fixed background space-time structure. General relativity is the first example of a totally background-free physical theory; in particular, the space-time structures are dynamical fields interacting with all other matter and fields in the universe. And the physics community (the Field) is still struggling with the implications of a background-free physics (see the discussion of quantum theory below for some additional remarks on this question).

The third key question was:

> Can the gravitational field and the electromagnetic field be grasped theoretically in a unified manner?

Einstein worked on the search for such a unified field theory for the last thirty years of his life, without bringing the work to a satisfactory conclusion. In particular, the major transformation of the domain of physics that he hoped to accomplish with a unified theory—the explanation of all quantum phenomena without the need to invoke the basic principles of quantum mechanics—has been abandoned by the community. Current work on a unified theory (often called a 'Theory of Everything' or TOE for short) is based on the need to apply some form of these quantum-mechanical principles.

After listing these three key questions, he added: 'Whatever else I occupied my mind with was more odd-job work ["*Gelegenheitsarbiet*"] ... and is related to the current problems of physics.' By this he meant that his work on such topics as Brownian motion, the effects of suspended particles on fluid viscosity, etc., important as they were and still are, did not exert a transformative effect on the domain.

Remarkably, he omitted from his list of key questions (and thereby seemed to relegate to the status of '*Gelegenheitsarbeit*') any question about the nature of light. Yet in 1905, his *Annus Mirabilis*, he characterised his paper on light quanta (and only that paper) as 'revolutionary'. And near the end of his life, he signalled the importance of this question:

> The whole fifty years of conscious rumination ['*Grübelei*'] have not brought me nearer to the answer to the question 'What are light quanta?' Nowadays, every scalawag ['*Lump*'] believes that he knows what they are, but he deceives himself.

---

[81] 'The Development of the Concepts of Space, Time and Space-Time from Newton to Einstein', in Abhay Ashtekar (ed.), *One Hundred Years of Relativity* (Singapore, 2005), pp. 3–36.

So I feel justified in adding this question to Einstein's list.[82] In my words, rather than his, the fourth key question is:

> What is the nature of light—and matter—quanta?

The best current answers to this question are given by the quantum theory of fields, which is based on the fixed background space-time structure of the special theory. For this reason, and quite aside from his other problems with quantum mechanics, Einstein could never accept such answers as final. And indeed, until some synthesis of background-free general relativity and background-dependent quantum field theory is achieved, one cannot say that our current answers are complete. The search for such a synthesis is called the problem of quantum gravity. Elsewhere, I have commented on the significance of Einstein's work.[83]

The creative individual: domain specificity

These few comments on what uniquely characterised Einstein's life work raise the question of the nature of human intelligence. Piaget regarded all aspects of symbolic activity as elements of a unique 'semiotic function'. Howard Gardner disputes this, maintaining that:

> human cognition is multifaceted and that the human intellect is best thought of as an ensemble of relatively autonomous faculties—ones that I have dubbed the various 'human intelligences'.[84]

> Whereas Piaget . . . had conceptualized all aspects of symbol use as part of a single 'semiotic function', empirical evidence was accruing that the human mind may be quite modular in design. That is, separate psychological processes appear to be involved in dealing with linguistic, numerical, pictorial, gestural, and other kinds of symbolic systems. . . . Individuals may be precocious with one form of symbol use, without any necessary carry over to other forms. By the same token, one form of symbol use may become seriously compromised under conditions of brain damage, without correlative depreciation of other

---

[82] For further discussion of all four questions, see John Stachel, *Einstein from 'B' to 'Z'* (Boston, Basel and Berlin, 2002).

[83] John Stachel, 'Albert Einstein: A Man for the Millenium?', in Lysiane Mornas and Joaquin Diaz Alonzo (eds.), *A Century of Relativity Physics: ERE 2005 XXVII Spanish Relativity Meeting: AIP Conference Proceedings*, vol. 841 (Melville, NY, 2006), pp. 195–227. Reprinted in Jean-Michel Alimi and André Füzfa (eds.), *Albert Einstein Century International Conference Paris, France 18–22 July 2005: AIP Conference Proceedings*, vol. 861 (Melville, NY, 2006), pp. 211–43.

[84] Gardner, *Creating Minds*, p. xii.

symbolic capacities. . . . Indeed, different forms of symbol use appear to be subserved by different portions of the cerebral cortex.[85]

Note Gardner's use of the plural: 'intelligences'. Perhaps, at this stage of our understanding of the processes involved, it is safer to speak of *domain-specificity*: 'Cognitive abilities are domain-specific to the extent that the mode of reasoning, structure of knowledge, and mechanisms for acquiring knowledge differ in important ways across distinct content areas.'[86]

Susan Gelman points out:

> Domain-specificity is not a single, unified theory of the mind. There are at least three distinct approaches to cognition that assume domain specificity. These approaches include modules, theories, and expertise. . . .
>
> The most powerful domain-specific approach is modularity theory, according to which the mind consists of [citing Chomsky] 'separate systems [i.e., the language faculty, visual system, facial recognition module, etc.] with their own properties'.

Within this approach there is disagreement on 'whether modularity is restricted to perceptual processes or affects reasoning processes as well, and whether modularity is innate or constructed'. Proponents of the three approaches

> make different assumptions concerning what is innate, the role of input, mechanisms of development, interindividual variability in performance, and what constitutes a domain ... Nevertheless, they converge on the proposal that cognitive abilities are specialized to handle specific types of information.[87]

Without going any further into these issues, one may already recognise the assertion 'that cognitive abilities are specialized to handle specific types of information' offers the potential for a much deeper understanding of such well-known facts about Einstein as his comparatively late development of speech, retention of a primarily aural relation to words throughout his life; and discomfort at penning them even while doing so to beautiful effect.

Here is Einstein's description of his reasoning process:

> Words or language, as they are written or spoken, do not seem to play any role in my mechanisms of thought. The psychical entities which seem to serve as

---

[85] Howard Gardner and Thomas Hatch, *Multiple Intelligences Go To School: Educational Implications of the Theory of Multiple Intelligences. CTE Technical Report*, Issue No. 4, March 1990, cited from <www.edc.org/CCT/ccthome/reports/tr4.html>.
[86] Susan A Gelman, 'Domain Specificity', cited from <www.psych.upenn.edu/courses/psych 172_Spring2003/domainspec.htm>.
[87] Ibid.

> elements in thought are certain signs and more or less clear images which can be 'voluntarily' reproduced and combined. . . . [T]he above mentioned elements in my case are of visual and some of muscular type. Conventional words or signs [he presumably had in mind mathematical symbols] have to be sought for laboriously only at a secondary stage . . . In a stage when words intervene at all, they are in my case purely auditory.[88]

As an example of how recent research may shed light on such a question, I cite an article from the 14 February 2005 online edition of *Nature*, entitled 'Different processes underpin the grammars of numbers and of language'. Study of three aphasia victims showed that they

> can understand 'grammatical rules' in mathematics even though they cannot handle analogous rules in language. . . . Although the patients were unable to decode such linguistic expressions [unable to differentiate the 'The boy chased the girl' from 'The girl chased the boy'], they were able to perform the mathematical calculations [such as $90-[(3+17)\times 3]$] accurately with pen and paper . . . The discovery challenges a commonly held view [by Chomsky, for example] that linguistic and mathematical mental processing draw on the same cognitive resources.

'Our findings very strongly turn that idea on its head', says Rosemary Varley, a cognitive neuroscientist at the University of Sheffield, UK. If this finding holds up, it sheds light on the compatibility of young Einstein's facile manipulation of algebraic and geometric problems at a time he was having difficulty learning French.

Stephen M. Kosslyn has begun the task of relating these advances in cognitive science to the question of Einstein's mode of thought:

> Perhaps the most striking advance of contemporary cognitive science and cognitive neuroscience is the differentiation of mental faculties. Virtually all faculties that we name with a single word, such as memory, language, perception and imagery, have turned out not to be a single 'thing' but rather, to have a complex underlying structure (p. 272). It turns out that Einstein probably would have been a good psychologist after all; as he reported . . . , images can be visual (with high or low resolution), spatial, or motoric (p. 282).[89]

---

[88] Albert Einstein, response to a questionnaire in Jacques Hadamard, *An Essay on The Psychology of Invention in the Mathematical Field* (Princeton, 1955); cited from its publication as 'A Mathematician's Mind', in Albert Einstein, *Ideas and Opinions* (New York, 1954), pp. 25–6.

[89] 'Einstein's Mental Images The Role of Visual, Spatial and Motoric Representations' [hereafter cited as 'Einstein's Mental Images'], in Albert M. Galaburda, Stephen M. Kosselyn and Yves Christen (eds), *The Languages of the Brain* (Cambridge, MA and London, 2002), pp. 271–87. I thank my colleague Fred Tauber for bringing this article to my attention.

Needed: a critique of cognitive science

Howard Gardner has opined that:

> Knowledge is accumulating at a phenomenal rate in both brain science and genetics. At the risk of seeming hyperbolic, I am prepared to defend the proposition that we have learned as much from 1983 to 2003 as we did in the previous 500 years.[90]

So the future of cognitive science looks bright. But in order to fulfill its destiny, I maintain that it must be subjected to a critique analogous to Marx's critique of classical political economy.[91] He pointed out that economists 'naturalize' certain social relations. For example, instead of understanding that capital is a social relation between people mediated by material objects, they regard any object used in production as capital, thus making the caveman with his flints and Bill Gates of Microsoft fellow capitalists.

Similarly, some cognitive scientists regard the brain as the source of behaviour, rather than as the material carrier of socially fashioned behavioural traits. By conjoining the insights of social psychology with those of cognitive science, we are reaching a point, at which it is becoming possible to flesh out Marx's brilliant *aperçu* that '[T]he human essence is no abstraction inherent in each single individual. In its reality it is the ensemble of the social relations.'[92] Aaron Cicourel has long argued the need for such a conjunction. In 1974, he insisted that:

> Social structure remains an accountable illusion of the sociologist's common sense knowledge unless we can reveal a connection between the cognitive processes that contribute to the emergence of contextual activities, and the normative accounting schemes we use for claiming knowledge as laymen and researchers.[93]

Ten years ago, he said:

> Social scientists tend to ignore the role of human information processing for the production of social interaction and more complex forms of social organization.

---

[90] 'Multiple Intelligences After Twenty Years' (2003) <pzweb.Harvard.edu/PIs/HG_MI_after_20_years.pdf>.
[91] For a discussion of Marx's viewpoint, see John Stachel, '"The Relations Between Things" versus "The Things Between Relations": The Deeper Meaning of the Hole Argument' in David Malament (ed.), *Reading Natural Philosophy: Essays in the History and Philosophy of Science and Mathematics* (LaSalle and Chicago, 2002), pp. 232–66.
[92] Karl Marx, 'Theses on Feurbach' (1843). English translation cited from Karl Marx, *Early Writings* (New York, 1975), p. 423.
[93] Aaaron V. Cicourel, 'Preface' to *Cognitive Sociology* (New York, 1974), p. 7.

> Cognitive scientists, however, tend to take for granted the influence and constraints that complex forms of social organization and locally-organized social interaction can have on information processing. ... Work on the neurobiology of human cognitive processes tends to pay only lip service to 'experience' or the role of the local environment or social ecology on brain maturation.[94]

A recent review points out that:

> Although social scientists have developed a rich theoretical and methodological framework for examining and understanding social cognition, they have only recently begun to consider its neural substrates.[95]

On the other hand,

> Cognitive science often carries on as though humans had no culture, no significant variability and no history. ... It is not an exaggeration to say that theories of cognitive structure are built mostly upon studies of the human mind as manifest in literate, postindustrial society and upon studies of the capabilities of computers.[96]

The Brazilian philosopher Marcos Barbosa de Oliveira has undertaken a critique of cognitive science, leading him

> to reject naturalism,[97] and in the course of this process I became aware—again with a certain surprise—that the conclusions, at which I was arriving, had a certain affinity with the Marxist dialectical tradition; or more exactly, in philosophy with the currents of Western Marxism, and in psychology with the school of Vygotsky and his followers.[98]

Such a critique is beginning to take shape within cognitive science itself. Kosslyn discusses the question of whether brain connections are hard-wired:

---

[94] Cicourel, 'Cognition and Cultural Belief', in Peter Baumgartner and Sabine Payr (eds). *Speaking Minds: Interviews with Twenty Eminent Cognitive Scientists* (Princeton, 1995), p. 50.
[95] David M. Amodio and Chris D. Frith, 'Meeting of minds: the medial frontal cortex and social cognition,' *Nature Reviews: Neuroscience*, 7 (2006), 268–77, at p. 268.
[96] Merlin Donald, *Origins of the Modern Mind. Three Stages in the Evolution of Culture and Cognition* (Cambridge, MA and London 1991), pp. 1 and 5.
[97] Elsewhere, he defines 'naturalism . . . as the methodological attitude in the human sciences that takes the natural sciences as the paradigm to follow. . . . The central thesis that I tried to establish, in contraposition to naturalism, is that there are essential differences between the natural sciences and the human sciences, so that the natural sciences cannot and should not be taken as a paradigm for the human sciences, or broadly construed, for the humanities in general' (Marcos Barbosa de Oliveira, Entrevista concedida aos Profs. Michael Wrigley e Maria Eunice Gonzales em 11 de junho de 1999).
[98] *Da Ciência Cognitiva à Dialética* (São Paulo, 1999), p. 10. I thank Dr Luciana Garbayo for help with the translations from the Portuguese.

> [Peter] Huttenlocher [*Neural Plasticity* (Cambridge, MA, 2002)] summarizes evidence that only a minority of brain circuits are defined by the genes; the rest are initially configured randomly, and only via experience are specific circuits formed. I am going a step further here, suggesting that in the adult brain at least some of these circuits are 'general purpose' and that the pattern of activity within them defines different modules in different circumstances (functionally, not structurally—the connections themselves are not changed, only the patterning within them). . . . [T]he current enthusiasm for 'evolutionary psychology' (for example Pinker [*How the Mind Works* (New York, 1997)]) relies on the idea that modules have been produced via natural selection. If many modules for higher-level cognitive functions are not predefined by the genes, then this story will require modification.[99]

David Buller asserts that: '[A]lthough an adult human brain can be characterized by "modular" information-processing structures, these are environmentally shaped, not "genetically specified" outcomes of development.'[100]

In an interview, Buller answered the question, 'Why do you say the evolutionary psychology paradigm is problematic?'

> There are three foundational claims that it makes. One is that the nature of [evolutionary] adaptation is going to create massive modularity in the mind—separate mental organs functionally specialized for separate tasks. Second, that those modules continue to be adapted to a hunter-gatherer way of life. And third, that these modules are universal and define a universal human nature. I think that all three of those claims are deeply problematic.
>
> If anything the evidence indicates that the great cognitive achievement in human evolution was cortical plasticity, which allows for rapidly adaptive changes to the environment, both across evolutionary time and [across] individual lifetimes. Because of that, we're not quite the Pleistocene relics that Evolutionary Psychology claims. [Regarding universality,] all of the evidence indicates that [behavioral] polymorphisms are much more widespread in all sexually reproducing populations than the idea of a universal human nature would require. So I think the theoretical foundations from which a lot of predictions get made, about what our mate preferences are going to be, or what the psychology of parental care is, are problematic because the theoretical foundation is mistaken.[101]

An article by David Buller and Valerie Gray Hardcastle presents a detailed critique of evolutionary psychology's concept of modularity.

---

[99] 'Einstein's Mental Images', pp. 283–4.
[100] *Adapting Minds: Evolutionary Psychology and the Persistent Quest for Human Nature* (Cambridge, MA and London, 2005). The review by Johan J. Bolhuis in *Science*, 309 (2005), 706 states that: 'It sets the standard for the continuing debates on evolutionary psychology'.
[101] 'Psyching Out Evolutionary Psychology', *Scientific American*, 4 July 2005.

> [E]volutionary psychologists treat environmental factors as 'triggers' that activate the development of a module in accordance with a 'developmental program' that is coded in the genes.... But environmental inputs and endogenous innervations do not simply 'trigger' the formation of various processing modules. Instead, during development we find a diffuse proliferation of connectivity, which later brain activity, guided by interactions with the environment, sculpts into its final form.[102]

Howard Gardner has summarised well the implications of the new approach to creativity for the study of Einstein:

> I think extraordinary people are really made. They're made in part by their ambition, in part by their times, in part by luck, and in part by where the particular domain is at a historical moment.
>
> Einstein, for example, came at exactly the right time, when all the assumptions of physics, which had survived for two centuries under Newton, were coming into question. Everybody knew it didn't quite work, but he was the guy who could see things in a new way, in part because of what I would say he had a particular blend of intelligence. He was able to think spatially about issues that people had often thought about just mathematically. If Einstein had been born 50 years earlier or 50 years later, it's quite likely he would not have been an outstanding physicist, and certainly would not have been as revolutionary as he was, being—coming into his prime at the beginning of the century.[103]

I would just add that the challenges Einstein faced were not unique. Many theoretical physicists were aware of the situation, and Henri Poincaré even said: 'There are all the evidences of a bad crisis' in physics.[104] What is unique, and in many ways still remains ineffable, is the depth and scope of Einstein's response. As the Bible says: 'For many are called but few are chosen.'[105]

---

[102] 'Evolutionary Psychology, Meet Developmental Neurobiology: Against Promiscuous Modularity', *Brain and Mind*, 1 (2000): 307–25, at pp. 315–16. See also chapter 4 of Buller, *Adapting Minds*, on 'Modularity', written in collaboration with Hardcastle.

[103] 'What makes a genius? Howard Gardner considers this question in his book "Extraordinary Minds"' interview on 27 Aug. 1997. Transcription available at <http://www.pbs.org/newshour/gergen/august97/gardner_8-27.html>.

[104] See Poincaré's 1904 talk to the International Congress of Art and Science, 'The Present and Future Status of the Mathematical Physics'. First published in *Bulletin des Sciences Mathématiques*, 28 (1904), 302; and then in English in *The Monist*, 15 (1905).

[105] Matthew 22:14, King James Version.

Abstracts and Notes on Lecturers

The Child in Poetry: Foundlings, Lostlings, Changelings
MARGARET REYNOLDS

With the print explosion of the eighteenth century, poetry written about, for, to and by children became a new industry which continues to the present day. Just as historical legislative and reforming social imperatives shaped the poems, so the poetry influenced contemporary attitudes to children, which, in turn, contributed to political change.

'The Child in Poetry' examines three key moments in the history of the 'invention of childhood'—the establishment of the Foundling Hospital by Thomas Coram in 1739, the Infant Life Protection Act of 1872, and the first Adoption Act of 1926. Alongside these three social, charitable, and legislative markers are placed three directly contemporary poetry texts—Isaac Watts's *Divine Songs for the Use of Children* (1715), Christina Rossetti's *Sing-Song* (1872), and A. A. Milne's *When We Were Very Young* (1925) and *Now We Are Six* (1927). By setting historical events alongside specific poetic texts, 'The Child in Poetry' considers the effects of the cross-currents of influence, both on poetic practice, and on the construction of the popular image of 'the child'.

2005 Warton Lecture on English Poetry

Margaret Reynolds is Reader in English and Contemporary Culture at Queen Mary, University of London and a Life Member of Clare Hall, Cambridge. Previous posts were at the University of Birmingham and the University of Leeds. She is the author of *The Sappho History* (Basingstoke, 2003), *The Sappho Companion* (London, 2000) and—with Angela Leighton—editor of *Victorian Women Poets* (Oxford, 1999). Her edition of Elizabeth Barrett Browning's *Aurora Leigh* (Athens, OH, 1993) won the British Academy's Rose Mary Crawshay Prize. She is the presenter of BBC Radio 4's 'Adventures in Poetry', and has a weekly column in *The Times* on Saturdays on Classic Books.

Coercion and Consent in Nazi Germany
RICHARD J. EVANS

Current orthodoxy amongst historians regards the Third Reich as a 'dictatorship by consent', in which coercion was not needed to keep the German population in order because Germans overwhelmingly supported Hitler's rule. This lecture argues that this view seriously underplays the coercive element in the Nazi dictatorship. The evidence often adduced by historians to demonstrate the regime's popularity is seriously flawed; contrary to many recent claims, for example, elections and plebiscites in Nazi Germany were accompanied by massive intimidation, manipulation and falsification, and their massive majorities in favour of the regime cannot be regarded as reliable indicators of its popularity. Denunciations to the Gestapo were in fact very rare. And the publicity given to the camps was an instrument of intimidation more than an index of popular acceptance. Nazi coercion was exercised by a substantial minority of Germans against the great majority. Only by recognising the willingness of millions of people to exercise coercion and intimidation, including violence, real and threatened, against their fellow-citizens before 1939 can we understand the extreme levels of violence meted out by German occupiers against subjugated populations in Central and Eastern Europe during the war.

The Raleigh Lecture on History

Richard J. Evans is a Fellow of the British Academy and Professor of Modern History in the University of Cambridge. He is a specialist on the history of modern Germany, and his books include *Telling Lies About Hitler* (1997), *The Coming of the Third Reich* (2003) and *The Third Reich in Power* (2005).

A. E. Housman's Rejected Addresses
ROBERT DOUGLAS-FAIRHURST

> Ask me no more, for fear I should reply;
> Others have held their tongues, and so can I . . .

A. E. Housman (1895–1936) has often provoked disagreement among his readers, but there is one aspect of his life and work on which almost everyone agrees: he was a reserved, even a repressed figure—'self-absorbed, self-contained' (Katherine E. Symons), 'reticent and stiff' (Lawrence Housman), 'a strange union of deep passion with severe restraint' (John Sparrow). Housman himself recognised his tendencies towards the withheld and withdrawn, noting in his lecture 'The Name and Nature of Poetry' that his poems usually emerged as 'a morbid secretion', neatly balancing the production and concealment of his voice on the page. This essay explores some of the different ways in which a tussle between reticence and release is played out in Housman's verse: in its unstable encounters of lyrical self-expression and formal restraints; in allusions that turn individual lines into minature models of human relations, caught between sympathetic approach and nervous recoil; in its sceptical attention to commonplaces and bits of received widom; in syntax that is pulled on by desire and tugged back by regret; in its wary circling around the idea that his 'unlucky love should last | When answered passions thin to air.' In particular, this lecture shows how the personal and cultural circumstances of Housman's poetry provoked him into the creation of an imagined alternative: a world in which his unlucky love would find an answer.

Chatterton Lecture on Poetry

Robert Douglas-Fairhurst is Fellow and Tutor in English at Magdalen College, Oxford. He was educated at Pembroke College, Cambridge, and Princeton University (Procter Visiting Fellow, 1991–2), held a Junior Research Fellowship at Fitzwilliam College, Cambridge (1995–6), and from 1996 to 2002 was Fellow and Director of Studies in English at Emmanuel College, Cambridge. He is the author of *Victorian Afterlives: the Shaping of Influence in Nineteenth-Century Literature* (Oxford, 2002), editor of Dickens's *'A Christmas Carol' And Other Christmas Books* (Oxford 2006), general editor of the Anthem Press series Nineteenth-Century Studies, and editor of the *Tennyson Research Bulletin*. He also writes regularly for the *Daily Telegraph*, *Observer* and *Times Literary Supplement*. He is currently editing *Great Expectations* for Oxford University Press, co-editing a collection of bicentenary essays on Tennyson, and researching a book on Victorian magic.

Condorcet and the Meaning of Enlightenment
LORRAINE DASTON

Condorcet's career as savant and social reformer epitomises one strand of the Enlightenment: how science could be harnessed to the ends of virtue, both public and private, as well as to those of power and prosperity. Central to Condorcet's vision was the calculation of probabilities. The probabilities might be used to quantify and compare risks—and thereby, Condorcet hoped, to combat unreasoning fear in the face of uncertainty.

Still more fundamental was the act of calculation itself: a practice that realised and affirmed reason even at the most elementary levels. The uses of calculation link many of Condorcet's interests, from political economy to public instruction. For Condorcet, calculation—or more precisely, the act of calculating—was an engine of enlightenment, an antidote to the everyday fear of lurking danger and the philosophical fear of falling into error.

Master-Mind Lecture

Lorraine Daston is Director at the Max Planck Institute for the History of Science, Berlin, and Visiting Professor at the Committee on Social Thought, University of Chicago. Her publications include *Classical Probability in the Enlightenment* (1988), *Biographies of Scientific Objects* (2000), and (with Peter Galison) *Objectivity* (2007).

The Search for Perfection: Atlantic Dimensions
BERNARD BAILYN

One of Isaiah Berlin's abiding concerns was the disastrous effects of the search for perfection: the horrors that perfectionists had wrought in their determination to force some portion of mankind, for their own good, into ideal molds. In this lecture I consider this 'recipe for bloodshed' in terms not of the formal discourses Berlin discussed but of popular derivatives of those doctrines; and I sketch the fate of perfectionist aspirations not in the dense, tightly meshed environment of Europe but in the open amplitudes of the Western Hemisphere. Reviewing several perfectionist projects of Atlantic dimensions—Spanish Catholic, British Puritan, Dutch, and German—I conclude that the horrors Berlin deplored derived not from the search for perfection, which had creative consequences, but from the uses and misuses of power.

Isaiah Berlin Lecture

Bernard Bailyn is Adams University Professor and James Duncan Phillips Professor of Early American History at Harvard University, where he received his Ph.D. in 1953 and where he has taught ever since. He has also served as Pitt Professor at the University of Cambridge, where he delivered the Trevelyan Lectures in 1971. He is an Honorary Fellow of the Royal Society of Edinburgh and of Christ's College, Cambridge. His books include *The Ideological Origins of the American Revolution*, *The Peopling of British North America*, *Voyagers to the West*, and *Atlantic History: Concept and Contours*.

The Origins of Fair Play
KEN BINMORE

Economists are commonly thought to believe that the operation of the free market should trump any considerations of social justice. This view is sustainable only if one subscribes to the naive view that real markets and other social systems only have one equilibrium. However, game theory shows that realistic social systems usually have many equilibria. It is therefore not enough to argue that people will strive to improve their individual welfare. Their behaviour needs to be coordinated so that they all end up playing the same equilibrium. I argue that fairness can be explained as one of nature's answers to such coordination problems. That is to say, fairness evolved as an equilibrium selection device. This hypothesis leads to a theory of the structure of the fairness norms that we use in solving the coordination problems of everyday life. The theory allows a new interpretation of John Rawls's famous *Theory of Justice* that reconciles the seemingly hostile approaches of egalitarians and utilitarians.

Keynes Lecture in Economics

Ken Binmore began his academic career as a pure mathematician. His mathematical textbooks are still in use. While holding the Chair in Mathematics at the London School of Economics, he became interested in game theory. Since that time, he has devoted himself to the subject and its applications in economics, biology, psychology, and philosophy. He has held chairs in Economics at LSE, the University of Michigan and University College London. A wide range of applied work includes the design of major telecom auctions in many countries across the world. He currently devotes his time to applying game theory to the problem of the evolution of morality. His recent books include *Natural Justice* (Oxford), *Does Game Theory Work?* (Cambridge, MA), and *A Very Short Introduction to Game Theory* (Oxford). He is now a Visiting Professor of Economics at the University of Bristol and a Visiting Professor of Philosophy at LSE.

Judicial Independence: Who Cares?
NEIL MacCORMICK

Recent developments, both in Scotland and in England and Wales, have given rise to some concern about the independence of the judiciary. Constitutional changes have brought about new relationships between ministers and judges, and have led to enactments or governmental declarations of resolutions to respect the rule of law and judicial independence.

The Human Rights Act forms part of the background to tensions between judges and ministers, yet it has proved to be a strong safety net against abusive acts of government.

The principles that justify judicial independence, and the underlying concept of separation of powers, need to be considered and re-asserted in this context. The constitution is not the property of the executive for the time being, though there may be a democratic mandate to pursue constitutional change. Yet there remains the issue of pious fraud. Are judges lawmakers in just the same sense as legislators? If their decisions are as political as those of ministers, what is the justification for the special standing that attaches to judicial decisions? The answer lies in an adequate theory of legal reasoning.

British Academy Law Lecture

Sir Neil MacCormick, QC, FBA, FRSE, is Regius Professor of Public Law and the Law of Nature and Nations in the University of Edinburgh, where he also holds a Leverhulme Personal Research Professorship in philosophy of law in support of a research programme on 'Law, State, and Practical Reason'. Recent publications include *Institutions of Law: An Essay in Legal Theory* (Oxford, 2007) *Rhetoric and the Rule of Law: a Theory of Legal Reasoning* (Oxford, 2007), and *Questioning Sovereignty: Law, State and Nation in the European Commonwealth* (Oxford, 2007).

Nation and Covenant: The Contribution of Ancient Israel to Modern Nationalism
ANTHONY D. SMITH

Though modern nationalism appears as a secular doctrine in Western Europe, it functions as an inner-worldly form of religion of the people which, as Professor Kedourie demonstrated, draws on some of the beliefs and practices of the Judaeo-Christian tradition. One of the most important of these beliefs is the ancient Jewish ideal of the Covenant between God and His people, and the associated prophecies of deliverance and restoration. Transmitted through the Hebrew Bible, mainly in the various Christian traditions, they have inspired both hierarchical and covenantal forms of public culture in medieval empires, kingdoms and ethnic communities.

The return to Old Testament study after the Reformation, with its stress on vernacular scripture, paved the way for the rise of the earliest nationalisms, notably in seventeenth-century England, Scotland and the

Netherlands. Though quite different in language and style from the French Republican and the German Romantic varieties of nationalism, these movements manifested similar territorial, cultural and political ideals. But they owed less to the quest for authenticity and popular sovereignty than to myths of ethnic chosenness and regeneration, traceable to the ancient covenantal ideal of Israel as mediated by Christian beliefs. The many links between these movements and the narratives, ideals and exemplars of biblical Israel, show them to be examples of an early modern 'covenantal' nationalism which in turn suggests an earlier dating for nationalisms and national sentiments than modernist accounts propose, and one more in accord with their pre-modern roots.

Elie Kedourie Memorial Lecture

Anthony D. Smith is Professor Emeritus of Nationalism and Ethnicity at the London School of Economics and Political Science. He is President of The Association for the Study of Ethnicity and Nationalism, and Chief Editor of its journal, *Nations and Nationalism*. His main academic interests are in the theory and history of nations and nationalism, and his publications include *Theories of Nationalism* (London, 1971/1983), *Nationalism in the Twentieth Century* (London, 1979), *The Ethnic Revival* (Cambridge, 1981), *The Ethnic Origins of Nations* (Oxford, 1986), *National Identity* (London, 1991), *Nations and Nationalism in a Global Era* (Cambridge, 1995), *Nationalism and Modernism* (London, 1998), *Myths and Memories of the Nation* (Oxford, 1999), *The Nation in History* (Boston, MA, 2000), *Nationalism: Theory, Ideology, History* (Cambridge, 2001), *Chosen Peoples* (Oxford, 2003) and *The Antiquity of Nations* (Cambridge, 2004). He is currently working on a book on *The Genealogy of Nations*.

Bonjour Paresse: Literary Waste and Recycling in Book 4 of Gower's *Confessio Amantis*
JAMES SIMPSON

Moments of historical rupture not only detest the waste of the past but also define it, the better to dispose of the past as idle waste. Many of us are the heirs of Protestant anxiety regarding work, and bourgeois detestation of waste. We find it difficult to recover the charisma of idleness of any kind, be it religious or aristocratic. That is an especial problem for the time-consuming and non-utilitarian study of literature. This essay takes a friendly look at the literary representation of erotic idleness, and at the lover's idle reading of past texts. Despite its attempted indulgence, however, the essay cannot help but see literary idleness as simultaneously dangerous and productive: it is dangerous because it leads to despair, but that very despair generates a productive recycling of old texts. Even apparently idle, wasteful reading turns out to be regenerative within an optimistic account of the psychology of reading. In contrast to the active waste creation and disposal activities of post-Reformation English culture, then, pre-Reformation culture practises recycling. My test case is Book 4 of Gower's *Confessio Amantis*, a book devoted to sloth.

Sir Israel Gollancz Memorial Lecture

James Simpson is Professor of English and American Literature at Harvard University (2004–). He was formerly Professor of Medieval and Renaissance English at the University of Cambridge (1999–2003). He is a Life Fellow of Girton College, Cambridge and an Honorary Fellow of the Australian Academy of the Humanities. He was educated at Melbourne University (BA) and Oxford University (M.Phil.). He holds a doctorate from the University of Cambridge. His books are as follows: *Piers Plowman: An Introduction to the B-Text* (1990); *Sciences and the Self in Medieval Poetry* (1995); and *Reform and Cultural Revolution* (2002).

Kinds of People: Moving Targets
IAN HACKING

New classifications can bring new kinds of people into being: this is called 'making up people'. People interact with the ways they are classified. There are 'looping effects': not only do classifications affect people, but also the people classified affect classifications. The lecture does not examine race and sex, even though making up people and looping effects are easily found there. Ethnic and sexual classifications have been with us always; the lecture studies new and evolving classifications in the human sciences. These include the social sciences, psychology, psychiatry and medicine.

A simple framework for analysis consists of (*a*) classifications, (*b*) people classified, (*c*) institutions, (*d*) knowledge, and (*e*) experts. Multiple personality provides an easy example of looping effects and of making up people within this framework. The two more difficult examples are then used to illustrate the remaining points: autism and obesity. In these and so many other cases we think there is a fixed target to be investigated, but looping effects keep the target on the move.

The human sciences are driven by ten imperatives that have emerged over the past two centuries. Seven of these present 'engines of discovery': Count! Quantify! Create norms! Correlate! Medicalise! Biologise! Geneticise! These imperatives do not just drive knowledge; they also drive making up people and they produce looping effects: Normalise! Bureacratise! Reclaim our identity! The last is an important engine of resistance against classifications and stereotypes.

The paper sketches how each engine works, using the framework of analysis (*a*)–(*e*), illustrated by obesity and autism. It concludes with three more examples of kinds of people and their behaviour: poverty, suicide and genius.

British Academy Lecture

Ian Hacking is Professeur honoraire, Collège de France, in the chair of philosophy and history of scientific concepts, and also University Professor emeritus, University of Toronto. His books include: *Historical Ontology*, *The Social Construction of What?*, *Mad Travellers: Reflections of the Reality of Transient Mental Illnesses*, *Rewriting the Soul: Multiple Personality and the Sciences of Memory*, *The Taming of Chance*, *Representing and Intervening*, and *The Emergence of Probability*.

Shakespeare, Jonson, and the Invention of the Author
IAN DONALDSON

Though the literary careers of Shakespeare and Ben Jonson were closely linked, the two men operated professionally in very different ways. Jonson consciously fashioned for himself a public role as 'author' that derived in part from classical precedent, yet was also strikingly predictive of modern practice. Shakespeare's more reticent mode of self-presentation generated notorious mysteries concerning the nature of his personal life and for some, a radical doubt concerning his very identity. Yet in the combined practice of these two writers, the modern notion of *author* was born.

Shakespeare Lecture

Ian Donaldson is Professional Fellow at the University of Melbourne. He is a General Editor (with David Bevington and Martin Butler) of the forthcoming *Cambridge Edition of the Works of Ben Jonson*, and is completing a life of Jonson for Oxford University Press.

'Now Shall I Make My Soul': Approaching Death in Yeats's Life and Work
R. F. FOSTER

W. B. Yeats sustained a lifelong interest in death, as a poetic subject and a philosophical problem—remarking that it was, along with sex, the only topic of abiding interest to a serious person. This lecture traces the preoccupation in its changing forms throughout his life, from his *fin-de-siècle* love-poetry through his poems of death as a political sacrifice to the anticipations of his own death in his middle and late poetry. This is linked to Yeats's interest in Celtic legend, magical ritual and psychic research, as well as to particularly Irish intellectual influences and conjunctions—including the appeal, of supernaturalism for Irish Protestants (a subject first addressed in the author's Chatterton lecture for the Academy twenty years ago). Yeats's approach to death in his later work is here considered in terms of more general ideas of 'late style', and the death-cults of other modern poets. The conclusion discusses Yeats's creation of a structured canon of work in the light of his own death and the work which he wrote on his deathbed. This not only responded to questions he had been addressing himself and his readers all his life, but did so by returning to his early investigations of the Otherworld. It is argued that he contrived to arrive at a final resolution, both personal and aesthetic, for which he had prepared himself in unconventional but effective ways ever since his first apprenticeship to poetry, philosophy and passion.

Warton Lecture on English Poetry

R. F. Foster is Carroll Professor of Irish History at Oxford and a Fellow of Hertford College. Previously he was Professor of Modern British History at Birkbeck College, University of London. He was elected a Fellow of the British Academy in 1989. His books include *Charles Stuart Parnell: The Man and His Family* (1976), *Lord Randolph Churchill: A Political Life* (1981), *Modern Ireland 1600–1972* (1988), *Paddy and Mr Punch: Connections in Irish and English History* (1993), *The Irish Story: Telling Tales and Making It Up in Ireland* (2001), which won the 2003 Christian Gauss Award for Literary Criticism, *W. B. Yeats, A life. I: The Apprentice Mage 1865–1914* (1997) which won the 1998 James Tait Black Prize for biography, and *Volume II: The Arch-Poet, 1915–1939* (2003); his most recent book is *Luck and the Irish: a Brief History of Change 1970–2000* (2007).

Recovering Maya Civilisation
NORMAN HAMMOND

The Maya created in central America one of the most notable and surprising civilisations of the ancient world. Great cities such as Tikal, Copan, Palenque and Chichén Itzá, reached their apogee in the Classic Period of AD 250–900.

Forest clearance by maize farmers began around 2600 BC in the Petén and Belize. The oldest villages on the Pacific coast are c.1700 BC; in Belize c.1200 BC, where the Cuello site documents the development of domestic architecture and subsistence based on maize, root crops, deer hunting and domesticated dog. Long-distance procurement of jade and obsidian attests interdependent communities ruled by élites who laid the foundations of Maya civilisation 650–400 BC.

Maya hieroglyphic script as a tool of governance is found on the San Bartolo murals of the second century BC, portraying rituals of royal accession. The coeval development of larger communities at Nakbe, El Mirador and Calakmul with massive public works demonstrate the Late Preclassic origin of kingship. At Copan tunnels into the Acropolis revealed superimposed Early Classic dynastic temples and royal tombs, providing concrete evidence that the dynasty portrayed on an eighth-century altar was an historical reality.

Hieroglyphic texts also document prolonged Late Classic conflict between Tikal and Calakmul's alliance, and internecine warfare between Maya polities persisted through the ninth century as a major factor in the collapse of Classic civilisation. Natural factors include severe droughts in AD 800–1000. The Maya collapse remains mysterious in its finality, but its multiplicity of causes is being clarified.

Albert Reckitt Archaeological Lecture

Norman Hammond is Professor of Archaeology at Boston University and Associate in Maya Archaeology at the Peabody Museum, Harvard University. He has worked in the Maya area since 1968, including major excavations at the sites of Lubaantun, Cuello, Nohmul and La Milpa in Belize. Books include *Ancient Maya Civilization* (1982, many subsequent and foreign editions), and *Cuello: an early Maya community in Belize* (1991); his papers include 'New Light on the Most Ancient Maya' (Curl Lecture of the Royal Anthropological Institute, *Man* 1986) and contributions on the scientific study of Maya subsistence and trade. He was elected a Corresponding Fellow of the British Academy in 1998.

The Devil in the Holy Water: Political Libel in Eighteenth-Century France
ROBERT DARNTON

This lecture investigates the vast but unstudied literature of libel that flooded the French book market in the eighteenth century. By concentrating on four interconnected *libelles* from 1771 to 1793, it combines an analysis of the genre with an account of a colony of French refugees in London, who churned out slanderous attacks on public figures in Versailles and grafted a blackmail operation on to their literary speculations. Their adventures and misadventures, along with the attempts of secret agents from the Paris police to eliminate them, provide a rocambolesque tale that leads directly into the French Revolution. The same genre, developed by many of the same authors, fuelled polemics right through the Terror, but its substance changed while its form remained the same. The literature of libel therefore shows how an ideological current eroded authority under the *Ancien Régime* and became absorbed in a new political culture, one that reached its extreme point under Robespierre but that drew on ingredients from the world of Grub Street under Louis XV.

2007 British Academy Lecture

Robert Darnton was educated at Harvard University (AB, 1960) and Oxford University (B.Phil., 1962; D.Phil., 1964), where he was a Rhodes scholar. He taught at Princeton from 1968 until 2007, when he became Carl H. Pforzheimer University Professor and Director of the University Library at Harvard. He has been a visiting professor or fellow at many universities and institutes for advanced study, and his outside activities include service as a trustee of the New York Public Library and the Oxford University Press (USA). He has written and edited two dozen books, including *The Business of Enlightenment: A Publishing History of the Encyclopédie* (1979, an early attempt to develop the history of books as a field of study), *The Great Cat Massacre and Other Episodes in French Cultural History* (1984, translated into sixteen languages), *Berlin Journal, 1989–1990*, (1991, an account of the fall of the Berlin Wall and the collapse of East Germany), and *The Forbidden Best-Sellers of Prerevolutionary France* (1995). His latest book, *Slander. The Art and Politics of Libel in Eighteenth-Century France* should be published in the winter of 2007–8.

Einstein
JOHN STACHEL

This lecture was part of the Academy's celebration of the Centenary of 1905, Einstein's Miraculous Year, during which he published five fundamental papers on stochastic processes, special relativity and quantum theory. The myth of Einstein as magus hinders us from assessing the true nature of his personality and achievements. The nature of creativity is discussed: rather than focusing exclusively on an individual, creativity is defined in terms of the interaction between the invidividual and the field of experts in a certain domain; this interaction determines the form and content of results that are admitted to the domain. We may speak of Creativity with a capital 'C', when, as in the case of Einstein's work, this process results in crucial changes in the domain. Some of the dynamical polarities in Einstein's personality that enabled him to contribute to such changes in the domain of theoretical physics are discussed. The nature of his cognitive processes is considered; contrary to the currently fashionable emphasis in cognitive science on genetic factors, evidence is presented supporting the crucial role played by social relations in shaping the domain-specific cognitive apparatus.

2005 Master-Mind Lecture

John Stachel has taught at Lehigh University, the University of Pittsburgh and Boston University, and served as visiting professor at King's College, London, the Institute of Theoretical Physics, Warsaw, the University of Paris, and Princeton University. He is currently Emeritus Professor of Physics and Director of the Center for Einstein Studies at Boston University. He was the founding editor of *The Collected Papers of Albert Einstein* (Princeton, 1987–) and edited the first two volumes. He is also editor of *Einstein Studies* (Boston, 1989–), *Einstein's Miraculous Year* (2nd edn., Princeton, 2005); and the author of *Einstein From 'B' to 'Z'* (Boston, 2002).

Lecture series published in the *Proceedings of the British Academy*

The holding of academic lectures, and their publication in the *Proceedings*, have constituted a key activity of the British Academy since its foundation.

There are currently 24 established series of lectures. Some are of long standing, but there are several recent additions which have extended the range of the programme. Distinguished speakers are invited on the recommendation of the Academy's subject-based Sections or specialist nomination committees.

There are ten annual lecture series, eleven biennial series. Another three series have become incorporated in the Academy's programme of symposia. The Academy also organises occasional special lectures.

The lecture series are detailed below in the order in which they were inaugurated. Recent published lectures are listed (with *Proceedings* volume and page numbers).

Lectures published in print in the *Proceedings of the British Academy* are also available in PDF format via www.proc.britac.ac.uk

Warton Lectures on English Poetry *Annual; first delivered 1910*

Mrs Frida Mond endowed this lecture series as a tribute to Thomas Warton, 'the first historian of English poetry, whose work not only led the way to the scientific study of English Literature, but also stimulated creative genius, and played no small part in the Romantic Revival'.

Recent published lectures:
2002   Angela Leighton, 'Elegies of Form in Bishop, Plath, Stevenson' (**121,** 257–75)
2004   David Womersley, 'Dulness and Pope' (**131,** 229–50)
2005   Margaret Reynolds, 'The Child in Poetry: Foundlings, Lostlings, Changelings' (**151,** 1–52)

Shakespeare Lectures *Annual; first delivered 1911*

In 1910 Mrs Frida Mond provided for a lecture to be delivered 'on some Shakespearean subject, philosophical, historical, or philological, or some problem in English dramatic literature and histrionic art, or some study in literature of the age of Shakespeare'. Delivered on or around 23 April.

Recent published lectures:
2003   H. R. Woudhuysen, 'The Foundations of Shakespeare's Text' (**125,** 69–100)
2004   Michael Pennington, 'Barnardine's Straw: The Devil in Shakespeare's Detail' (**131,** 205–27)
2005   Alan C. Dessen, 'Staging Matters: Shakespeare, the Director, and the Theatre Historian' (**139,** 35–54)

Philosophical Lectures *Symposia; first delivered 1914*

The will of Miss Henriette Hertz made provision for a lecture 'on a philosophical problem or some problems in the philosophy of Western or Eastern Civilisation in Ancient or Modern times or discussions of theories of the Phenomena of life to Eternity'. Since the early 1990s, the lectures have been grouped together to form symposia, which are published in their own *Proceedings* volumes.

2001   *Bayes's Theorem* symposium:
         Elliott Sober, 'Bayesianism—its Scope and Limits' (**113,** 21–38)
         Colin Howson, 'Bayesianism in Statistics' (**113,** 39–69)
         A. P. Dawid, 'Bayes's Theorem and Weighing Evidence by Juries' (**113,** 71–90)
         John Earman, 'Bayes, Hume, Price, and Miracles' (**113,** 91–109)

Aspects of Art Lectures *Biennial; first delivered 1916*

Established by the Henriette Hertz Trust, the lecture is intended to be 'on some problem or aspect of the relation of Art in any of its manifestations to human culture; Art including Poetry and Music as well as Sculpture and Painting'.

Recent published lectures:
2001   Paul Binski, 'How Northern was the Northern Master at Assisi?' (**117,** 73–138)
2003   Stephen Banfield, 'Scholarship and the Musical: Reclaiming Jerome Kern' (**125,** 183–210
2005   Joseph Leo Koerner, 'Everyman in Motion: from Bosch to Bruegel' (**139,** 297–328

Master-Mind Lectures *Biennial; first delivered 1916*

Miss Henriette Hertz provided for a lecture on 'some Master-Mind considered individually with reference to his life and work especially in order to appraise the essential elements of his Genius: the subject to be chosen from the great Philosophers, Artists, Poets, Musicians'.

Recent published lectures:
2000 M. F. Burnyeat, 'Plato' (**111,** 1–22)
2004 Terence Cave, 'Montaigne' (**131,** 183–203)
2005 John Stachel, 'Einstein' (**151,** 423–58)

Italian Lectures *Biennial; first delivered 1917*

In 1916 Mrs Angela Mond offered funds for a lecture series 'to be on some subject relating to Italian literature, history, art, history of Italian science, Italy's part in the Renaissance, Italian influences on other countries, and any other theme which the Council may consider as coming within the scope of such a Lecture'.

Recent published lectures:
2003 Brian Pullan, 'Charity and Usury: Jewish and Christian Lending in Renaissance and Early Modern Italy' (**125,** 19–40)
2005 Carlo Ginzburg, 'Dante's Epistle to Cangrande and its Two Authors' (**139,** 195–216)

Raleigh Lectures on History *Annual; first delivered 1919*

In 1918 Sir Charles Wakefield (formerly Lord Mayor of London) offered the Academy the sum of £500 a year for at least five years to commemorate the tercentenary of Sir Walter Raleigh; from this fund, a history lecture was founded. Since 1974 the subject has rotated between the medieval, early modern and modern fields.

Recent published lectures:
2003 C. A. Bayly, '"The Nation Within": British India at War 1939–1947' (**125,** 265–85)
2004 Alexander Murray, 'The Inquisition and the Renaissance' (**131,** 91–126)
2005 Keith Wrightson, 'Mutualities and Obligations: Changing Social Relationships in Early Modern England' (**139,** 157–94)

Sir Israel Gollancz Memorial Lectures
Biennial; first delivered 1924

Endowed by Mrs Frida Mond in 1924, this lecture deals with 'Old English or Early English Language and Literature, or a philological subject connected with the history of English, more particularly during the early periods of the language, or cognate subjects, or some textual study and interpretation'. The lecture series was subsequently named after Sir Israel Gollancz (Secretary of the Academy 1902–30).

Recent published lectures:
2002 Ralph Hanna, 'Yorkshire Writers' (**121**, 91–109)
2004 Joyce Hill, 'Authority and Intertextuality in the Works of Ælfric' (**131**, 157–81)

Sir John Rhŷs Memorial Lectures
Biennial; first delivered 1925

In May 1924 a memorial fund was offered to the Academy 'for the promotion of Welsh and other studies', to commemorate the services of the Rt Hon. Sir John Rhŷs, FBA, Professor of Celtic, and Principal of Jesus College, Oxford.

Recent published lectures:
2001 Ralph A. Griffiths, 'After Glyn Dŵr: An Age of Reconciliation?' (**117**, 139–64)
2003 Fergus Kelly, 'Thinking in Threes: "The Triad in Early Irish Literature"' (**125**, 1–18)

Albert Reckitt Archaeological Lectures
Biennial; first delivered 1951

The Reckitt Archaeological Trust, established by the late Mr Albert L. Reckitt for the furtherance of archaeological research, was transferred to the Academy in 1950; it was decided to establish a lecture series in memory of the founder.

Recent published lectures:
2002 Charles F. W. Higham, 'The Origins of the Civilisation of Angkor' (**121**, 41–89)
2004 Joan Oates, 'Archaeology in Mesopotamia: Digging Deeper at Tell Brak' (**131**, 1–39)

Chatterton Lectures on Poetry *Annual; first delivered 1955*

Established in 1954 under the will of E. H. W. Meyerstein of Gray's Inn, this annual lecture is to be given by a lecturer under the age of 40 on the life and works of a deceased English poet (interpreted as 'a deceased poet writing in the English language').

Recent published lectures:
2003 Andrew Hadfield, 'Michael Drayton's Brilliant Career' (**125,** 119–47)
2004 Fran Brearton, 'Robert Graves and *The White Goddess*' (**131,** 273–301)
2005 Jane Stabler, 'Byron, Conversation and Discord' (**139,** 111–35)

Dawes Hicks Lectures on Philosophy *Symposia; first delivered 1955*

Established in 1954, under the will of George Dawes Hicks (Professor of Philosophy at the University of London), these lectures were to be given on 'subjects relating to the History of Philosophy, either ancient or modern'. Since the early 1990s, the lectures have been grouped together to form symposia, which are published in their own *Proceedings* volumes.

2000 *Henry Sidgwick* symposium:
       Stefan Collini, 'My Roles and their Duties: Sidgwick as Philosopher, Professor, and Public Moralist' (**109,** 9–49)
       John Skorupski, 'Three Methods and a Dualism' (**109,** 61–81)
       Ross Harrison, 'The Sanctions of Utilitarianism' (**109,** 93–116)

Maccabaean Lectures in Jurisprudence *Biennial; first delivered 1956*

This lecture series, which may be on any aspect of Jurisprudence, was endowed in 1956 by the Maccabaeans, a society of Jewish professional men with a strong interest in the law, to mark the tercentenary of the Jewish resettlement in England under Cromwell.

Recent published lectures:
2003 Brian Simpson, 'The Rule of Law in International Affairs' (**125,** 211–63)
2005 Lord Bingham of Cornhill, 'The Judges: Active or Passive?' (**139,** 55–72)

Sarah Tryphena Phillips Lectures in American Literature and History

Biennial; first delivered 1961

Dr Carl Bode, Cultural Attaché at the US Embassy in London 1958–9, proposed a series of lectures on American Literature. In 1960 a lecture series was endowed by the Ellis L. Phillips Foundation—the scope of the series to include American history, though the emphasis was to be on literature.

Recent published lectures:
2003   Eric Foner, 'Abraham Lincoln: The Great Emancipator?' (**125**, 149–62)
2005   Richard Gray, '"They Worship Death Here": William Faulkner, *Sanctuary* and Hollywood' (**131**, 251–71)

Thank-Offering to Britain Fund Lectures

Biennial; first delivered 1966

In 1965 the proceeds of a 'Thank-you Britain' appeal, initiated by the Association of Jewish Refugees, were presented to the Academy as a token of gratitude from the people who had sought refuge in this country from the oppression of the Nazis. One of the purposes of the fund was to establish a 'Thank-offering to Britain' Lecture.

Recent published lectures:
2002   The Right Honourable Lord Woolf, 'Human Rights: Have the Public Benefited?' (**121**, 301–14)
2004   Lord Moser, 'The Future of Our Universities' (**131**, 303–30)

Keynes Lectures in Economics

Annual; first delivered 1971

Proposed by the economists within the Academy, these lectures are devoted to an up-to-date survey of theoretical research and trends of thought in the field of economics. In recent years, the lectures have been followed by formal discussion.

Recent published lectures:
2002   Nicholas Stern, 'Development as a Process of Change: Toward a Dynamic Public Economics' (**121**, 277–99)
2003   John Vickers, 'Economics for Consumer Policy' (**125**, 287–310)
2004   Timothy Besley, 'The New Political Economy' (**131**, 371–95)
2005   Stephen Nickell, 'Practical Issues in UK Monetary Policy, 2000–2005' (**139**, 1–33)

Mortimer Wheeler Archaeological Lectures

Symposia; first delivered 1971

On the proposal of Council a lecture series was established to commemorate the eightieth birthday (in September 1970) of Sir Mortimer Wheeler (Secretary of the Academy 1949–70). Since the early 1990s, the lecture has been subsumed within a number of Academy symposia on archaeological subjects, published as distinct volumes of the *Proceedings*.

Recent published lectures:
2001   Robin Osborne, 'Urban Sprawl: What is Urbanization and why does it matter?' (**126**, 1–16)

Radcliffe-Brown Lectures in Social Anthropology

Biennial; first delivered 1972

This series was established in 1972 by the Academy and the Association of Social Anthropologists and named after the Association's first President, A. R. Radcliffe-Brown, FBA, who was also the first Professor of Social Anthropology in the University of Oxford.

Recent published lectures:
2003   Gillian Feeley-Harnik, 'The Geography of Descent' (**125**, 311–64)
2005   Philippe Descola, 'Beyond Nature and Culture' (**139**, 137–55)

Elie Kedourie Memorial Lectures

Annual; first delivered 1996

In 1993, a Fund was set up by appeal, in memory of the modern historian and political philosopher Elie Kedourie, FBA, in order to establish a lecture in modern history, preference being given to subjects in Middle Eastern and modern European history.

Recent published lectures:
2003   Noel Malcolm, 'The Crescent and the City of the Sun: Islam and the Renaissance Utopia of Tommaso Campanella' (**125**, 41–67)
2004   James Piscatori, 'Imagining Pan-Islam: Religious Activism and Political Utopias' (**131**, 421–42)
2005   Dominic Leiven, 'Empire, History and the Contemporary Global Order' (**131**, 127–56)

British Academy Lectures *Annual; first delivered 1998*

Established to mark the Academy's move to Carlton House Terrace in 1998, the keynote British Academy Lecture is intended to address a wide audience and to promote understanding of the humanities and social sciences.

Recent published lectures:
2002 E. A. Wrigley, 'The Quest for the Industrial Revolution' (**121**, 147–70)
2003 Gillian Beer, 'Revenants and Migrants: Hardy, Butler, Woolf and Sebald' (**125**, 163–82)
2004 Mervyn King, 'What Fates Impose: Facing Up to Uncertainty' (**131**, 397–420)
2005 Colin Renfrew, 'Becoming Human: the Archaeological Challenge' (**139**, 217–38)

Isaiah Berlin Lectures *Annual; first delivered 2001*

Established under the will of Sir Isaiah Berlin (President of the Academy 1974–8), the lecture is intended to appraise the contemporary condition of any one of the fields of learning with which the Academy is concerned.

Recent published lectures:
2003 J. G. A. Pocock, 'The Re-Description of Enlightenment' (**125**, 101–17)
2004 Lord Sutherland, 'Nomad's Progress' (**131**, 443–63)
2005 Marilyn Strathern, 'Useful Knowledge' (**139**, 73–109)

Elsley Zeitlyn Lectures on Chinese Archaeology and Culture *Annual; first delivered 2001*

Through a bequest from Miss M. H. Zeitlyn in memory of her father, this lecture series was established 'to support the understanding and appreciation of Chinese Archaeology and Culture and to stimulate new programmes of high quality research in this field'.

Recent published lectures:
2003 Lothar Ledderose, 'Carving Sutras into Stone before the Catastrophe: the Inscription of 1118 at Cloud Dwelling Monastery near Beijing' (**125**, 381–454)
2004 Robert Bagley, 'The Prehistory of Chinese Music Theory' (**131**, 41–90)
2005 Lothar von Falkenhausen, 'The Inscribed Bronzes from Yangjiacun: New Evidence on Social Structure and Historical Consciousness in Late Western Zhou China (*c.*800 BC)' (**139**, 239–95)

Joint British Academy/British   *Annual; first delivered 2001*
Psychological Society Lectures

In 2001 the Academy held a lecture to mark the centenary of the British Psychological Society. The Academy's Psychology Section subsequently recommended that a joint lecture should be added to the Academy's lecture programme.

Recent published lectures:
2001   Annette Karmiloff-Smith, 'Elementary, my dear Watson, the clue is in the genes . . . or is it?' (**117,** 525–43)
2003   Susan E. Gathercole, 'Working Memory and Learning During the School Years' (**125,** 365–80)

British Academy Law Lecture   *Biennial; first delivered 2004*

In 2003 the Academy approved the proposal of the Law Section for an additional Law Lecture, to complement the Maccabean Lecture.

2004   Edwin Cameron & Jonathan Berger, 'Patents and Public Health: Principle, Politics and Paradox' (**131,** 331–69)